Beginning Relational Data Modeling

Second Edition

SHARON ALLEN AND EVAN TERRY

Beginning Relational Data Modeling, Second Edition

Copyright © 2005 by Sharon Allen and Evan Terry

ISBN (pbk): 1-59059-463-0

Printed and bound in the United States of America 9 8 7 6 5 4 3 2 1

Lead Editor: Tony Davis
Technical Reviewer: Evan Terry
Editorial Board: Steve Anglin, Dan Appleman, Ewan Buckingham, Gary Cornell, Tony Davis,
    Jason Gilmore, Jonathan Hassell, Chris Mills, Dominic Shakeshaft, Jim Sumser
Assistant Publisher: Grace Wong
Project Manager: Sofia Marchant
Copy Manager: Nicole LeClerc
Copy Editor: Kim Wimpsett
Production Manager: Kari Brooks-Copony
Production Editor: Ellie Fountain
Compositor: Dina Quan
Proofreader: Sue Boshers
Indexer: Kevin Broccoli
Artist: Kinetic Publishing Services, LLC
Cover Designer: Kurt Krames
Manufacturing Manager: Tom Debolski

Distributed to the book trade in the United States by Springer-Verlag New York, Inc., 233 Spring Street, 6th Floor, New York, NY 10013, and outside the United States by Springer-Verlag GmbH & Co. KG, Tiergartenstr. 17, 69112 Heidelberg, Germany.

In the United States: phone 1-800-SPRINGER, fax 201-348-4505, e-mail orders@springer-ny.com, or visit http://www.springer-ny.com. Outside the United States: fax +49 6221 345229, e-mail orders@springer.de, or visit http://www.springer.de.

For information on translations, please contact Apress directly at 2560 Ninth Street, Suite 219, Berkeley, CA 94710. Phone 510-549-5930, fax 510-549-5939, e-mail info@apress.com, or visit http://www.apress.com.

I would like to dedicate this book to the three wonderful women who have become very special to our family, a.k.a. "The Girls": Julie Allen née Herlehy, Leslie Teeter (soon to be Allen), and Christy Bourdaa.
—Sharon Allen

I would like to dedicate this book to our new instance of FamilyMember, Caitlin Elizabeth Terry, who provided much feedback during the book's revision.
—Evan Terry

Contents at a Glance

Contents

About the Authors

SHARON ALLEN has enjoyed learning the intricacies of several careers since 1975, including medical assistant, inventory control supervisor, data administrator, HTML and PL/SQL programmer, and data warehouse architect. This may sound a bit confused, but it has given her a unique perspective and sensitivity to the goals and pressures of both business and information technologies. This has been a huge asset for her as a data modeler; she works as an ambassador and interpreter of both business and information technologies in order to successfully build data requirements and design data solutions.

Sharon could be role-named as Wife, Mother, Daughter, Sister, Friend, Author, Data Modeler, Programmer, Stained-Glass Crafter, Crocheter, Playwright, Storyteller, Gardener, Teacher, and World Traveler. Recently added roles include Mother-in-Law, Conference Speaker, Wedding Planner, and (soon to be) Grandmother. She knows she doesn't fulfill any of these roles nearly well enough, but she has a great time trying.

EVAN TERRY has been in the IT industry for more than 15 years as a programmer/analyst, systems engineer, custom software consultant, senior developer, data analyst, and data architect, serving government and the private sector. He firmly believes that in order to succeed at developing complex systems, the IT professional must *truly understand the business processes* he supports. Evan tries to bridge the gap between the technical and the nontechnical by understanding the perspectives of both and helping the two groups communicate effectively.

In addition to a fascination with North American international relations, the following entities would be included in Evan's logical subject area: Charitable Organization, Ice Hockey, Trail Running, Hiking, International Travel, Vocal Music, Foreign Language, and Labor Day Weekend (although this subject area would likely still be considered incomplete).

Data Modeler Blessings

May the Creator gather us into one entity defined as members of the set Humanity.

May our primary key help us to recognize ourselves as irreplaceable and unique for all time.

May all our mandatory attributes be filled with good values and our optional attributes be generously supplied.

May all our relationships be for good, gainful, and positive purposes for building strong connections in our travels as foreign keys both as recursions to ourselves and as intersections with other entities in this universe.

And may any categorization be recognized as less a division, separating us from each other, and more a highlighting of what makes us special.

—Sharon Allen, 2002

A bad design is the bulldozer of ideas. Inelegant and ruthless. It leaves you to sift through the rubble of what might have been. A good design, done with style, takes longer but will always serve you better in the end.

May your teammates be open to new ideas.

May your management allow you the time to do your job.

May your encounters with bulldozers be few and your designs be elegant.

—Evan Terry, 2005

Acknowledgments

To John Baker and Paul Yamor, who let me try data modeling in the first place: thanks for giving me a chance! And to Shan Pao who graciously read through the raw material.

To the gang who helped me learn this craft and how to wield it wisely: Wendell, Ted, Paul, Janet, Karen, Drew, Cindy, Ron, Dennis, Charles, Cory, Camelia, Sanjiv, Geraldo, Richard, Ella, Jan, Paul, David, Stuart, Wendell, Rich, Phil, Michael, John, Dave, Daryl, Danny, Brad, Yamile, Cindy, Rex, Arno, Steve, Rick, Jane, Susan, Arun, Evan, and Les. Thanks for taking the time to explain "one more time" and share your wisdom and experience.

To the people who bought the first edition and critics on Amazon.com: thanks for inspiring me to go through the process of a second edition. I hope you like this one better; I do!

To the IT writers who gave me an encouraging word: Sid Adelman, Larry English, David Marco, and Michael Brackett. Thanks for the vision of possibility!

To the special people who kept me going when the going got rough: Doug, Dan, Julie, Tim, Leslie, and Mike (my gang), as well as Mom, Charlie, Evan, and Suzanne. I wouldn't have gotten here without you!

To Evan Terry, my coauthor, who helped me realize a much better version of my dream.

To everyone who had to put up with me through yet another odyssey: thanks for all the understanding and patience during my roller coaster highs and lows.

—Sharon Allen

To Sharon, for allowing me the opportunity to be a part of this work.

To my wife, Jen, for supporting me in taking on this project.

To Russ Robinson and the gang at CFS, who got me going in the first place.

To Mike Elsesser, who allowed me to grow from programmer to data architect.

To Jay Flynn and Robert Kreznarich, whose friendship and whose input into UML and object-relational mapping techniques were critical to me retaining my sense of humor amid the boots to the head. I really appreciate it.

To those who helped me learn the art and science of data modeling: Chris Dufour, Joe Mayer, Loren Brewster, Christopher Thames, Robert Kreznarich, Jay Flynn, Sharon Allen, and Arun Yarlagadda.

—Evan Terry

To the team who made something out of our first attempts: the editors, reviewers, and development team. Three cheers!

—Sharon Allen and Evan Terry

Introduction

Data modeling is a skill set that has a long history and yet is often not immediately recognized in the IT world. Although jobs for programmers and database administrators are regularly advertised, few companies employ people in a role titled *data modeler*. However, data design, which is an awareness of how data behaves and what it means within an organization, is supremely important in ensuring that company data systems work efficiently. It's often only when systems start misbehaving, or can't cope with the data in a way that the clients want it to, that poor database design and incomplete data understanding is exposed. How many times have you tried to cancel a gas or electric utility account only to find that the phone operators can't erase your records because of constraints in their data system? Instead of modifying or removing your details, you're forced to set up another account. This is not only time consuming but also a poor use of existing data. Accurate data modeling and subsequent database design can minimize these problems and ensure that each system is truly tailored to the needs of the clients.

Relational databases provide a powerful means by which to store and manipulate vast volumes of data. The design of such systems is based on the mathematics of relational theory, which was advanced in its initial stages by E. F. Codd. This mathematical basis has meant that many of the standard database design titles aren't easily accessible to many would-be modelers who want to know how to practically implement the theories they read about. This book focuses on giving the reader a background in the field of relational data modeling. The final physical implementation of these designs is beyond the scope of this book (it merits a title of its own), thanks to the complexities that can result in performance tuning a database application. The aim of this book is to provide a practical guide to the what and how of data modeling in a day-to-day, task-oriented way, rather than from a purely theoretical viewpoint. It has been more than 40 years since Codd's initial work, and yet we're still waiting to see a commercial relational database that can be said to be truly relational. In the real world, theoretical perfection, as prescribed by Codd's own rules for a relational system, has to be compromised by system performance. The most useful aspect of the art of data modeling is understanding the data better so you can suggest compromises and understand the risk factors that accompany them.

What This Book Covers

The book is split into three sections. The first seven chapters of this book deal with the basic skill set that a data modeler has to have.

> **Chapter 1** begins your journey into data modeling by covering the nature of data and data modeling, as well as its use within an enterprise. It recognizes the various guises in which data modeling makes its way into job descriptions within business and gives an overview of the ultimate goals of modeling.

Chapter 2 delves into the theory underpinning the relational model and covers the rules by which a database is assessed as relational. It then covers the process of normalization by which data is broken down so as to adhere to the premises of relational theory. It also briefly touches on the practical nature of modeling and where Codd's rules need to be bent so as to improve the performance of the given application.

Chapter 3 looks at the terminology involved in Conceptual, Logical, and Physical relational data modeling. This is where the mathematical basis of relational theory is left to others to expound; the focus is on what the various concepts equate to in a real-world setting. We also introduce the syntax by which we graphically represent data models, focusing primarily on the notation we'll use throughout the book.

Chapter 4 looks at the world of Logical and Physical modeling using graphics. This is where various database structures are designed to store data for various purposes. Again, we review the physical graphic syntax used throughout the book.

Chapter 5 briefly compares relational modeling and object-oriented data modeling. We cover the differences and overlaps using UML as a basis of graphic syntax comparison. This chapter tries to provide a simple translation technique you can use to deploy an object model to a relational database.

Chapter 6 provides a guide to the various types of analytical models that you can be asked to produce as a data modeler and the level of detail you can choose to deliver. Tailoring your model to the needs of your audience is of key importance since a lack of comprehension of the model makes the exercise itself entirely futile. Knowing what level of detail is appropriate in different circumstances is important for a modeler; by providing the right information at the right time, you make yourself an indispensable part of any development team. For example, while project managers will want an overview of the data model you've devised, programmers will need more detail in terms of the data types and size constraints they need to use in implementing your model. You need to be flexible in providing models for a variety of needs.

Chapter 7 covers how models fit into development projects. The design of a new application passes through several iterations, from the beginning of the project where the data elements that need capturing are outlined at a general level of detail to the final model provided for physical implementation as a database system, which is highly detailed and often complex. Ensuring that the model meets the needs of the project requires careful management as well as effective communication between the modeler and client.

The next portion of the book puts the knowledge gained in the first half of the book to practical use by covering how to build a sample system. And in order to emphasize that the modeling techniques presented here are applicable to whatever system you happen to be working on, the chosen system isn't a sample proprietary database such as Oracle 8*i* or SQL Server 2000 but rather the electronic version of the card game Solitaire.

Chapter 8 begins the process of modeling by capturing the scope of the modeling project. This is where the initial boundaries of the model are drawn and the important concepts of the game are captured in graphical format. By the end of this chapter, we present a general model of the game for further analysis. In the course of drawing up this model, we show how to create a general checklist of tasks that you can apply to any general project.

Chapter 9 picks up this model and iterates through many of the same steps outlined in the previous chapter in developing the level of detail further. It takes the concepts of the previous chapter and converts them into logical entities on the model. This process is something of a "drill down"—the Conceptual model of the previous chapter is fleshed out with more detail regarding the nature of the data in the system.

Chapter 10 illustrates the basic principles needed to take the Logical model from the previous chapter and turn it into a model capable of being implemented as a physical database system. This is where the fine detail must be documented and room for errors is greatly diminished. If you have a poor design here, the implementation problems for the development team may be myriad. It's important at this stage in the model development to be clear about the definitions of the various data elements and how they relate.

Chapter 11 considers the situation where budget and time constraints mean you have to skip the work highlighted in earlier chapters and move straight to a Physical model. This isn't an ideal situation for a modeler, but it's one where you can still apply basic practices to improve the model's integrity and longevity. This chapter outlines how you can take appropriate shortcuts and still provide verifiable detail in the model.

Chapter 12 covers the basics of Dimensional modeling techniques. This presents a different challenge to those of the previous chapters since the data is structured differently to improve the efficiency with which users can sum, aggregate, and manipulate data to provide reports and summary sheets. This chapter also introduces all the necessary terminology along with two sample applications that illustrate how you can develop such ad hoc analysis designs.

Chapter 13 explores a different scenario altogether. While all the work until this point has focused on building systems from scratch, this chapter covers the process of reverse engineering, where you attempt to model an existing system. This, in many ways, is the reverse process of the previous chapters since you have to work your way back along the development chain, starting with the physical elements in the database, in order to return to a Logical or Conceptual model. This is often necessary in the reappraisal of systems, such as when companies merge and need to verify what data is being collected in each system or when looking to expand or enhance an existing system.

The final section of the book covers the added value that the modeler can bring to a development team.

Chapter 14 covers what enhancements a modeler can provide to make the graphical models they produce for their clients more readable. Simple additions of text, abbreviations, icons, and color can greatly enhance the readability of a model and give it a life beyond the point when you're no longer associated with it. The more clarity a modeler can bring to their work, the easier it is for others to both follow and utilize their work.

Chapter 15 looks at additional value issues in terms of the integrity and security issues surrounding the system data. Data integrity is of key importance to a system since nonsensical values naturally reduce the effectiveness of the application and user confidence in its viability. A modeler can do a number of simple tests to consider the nature of the data in the system and flag any obvious problems for the rest of the development team.

In cases where company-sensitive information is involved, you may need to modify the model design to protect the data from being publicly exposed. While the database administrator (DBA) is often the first port of call in restricting access to the databases being used, the modeler can help protect the data.

Chapter 16 looks at the nature of metadata, or data about data. It discusses the need to document descriptive information about data, which often appears of little value within the development team and which is generally lost over time since it often exists only in the heads of the team and not in paper or electronic format. This chapter also covers how to distribute data, and its use in repositories, for easy reuse. As the number of database systems grows, the number of model designs also increases. While each system will have its own special requirements, often previously modeled structures can be reused. This requires both easy access to previous models and good documentation of such models, which is where metadata repositories can prove to be valuable assets.

Chapter 17 is the final chapter in the book and summarizes some of the best practices modelers should aim for in their working environment. It highlights what traits a modeler should avoid in order to ensure that the project succeeds, and the chapter reinforces this with some best practices. It then covers some further project details, such as how long each of the various modeling tasks will take and some of the pitfalls to look for as you work your way through a project.

Finally, Appendix A shows where you can find more information about the topics in the book, and Appendix B includes a glossary of terminology related to data modeling.

Who Is This Book For?

This book assumes no prior knowledge of relational modeling or programming constructs. It's aimed at anyone who has a need for an easy-to-read, practical guide to relational data modeling. To that end, it has a broad appeal not only for developers and DBAs taking their first steps into database design but also for people such as data architects, information officers, and knowledge managers who simply want a greater understanding of how to analyze their data efficiently. To follow along with this book, there are no specific software needs since it shies away from a specific database platform. Access to a computer with a version of Solitaire, or even a pack of playing cards, may aid your understanding of the Solitaire example, but it isn't essential.

Conventions

We've used certain styles of text and layout in this book to help highlight special kinds of information. For example, program code will appear in a block formatted like the following:

```
ALTER TABLE Suit
    ADD ( FOREIGN KEY (ColorNm)
            REFERENCES Color ) ;
```

In addition, we've made every attempt to distinguish entity names for Physical data models, table names, and attribute names using a monospaced font.

Finally, *notes* (shown here) consist of incidental information of one type or another that defines, explains, or elaborates upon the main discussion. *Tips* contain information that should make your life easier. *Cautions* indicate a potential danger.

▓**Note** Remember that you're developing models for clients, not to suit your own needs.

■■■

CHAPTER 1

Understanding and Organizing Data: Past and Present

In this chapter you'll look at a bit of history of how humans have strived through the ages to find a good way to organize, locate, and understand the knowledge they gather. We'll show how data modeling has become the current industry standard in documenting what we know about data, its intrinsic nature, and business uses. And we'll review what data modeling involves and who, within any given organization, actually does the modeling. You'll look at the following:

- The nature of data vs. information vs. knowledge

- The ancient history of data management

- What data modeling is today

- How data modeling helps in dealing with the life cycle of enterprise data

- Who actually performs data modeling tasks in the organization

- In what activities the data modeler participates

What Is Data?

We're sure many term papers and master's theses attempt to answer this very question. The nature and importance of specific data elements are being challenged every day. What we've discovered over time is that we can't architect a good storage solution that supports creation, movement, management, integration, and storage functionalities without knowing more than the basic values, shapes, and sizes generally found in the element. You need to understand its meaning, use, importance, and security aspects as well.

If we were to describe the various characteristics of data in terms of its physical syntax (which you need to understand to design a basic "holder" for it), we would probably list something like this:

- **Data type**: Binary, numeric, textual, video, and so on

- **Size**: Maximum length or volume of memory required to store it

- **Precision**: Decimal allowance

- **Necessity**: Null or not null

- **Language**: English, Spanish, Japanese, and so on

- **Restricted domain**: The day names in a week, the numbers 0–9, Yes or No

You probably recognize these characteristics as ways to describe the rules for a data holder (column, field) in a screen or database. Describing how a data holder needs to be built is one way for you to understand data. Unfortunately, it's often the only aspect of data on which any emphasis is placed.

But it isn't hard to grasp that data is more than that. Each value means something to a person who understands its use. In other words, *data*, as we use the term, is both a logical building block that we call a *data element* with a shape and size as well as a bit of communication conveying a meaning that represents a single measurement, fact, or concept. You can't map data values as being the same data element with the same meaning based on shape and size alone. You can do that only if you're completely confident of what the value is trying to communicate. You can always change, or *transform*, data values to look the same if they can be counted on to mean the same thing.

This book is all about understanding and documenting data mostly from the perspective of a single theoretical abstract notion of meaning. We often analyze data values to gain understanding about that theoretical concept. Here are two definitions that note the differences between data and data elements:

- *Data* is a unit of readable language (such as numbers, characters, images, or other methods of recording) on a durable medium. Data on its own may carry no (or little) meaning. It needs an interpretation to fully process meaning.

- A *data element* is the smallest autonomous communication definition that imparts meaningful information, generally corresponding to a field in a database column of a spreadsheet or to a blank on a paper or electronic form. For example, names, addresses, work titles, Social Security numbers, record series titles, and record group numbers all represent data elements.

As a simple example, the meaning *yes* or *positive* in data could come in many data value forms: different human languages (ja, sí, da, yes), different computer languages (0, 1, ASCII codes), abbreviations (Y, N), full words (true, false), and even graphical symbols (+, –). A data value, such as these, when used in a well-defined data element, represents a meaning to someone using it. You need both halves in conjunction to communicate, which underscores the importance of understanding the data vs. accommodating the necessary means to store it. One of the things often missing in information technology (IT) is the desire to *understand* the nature of the data being used (and the business processes that use the data). Data modeling is the process we use to review and capture the data element and their relationships to each other. Frequently we review data values in order to gain understanding.

You should note that the terms *data*, *information*, and *knowledge* all have different meanings. *Data* are the values describing facts, *information* is the useful interpretation of data, and *knowledge* implies the ability to act on decisions based on that interpretation. Because the ultimate goal of data is to provide useful information that can be built into working knowledge, it must be modeled in such a way to aid that aim.

- *Information* is data that has been organized in a coherent and meaningful manner.

- *Knowledge* is information associated with rules, which allow inferences to be drawn automatically so that the information can be employed for useful purposes.

Data values used to be represented simply by text and numbers in a database; today data is captured as abstractions in digital format. It has expanded to include pictures, sounds, virtual 3D objects, and complex multimedia that blends all those things. The evolutionary growth of the very nature of data is challenging us all to figure out how to use technology to its maximum effectiveness, including how to properly use technology as a laborsaving device and as a means to enhance our information-processing ability.

Knowledge—that blend of familiarity, awareness, and understanding gained through pattern recognition—could be defined as the supposition that information will always support a specific conclusion. You may "know" it takes ten minutes to bring water to boiling using your current method of heating it. Therefore, you may stop measuring that time duration of a process because you "know" it to be true. You may know that political unrest in the Middle East will result in the price of crude oil rising, which leads you to believe gasoline prices will be going up next, which again leads you to include political climates as a variable for next year's budgets. Knowledge is an expected extrapolation based on collections of information.

Data is the raw material for information, and information is the raw material of knowledge.

We're pointing this out because data management (DM), information management (IM), and knowledge management (KM) are different, but they do have connections and dependencies, most notably to the quality of the data and the ability to decipher it back into its underlying meaning.

Data subjects, focus areas, and methods of data and data capture have changed. We used to think of data mostly in terms of inventory and accounts payable systems. We've added dynamic assessment of complex spatial data using dynamic uplinks to satellites that help us find our way around matching urban map data, noting locations of gas stations with the global positioning system (GPS) coordinates of our car to keep us from running out of gas. Online shopping applications remember either in databases or as cookies on customer systems exactly who we are and what we might be interested in buying. We even find ourselves under the scrutiny of cameras on public buildings that match our features with face recognition software to see if our location may need extra attention.

While people seem to want to collect ever-increasing amounts of data values, they also want to have it manipulated into information and knowledge in order to provide aggregates, trends, logic-driven prioritizations, derivations, and associations to other aspects of importance about the data (metadata). To support those desires, we need to analyze and model the targeted data in order to document meaning and build storage structures that support different styles of software design and functionality, such as the following:

- **Online transactional processing (OLTP)**: Event-by-event-driven data capture

- **Online analytical processing (OLAP)**: Specially organized data sets to support analytical pattern assessment

- **Operational data stores (ODS)**: Timely data collections usually used for reporting

- **Data warehousing (DW)**: Historic data collections used for any number of uses

To support these increasingly complex analyses, we need to better understand, manage, anticipate, and control data. The software that allows all these increasingly complex algorithms requires that the data is highly consistent and predictable. The understanding, management, anticipation, and control of data are all enhanced by proper data modeling and proper database design.

Our current view of data value management tells us that we need to collect and store data in the most elemental, atomic, basic, and reusable parts possible. Only by doing that can we isolate data meaning and build relationships that support the creation of newly defined information. And since we frequently need to combine those basic data elements, we need to design appropriate storage and processing facilities that allow this to be accomplished. For instance, look at any date we use. The data value is made up of three pieces combined: the day number, month number, and year number. We hardly even consider that all dates are really three distinct data elements. Data modeling is concerned with recognizing and separating the meanings of those data elements so that you can easily relate, group, locate, or just recognize all the 2004 dates without having to separate that part of the meaning from the full data value of a date.

The process we use to discover those basic data elements, determine how they relate to each other today, and define them so that they can be recognized and interpreted in the future is called *data modeling*.

Data Management in History

Let's look at a severely abbreviated history of data to show our drive to find more efficient ways of recording, collecting, ordering, searching, and protecting data. People have been working on these tasks for more than 5,000 years, and these tasks are still relevant today. Data management isn't just about computers and electronic information. It's also about our need to find and reuse information and to build knowledge that can be shared with future generations.

Language: The Origin of Data

Language, in its most generic interpretation as a useable communication medium, is the most recognized raw material from which data is created. Spoken language is much older and more mysterious than written language. It took quite some time for humans to discover a method of capturing the content and meaning of what was said in a form that would support gathering collections of persistent "data." In other words, it was a while before we started writing things down.

Writing became an important tool for dealing with the practical day-by-day economic, social, and administrative affairs of urban collections of people around 3500 BC. To continue to survive and flourish, people realized they needed better records and data management capabilities than the soft tissue between their ears permitted.

Sumerians developed the first widely used written language. Called *cuneiform*, it consisted of a series of little arrowhead shapes pointed in different directions. A shocking 95 percent of the document samples from that era, accumulated by archeologists, is economic in nature. Existing cuneiform records, in the form of stone tablets, are largely tallies, accounts, and records relating to personal property and temple business—data values that needed collection and maintenance to allow assessment and reporting on the local economy.

But early languages, such as cuneiform, weren't sophisticated enough for people. Symbols and pictograms weren't flexible enough to represent all the data people wanted to capture.

So written language transformed further, from pictograms to hieroglyphs and ultimately to symbols that could represent phonetic sounds. With these phonetic symbols, a spoken language and written language became much more closely tied. Now people could record songs, stories, and descriptions of life processes in subject areas from medicine to metallurgy, and they could develop sophisticated cultural artifacts such as poetry and literature.

Around 3200 BC the process of writing further evolved with the invention of a flexible writing material, made from the pith of the papyrus plant. This new material (the first type of paper) was much lighter than stone tablets but could still be awkward since it was generally used in the form of long strips, rolled up into scrolls. This meant you'd basically have to search an entire document to locate the single piece of information for which you were looking. Every request for data was pretty much a full document search!

Collecting and Organizing

As certain civilizations thrived, and in their growth absorbed other groups, reading and writing became even more important as a critical communication tool. As more and more data was recorded, people started to create larger and larger collections of it. The gathering piles of scrolls containing an ever-increasing quantity of information became rather like sand dunes. Each fact was a grain of sand that grew over time into mountains of great width and depth. They became proof of the human need to remember—and the databank came into being.

In the dictionary, a *databank* is defined as "a large collection of stored records from which data may be extracted or organized as desired." The operative words here are *extracted* and *organized*. Great collections of data weren't enough. There needed to be a way to easily extract key pieces of information from the mounds of scrolls.

In early 600 BC, King Ashurbanipal of Assyria wanted to accumulate and organize written records of Babylonian history in his library in Nineveh. When he finished, his library supposedly contained at least 5,000 stone tablets and scrolls, physically arranged by subject or type and organized in alcoves. A summary list of contents of each alcove was painted or carved on the alcove's entrance to serve as a catalog. While this was obviously not a very flexible design, he knew that having a large collection of data wasn't useful if you couldn't find the information for which you were looking.

Having data and being able to use it are two different things. Book and periodical catalogs, tables of contents, bibliographies, and cross-referencing indexes sprang into being almost as soon as collections of data were created, probably as a defensive measure by the information curators. Customers have always wanted data retrieved as quickly and successfully as possible.

Even within an individual scroll there were problems finding specific data. Locator structures such as book name or number, chapter number, and verse numbers were created to provide an address of sorts for specific information. These techniques were constantly evolving and being fine-tuned so that a librarian could accurately reference specific data using a location notation.

At the height of the Roman Empire, data storage evolved. The Romans found reading and writing those long, rolled-up scrolls to be troublesome, so they cut the parchment into pages and bound the pages together into the book form we still use today. They called it a *codex*. The design of the storage media (pages in a book) created a structure for the written material captured upon it. A page number could be used as a locator number for data values. You could navigate straight to the general location of the data without having to unroll the whole scroll.

In the tenth century, the Grand Vizier of Persia took his 117,000-volume library on the road with him. He insisted that the camels carrying his precious library be trained to walk in alphabetical order to preserve his ability to find his favorite volumes, even during the trip. Again, organization and knowledge of what was in the collection was of paramount importance to him.

After the Jesuits were dissolved in 1773, all the books they had collected were moved to a vacant church for storage. When the mice that plagued the church kept chewing on the books, the books were sorted by importance, with the most important being placed on shelves in the center of the storage room. All the other books were then stacked on the floor encircling the center shelves. The strategy was to let the mice gnaw away at the books on the floor, leaving those on the central stacks, which had been identified as being more important, alone.

Data organization and management has evolved throughout history. It has become easier and easier to discover the answer to our ever-expanding list of questions. Our insatiable need for information has increased as the media and processes that are used to capture and copy data become faster and less expensive. How many of us use the text search functions on the Internet to find information about just about anything? Data collection and storage have become part of our daily lives, and we're not just interested in mission-critical data but also in little details once thought unimportant. We're now able to capture, store, and retrieve detailed data, such as what products are bought together at grocery stores at 10 a.m. on Mondays or how many adult tickets were purchased for G-rated movies. We admit to having difficulty in subjectively calling any data unimportant—importance is in the eye of the data customer. We collect, organize, and correlate data about almost everything. It seems to be part of human nature.

Note Human data needs are getting broader and richer all the time.

Libraries and the library sciences have been at the forefront of data and information management. They were the first to tackle the challenges of managing collections of data, information, and knowledge. Even today many terms from the library sciences and the book publishing communities are used to describe facets of computer science and computerized data management, such as *coding*, *paging*, *indexing*, *cataloging*, and *referencing* data. Thus, today's media (electronic storage) and techniques (database management systems) are really just the tools and techniques of a point in time of the evolution of data management.

Data values, which began as a physical record used to remember something important about an event or thought, were handwritten, painstakingly reviewed, and artistically illuminated. What were at first rare and special artifacts of the educated and elite have became natural and unavoidable products of our lifestyles. We struggle now because so much data exists that it is hard to care about all of it. This makes the ability to target specific values or filter large collections an increasingly important task.

In today's world of data collecting, not all data passes through human hands anymore. Sometimes this is good, since it eliminates transcription errors and inherent subjectivity or bias. On the other hand, in doing this we have removed the natural quality checks such as human reasonability factors and judgment.

The following is a quote from Sir Josiah Stamp (1880–1941), who was head of the Inland Revenue Department of the United Kingdom:

The government are very keen on amassing statistics. They collect them, add them, raise them to the nth power, take the cube root, and prepare wonderful diagrams. But you must never forget that every one of these figures comes in the first instance from the village watchman, who puts down what he damn well pleases.

These days, we try to avoid the village watchman technique of gathering data. We've invented mechanical servants to do those mundane tasks for us. Machines count at turnstiles, record temperatures, log site visits, and capture data for our use without a single complaint. (OK, they do fail us from time to time, but you never hear them griping about writing yet another copy of data, do you?) They've created mountains of distinct facts that never get used except as members of an aggregation.

So how important is it to be careful about organizing and managing all that data? After all, how problematic is it if we're left with data that doesn't easily satisfy the data customers' needs? Only your data customers can really answer this type of question.

So, again, why talk about the origin and history of data management? Well, this book will cover only one of the current techniques you can use to make sure data is high quality, reusable, and the right raw material to support the creation of information and knowledge. That technique is to model the data relationally before you begin collecting and storing it and to design repositories for data with a full understanding of how your data customers need to be supported. Relational modeling is one technique that allows you to manage your electronic data effectively, to communicate concepts, and to leverage approximately five millennia of experience organizing and accessing data.

What Is Relational Data Modeling?

Relational data modeling is a skill set, a collection of processes, and a set of techniques that records the inventory, shape, size, contents, and rules of data elements used in the scope of a business process to build a complete representation of that scope. The business process scope may be as large as a multidiscipline global corporation or as small as receiving boxes on a dock. The final product is something like a map accompanied by all the backup documentation needed to interpret the data used by that business process with complete clarity.

Some models are built to document high-level business concepts and are termed *Conceptual* models. Some are built to document the theoretical purity of data element rules and structure and are called *Logical* models. And maybe the best-known type of data model, called a *Physical* model, is the type that determines the actual design of a database. This model is the basis of the code written to create tables, views, and integrity constraints. These three basic types connect to each other loosely and can support each other as different views of a single business process.

Many other types of models are in use to analyze what needs to be known in a software development or process improvement project, including the following:

- **Activity modeling**: Decomposition of high process to details with triggers and products

- **Process flow**: Sequencing and dependencies of hardware, software, and networks

- **Use case**: Functionality descriptions

- **Data integration**: Mapping source and target

We're focusing on basic data modeling—what data we are talking about (inventory of elements), how it fits together (rules of behavior and relationships), and what it looks like (shape, size, and so on).

A data model doesn't provide the full complement of back-end code that needs to be built to support an application. It doesn't contain security grants or database link code. It doesn't show sizing and space needs (although some modeling software will let you add those aspects). The data model is a basis for developing the blueprint for a database, *not* the database itself. It's a cornerstone of the development effort but only one of the building blocks of designing an application.

The process of modeling can capture a representation of something that exists, the *As-Is* state of your physical data, so that you can view how the data is structured in an existing database and what rules the database manages in an environment today. These views are generally restricted to a single application or a set of tables in a restricted schema such as a database. It could take hundreds of them to fully document the scope of an enterprise, for example. It could also take hundreds of Logical models to describe the more theoretical rules of the data, rather than how they were physically implemented. Similarly, many Conceptual models could cover all the business processes, but it's more likely at the higher level of the Conceptual model than it is at the other stages to attempt to cover all the enterprise activities in a single view.

Note A model helps you view how you want to manage data in the future, how you do it now, or how you did it in the past (change control).

Data modeling is also used to create designs for something new, the *To-Be*. Sometimes we create multiple To-Be designs and the development team chooses which one to implement.

Note You model to try options. It isn't always easy to know the right one. Heed the words of H. L. Mencken: "For every problem, there is a solution that is simple, neat, and wrong."

However, whatever it's used for, data, in its elemental form, needs to be understood and should be cared for with a disciplined approach to its management throughout its term of usefulness for the business. Before we continue covering data modeling techniques, we'll present the life cycle of a typical data element.

Understanding the Data Life Cycle

What follows are the stages that new data goes through on its way from being used as a recent fact to becoming a historic fact and eventually to becoming a forgotten fact. (The latter is a stage in the life cycle that we're having increasing difficulty believing in because of repeated requests by clients to unearth their archived data or restore it from backups.)

This isn't the life cycle of an application development project, but many other processes can go through similar stages. Figure 1-1 shows the steps through which every data element goes.

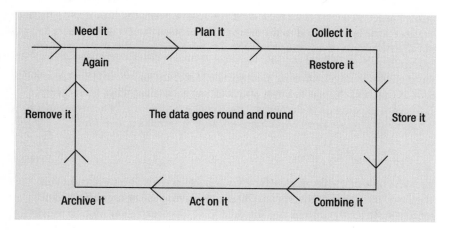

Figure 1-1. *Data values and data element life cycle*

Need It

This is the point in time where someone asks for some data. What was the temperature in Des Moines, Iowa, yesterday? How many candy bars were bought before the PG-rated movies last week? How many parking spaces are going to be available before second shift shows up?

Let's consider the example of a credit card transaction charge-back fee amount. Say you're a small retail firm, and you want to begin accepting credit cards to pay for purchases. You contact several credit card companies to find out how to do this. You discover that different companies charge different fees for using their services, and even the fees differ under different circumstances such as cash advances vs. payment overdue fees. You realize that to understand what the provision of this service to your customers is going to cost you, you need to collect the service fee for each transaction separately to be able to better analyze profitability. This recognition of the need for a data element is step one.

Almost no data element is captured just because it exists. To bring it to life, it needs to be of value to someone, or there at least needs to be belief in a future value. As you find out what impact the new data element has on the organization, you may discover other data elements also need to be available.

The Need It phase is the recognition of a new fact, which needs to be available in order to accomplish a task. You now know you need a Credit Card Transaction Charge-Back Fee Amount to assess profitability in your business, determine return on investment (ROI) by looking at service usage and cost, and even plan next year's budget. So what happens after you know you need it?

Plan It

In this stage, you explore and analyze the data element you need to collect. You ask questions about frequency, size, and business rules. You explore methods of capturing and storing it. You investigate security, reliability, and quality issues.

You ask questions such as, how much can a credit card transaction charge-back fee amount be? Is it determined by the amount of the sale and so presented as a percent? Is it a flat fee per transaction? Do you know what the service charge to your store will be when the customer makes a credit purchase using their charge card? Is it applied transaction by transaction, or is the store charged at a later time in bulk? If you're charged later, how do you tie it to the individual transaction? Is it credited to the store so the amount could be a plus or a minus value? Generally, hundreds of questions arise to discover and plan for the true nature and business requirements of the data element.

When you're in this Plan It stage, you look at all sorts of different aspects of the data element and document as much as there is to know about this new data element, including where you think it fits with existing data elements. This may be in the form of a formal specification or a lively brainstorming session. What happens after you make a plan for it?

Collect It

The Collect It stage is the part of the life cycle where you check to see if you were right and then implement the plan. It's a time of testing and finally deploying the chosen method of data creation. You must sufficiently understand the data to at least draft a solution to the data requirements and to be able to verify that the plan is going to work.

For this example, you start a collection of credit card transaction charge-back fee amounts and see if you learned enough to manage them properly. Sometimes this means you end up discovering you need more data elements or you didn't plan for this one properly. This testing happens every time a new value (a real instance of the data element) comes into your hands to manage. You may find that things run smoothly for a period of time and then changes in the billing style of the credit card company impact your understanding, use, and definition of this data element. When that happens, the plan for the data element changes. None of these stages in the life cycle has to be sequential. Loopbacks can happen innumerable times.

So now you feel comfortable that you have the process of collection of credit card transaction charge-back fee amounts right. What next?

Store It

After collecting a certain amount of data, you must decide how to store it, possibly using different techniques to support different processes. For example, you may need a focused, simple, little data store, such as an Extensible Markup Language (XML) file to collect real-time data. However, you also need a larger, more complex one to support the compilation of all the little data sets into one for corporate reporting. Imagine that the data elements are originally collected in dozens of little individual credit card scanners that are polled on a periodic basis. Those data values may need to be applied correctly to the sales data from the cash registers and finally aggregated and sent on to a different environment. Security or accessibility issues may require parallel storage (in case of power or equipment failure).

This is another point at which it's critical to monitor the process by which you'll collect this data element, with particular regard to correctness and to performance requirements. You're striving for a process that's accurate and reliable so that the Credit Card Transaction Charge-Back Fee Amount is correctly collected and stored each time, but at the same time you may be required to be sensitive to adding undue complexity (and therefore time) to the sale completion process.

But once you've collected and stored it to your satisfaction, what happens next?

Combine It

This is where you start to use the data element to your advantage. This is a maturing of the data element itself. After it has been defined to the team's satisfaction, new ways to use it should start to spring up, especially if the data element is a timely and reliable addition to the inventory of business data elements. Equally, any problems with the original analysis will have become apparent and need revising. This is a time of integration with other data elements, sometimes even in other data collections with a new generation of highly complicated report writing. The more the data element is requested for use, the more confident you can be that it was well-defined to satisfy the requirements.

The Credit Card Transaction Charge-Back Fee Amount becomes a new variable, additive fact, or decision point in the sales, marketing, finance, and accounting departments. The new data element could become a popular new addition to the data element resource pool for the enterprise. It's referred to in the formula for gross sales and net sales. The data warehousing team is asked to provide it in the monthly sales fact table. It becomes a part of the never-ending thirst for better understanding of the enterprise's health.

So after it's aggregated, averaged, sliced, diced, racked, and stacked in reports and on screens all over the company, what can it do?

Act on It

Data elements can become the foundation for business action. They can even become the foundation for a new series of data elements that are used like a dashboard of combined data elements provided to influence decisions. You can achieve this stage only if you understand the data and it becomes a cornerstone of the data collection for the client. In combination, data elements can be the basis for business information and ultimately business knowledge. This is the crowning achievement for a piece of data. It has been proven to be a quality fact and can be relied on to support a decision. This data should have an auditable pedigree (traceable origin and processing) in order to stand the scrutiny of doubt if the action doesn't get the expected results. In other words, you'd better know where it came from and who thought it was a true fact.

This is, of course, the targeted goal of data: to be useful.

The Credit Card Transaction Charge-Back Fee Amount can become the basis for a large decision, such as another new program to provide a bank debit function for customers, which could be less expensive to the company than the charges from credit cards. It can become the basis for daily small decisions, such as offering discounts for cash sales of less than a certain value. It may even become the basis for a decision to cancel the credit card program and become the reason for its own removal from the data element inventory.

However, once the data element has established itself as a useful addition to the company data resource, what do you do with it?

Archive It

Now the data values have become a sizeable data set. The next step in the life cycle is to begin the process of archiving or preserving backup and historic copies for security, for restorability (in the case of disasters), and for reducing the bulk in the production data sets. Once data values have depreciated in relevance and value (sometimes that just means they're too old to be referenced daily), they're usually transferred to a nearby storage area. Only the data clients (people who use the data values) can determine how old a data value should be to be archived. Archiving data is fraught with its own challenges. How should the data be archived? How accessible should it be? How safe should the archive be? Should it be saved in the same format, in the same structure, and according to the same rules as the "live" data?

The `Credit Card Transaction Charge-Back Fee Amount` from the current week are critical to have available; the ones from last month are less so. The individual values from two years ago have almost lost their value. They may have value now only in an aggregated form for trend reporting.

You can begin to take slices of data from the production systems and archive them in several ways. A data warehouse may keep a larger set of older data than any other application in the company, but even it may need to resort to removing transaction-level details into various data storage tools that support accessibility performance at an appropriate level.

This is the golden retirement stage of data values. They can still be useful but are no longer of immediate relevance. What happens when the data values or whole data elements finally become obsolete?

Remove It

Well, you delete them from all live environments. They fall off everyone's list of responsibilities. They may not be deleted the way you think of a transaction deleting a record, but they're gone for all intents and purposes from anyone's ability to use them. Over time their very existence fades away. Data values and data elements get tossed out when they're no longer of value. Tapes are erased, backups deleted, and whole collection tools (such as old applications, measuring devices, and storage devices) are scrapped. Even if the data still exists (say, on an 8-inch floppy), the means to retrieve it may no longer be available.

This is the "rest in peace" stage of data. The amount of data in our landfills is probably staggering, but our perception of the value has changed over time. It's hard now to conceive of any data being worthless. But we do know that we still come across bone piles of tapes, disks, and clunky old machines that contain data values and collections that exist nowhere else, so it seems appropriate to note that this stage still exists in the life of a data element.

When credit cards no longer exist, the `Credit Card Transaction Charge-Back Fee Amount` will be as useful as a collection of payroll information from 1912. Only historians will be interested, and they will be interested in only samples, not all of it. But that leads us into the next step that can happen to a data element.

Need It Again

This is where the data archeologists come in. Sometimes a need shows up for old data values and data elements, or at least for the ability to pull a restricted selection of data elements out of data sets no one thought anyone would need and were deleted.

The data miners want to get a view of data over as much as ten or twenty years to look for trends between outlying factors and the behavior of company data. It seems that as soon as we decide no one needs something anymore and we toss it into a deep ocean trench, someone wants it back again. It was this need that really brought data warehousing to the importance it has today. Unfortunately, even a data warehouse team has to pick and choose what it keeps based on the *known* understanding of need. You still lose data from lack of having an identified customer for it.

So you could say this is a rediscovery stage of data. It's usually extremely painful, and often expensive, to try to satisfy, because nobody planned for it. It's seldom that you can find a map of where data treasure is buried. Almost no one archives the metadata with the data sets. But once you sift through enough and rediscover what you're looking for, you need to restore it.

Restore It

The Restore It stage is the hard part if you haven't planned for an eventuality of this nature. This is the point where someone has to figure out how to get data from files or media where the access tools don't exist anymore. Here you try to bring it back to life. You usually have to deal with the extra burden of lost understanding about the nature and rules of the data (in other words, it may have to be analyzed to be understood again) as well as media corruptions and lack of usable tools.

Just think of how expensive it has become to read, collate, understand, and use all that rediscovered Sumerian financial data!

How a Data Model Helps

We've talked about the life cycle of data because helping to manage and understand the company's use of data elements is what data modeling is. Data models can help you in every stage of the life cycle of data, bearing in mind that they need to be built differently according to the support requirement of the task in mind. Throughout iterations of these steps, you can use the model to help explain your understanding of the data to the client. This works both as a reality check (do I understand your business properly?) and as a prompt to show what's missing in your understanding. This is particularly important during the first few stages of the life cycle.

In the Need It stage, when the requirements are being gathered, you can build a high-level concept model to explain high-level business processes and the data elements needed to support them. It captures the definitions, descriptions of "business world" vocabulary, and interview notes about the basic rules and known exceptions.

In the Plan It stage, you assess all the little details of each data element needed to support the requirements in the preliminary analysis. You discover and document them in the data model with focus on their data domains, definitions, and nullability. You can gather enough information to build actual data structures for the design and test stages of a project. The model in this stage is an evolving blueprint of the design and definition of many aspects of a data element.

In the Collect It stage, the data model can define test and verification scenarios for business rules you defined earlier where you exercise actual data values in insert, update, and delete processing. You can actually build small subsets of the model that ease the ability to trace "what if?' examples through the boxes and lines, discovering timing and security issues before trying it with an application.

In the Store It stage, you can use many data models of the various local data structures as a part of the requirements document to create a separate global repository. It's also the real test of whether the estimates are correct that those concerned with hardware and physical storage made to determine how much disk space is necessary. If data needs to be relocated, the model will confirm the basic rules required for the storage system.

In the Combine It stage, a model can act like a menu and list all the ingredient options and how they can be combined. Without a model as a map of what to choose, you're dependent on what the person assigned to help remembers. You can create a submodel with all the necessary elements to visually document the combination.

In the Act on It stage, a model can be one half of the pedigree map. It can document from which application, table, and column the data was pulled. You can document the original creation process in the form of an external (screen field) to internal (table column) map. The data definitions and rules can document the quality and integrity goals of the structure. Stewardship and security measures may also be a part of the model documentation. You therefore can add the model as part of the backup documentation for audit purposes.

In the Archive It stage, the data model can show the original and archived resting spots of the data element. It can show the structure with its rules and definitions of the data elements at the time of archival for later review in the case of restoration.

In the Remove It stage, the data model can document the targeted full database, selected tables or columns, or locations of data being proposed for surgical removal. You can use it as a map or catalog of the chosen deletions to be able to understand what they were when they were used.

In the Need It Again stage, models that were archived along with the data can refresh everyone's memory of what was actually archived. It can assist in targeting one specific area of data need rather than having to simply bring everything back from the grave.

In the Restore It stage, you can use the data model to build new data structures to which the data can return. They may not be named exactly the way they used to be because of uniqueness conflicts. You may need to plan a whole new structure for the return engagement.

We've covered what data is and how you can use models to manage it. Now let's put a face on the data modeler role.

Who Are the Data Modelers in Most Organizations?

This can be a tough question to answer. Finding the people in your organization with data modeling skills in their toolbox can be a challenge. Different companies use different titles for this position and frequently append this skill to the job description of different job titles.

■**Note** Data modeling is often an additional skill set rather than a full-time job (not because there isn't enough work to keep a modeler busy, more because of the way department responsibilities have evolved).

Defining the Role

Data modeling as a profession doesn't seem to have established its own persona like database administrators (DBAs) or programmers. We've completely given up writing *data modeler* in occupation blanks on forms. Yet it's a profession unto itself, with its own internationally recognized professional organization, Data Management Association (DAMA), at www.dama.org. Plus, the skill of data modeling is brought up over and over in database development books as the discipline of choice toward building a quality database. You can find data modelers doing the following, with or without a title that highlights the modeling skill set:

- Documenting, designing (conceptually, logically, or physically), and improving

- Guiding and advising

- Auditing/enforcing

- Analyzing and researching

- Communicating

You'll now look at a few metaphors that could be used to describe the data modeler's role.

Photojournalist

Think of data modelers as photographers for *National Geographic*. Depending on the assignment, the photographers are taking pictures of deep space nebulas or inner space neutrons. They take pictures documenting reality at any level of detail and give the viewer the ability to find answers. Those beautiful, colorful, simple images provide easily recognized documentation that captures the drama happening at that moment or explains a natural phenomenon about the subject. What would you do without pictures of your As-Is (current state) life?

A photographer does a similar job of someone *documenting* data structures already in existence (so-called As-Is data structures). The art of photography doesn't simply reflect true life but adds a little something, helping your understanding of the subject. Photographers use their skills to highlight and emphasize aspects that show the subject from a particular viewpoint and focus your attention on something they've found to be important.

The data modeler working to document the current state of the enterprise data is constantly updating a library of information relating to data elements, what they are, where they're used, how they're built, what they mean, and all the details referring to their physical nature (data type, size, precision, default values, and so on). The level of detail varies depending on the audience and purpose of the model, and much of the documentation can be shown in a graphic, as you'll see in examples throughout the book.

Architect

Now think of the data modeler as an architect. Architects work to understand the owner's requirements, intended use, budget, resources, and future plans for a building. An architect would develop the blueprints for a museum and research facility in a way that would differ from a bakery or auto factory, since each design has to take into account multiple parameters. Then the architect oversees construction from a consultant and validation point of view. The architect stays a part of the build team and iteratively changes the design if problems arise.

A data structure architect describes someone *designing* a new data model, as you would in custom development projects. That architect may have to balance all sorts of conflicting requirements. The design ultimately chosen is a professional suggestion of how to mitigate the risks and enhance the strengths inherent to the data. These are To-Be (future state) designs. Quite frequently, several are offered to the clients and reviewed to find the appropriate final choice.

The data modeler working to build for the future is trying to design the best solution to a business problem. The solution may need to focus on flexibility, security, process improvement, data quality, or all of these. Solutions can be elegant or inelegant. Data modelers are trying to find the best solution that balances elegance, simplicity, flexibility, and so on, and also the strengths, weaknesses, and understanding of the development team that must consume the model. (A perfect design that the development team is unable to understand or unwilling to accept isn't helpful.) Architects have to come up with the "best" design they can, given the constraints imposed upon them. They use their models of the As-Is state of the data elements to discover the shortcomings and new data elements that are now needed. They may create a new solution or create a delta design that's an upgrade.

R&D Engineer

Research and development (R&D) engineers (say, in the auto or aerospace industry) frequently take existing machines, tools, or systems and try to make them better. They find ways to streamline steps and lower the energy requirements. They're constantly looking for ways to reduce moving parts to simplify construction and increase maintainability. They want to increase safety and reliability and satisfy new standards. And they want to reduce failure points to the lowest possible level while supporting critical parts with the highest amount of protection. Their prototypes are usually mini To-Be proposals of solutions sent to a committee for review and approval.

This metaphor describes the enterprise focus of an *improvement* style of data modeling. Data is an asset of the company. Ask any members of the finance department if they wouldn't prefer all assets be maintained as inexpensively for as long a life as possible. A data modeler acting as an R&D engineer will generally work only with Physical data models. They will probably start with an As-Is issue of some kind and follow it with one or more proposed To-Be solutions.

Reference Librarian

Data modelers are people who it would be appropriate to approach if you were looking for a specific type of data. They can be the reference librarians of corporate data elements, especially if there's no metadata management team. At the very least they know all their own designs inside and out.

Librarians ask you all sorts of questions about what you need. They head off to the various indexes and files and pull up all sorts of interesting references and descriptions of what you're looking for along with the locators of those references. They help point you in the right direction. The data reference librarian can be analytical and frequently creates several custom submodels, incorporating data elements from multiple systems and sources, to be used for *guidance* to lead the way to new questions, research, and discoveries.

Business Consultant

Given a complete and detailed enough set of requirements, a data business consultant can look at the specs of a project and provide feedback as to the company's ability to meet them, especially from the relationship rules built into a database design. The data business consultant can help solve a "make or buy?" decision. They provide *advice*, or perhaps a complete functional review of a software tool, from a content and data restriction viewpoint. Frequently this has to be done with the help of a vendor if the database design or Logical model of the tool is unavailable or private.

Buildings Inspector

Another metaphor of a data modeler can be that of an inspector. Inspectors enforce rules issued by a higher authority in regard to a process, structure, or environment. Data modelers can do the same thing in an organization. They're frequently part of a review team that enforces naming, structure, use, integration, or data element definition standards for an enterprise.

Data buildings inspector is one of our least favorite roles to perform. It doesn't help you make friends, but it can be as vitally important as any of the other policing and monitoring functions that are needed to keep everyone honest. However, it's a part of the world of modeling, and you may find inspectors in an *audit* function in your corporation, attempting to enforce data management department development rules.

Private Investigator

Data sleuthing, or *researching*, is another major role that data architects play during the analysis phase of a project. Actually, this is one of our favorite roles to play. Digging into existing data stashes and coming up with real rules as to how the data is actually working to make the business successful is a great feeling. We're constantly finding ourselves in a state of awe and respect for how the business clients have managed to take an existing inflexible software application that no longer is in line with their processes and force it into doing what they need it to do.

Interpreter/Negotiator

Sometimes the most important role is making sure that the business, the developers, the DBA, and the clients are all talking and understanding each other. The interpreter/negotiator works to *communicate* problems, issues, and solutions in a way that can be well understood by all parties while resolving potential problems because of vocabulary choice. Business terms are strewn with language challenges, and the data modeler is in a perfect position to recognize the potential conflicts and mitigate them. Some of our favorite culprits are the following:

- **Acronyms**: Abbreviated title generally using first letters (generally not really understood or reused for different meanings based on context)

- **Synonyms**: Different words with the same meaning

- **Homonyms**: Same word with different meanings

A Data Modeler Charter

The metaphors listed previously for the skills a data modeler may have are just examples. Many groups responsible for these skills have to include many more aspects to their department charter. However, it's important to be careful about the wording of a department charter. You have to have the authority as well as responsibility to be able to be successful.

Mostly, a data modeler just wants to make life easier for people who need to use data as a second language so they can leave at 5 p.m. every day to go play baseball with their kids, for example. If people can depend on the documentation and designs that the data modeler can provide, they can cut their R&D time down considerably.

Enterprise Data Modeler Charter

Data modelers who are chartered to work from an enterprise overview perspective take on responsibility for more strategic goals in the company, including the following:

- Taking responsibility for the enterprise data element inventory (as opposed to data value inventory, which would be the data stewards) and structure of the past, present, and future

- Documenting, designing, researching, guiding, auditing, and/or inspecting enterprise data elements and creating a high-quality set of metadata to describe the As-Is environment

- Enabling and empowering efficient, safe, maintainable, reliable, quality data structure development for the creation, maintenance, and accessibility of To-Be enterprise data assets

Project Data Modeler Charter

Data modelers who are working on OLTP systems often have a very different charter, involving balancing complexity, maintainability, efficiency, and other attributes. These goals may be quite different (and sometimes conflicting) from the goals and objectives of an enterprise data group. Their success factors are generally more tactical in nature.

- Taking responsibility for tasks in a data project regarding the data element inventory and structure of the past (As-Is) and future (To-Be). These tasks should be completed within the enterprise standards and project schedule. They should satisfy business requirements as completely as possible or manage deviations by providing viable alternate solutions to the development team.

- Documenting, designing, researching, guiding, auditing, and/or inspecting each project data element and creating a high-quality set of metadata as a part of the project deliverable to support enterprise goals.

- Encouraging, enabling, and empowering efficient, safe, maintainable, reliable, quality data structure development for the creation, maintenance, and accessibility of To-Be enterprise data assets.

Job Titles

It's always fun to find out what the world calls people with your skill set these days and find out what skills they bundle with it. We did a simple search for *data modeling* on Monster.com for the United States, and the following is what we found for one day of listings. It has gotten so that we don't know what to call ourselves anymore.

- Application developer/architect

- Business enterprise architecture data modeler

- *Data administrator*

- *Data architect*

- Data engineer

- Data manager

- *Data modeler/analyst*

- Data modeling engineer

- Database administrator

- Enterprise data architect

- *Information analyst*

- Programmer/analyst

- Software developer

- Systems analyst

The job titles in italics are the ones we consider the better titles for data modelers. The key point to note is that most modelers don't perform just one task. Their jobs are combinations of tasks, and data modelers are found all over an enterprise. They often span the design/analysis/maintenance of databases, hardware/software/network architecture, application development, data management department standards, and policy management. In fact, data modeling is bundled with a wide and varied set of skills. Some of the core skills of data modeling (ability to conceptualize, ability to analyze, and ability to make design judgments) are really critical skills for the entire IT industry.

■**Note** Data modeling is often combined with other skills to create composite job titles and descriptions. This can make figuring out if you should apply for a data modeling job difficult to assess.

Understanding As-Is Support

Data modeling tasks generally fall into one of two areas. They deal with what's now or what could be in the future. We call these areas *As-Is* and *To-Be*.

■**Note** As-Is tasks require discipline and orderliness. They're often repetitive, such as auditing the current state of a database, and systematic, such as profiling all the data values in a production system.

As-Is tasks tend to be included in several areas such as supporting configuration management, providing impact analysis, promoting data management departmental standards, providing data integrity analysis, and researching existing techniques and tools. The data modeler also answers questions about existing data relationships or metadata. When they really know a subject area, they can sometimes become de facto subject matter experts (SMEs) to support other analysis efforts.

Support Configuration Management

Configuration management is the process of controlling what an environment is. It may be the hardware/software complement or the data elements in the databases loading on a piece of hardware. Sometimes it can even be the data values themselves—especially when special list values are crucial to the ability of the application to perform. Some companies have a whole department chartered to manage the configuration of at least the production data environment, but they may be managing the tools and content of several test environments as well. Data modelers participate in controlling data environment change, often through very detailed processes called *change control*. They maintain many different kinds of documentation tailored to fit the needs of the audience. These are the models, definitions, and mappings. They build and maintain the following:

- Enterprise-level conceptual data documentation

- Project logical data documentation

- Maps of data (Logical/Physical) objects into an enterprise data library

- Physical data object documentation

- Data element relationship rule documentation

- Risk assessments

- Documentation of data element security needs

- Extraction, transformation, and loading (ETL) source to target mappings and logic

Sometimes this documentation is kept under the same controls as production code. It may be assessed, but not updated, without going through the correct procedures of check out, change, test, QA review, approve, and check in.

Provide Impact Analysis

The data model library and metadata repository should be the first place an organization notices the ripple effects of enterprise data that has changed. Y2K would have been much easier for most of us if there had been a reliable central repository from which to start. The modeler can look for impacts to and from the following:

- Alterations to data element definition and physical details

- Alterations to existing functions changing data deliverables

- Retiring applications, procedures, interfaces, and concepts

- Incorporation of new applications, procedures, interfaces, and concepts

Promote Data Management Departmental Standards

Data modelers are card-carrying members of the data quality team. They constantly promote data and data design standards and are frequently called upon to participate in code, procedure, and document reviews. They frequently provide their expertise in the following areas:

- Assist in test plan creation to test for quality

- Plan integrity checks for denormalizations

- Promote proper relational integrity

- Promote standardized project documentation

- Promote names based on departmental standards and platform requirements

- Build definitions provided by the data element owner

- Promote standard sizes and data types

- Promote standard abbreviations

- Promote security for documented sensitive and critical data objects

- Promote standard nullability options

- Promote the creation and maintenance of documentation

Data modelers promote repeatability, consistency of data structure/content and consistency of use, data integrity, software-oriented data recoverability, and other features. The data modeler provides a holistic view of data and data management.

Provide Data Integrity Assessments

Data modelers may assess the suitability of data design to highlight necessary concerns over the existing data management environment, looking for areas of improvement in the following:

- **Supportability**: Is this structure appropriate for future needs?

- **Quality**: Does the existing structure promote quality data creation and updates?

- **Integrity**: Are there business rule checks at the database level?

- **Consistency and accuracy**: Do the data values make sense?

- **Enterprise appropriateness**: Is this structure suitable for your company (are you trying to force a manufacturing application to manage contract documentation)?

They may also participate in the quality assurance (QA) team by testing existing data sets or newly created processes for expected levels of integrity and quality. They frequently participate in testing data movement designs (extraction, transformation, and loading, or ETL) for source and target consistency. This is especially true if they helped design the mappings from one place to another and documented any transformation that needs to happen along the way.

Research Existing Techniques and Tools

Sometimes data modelers are tasked to be way out in front of the pack to review tools (including purchased software tools). These tools may be any data-related tool, such as ETL, data quality monitoring, metadata management, and others. They're often involved in doing early analysis and finding hidden or currently unknown data sources. This may mean they have to be proactive and nosy instead of just working by request. This may also mean they need access to people, applications, machines, and documentation from all levels in order to accomplish the task. They may need to be able to interview both the CEO and a local machinist, use the HR system in a test environment, or exercise a department's PC that they've set up to behave "just so." The data modeler needs an entrée to get their job done right, and without that, critical manually managed enterprise data in the form of spreadsheets, text documents, or local databases (and our favorites, the Post-it note stuck to the monitor or the laminated sheet of paper thumbtacked to the cube wall) can be overlooked, as those data sets are under the horizon of the data management department.

- Documenting business process/scope

- Document user requirements

- Mapping business processes to data objects

- Discovering critical data values not managed in enterprise-controlled tools (in other words, finding and documenting the local desktop application development)

Understanding To-Be Support

To-Be support is different. This looks at enterprise data with a view to the bright future of data management. To-Be support means designing, advising, and suggesting alternatives to the As-Is environment, which should be already fully documented in a three- or five-year plan put in place by senior management.

Note To-Be tasks involve creativity, vision, and innovative problem solving. They're less serial and more iterative, requiring a level of self-motivation, management, and a passion for problem solving.

Design New Data Structures

With the advent of object-oriented programming, data structures don't need to be necessarily persisted in a database. There may be data modeling work required during the creation of an XML schema or during the design of a series of internal memory-oriented structures that will be used by an application. Usually application developers do this work, but it's often as critical to the design of the application to get these data structures modeled accurately.

- Creating the planned enterprise Conceptual/Logical data view

- Designing data element structure fixes for change requests

- Designing new database architecture for custom development projects

Provide Expert Advice

Data modelers are often required to provide advice about proposed changes and may be asked to be responsible for at least documenting expected redundancy in data and/or duplication of effort when integrating new plans into the company's data environment. A data modeler's constant research of and exposure to the business data often makes them valuable sources of knowledge and options. Any advice you offer will need to be backed up with explanations and examples of what could happen if the choice goes one way or the other.

- Researching data element scope and provide options

- Providing recommendations about designs

- Suggesting a "make or buy?" decision

- Researching and providing a recommendation on data manipulation or software design tools

- Suggesting risk mitigation options, especially for denormalization decisions

Provide Alternatives

Often you're asked to provide a summary of choices, recognized deficiencies, and unresolved needs. You're also asked to provide data design alternatives, showing different ways that a potential change/improvement/fix can be represented, so that a decision can be made by all the interested parties (application developers, DBAs, data modelers, business analysts).

- **Plan integration**: Identifying and suggesting candidate data elements for integration

- **Plan of data organization**: Providing options in a one/five/ten-year enterprise data management plan

- **Plan of phased growth**: Group and document further enhancements in the form of phased rollout approached to gradually tackle large enterprise changes

Provide Expectation Assessments

You may assess the suitability of new data designs (purchase software decision support tasks) and check database designs for the following:

- Risk analysis

- Supportability

- Quality

- Integrity

- Enterprise appropriateness

Research New Techniques and Tools

The world of data management is broad and full of growth. Data modelers need to keep up with current developments to know if they're still making the right decisions and providing the best advice possible to their enterprise. They need to attend conferences, read journals, and develop a good network of others who can share experiences. They need to pay attention to the following new and evolving elements:

- Tools, including hardware and software

- Techniques, including modeling, programming, and designing

- Directions of the enterprise market

- Client goals

- Enterprise goals

- And whatever else might come in handy

Summary

You can use data modeling for much more than just building a new database. It can be an integral process in the management of the data life cycle. The model can be there at the conception, birth, life, death, and restoration of data. It's certainly a great design technique, but it's also a great cataloging technique. It has become more prominent in recent years, thanks to the increasing volume and complexity of data stored by individuals and businesses.

We've discussed the varied goals and team positions of data modelers and shown how they can be just about anyone involved in data management, since data modelers are involved in all aspects of data design, build, maintenance, and rediscovery.

You also looked at how to use modeling in an As-Is environment for the following:

- **Configuration management**: Every change is drafted, reviewed, approved, and acted on.

- **Impact analysis**: Every change is analyzed for ripples and given a cost.

- **Development standards**: Every structure is designed and reviewed for corporate consistency.

- **Quality review**: Every existing data element can be assigned a steward for quality, security, criticality, sensitivity, and integrity issues.

- **As-Is review**: The current enterprise data environment is researched.

And you learned how you can use it in To-Be conceptualization so that you can do the following:

- **Design new data structures**: Provide new solutions to data challenges.

- **Provide data design "make or buy?" advice**: With a data model of the business rules, you can compare the data model of a proposed vendor solution to verify a good match.

- **Provide alternatives**: Help to map directions for the future.

- **Assessments of what to expect**: Create risk analysis, supportability, quality, and integrity because of proposals.

- **Keep up with best practices**: Research new directions for data management.

■ ■ ■

CHAPTER 2

Introducing Relational Theory

In this chapter we'll introduce the realm of relational theory. Although relational theory is based on relational algebra and calculus, we won't go into any actual math or logic proofs of relational algebra, and we won't go into a complete discourse on set theory; however, we'll cover the foundation principles relational theory uses. We'll concentrate on the implications set theory has for data organization in order to illustrate the solid foundation upon which relational modeling is based.

We'll then review the process of normalization and the series of rules (the tests for normalization or normal forms) by which you can test the relational nature of your data organization. We'll finish by briefly introducing *denormalization*, the process by which you deliberately break some of the normalization rules in your design, to contrast ideal data organization based on normal forms with some of the more practical compromises (denormalizations) physical database designs frequently require.

In summary, this chapter covers the following:

- The nature of relational databases and how they differ from hierarchical and network database management systems (DBMSs)

- A brief overview of the relational approach to data modeling

- Codd's data management objectives and 12 rules of a relational database management system (RDBMS)

- Normalization, which includes working with data so that it adheres to the following:

  - Universal relations

  - First Normal Form

  - Second Normal Form

  - Third Normal Form

  - Boyce-Codd Normal Form

- Denormalization, including what it is and why you may want to do it, including examples of the following:

  - Derived columns

  - Deliberate duplication of data

  - Disabling constraints

Understanding Database Models

Before covering relational databases in more detail, we'll briefly cover hierarchical and network DBMSs. Understanding their limitations will help you understand the relational approach and how the approach attempts to address these limitations.

Hierarchical Databases

One of the hierarchical DBMSs still in use today is an IBM product called IMS, which stands for Information Management System. Its paradigm is to use a tree structure and a series of links to navigate from record type (a table) to record type. Records (single rows) include one or more fields (columns). Each tree must have a single *root*, or parent record type. The relationship between the record types is the same as the directory structure on your computer: parent to child, continuing onto lower and lower levels. The relationship is maintained as a DBMS *pointer* structure from one record to another. That pointer is valid for only one level of connectivity, and maintaining the order of the rows is required for the pointer to work.

As an example of this type of system, consider Figure 2-1, which illustrates a class-scheduling system at a college.

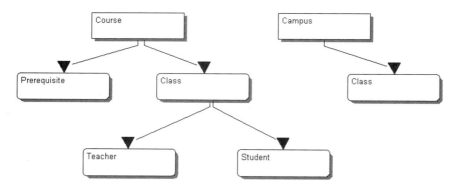

Figure 2-1. *Hierarchical class scheduling: record types connected in a tree structure*

This type of data management system has several challenges. One is the direct result of the restriction of being able to link only one parent to any children record types (such as Class in Figure 2-1). Look at the necessary duplication of Class because of its need to relate to both Campus and Course. A hierarchical DBMS (such as IMS) assumes the world can be viewed as a series of unrelated, strictly applied hierarchies, with one parent having many children within a tree structure. When this doesn't work (and there are many cases when you don't have exclusive classification), you end up with duplication of data across different tree structures. Workarounds for this usually require creating duplicate records or tables to satisfy each different use of the same data, which can lead to data synchronization problems, since the same records appear in numerous places within the database.

Another challenge with this type of design is the unnecessary duplication of records within a single record type and hierarchy. Look at the relationship of Student to Course. A student will often enroll for many courses, and the details of that student will be stored as a child of every course for which the student is enrolled.

One of the major limitations of this technology is that because of the technical difficulty inherent in setting up and navigating complex hierarchies within the physical database, the physical design is often implemented as a series of single-level parent-child relationships (root-child, root-child2, and so on), regardless of whether this actually represents the business rules of the data. The technological limitations with which the database administrators (DBAs) and programmers must work bias the implementation to the point where the hierarchies aren't implemented in the way the designers intended.

And unfortunately, because of the linage structures connecting the tables, you can't skip a level of relationship to find data. So, to get from Course to Teacher, you must perform additional input/output (I/O) operations and walk the tree down through Class. You can imagine that for a large database with complex hierarchies this would be a very long path. Furthermore, because these relationship paths aren't easy to change and new ones aren't easy to add, these databases become rather inflexible once the database is created.

However, in spite of these types of challenges, hierarchical DBMSs are still regularly used. They were popular in the 1960–70s, can still deliver high-performing systems, and are prevalent in legacy systems still in use today.

Network Databases

One of the big network databases still fairly common in data management is IDMS, which stands for Integrated Database Management Systems. Network databases were a logical extension of hierarchical databases and resolved the problem hierarchical databases had with child records having multiple parents.

The Conference on Data Systems Languages (CODASYL) in 1971 formally introduced the network model. Under this system, data management is based on mathematical "set" theory. A *data set* consists of an *owner record type*, a *set name*, and a *member record type*. A member record type basically corresponds to a data element in a row. The member record types can belong to various owner record types, thereby allowing for more than one parent relationship for a record. The owner record type can also be a member or an owner in another record type.

To address data sizing issues, data elements making up a record of a network design can be "redefined" to mean different things. This means that if a record has been defined as containing four data elements, such as A, B, C, and D, under some circumstances the fields within the record may be redefined to actually store the elements A, E, F, and G instead. This is a flexible construct, which reduces the amount of database structures and the amount of disk space required, but it can make locating and identifying specific data elements challenging. Also, one data element can be defined to "occur" more than one time on a record, allowing for the creation of a specific (and usually restrictive) number of multiples of a value or group of values to exist within a single record. The record type can be a complex structure even when looked at as a single construct and may hide some of the complexity of the data through the flexibility of its definition.

From a high level, the database design is a simple network, with link and intersection record types (called *junction records* by IDMS). The flexibility of this design provides a network of relationships represented by several parent-to-child pairings. With each parent-child pair, one record type is recognized as the owner record type, and one or more record types are recognized as member record types.

Revisiting the college database example from Figure 2-1, you could alter a network database design from the previous hierarchical example to allow Campus to be directly linked to Class through a second owner/member link, as shown in Figure 2-2.

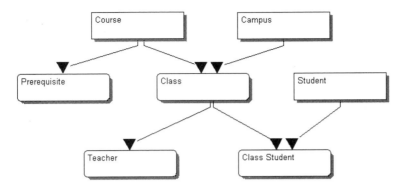

Figure 2-2. *Network class scheduling: record types connected in a modified tree structure and allowing more than one parent*

Network databases still have the limitations of pointer-type connections between the tables. You still need to step through each node of the network to connect data records. In this example, you still need to navigate from Campus to Teacher by way of Class. And the rows still have to be maintained in the order the pointer is expecting so that they function properly.

Relational Databases

Relational databases such as Oracle, Microsoft SQL Server, and IBM DB2 are different from both network and hierarchical database management systems in several ways. In a relational database, data is organized into structures called *tables*, and the relations between data elements are organized into structures called *constraints*. A table is a collection of records, and each record in a table contains the same data elements, or *fields*. Relational databases don't generally support multiple definitions of the fields or multiple occurrences within a single record, which is in contrast to network and hierarchical databases. The high-level properties of RDBMS tables are as follows:

- The value in a data element is single and atomic (no data replicates within a field, and data contained in a field doesn't require any interpretation).

- Each row is unique (no wholly duplicated records should exist within a set).

- Column values are of the same kind (a field's data doesn't have multiple definitions or permit "redefines").

- The ordinal sequence of columns in a table isn't significant.

- The ordinal sequence of rows in a table isn't significant, eliminating the problem of maintaining record pointers.

- Each column has a unique name within its owning table.

By connecting records through matching data contained in database fields rather than the pointer constructs (unlike network databases), and by allowing for child records to have multiple parents (unlike hierarchical databases), this type of design builds upon the strengths of prior database systems.

You'll see in more detail how this is achieved in a moment, but let's consider how the example would be represented in a relational database (see Figure 2-3).

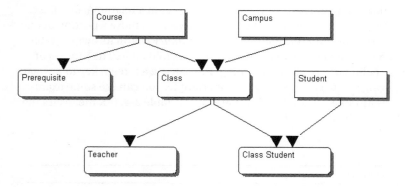

Figure 2-3. *A relational class scheduling—if all the business rules are the same*

It looks the same as the network database model, doesn't it? The network database management systems allow almost the same flexibility as a relational system in terms of allowable relationships. The power of this database paradigm lies in a different area. If you follow the rules of normalization (which we'll cover in detail in the "Introducing Normalization" section), you'd probably end up with a model that looks more like Figure 2-4.

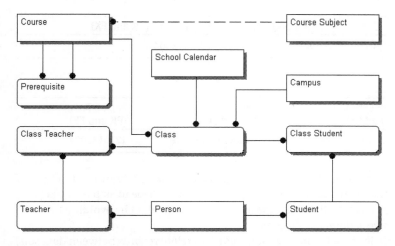

Figure 2-4. *A relational class scheduling—in Third Normal Form*

So, why is this model so different from Figure 2-3? This model ensures that only one set named Course is necessary, since it can be related to other courses in the event you need to set up a Prerequisite. In a similar fashion, teachers and students are recognized as being part of the single set Person, allowing a person, Isaac Asimov, to be both a Student and a Teacher of a Class. Relational design emphasizes storing information in one and only one place. Here, a single teacher record is reused for as many classes as necessary, rather than duplicating the teacher information for each class. We also created two new sets, Course Subject and School

Calendar, to group courses. This creates two new small sets to manage certain business rules in the database, rather than a code domain structure for subjects in the network database and a data format restriction to restrict Begin Date values to dates in Class.

The other big gain is that accessing records can also be simpler in a relational database. Instead of using record pointers to navigate between data sets, you can reuse a portion of one record to link it to another. That portion is usually called the *primary key* on its owning table, because of its identifying nature. It becomes a *foreign key* on the child table. The process of propagating the key to the child table is called *migrating*. You can use a foreign key to navigate back into the design, allowing you to skip over tables. For example, you can see some examples of possible data values in Table 2-1, Table 2-2, Table 2-3, and Table 2-4. (PK means it's the primary key, and FK means it's the foreign key.)

Table 2-1. Teacher

Teacher Name **(PK)**	Rating
Isaac Asimov	Most Excellent

Table 2-2. Campus

Campus Name **(PK)**	Campus Phone Number
Anaheim Satellite	714-663-7853

Table 2-3. Class

Course Name **(PK)**	Campus Name **(PK and FK)**	Begin Date **(PK and FK)**
Creative Writing 101	Anaheim Satellite	12/01/2004

Table 2-4. Class Teacher

Teacher Name **(PK and FK)**	Course Name **(PK and FK)**	Campus Name **(PK and FK)**	Begin Date **(PK and FK)**
Isaac Asimov	Creative Writing 101	Anaheim Satellite	12/01/2004

If you want to know the phone number of the campus where Isaac Asimov is attending the Creative Writing 101 class, you can use the foreign key of Campus Name to skip over Class and link directly with Campus. We've shortened the access path to the data by avoiding the pointer design used in network database designs.

The design characteristics of using natural data values to relate records between data sets, and the philosophy of building of simple understandable List of Values (LOV) sets for reuse as foreign keys, may be the most important characteristics contributing to the success of relational databases. Their potential for simplicity and understandability can make them nonthreatening and an easy technology to learn.

Notice the evolutionary nature of the database systems. Over time, each database management system built on the strengths of existing systems while attempting to address their restrictions.

Taking a Relational Approach to Data Modeling

Relational theory, which is used in relational database design and documented by a relational model, centers on the mathematical term *relation*. A relation, in this context, refers to two-dimensional tables that have single-valued entries, such as a spreadsheet. All data entries exist on a row in one or more columns. Data existing in a column is the same data element, which can be defined by a unique name, and has no positional or ordinal significance whatsoever. You may think the term *relational* is in reference to the use of relationships to link data sets (entities) and tables, but this isn't the case.

In spite of being referred to as a relational theory, it isn't a theory in the normal sense. It doesn't have a succinct, well-defined list of premise-conclusion statements. It wasn't originally written to explain data behavior in the context of data storage structures in place at the time (prior to relational theory, no RDBMSs existed). Relational theory was developed to propose rules for organizing data in a new way. The priority for this new data organization was to reduce redundancy and data maintenance anomalies. The reason it was called a *theory* was that these rules for organizing and storing data are based upon the mathematical concepts of relational set theory, which began to be explored in depth by George Cantor in the 1800s. This means that relational theory isn't just a database design standard, as you can use relational set theory techniques to document data characteristics without considering any physical deployment of a database platform. In fact, the mathematical set theory upon which relational databases are based predates modern electronic data storage. The concepts used by Dr. Edgar F. Codd to apply relational set theory to data storage provide sound analysis and documentation goals for describing the details of data element behavior in a business activity.

The relational model provides a data organization technique that allows for consistency in storing and retrieving data by using recognized mathematical operations. A good point to remember is that scientific models reflect a sort of theoretical perfection that no one ever achieves in reality (which results in the need to sometimes break the rules once you know when it's a good idea to do so).

■**Note** You can read more about the mathematics of relational theory in *An Introduction to Database Systems*, Eighth Edition (Addison-Wesley, 2003) by C. J. Date.

Origins of Relational Theory

In 1969, Codd, an IBM mathematician, wrote a groundbreaking report for his employees regarding storing large amounts of data. He expanded on these original thoughts in an article published the next year in *Communications of the ACM* (June 1970, pp. 377–387), which is usually considered as having been the starting point for research into relational modeling.

■**Note** You can find this article, "A Relational Model of Data for Large Shared Data Banks," at `http://www1.acm.org/classics/nov95/toc.html`.

A database, by Codd's definition, is "a collection of time-varying relations . . . of assorted degrees." *Relation* is used here in its mathematical sense as being simply a set of data, comprised of records. So, today we may say that a database consists of tables, which can contain records. These collections of records can change over time by insertion, deletion, and modification. These sets may have references to members of other sets through relationships. An instance or record of data is created and managed in only one set and is referenced everywhere else.

Notice that Codd doesn't mention computers or electronic formats in this definition. Databases, by this definition, are simply collections of data that can be organized relationally. You should also note that the writings of Codd didn't give us the art of data modeling, a graphical syntax for representing relational models, or a completely developed approach to relational modeling. He described only the concepts and laid the foundation, and that foundation has been built upon ever since.

Relational DBMS Objectives

You saw, from your brief look at nonrelational DBMSs, some of the challenges of both hierarchical and network database systems in terms of storing large amounts of data. Codd, while seeking to improve these database models, outlined a series of objectives for a "relational" DBMS in an invited paper to the 1974 International Federation for Information Processing (IFIP) Congress.

■**Note** You can find the article "Recent Investigations in Relational Data Base Systems" in *Information Processing 74, Proceedings of IFIP Congress 74*. Stockholm, Sweden: August 5–10, 1974 (ISBN 0-7204-2803-3).

These are the objectives for which he was striving:

- To provide a high degree of data independence

- To provide a community view of the data, of Spartan simplicity, so that a wide variety of users in an enterprise (ranging from the most computer naive to the most computer sophisticated) can interact with a common model (while not prohibiting user-specific views for specialized purposes)

- To simplify the potentially formidable job of the DBA

- To introduce a theoretical foundation (albeit modest) to the activity of database management (a field sadly lacking in solid principles and guidelines)

- To merge the fact or record retrieval and file management fields in preparation for the addition, at a later time, of inferential services in the commercial world (in other words, finding a new way of retrieving data other than using the single-level pointer structures)

- To lift data-based application programming to a new level, namely one in which sets (and more specifically relations) are treated as operands instead of being processed element by element

He goes on to list the four main components of his relational model. Codd said the motive for the establishment of data collections isn't to store knowledge altruistically for its own sake but to benefit the business by providing business clients with the data they need for their activities. And since this is true, why not treat the client data needs as the drivers for database development in the future? So, he therefore suggests that data should be organized to do the following:

- To simplify, to the greatest practical extent, the types of data structures employed in the principal schema (or community view)

- To introduce powerful operators to enable both programmers and nonprogrammers to store and retrieve target data *without having to "navigate" to the target*

- To introduce natural language (for example, English) methods with dialog box support to permit effective interaction by casual (and possibly computer-naive) users

- To express authorization and integrity constraints separately from the data structure (because they're liable to change)

Although the first commercial RDBMS was the Multics Relational Data Store (MRDS) launched in 1978 by Honeywell, it wasn't until the early 1980s that RDBMSs became readily available and Codd's concepts began to be tested.

What Are Codd's Rules of an RDBMS?

Several years after his IFIP paper, Codd came up with 12 rules, which are still used today as the measure of the relational nature of databases. It's important to note that many of the DBMSs we consider to be relational today don't conform to all these rules. Although these rules act primarily as a measure of the degree to which a database can be described as relational, it's also possible to use them in highlighting the importance of some of the aspects of Physical modeling.

Although most database designs (the physicalization of a Logical data model) almost never follow all these rules religiously, it's good to understand the foundations from which you're working. These rules provide an indication of what a theoretically perfect relational database would be like and provide a rationale for organizing data relationally. However, as you'll see in the course of this book, when physically implementing relational databases, we often break some of these rules to tune the database's performance.

Rule 0: The Proviso

The proviso to these rules is a Rule 0: any system that claims to be a relational database management system must be able to manage data entirely through its relational capabilities.

This means that the RDBMS must be self-contained as far as data management is concerned. It must not require any hardware- or software-specific commands to be able to access or manage the data. All data management activities must be command oriented and accessible through the RDBMS's relational commands. In other words, although the RDBMS software is loaded on a given piece of hardware and is under the control of an operating system, the RDBMS doesn't directly reference any of the capabilities of the hardware or operating system for data management. Although a front-end tool such as Enterprise Manager in SQL Server 2000 may help create database objects, the actual management of these objects happens within the database itself. This is accomplished using internal catalog tables to locate and manipulate all the data structures within the database. The actual location of this information on disk, tape, or in memory isn't relevant.

Rule 1: The Information Rule

Rule 1 states that all information in a relational database is represented explicitly at the logical level in exactly one way—by values in a table.

This means that data elements (and data values) aren't kept in a code block or a screen widget. All data elements must be stored and managed in tables. Keeping a restricted value set in the front end, using things such as LOV functions, or in the back end, using restricted domain sets such as the 88-code description level of IMS or SQL triggers, violates this rule. Again, all data values and program constants have to be stored in a table.

Rule 2: Guaranteed Access Rule

Rule 2 states that each and every datum (atomic value) in a relational database is guaranteed to be logically accessible through referencing a table name, primary key value, and column name.

This means that every value in every record in the database can be located by the table name, column name, and unique identifier (as a key, not as a physical storage locator number) of the record. It emphasizes the following two points:

- First, the importance of naming in modeling. Every table must have a unique name (we hope across the enterprise but at least in the database), but meaningful names aren't required—they're simply helpful to those accessing and maintaining the data. Some RDBMSs allow duplicate tablenames as long as the creating owner is different, as in DB2.

- Second, the importance of choosing the data element(s) that will act as each table's primary key.

Rule 3: Systematic Treatment of NULL Values

Rule 3 states that NULL values (distinct from an empty character string, a string of blank characters, or a numeric zero value) are supported in the RDBMS as a systematic representation of missing information, independent of the data type of the column containing the NULL value.

This means that the database engine has to allow NULL values for any data type, as distinct and different from zeros, spaces, and N/A. This emphasizes the importance of the database supporting defined *nullability* (the ability to not have any value at all) and *optionality* (the ability for optional relationships to other data sets).

Rule 4: Dynamic Online Catalog Based on the Relational Model

Rule 4 states that the description of the database structures is represented at the logical level in the same way as ordinary data so that authorized users can apply the same relational language to database structure interrogation as they apply to regular data.

Also, metadata about the actual data structures themselves should be able to be selected from system tables, usually called *system catalogs*. For example, in Oracle these tables make up the Oracle Data Dictionary. These catalogs or library tables contain the key pieces of data about the Physical model in data element form. Some even store the definitions of the tables and columns. This emphasizes that the data model and database structures are available for public use.

Rule 5: Comprehensive Data Sublanguage Rule

Rule 5 states that a relational system may support several languages and various modes of terminal use (for example, the fill-in-the-blanks mode). However, there must be at least one language whose statements are expressible, by some well-defined syntax, as character strings and whose ability to support all the following is comprehensible: data definition, view definition, data manipulation (interactive and by program), integrity constraints, and transaction boundaries (begin, commit, and rollback).

This means that a relational database must work with one or several programming languages (SQL, T-SQL, and PL/SQL, for example) that are extensible enough to cover all the functionality requirements of managing the environment. They must support any number of changes to be treated by the DBMS as a single unit of work, which must succeed or fail completely.

For a modeler, this means you need to be aware of the rules of the programming languages being used in your world before you generate your physical database design. There will be a list of restricted words you can't use for naming, for example.

Rule 6: View Updating Rule

Rule 6 states that all views that can theoretically be updated can also be updated by the system.

Views are temporary sets of data based on the results of a query. Rule 6 proves that Codd was very forward thinking. This rule means that if a view can be changed by changing the base values that it displays, then it should also be possible for the data represented to be manipulated directly, and the changes should ripple through to the base values. It also means that each view should support the same full range of data manipulation options that's available for tables.

Up until recently, views were temporary arrays of data, accessible like a table but "read-only" as the answer to a query. This meant that the data really lived elsewhere, and a view was simply a report-like display. Updating data through views was impossible. You could update only the base data to impact the view. Materialized views (available in Oracle 8), indexed views (available in Microsoft SQL Server 2000), and some other new functionality (such as INSTEAD OF triggers in SQL Server 2000, which can take control as soon as any data manipulation commands are executed against the view) changed all that. Given that a view should know where its data comes from, it can now push an update backward to the origin.

Of course, restrictions still exist. Basically, a view can be updated only if the Data Manipulation Language (DML) command against the view can be unambiguously decomposed into corresponding DML commands against rows and columns of the underlying base tables. At the time of this writing, using a GROUP BY or UNION, and so on, will take away the ability of your view to be updated, as there's no one-to-one correlation between rows in the view and in the base table. Inserting rows through views is usually problematic, as there may well be columns outside the view scope that are NOT NULL (but with no default value defined).

Rule 7: High-Level Insert, Update, and Delete

Rule 7 states that the capability of handling a base relation or a derived relation as a single operand applies not only to the retrieval of data but also to the insertion, update, and deletion of data.

This rule underlines the mathematics of set theory upon which the relational database is built. It says that records have to be treated as sets for all functions. First the set of records (a set of one or more) is identified, and then the set is modified as a group, without having to step through single row processing. This rule states that data manipulation processes occur independently of the order of retrieval or storage of records in a table. All records are manipulated equally.

Rule 8: Physical Data Independence

Rule 8 states that application programs and terminal activities remain logically unimpaired whenever any changes are made in either storage representation or access methods.

This means that the data customer is isolated from the physical method of storing and retrieving data from the database. They don't need to worry about factors such as the physical location of data on physical disks or the disk space management for each table. In other words, the logical manner in which the user accesses the data must be independent from the underlying architecture (storage, indexing, partitioning, and so on). Such independence ensures that the data remains accessible to the user no matter what performance tuning of the physical architecture occurs.

Rule 9: Logical Data Independence

Rule 9 states that application programs and terminal activities remain logically unimpaired when changes of any kind that theoretically permit unimpairment are made to the base tables.

This rule strongly suggests that the logical understanding of data organization and the physical design choices of that data are completely independent. You should be able to change the database-level design of data structures without a front end losing connectivity. This is sometimes difficult to implement. We often buffer applications from database changes by restricting access through views only, by setting up synonyms, or by renaming tables if they need to change drastically, but applications depend on the names of physical structures. The term *unimpairment* that Codd uses refers to changes that aren't destructive. For instance, dropping a column is destructive and likely to cause impairment to the application whereas changing a name isn't from a logical perspective (although if not buffered by a view, the name change can cause havoc).

Rule 10: Integrity Independence

Rule 10 states that integrity constraints specific to a particular relational database must be definable in the relational data sublanguage and storable in the catalog, not in the application programs.

A minimum of the following two integrity constraints must be supported:

- **Data set integrity**: No components of the identifying factor of the set are allowed to have a NULL value (or a value representing a NULL, such as N/A).

- **Referential integrity**: For each distinct non-NULL foreign key value in a relational database, a matching primary key value from the same domain must exist. So, in other words, no parent record can be processed without all the impacts to the children records being processed at the same time. *Orphan* records, those not related to others in the database tables, aren't allowed.

These integrity constraints must be enforceable at the database level—not in the programming. So not only must they be enforceable by the RDBMS, these constraints must also be *enforced* by the RDBMS, not by any application program that uses this database.

Rule 11: Distribution Independence

Rule 11 states that an RDBMS has distribution independence. Distribution independence implies that users shouldn't have to be aware of whether a database is distributed.

This means that anyone using data should be totally unaware of whether the database is distributed (in other words, whether parts of the database exist in multiple locations). Even from the Physical model, it shouldn't make any difference where the DBA chooses to set up the data storage, but it most certainly doesn't matter to the Logical model. This was very forward thinking, as relational database vendors are only just now producing features that support fully distributed databases.

Rule 12: Nonsubversion Rule

Rule 12 states that if an RDBMS has a low-level (single-record-at-a-time) language, that low-level language can't be used to subvert or bypass the integrity rules or constraints expressed in the higher-level (multiple-records-at-a-time) relational language.

All this rule is saying is that there should be no way around the integrity rules in the database. The rules should be so intrinsic that you have no way to violate these rules without deleting and re-creating the database object.

Advantages of Using the Relational Model

The following list came from *Professional Java Data* (Apress, 2001). It's a nice overview of what relational modeling is trying to achieve.

- It describes data independent of the actual physical representation of the data.

- The model of data is simple and easy to understand.

- It provides high-level operations for querying the data.

- The model is conceptually simple, allowing application programmers to be able to quickly grasp the important concepts they need to get started with their work.

- The model is based on a mathematical structure, which allows many operational aspects to be proved, and the operations have well-defined properties.

- It's easy to modify and add to relational databases.

- The same database can be represented with less redundancy.

This is a pretty comprehensive list of the advantages of modeling your data relationally before you commit yourself to a physical design. We have to add a few things here, though. Codd was trying to say that understanding your data is paramount to designing a data management solution. You need to divorce your analysis from the restrictions and characteristics of any DBMS and concentrate on understanding the realities of the data you're expecting to build and store. You need to document this in a way that you can communicate your conclusions to all members of the development team no matter how technical they are—so your analysis needs to be simple and yet comprehensive.

The details of the rules of normalization upon which relational modeling is based form one part of the Logical modeler's task—understanding the atomic data organization needed to document all the rules the business takes for granted. The communication and documentation language of modeling, which is graphic in nature, comes in a variety of syntaxes, one of which we'll cover in detail in Chapter 4 and use later in the book as we show how to build a variety of relational models in the tutorial.

Introducing Normalization

Having covered the rules by which you determine the relational nature of a database, we'll now cover the process of normalization used in designing relational systems.

Normalization is a data modeling technique, the goal of which is to organize data elements in such a way that they're stored in one place and one place only (with the exception of foreign keys, which are shared).

Data sets, or *entities* (in relational modeling vocabulary), are business concepts, and data elements, or *attributes*, are the business data. Every data element must belong to one and only one data set (with the exception of shared data values, called *foreign keys*), and every data set must own at least one data element. The test to make sure you've done this correctly is often referred to as the process of, or testing for, *normalization*. If you've been diligent about creating atomic (single-meaning and nonconcatenated) data elements, then this process will be much simpler. Don't try to normalize a model before you've taken it to the greatest level of detail possible, having called out all its data elements separately and having understood each one well. Seven normal forms are widely accepted in the modeling community, sequenced in order of increasing data organization discipline.

▪**Note** A *normal form* is a state of a relation that can be determined by applying simple rules regarding dependencies to that relation. Normal forms are designed to prevent update and delete anomalies, data redundancies, and inconsistencies.

By the time you're testing for Domain Key Normal Form, you must have tested and organized the data elements to support the previous six normal forms and the universal properties of data records. These rules are cumulative, and Table 2-5 summarizes them.

Table 2-5. *Normal Forms 1–5, Boyce-Codd, and Domain Key*

Name	Tests for the Previous Normal Forms And . . .
Universal properties	No duplicate members of the set.
	Record order unimportant (top to bottom).
	Attributes order unimportant (left to right).
	All attribute values are atomic. No single attribute is allowed to hold more than one value at one time.
First Normal Form (1NF)	The appropriateness of the primary key.
Second Normal Form (2NF)	The dependence of all attributes on all aspects of the primary key.
Third Normal Form (3NF)	The dependence of any attribute on any attribute other than the primary key.
Boyce-Codd Normal Form (BCNF)	Verifies that all data sets are identified and segregated.
Fourth Normal Form (4NF)	Verifies that all attributes are single valued for a member of the set.
Fifth Normal Form (5NF)	Verifies that if the constituent parts of a data set were divided, they couldn't be reconstructed.
Domain Key Normal Form (DKNF)	Verifies that all constraints are the logical consequence of the definition of the keys and the domains (data value rules).

We'll cover only the first three normal forms in this chapter, as well as BCNF. This isn't because we don't think the others aren't interesting, but we're simply trying to reduce the complexity of normalization to make it more accessible here. On a more practical note, just getting to 3NF or BCNF is the goal of many project teams.

Up until now we've talked about data modeling with an emphasis on concepts, relationships, and data understanding rather than data element organization. Normalization is all about organizing data elements into a format where relational data integrity is maintained as strictly as possible. Logical data models should adhere to the normalization rules so that you can translate them into functioning Physical data models. However, as we mentioned earlier, in implementing Physical models you'll almost inevitably break some of the normalization rules to optimize the performance of the system.

Universal Properties of Relations

The universal properties of relations are the preconditions that must be in place prior to the test for normal forms. They refer to that two-dimensional math form called a *relation* upon which relational design is based.

- There must be no duplicate instances (duplicate members of the set).

- Instances are unordered (top to bottom).

- Data elements are unordered (left to right).

- All data element values are atomic. No single column describing a single instance is allowed to hold multiple values at one time.

These concepts underpin the way you define data sets and data elements. The identifying factor (primary key) must ensure that no duplicates exist. Not only that, but a primary key must be defined and the unique values must exist for a member to be added to the set. There must be at least enough data elements to make a member of the set unique. In addition, it shouldn't matter in what order the instances (members of the set) of a data set are created.

The same goes for the order of the data elements. They end up being stored in some order, but it shouldn't matter what that order is (except for RDBMS needs). The sequence of the data elements is as independent as the sequence of the instances. Figure 2-5 illustrates that once the universal properties are true (as supported by RDBMS and your analysis), you add layer upon layer of tests for potential anomalies in the data organization. Each subsequent test depends on the universal properties already being satisfied.

Think of building on normal forms as analogous to painting a house. First you prepare the surface, then you seal the wood, then you add the primer, and finally you apply two top-coats of paint. Similarly, in building data models it doesn't make sense to apply 3NF tests until 1NF and 2NF have already been reflected in the design. Each normal form test represents a layering of data structure quality testing. Figure 2-5 shows the cumulation of forms.

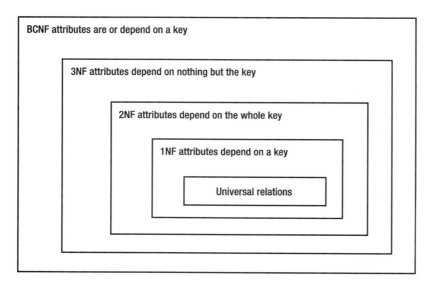

Figure 2-5. *Cumulation of forms*

So, you satisfy the generic universal relations by concentrating on the duplicate instances within each set. For example, in the set of Orders, Order 6497 isn't allowed to appear more than once. In a similar fashion, no data elements are allowed to represent multiple values at the same time. For example, you can't store the data values *Spokane*, *Miami*, and *LA* as a single City data element; each value must be stored as an individual data element. You can test this by getting sample data and combing through it. You have to resolve data issues such as this before you can finalize your logical design that a physical database can be built from.

Why Check for Universal Relations?

Unwanted or unmanaged duplicates create serious issues in physical data management. They cause the following problems:

- You have to worry about consistent and concurrent updates in all the places where the data is stored.

- You have to customize code for data retrieval issues when there may be possible inconsistent multiples of the same data element in the return set.

- You have to customize correct values in data generalizations, especially in math functions such as sums and averages.

- You have to parse and customize code for multiple values stored in one column.

For example, if your bank account current balance is stored as several duplicated values in several different data stores in the bank's database, then there's a chance that, if the relevant integrity constraints are compromised in some way, your balance will be updated in only one location. All these values need to be updated in a synchronized fashion, or your latest salary payment may be missed!

If these rules aren't followed, there's a chance of providing incorrect answers to simple data questions needed by the clients. The inability to provide correct answers lowers the value of the data. Having to be creative about getting correct answers because of these kinds of data storage issues increases the cost of managing the data. In practice, a lot of code randomly picks the first instance of a duplicate row just because there's no other way of filtering out duplicate records. There are also complicated blocks of code, involving complex query statements and coupled with IF...THEN...ELSE case statements, that are devised to custom parse through multiple values buried in one unstructured column in a table just to be able to access data and report correctly.

Keeping all the instances unique and the data elements atomic provides a huge increase in data quality and performance (in part because you can now use indexes to access data). Let's say you're analyzing orders at a new car dealership. You learn that each customer places a separate order but that they can buy multiple cars on one order. A customer can place their order in person, over the phone, or via the Web page, and to finalize the order, one of the staff members must verify all the information. Having discovered these data elements, you test for the universal relation rules and use the results of those tests to reorganize the data into a preliminary normalized structure, as shown in Figure 2-6.

Figure 2-6. *Preliminary normalized structure of a car dealership*

Try to figure out what makes each sale unique so that you can determine the unique identifiers that are possible primary keys. In this case, you can come up with two options (candidate keys), namely, Order Number as a single unique piece of information or the coupling of two values, Customer Name plus Order Date. However, although it's improbable that a customer will make two orders on the same day, it isn't impossible, so you can't use Customer Name and Order Date in combination as a primary key. This leaves Order Number that can be used to uniquely identify each Order, and this data element moves into a position above the line to note it's the primary key, as shown in Figure 2-7. Now you've met the requirement for a unique method of recognizing the members of the set.

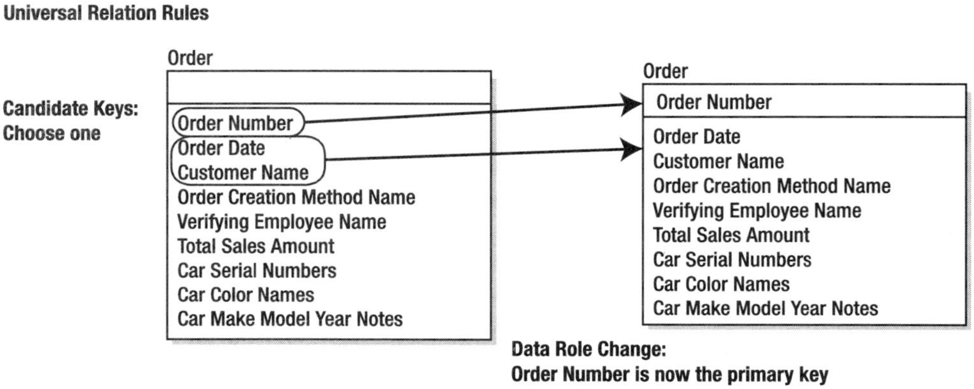

Universal Relation Rules

Figure 2-7. Order Number *is chosen as the primary identifier (primary key).*

Now look at the sequence of the orders. Can you still find one specific order if you shuffle the orders? Yes. Then it doesn't matter what order the data is in the table. That requirement is fine. Would it matter if you reorganize the values for an order as long as you still knew they represented the Order Number, Customer Name, and so on? No, you could still find one specific order, and it would still mean the same thing. That requirement is OK.

Next, you notice that Car Serial Number, Car Color Number, and Car Make Model Year Note are noted as plurals. You look through the data and find that indeed there are several orders with two car purchases and one (out of the 100 examples you looked through) that has three cars. So you create separate data elements for the potential three car sales on the Order. This requires the structure changes shown in Figure 2-8.

Now you need to carry out the same checks on the revised data structure. Does this relation have a unique identifier? Are there any sequencing issues? Are there any multivalue data elements? The answer to this last question is of course "yes," which you probably spotted by reading the descriptive names. The Car Make Model Year Note data elements have been duplicated to support car 1, 2, and 3. So, although they no longer have duplicated values for different cars, they contain an internal repeating group of make, model, and year. Since the process of normalization focuses on creating atomic data elements, leaving data elements such as this breaks the normalization rules. In the case of Logical modeling, you'll want to separate these concepts into distinctive data elements, as shown in Figure 2-9.

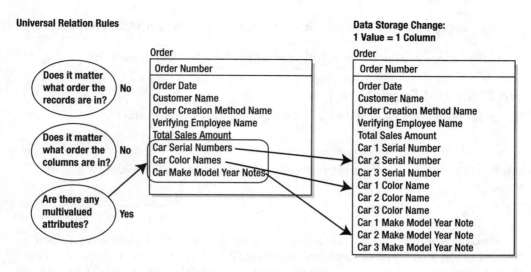

Figure 2-8. *Continued tests resulting in a change for multivalues*

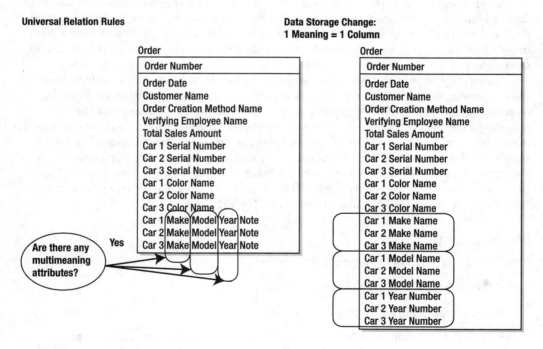

Figure 2-9. *Continued tests resulting in a change for multimeaning*

You must continue to review your data set design until you've met all the universal rela-tion rules.

Let's now look in a little more detail at the nature of the first four normal forms.

First Normal Form (1NF)

Having obeyed the demands of the universal relations, you can move onto 1NF.

■**Note** 1NF demands that every member of the set depends on the key, and no repeating groups are allowed.

Here you're testing for any data element, or group of data elements, that seem to dupli-cate. For example, any data element that's numbered is probably a repeater. In the earlier car dealership example, you can see Car Serial Number 1, Car Serial Number 2, and Car Serial Number 3 and the corresponding Color data elements.

Another way to recognize that data elements repeat is by looking for a distinctive grouping that's within a differentiating factor such as types or series numbers. You could find something such as Home Area Code and Home Phone Number, then Cell Area Code and Cell Phone Number, fol-lowed by Work Area Code and Work Phone Number, or just a simple Area Code 1, Area Code 2, and Area Code 3.

Repeating groups of data elements denote at least a one-to-many relationship to cover the multiplicity of their nature. What do you do with them? You recognize this case as a one-to-many relationship and break the data elements into a different data set (since they represent a new business concept). Then you change the data element names to show they occur only once. Finally, you have to apply the universal rules for the new data set and deter-mine what the primary key for this new data set would be. In this case, each member of this set represents a sale of a car. You need both the Order Number and the Car Serial Number in the primary key. In many order systems this will be an order-to-order line structure, because the sales aren't for uniquely identifiable products (see Figure 2-10).

Why Check for 1NF?

You check for 1FN in order to ensure the following:

- Consistent updates in all the places the data is stored

- Correct reporting with multiples in the mix

- Correct generalizations especially in math functions such as sums and averages

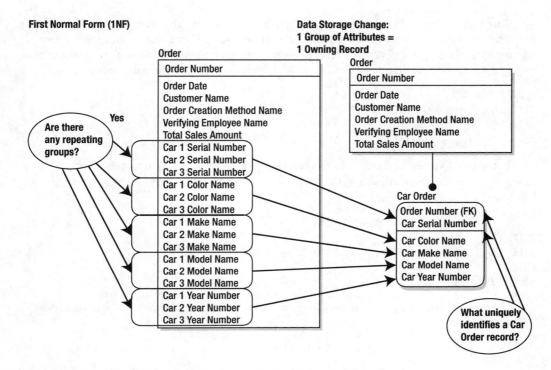

Figure 2-10. *1NF test resulting in a new data set for multivalues:* Car Order

Imagine trying to update all Color Name records in your Orders table from *Dark Red* to *Burgundy*. You have to find all the right places under all the right circumstances to perform the update and issue code that looks something like this:

```
UPDATE Order
SET Car_1_Color_Name = 'Burgundy'
WHERE
Car_1_Color_Name = 'Dark Red';

UPDATE Order
SET Car_2_Color_Name = 'Burgundy'
WHERE
Car_2_Color_Name = 'Dark Red';

UPDATE Order
SET Car_3_Color_Name = 'Burgundy'
WHERE
Car_3_Color_Name = 'Dark Red';
```

This approach means it'll be more likely that an instance of Color Name is missed, resulting in a loss of data integrity. By creating a data set that contains information relating to just one car order, rather than keeping three recurring sets of data elements within the Order table, you can update this data with a single database call, which would look something like this:

```
UPDATE Car_Sale
SET Car_Color_Name = 'Burgundy'
WHERE
Car_Color_Name = 'Dark Red';
```

In the pre-1NF-normalized table, finding the distinct list of car color names sold in a given month is complicated, since you would have to issue a query that looked something like this:

```
SELECT DISTINCT Car_1_Color_Name FROM Order
UNION
SELECT DISTINCT Car_2_Color_Name FROM Order
UNION
SELECT DISTINCT Car_3_Color_Name FROM Order
```

However, having modified the data to conform to 1NF leaves you with a single statement of the following form:

```
SELECT DISTINCT Car_Color_Name FROM Car_Sale
```

Now imagine what happens to the reports, screens, and related procedures when the clients need to increase the number of Car Orders allowed on an Order. Suppose the clients want to be able to sell 100 cars at a time in the case of a bulk order. If you remove the repeating group from Order to satisfy the 1NF tests, then there's no impact to this change at all, and a huge order of 500 separate Car Orders is no issue whatsoever.

Second Normal Form (2NF)

Having met the demands of the universal relations and 1NF, you can move onto the next test: 2NF.

■**Note** 2NF demands that every aspect of every member of the set depends on the whole key.

Look at the Car Order data set in Figure 2-11, which violates 2NF. If you assume that car serial numbers are unique around the world and never repeat, then car buffs would tell you that you can determine the make, model, and year just by knowing how to read the serial number. None of the values for those data elements should change during the course of a sale. Also, the color of the car probably doesn't change during the course of a sale; most of us choose the color of the car when it's on the lot. Figure 2-11 shows a new data set whose purpose it is to manage cars, whether they're sold or not.

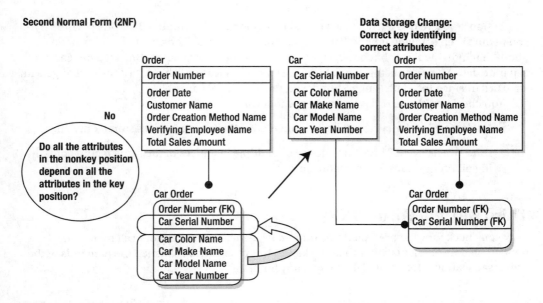

Figure 2-11. *2NF test resulting in a new data set for owned data elements (attributes)*

The normal forms between 2NF and BCNF work with this issue of data element ownership. Every data element needs to be "owned" by the correct data set. They need to be completely identifiable by one and only one primary key, namely, the key of the owning data set. They're then shared by relationships to other data sets.

In this case, testing for 2NF has caused you to move the information about cars to a separate Car data set with an identifying relationship back to the sale event of the car.

Why Check for 2NF?

This time you don't need to worry about repeating nonatomic data element values (such as Car Make Model Year Text), repeating instances in a data set (such as the Order table without a primary key), or repeating occurrences of a data element in a data set (such as Car 1 Color Name, Car 2 Color Name, and Car 3 Color Name). This time, it's repeating information across *instances* of a data set that concerns you. In the Car Order instance table (examples of what data could look like in a design), the data would look like Table 2-6 before applying the test for 2NF.

Table 2-6. *The* Car Order *Instance Data*

Order Number	Car Serial Number	Car Color Name	Car Make Name	Car Model Name	Car Year Number
001	928374	Silver	Toyota	Camry	2002
002	928374	Silver	Toyota	Camry	2002
003	928374	Silver	Toyota	Camry	2002
004	928374	Silver	Toyota	Camry	2002

Suppose you've had a whole rash of bad luck selling serial number 928374. For some reason people keep bringing it back. You've sold it four times now. Look at all the information about that individual car that has been duplicated over and over again. Breaking out `Car` as a separate data set prevents this type of interinstance duplication. This data doesn't change with each `Order`, since this data is now stored with the individual `Car` itself.

You check for 2NF in order to ensure the following:

- **No data redundancy**: If you knew it once, you still know it, and it's stored only once.

- **Data consistency**: There's no chance of multiple instances of the same record containing different values for common facts.

Third Normal Form (3NF)

Now you check for what are called *transitive dependencies*. These are data element values that depend on data elements other than the key. In this case, having satisfied the demands of the universal relations, 1NF, and 2NF, you're ready for 3NF.

▩**Note** 3NF demands that every data element of every member of the set depends on nothing but the key.

Look at the `Car` data set. Can a `Car Model Name` of `Camry` have a `Car Make Name` of `GM`? No, only Toyota makes `Camry`. Can a `Camry` have a `Car Year Number` of 1975? No, the Toyota Camry wasn't offered until 1983. Dependencies exist between the values of `Make`, `Model`, and `Year` of a `Car`. These dependencies create a set of *true* facts about cars that can be used repeatedly by many different members of the set of cars. That means they need to be kept in a new data set that you can call `Car Manufacturer Type`. You can change the organization to include this new data set and relate it to `Car`, as shown in Figure 2-12.

Resolving the transitive dependency gives you another clue that another data set was needed. This process creates simpler, more atomic sets of data for you to manage.

Why Check for 3NF?

You're reducing duplication again and adding quality checks. This time let's look at an instance table of `Car` (see Table 2-7).

Table 2-7. `Car` *Instance Data*

Car Serial Number	Car Color Name	Car Make Name	Car Model Name	Car Year Number
928374	Silver	Toyota	Camry	2002
876978	Black	Toyota	Camry	2002
987678	Red	Toyota	Echo	2002
986765	Blue	Toyota	Camry	2002
234590	Purple	Chrysler	PT Cruiser	2002
093485	Black	Volkswagen	Beetle	2001

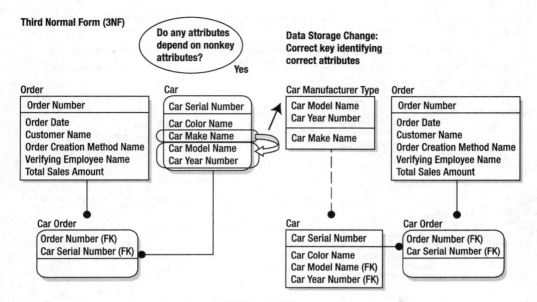

Figure 2-12. *3NF test resulting in a new data set for further defined owned data elements (attributes)*

Just knowing the Model Name of the car should tell you the Make Name. Volkswagen can't be the Car Make Name of a Camry. And a PT Cruiser can't be a Toyota. The relationship of Make to Model is a concept unto itself. You also know that Camry wouldn't be valid for any car older than 1983, so the Car Year Number is also part of the concept about Make and Model.

You check for 3NF in order to ensure the following:

- Only one version of a collection of data values (which refer to one thing at one point in time) exists. Once they're established, you've reduced the risk of incorrect values such as instances of Chrysler Echos or Toyota PT Cruisers existing in the Car Order set.

Boyce-Codd Normal Form (BCNF)

Having met the demands of the universal relations, 1NF, 2NF, and 3NF, you check for BCNF.

■**Note** BCNF demands that every data element must be a fact about the data set whose members are identified by the key and that all keys are identified.

Look at the Order data set again. Order Date is a fact about the Order Number key, but Customer Name isn't, since the name of the customer is a fact about customers. Orders just reference customers, so any information about the customer would be inappropriate in the Order data set. How about Order Creation Method Name? It's actually one of a small set of order creation methods. Finally, you need to recognize that Verifying Employee Name isn't a fact about the Order Number key and that employees are another data set that should be referenced by the order.

If the values are part of a restricted list, they need to be analyzed for their identifying characteristics. This process builds reusable data sets that add a great deal of quality to the data sets (see Figure 2-13).

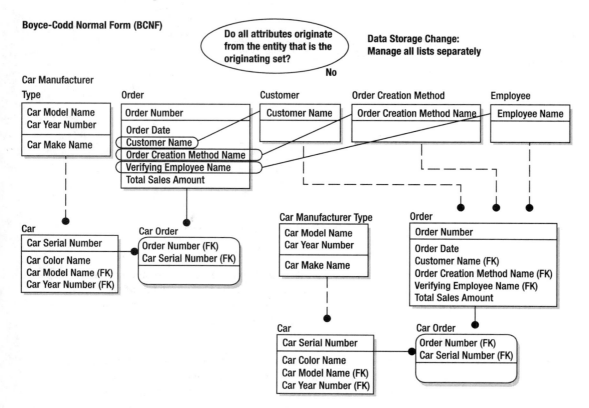

Figure 2-13. *BCNF test resulting in a more distinct group of data sets*

BCNF says that every data element must be a fact about the data set identified by its primary key or that the data element is a foreign key originating elsewhere. It's very much a test for the saying "a place for everything and having everything in its place." Think of the BCNF test as the final sweep for the restrictive LOV that the application will want to provide for the clients. It segregates all data elements into sets and tests to see whether they stand alone.

So, you pull out the concepts of Customer, Order Creation Method, and Employee and build three new data sets. You may wonder how Employee Name changed into Verifying Employee Name. That occurred through a process called *role naming*, where the migrating primary key changes its name in the new data set to clarify the role it plays. You'll look in more detail at role naming in Chapter 3.

If you can take your data sets and data attributes through to BCNF, you've done a pretty thorough job of capturing the essence of relational modeling. From here it's simply a question of translating the logical design into a physical design and adding enough physical characteristics to the model to turn it into a complete blueprint for creating database objects.

This seems to be a really tedious exercise, especially if you're analyzing a subject area that contains more than nine data elements. After a while you'll get so good at this activity that it will come to you automatically. In practice, you don't test each data set over and over again like you just did in this chapter. If a normal form violation exists in your model, the resultant structure will "just not feel right," and you'll fix it without giving any real thought to whether the correction fixed a 2NF or BCNF violation.

You check for BCNF in order to ensure the following:

- All data is managed in the correct "set."

Introducing Denormalization

Denormalization is a process that generally occurs during the final Physical model design and testing phases of a development project. It purposely undoes some of the modifications to the model that were made to ensure support for one of the normal forms. These denormalizations always address specific physical hardware or software constraints, including application performance. It may, for example, be more convenient to have some degree of redundancy in your physical design, such as having `Customer Name` in both the `Order` and `Customer` tables in the previous example. Or you may want to use a trigger for the `Order Creation Method` rather than build a table of three records.

Denormalization is performed after weighing the benefit it will bring to your application's performance against a loss of relational integrity and ease of data value management. As such, it can be a powerful technique in physical database design. Denormalization can be helpful or harmful, or both simultaneously, depending on the perspective you take of different aspects of managing the data in the model. Without an understanding of what denormalization is trying to achieve, all the hard work you've put into adhering to the various levels of normal form could be undone, causing the system to suffer as a result. Equally, if you're unaware of how denormalization can be used to optimize the performance of the physical implementations of your designs, then you won't always produce the best possible performing database design. Bear in mind that *denormalized* doesn't mean *unnormalized*. Unnormalized database designs (those that never went through the rigors of logical analysis) can't be said to be denormalized, since they were never normalized in the first place.

Denormalization should be done with the delicacy of brain surgery and should involve experience and input from all affected parties. But the affected parties should only be providing *input* to this process. Denormalization is best done by the data modeler and the DBA, but sometimes you have to include others from the development team for purposes of understanding functionality requirements. The DBA will be heavily involved, and programmers will also have suggestions. Some enterprise oversight committee may even review and approve the final physical design. We've introduced this topic here so that, as a data modeler, you won't be taken by surprise when the logical designs you created and built to support the documented and proven worth of normalization seem to be mangled in their physical implementation, without appearing to address any data anomalies these decisions could cause. Denormalization, when carried out efficiently, includes built-in safety nets to ensure that data integrity and data value management functions are still maintained and available.

Let's look at a few examples of "normal" denormalization in the next section.

Derived Columns

Although you don't logically model derived values, you deal with them all the time in reports and on screens. You want to see values such as Order Total Amount and the Expected Arrival Date, which are probably derived from other base elements. It's often tempting to store these values in data elements, rather than waste I/O re-creating them at every request. This, however, necessitates creating custom coding (in the form of stored procedures or triggers) to ensure that any change in the base values is reflected in those values derived from them. This safeguard must be maintained at all times, or the data passed on to the client may be inaccurate and worthless.

Derived columns can be good choices, especially in the cases of nonvolatile, complicated, time-consuming, high-use formula results. Storing last year's budget at the department level, rather than the general ledger (G/L) level, would probably be a good candidate. There's a pretty small chance that someone is going to change the proposed value now, and everyone wants to know what the target value is. Keeping the department level proposal rolled up from lower-level details may be an appropriate storage of derived data. The Order Total is another matter. While the RDBMS may be wasting I/O time to get you a total, it depends on how the Order Total is used by other operational processes. If the total value can be arbitrarily adjusted by users (so that an order total no longer represents the clear sum of its line items), then you may want to denormalize this value.

Remember that you may not need to consider storing derived data, if you can generate derived values by some other means, such as materialized views. If you're able to use database views, then you can maintain the highly normalized form of the database and simply update the view when the base values change.

Deliberate Duplication

Another thing you don't model logically is duplicate data elements. Remember that, from the point of view of normalization, you want each data element owned by one data set. On the other hand, you may have six pairs of scissors in your house, even though they duplicate each other's functionality. You can denormalize them because nobody ever seems to put them back where you can get to them and you waste time searching for them.

Some database table structures are huge and complicated. It may take five or more table joins to get the Product Code of a product or the Hire Date of an employee. Duplicating columns incurs the same risk as storing derived columns, since you're deliberately introducing redundancy into the database. You need to evaluate the cost of obtaining the value dynamically against the cost of refreshing the duplicates every time the base data elements are updated for a specific record.

Another risk similar to the case of derived columns is that you must have code in the form of stored procedures or triggers to ensure that the duplicated data values are updated whenever the base value changes. Duplicated columns should be protected from being updated by any other custom process, and the data should be retrieved from a single, approved source.

Deliberately Removing or Disabling Constraints

In referring to disabling constraints, we're not referring to temporarily disabling constraints for data loading or emergency data management. What we're referring to is the full-time, deliberate removal of relationships that have been discovered in the logical analysis. This is usually proposed to enhance insert, update, or delete transaction speed.

Every time an insert, update, or delete is performed on a table that's implemented with enforced constraints, the constraints must be checked, which takes some time. Sometimes this isn't an optimal physical implementation, as some tables are subject to almost continual processing. Transactional tables, in particular, may have data updated or inserted every couple of milliseconds. Other tables may need a looser rule implementation in order to be able to take in less than high-quality records under the assumption that this data can be cleaned up later.

This seems a little like removing the seat belt from your car because it wrinkles your tie. The whole purpose of the analysis is to document the rules of the business. All denormalization should be considered an "option of last resort," since denormalizations are design changes made to get around existing physical constraints of the hardware or software. All other design options should be tried first, including configuration modifications and application tuning, before the data model is denormalized. The best you can do if this denormalization choice is inevitable is to create a regular batch job that checks for data integrity and communicates the results to individuals who care enough about data integrity to fix things.

Deliberate Undoing of Normalization Forms

The deliberate undoing of normalization forms is another form of denormalization. This is the process of going backward through the normal form exercises and undoing all the changes that made the model normalized. As you do this, you'll get closer and closer to one huge flat file. We're not saying that a huge flat file can never be the right database design, but we haven't come across a flat file design that's used in a transactional system. Data warehouse dimensional designs are another question entirely. They generally come much closer to this flat data organization by design. You'll look at the benefits of Dimensional modeling in Chapter 12.

Denormalizing using this technique requires you to deliberately go back to repeating groups, transitive dependencies, partial key dependencies, and even keyless tables. Each of these denormalization decisions has to be made with the knowledge of what could happen to the data in the resulting data structures. The basics of this knowledge were listed earlier in this chapter. Simply reversing the process you went through is the basis for most denormalization decisions. The particulars will, of course, depend upon the specific situation.

Summary

A relational database adheres to a greater or lesser extent to the 12 rules of an RDBMS drawn up by Codd. In developing a relational system, you use the process of normalization, which is verifying the relational nature of your data organization against the various degrees of normal form. We covered 1NF, 2NF, 3NF, and BCNF and showed how they help you verify the following:

- Single membership of an instance in a set is recognized by a stable unique identifier.

- All the data elements in a data set depend on all the identifying data elements.

- None of the data elements depend on any other attributes other than the identifying data elements.

- Any data elements that can be recognized as a set have their own data set and identifying factors (primary key).

You then looked at the power and risks of denormalization, the process by which you break the rules of normalization in order to improve application performance. This is something that requires experience in order to tailor its use appropriately for any given application, but it can prove invaluable in enhancing the user experience of your application.

CHAPTER 3

■■■

Understanding Relational Modeling Terminology

To be able to create relational data models and develop truly relational databases, you need to understand the terms used to describe the objects involved in describing relational systems. In this chapter you'll look at both sides of modeling—the Conceptual/Logical side and the physical structure side. To this end, in this chapter you'll consider terminology for the following areas of relational modeling:

- Entities

- Attributes

- Keys (candidate, primary, and foreign)

- Relationships

- Tables/views

- Columns

- Keys and indexes (primary, surrogate, alternate, and foreign)

- Constraints

Introducing Conceptual/Logical Modeling Concepts

The data models capturing the Conceptual/Logical side and the physical structure side are tied together. Conceptual/Logical data modeling is generally a first step to building a relational physical database design. Since one evolves through a maturing process into the other, the concepts are linked when introducing design.

Conceptual/Logical modeling captures the rules of data in a business activity. The emphasis is on how the data actually exists in the world and how it's used in a business environment. From a logical perspective, if a vendor has multiple e-mail addresses and the business needs access to them, it's immaterial that the current software application allows only one e-mail address per vendor. It doesn't matter if today's form has no space for a Web site address if the business needs to know this information. Conceptual/Logical modeling concentrates on documenting what's really happening with data, how it's being used, and what it needs to do in the future. This type of modeling completely ignores what a physical implementation would look like.

From this analysis, you can then move into Physical modeling and support by building software applications that make using business data correct, easy, and fast. The physical database design will have logical data rules built into the actual structure that promotes high-quality, simple data value maintenance and growth. The idea is that the business policies governing the business processes may change often. The challenge lies in whether you can break down the necessary structures to minimize the potential for massive rewrites when fundamental and arbitrary business policies change. Knowing the logical rules of the data sets, data elements, and data values in the context of the business is the first step in designing an appropriate physical table design that can be deployed in a relational database management system (RDBMS).

Entities

Entities are the foundation of relational data modeling. The industry definition of *entity* is that it's a person, place, thing, or concept that has characteristics of interest to the enterprise about which you want to store information.

Note that entities aren't tables. They're often physically implemented as tables and are depicted in a similar manner to tables in data model graphics, but they're not tables. Tables are always physically implemented, but some entities are too conceptual to ever become actual tables. Let's repeat that: physical structures are never entities. They may be physical representations of entities, but entities by definition are references to real-world things, ideas, and concepts. Tables are physical data storage constructs that often represent entities.

Think about your house. When the earth rattles too much, those of us in California find ourselves picking our wares (books, CDs, wine bottles, pencils, and so on) off the floor. Everything that had once been organized is now lying in heaps on the floor. When you're faced with that kind of chaos, your natural instinct is to create organized piles of belongings; CDs go in one corner, the books stack up in another, and so on. Data modeling organizes distinctive data sets (entities) and the data elements they contain in a similar manner, grouping concepts that represent a person, place, thing, or concept. Fortunately, data isn't generally found in this chaotic a state in your company. You have to determine the needs of the system you're looking at and build suitable storage structures from scratch.

When clearing up your house, you'd begin by quickly organizing your belongings, probably by subject. All the multimedia goes in this corner, the kitchen stuff goes over here, and you place broken bits in a bin. In data modeling this would be analogous to the *conceptual analysis* phase. You have the elements you're going to keep in large, general, still unexplored piles (*conceptual entities*) and a pile of stuff that's out of scope (purposely set aside for now). After this conceptual organization, you go onto a more detailed organization. This time, you sort the multimedia pile into more distinctive groupings titled Music, Movie, and Game. In data modeling terms you've identified your conceptual Multimedia entity, representing this set of things, and you're now refining your understanding by developing logical entities in the form of Music, Movie, and Game. Each subpile is a distinctive set with different important attributes. The composer or artist is important to how you store and retrieve music, but subject and title are the important factors in movies.

This is the stage where you can make mistakes. In this example, the subject matter isn't related to the media but is related to the entertainment matter that's stored on the media. If you had a DVD with multiple movies on it, you'd need to recognize this distinction. People tend to collapse entities together and migrate convenient attributes from one entity to the next. Before creating entities, you should carefully consider what the *real relationships and entities are*.

Data modeling starts by organizing, in a conceptual abstraction, sets of relevant data. By using *normalization*, which we just looked at in Chapter 2, you purify and isolate the data logically into distinctive, reusable, elemental sets that can be related and combined for different purposes. Finally, you design physical storage structures (tables) to hold the data and manage it appropriately.

Entities are generally thought of as sets of entity classes, representing a person, place, thing, event, or concept. Entities are usually *nouns*. If you were to list all the *things* affected by the business, you'd have a good starting point for entity identification. It's good to use this list to check against when you're looking at a group of instances to see if they could be an entity. So, if you think of an entity as a noun describing multiple instances that create a set, then both Figure 3-1 and Figure 3-2 represent entities, one from a more conceptual (business-process-oriented) viewpoint and one from a logical (data element relations) viewpoint.

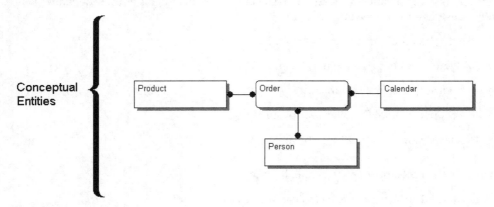

Figure 3-1. *Conceptual entities*

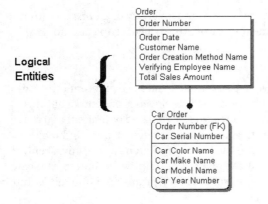

Figure 3-2. *Logical entities*

What entities are relevant to your project depends on your perspective. Are you interested in modeling the sales order *document*, or are you trying to model the event where the item is sold? If you're modeling the document, the Order and Car Order item are entities. If you're modeling the sales event or sales activity, an order might be a purchase request that's initiated by a customer to obtain a product. The system's focus is important when you try to determine your lists of entities.

Equally, concepts such as Employee, Project, Department, Part, and Vendor could all qualify as entities.

▉**Note** You need to be careful with names in data modeling. Employee may be better titled as Person, Worker, or even Support Staff, depending on the context of the model.

The model perspective is important. In the Conceptual model, it may be better still to model the entity as Person (see Figure 3-1) and role-type the activities people perform. This depends on the variability of the roles and the duplication of an employee as a participant in different parts of the business process. So what constitutes an entity is entirely dependent upon the business process system being modeled. For example:

- To a dog breeder, Collie may be an entity.

- To a veterinarian, Large_Dog may be an entity.

- To a pet shop, Dog may be an entity.

- To a property rental firm, Pet may be an entity.

- To Animal Control, Animal may be an entity.

On a similar note, the following could be true:

- To a legal firm, Advice may be a billable service or entity.

- To a car dealer, Advice may merely be an attribute of a Salesperson entity.

The real trick to entities is deciding whether you've found an entity or an *instance* (one member of a set), or both; the way to determine this is from the project scope and domain.

Conceptual or Logical Entities

It's good to remember that entities come in two major varieties that have different purposes. The *conceptual entity* is an idea that will never be physically deployed. Conceptual entities don't often have further characteristics (known as *attributes*) associated with them and are mostly used as communication tools for teams to learn about the subject areas and major concepts to be analyzed further. Almost no rules exist about what can be a conceptual entity. If you think an entity helps tell the story, and you can give it a descriptive definition, you can generally use it as a conceptual entity. These may never be directly translated into tables, but if the concept is important, a conceptual entity will still be represented by a collection of attributes contained within a table representing another entity.

Figure 3-3 is a little model showing conceptual entities; it captures a few thoughts about the order system. These entities are at a very high level. Order here will probably encompass individual orders as well as supply chain contracts. Product could be services, as well as audit functions or processes that help fulfill orders. It all depends upon what you discover from your analysis.

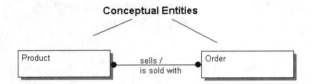

Figure 3-3. *Conceptual entities with relationship names*

At the conceptual level the details are blurred. You may not actually fully understand the scope of the concepts when you use these structures in your model. You'll have to work with a person who is knowledgeable in the area of your analysis to build and validate your model.

Logical entities are a little tougher, since, having been fully detailed and documented, they will quite often be the structure that leads to a design of a table or physical object. You want your logical entities to include attributes to ensure you fully understand how these entities are being used. But you don't necessarily want to use this model to communicate a physical design. These Logical models are hybrid models that show an in-between state. They exist between truly implementation-neutral Conceptual models (which can be attributed if necessary) and Physical models that show a database design. When Logical models are fully attributed, they look like Figure 3-4.

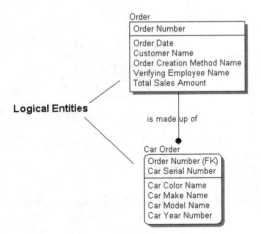

Figure 3-4. *Fully attributed logical entities*

From this point on when we talk about entities, we're referring to logical entities.

Instance or Entity?

An *instance* (or member of the set) defined by an entity correlates roughly to a row or record in a table, in the same way that an entity correlates to a table but isn't strictly defined as such. For example, in a `Jazz Records` entity, you might find instances such as Kind of Blue, Porgy and Bess, or Time Out.

■**Note** *Instance* means a single member (sample of values) of an entity or a member of the set. It may ultimately be a row or record in a table but isn't defined as such. In math it's called a *tuple*.

Category Entities

Category structures, or *generalization hierarchies,* partition an entity into subsets. Each subset is part of the whole; for example, `Truck`, `Car`, `Ship`, and `Airplane` are all subsets of `Vehicle`. Figure 3-5 shows the order system. Now you can see that you sell vehicles, which can be broken down into cars, trucks, and vans.

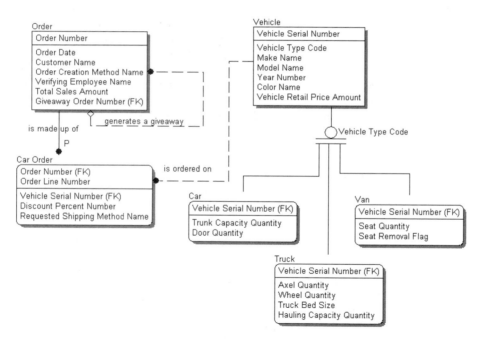

Figure 3-5. *Small portion of an order system's Logical model highlighting the category structure of Vehicle*

The entity whose set includes all the members (in this case, `Vehicle`) is referred to as the *supertype*. The divisions (in this case, `Car`, `Van`, and `Truck`) are *subtypes*. Subtyping is also important in object modeling and is a subject we'll cover in Chapter 5. The activities are the same in both types of models. All subtypes share the data elements found in the supertype, but each subtype may have unique data elements. You use a category modeling structure to document a cohesiveness that would otherwise be lost.

Child category entities sometimes seem like instances because each subdivision gets more and more detailed. Once in a while you'll even have a subtype entity that's the only member of its set, so the difference between the instance and the entity gets very slim. Remember that an instance is a *member* of a set whereas an entity is an *idea* or the *set itself*.

■**Note** A category structure manages a single set of instances by dividing them into types. This generally occurs because of differences in the definition, the owned attributes belonging to each type, and, to some extent, the entity's use.

Obviously, a Collie can be an instance of Dog, and Truck, Car, and Van can be instances of Vehicle. So how do you know if a noun is an instance or member of a category? You have to observe or discover the "natural use" of the set; in other words, you have to observe how and why things behave the way they do in a given set, using guidelines we'll cover now.

Defining Signs of a Category

The following are the main clues to knowing whether you need to document a category structure or just note a descriptive division of the instances in an entity:

What the customers think: This is your first and best check to see if you're working with an instance or an entity. Find out how the clients think. But note that sometimes the customers are wrong: they call things out as being different when they differ only in the values of attributes, and they consider things to be the same when they're fundamentally different in nature and attributes. Listen to what they say, but be ready to challenge them. If you ask them what a truck, van, or car is, do they think you're referring to a vehicle? If they do, then trucks are just instances of the set Vehicle. Or is Truck an entity in its own right, considered different enough because of its use or structure, needing to be categorized separately with useful attributes uniquely its own?

How they define it: Write down the definitions of the concepts you think could be an entity. Audition the concepts to be entities in textual form. Review the definitions with your customers, and look for similarities. You may find concepts that seem dissimilar that are actually part of the same entity family. If so, these entities could be subtypes that are part of a supertype encapsulating the similarities. For example:

- Car: A wheeled vehicle, especially an automobile.

- Truck: A strong, usually four-wheeled vehicle used for road transport of heavy loads.

- Van: A large, covered vehicle for carrying furniture and other goods by road.

Notice the similarities between these three items; all have the term *vehicle* in their definition, all have wheels, and all seem to be used on a road. Notice the differences: Truck is specifically used for heavy loads, a Van is covered, and a Car is an automobile. If your clients emphasize the similarities, you probably have instances. If they emphasize the differences, you probably have subtypes of a category.

Look at sample data: Do the same for data that the client will want to capture about the candidate entity. Create a list of descriptive data elements. If you start to see repeating patterns of attributes such as name, weight, and description, you probably have a collection of instances rather than entities. Instances won't need a distinct enough structure to make it necessary to identify them as different entities. On the other hand, if only trucks require government inspections to be tracked, then trucks have at least one different attribute from other vehicles and therefore may warrant their own category entity.

Count how many there are: Another check is to find out if there's more than one instance of the candidate entity. But be aware this isn't a foolproof check. Some entities may include only one instance at the time of analysis, but they may have the *potential* for more instances later. For example, the Company entity that refers to the enterprise itself may be a single instance now, but a future merger may require the identification of new companies. Sometimes it's important to recognize that a single instance is a distinct concept and therefore should be defined as an entity. Doing so can increase flexibility for the future.

Complete or Incomplete

Categories can be either *complete* or *incomplete*. Complete categories have all subtypes defined whereas incomplete categories don't. A category may be incomplete because all of the categories aren't known, the number of subcategories can increase over time, or you choose not to show all the subcategories. The decision to show them all is based on the importance of identifying the subtypes to the customers and/or the information technology (IT) development team. If a subtype needs to be treated differently for security or processing, you may need to display it in the Logical model so that you can capture those types of requirements.

▓**Note** A complete category structure creates a subcategory into which every instance in the set fits. An incomplete category structure creates some but not all subcategories into which the instances fits.

A child category entity can be a parent category in another level of categorization, and this can be extended for an unlimited number of levels. Just remember that every instance of every level must also be part of the set defined by the topmost parent category. If you find yourself able to arrange a category hierarchy tree in different ways, you may have blended two concepts together, or you may be looking at a matrix rather than a hierarchy.

Inclusive or Exclusive

Categories can also be *inclusive* or *exclusive*. When a category is inclusive, any of the members of the supertype can be members of any (or all) of the subtypes. When a category is exclusive, each set member can be a member of only one of the subtypes. For instance, in a bakery where the different styles of dessert are important, you could define an inclusive category that's broken into four subtypes: Frozen, Baked, Fresh, and Flambé. The instance of Dessert named Cherries Jubilee would be a member of both Frozen and Flambé. However, for an exclusive category, you'd have to choose into which category to place the instance, probably Flambé since the fire is the most distinctive feature. Choosing this aspect of the category can be important to the flexibility of the future application development. Exclusively defined categories have much more rigid instance management.

Associative, or Intersection, Entity

An *associative*, or *intersection*, entity is a juncture between two entities. This is generally created as a resolution of a many-to-many relationship. You'll see more regarding these relationships later in this chapter. For now let's consider a simple example. Suppose there are people in your sales department who have to follow up on order issues. Each order may require more than one "call back" in order to resolve the problem. Each member of the sales staff can assist in the resolution of many orders. You have an entity named Orders and one named Sales Staff, but you need a further entity, Order Call Backs, to record the call back events (see Figure 3-6).

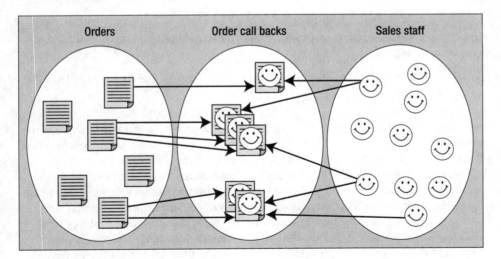

Figure 3-6. *The overlapping concepts in the event of a call back*

It would look like Figure 3-7 in a model.

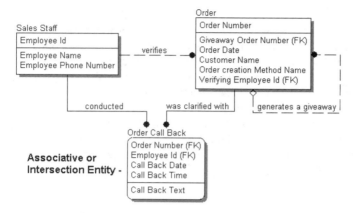

Figure 3-7. *Associative, or intersection, entity*

Example of Identifying an Entity

Identifying entities depends upon the circumstances, scope, and purpose of the analysis. Let's consider a sample wallet and document its contents. Say you have one black, plastic, trifold wallet. The contents are as follows:

- **Cards**: Two business cards, one driver's license, two club memberships, one bank card, and four credit cards (one company, one store, and two generic)

- **Paper**: Five store receipts, one canceled check, two deposit slips, four ATM slips, and three pictures of kids

- **Money**: Seventeen pennies, three nickels, one five-dollar bill, and four one-dollar bills

Some of these nouns are instances, some are entities, and some are entity concepts that haven't been named or discovered yet. The distinction between entities and instances will be different for each different business client. The requirements of the business process are completely different for a client who is an archeologist digging up the wallet 3,000 years in the future from the client who runs the Lost and Found department at a college now. Both will care about finding the wallet and will find capturing some information about its contents useful. However, each will require a different level of detail, and, as such, the definition of an entity is in the eye of the beholder. Both will have an entity for the event (the finding of the wallet), which wasn't even on the list but is important nonetheless. It may be the Recovered Property event entity. It would include attributes concerning time, location, discoverer, and other event type information. The rest of the entities are specific to the needs of the clients.

To the Lost and Found department staff at the college, Wallet is probably an instance. Does it matter that the property is a wallet rather than an umbrella? It matters only because they need to put the wallet in a safe and the umbrella in a box. This client just sees each object as someone else's property and logs each item into the system accordingly. For them, the entity is probably Property with Wallet as an instance of property. The $9.32 recovered and the name on the driver's license may be enough for them to identify the item, so `Property` and `Recovered Property` may be all they want to capture. In fact, they may be satisfied with tracking only `Recovered Property`, which is kept in a logbook on the desk. Their Logical model could look something like Figure 3-8.

Lost and Found Department

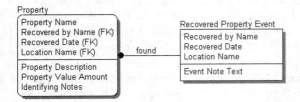

Figure 3-8. *Lost and Found department's Logical model of finding a wallet*

To archeologists, on the other hand, `Wallet` may be important and distinctive enough to have its own entity. They may want to describe the size, material, and style that will make it different from other property. The contents of my wallet may even yield enough information to become part of someone's doctoral thesis about the inhabitants of Southern California in the early 2000s. Figure 3-9 is a higher view of what would be a complex model for finding a wallet.

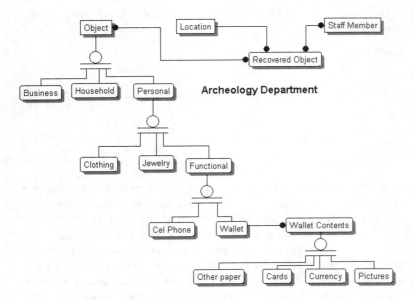

Figure 3-9. *Archeological department Logical model of finding a wallet*

Attributes

Attributes are what most people think of as data. They exist as numbers, codes, words, phrases, text chunks, and even sounds and images that combine to be an instance in an entity. Attributes *aren't* columns in a table, although they may grow up to be implemented that way some day. Attributes are simple, separate, distinct, singular characteristics that describe or identify an entity. Attributes are the genes, or the DNA, of an entity. An attribute can be defined as a distinct characteristic for which data is maintained.

Here again, we'll make a distinction between the logical world and the physical world. Attributes don't store data; they describe it. Some attributes never make it to being table columns in their own right. It's rare to see `Century Number`, `Year Number`, `Month Number`, `Day Number`, `Hour Number`, `Minute Number`, and `Second Number` all physically implemented separately. Our point is that all these distinctive elements could qualify as attributes, since each has a meaning that's different from a combination of them. However, under some circumstances it's only the full combination that's important. Each separate data element may be important to know and be defined by itself.

So, what's an attribute? If you consider the `Order` entity from earlier, then all the labels inside the entity (`Order Number`, `Order Date`, `Customer Name`, `Order Creation Method Name`, and `Verifying Employee Number`) are attributes. Every attribute has to be *owned* by an entity. And in the world of logical relational modeling, every distinct attribute is owned by one entity. It can be *migrated* through relationships and shared, but it's created and maintained in one place.

Group Attributes

A *group attribute* is a combination of distinct logical attributes describing a single characteristic of an entity. `Address` consists of many distinct data elements, as does `Phone Number`. If you listed every phone number in terms of the following:

- Long distance operator number

- Country code

- Area code

- Phone number

- Extension number

you'd need to add all those attributes to each entity that required a phone number. If you can use a `Phone Number` as a defined group attribute, it saves you time later, especially if you need to redefine addresses and phone numbers to comply with different regional formats. Is an address or phone number a composite of characters, or is it a label and therefore complete unto itself? Defining these everyday bundles of attributes as a group can save complexity at the beginning of the modeling process when you may not want to overwhelm your audience with details. We should point out here, though, that if an attribute is part of a group, it can't be part of any other group. It has been absorbed into the larger attribute completely.

It's also possible, though less common, to use *conceptual attributes*. These can be defined as an abstraction of a characteristic of an entity. So, for example, you might add an attribute `Person Full Name` to your `Client` entity as a conceptual attribute placeholder. When it's finally fully logically attributed, you may find it to be made up of five or more different logical attributes, such as these:

- Title Code

- First Name

- Middle Name

- Last Name

- Generational Qualifier Code

Dr. Martin Luther King Jr. is an example. In fact, you may need several middle names or titles in order to fully describe a name, depending on your clients' need.

■**Note** You may generate a Logical model that breaks out the definitive data elements of Name, only to have them compressed back together again during physicalization as a full name. However, keeping the logical attributes atomic during physicalization will allow simple access to the data, such as sorting on Last Name. Compressing the name back together into a full name makes it much harder to do that.

If you aren't ready to break an attribute into its most basic parts, or you're going for simplicity in the early stages, use conceptual or group attributes. Not every modeling software package can help you manage both the details and the group attribute name. You may have to manage this kind of association outside the model.

Now that we've talked about what attributes are and how much detail they can hold, we'll talk about another aspect of attributes, namely, the type of data they describe.

Attribute Classes (Types)

All logical attributes (note that conceptual and group attributes aren't precise enough to need this level of definition) must be of one type of data or another. In the Logical model, this is a high-level classification of data meaning considering an attribute's use and definition. It's different from the domain of the attribute or the target data type in physicalization, such as VARCHAR, DECIMAL, and so on. However, profiling the actual data values of an attribute and noting their shapes, character values, and sizes is a good test of your logical analysis and your definitions for the attributes. So, for example, in the Order entity from earlier, you have attributes such as Order Number, Order Date, and Customer Name. You'd expect the Order Number attribute to contain a number value, and Order Date should contain a date value. Similarly, the Customer Name attribute should contain a text value.

But what happens when, for example, you think you're looking at a list of sale amount values in a spreadsheet someone compiled from a pile of paper invoices and you discover dates mixed with the dollar amounts? You ask around. Chances are, a field on a paper form was used for several purposes, and the data contained on your spreadsheet has two or more meanings. It could be that you've discovered a new business rule no one thought to tell you about, or you may have found one of the areas where the data elements can be clarified.

The business process may be supporting a strange rule that states, if an invoice is a real invoice, the field contains the billing amount, but if the invoice is really a return for maintenance, then it contains the proposed return date. Stranger things have happened.

Every attribute must be able to be defined as one, and only one, data type. If, for whatever reason, you have values with multiple data types with similar meanings, stored in the same attribute, then choose the most specific type possible that applies to all occurrences. You may find that you need a more general class, such as Number instead of Quantity or Amount, because the data values are too inconsistent to qualify for a more definitive class. You may even need to use a really generic class such as Text if you're merging attributes that seem to have many meanings. This often happens when you have to consolidate legacy applications. While no one wants to exclude the data, sometimes they can't tell you what all the values mean either.

Table 3-1 shows our shortlist of attribute types, but you may want to add your own in time.

Table 3-1. *Class Word List*

Type Word	Meaning	Logical Data Domain
Amount	A monetary number.	Number
Code	An alphanumeric meaningful abbreviation.	Text
Date	A calendar date—month, day, year.	Date
Description	A textual account or portrayal.	Text
Flag	A one letter or number Boolean set.	Text
Identifier	A unique recognition tag in the form of a character and/or number, system-generated ID, or a globally unique identifier (GUID). This may be process driven or nonsensical and insignificant to the data user.	Text
Image	A nonlanguage visual object.	BLOB
Name	A textual label.	Text
Number	A place in a sequence.	Number
Quantity	A number totaling a measurement by a unit.	Number
Sound	An aural resonating object.	Blob
Text	An unformatted language segment.	Text
Time	A moment such as hour, minute, second, and so on.	Time

Notice that identifying every attribute with its data type isn't the same as defining a logical data domain. We reuse the domain (Text, Number, and so on) of the data for many different classes or data types. This classification becomes important when we talk about naming standards of attributes.

Keys

In addition to describing the characteristics of an entity, attributes also identify unique instances of the entity, either as part of a key value (described as a candidate, primary, or alternate key) or to reference one entity from another entity (foreign key). These attributes, or groupings of attributes, are called *keys*. When determining your entities' keys, you also have to decide whether to use existing attributes to form the key (a *natural* key) or to use a made-up key with nonbusiness attributes (a *surrogate* key).

■**Note** A *logical model key* is one or more attributes used to uniquely identify an instance in an entity, either as part of the entity or in reference to another entity.

We'll cover each type of key in turn, beginning with candidate keys.

Candidate Keys

A *candidate key* is an attribute, or a combination of attributes, that can uniquely identify an instance of an entity.

During the development of the Logical model, you need to discover all the candidate keys. Candidate keys are the possible choices for unique identification of an entity using natural keys. See the two choices you have for Order in Figure 3-10. Candidate 1 consists of a single attribute, and Candidate 2 consists of multiple attributes.

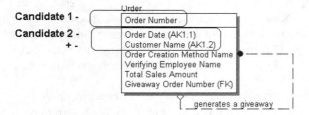

Figure 3-10. *Candidates, or options, for the primary key of* Order

Candidate keys are expected to be unique forever, as well as stable and never changing. In the previous example, you have two candidate keys. Instances in the Order entity could be identified by the following:

- A unique number that the business has given the instances (Order Number)

- The combination of Order Date and Customer Name (assuming a customer can only order once a day, and each customer has a different name)

■**Note** In ERwin 4.1, a candidate key is also known as an *alternate key*, which is represented by AKx.y notation in Figure 3-10. The first number (x) tells you to which alternate key the attribute belongs. The second number (y) tells you what position in the key the attribute occupies. Other software packages may adhere to different conventions.

Identifying the candidate keys provides you with some options for instance identification. It may be that your project includes interfaces that would lead you toward one method of identification over another. You'll want to get sample data and test for each candidate key's uniqueness and stability.

You can document as many candidate keys as you discover. An attribute can be a member of multiple candidate keys. Any attribute or combination that could act as an identifier should be identified as a candidate.

Natural and Surrogate Keys

Logical modeling focuses on attributes that are actually used in the business world, such as numbers on invoices and checks, names of places and countries, and longitude and latitude coordinates of reefs and landing strips. You generally don't make up attributes for a Logical model. Natural keys are built out of attributes that exist in the real world.

▓**Note** A *natural key* is a collection of one or more attributes that can be used to uniquely identify an instance in an entity, where the attributes exist in the business world.

Quite frequently, however, natural keys aren't stable or consistent enough to use in a physical design. The danger in using natural candidate keys is that usually these attributes (or collection of attributes) depend on a business convention or the business process that creates them. This business convention or process is often outside your control. You should be careful when using these to enforce uniqueness, as natural keys can change without notice. For example, the U.S. Postal Service owns ZIP codes. The U.S. federal government owns Social Security numbers. Therefore, these don't make good candidates as natural keys. You have no say in changes to them over time.

Fortunately, database platforms have the ability to autogenerate numbers and apply them to records being created in a table. They have no meaning in themselves, but they provide a means of identifying a row. They're called *surrogate (substitute)* keys.

▓**Note** A *surrogate key* is a single attribute created and maintained by the system to be used in uniquely identifying an instance in an entity. It has no natural occurrence in the business world.

A simple example of a surrogate key is an order identifier. A surrogate key can be created and managed by the database. If you choose to use one to manage the uniqueness of the instances in an entity, you need to take some special precautions to prevent duplicate data entry, since all surrogate keys do is identify a row instance as being unique (rather than the member of the set). For example, with an order ID, and no forethought, you can insert the same order over and over again. As a database convention, when using unique surrogate keys as a table's primary key, it's *critical* to ensure that all the other constraints (unique constraints, check constraints, and so on) are implemented so that the necessary business rules about the uniqueness of the instances are being enforced by the database.

Primary and Alternate Keys

A primary key is the candidate key that's chosen to uniquely identify an instance in an entity.

The identifier you choose to be your primary key becomes the unique record identifier and as such may migrate through your system and be referenced by other systems as a foreign key. That identifier is what will be used to find the rest of the attributes owned by this entity. This means that whatever you choose to be your primary key should never be allowed to change. Otherwise, anything referencing it could potentially lose its link to the other owned attributes. New functionality in some RDBMSs allows for the migration of any key defined as an alternate key—so some of the link constraints may not be using the primary key to refer to other entities. This will increase the need to be sensitive to changes in your design. Now you have to watch any attribute in a key that's being used in a relationship and realize the impact of changing that key.

The single most common database design misstep is an incorrectly chosen primary key. Our rule is that using anything not directly under the control of the application/database in question shouldn't be chosen as the primary key.

The modeling syntax used throughout this book will always show the primary key above a line in the entity to give it prominence in the list of attributes, as shown in Figure 3-11.

Primary and Alternate Keys

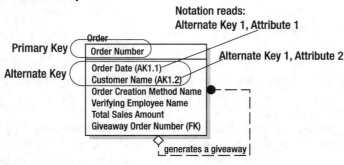

Figure 3-11. *Primary and alternate keys in an entity*

Whatever candidate keys are left over following the designation of the primary key are now called *alternate* keys. Note that although the primary key is never referred to as a candidate key after this point, it still fits into that definition.

■**Note** An *alternate key* is one of one or more sets of single or multiple attributes not chosen to primarily identify an instance in an entity but that could uniquely identify an instance as well.

Foreign Key

A *foreign key* is the complete complement of attributes designated as the primary key of another entity that has migrated (or is shared) through a relationship to an entity (see Figure 3-12).

Foreign Keys

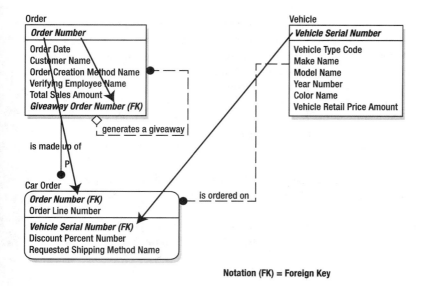

Notation (FK) = Foreign Key

Figure 3-12. *The migration of a primary key into a foreign key*

In this example, Order Number has migrated to be part of the primary key of Car Order. Vehicle Serial Number has migrated to Car Order as well. There are no limits to how many attributes you may need to migrate to an entity.

Foreign keys allow you to look backward to their source. You'll find references to other entities, and by doing so you'll have the information needed to access that entity and the attributes that are contained in that entity. From Car Order you can get Customer Name by following Order Number to Order. From Car Order you can also get to Vehicle Model Name by tracing the foreign key attributes. As long as an attribute has been identified in the parent entity as a primary key, then a foreign key (the entire set of identifying attributes chosen to be the primary key) will become part of the set of attributes in any related entity.

Role Names

Foreign keys don't have to keep the name of the attribute belonging to the entity from which they originate. Note how Employee Name becomes a foreign key named Verifying Employee Name in Order and Order Number became Giveaway Order Number in Figure 3-13 by following the arrows. Role naming generally includes a definition change as well. Using data in a new place may change the definition of that data entirely. However, a rule of thumb is that they will retain their size and data domain definitions. The only time there may be differences is during column *unification* (which I'll talk about later in Chapter 10).

Role naming is a form of self-documenting the model. The new name denotes the use of the instance to which the foreign key is referring. Just letting the attribute name retain the exact form of the point of origin can be sloppy and shortsighted. If you left the attribute as

Employee Name in the Order entity, you'd probably have assumed, incorrectly, that the Employee being referenced was the creator of the Order. You can see from the list in Figure 3-13 you could actually have many references to Employee in the Order entity—all providing different meaning for the processing of the order. The same issue applies for relating an Order to other instances of Order.

Role Names

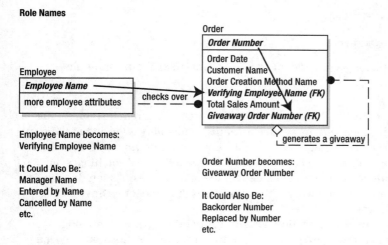

Figure 3-13. *How role naming happens*

Relationships

Relationships are the logical links between entities.

Relationships connect one entity to another. While these are potential physical database constraints for when you design a database for your Logical model, in a Logical model they just note the logical links between entities. Active verb phrases show the dynamic nature of relationships as well as the business process being supported by that link. The entity-relationship sentences created by the noun and verb phrase are sometimes called *business rules*.

Relationships are two-sided. They show a link from one entity to another, or they link an entity to itself.

It's by defining relationships that foreign keys are migrated to other entities, creating links by which instances connected together can be traced. These are generally referred to as a *parent* (the source) and *child* (the target). Relationships are either identifying or nonidentifying.

- **Identifying**: The parent primary key migrates into a primary key position of the child and is therefore needed to identify the child instance.

- **Nonidentifying**: The parent primary key migrates into a nonkey position where it isn't needed to identify the child but instead describes a fact about the child.

Each side of the relationship has a *cardinality* and *nullability* symbol. Cardinality tells you *how many* instances can be related to each instance in a parent entity. One parent entity can be related to child entities with a cardinality of the following:

- Zero or one

- One and only one

- Zero, one, or many

- One or many

- Specifically <Number>

- A range of <Number>–<Number>

- Whatever it says (either in a comment or by noting a formula) about a multiple relationship

Nullability tells you whether child instances *must* be related to a parent instance. If the migrated key in the child instance *must* exist, then an entity's nullability is termed *mandatory*, and NULL values aren't allowed. If the migrated key in the child instance *may* exist, then the nullability is termed *nonmandatory*, and NULL values are allowed. The decision hinges on whether the child entity is dependent or independent of the parent. The question that needs answering is whether this is a situation where the parent owns the child, or is the child just sometimes "related" back to the parent?

So, the relationship combines information describing (Identifying/nonidentifying) + (Nullability) + (Cardinality) + (Active verb phrase). When you read the relationship between two entities, you get sentences that are easily determined to be true or false rules about how the data sets behave. Look at Figure 3-14, and note all the different shapes and text involved in defining a relationship.

Relationships - Business Rules

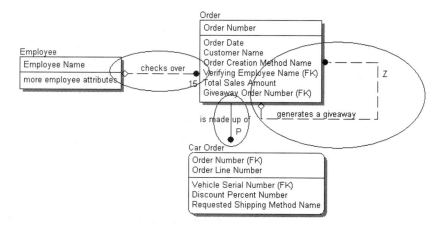

Figure 3-14. *Examples of relationships*

Each Car Order can be identified only if the Order that generated it is known. True or false? True. How about the verifying Employee Name? Do you need to know the employee who verified the order to be able to identify the order? No, you don't, since orders are identified by a unique number (although you can select a smaller set of them by restricting the list to the person who verified them). If you were able to identify an order by knowing the verifying employee name, you wouldn't be able to use a nullable nonidentifying relationship (noted by the diamond in this modeling syntax). NULLs aren't allowed in a primary key, which is where the primary key of the parent entity would be migrating to in an identifying relationship. You allow this relationship to be NULL because for a period of time an order can exist without having gone through the process of verification. You need to watch things such as this when you model.

Don't get too involved in the symbols we use to describe these characteristics of a relationship. This is only one of the graphic syntaxes (IDEF1X) used in the modeling world. But it does happen to be the one we're using in this book. The important thing is to note that the relationships between entities are also rich with characteristics that need attention.

Now let's look at the nullability and cardinality rules in Table 3-2. The "may" or "must" part of the sentences invokes the nullability rule. The multiplicity allowances are the cardinality.

Table 3-2. *Detailed Relationship Rules*

Relationship Rule	True or False?
Each Order may own zero or one Car Order	False
Each Order may own zero, one, or many Car Order	True (if we can build orders before we make up our mind about the vehicle)
Each Order must own one and only one Car Order	False
Each Order must own one or many Car Order	False
Each Order must own 7 Car Order (but no more and no less)	False
Each Order must own 1–7 Car Order (but no more than seven and no less than one)	False
Each Order must own the quantity of Car Order equal to today's calendar day (but no more and no less)	False

Note that only cardinalities that allow for a zero can be of NULL cardinality. So by combining nullability and cardinality, you can specify the business rule exactly.

Many-to-Many

In Conceptual modeling you can combine any of the cardinality choices on either side of the relationship. There are no parents or children in a relationship such as the one shown in Figure 3-15. The entities are simply noted as being related and must be resolved by an associative or intersection entity (like you did with Car Order and Order Call Back earlier) when greater detail is necessary.

Many-to-Many Relationship

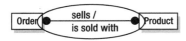

Figure 3-15. *A many-to-many relationship*

We'd classify this as the one truly conceptual relationship that we deal with (although it's allowable on entity-relationship-level Logical models as well). It covers a broad concept and needs to be analyzed further to be of much use.

Recursive (Hierarchical) Relationships

A *recursive relationship* is a relationship of an entity to itself. The relationship line loops from itself to itself, creating a funny-looking structure sometimes called a *pig's ear*. To continue the example, let's say that every tenth order more than $50 gets a special giveaway. However, because the marketing department is financing the giveaways, it needs a separate order to maintain tax and finance autonomy from the customer. The business rule is determined to be that a giveaway order must be the result of an order counting process, and only one giveaway can be created by any one order. The result is a *recursion* from order to order, as shown in Figure 3-16.

Recursive Relationship:
The Entity to Itself

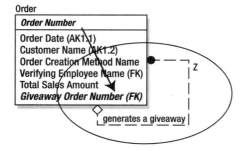

Figure 3-16. *Recursive relationship*

A recursion creates a hierarchical tree, where a child can have only one parent. Using the Z for "zero or one" in this example, the recursion is a single link downward.

Network Relationships

A network-style relationship involves the same principle of bringing two or more of the same entity together but is much more flexible than a recursive relationship since in this case a child can have many parents. We use them all the time to build organizational charts and parts trees. Figure 3-17 shows an example of an organizational chart.

Network Relationship:
Two Identifying Relationships from the Same Parent

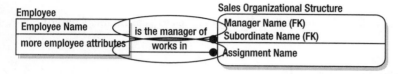

Figure 3-17. *A network relationship*

Let's say you want to build a matrix of the people who manage teams and those who participate in them. The recursive relationship wouldn't work, since it allows only a single relationship for the set members and is too restrictive. In this case, Employee can be both a Manager and a Subordinate. They can be on many teams, manage many teams, and participate in many teams.

This type of dual relationship has limitless possibilities for depth and breadth of the network. It has one risk that will need to be dealt with physically—namely, that no record can be its own child or parent. This situation would cause an infinite loop when the resultant data structures are queried, since to get the details, the query goes around and around the recursive relationship, chasing its tail like a puppy.

Relational Model Business Rules

Business rules combine the entity and the relationship into sentences that can be reviewed by the clients for truth and accuracy. Since everything is usually so atomic in the model, they can seem pretty silly at times. For example, you may well think that everyone knows that "one week must have seven days." However, if a week is defined as a "Sunday-to-Saturday period of time," then chances are that you have two weeks every year that aren't exactly seven days long: the first week in January and the last week in December. The first time we ran across 54 weeks in a year we were stunned, and we didn't catch it with the business rule review because we thought rules such as this didn't warrant review. This little oversight caused a week's worth of discussion because of the need for a "week over week" analysis report. We obviously broke the rule of making sure that you come to your analysis without preconceived notions and that you remain objective during the modeling process.

Business rules are built to read in both directions.

- Each || parent entity name || relationship verb phrase || cardinality || child entity name

- Each || child entity name || relationship verb phrase || cardinality || parent entity name

In the modeling syntax we'll use in this book, the standard way to write the verb phrases is in third person singular. A second business rule is then added to include the rules about nullability. They look as follows:

- No null allowed: Each || child entity name || belongs to || cardinality || parent entity name

- Null allowed: Each || child entity name || optionally belongs to || cardinality || parent entity name

Let's consider the example in Figure 3-18.

Elements of a Business Rule

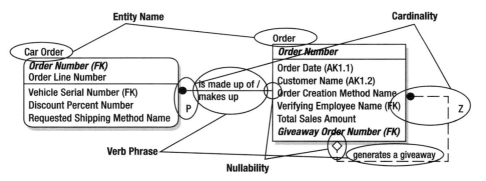

Figure 3-18. *Business rule components*

So you'd build business rules such as this:

- Each Order consists of zero, one, or many Car Orders.

- Each Car Order makes up one and only one Order.

- Each Car Order must belong to one and only one Order.

In this book we'll use a combination that departs slightly from the IDEF1X standard but allows you to review the business rules with the nullability factor included.

- Each || parent entity name || nullability || relationship verb phrase || cardinality || child entity name

- Each || child entity name || nullability || relationship verb phrase || cardinality || parent entity name

This gives you the following rules in the previous example:

- Each Order may be made up of zero, one, or many Car Orders.

- Each Car Order must make up one and only one Order.

In reading these it's implied that a Car Order can't exist after the Order that it's part of is deleted. Not only that, but a Car Order can't be part of more than one Order, and Car Orders can't be created until the Order exists.

■**Note** Sometimes reading the implications derived from the rules is more important than the rules themselves, because you see how restrictive the rules actually are and you realize that there are specific circumstances when the rules aren't true. Business rules must allow for every possible circumstance over the course of time.

There's some disagreement in the world of modeling right now as to whether entity-relationship phrases are business rules. We'd say they're just one type of business rule. A sentence such as "An employee may be assigned to zero, one, or many projects" sounds very much like a business rule. However, so does "A customer can earn credit toward a free giveaway by purchasing $100 of product within three months of their first order." Given the correct Logical model, this business rule can be derived from several true/false decisions, but it isn't represented as a simple entity-relationship phrase. Business rules are more than just what can be modeled, but it's important that the model supports them. *Business rules*, as a term, has evolved with the creation of "rules engines." There are *data integrity rules* (the kind of rules described here), and *business rules*, which relate to business policies that are important to the business process (in other words, an order must be filled within seven days or it's automatically canceled).

Introducing Physical Modeling Concepts

It's in developing a Physical model that all the care and concern you put into analyzing data elements and business processes really pays off. Entities are promoted to candidate tables, attributes to candidate columns, and relationships to candidate constraints. Many times there's almost a default "take it like it is" process that happens in the first pass at developing the Physical model. This is where the rubber hits the road, so to speak. The fine-tuning you thought you did in your Logical model needs to happen again but with a much greater awareness of your model's permanent impact on the business. You can build Logical models all day without affecting too many people. That isn't the case now with physical database designs. Every name you choose, misspelling you make, data size you make too small, data type you misjudge, and constraint you define incorrectly is going to have an impact on the entire development and maintenance teams for possibly years to come. Fortunately, the data modeler isn't alone in building the physical design; the DBA and programmers are also generally involved in brainstorming and reviewing the model before anything is built. While there are still corrections and alterations made at this stage, it's crucial to have as well developed a design as possible, even in the case of development and test databases built to "road-test" the design with a reasonable set of test data and queries.

Tables

Tables are called *files* or *records* in network and hierarchical DBMSs. They're the physical equivalent of entities. When we speak to a business client who doesn't have any database background, we equate tables to their spreadsheets or ledgers. A table is a singular container for data organized in rows and columns. And just like spreadsheets, tables can be linked together to provide a foreign key connection from a record in one spreadsheet to a record in another one.

Promoting an entity into a table isn't hard. In a data modeling tool, it can simply be a toggle of preferences from logical to physical. When moving to Physical models, we actually have to remind ourselves that everything needs to be looked at from a new direction, namely that of the chosen RDBMS platform on which the Physical model is expected to be deployed. DB2 has name length constraints, and older versions of SQL Server didn't support comments on the tables and columns for saving definitions at the database level. Every RDBMS we've worked with has some personality quirk that impacts how we create the Physical model. You need to learn your RDBMS to know its strengths and weaknesses.

■**Note** We used the Oracle RDBMS option in the following examples and are using underscore notation, replacing spaces in the column names with underscores.

In a simple logical-to-physical transformation, logical entities become physical tables, as shown in Figure 3-19.

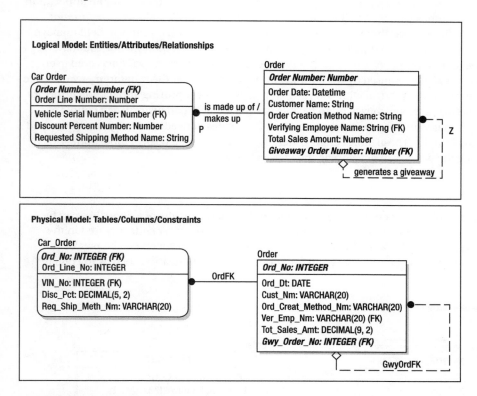

Figure 3-19. *Simple transformation of logical to physical*

We've made the attribute data domains visible so that you can compare them with the default data types that are created in the physical tables. As you can see, there have been few other changes during the transformation, other than the replacement of spaces with underscores. Sometimes getting physical is as simple as this. Remember that there are some rules you need to bear in mind regarding restricted words, depending on the programming language being used to code. You can't use certain simple words such as *Date* or *Column* as column names, for example. You may also want to shorten lengthy column names by creating a standard list of abbreviations. Different companies have different standards and approaches to the naming conventions of database objects.

You'll see more details regarding the transformation of a Logical into a Physical model in Chapter 10.

Operational Tables

The logical entities may not represent the only tables that need to be created for an application database. Sometimes you need tables that have no entity source. We call these *operational* tables, but you'll also hear them referred to as *utility* tables. They exist simply to help manage the processes that need to happen in order to support the system requirements. You may, for example, need to model a table that deals with user security details, such as encrypted usernames and passwords required by the administrator. It may be that the programmer would like a table to store values that deal with counting Web page hits or capturing application errors for historic reference. Perhaps they want to be able to keep a batch load history for a couple of weeks before archiving it. There are thousands of these types of needs that may be represented in the Physical model. These tables aren't generally modeled on the Logical model but are added during the process of developing the Physical model.

Views

A *view* is (generally) a temporary structure that's based on the results of a query but can be used in the same fashion (with a few restrictions) as a table. The view code is stored in the catalog tables of the RDBMS and is launched upon use in a query. Views can be part of your design, supporting the requirements and functionality of an application such as the one in Figure 3-20.

View Structure Design in a Physical Model

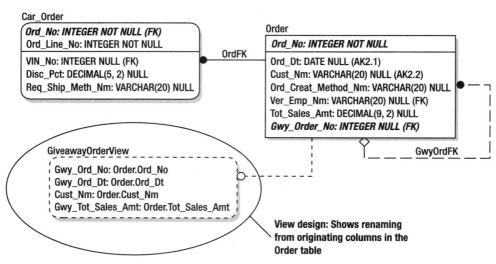

Figure 3-20. *A view design*

Notice that the column names in the view don't have to match the column names from their original tables. Many views are created simply to give clients names that are easier for them to recognize. This view has been created to support a giveaway order screen for the marketing department to be able to report on just the giveaway orders in their ad hoc query tool.

It's important to remember that views are database structures that abstract away some of the complexity of the underlying tables or provide a consistent interface to the tables, or both. Views serve many purposes, including the following:

- Pre-combining data sets for performance—(using materialized views)

- Managing complex algorithms for consistent use

- Restricting access to tables, columns in tables, or even data values by filtering the data set

- Buffering the application from changes to the actual tables

- Renaming tables and columns for a more client-friendly interface

Columns

All attributes that represent business data elements should be considered candidates to become columns. Few extra qualifications need to be reviewed before these candidate columns are included in the physical design. To be columns, attributes need to have a method of creation and maintenance and should have a steward to verify the values. This is especially true in the case of independent entities, such as lists of values, or sources of heavily relied-on data such as ZIP codes and country names that become tables. Theoretically, most if not all logical attributes should become columns. If the data represented by these attributes aren't valuable, they should probably not be in the Logical model or ultimately in the database.

Try not to send an attribute onto a database design if no one is going to accept responsibility for the quality and maintenance of it. The modeler does have some responsibility in verifying that the attribute has some chance of being a corporate asset rather than yet another bit of data dead weight to clog the RDBMS and lengthen the time for database diagnosis, backup, or recovery. We would have mentioned this earlier, at the table level, but it's at the attribute level where this is really important. Reviewing the attributes one last time with the business clients and determining whether they're important enough for someone to audit them for quality is a good test to conduct before you add them as columns of a database table.

Operational Columns

Operational columns are similar structures to operational tables. They're needed by the IT development team members to be able to do their job easily and well. Almost all tables could use a set of columns that record their creation and modification date and time. Sometimes you may need to include a flag column that a programmer uses to trace the stage of complex processes. As an example, consider the physical design for the Order table shown in Figure 3-21.

Operational Columns

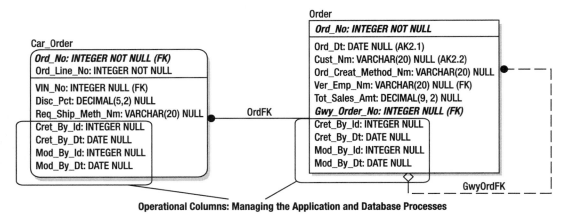

Operational Columns: Managing the Application and Database Processes

Figure 3-21. *Physical-only columns to support application management*

Operational columns don't show up in the Logical model but are added to the physical design.

Constraints

A simple way to think of a constraint is as the physical deployment of a logical relationship, which represents a business rule. The more sophisticated software tools can actually build a constraint directly from the definitions you built in the Physical model. The neat thing about RDBMS constraints is that they act like gravity; you can't break constraints unless you disable them. This is one of the places where having experience in physical transformation is really useful. Some logical relationship rules (constraints) are part of the physical design, and some aren't. An important design question is that of where data constraints are best applied or implemented. Sometimes this is in the front end (the application or screens) and sometimes in the back end (database or other nonvisible processes).

■**Note** Some seriously complicated constraints can also be created in the RDBMS. Generally, they can't be shown as a simple line between boxes on your data model. These constraints, as database objects, are beyond the scope of the discussion here.

The following is an example of a foreign key constraint:

```
ALTER TABLE Order_Line
      ADD constraint OrderLineFK ( FOREIGN KEY (Order_Number)
                             REFERENCES Order (Order Number) ) ;
```

If your constraint says that a parent must have at least one child, then the RDBMS will actually prevent the insertion of a parent record without a corresponding child record. Deletions of records are prevented if they're connected through foreign keys to other tables. So the previous constraint prevents the deletion of an Order record unless all the corresponding Order_Line records are deleted as well. This prevents the occurrence of *orphan* records, unrelated to any other values in the database, which violates referential integrity.

Summary

In this chapter we introduced relational modeling terminology and the concepts used every day to build Conceptual, Logical, and Physical data models. Specifically, you looked at the following:

- Entities (independent, dependent)

- Attributes (singular, group)

- Keys (candidate, primary, foreign)

- Relationships (identifying, nonidentifying, category, view)

- Relationship terminators (cardinality, nullability)

- Tables/views (customer data sets, operational data sets)

- Columns (customer data elements, operational data elements)

- Keys (primary, surrogate, alternate, foreign)

- Constraints

∎∎∎

CHAPTER 4

Understanding Data Modeling Methods: Graphical Syntax

Having covered the conceptual building blocks of entities, attributes, keys, and relationships, let's now look at the various methods and the graphical symbols used to draw a relational data model. We'll cover the following:

- Integration DEFinition (IDEF1X) modeling syntax and other notations available for a modeler's use in documenting data elements and business rules (used throughout the book)

- Entity-relationship (ER) diagramming (Chen notation)

- Information engineering (IE) modeling syntax

- Barker notation

A number of different data modeling standards exist, and choosing which one of them to use in performing your data analysis can be one of the most interesting (and confusing) issues that you'll have to address. Although each style is similar, the standards have differences when it comes to the details of what data characteristics you can capture in a picture and how you document each building block. Just keep in mind that no method is perfect.

Usually, once the choice is made about the model drawing style at your company, it's almost set in stone. You'll quite likely need to train clients and programmers how to read the model, so you may want to do this for only one drawing style. However, knowing the strengths and limitations of a variety of different styles will help decide which style is most useful in your work. Don't make up your mind too soon. Although our focus here will be on the IDEF1X standard, we'll introduce three other modeling styles for you to review.

Integration Definition (IDEF1X)

We'll begin with IDEF1X because that's the notation we'll use throughout the book. It's found in most CASE and modeling tools and is the language used in U.S. government projects, having been developed in the 1970s by the U.S. Air Force and revised by D. Appleton in 1993. It has gone through its testing period and is able to document most discoveries about how data relates. But unlike Latin, it isn't a dead language and is growing to encompass some of the new Unified Modeling Language (UML) and object modeling needs in the form of its latest incarnation, IDEF1X$_{97}$.

Note   Using IDEF1X is a personal preference; you can generally draw the same analysis in many different notations. Some notations have symbols that cover concepts others don't. For instance, Barker notation can denote either/or relationships, but IDEF1X can't. Whatever notation you use, you should practice it until you're comfortable using it.

The symbols used in IDEF1X are close enough to the symbols used by other modeling styles to be recognizable, and they're different enough to be confusing if you haven't used other modeling styles. The following list describes the elements you need to master in order to document data characteristics in this graphical language:

- Entities, tables, and views are both square- and round-cornered boxes. Square corners denote a lack of dependence for identification on another entity. Round corners denote the opposite.

- Relationships are solid lines if the foreign key is identifying and dashed if it's nonidentifying. Solid and dashed lines are completed with a set of terminating symbols that can be combined to cover a variety of cardinality and optionality rules.

- Entities that are categories have symbols signifying whether the subtypes represent a complete or incomplete membership.

- Attributes and columns are displayed depending on the view with an optional set of characteristics.

- Primary keys are segregated from other attributes above a dividing line in an entity box.

- Foreign, alternate, and inversion entry keys/indexes are optionally displayed with text notations.

No matter the choice of drawing style, what you're capturing is essentially the same. You may just draw it a little differently depending upon the syntax you use. You'll now take a closer look at this notation.

Boxes

Boxes denote three different concepts. Logical models contain entities, and Physical models contain tables and views. It's often hard at first glance to be able to decide whether you're looking at a Logical or Physical model for this reason (see Figure 4-1).

Assorted Data Modeling Boxes

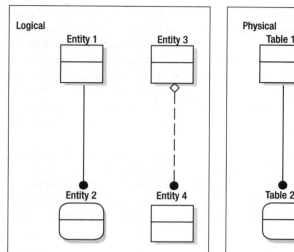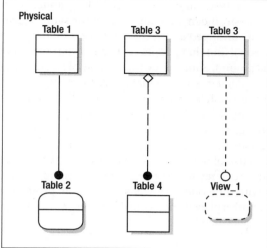

Figure 4-1. *The box shapes in IDEF1X*

The following are some pretty basic rules about boxes on a model.

Dual Syntax

All the boxes on a model represent either entities or tables/views. They can't be mixed. Although they may look similar, logical and physical objects are *never* used in the same model. The only boxes used in both logical and physical diagrams are cosmetic drawing objects used to frame and highlight text.

Singular Purpose

Boxes have one purpose. They're visual boundaries surrounding a data set. On a relational model, this basically means the following:

Boxes don't represent anything other than entities (in a Logical model) or tables or views (in a Physical model).

All entities or tables/views are represented as a box. They aren't represented any other way. Even discoveries from other logical analyses or actual objects in other databases, which won't be deployed, are still boxes on the model. They're usually noted with a distinctive color, text format, or naming convention to identify them appropriately.

Location Indifference

In IDEF1X, boxes aren't in any order. They aren't arranged in any special way, and their placement doesn't mean anything. You get the same logical or physical design no matter how the boxes are arranged on the model. They should be arranged to best communicate data discoveries. You'll find that people get used to your placements and react negatively when you move things around. Some argue that the physical creation order should order the boxes on the model so that everything that needs to be built first should appear above those objects that need to be built later. Others claim all relationship lines should either be "in the top and out the bottom" or on the sides noting the migrating key (but not all directions at once). But these are conventions, not hard-and-fast rules.

Concentrate on making the arrangement of the objects on your model part of the way to create a useful product for your customers. We have a tendency to try to use as little paper as possible so that we can print our models more easily. This won't be useful if you're trying to work with someone who needs the creation precedence clearly noted and wants the independent entities placed above the dependent entities. Use your best judgment, and be sensitive to your clients' needs.

Corner Meaning: Dependent/Independent

The corners of the boxes denote their degree of dependence. Square-cornered boxes denote independent entities or tables, and rounded-cornered boxes denote dependent entities or tables. You can determine this dependency by whether the primary key attributes needed to identify an instance in the member set also identify an instance in another entity's member set. If you look at Figure 4-2, you can see that Entity2 and Table_2 are *dependent* on their parents. On the other hand, Entity4 and Table_4 are *independent* of their parents. The same occurs with tables in the Physical model. Database views are always dependent because they can't exist without the tables from which they're derived.

Corner shape notes dependence or independence on a parent entity or table

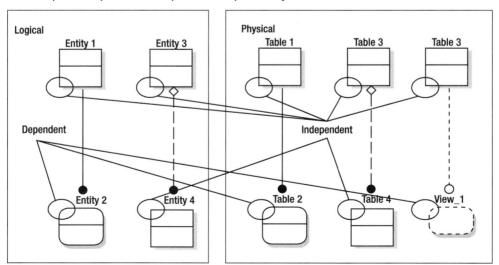

Figure 4-2. *Corner shape meaning*

For example, Figure 4-3 shows the little model from Chapter 3.

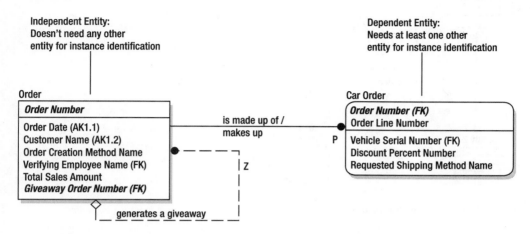

Figure 4-3. *Entity dependence*

You can see from this example that a Car Order depends on Order for a portion of its identity. You need the Order Number identifier to be able to complete the identifier (or primary key) of the Car Order.

Remember that dependence results in having a portion of the parent's complete identifier created in the child entity or table and is important to the sequencing of some data creation and deletion. We'd like to say that it will be your visual clue to all sequential dependence, but that isn't true. Certain mandatory nonidentifying relationships will also impact sequential tasks of creation and deletion of objects, constraints, and data, yet in IDEF1X they aren't shown with soft corners.

Lines

Line styles are the same on both the Logical and Physical model. The only exception is the line noting the relationship of a table to a view, which has no counterpart in Logical modeling. Lines in the model are used to segregate, connect, and note membership.

Lines Within Boxes

Lines in boxes segregate the data elements into two types: those that act as a primary key or identifier and those that don't. Every text label above the line notes one separate data element that has been chosen to either partially (in combination with other data elements), or uniquely, identify each member of the entity. That separator line divides the data elements into two groups: the group of primary identifying attributes and the group of attributes not used as part of a primary identifier. Those data elements under the line could still be defined as candidate keys and could therefore be identifying attributes—they just aren't part of the primary key. You should only ever see one line in a box, as shown in Figure 4-4.

Line Inside a Box

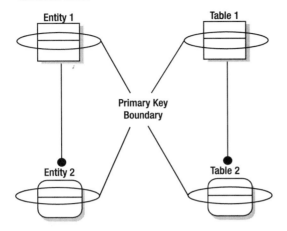

Figure 4-4. *Primary key boundary line*

Relationships Between Boxes

Relationships, or constraints (as you saw earlier), tie entities and tables together and are also depicted using lines. These lines often have a verb phrase explaining why the tie is there or showing the name of the constraint. These lines also terminate using a specific symbol set to depict quite a bit of information about the relationship. But focus for a moment on the simple line definition shown in Figure 4-5—solid, dashed, and dots.

Assorted Data Modeling Lines

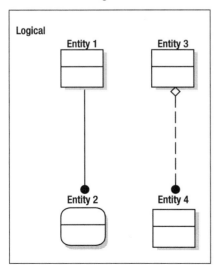
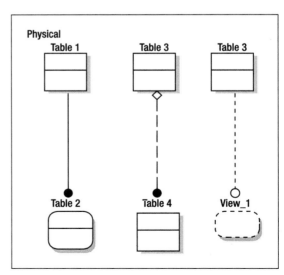

Figure 4-5. *Logical and physical relationship line graphics*

You can read these examples to mean the following:

Solid lines denote that the entire complement of data elements above the line (the primary key of the parent entity or table) is migrating to the primary key position of the entity (or table) to which it's being related. This is called an *identifying* relationship. You can look at one between Order and Car Order in Figure 4-6. A Car Order can't exist without an Order.

Long, dashed lines denote that the entire complement of data elements above the line of the parent entity or table is migrating to a position below the line of the entity or table to which it's being related. This is called a *nonidentifying* relationship. The relationship between Order and Order to denote a Giveaway Order is nonidentifying. Specifically, an Order could exist without a Giveaway Order, and one doesn't need the Order that caused the Giveaway Order creation to find the Giveaway Order.

The last line style is a series of dots or short dashes. It's a physical notation only, since it notes that a view uses a table for source data. Views can use any or all the columns in the table they reference. The GiveawayOrderView in Figure 4-6 is an example.

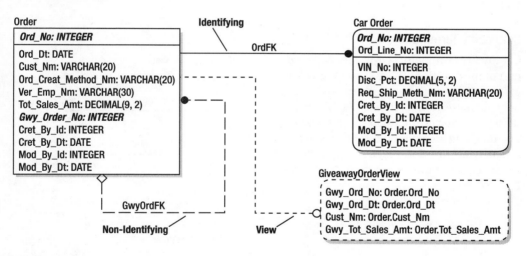

Figure 4-6. *Various line types in a small Physical model example*

Another type of line notation that's used solely in Logical modeling denotes a category grouping, as shown in Figure 4-7. As a reminder, when using a category structure, you have one parent (supertype) entity with as many subtype entities as required to document your analysis. The solid lines tell you that the relationship is identifying or, in other words, that all the category entities share the same primary key. The single or double lines at the intersection tell you whether the entire set of category subtype divisions is noted. A complete category notes all the subtypes, and an incomplete category notes only some of them.

Category Line Options

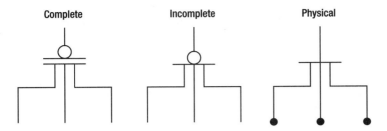

Figure 4-7. *Lines representing category relationships*

The physical notation for categories is the default notation used on the Physical model. For Physical models, the same notation is used for both complete and incomplete categories.

Terminators

Terminators show up at the end of lines. They tell you how many instances of an entity or table are subject to the relationship.

Cardinality Terminator

Cardinality terminators cover the "how many?" part of the question. These symbols give you lots of flexibility in defining relationships. They also help database administrators (DBAs) figure out ratio and sizing estimates in the physical world. The meaning is conveyed through a simple terminated line or a dot, which can be enhanced with a letter or number notation, as shown in Figure 4-8.

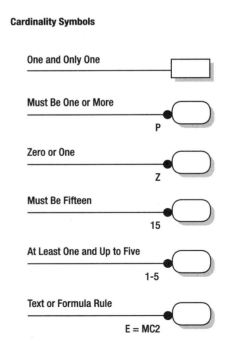

Figure 4-8. *IDEF1X cardinality graphics*

Table 4-1 shows how you read these rules.

Table 4-1. *IDEF1X Cardinality Graphics Meanings*

Relationship Line Terminator Symbol	Meaning	Infers	Example
Plain line	One and only one	Generally the parent or source.	This is the parent terminator. It's used for child to parent business rules, such as "Each order line makes up one and only one order."
Z plus dot	Zero or one	Boolean decision.	This is a child terminator. It's used for parent to child business rules, such as "Each order generates zero or one order."
P plus dot	One or many	Mandatory requirement of at least one.	This is a child terminator. It's used for parent to child business rules, such as "Each order is made up of one or many order lines."
Dot	Zero, one, or many	Most flexible rule.	This is a child terminator. It is used for parent to child business rules, such as "Order is made up of zero, one, or many order lines."
\<Number\> plus dot	Specifically \<N\>	The most restrictive. That quantity only (always).	This is a child terminator. It's used for parent to child business rules, such as "Each calendar year is made up of 12 months."
\<N–N\> plus dot	The range Number–Number	A range rule. Must be at least at the lower but may be as high as the higher of the two values.	This is a child terminator. It's used for parent to child business rules, such as "Each calendar month is made up of 28 to 31 days."
\<note\> plus dot	Whatever it says about a multiple relationship	A very complicated "how many?" that can't be stated any other way. (This is a good example of a logical modeling notation that doesn't translate simply into a physical implementation.)	This is a child terminator. It's used for parent to child business rules, such as "Each customer younger than 12 and older than 65 is offered a ticket discount."

■Note This table includes two notations (*\<N–N\> plus dot* and *\<note\> plus dot*) that aren't standard IDEF1X.

Nullability Terminator

The nullability terminator symbol denotes whether a relationship is required from all the child instances. This is read from the child to the parent, and in the case of a mandatory relationship will read as follows:.

- Every child <Entity / Table> instance *must* be related to a parent <Entity/Table> instance.

In the case of a null-allowed relationship, it will read as follows:

- Every child <Entity / Table> instance *is allowed not be* related to a parent <Entity/Table> instance.

The symbol to denote this latter relationship type is an open diamond at the end of the line closest to the parent. For example, in the little Order model you can see in Figure 4-9, the diamond is at the end of the relationship noting the connection of Order to Order and Employee to Order. You'll see this symbol only at the end of a nonidentifying relationship (the dashed line). No nulls are allowed in an identifying relationship, and it isn't used in view notation.

Nullability Symbol

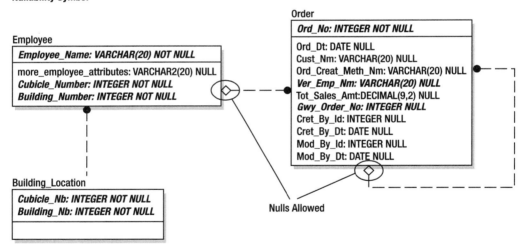

Figure 4-9. *Notation for nullability*

See in Figure 4-9 how we've used the nullability symbols to say that every Employee must have a Building_Location? However, not every Order generates a Giveaway Order; an Order *may* have a Giveaway_Order, but this relationship isn't required.

View Terminator

The small dashed line and a hollow dot terminator denotes a view (see Figure 4-10). As a reminder, views are found only on Physical models, and they contain prepackaged or filtered data from source tables. Everything in them depends for existence on the original sources.

We tend to look at that empty dot as a ghost terminator; for example, you model views for many different reasons, but they have no substance on their own. It shows up as an empty terminator since the notation shows a dependency only between the view and the source tables. You may find views on Physical models that have no visible relationships if these views are referencing tables that aren't on the model.

View Line Terminator

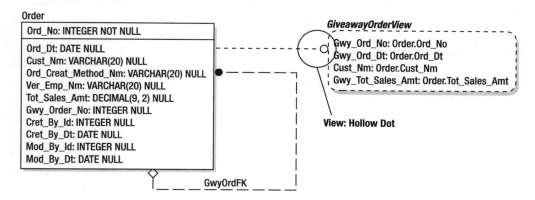

Figure 4-10. *Terminator for a view*

Entity-Relationship (ER) or Chen Diagramming

ER has been very popular, especially for Conceptual modeling, and is one of the oldest modeling styles, having been first developed by Dr. Peter P. Chen in 1976. Some modern modeling software has dropped ER from the choices offered in recent years, but you may come across it in your company's archives. Figure 4-11 shows the symbols generally used in this type of diagramming.

ER Diagramming Symbols (Chen Notation)

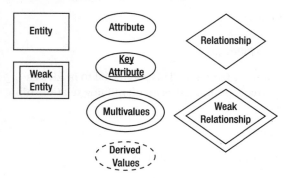

Figure 4-11. *ER symbols*

ER modeling uses the following common constructs:

- Independent entities are in square-cornered boxes.

- The name of the entity is attached to the box.

- Attributes are described in reference to an entity.

Figure 4-12 shows characteristics similar to those you've looked at for IDEF1X of relation-ships (such as nullability or ordinality in ER terms) and cardinality.

ER Relationship Symbols (Chen Notation)

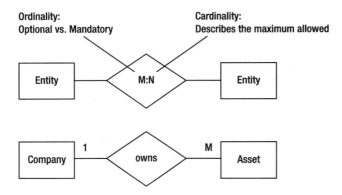

1:M = One to Zero or More
M:N = Zero or More to Zero or More (Many to Many)
1:1 = One to One

Figure 4-12. *ER relationship symbols*

Similarities include the following:

- Relationships connect the boxes with a line.

- A letter or number code denotes cardinality.

Notations that are unique to ER include the following:

- Dependent entities are noted as a double-bordered box. This is referred to in ER as a *weak entity type*, or one whose key is partially populated as an identifying relationship to another entity and can't exist alone.

- Relationships are designated with diamonds.

- The relationships are frequently nouns, rather than verb phrases.

- Rules should be read in a definite direction (left to right, top to bottom).

Figure 4-13 shows an example of a Chen diagram; the following list describes the information it portrays:

- An Employee can do project work (proj-work) on many (M) Projects.

- An Employee can be the project manager (proj-mgr) of one (1) Project.

- A Dependent is a dependent (emp-dep) for only one (1) Employee. Since Dependent is a weak entity type, each instance of Dependent must have an Employee instance that identifies it.

- A Part can be a Component of many (M) parts.

- A Supplier supplies one or more Parts for one or more Projects.

- A Part may be supplied by many Suppliers.

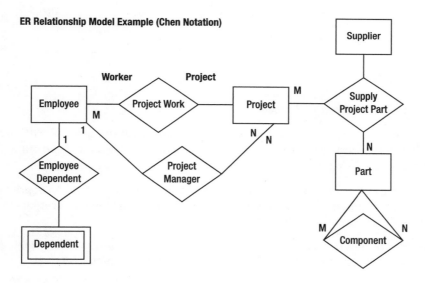

Figure 4-13. *Example of ER data model*

Chen (ER) is still used quite a bit and is good at capturing the details required for summary or conceptual analysis.

Information Engineering (IE)

IE, developed by Clive Finkelstein and James Martin in 1976, is popular today among modelers and is generally an option in the popular modeling tools. Note the similarities to the IDEF1X box symbols in Figure 4-14.

IE: Entity, Table, and View Boxes

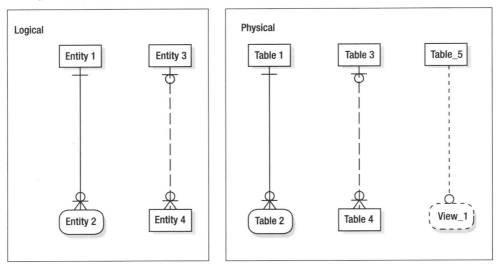

Figure 4-14. *IE box symbols*

IE symbols have the following characteristics:

IE models use square- and round-cornered box conventions like you saw in IDEF1X for entities. The square-cornered boxes denote an independent entity or table; the round-cornered boxes denote a dependent entity or table. The dashed box is a view.

The entity/table box can be shown with a dividing line to show the distinction of primary key and owned attributes. You also have the option of viewing attributes or keeping them hidden, but they're contained within their owning box.

Relationships are lines between boxes using the same conventions of solid lines for identifying relationships and dashed lines for nonidentifying relationships.

The distinctive feature of IE models is the terminator of the relationship lines. IE uses the famous "crow's foot" symbol to denote multiplicity (cardinality), allowing for many rule combinations between parents and children. An interesting point to note here is that different versions of IE actually have subtle syntax differences. Some allow for an exclusive either/or notation, and some don't. You'll need to get familiar with your own version. Figure 4-15 shows the symbols used in ERwin 4.1.

One of the places where the syntax of one modeling notation is different from another is in the difference in meaning of categories between IDEF1X and IE. Where IDEF1X notes complete and incomplete categories, IE notes categories as exclusive (where one instance must be grouped into one and only one subtype) and inclusive (where an instance can be noted as part of one or more subtypes), as shown in Figure 4-16. These can look similar, so you need to pay attention to notice these subtle differences in meaning.

IE Cardinality Symbols

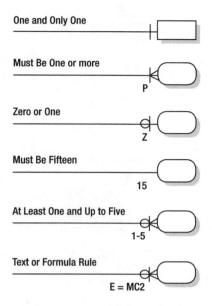

Figure 4-15. *IE cardinality symbols*

IE Category Symbols

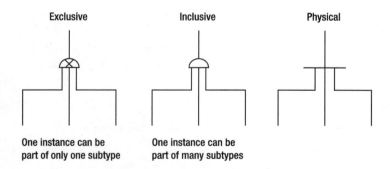

Figure 4-16. *IE category symbols*

Figure 4-17 shows the example Order model reworked as an IE diagram. You'll notice that the IE notations map to IDEF1X notations fairly well. Both of these notations are similar, other than the differences in category notation.

IE Logical Model Example

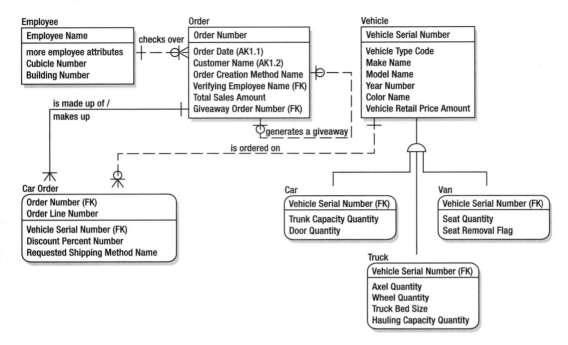

Figure 4-17. *IE logical model example*

Barker Notation

The last notation style we'll cover is Richard Barker's notation, developed in 1990. It's used in Oracle's CASE design tools as well as some other data modeling software. In this syntax language, the following happens:

- The entity boxes all have round corners.

- The relationship line shows optionality as a dashed line, rather than a terminator symbol.

- Attributes are shown, but a line doesn't segregate the primary key. The primary key is coded with a pound (#) sign.

- Relationships are restricted to binary (true or false).

- The exclusion (either/or constraint) is represented as an arc, spanning relationships on the diagram.

- Category or subtype/supertype relationships are shown as nested boxes.

Figure 4-18 shows an example of what Barker looks like. And you can read the following business rules from this model:

- Each LINE ITEM is bought via one PRODUCT or one SERVICE.

- Each PRODUCT is for many LINE ITEMs.

- Each SERVICE is for many LINE ITEMs.

- The Product code is the primary identifier of PRODUCT.

- The Description, Unit price are optional attributes of PRODUCT.

- Each PURCHASE ORDER is composed of many LINE ITEMs.

- Each LINE ITEM is part of and at least partially identified by a PURCHASEORDER.

- Each PARTY is either a PERSON or an ORGANIZATION.

Barker Notation Logical Model Example

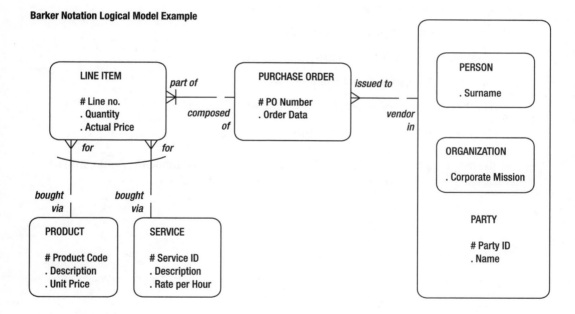

Figure 4-18. *Barker notation*

■**Note** Figure 4-18 came from www.essentialstrategies.com/publications/modeling/ barker.htm; you can read more about Barker notation at this site.

Summary

We covered some alternatives in data modeling graphic syntax languages, focusing on the IDEF1X notation we'll use in all the models throughout this book. Many of the concepts that the symbols represent are the same. Although some symbols are unique to one style or another, the higher-level concepts are largely independent of the graphic symbol sets used in these languages. The symbols cover notations for many different aspects of set members and their attributes, which can be read as sentences when you know what the symbols represent. The symbols cover meaning for the following:

- Dependent (weak) and independent (strong) entities or tables

- Views and their dependencies on tables or other views

- Identifying and nonidentifying relationships or constraints

- Null ability of migrating keys

- Cardinality (how many allowed) of entity relationships

- Supertype and subtype category members

- Inclusive or exclusivity within category members

- Exclusivity between optional relationships

- Whether the category is complete or incomplete

- Primary key attributes and other owned attributes

In the next chapter, we'll cover how UML, an object-oriented modeling syntax with its own distinctive modeling symbols, relates to relational modeling.

■■■
Introducing Object-Oriented Data Modeling

While the focus of this book is on relational data modeling techniques, it's relevant at this point to discuss the subject of object-oriented modeling (OOM). The widespread acceptance of relational databases and the popularity of object-oriented programming languages often require that object models be converted into, and supported by, a relational physical database design. Therefore, the techniques of OOM and relational data modeling need to coexist, and it's entirely possible that at some point you'll be asked to support an object-oriented development process with a relational database. Certainly, we've seen both styles used concurrently by software development teams (with varying levels of success).

A full discussion of the scope of OOM and techniques is outside the scope of this book. This chapter will explore the basics of OOM and show how it compares to relational modeling. Although at first glance the two techniques might appear to be largely incompatible, the object modeling process captures the "data-centric" portion of a business process in much the same way as relational data models do.

In this chapter, you'll look at similarities and differences between the object and relational models, including the following:

- A basic description of object-oriented analysis and design

- The syntax and purpose of object-oriented models

- A comparison of object-oriented models and relational models

- Supporting object models with relational databases

Introducing Object-Oriented Design

Three design paradigms exist for constructing software systems. The paradigm you choose largely depends on the style of analysis you perform and the way you prioritize your system's components. Given that the software side of a system consists of data and programs, traditional design methodologies focus either on the data or on the functionality of the software, depending on what's considered to be important or complex. The following are the schools of thought:

- **Data-oriented design**: Also known as *information engineering* (IE), this focuses the analysis of software requirements on the system's data requirements. These data requirements then determine the software design.

- **Function-oriented design**: Also known as *structured analysis,* this uses process decomposition to break down the requirements of the system's functionality into a procedural hierarchy. The functional requirements then determine the software design.

As software development capabilities have matured, these design methodologies have evolved and merged to become object-oriented design (OOD). OOD combines elements of data-oriented and function-oriented design techniques, and it models systems as collections of cooperating objects. The design of the system's objects, which include functional and data requirements, then determine the software design.

OOD is a hybrid methodology that breaks a system down into objects, embodying both *data* characteristics in the form of attributes and *process* characteristics in the form of methods. Software programs become collections of interconnected objects, where those objects perform their individual functions and store their particular data independently of each other. These interconnected objects are then integrated into a program that performs some meaningful task.

Relational data modeling activities focus on the "data-oriented" analysis and design tasks, applying relational theory to collections of entities (data sets) and focusing on the interrelationships between them. Object-oriented analysis and modeling, in contrast, takes a more holistic view of software development by classifying all the distinct system and business components as objects, and then it focuses on their behaviors and attributes. In this sense, "objects" can be system components, such as screens or shared subprocesses, or they can be business objects, which are similar to relational entities. The big difference between objects and entities is the inclusion of functions or behaviors in the object definition.

The benefits of OOD are that, with carefully constructed object models, the reusability and interchangeability of the objects allow for very flexible software designs. Think of software objects as self-contained building blocks of functionality and data, where the combination of data elements and programmatic behavior allows objects to be relatively easily reused or recombined into different configurations. Each configuration can then perform a different function.

Object-Oriented Models: Class Diagrams

Since discussing how object-oriented models fit into data modeling and relational databases, we'll focus on how object-oriented models document the business subject area and its processes in much the same way as relational models. Unified Modeling Language (UML) object models are referred to as *class diagrams*, where classes encapsulate the data and behavior of the relevant business objects. Objects always combine data and behavior.

Class diagrams are the logical equivalent to relational data models. They show the important business concepts, including the following:

- The data attributes needed

- The behaviors each object exhibits

- How the different objects are related

When comparing relational models to object models, you're really comparing relational models to class diagrams.

The following types of class diagrams can capture information about the business data:

Business information models: These document a business subject area's objects and attributes, as well as how these objects are conceptually related. These models generally don't capture behavior or are process oriented, and as such they're analogous to Logical data models in the relational world.

Business analysis models: These document a business subject area's objects, attributes, and methods, as well as how the objects are conceptually related. These models include object behaviors in addition to data attributes. Because relational data models don't capture behavioral characteristics of the business entities, they're also analogous to Logical data models in the relational world.

Business object models: These represent the physical realization of a business analysis model, and they model the software objects, including attributes, methods and interobject relationships, as they're designed to be built. Because business object models document the physical design of the software to be built, they're analogous to Physical data models in the relational world.

You can create other object-oriented models that show how the software is intended to function from a nonbusiness perspective, including infrastructure and communication components; these are beyond the scope of this chapter. The three model types described previously provide the basis for comparison against relational data models.

Unified Modeling Language (UML)

UML was first published in 1997 by the Object Management Group (www.omg.org) and was an attempt to create a single syntax with which data and application components could be modeled. UML represents a compilation of "best engineering practices" that have proven successful in modeling large, complex systems.

As you'll note in the timeline shown in Figure 5-1, UML grew into a single, common, widely usable modeling method and was the product of many individuals from a variety of backgrounds, including corporate information technology (IT) departments, software tool developers, industry experts, and others. UML's goal is to be a standard modeling language that can model concurrent and distributed systems.

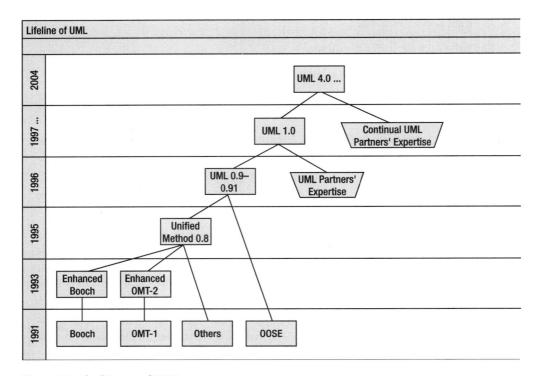

Figure 5-1. *The history of UML*

However, in the context of modeling the business process, UML is more than just a graphical syntax for generating class diagrams. You can use UML to model the static structure of the system as well as activities that occur within the system. Note, in Table 5-1, how the purposes of UML diagrams correspond with the existing Integration DEFinition (IDEF) family of modeling syntaxes.

Table 5-1. *Comparing UML Diagrams and IDEF Diagrams*

UML Diagram	What It Contains	IDEF Model Equivalent
Structural Diagrams		
Class diagram	The static objects with their attributes and their relationships to other objects	IDEF1: Conceptual Modeling IDEF1X: Logical Modeling IDEF1X$_{97}$: Logical Modeling with Object Extensions
Component diagram	Physical software and hardware component dependencies and organization	
Object diagram	Relationships between system objects	
Deployment diagram	Physical system runtime architecture, which can include hardware and software details	

UML Diagram	What It Contains	IDEF Model Equivalent
Behavior Diagrams		
Activity diagram	System activities or business processes and the workflows that connect these processes	IDEF0: Activity Modeling
Use case diagram	Business processes that will be implemented and the people who will interact with them	IDEF3: Process Modeling
State chart diagram	The details surrounding the transition of objects from one business state to another	IDEF3: Process Modeling
Collaboration diagram	The details of how individual objects collaborate and interact	
Sequence diagram	The details of the specific sequencing of messages sent between objects in the system	IDEF3: Process Modeling

Notice that the IDEF notations can't capture the same richness of information about the physical software implementation as UML. Also, the shortcoming of the IDEF suite of models is that the information gathered about a process can't be easily shared with other processes. The IDEF models were designed to be used independently from each other, but UML tries by design to keep the information together and integrated. This allows for multiple different views or perspectives of the same base system information.

UML Syntax

When comparing UML class diagrams to relational data models, it's important to understand what's common to the two styles of modeling and what isn't. Because of the nature of OOD, some of the concepts you're able to model in class diagrams, such as class behaviors or complex object data types, aren't easily represented in a Logical data model. But although the notations aren't 100 percent compatible, a significant degree of overlap exists in the fundamental areas.

Later in this chapter, in the "Example UML Transformation" section, we'll show how to convert a Logical data model into a UML diagram, but before we do that, we'll discuss some of the conceptual similarities between object models and relational models.

Classes vs. Entities

Classes are roughly equivalent to Logical modeling entities, as shown in Figure 5-2. When looking at a business-oriented model, they're the items that are important to the business.

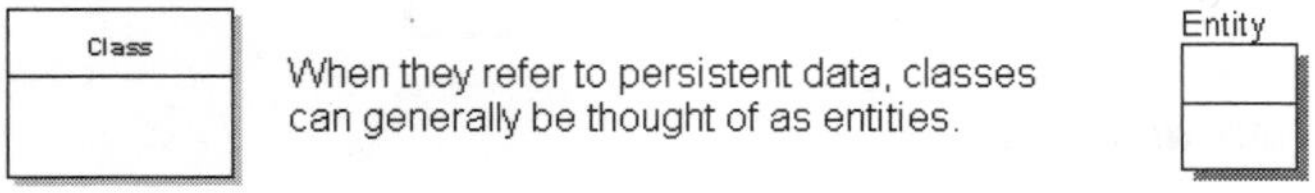

Figure 5-2. *How classes and entities are similar*

Class is a named rectangle with compartments for attributes, operations, and other characteristics, as shown in Figure 5-3.

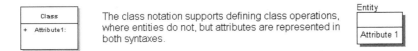

Figure 5-3. *Classes and entities with attributes*

For object classes, you'll see three distinct areas for each class in the diagram. The top section names the class, the middle section shows the attributes that are part of the class, and the bottom section shows the behaviors or operations that can be performed on that class. Note that no key determination appears on a class, just as no operations appear as part of an entity's definition.

Generalizations vs. Categories

In Chapter 3, you saw how slightly different entities with common attributes can be represented by a category structure, where each subtype is related to its supertype by an "is a" phrase. In UML, categories are represented by generalizations. In both relational and object models, these constructs denote a categorization mechanism representing a hierarchy of supertypes and subtypes (see Figure 5-4).

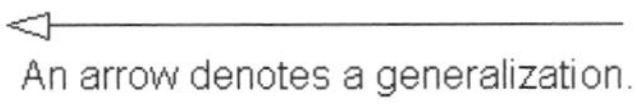

An arrow denotes a generalization.

Figure 5-4. *UML generalization notation*

See Figure 5-5 for an example of how this type of relationship is represented in both object and relational models. These hierarchies are always read with an "is a" phrase between the subordinate and generalized Class. For example, Motorcycle "is a" Powered Vehicle. Truck "is a" Powered Vehicle. Cookie "is a" Dessert. Ice Cream "is a" Dessert.

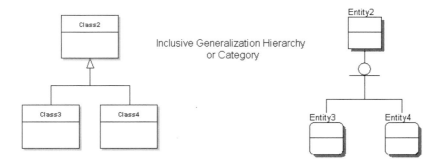

Figure 5-5. *Inclusive hierarchies in UML and IDEF1X*

Generalizations denote the distinctness of recognizably different members within a larger, more generic grouping by using an arrow to point to the higher, more encompassing class. An object that's a single instance of the class in Figure 5-5 may actually be both of the subtypes simultaneously. In relational modeling this is equivalent to an inclusive category. For instance, a Ford Ranchero may belong to both Truck and Automobile depending on the definition of each.

To show that an instance of a class may be one and only one of the listed subtypes, use the OR notation, as shown in Figure 5-6.

----------{OR}----------
(OR) between associations indicates one or the other, not both.

Figure 5-6. *UML exclusive generalization notation*

This notation is equivalent to the IDEF1X double-line category symbol, as shown in Figure 5-7.

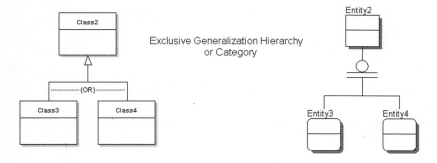

Figure 5-7. *Exclusive generalization in UML and IDEF1X*

A generalization notation with the dotted line and OR statement notes that a member of the generalized class may belong to only one or the other of the subordinates. This is referred to as an *exclusive hierarchy* in both UML and IDEF1X. You'd use this notation to show that a Dachshund, for example, can only ever be classified as Dog in the category of Pet.

Relationships vs. Associations

Similarly to relational models, UML models allow objects to be related, and UML has notation that allows a slightly richer set of relationships to be documented in a UML class diagram. UML has three types of relationships.

- *Associations* connect objects that are related but where no dependency exists between the classes taking part in the relationship. For example, an employee is related to an employer, but no existence dependency exists between them.

- *Compositions* show that a parent-child relationship exists and that the child entities depend on the parent for their existence. For example, a building contains a series of rooms. If the building is demolished, the rooms that were part of the building also cease to exist.

- *Aggregations* show that a group-member relationship exists and that the group entities depend on their members for their existence. For example, the chess club is an aggregation of students, but if the chess club ceased to exist, the students would still exist. If the students ceased to exist, the club also would cease to exist.

Relational graphic notations, such as IDEF1X or IE, don't have a method for noting aggregations. Other than in text blocks or diagram notes, IDEF1X lacks the ability to show that some relationships are built because of a "binding" of the elements for the purpose of creating a grouping entity. Relational modeling techniques recognize only entities connected in some kind of a parent-child relationship or a supertype-subtype hierarchy. These techniques make assumptions regarding the dependence of the child on the parent or regarding the subtype on the supertype. They're missing the notion of a high-level group that depends on its members for existence.

Associations

As mentioned, associations show that two objects are connected in some way. An association is equivalent to a relationship line between entities on a relational data model. A solid line shows an association relationship between two objects (see Figure 5-8).

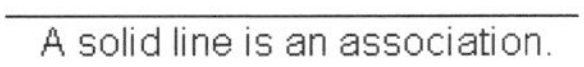

A solid line is an association.

Figure 5-8. *UML association notation*

The lack of specific diagram notation at either end of the relationship indicates no dependence between these entities (see Figure 5-9).

Figure 5-9. *Ordinary association in UML and IDEF1X*

In a class diagram, the cardinality of the relationship is shown through the use of the numbers at either end of the association line. In Figure 5-9, ClassA is related to ClassB in a one-to-many relationship. Exactly one ClassA object must exist for every ClassB object, and zero or more ClassB objects may exist for every ClassA object.

Compositions

Composition relationships, also known as *strong associations*, are the type of relationship that's most easily translated between UML and relational models. Composition relationships establish a parent-child relationship, where the child depends on the parent for its existence. The dependence is strong enough that it implies that by deleting the parent instance, any child instances will be deleted as well (see Figure 5-10).

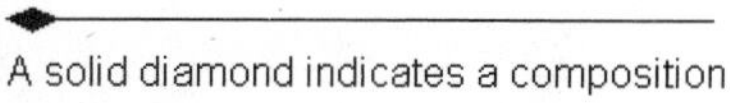

A solid diamond indicates a composition.

Figure 5-10. *UML composition notation*

A composition relationship uses a solid diamond notation to identify the owning, parent class. Cardinality symbols as used in association relationships are also used in this example to show the cardinality of the relationship, although the use of a composition requires that the parent entity be marked with a one (see Figure 5-11 and Figure 5-12).

The examples in Figures 5-11 and 5-12 show both a recursive composition relationship and a regular nonrecursive composition relationship. In the model, the solid diamond indicates that a Room is dependent on its associated Building for the Room's existence. If the building were to cease to exist, any Room objects related to it through this composition would also cease to exist.

Figure 5-11. *Recursive composition in UML and IDEF1X*

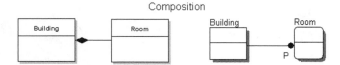

Figure 5-12. *Nonrecursive composition in UML and IDEF1X*

Aggregations

Aggregation relationships, also known as *weak associations*, establish a group-member relationship between objects, where the parent entity depends on the children for its existence. This type of aggregation is noted with a hollow diamond (see Figure 5-13).

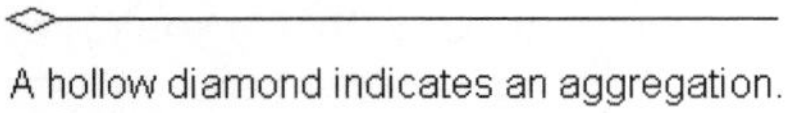

A hollow diamond indicates an aggregation.

Figure 5-13. *UML shared aggregation notation*

An aggregation relationship uses a hollow diamond notation to identify the parent class. Cardinality symbols, as used in association relationships, are also used to show the cardinality of the relationship (see Figure 5-14).

Figure 5-14. *Shared aggregation in UML and IDEF1X*

A member of an aggregation may be included in several aggregates simultaneously. This "weakened" relationship allows the child members to survive a deletion of its aggregate. This concept isn't completely compatible with IDEF1X notation, but Figure 5-14 shows as close an equivalent as you can get.

Supporting Object Models with Relational Databases

So, what's the best way to support a UML model with a Physical data model of a relational database design? The trick is to establish a set of ground rules or patterns for transforming your UML Class model. By establishing a set of basic patterns, you then have a default transformation mechanism that the team can use to follow the translation of your model, class by class and association by association.

General Transformation Rules

Our suggested steps of default transformations are as follows:

1. Set the model's scope.

   • Segregate the persistent objects; your business classes will most likely be the ones you need to persist (store) in your database.

2. Transform UML classes to relational tables.

   • Every UML class becomes a table.

   • Every UML attribute becomes a column.

   • Every UML attribute type maps to a default data type, size, and precision controlled by the specific relational database management system (RDBMS) you're targeting (Oracle, SQL Server, DB2).

   • All nullability defined in the UML attribute is maintained in the column specs (NULL, NOT NULL).

   • Every UML attribute "initializer" becomes a DEFAULT clause.

   • Every UML class with no "generalization" or "implicit identity" defined will have a primary key.

   • Consider using surrogate keys for objects with no obvious primary key.

3. Transform UML associations to relationships.

- Every table will define primary key to foreign key constraints for data integrity and connections for each role in an association (between parent-child or independent-dependent relationships).

- Every associative class will be deployed as a cross-reference or intersection table. It will have a multipart candidate key made up of (at least) the primary keys of the parent tables.

- Every composite aggregation will have a foreign key to the aggregating tables.

- Every many-to-many association that wasn't resolved with an association class will be deployed as a cross-reference or intersection table.

4. Transform UML class hierarchies to relational category implementations.

- Choose the default method of handling classes defined as a "generalization" with subclasses. Use rolled-up categories, rolled-down categories, or expansive categories for your physical deployment method (see Chapter 10). Your choice will depend on the similarity the structure and use of your subclasses.

- Every different role-named relationship should be considered as a candidate for an independent list–type table.

- For complex class definitions used for attributes, duplicate the complex class's basic attributes and data types everywhere that class is used.

Later in this chapter, in the "Example UML Transformation" section, you'll follow this process in a small example to show how you can use these transformations to create relational data models. However, it's important to note that following this process will result only in the creation of a draft Physical data model. You may still need to examine denormalization opportunities or add extra indexes for performance tuning. You can work out these details of deploy-ment, or tune the physical design, later with the help of the database administrators (DBAs) after you use a formulaic method for transforming the model.

Transforming UML Classes into Entities

Next, let's look at some case-by-case examples of how certain partial UML diagrams can be represented in logical IDEF1X formats. These mini-examples will provide a blueprint for performing larger transformations.

General Class

This is the simplest set of transformations. Make sure every persistent class is represented by a table or entity, depending on whether you're creating a Logical or Physical relational data model. Also, make sure all data attributes shown in the UML diagram are represented as columns or attributes in your relational model. A persistent class is any class where the data contained in that class needs to be stored in the database. Most, if not all, of the classes on your business-oriented class diagram will be persistent (see Figure 5-15).

Figure 5-15. *Transforming UML classes to IDEF1X*

Association Class

An association class denotes that for a given association of two classes, there can be only one resultant association class. This is transformed similarly to a many-to-many association (see Figure 5-16).

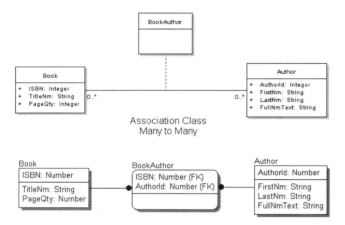

Figure 5-16. *Transforming UML association classes to IDEF1X*

Note the added subtlety here that, unlike a simple many-to-many relationship, the Book's primary key and the Author's primary key have migrated to be the primary key of the BookAuthor table, ensuring that only one combination of the two is permitted.

Transforming UML Associations into Relationships

Now that you've transformed the UML classes into relational entities, let's look at how to represent the UML associations in a relational model.

Associations: One to Many

General associations indicate two objects are associated but that no dependence exists between the connected objects. As noted earlier, this doesn't translate perfectly into relational modeling syntax, but it can be represented effectively as a foreign key constraint linking two tables (see Figure 5-17).

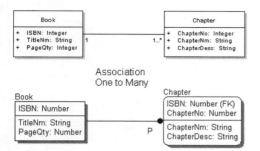

Figure 5-17. *Transforming UML associations to IDEF1X with one-to-many cardinality*

In Figure 5-17, each class is represented by a table, and each association is represented by one foreign key constraint.

Associations: Many to Many

Many-to-many relationships, as shown in UML, are transformed into Physical data models in the same way as many-to-many relationships that are part of relational Logical models. In either case, many-to-many relationships require an intersection entity when physically deployed (see Figure 5-18).

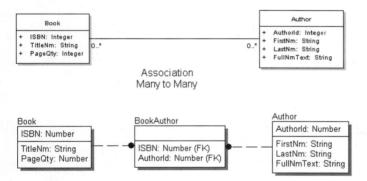

Figure 5-18. *Transforming UML associations with many-to-many cardinality*

To resolve the many-to-many relationship, we've created an intersection table to store the existence of the many-to-many relationship between Book and Author.

Compositions

Composition associations are the most straightforward of UML associations to transform, since they closely mirror the available relationships in IDEF1X (see Figure 5-19).

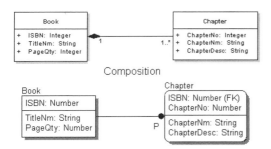

Figure 5-19. *Transforming UML composition associations to IDEF1X*

The composition association is translated into a one-to-many relationship in the relational model.

Aggregations

Aggregation associations imply that the members of the aggregation are independent of the aggregation itself. For example, a high-school chess club is an aggregation whose aggregation members are the people in the club. However, if the club disbands, the members still exist (see Figure 5-20).

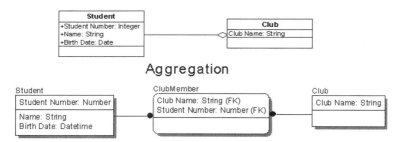

Figure 5-20. *Transforming UML aggregations to IDEF1X*

The aggregation association is represented by a many-to-many relationship. Any specific control on the cardinality of the relationship will need trigger code or check constraints to perform the verifications.

Class Hierarchies

Now that we've addressed how to transform UML classes and associations into relational structures, we'll cover *categories,* or UML generalizations.

UML generalizations are equivalent to relational categories. There are several ways to physically implement relational categories (rolled-up, rolled-down, and expanded solutions), and you can refer to Chapter 8 to see the options for a category's physical design in more detail. The development team needs to evaluate the physical implementation options and choose a preferred category of physical design. These same options exist when creating a physical design for UML class hierarchies. Figure 5-21 shows an example of a UML class diagram, a Logical IDEF1X relational model, and a Physical IDEF1X relational model.

Generalization

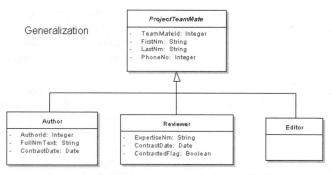

Italicized names note the class is abstract rather than
persistent. It is not expected to be instantiated.

Logical Representation

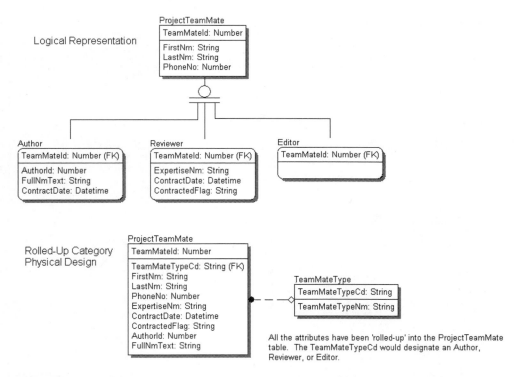

Figure 5-21. *Transforming UML generalizations to IDEF1X (rolled-up categories)*

In Figure 5-21, you first see a UML representation of a project team member, implemented as a hierarchy. A project teammate can be an Author, a Reviewer, or an Editor, and the grouping isn't mutually exclusive (a teammate can be a Reviewer *and* an Author). However, the italics in the supertype ProjectTeamMate indicates that it's *abstract*, meaning that each team member must be at least one of the subtypes.

Next, you can see how the UML supertypes and subtypes have been transformed into an IDEF1X Logical model. The UML generalization and the IDEF1X Logical model are similar when it comes to representing this kind of structure.

Lastly, Figure 5-21 shows the UML and IDEF1X Logical model represented in a Physical model. The three subtypes have been "rolled up" into the ProjectTeamMate table, and the attribute of TeamMateTypeCd indicates which of the three subtypes apply to a given team member. In this case, we've chosen a rolled-up category structure for the physical implementation, but other options are also available.

Figure 5-22 shows a slightly more complex example so you can actually see the UML notations being translated into the IDEF1X physical design.

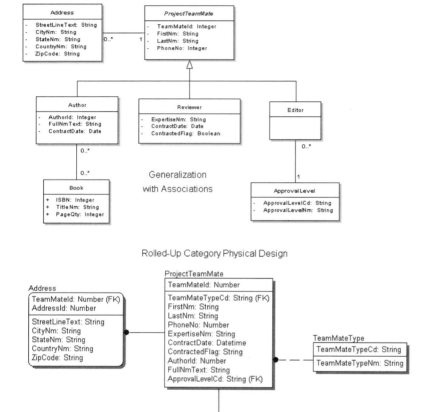

Figure 5-22. *Transforming UML generalizations with associations to IDEF1X*

In Figure 5-22, you can see a similar example to Figure 5-21. In this case, we've complicated the model somewhat by creating an Address class that applies to all team members, including a Book class that's related to the Author subtype and an ApprovalLevel class that's related to the Editor subtype.

In this example, we skipped transforming the UML class diagram to an IDEF1X Logical model, and instead we went straight to a Physical model. We again chose a "rolled-up" physical solution for our categories and combined the subtypes and supertype into one physical table called `ProjectTeamMate`. Note that in this case, we've added an `Address` table that's mandatory for each team member and an optional `ApprovalLevel` table that will represent the approval level given by the `Editor`.

Example UML Transformation

Now that we've covered the basic rules of transforming UML class diagrams to relational models, we'll take the Logical data model of a vehicle order system example that we presented in Chapter 3 and show how it can be represented in UML. Then, we'll take the UML diagram and build a Physical data model that could be deployed in an RDBMS that could support the UML class diagram. Although this process may be slightly counterintuitive, we want to show that a Logical model can be transformed into a corresponding UML model and that if the Logical and UML models can represent the same concepts in different formats, the transformation between UML and a relational database design is reduced to the problem of transforming a Logical model into a Physical model.

Initial Logical Data Model

Figure 5-23 shows the IDEF1X Logical model example for the vehicle order subject area.

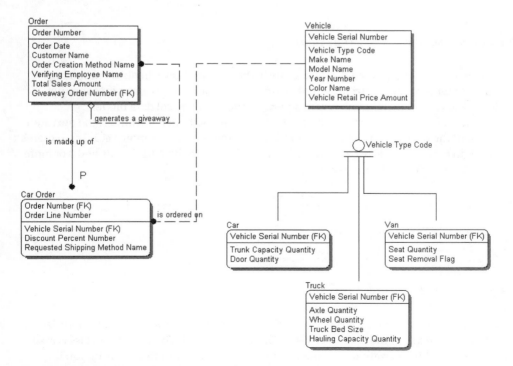

Figure 5-23. *IDEF1X vehicle order system's Logical model*

This model represents a vehicle ordering system, where an Order consists of one or more line items, and each line item is always a Vehicle. Vehicles must be a Car, a Truck, or a Van. Each order may trigger a Giveaway Order, if the appropriate business rules are met. This Giveaway Order is an Order separate from the original order, but it's important to keep track of which order triggered the giveaway.

Now, let's see what this IDEF1X model looks like in UML!

Transformation to UML Class Diagram

Let's take the IDEF1X Logical model and transform the entities into classes. All six entities will become classes: Order, Car Order, Vehicle, Car, Van, and Truck. The first step is to create classes for these, with attributes (see Figure 5-24).

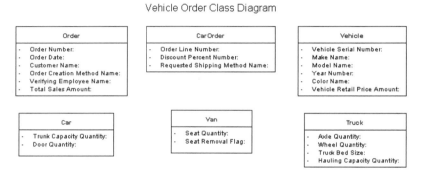

Figure 5-24. *Vehicle order system's UML classes*

Note that the classes created don't have any of the migrated keys. In object modeling, each class contains only the attributes that belong to that class. In this way, you construct an object model in much the same way as a pure, normalized Logical data model.

Now that you have the six classes on the class diagram with their attributes, the next step is to represent the relationships as associations. A Car Order has one or more Vehicle, so there's an association between these two classes with cardinality of 1 on the Vehicle side and 0 or more on the Car Order side (see Figure 5-25).

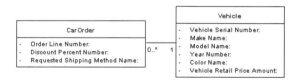

Figure 5-25. Vehicle *to* Car Order *association*

Notice that even though we've created the association between Vehicle and Car Order, there's no migrated key in the Car Order class. This is intentional. The Car Order class is associated to a Vehicle. If you want to find the Vehicle Serial Number of that Vehicle, you'll traverse the relationship to Vehicle. Keys don't migrate in object models; associations exist and can be used to navigate from one class to another.

Next, Orders contain one or more Order Line (represented by the Car Order entity). Since the Car Order class is identified by an Order Number and an Order Line Number, Car Order is owned by the Order class. Can the Car Order entity exist independently of its Order? No, it needs its associated Order class. Since the Car Order class can't exist without its associated Order, this relationship is a *composition aggregation*. The cardinality of this association is 1 on the Order side, and it's 1 or more on the Car Order side (see Figure 5-26).

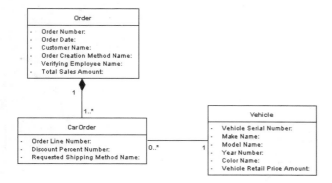

Figure 5-26. *Connecting* Car Order *to* Order

The last relationship you need to address is the optional recursive relationship between Order and itself. An order can generate a Giveaway Order. Can both Orders exist independently of each other? Technically, the Giveaway Order is created by the first Order, but once it exists, is it an independent Order? In this case, we'll assume that the Giveaway Order is treated as an independent instance of an Order once it has been created and isn't "owned" by the creating Order. Some complex logic may trigger the creation of the Giveaway Order, but once it has been created, we'll treat it as a regular Order. The relationship is then a simple association between two independent classes, represented as a recursive association, with 0..1 on one side of the association and 1 on the other side of the association (see Figure 5-27).

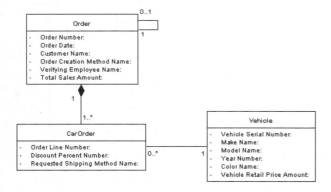

Figure 5-27. *Adding the* Giveaway Order *association*

The last part of this particular transformation is to create a class hierarchy for the Vehicle category represented in the Logical model. From the Logical model, the hierarchy is an exclusive hierarchy, meaning that each instance can be an instance of only one of the subtypes. In UML notation, subtyping is shown through generalizations. Let's create a generalization with Vehicle being the supertype for Car, Truck, and Van. This class hierarchy is exclusive, so you need to use the OR operator to indicate the mutual exclusivity of the subtypes (see Figure 5-28).

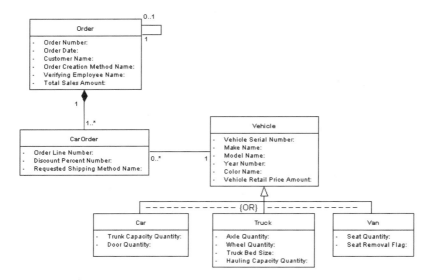

Figure 5-28. *The completed UML model*

The UML model is complete, and you can now move onto creating a Physical model to support this class diagram.

UML Class Diagram to Relational Physical Model

Let's suppose you were given this UML class diagram and were asked to create a relational database design that would support it. Falling back on general rules, you'd start by creating tables for each of the classes. Therefore, let's start by creating tables for the Order, Car Order, and Vehicle classes (see Figure 5-29).

Figure 5-29. *Classes to relational tables*

You'll also have to choose the strategy for addressing the generalization in the class diagram. Given that these subtypes are fairly straightforward and that you're likely to use the Car,

Truck, and Van subtypes in the same way, we'll choose a rolled-up category implementation (covered in Chapter 10). Implementing rolled-up categories involves collapsing the classes into one physical table, with a union of all the required attributes (see Figure 5-30).

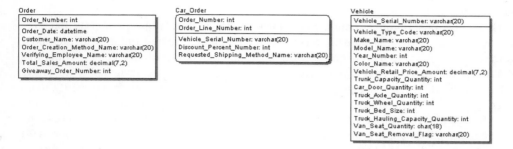

Figure 5-30. *Adding the* Vehicle *hierarchy*

Now that you have your tables defined, let's work on the associations. When connecting foreign keys in the relational model, remember to migrate the appropriate columns from the parent table participating in the foreign key. The composition association between Order and Car Order is transformed into a foreign key relationship between these two tables, with Order being the parent and Car Order being the child. A nonidentifying relationship exists between Vehicle and Car Order, since every Vehicle could be on more than one Car Order. Connect Vehicle to Car Order with a foreign key relationship, with Vehicle being the parent and Car Order being the child. The recursive association between Order and itself can be represented as a nullable, recursive, foreign key relationship on the Order table. Make sure to create a second column in this table, with a different name, to keep track of the original Order Number that triggers the Giveaway Order (see Figure 5-31).

Figure 5-31. *The complete Physical model*

You've now created the Physical model for your vehicle order model! By transforming the Logical model to a UML diagram and then creating a Physical model, you've seen how the Logical model and a UML class diagram can represent the same thing, in their own notation and format.

Lost in Translation: Impedence Mismatch

Before you start to think, however, that object modeling and relational modeling are completely compatible, it's important to note the philosophical differences between the two approaches.

One of the most significant differences between relational and object models is that relational models are based upon the notion of sets of data that are related and that are queried to return results. Object models are based upon the notion that objects are associated with other objects and that, in order to return information, these associations are navigated or traversed. In relational modeling, the foreign key is meaningful and helps to enforce data integrity. In the object model, referential integrity isn't an issue, since objects simply refer to other objects.

At first glance, this may seem to be splitting hairs. After all, you can traverse a set of keys within a relational database to find information, and you could argue that you can query a set of objects. Although it's against the principle of object-oriented modeling, you could engage in denormalization activities and store data in objects where they don't really belong. A Third Normal Form (3NF) relational model with surrogate keys will need to be traversed by the SQL query that accesses the data.

The difference here has more to do with the action of obtaining data and the conventions of data organization and access. When you're querying a relational model, you construct general query statements that return a collection of data in a result set. When you're using a set of interconnected objects, you navigate the relationships to obtain information piecemeal.

You can use the Car Order example to illustrate this subtle difference. If you wanted to find the model years for all of the vehicles on a given order—say, Order A—you could write a SQL statement like this:

```
select   v.Vehicle_Serial_No, v.Year_No
from     Vehicle v, Order o, Car_Order co
where    v.Vehicle_Serial_No = co.Vehicle_Serial_No and
             v.Order_Number = o.Order_Number and
             o.Order_Number = A
```

If you were trying to navigate the Car Order UML model, you'd find Order A, and then navigate to the model year using syntax such as the following for as many Car Order objects that exist for the given Order:

```
Order.Car_Order(1).Vehicle.Year_Number
Order.Car_Order(2).Vehicle.Year_Number
etc.
```

What we're trying to show here is that the philosophy of the two styles are very different but that they can ultimately coexist and even support one another. It's important to understand what isn't easily translated so you can avoid misinterpretations.

In addition to the way objects are associated, the fact that UML class diagrams are intended to show *methods* is at odds with the notion of relational modeling. Relational models don't attempt to capture the procedural operations that are performed, since relational data modeling is based purely upon the data and its interrelationships—the manipulations of this data are left to the programs that query and access this data.

This type of philosophical difference between these "worldviews" is called the *impedence mismatch*. Relational sets query relationships; conversely, object associations are traversed.

Objects show methods, and relational modeling leaves that to the programs accessing the data. Relational sets exist in a nonhierarchical structure, and objects are intended to be hierarchical, with subtypes inheriting all the data and operations of their supertypes.

What impedence mismatch means is that relational and object modeling approaches aren't entirely compatible but can coexist and support each other within the same project team. With a good understanding of the limitations and advantages of each approach, a data modeler can successfully navigate situations when a UML design needs to be supported by a relational database.

Summary

As a data modeler, your task is to analyze your data using a systematic and disciplined approach. Only once you truly understand the scope, meaning, and interactive rules of the data you're working with can you be in a strong position to architect a solution that supports quality, integrity, flexibility, and future growth.

Relational data modeling has been chosen for this book because it serves as a good starting place and is the foundation you can use regardless of the modeling technique in place on a given project. All disciplined techniques, by the very nature of being disciplined, will allow you to create a better design than by jumping straight to a physical solution without adequate analysis.

As a basic foundation technique, relational modeling is well established and has been used for more than 30 years. RDBMSs have also grown into robust, dependable tools. Hierarchical and network systems are still around but are slowly fading as legacy systems go offline.

In the past 15 years there has been incredible growth and development in the area of object-oriented programming languages and development tools. But object-oriented databases haven't caught on with the same enthusiasm as programming languages such as Java and C++, and it's entirely likely that any system written in an object-oriented programming language will ultimately have to rely on a relational database for storing data, managing transactions, and querying data. While impedence mismatch does cause some problems in translating between relational and object models, these two approaches aren't incompatible.

If you become embroiled in a philosophical battle between the relational and object camps, try to maintain an objective perspective. Few black-and-white answers exist in this world. There have always been alternative techniques to almost every human activity, and most practices that result in positive, constructive results will evolve over time to create new alternatives.

Data modeling is no different. You're just starting to resolve the problem of information management. You'll be developing, evolving, discarding, and exploring new solutions one after the other for a while yet.

Relational and object modeling techniques are indeed different, but their goals are the same: to analyze the problem space and to develop quick, speedy, efficient data structures to be used in representing that problem space. Fortunately, this similarity allows for a coexistence of these two technologies. No matter which side of the object-relational debate you support, everyone should support thorough analysis and intelligent design.

CHAPTER 6

■ ■ ■

Examining Levels of Analysis

You've looked at the theory behind relational data modeling, the terminology used in discussing relational models, and a sampling of the notations used to build data models. In this chapter, we'll review the types of data models you can construct and the level of data element detail you can include in those models. This will allow you to decide which type of data model you want to provide as a deliverable. Data models can and should be tailored to the specific needs of the client or phase of the project, focusing on the appropriate level of required detail.

You'll learn about the following types of model in this chapter:

Conceptual: This model type relates thoughts or big subject areas together. The entities in this model are generally named and defined as generically and inclusively as possible. The goal is to support project scope reviews or create a data subject area table of contents, and it involves creating logical groups for a greater understanding of the subject area.

Logical: This model contains detailed subject areas and relates them together. The objects in this model are named and built with as much detail as necessary for the logical data requirements to be understood. The goal is to isolate and present each distinct data element, documenting as much about it as possible. Business rules documented in the relationships (rules relating entities) can be used as a true/false test of the model prior to writing code.

Physical: This model contains table structures designed to manage the detailed subjects. Database object naming standards are applied here, and these models provide a blueprint for database design.

Reverse engineering: This is a special case of a Physical data model. Reverse-engineered models are the product of analyzing data management structures that already exist (either as a custom development or a vendor product). What separates reverse-engineering analysis from conventional physical analysis is that you may need to include items on the model that don't necessarily exist physically at the relational database management system (RDBMS) level. For example, you might include relationships that never make it into the database as constraints and are instead managed in screens or procedures.

In creating Conceptual, Logical, and Physical models you'll see a progression in the level of detail you need to provide. The closer you get to a Physical model, the more you need to define the data elements in detail and the more design choices you have to make. This is what makes modeling such an iterative process. Double-checking details in the definitions within your Physical model may cause you to have to refer to your Logical and Conceptual models to verify the existence of data elements and the relationships between them. In this chapter, you'll look at the level of detail provided in each of these modeling phases in terms of the following:

- **Entity-level analysis**: Logical high-level analysis used for scope and planning or a simplified review at the beginning of a project. This view contains only (core) entities, their definitions, and (preliminary) relationship lines.

- **Key-based analysis**: This analysis contains only entities/tables, primary keys, (preliminary) relationship lines, and foreign keys and their definitions.

- **Fully attributed analysis**: This is the most detailed level of analysis, containing entities/tables, primary keys, (preliminary) relationship lines, foreign keys, attributes/columns, and definitions.

Developing Models

In most professions, multiple iterations of work occur as part of a creative process. Photographers, for example, will often work with a fast, self-developing Polaroid in order to get a feel for lighting and to perform other checks before they move onto using high-cost film. Design engineers progress from sketches and drafts to the final release of a drawing. Even your doctor will probably work up a diagnosis of your symptoms and treatment by starting with simple diagnostic tests before determining whether more work is required.

Data modelers follow the same pattern. They gather information in an iterative process, moving the knowledge from conceptual representations to logical designs to physical designs. This iterative approach is the safest and most commonly taught method of modeling. Yes, you'll find shortcuts being taken daily, but an iterative approach is still the best way to analyze and develop data structures.

You should also know that the process can be executed backward. This is generally called *reverse engineering*. If you're starting with the finished product of a data management tool (sophisticated software or even simple forms), it's possible to work backward and create a Logical model from a Physical one and a Conceptual model from a Logical one. This kind of analysis and modeling can be quite useful when trying to extract data from an old system for use in a new one.

In creating a data model, several stages of development exist depending upon the project goals that have been set for you. Sometimes you're developing models to capture currently undefined data dynamics in order to support building a new application. In these cases, you're moving through a fairly well-defined life cycle of analysis: the development of a future (To-Be) model, as defined next.

■Note These steps are listed in general order, and not all projects work through all of them. Bear in mind that as you acquire a greater understanding of the system, it's often necessary to return to one of these steps to verify particular details or document your greater understanding.

Pre-scope and discovery: This is brainstorming time. It may be that a series of "change requests" or "enhancement suggestions" have been gathered into a group, and you need to put together a model that will document the scope of the changes. It may also be a task necessary to fulfill a five-year plan. This step puts together a "rough draft" of the impact of doing the project. The model will need to be built according to the level of detail understood at this point in time; however, it's usually very conceptual in nature. This phase sometimes involves data scoping and data analysis as well, including activities such as data profiling and data discovery. Often a series of higher-level architectural diagrams are created in this step to show data flows and the potential technology and hardware implications.

Proposal and planning: The team of people chartered to review proposals (a guidance or review board) usually needs a conceptual or logical design to explain the intended scope of a project. This helps to justify funding for your project, especially if you can show what enterprise concepts will be added, deleted, or modified. Sometimes you're helping the business understand and document its intended business process or business policy changes in a way that's similar to business process consulting or reengineering.

Detailed requirement gathering: Building on your initial requirements gathering activities, this stage verifies and enhances the conceptual design to reflect new knowledge or provide confidence that the scope was originally well-defined. You may even decompose very high-level concepts to produce several conceptual designs if the project is large enough to have the work divided between smaller teams.

Logical design: Based on the conceptual design, this phase gathers and defines specific data elements (attributes) and organizes them into entities that comply with the normal form rules (as set out in Chapter 2). You need your nontechnical clients to review what you've discovered along the way. They need a Logical model with full names and descriptive relationship verb phrases to be able to read and comprehend what has been analyzed so far.

Physical design: The next phase changes the logical design into a concrete, database-specific physical design. The full logical names are often too long for RDBMS use and have to go through a process of renaming (to support the target RDBMS standards). You also may have to create "physical-only" objects to help manage the application. These physical objects may not stem from any logical entities. This process results in the model that can be used to create RDBMS objects. Programmers working to create, or maintain, a set of tables need a completed and up-to-date Physical model to learn from and eventually write code to access. Depending on the degree of physical transformation, the logical design can still be necessary to the developers, especially if the Logical model has been severely compromised by physical constraints to the extent that the business concepts have been obscured.

Design review: This evaluation phase focuses the team on the transformation of the Logical model into the physical design. This meeting (or set of meetings) becomes the communication method for explaining how the business concepts documented in the Logical model were transformed into a database design. The team will then discuss the various design choices made and why these options were chosen. This review is especially useful in an experimental, rapid prototype development environment, as the team can review various physical database design options to see which solution works best.

Implementation: Finally, the design goes into production. The whole set of Conceptual, Logical, and Physical models, definitions, and mappings become part of the department-controlled reference documentation. This set of documents is the most difficult to keep synchronized with reality since production databases often change without your involvement.

Vendor or legacy solutions: Reverse-engineered analysis models generally produce physical designs. Sometimes it becomes necessary to add relationship lines for improved diagram clarity even when the constraints don't exist in the database. These deliverables need to be more than simply an inventory of physical objects. As company mergers become more frequent, reverse-engineered analysis of similar existing systems are necessary to be able to compare system similarities and differences. Vendor packages may need to be compared with existing company business rules and policies to verify a good fit before purchase. You may need to fully understand legacy systems before targeting them for replacement or enhancement. Developers can already get an inventory of objects from the RDBMS, but what they really need is the metadata and business understanding that comes from a properly created data model (Conceptual/Logical). Even the Physical model can be more than an inventory of database objects, since it can document design decisions that were made to address physical constraints.

You'll sometimes find yourself working on a custom development project that allows you to begin with a fairly clean slate. Under other circumstances you may find yourself starting with a complex systems' integration project, working to integrate several systems that are in place and functioning in full production support. Some projects require you to identify and retire specific components determined to be redundant or too costly. In cases such as these, you may be alternating between some of the steps noted in the previous list. Sometimes you'll compare the current view (often referred to as the *As-Is*) with the future view (referred to as the *To-Be*) to identify the required changes. Sometimes you'll be operating in an iterative and reactive mode, which isn't as neat and linear as you may like.

A Data Model Isn't a Flow Diagram

A data model, at any level of analysis, isn't a process or business flow diagram. We hope your project team is developing process diagrams on its own, as these diagrams provide another level of analysis that will contribute to the success of the project. Although relational data models perform some of the same roles as a flow diagram, insofar as they act as a representational graphic of the details discovered during analysis, they don't tell a comprehensive, coherent story from start to finish. In fact, relational data models don't have a "Start" and "Finish" box. In Chapter 4 you learned the graphical symbols that "tell the story" of a model to the reader, but some layers of information in a model don't show up on the diagram. These include, but aren't limited to, items such as long informative definitions for each of the textual labels on the model, lists of allowed values, notes, critical data rules, data mapping for data movement, and quality checks that are documented and available for the enterprise.

■**Note** Data models provide a data structure in terms of the mathematics of relational algebra. In a data model, the business organization's rules are noted as a function of the connection, identification, cardinality, and nullability of data.

Data models capture rules at a much more granular level of detail (individual field-level rules) than most documented business processes. This is initially one thing that seems to be the most confusing about data models, since most people tend to think that a model should explain all the business rules. A data model can document primary business rules and meta-data of the modeler's choosing only. The business rules in a data model are so basic that no one actually thinks about them as business rules. More complex business rules probably can be inferred from the model but can't be captured in the graphical format. To understand this kind of rule, you need to examine the documentation accompanying the graphical data model.

Take the following business rule as an example:

- Each `Customer` must have a `Credit Rating` of Satisfactory or better to be notified by `Marketing` of a `Product Promotion`.

A data model can't document the portion of the rule that narrows the triggering of action to finding customers with a credit rating value of Satisfactory. And it can't show how to determine the business rule that needs to ascertain whether another credit rating value is "better" than Satisfactory. Look at Figure 6-1. Can you find that level of detail?

Figure 6-1. *Conceptual model of promotion notification rule*

The credit rating "values" are members of the data set `Credit Rating`, and those values are what support this rule. This information isn't visible in Figure 6-1. This can cause some distress among your clients if they expect to find this kind of rule in the data model. Those rules will probably be managed in code, based on requirements and business rules documented elsewhere (although the modeler can add them to a data model's notes to capture this knowledge).

■**Note** You need to manage the team's expectations as to what the model can and can't provide at different stages of the development process.

Data Relationship Rules

The data model does an excellent job of noting primary business rules, as shown in Figure 6-2. This little model notes 16 rules.

- Each Customer must have a Credit Rating.

- Each Credit Rating may describe the status of zero or more Customers.

- Each Product may be advertised by zero or more Promotions.

- Each Promotion may advertise a Product.

- Each Customer may receive zero or more Product Promotion Notifications.

- Each Product Promotion Notification may be received by a Customer.

- Each Product Promotion is developed by a Marketing Department.

- Each Marketing Department develops zero or more Product Promotions.

- Each Marketing Department Representative may deploy zero or more Product Promotion Notifications.

- Each Product Promotion Notification is deployed by a Marketing Department Representative.

- Each Credit Rating must be attained for a Product Promotion.

- Each Product Promotion can be released upon the attainment of a Credit Rating.

- Each Product may be advertised by zero or more Product Promotions.

- Each Product Promotion may advertise a Product.

- Each Marketing Department is staffed with zero or more Marketing Department Representatives.

- Each Marketing Department Representative staffs a Marketing Department.

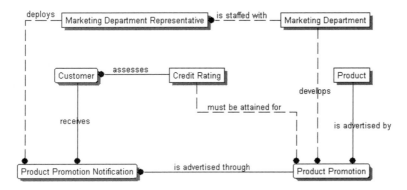

Figure 6-2. *Conceptual model of promotion notification rule*

Note that this model shows many rules at a simple level by pairing concepts or (eventually) sets of data values such as those in `Credit Rating` (such as Satisfactory, Unsatisfactory, Outstanding, and so on) and `Customer` (such as John Smith, Jane Doe, and so on). These are referred to as *binary* relationships. Exceptions exist when a concept is complex enough to need three or more relationships in order to describe it. However, at this level, even these can be read as pairs, as you can see in the following example.

The `Product Promotion` and `Product Promotion Notification` entities have at least three relationships to other entities. Even though these entities have many relationships, you're able to read each of the relationship lines as simple relationships between two entities. You may not even recognize that `Product Promotion` should be connected to so many other entities without graphically highlighting this fact.

■**Note** Data models don't document the underlying data or concept connectivity in the way they're exercised in business situations.

To show the way concepts are exercised in business situations, you need "scenarios" to show typical business situations and how the data might be represented. This is important in Unified Modeling Language (UML), as a highly normalized and generalized model may be too difficult to understand without these scenarios illustrating real-world situations.

Performing Conceptual Analysis

Conceptual models are "reference-only" documents. They capture and document the project team's first look at a data subject area. Ideally they're built without a single thought as to what, how, and where a physical database might be deployed.

Conceptual modeling is often overlooked or even dismissed as having little intrinsic value, but it's really worth a second look. Someone has to become acquainted with the project scope. They have to interview the creators and processors of the data elements. They have to trace documentation through paths of creating, auditing, publishing, saving, and distributing. They have to understand both the normal business process as well as the document anomalies. Then they need to jot down process improvement opportunities. They have to take all that knowledge back to their desk, mull it over, and create a simple, easy-to-read graphic that conveys this information. Without this type of analysis and documentation, the details quickly fade, and the risks of project failure, angry recrimination, and ultimately loss of faith increase.

A *concept* is a thought, opinion, general notion, or idea, especially one formed by generalization from particular examples. And that's exactly what you're aiming to capture in a conceptual level of analysis. You're documenting unique and identifiable data set types, which are intrinsically necessary to successfully managing your project's data. One or more business processes should support concepts, and concepts could be almost anything that requires gathering and managing high-quality data. This is really the only time during the modeling process that you get a chance to really model business concepts without having to worry about how data will be stored, managed, transmitted, or accessed.

Conceptual modeling isn't a trivial task. This type of model centers on discovering and analyzing organizational and user data requirements. You're focusing on what data is important to the business. When the data model encompasses the entire enterprise, it's called an *enterprise* or *corporate* data model.

This type of model can document the current environment (As-Is) or future plans (To-Be). A Conceptual model can support strategic or tactical analysis of the corporate data inventory. When data modeling includes the involvement of senior-level managers, it can help them focus on current data management and look for opportunities to improve. For example, a Conceptual model that spans more than one project, department, or business process can show in a simple fashion the most fundamental, highly used, and integrated data concepts (such as a calendar or an employee) simply by the number of relationship lines linking them to other conceptual entities.

Entities in a Conceptual Model

Remember from Chapter 3 that entities aren't tables. They represent nouns that capture an idea that's a necessary ingredient in a process. Entities are things such as the following:

- People or mechanisms that do things

- Material or requests that need to be changed

- Product or deliverables that need to be created

- Thresholds or control concepts that need to be applied

- Time, geography, budget, and organizing structures that need to be referred to

- Logic points that need to be used to govern "if this, then that" decisions

Entities shouldn't be too specific, since you're capturing information at a high level, but at the same time, they shouldn't be too general, because then you lose sight of the detail of the data you're capturing. *Envelope* may be too specific a noun, but *paper thing* is too general. Conceptual entities should have singular noun names and a good definition that encapsulates all the information you discovered when analyzing the environment. Conceptual entities are guides to the more detailed logical entities that come next.

Relationships in a Conceptual Model

Relationships are the verbs that tie the entities together. They're also not physical constructs but notes describing the dependencies that appear to exist between entities. In addition to any information you need to document regarding specific business rules, these relationships should capture the following details:

Category: We introduced categories in Chapter 3. Conceptual categories can be useful to note big separations in concepts that need to be treated one way as an aggregate and another way as a specific member. Geography is a great example of a conceptual category. An enterprise may use data sets such as Continent, Nation, State, Province, and City as part of the set Geography. Yet each one may need to be broken out as a subtype to be able to document different business rules relating to their particular group. For example, a Film Company makes contracts with Nations to release rights to a Film. However, the Films are shown in Cities.

Note You'll see many categories throughout the book. Categories are useful data model constructs to display the similarity and differences of entity families.

The ability to properly distinguish between things that are basically the same but differ in data values and those that have similar data values but are fundamentally different concepts is the most important ability a data modeler can have. Categories are how the modeler documents show that concepts are similar or different. A modeler should be familiar with the power of categories, even when they don't directly translate to an RDBMS database implementation.

Verb phrase: Generally you want verb phrases to be simple connective phrases that note that this "happens" to that, creating simple sentences. In the Conceptual model it may not be as easy as a simple verb. Parts may be used as spares or to build, or rework, a product. For example, people can *manage, support, be assigned to, assist, train,* and *hire* other people. Draw a line for each to show the separate business rules binding the entities together. Try to stay away from generalizations in your verb phrases such as *is, has, belongs to,* or *is associated with*; this is generally considered lazy modeling, so be as specific and descriptive as you can.

Cardinality: This is the choice you need to make for the line terminators. It notates "how many?" of one entity are related to another. This is the cardinality definition. Every relationship has two terminators. Conceptual models tend to use the most generic types of relationships, the "one" or "many" notations, but you can use any of them you think you need. If you need a refresher as to the notation used to denote cardinality, then refer to Chapter 4.

Conceptual Model Example

Figure 6-3 shows what a Conceptual model could look like for an advertising and marketing department.

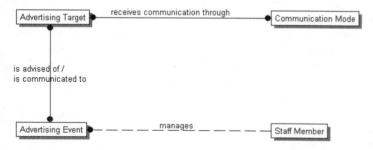

Figure 6-3. *Conceptual model for an advertising and marketing department*

You can see that this is a pretty high-level view. Notice that all you're looking at are the entities and relationships. The model has really only four basic concepts—namely, who does the task, what the task is, who the targets are, and how you communicate with them.

In this model, we kept the names specific enough to help the client see the process, and yet these names are generic enough to cover large areas of data. The relationship names are simple and instructive to someone who isn't as familiar with the business area.

Performing Logical Analysis

Logical analysis uses conceptual analysis as a launch point and drills down to the details that fully document the "sets" or entities that must be created and related together. This analysis is the activity where the conceptual purity of the design must be balanced against detailed instance and data element constraints supporting business processes.

You discover and document each separate data element. They're all recognizable in their entities, and every aspect of that entity that the clients are interested in becomes an attribute. You then determine how to manage those attributes, often by developing unique entities to manage them in simple List of Values (LOV) type sets and by building relationships for them so that they can be used as foreign keys. You need to create all the different combinations of data elements that are required to satisfy the project needs.

Beginning with a Conceptual model can give a certain feel for entity differentiation. This process is iterative, since in the course of analysis you may change your mind as to how to group data elements into entities. This is the nature of the process, and you refine your definitions until all the data elements are members of the appropriate entity and defined correctly to support that membership.

We call this process *logical* analysis because of the mathematics on which it's based. Whether you're talking about the Logical model of a network or hierarchical, object-oriented, or relational analysis, you're using the math that started the whole thing.

Note A well-documented logical analysis provides a framework for organizing sets of data to provide consistent answers to questions.

The conceptual analysis groups the data elements that are necessary to support a set of business processes. The logical analysis delves deep into the nature of these conceptual data elements. Because of that need for depth and details, you add a new level of detail to the model in the form of the actual attributes or data elements of each entity. You'll find the entity identifiers in the form of candidate keys and promote one of these keys to be the primary key of each entity. You'll also begin the process of defining domains and tightening up the relationship aspects such as cardinality and nullability. And then you'll test it against the normal forms for quality and accuracy.

The logical analysis is probably the most taxing portion of modeling for a project. This is where you lay out the foundations for the physical design. Mistakes made here are serious. The ripple they create when mistakes are discovered can cripple a project's ability to deliver on time or on budget. What makes logical analysis troublesome is that it's difficult to accurately transform the conceptual analysis into the true data elements and true data sets. And once you do, validating it (explaining your conclusions to your customers and team) is still a surprising and enlightening experience. Not only that, but you must allow yourself enough time in this phase of your analysis to prevent going from logical design to physical design too quickly. Once the physical design has been implemented, the ripple effects of a new under-standing or key concept can be costly. Take some time to make sure the Logical model is stable by doing everything you can think of to verify, validate, test, and attempt to break your understandings of the sets (entities) and business rules (relationships).

We'll go over the detailed steps required in developing a Logical model from a Conceptual model in the tutorial, which starts in Chapter 8. The process of building a model is complex and iterative. In the tutorial, you'll follow one example exhaustively to help introduce you to that process. Right now we just want you to get familiar with the finished products of various data modeling efforts.

Entities in a Logical Model

Entities represent data sets in logical analysis. Each one is a pure set of building blocks grouped to create information. For example, to answer the question "what number is valid to call a person at work?" you need to relate Person + Company + Phone (the type Company Phone) correctly. Look at Figure 6-4. The little four-entity Conceptual model you saw in Figure 6-3 has really exploded, hasn't it?

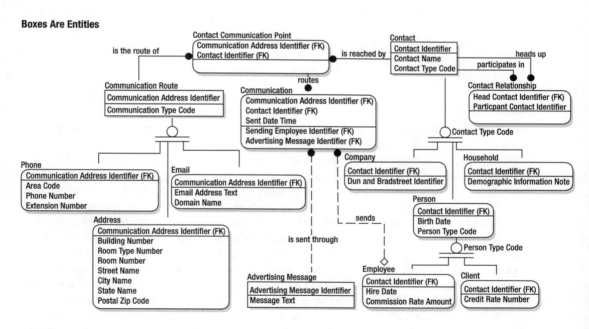

Figure 6-4. *Logical model for an advertising and marketing department*

Whereas the conceptual entities were broad ideas, these entities are narrower and more focused. In fact, we'd say (within reason) that the narrower the focus, the better. You have to drive the logical analysis down until you can actually see the business data elements in their most atomic form.

Attributes

Attributes are all the things that the clients think they need to store to be able to do their jobs. The attributes are the things you want to remember about the entities. They're the descriptors that define the individual bits of data. You may find them originally in reports or spreadsheets that the clients use now to manage a process. You have to find every one of them and add them to the model in the correct entity. When you do the tests for normal forms, you're really verifying the placement of the attributes into the proper "owning" entity.

Candidate Keys

You must review the attributes to see if they can act as a nonchanging unique identifier of a member of the set of rows in the entity. Candidate keys are usually the natural identifiers of things in the world, which you've discovered at this stage of analysis. However, you may have to add a surrogate key at this point if nothing else is available. Candidate keys can be single attributes such as serial numbers that stay with a railcar for its entire life. However, some keys are composites made up of combinations of attributes such as date, time, route, location, airline, and seat class for your airline reservation for your vacation. Remember from Chapter 3 that an entity can have more than one candidate key, but only one of these (or the choice of a completely new surrogate) is then selected to be the primary key; the rest are noted as alternate keys.

In Logical modeling it doesn't matter what order multiattribute keys are in. But it will matter when you physicalize the model, since the primary key will be deployed as a physical index that could impact the eventual performance of the application.

Logical Domains

Your attributes will have to be of a particular data type, or *domain*, such as integer, string, boolean, and so on. Specifying the data domain here, before you get to the Physical model, makes creating the Physical model much easier and also highlights anomalies in the data by providing an expectation of what the data will contain. With that expectation defined, you have the means of testing reality to see if it's what you thought it would be. For example, if you have an attribute designated as a time domain, and you find the word *noon* (as opposed to the time value 12 p.m.) or *after 6* in the real data, you'll have to rethink the definition of the attribute with the clients. Either it's a Time attribute or it's a Text attribute. Programmers count on numbers, dates, and time being what they say they are. Otherwise they have to put in all sorts of complicated translation and check code into their programs. Sometimes they have to do this anyway, but they'd rather know about it up front, rather than finding out by trial and error. Of course, if you can't find anomalies such as this in the current data set, it doesn't mean a user in the future won't want to enter data in this way. You have to try to foresee these kinds of issues and resolve them with the client as early as possible. The best way not to get tripped up is by modeling reality as closely as possible and then denormalizing or physically compromising the model where necessary.

Logical domains represent the lowest common denominator among RDBMS data types and may be one of the following:

- **BLOB, CLOB, LOB**: A Binary Large Object (BLOB) is generally a picture or graphic-formatted object. A Character Large Object (CLOB) is generally long text blocks with some formatting. Large Objects (LOBs) are usually music or video.

- **DateTime**: These are values that must fit within the Gregorian calendar and a 24-hour clock.

- **Number**: This is an entire set of symbols noting sequencing at any precision. This data type includes symbols for positive and negative values.

- **String**: This is any character, including numbers and complex characters such as accent marks and tildes.

- **Unknown**: This means no domain is specified.

Remember that these are simple in comparison to physical RDBMS data types. So, for example, the logical data type NUMBER(5,2) would in one RDBMS translate to NUMERIC(5,2) and in another to DECIMAL(5,2). Logical analysis is done without any thought about the tool or platform that will be used in building and deploying the database.

Role Names

Either you'll be forced into creating role names (because the same attribute name can't exist in any entity more than once) or you may simply want to role name for clarity. Either way, this is an important element of logical analysis. Employee ID makes perfect sense in the Employee entity, but what is it doing in an entity concerned with advertising campaign attributes? Is it the employee who launched the campaign, the author of the campaign, the person who approved it, the manager of a department, or the Webmaster in charge of the Web site? Role names clarify just what a migrated key is doing there.

In a similar manner, Employee ID may have a recursive relationship to itself, such as employee to their manager (an Employee must be managed by one, and only one, Employee). You can't have Employee ID noted twice with the same name (once for the employee record identifier and once for the manager). If you want those recursions to exist, you *have* to role-name the foreign keys so that they can exist. Besides, you have the same problem of the purpose of these attributes. Why are they there? You can't tell if they all are named Employee ID. Is this a manager or an administrative assistant, and is it the person who hired them, gave them their review, or recommended them for promotion? Who do these Employee IDs represent?

You may find that the verb phrase of the relationship can help in choosing the name you want to use for the role name. Take, for example, "Each Employee must be managed by one, and only one, Employee." In this case, the verb *managed* changes the EmployeeID into ManagerID as the name of the foreign key using a role name.

Relationships in a Logical Model

Logical analysis evolves from the generalities of conceptual analysis. So, although the many-to-many relationship is a legal one, the point of logical analysis is to get the data elements organized in whatever normal form you're targeting. Many-to-many relationships must be resolved at some point along the way. Entity detail models allow the many-to-many notation, but all other detail levels require it to be resolved. You saw how to do this by using intersection (associative) entities in Chapter 3.

Other than that, relationships are pretty much the same as they are in a Conceptual model. They're the paths that primary keys travel in order to connect the data sets.

Categories

Categories in logical analysis identify the subtypes of an entity so that you can model more detailed attribute ownership or relationships. For example, when you're talking about types of phone number, only Company Phone Number is allowed to have an Extension Number, but Mobile Phone Number isn't. Showing this in a category structure provides an insight during physicalization as to why an attribute should be NULL allowed. In this case, the Extension Number attribute should be NULL allowed since some phone numbers won't have one.

This is also an extremely useful technique in exposing anomalies. Bringing the seven different types of vehicles to the attention of the owner of a classic car business that you're doing a sales system for may jog her memory into remembering that sometimes she sells motorcycles, too. You unearth a portion of the current business data that has been shoehorned into tables and columns in which they don't fit very well.

Categories may also highlight different business rules. The category for Book at a library may note that they have subtypes of Public Access and Private Collection books, with only Public Access books allowed to be checked out. To reflect this business rule onto the Logical model would require that only Public Access books should be provided to the Checkout entities through a relationship.

Identifying or Nonidentifying

The conceptual analysis has only a limited understanding of whether relationships between the concepts are identifying or nonidentifying. There is no concept of key migration. You simply do your best to capture your understanding of existence dependencies. It isn't until you start to get the migrations of the foreign keys and the definitions of the primary keys analyzed that this differentiation becomes important.

As a reminder, if you need the identifying attributes from one entity to identify a different entity, then this is defined as an *identifying* relationship. For example, you need to know the State Identifier from the entity State to uniquely identify a record in County entity. Otherwise, you couldn't distinguish between the record for Orange County, California, and Orange County, Florida. Other times you're just making reference to another entity in a nonidentifying fashion. For instance, in the example coming up you'll see that Employee has a nonidentifying relationship to Communication. The Person getting the message, how it was routed to them, what message it was, and the date/time it got to them all identify a single row of Communication. Who sent the message is informational only.

Verb Phrase

Every different verb needs a different relationship in order to capture the multiple roles that the migrating member of the data set can play. Notice how many relationships you have in the tiny model from a taxi company in Figure 6-5.

**Employee Identifier is here six times:
once as a primary key and
five times as a foreign key**

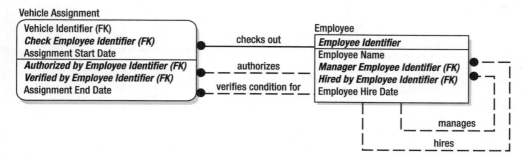

Figure 6-5. *Logical model showing various activities in which an employee participates*

Often you'll find a key entity loaded down with relationships. Keep them as simple as possible, but try to avoid *has* and *is* unless you're stumped. Most relationships aren't all that hard to describe. You may discover them in the way people refer to them. A part becomes an accessory; therefore, it *accessorizes*. A person is called a *manager*; therefore, it's safe to say they *manage* people.

The business rule is much clearer when you find the correct verb phrase. Think about how little you know about a business rule such as "An Employee is zero, one, or many Employees." It hardly makes sense. But "An Employee manages zero, one, or many Employees" is clear.

Cardinality

Now the detail levels of cardinality ("how many?") come into play. Detail the terminators of the relationships as much as possible, and make the rules as restrictive as the data rules are. The objective is to determine a representation of how the data is shaped that will help in the physicalization, and give the clients a black-and-white view of the world you're creating in which to store their data. As a result, your data structures need to be as restrictive or nonrestrictive as the things in reality you're modeling. Remember that rules noted in the structure now can result in huge advantages in quality and integrity as you progress to a physical analysis.

May or Must

The logical analysis is the place to focus on the finishing touches to the relationships, including restrictions on the allowed nullability. As a reminder, we use NULL to denote the absence of any value, in other words, an empty data element. Values such as N/A, Unknown, or --- aren't NULLs but data values representative of meaning to someone. If a relationship is possible but not mandatory, such as "A Communication may be sent by an Employee, and an Employee may send zero, one, or many Communications," then you say that the relationship is NULL allowed and denote it as shown in the sales and promotion Logical model in Figure 6-6.

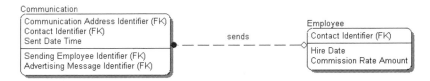

Figure 6-6. *Logical model showing nullability*

Logical Analysis Example

Look at Figure 6-7 and Figure 6-3. Compare how the evolution from conceptual to logical entities created distinctly and detailed sets of values that need to be managed and grouped to allow maximum integrity and flexibility. You'll see more about the development of such models in the tutorial. It's sufficient here to point out the inclusion of category structures, the resolution of the many-to-many relationships, and the inclusion of attributes with key designations.

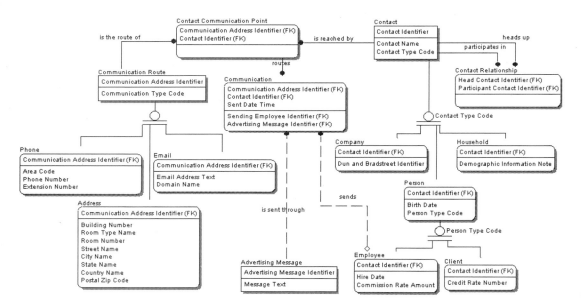

Figure 6-7. *Logical model of an advertising and marketing department*

Table 6-1 shows a conceptual to logical mapping just for curiosity sake while noting that most of the Staff and Advertising Event entities aren't in this submodel. It expands to be even bigger than this!

Table 6-1. *Conceptual-to-Logical Mapping*

Conceptual	Logical
Staff	Contact
Staff	Person
Staff	Employee
Advertising Event	Advertising Message (subset of the Event entities)
Advertising Event	Communication
Advertising Target	Contact
Advertising Target	Company
Advertising Target	Person
Advertising Target	Household
Advertising Target	Client
Advertising Target	Client Relationship
Advertising Target	Client Communication Point
Communication Mode	Communication Route
Communication Mode	Phone
Communication Mode	Address
Communication Mode	Email

Performing Physical Analysis

Now that we've covered the logical analysis, we'll cover the next step, physical analysis. If you've done the due diligence of serious logical analysis, physical analysis is more a continuation of the process aimed at building database objects. However, as we've emphasized, if your understanding of the data increases during this phase of the analysis, then you may have to revisit the Logical model to verify entity or relationship definitions.

In this phase, you need to decide what tools to use to write the front end and which RDBMS to use in deploying the tables (SQL Server, Oracle, Access, or DB2, for example). You can't go very far until you do that. Different RDBMSs and programming tools have different quirks you need to know, such as the size constraints of the table and column names, the system's reserved words (such as SELECT, INSERT, DELETE, and so on), and quirky database-specific things such as being unable to migrate more than one column in a foreign key.

■**Note** Being familiar with the database and programming language domain you're designing will assist you in proceeding with the physical design.

We call it *physical* design because, unlike a Logical model, you can build a real RDBMS database from a Physical model. It's going to be a tool to provide a means of saving time, effort, pain, money, and headaches. You'll now take all the logical analysis that you so faithfully documented and figure out how to create a real working data storage environment. This analysis takes the plan drawing and transforms it into the final database blueprint.

The first default action in moving a model from Logical to Physical is to change entities to tables and to change attributes to columns. That's a first draft of the structure, but you need to figure out a whole lot more before deploying it. You need to determine exact parameters for the naming standards, sizing, and data types. (These items are specific to the RDBMS; we just spent a section on logical analysis that involved choosing domains and attribute names.) You may also want to expand the model to include operational tables or columns. None of these things have been included in the analysis yet. And then you need to test the model for quality against the normal forms again. Normalization should have been completed in the logical analysis, but additions to the model discovered in this phase need to be retested.

Tables

Tables are the file structures where data will be organized and stored. Each row is one member of a set. Each column is one fact about that member. You'll see the words *entity* and *table* used interchangeably in some books, but, as we've previously stated, they aren't the same. Tables are physical implementations of the logical definitions contained in entities. The first task here is usually renaming the logical entity name with a proposed table name.

Entities don't care where they may end up someday. In fact, one logical analysis could be the basis for several different physical analysis designs depending on different deployment platforms with different structures and different naming conventions. Entities are independent of physical constraints since they're theoretical; tables are practical and are therefore dependent on the physical constraints of the target RDBMS.

Columns

Columns have a similar relationship to attributes as entities have to tables. Attributes are transformed into columns by default if you're using modeling software to assist you in the move from Logical to Physical models, since attributes are usually transformed into columns without much impact. The only significant issue in defaulting attributes into columns is that physical columns need to know if their data is optional. In other words, if a data value has no data, you need to state that it's NULL; you can't simply leave it as a series of spaces or blanks. Blank values in legacy systems or flat files, and NULLs in an RDBMS, represent the same thing. Both indicate that no data has been supplied for that attribute.

Your first task with columns will probably be changing their full logical attribute names to shorter, abbreviated forms to comply with whatever name length restrictions or naming rule restrictions may exist in the RDBMS you're targeting. You'll also need to take into account any applicable enterprise database naming standards in creating physical column names.

Quite frequently, a development group has standards that include adding columns (termed *operational columns*) that weren't in the original inventory of attributes. Other times, you may also need to satisfy business-side requirements for an audit trail to track inserts/updates. You might be asked to add a set of columns like the ones in Table 6-2 to every table.

Table 6-2. *Operational or Application Management–Only Columns*

Column Name	Definition
CreateId	The person or process who created the record
CreateDtTm	The date and time the record was created
CreateLocationId	The environment identifier from where the record insertion request originated
ModifiedId	The person or process who last modified the record
ModifiedDtTm	The date and time the record was last modified
ModifiedLocationId	The environment identifier from where the record update request originated

Such columns provide the programmers, database administrators (DBAs), and extraction, transformation, and loading (ETL) team members with the means to troubleshoot data and processing issues by allowing them to see who created a record, when it was created, and from where it came. These are generally not logical attributes from a client perspective, since they don't represent anything that's business oriented. Columns of this type are frequently referred to as *operational columns*, meaning that they assist in the operations involved in managing the rows.

After renaming and adding new columns, you have another set of analysis to perform. This time you need to add new information at the column level.

Primary Keys

This is the last change point for primary keys.

■**Note** After the tables have been built, the impact of changing a primary key is really painful.

Check one last time for the appropriateness of the current primary key choice. The team may want to go with surrogate keys rather than natural keys. Every table needs to be thoroughly reviewed and have the primary key approved from the perspective of current use and future needs.

Physical Domains

Creating physical domains is a detailed task. You can profile existing data, if it's available, in order to give yourself a leg up, but ultimately the client should be responsible for the answers (see the following questions), since it's is going to be their new application or software tool. Some of these questions will have been asked during the logical analysis. Now is the time to verify and really emphasize the need to finalize the decisions.

- Is this a fixed- or variable-length field?

- If it's a date field, will you ever want to see time also?

- How big do you want the column be?

- What kind of number do you need to store (-/+)?

- How many digits after the decimal do you need?

- Should you restrict the values?

- Is there a way to prevent incorrect data?

- Do you want to set up a default value on insert?

Relationships/Constraints in a Physical Model

Relationships in the Physical model are candidates for implementation as constraints in the RDBMS. Unfortunately, some platforms aren't able to deploy them. The rules in a constraint can be deployed in triggers, scripts, and stored procedures. If database constraints aren't going to be used, you may want to map the rules from your logical analysis to whatever mechanism has been chosen to prevent data integrity and quality errors. These types of rules can also be implemented as check constraints. The location for the code necessary to implement these constraints is an architectural decision; sometimes it's better to do it in stored procedure code, and sometimes it's better in triggers. The project team will have to decide what approach makes the most sense in your situation.

An example (using Oracle as the RDBMS) of the constraints from the model you just looked at is as follows:

```
ALTER TABLE Employee
      ADD   ( PRIMARY KEY (EmployeeId) ) ;

ALTER TABLE Employee
      ADD   ( FOREIGN KEY (HiredById)
                        REFERENCES Employee ) ;
```

Security

And finally, once you have all the tables, columns, and extra information available, you need to create a "Roles and Privileges" matrix of the client community, noting what rights they can have. You need a way to group the clients to provide specific privileges for functions in their system. They generally have groupings something like this:

- **Owners**: Can do anything

- **Administrators**: Can do almost anything

- **Special groups**: Have restricted power to carry out certain operations

- **Viewers**: Can only see

DBAs may implement security by giving clients access only to tables by granting appropriate INSERT, UPDATE, and DELETE privileges. It's up to them to devise the specifics of the security policy that needs implementing, but you need to give them an overview of what's needed. Once you establish the general groups the clients want to maintain, you set up a

CRUD diagram for all the tables and columns. (CRUD stands for Create, Read, Update, and Delete.) These are the general privileges that the DBA can set up for them. From this diagram, all the security roles can be created in whatever security method is being developed. You may want to do a separate or combined view of this type of grid (see Table 6-3).

Table 6-3. *CRUD Diagram of Marketing Group Security Privileges*

Security Analysis: Marketing Group

Table/Column	Create	Read	Update	Delete
Emp.Emp_id		X		
Emp.Hire_Date		X		
Emp.Cons_Rate_Amt				
Emp.Emp_Name		X		
Emp.Emp_Birth_Date		X		

You'll see here that the marketing group isn't allowed to change any data and can't view the commission rates of employees. The other thing this analysis will bring out is whether the clients need to partition the data in some way other than by table and column. Quite frequently you'll find clients needing to restrict even read access to the data based on geography or department. Cases such as these may cause you to return to the model and perhaps develop other views to be able to support this requirement. You'll probably hope this isn't something that's newly discovered at this stage of development; you'll want to know it was coming all along. Sometimes developing the solution required to support this set of rules may not involve database security concepts but may involve creating another set of entities, tables, or views to identify the security constraints.

Unfortunately, the model itself isn't very good at documenting this portion of the analysis; it's generally another mapping document separate from the model itself.

Physical Analysis Example

We'll leave a fuller discussion of the issues involved in developing a Physical model from a Logical one to the tutorial in Chapter 10. At this point we'll simply present a Physical model, based on our earlier logical one, that we drew up for our marketing department. To give some insight here, Table 6-4 shows how we mapped the logical entities to physical ones.

Table 6-4. *Conceptual-Logical-Physical Entity Mapping*

Conceptual	Logical	Physical
Staff	Contact	Contact
Staff	Person	Contact
Staff	Employee	Employee
Advertising Event	Advertising Message (subset of the Event entities)	AdvertisingMessage
Advertising Event	Communication	Communication

Continued

Table 6-4. *Continued*

Conceptual	Logical	Physical
Advertising Target	Contact	Contact
Advertising Target	Company	Contact
Advertising Target	Person	Contact
Advertising Target	Household	Contact
Advertising Target	Client	Contact
Advertising Target	Client Relationship	ContactRelationship
Advertising Target	Client Communication Point	CommunicationPoint
Communication Mode	Communication Route	CommunicationRoute
Communication Mode	Phone	CommunicationRoute
Communication Mode	Address	CommunicationRoute
Communication Mode	Email	CommunicationRoute

Compare Figure 6-8, the Physical model, to Figure 6-9, the logical design.

The key decisions made in this case are as follows:

- All the Contact attributes were rolled into Contact (a choice in category structure physicalization) except in the case of Employee, which means almost all the attributes are NULL allowed. The logic for what columns can be filled in is being managed through code based on the Contact_Type_Cd.

- The choice was made to give Employee its own table for security reasons rather than roll it up with the rest of the contacts. This means the relationship to Comm_Route (which holds their addresses, phone number, and e-mail addresses) needed a new intersection table called Emp_Comm_Point.

- All the communication routes were rolled into one table (a choice in category structure physicalization), which means that except for Comm_Type_Cd, all the attributes are NULL allowed. The logic for what columns can be filled in is being managed through code based on the type code.

Performing Reverse-Engineered Analysis

We devote Chapter 13 to reverse-engineered modeling since it's a necessary modeling activity. The goal of reverse-engineered analysis is to develop a graphic that identifies the existing database objects to aid tasks such as redevelopment, redesign, or performance tuning. What makes this kind of analysis tough is that you're working backward from the existing system implementation and don't have any of the development notes or models to use. Instead of coming "top down" from the Logical model, you're moving "bottom up," beginning with the Physical model and working backward to develop and document a Logical (and possibly even a Conceptual) model.

Marketing/Advertising Target Submodel
Logical Model

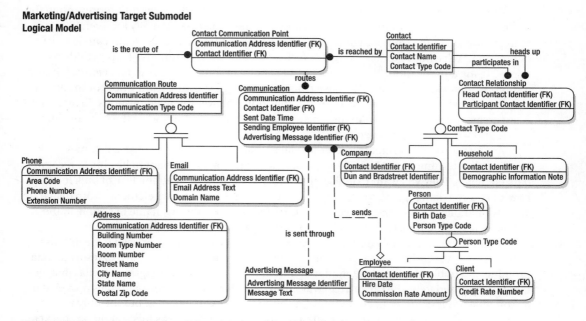

Figure 6-8. *Logical model of an advertising and marketing department*

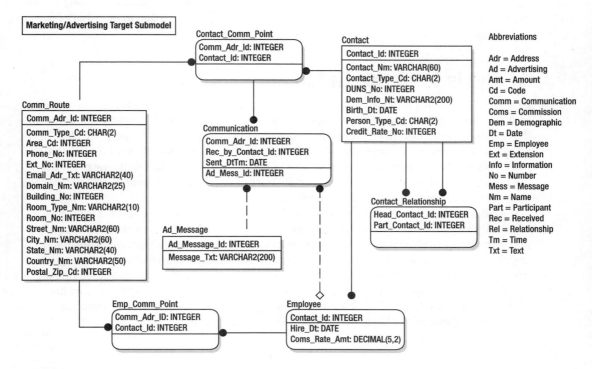

Figure 6-9. *Physical model of an advertising and marketing department*

You almost need two Physical models: one that's the exact Physical truth representing the current database and another that documents what the data rules actually are even if they're being managed in the front end or through stored procedures. The exact truth can be most depressing. We've built models using this technique that show hundreds of tables and are named using abbreviations that no one has the ability to translate back to real words, without a single primary key and not a database constraint in sight showing from where or to the keys migrate. Models such as this have a use, but they don't answer the real questions. In fact, they often create more questions than they answer, but they do show you what the current situation is and what you have to use.

You may also need to create a semi-logical model and translate the physical names back into business terminology. Most of your data model customers will want to be able to recognize data elements. They will want to look at the model to see how difficult the task of bulk loading newly acquired data is going to be. The necessity of matching like data elements from disparate systems in order to check the size constraints of, for example, the last name of people in the system, will require translating the physical name L_NM into the logical Last Name.

Definitions can be really difficult to create. Who knew what was supposed to be in those tables or columns compared to what you actually find in them? You may have to resort to data profiling and publishing what you find rather than using a textual description of what that element is supposed to be. Be sensitive to ways the clients have broken the data rules provided in the original implementation. For example, a column may be mandatory, but the only values actually found in it are spaces or N/A (rather than NULL). Things such as this should be checked for and can be prevented in a check constraint, but you'll find that the clients who are providing the business rules often forget to add that level of detail to the requirements. In the process of reverse engineering an As-Is Physical model, it's more important to document what's real rather than what was intended.

Analysis Is in the Detail

In the first half of this chapter you've looked at the different types of models you can develop as you move from the initial design phase toward your Physical model, iterating through your definitions in order to verify their accuracy and validity (a top-down approach). We also touched on reverse-engineered models, where you look at an existing Physical model and work backward to determine a Logical model (a bottom-up approach). Each type of model has a particular role to play in representing the state of the data you're modeling, and you can give different levels of detail in such models, as you'll see now.

At one time we thought entity level models were always the beginning place for a new design. We've learned over time that it's really up to the modeler as to how they want to approach a data problem. Top-down analysis has a tendency to begin with concepts that fit better into an entity (simple) level of detail model, and bottom-up analysis tends to begin with a fully attributed (FA) detail level. Most models have the ability to be translated into all detail levels, no matter where the analysis started. In practice you may end up performing both top-down and bottom-up analysis at the same time, with the hope of verifying your process by the meeting of these two analyses at some midpoint.

Entity-Level Detailing

Entity-level models tend to have simplicity in the measure of both the entity quantity and the complexity of the relationships. It's not necessary to resolve the many-to-many relationships by building intersection/associative entities at this level. But don't think that this is a hard-and-fast rule since you can create entity models that have no many-to-many relationships. The decision of whether you should have many-to-many relationships should follow from an importance or prioritization goal of your own. Often the determining factor is whether the intersection of two entities has attributes of its own that need documenting (such as a time-frame during which the relationship is valid). If the intersection has its own attributes, it should be its own entity.

Entity models are generally not Physical data models because of this high degree of flexibility. Physical data models must adhere to the rules of creating RDBMS objects, and entity modeling allows syntax that's simply not physically deployable. Let's consider the marketing department example once again. An entity level diagram in this case would look something like Figure 6-10.

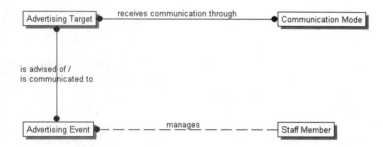

Figure 6-10. *Conceptual model of an advertising and marketing department*

An alternative view of this model includes definitions along with the conceptual entity names, providing an additional level of detail with which to work. This is particularly useful in team review meetings; see Figure 6-11 for an example.

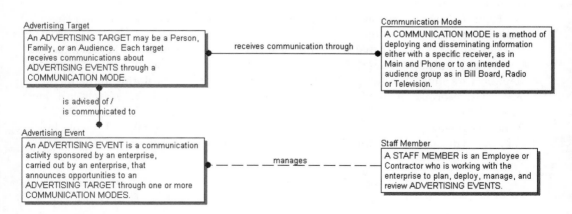

Figure 6-11. *Conceptual model using a definition view*

When to Use Entity-Level Detailing

This level of detail is suitable for the following:

- Scope documentation, such as projects

- Beginning business client reviews

- Overview documentation, such as enterprise models

- Top-down analysis

Sometimes details can overwhelm an audience, whether it's your project manager, your business client, or a review committee. As we said earlier, an entity model can be backed into from a detailed design or, indeed, used as a starting place for original analysis. However, keeping everything synchronized can be a real challenge. Either way, the entity model should be the best choice for reviewing general content and rules of use. An entity model is most useful as a tool to communicate with the members of the team who are more interested in that their business requirements have been captured.

Key-Based (KB) Detailing

Data models detailed to the key-based level concentrate on keys and their migrations along the paths of relationships. Why concentrate on keys? Keys are powerful indicators that you've separated out similar concepts and ensured that there's no duplication of entities in your model. They confirm you've separated similar *but different* concepts. They must be understood for integration and extraction efforts and should be chosen with care and thought for future of enterprise data. What makes a set member distinct should matter to you, and you may need to work with a set of sample data for each entity to verify this level of analysis.

However, we admit that this level of analysis is seen least often in data modeling circles. Entity-level models are used constantly to create the simple view, but a fully attributed model is the ultimate goal for anything that's going to be deployed (as you'll see shortly). Key-based should be the model used to review the entities and their identifying attributes and to watch for redundancy, incompatibility, and inconsistency. That step is often combined into the creation of the fully attributed model.

Figure 6-12 shows an example of a Logical key-based model, again based around the marketing department example.

You can see at a glance that some entities are using the same identifier. For example, the Phone, Email, and Address entities all use Communication Address ID as their identifier. Such identifiers are often opportunities to aggregate entities into one table during the logical to physical transformation. In this case, you could combine Phone, Email, and Address in a single Communication Route entity. The choice to roll up a category structure is visible this way. Obviously, you have other considerations and other options for designing such a table, but a key-based detailed model provides a useful means by which to carry out such a review.

Keys Only

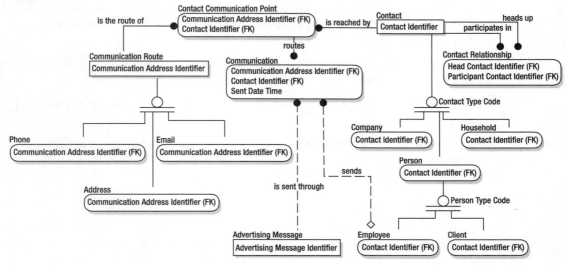

Figure 6-12. *Logical model using a key-based view*

Figure 6-13 shows the key-based Physical model. Now you can even review the data types and sizes of the primary key. The model shown in Figure 6-13 would be useful for index order or naming convention reviews.

Physical Data Model - Primary Keys Only

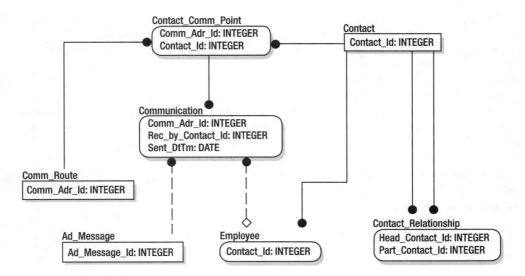

Figure 6-13. *Physical model using a key-based view*

When to Use KB Detailing

The goal of the key-based level of detail is to display and concentrate on the identifiers of the instances or rows. Identifiers are hugely important to anyone needing to work with the data without using the front end. This style is suitable for showing the following:

- **Proposed or actual keys of a system**: To highlight the currently chosen primary keys to check their suitability

- **Integration opportunities and issues**: To see what other systems are using as the PK of the same entities

- **Merging data (retiring systems and acquiring new data)**: To map source to target transformation issues

Fully Attributed (FA) Detailing

A data model with the full complement of attributes is termed *fully attributed* (FA). Logical and Physical models can be taken to this level of detail, and it's the detail level that most often is associated with a data model; it's the one that has all the attributes or columns clearly defined.

We don't really believe in fully attributed Conceptual models, so we won't try to show you what one would look like. They can become immense, with too much information to be able to find what you're looking for easily. In general, all the entities would be conceptual and so would the attributes. But it could be a useful strategic tool if used correctly. Fully attributed Conceptual models can show that you've captured all the information (in both entities and attributes) that's necessary to properly separate different business concepts. They're sometimes useful to verify with true business users who have no knowledge of the physical implementation.

The fully attributed Logical model is the final level of analysis of capturing the business rules and data elements of a business process (see Figure 6-14). You can use this model to walk through all the requirements that deal with creating, modifying, deleting, or displaying data. There's an enormous wealth of other information (especially the definitions) that isn't visible on the graphic but that's also a part of the fully attributed model.

Figure 6-15 shows an example of a fully attributed Physical model.

The fully attributed Physical model is the database schematic, also known as the *database diagram*. It should show all the tables and columns needed to support both the business process and the operational management of the application. The fully attributed Physical model is the source of information used to generate the Data Definition Language (DDL) and create database objects and must be developed with the rigor needed to successfully accomplish that task. A reverse-engineered fully attributed data model ought to have captured the details to be able to rebuild the physical database structure if necessary.

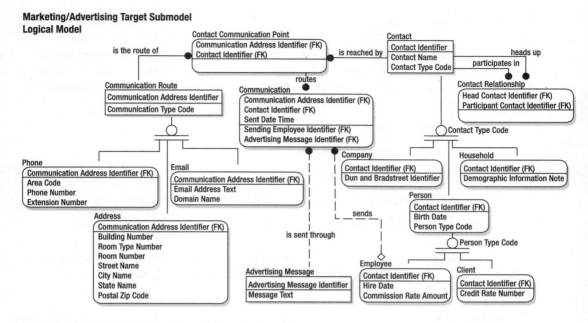

Figure 6-14. *Logical model using a fully attributed view*

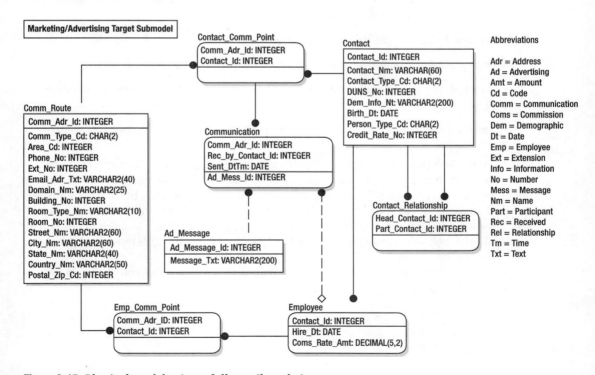

Figure 6-15. *Physical model using a fully attributed view*

When to Use FA Detailing

The goal of the fully attributed data model is to capture and present all the data elements necessary to satisfy the charter of the project. The charter may be a development project for a new custom application, or it may be to create a model of a legacy system. Fully attributed models are generally the most important models for the information technology (IT) community. This modeling style is suitable for many tasks, including the following:

- Fully analyzed data element requirements (logical)

- Blueprints for databases (physical)

- Delta points for change control (logical and physical)

- Visual data load/unload ordering documents (physical constraints)

- Impact analysis (data type, data element, data size)

You can also use this fully attributed model to validate business process changes in order to ensure that the data and the business process or policies can be supported.

Summary

This chapter covered the various analysis styles you can use as data models in data analysis and design. These can be summarized as follows:

- **Conceptual**: The highest-level beginning place

- **Logical**: The most important model for developing a good physical design

- **Physical**: The most detailed model that's the source of the DDL to generate database objects

- **Reverse engineered**: A Physical model that shows the As-Is of a deployed database

A *top-down* approach to the modeling of a system will begin with a Conceptual model and work down through a Logical model to a Physical model for implementation. This process documents details regarding the conceptual entities that you begin with, breaking out attributes and relationships as you progress toward a Physical model. Sometimes you have to work with a *bottom-up* approach, working backward from an existing system, in order to develop a Logical model (and sometimes further back to a Conceptual model). This type of approach is *reverse-engineering* analysis.

At each of these stages of analysis, you can choose the level of detail you display in the model you develop.

- **Entity level**: This is a high level of detail used for scope and planning or a simplified review at the beginning of a project. It shows only entities and attributes.

- **Key-based**: This is an intermediate level of detail, which includes entities and primary key attributes (usually natural keys if possible).

- **Fully attributed**: This is the most detailed level of analysis. All attributes are listed, including all foreign keys migrating from the parent table.

It's important to use the appropriate type of model and level of detail and to tailor the model to the needs of your particular situation. You'll consider the scope of projects in the next chapter.

CHAPTER 7

■■■

How Data Models Fit Into Projects

In this chapter you'll see how everything you've been looking at comes together in a project and drives the creation of a data model. You'll look at how a project methodology helps organize different model deliverables throughout the life cycle. You'll look at what you need before you begin modeling and what model or models you may want to build at different stages to make the project a success.

This isn't a book about project management, so although we'll cover some of the tasks and stages of a project, we won't go through a software development methodology in detail. What we'll do is cover all the stages in light of the data modeling tasks that accompany them. To that end, you'll learn about the following:

- **Setting project parameters**: The scoping, standards, and restrictions that a project team needs to know in order to satisfy expectations successfully

- **Selecting the right model for the job**: Conceptual, Logical, or Physical at the varying levels of detail that we covered in the previous chapter

The Project

Up until now we've been focusing almost exclusively on data modeling, its history, its techniques, and its definitions. Now you need to look at how to launch a data model into the furious currents of enterprise activity. Most often a modeling task will be nested inside a formal application development project, although from time to time you'll model outlying structures that may help the team determine interface and integration options, such as when you create reverse-engineered models of legacy or vendor systems.

Application development projects arise because someone somewhere in the enterprise has determined that business needs for data have changed and the data needs to be managed differently. Understanding this data need is extremely important for you to be able to help provide a new or modified data storage solution. The person suggesting the project may have done a preliminary business process study and determined that productivity could be increased with a new automated way of capturing and reporting on data that's currently being managed manually. They may have read about a new business process they think will make the company more profitable. They may be required to change certain internal data rules to respond to external data rule changes. They may also have to react to regulatory changes or externally imposed requirements, such as the new federal data management rules imposed by the Sarbanes-Oxley Act in the United States. The proposal may or may not have focused on data storage structures. Many times the data element inventory and design changes are just one (critical) part of the overall enterprise changes that need to happen to support a business process change.

As a data modeler determining how to best respond to data storage requests for an enterprise, you must always keep in mind that you serve two masters. You need to help achieve the short-term goals of the project, and you need to pursue the long-term goals of enterprise data management. Balancing these two goals often takes some creative compromising. You'll generally find that project success is judged in terms of adherence to time and budget constraints or preconceptions of what the solution should be, but enterprise success is more focused on whether the solution met its strategic functional objectives using a high-quality and extensible design that's in alignment with corporate long-term plans. As a result, you have to balance strategic objectives (quality and functionality) against tactical objectives (time and cost). This tension is often referred to as balancing *tactical* vs. *strategic* needs.

Project Management

Before starting to think about building a data model, you need to learn about the project. You can't begin without knowing the basics. You need to complete a survey of intended enterprise-level data management strategies (financial, quality, growth, simplification, and expansion) and the high-level expectation of how to achieve them in order to guide the project. What's also important at this stage is to determine the methodology the project will follow. In meeting the project goal you may well follow a formal project methodology that involves systematic, planned undertakings with clear goals, teams, budgets, and stages. On other occasions you'll head toward the goal in a more spontaneous manner, taking action to supplement and enhance productivity or to fight one of the short-term data "fires" that crop up every day in an enterprise. However, bear in mind that quick fixes have a habit of staying around for a lot longer than generally anticipated, and you should still endeavor to approach seemingly informal projects with the same care and process as larger ones. It can be like a chess game, where even the moves made by the pawns, if not fully thought through, may end up causing a checkmate situation later.

In a formal project, a feasibility study probably determined a set of generic goals and assessed whether the goals were reasonable, accomplishable, and appropriate to the strategy of the enterprise. You may be given this information in a charter/kickoff/formal project meeting that brings all the key team members together for the first time to begin detailed project planning. In a less formal project, your team may have to gather and write down their own understanding of the goals in the form of a list of assumptions. Either way, at this point you need to draw up an initial scope for the project, outlining the expected results as the boundary markers for exploration.

All the project documentation needs to be kept up-to-date and relevant to ensure that the entire team is working from the most recent revision. It's a good idea to determine how you intend to ensure that everyone has the correct copies at the beginning of a project: the version control strategy. A numbering, dating, and/or location standard may help prevent the confusion caused by having 20 versions of the scope statement floating around the office.

Scope

We'd say that the *most* critical factor to the success of any project is defining and managing the scope. This is an iterative process, since the scope may need to be modified over the life of the project as the analysis clarifies and decides on the validity of more and more detail. This new understanding drives the direction of the exploration, which in turn results in a tighter control of the direction. Don't expect the first draft of the scope to survive without alterations.

We're sure you could come up with several instances of incorrect or misunderstood scope (and by association, requirements) that caused incorrect decisions to be made that wasted time and money. We've seen requirements documents, software prototypes, and even (as painful as this was to witness) complete alpha test systems shared proudly with the clients, only for the team to be told the solution was insufficient to meet the intended scope. This seems to happen most often when the business clients and the project team don't stay in close communication with each other, at least through the design phase. The scope needs to be interpreted, clarified, tested, and detailed by both the customers and the development members of the team. Scope, assumptions, definitions, and outcomes are elements best confirmed with the customer in writing or in e-mail to verify that there's "project clarity" amongst the respective parties. Critical amendments and iterations also need formal acknowledgment since ambiguity, misperception, or vagueness can often lead to expensive overruns. The initial scope document will include the following:

- **Definitions of goals to be included**: For example, a business goal could say, "Create a central, managed list of customers with a purchase history."

- **Goals to be excluded**: For example, a business goal that the team deliberately chose to leave out could read like this, "Not in scope at this time—the marketing department's potential customers and the sales department's canceled customers."

- **Assumptions made**: For example, a business assumption could be that "This list of customers will be a list available for enterprise use, managed by the accounts receivable department."

The scope statement is usually a short document describing the goal of the project. Descriptions of what isn't being dealt with are as important as what will be, especially if there could be any confusion among those who aren't as close to the analysis. Product customers are the most important to keep up-to-date. The language used to describe scope can be critical. Saying that the project will automate "inventory processes" is probably too broad. Does that include receiving, shipping, rework, manufacturing, scrap, return, credit, restock, samples, and supply chain management? It's imperative to clarify this. It may be all of that, or it may be just the conjunction of those processes where they impact "on-hand" quantities. The scope should contribute heavily at the beginning of the project to a glossary to ensure that the whole project team understands the project terminology. We usually include all acronyms as well, since we have, for example, used acronym lists in aerospace projects where the same letters can mean as many as 15 different things depending on the context.

To support the scope phase of a project, the data modeler may provide models and data description documentation. Consider using as many models as you need as communication tools during this volatile phase of brainstorming and exploration. The best thing you can do is to provide deliverables for the express purpose of being used for pinning on walls, being scribbled on, highlighted, and annotated with notes and references. You may need the following:

- A new Conceptual model describing the scope of the project

- Existing Logical models of various subject area you plan to tackle

- Newly reverse engineered or existing Physical models that describe the current As-Is relational database management system (RDBMS) structures of areas you need to integrate to or replace

Project Standards

Standards are the ground rules that govern the process of any project. They may cover the available development methodologies, enterprise-level governance standards describing preferred hardware/software choices, deliverable formats for project plans, requirements, functional specifications, and even data element naming on the models. They may be developed internally or adopted from external sources such as government, military, or international customers.

Many shops don't worry about creating such formal rules to manage their processes. On the other hand, even small companies may need to use some formal development guidelines to be eligible to participate in bidding for certain contracts (such as government or military contracts). The development and management processes of the enterprise's data may also be part of the judgment criteria used in external quality rating systems of enterprises.

Methodologies

Formal methodologies, when used correctly and, maybe more important, consistently, can become an awesome tool for getting the best results possible out of a project. They will impact not only the final deliverable of the project but also the plan for delivering, maintaining, enhancing, monitoring, and judging the effectiveness of it. When used incorrectly, formal methodologies may steal the focus of the team from solving a problem for a client and redirect the effort into a document generation process.

Methodologies need to be used correctly. It's crucial to being able to make them work well for you. When used incorrectly, ISO 9001, CMM (described shortly), or any other documentation/checklist methodology can stifle creativity and deadlock design decisions. When this happens, project managers and developers make decisions designed to avoid the documentation or approval processes, and the project suffers as a result.

Some big companies such as large aerospace firms may have developed their own software project management methodology. Computer-aided system engineering (CASE) tools exist that have inherent processes. And some consulting firms have created their own methodologies, which they will teach and share. You'll find most methodologies need enterprise sponsorship, training, and support to make them an integral part of the software development process.

Formal methodologies are like checklists. They remind us of all the myriad aspects of analysis and planning that you should do even if you don't have the time or resources to do them. The nice thing about formal methodologies for a modeler is that the various stages of model development are often actually called out as deliverables at established steps in the process.

You'll now briefly look at the following formal process controls that could be used as standards in a project:

- Dacom methodology

- International Standards Organization (ISO): standard 9001

- Capability maturity model (CMM)

The data modeler needs to be familiar with the formal steps, milestones, reviews, and deliverables of the chosen methodology. You'll use every type, style, and detail level of data model depending on the circumstances. Not all your models will be formal deliverables, but you should consider them all to be tools at your disposal that may be necessary to make headway through a defined methodology phase.

DACOM Methodology

We've used many methodologies. Our first was a top-down approach starting with a formal set of analysis steps developed in the 1990s by DACOM. The requirements analysis planning (RAP) stage discovered current business processes, identified deficiencies, and scoped one or more projects to mitigate them. The emphasis was on documenting everyone's viewpoint (current and future), from the business client, through the technical team, and into the enterprise. This provided the tactical, technical, and strategic dynamics at play in the project. This stage developed documentation from scope to detail requirements (including activity and high-level data models).

Each project that the RAP identified was then planned and deployed using another set of formal steps. The prototype development methodology (PDM) built on the analysis of the RAP to develop software and business process enhancement for the enterprise. The emphasis was to provide a framework for iterating through designing, developing, and maintaining an automated system and utilizing prototyping as a means to refine the definition of requirements and to allow the business clients to experience the functionality of the system in a timely fashion to fine-tune it to meet their needs. This stage developed from further enhanced project plans to fully tested, deployed, documented software (including Conceptual, Logical, and Physical data models).

ISO 9001

Bidding for some contracts (government or industry) requires that a company must comply with standards established by an outside regulatory department. One of the most common that you in information technology (IT) are being judged by is ISO 9001. ISO 9001 is a quality standard in the industry, which has been established by the ISO, and is equally applicable to anyone producing furniture, rocket ships, or video games. The emphasis is in management of processes. It has a two-step approach, which requires that a company record the following:

- Defining and documenting what they're going to do

- Auditing what was done against the plan

You can visit ISO's Web site at www.iso.org, where the ISO series is described as follows:

A network of national standards institutes from 140 countries working in partnership with international organizations, governments, industry, business, and consumer representatives. A bridge between public and private sectors.

This certification doesn't put an auditor or ISO committee in the company. It verifies that good practices were being used consistently at the time the company was certified (and we hope are still being used). It gives customers a certain level of confidence in the level of documentation and support they can expect.

You can see the benefits immediately. Using this type of standard the project team takes the time to plot the detailed tasks necessary to accomplish the goal and then uses that as a checklist to verify that all the tasks have been accomplished. And since all projects have an iterative understanding of the plan, a simple feedback mechanism sets up self-correcting documentation.

Getting an ISO-compliance rating (15,000 exist) is a big deal, and you'll see companies putting banners on their buildings noting that they're certified. For a company to claim it's ISO 9001 compliant, it must go through a series of audits leading to certification. The company may need to go through a lengthy process of training, analyzing, and altering current practices, and then set up a self-correcting audit function to maintain ISO requirements. Your data models may become part of the documentation proving the level of data management and software tool development.

Capability Maturity Model (CMM)

The CMM for software is a software process maturity framework that helps organizations assess and improve their software development process. The Software Engineering Institute (SEI) at Carnegie Mellon University developed it in response to a request by the U.S. government for a method of assessing software contractors. This gives everyone the ability to compare projects and products against an objective, common measurement and takes some of the "gut feel" factor out of the judgment of success.

Again, it doesn't have standard process steps. These are levels of compliance and achievement, like a ladder or staircase leading upward to higher-quality levels. It's a great way to assess how your team is managing data and gives you a "next level" of control for which to shoot. Here are the five levels defined:

- **Initial**: The software process is characterized as ad hoc, and occasionally even chaotic. Few processes are defined, and success depends on individual effort and heroics.

- **Repeatable**: Basic project management processes are established to track cost, schedule, and functionality. The necessary process discipline is in place to repeat earlier successes on projects with similar applications.

- **Defined**: The software process for both management and engineering activities is documented, standardized, and integrated into a standard software process for the organization. All projects use an approved, tailored version of the organization's standard software process for developing and maintaining software.

- **Managed**: Detailed measures of the software process and product quality are collected. Both the software process and products are quantitatively understood and controlled.

- **Optimizing**: Continuous process improvement is enabled by quantitative feedback from the process and from piloting innovative ideas and technologies.

Note You can find out more about this standard and how to implement it at www.sei.cmu.edu/cmm.

If your organization is using CMM to understand and improve their process areas, you may already understand the current level. You need to identify key process areas to achieve the next level. So, for example, the key process areas at the second level focus on the software project's concerns related to establishing basic project management controls. They are requirements management, software project planning, software project tracking and oversight, software subcontract management, software quality assurance, and software configuration management. Modeling standards and model management may be a part of that process.

Project Team Needs

Data models are communication tools, so they need to be able to depict information in a form that can be understood by all the members of the project team: no matter how technical or nontechnical they may be. As discussed in the previous chapter, you can develop Conceptual, Logical, and Physical models with different levels of detail (entity, key-based, or fully attributed). This allows you to create submodels—covering specific subject areas—where some levels of detail are invisible (such as data types and relationship verb phrases in an entity-level model). These smaller, more focused models are useful for discussion with your business clients. If the full model is too large, your clients will be overwhelmed by the complexity and may be unable to provide the feedback you need. You may want to concentrate on just displaying the data element names and leaving the domains invisible at this stage in your discussion. You have to choose how to present your analysis in the most constructive way possible. Sizing up the audience is so important. Just like any presentation, the data model presentation must take into account what the audience is able to absorb and to whom the material is being presented.

With this in mind, let's look at the data model customers and what the modeler does to support them.

Project Initiators/Sponsor

The project initiators are generally the group of people who are sponsoring the project. They're frequently management business-type customers who have a limited understanding of what the data model is trying to capture. They will probably need a simpler model to follow what you're saying, generally a Conceptual or Logical model, pretty tightly focused on their area of knowledge. You may even need to have a model that uses their business terms or provides a definition view so they can follow along.

These people don't need to know the internal workings of your model, but they do need to know the general outline, as well as any indications of the bottom line of cost and resource allocation that you can provide. They will probably have different priorities than your organization will. Be careful how you explain your analysis to prevent misunderstandings. Their priorities are important, so make sure they know you're aware of that. Be aware, though, and don't misrepresent complexity as being simple or indeed simplicity as being complex. One can cause a completely unreal expectation about time and budget, and the other can cause a devastating loss of faith in your integrity.

For these team members, the data modeler will do the following:

- Provide copies of finalized deliverables (data models and supporting documentation).

- Act as a mentor to make any details that are in question clear and understandable.

- Act as a reviewer to ensure all standards and guidelines imposed by the team are used in the development process.

Business Team

The business team generally represents the group of people who will be impacted the most by the project's deployment. They're the development team's contact with the business world. Although the development team may be involved in the initial series of interviews and fact-finding sessions with the actual users of the final product, the business team will spend much of their time answering data and process questions. They resolve these questions by taking them back to their management (the project sponsors) or further exploring details in the user community. The people they represent will either have their process impacted by a new tool or have their data sources impacted by your project. This means that the business team generally has a *huge* vested interest in the success of the project.

At the least, business team members need to learn how to read detailed models at the logical level. They need to understand these models down to the level of data element size and nullability to decide whether you've captured their requirements adequately. However, the fact that they need to learn how to read your models means you have to be doubly sensitive to their frustrations and will need to help them recognize the mappings of model elements to screen and report designs. Only the business team can tell you if your analysis and design are wrong for their needs. These are the people with whom you'll be doing most of your upfront model reviews.

For these team members, the data modeler will do the following:

- Provide copies of interim working documentation for review and enhancement (data models and supporting documentation).

- Act as a mentor to make any details that are in question clear and understandable.

- Act as an advocate to the business community in documenting and understanding all rules/restrictions/quirks of the data without deciding on the physicalization of the design.

- Provide objective assessments as to options and risks in terms of data management: existing and future.

Development Team

The development team may also have a sort of liaison to the data modeler (often the database administrator [DBA] and/or a senior programmer or lead). At some level the team will have to work with the results of the model (especially in decision making for table design) and will want to know all the rules of storing, processing, retrieving, updating, and deleting data (the same way the business team needs to do). We hope the team will want to understand the data model even if they've never worked with one before. They should recognize how the model maps to the structures in the database. Still, especially in large projects, you'll want to create submodels to reduce the clutter and allow them to focus on their assigned portions of the tasks in the same way you restricted views by subject areas for the business team. The development team is often not as interested in the logical model as they are the physical model. Once you've completed your analysis of the Logical rules with the business team they're itching to see a Physical design. You may need to do several physical designs in order to point out different options for category structures and physical implementation denormalization options. Make sure they're clear about the pros and cons of each option when you need to work with them.

For these team members, the data modeler will do the following:

- Provide copies of interim working documentation for review and enhancement (data models and supporting documentation).

- Act as a mentor to make any details that are in question clear and understandable.

- Act as an advocate for the business community to provide a management solution for as many of the rules/restrictions/quirks of the data in the application design.

- Provide objective assessments as to options and risks of physicalization solutions.

Extraction, Transformation, and Loading (ETL) Team

These team members are responsible for moving data values from place to place using repeatable tasks or scripts, generally on a schedule of time or sequential dependencies. The ETL team may be involved in building batch jobs that run at the end of the day or fast-paced interim loads to support a more timely delivery. As such, they need an intimate knowledge of what to expect of the data values themselves along with the more theoretical description of what that data means. The data modeler probably has a more intimate and complete understanding of the nature of the data as a result of all the analysis and profiling they've done in various systems or with the business community. The data modeler will have gathered all that information and documented it in a variety of deliverables. Modelers often act as the "go to" guy for the ETL team to begin and develop their processes.

For these team members, the data modeler will do the following:

- Provide copies of interim working documentation for review and enhancement (data models and supporting documentation).

- Act as a mentor to make any details that are in question clear and understandable.

- Act as a designer and guide to solving for as many of the rules/restrictions/quirks of the data as possible in the data movement processes (including exception processing), providing the following:

- **Extraction guidelines**: How to find the best, fastest, and most reliable selection sources

- **Transformation needs**: Identifying decoding and parsing rules, data value mapping between nonintegrated lists, and mathematical formulas for derived data creation

- **Loading to target requirements**: Mapping source to target rules

Business Intelligence (BI) Team

The job of the business intelligence (BI) team is to properly develop crafted data sets to support the decision-making processes of the company. Sometimes this data is historic in nature to support looking for data trends, such as reports from a data warehouse spanning long periods of time. Other times this data is needed to make moment-by-moment decisions that affect the daily processes of the enterprise. Both of these reporting types (or some combination of both) require a deep understanding of the right data source, the right data elements, the right time to select them, and the right rules to apply to configure and correlate the data to best support the reporting function. Again, the data modeler is a good resource for providing that guidance and designing easy-to-use reporting data storage structures.

For these team members, the data modeler will do the following:

- Provide copies of metadata documentation for review to assist in targeting the correct data source.

- Act as a mentor to make any details that are in question clear and understandable.

- Design quality, well-performing data storage solutions to support BI reporting tools.

Extended Development Team

Don't forget the members of the team who aren't full-time on the project but are critical to its overall success. The infrastructure team is going to need estimates of bandwidth to move the data. The training group may need to see how complex this is going to be to teach. The help desk may need to add extra operational data elements to be able to troubleshoot issues. Project managers will want to look at how the design is coming. The test team will want to begin making test scenarios based on the business rules. Even the software quality team may want a model to explore.

For these team members, the data modeler will do the following:

- Provide copies of finalized deliverables (data models and supporting documentation).

- Act as a mentor to make any details that are in question clear and understandable.

- Act as an advocate for the business community to provide a management solution for as many of the rules/restrictions/quirks of the data in the application design.

- Provide objective assessments as to the options and risks of physicalization solutions.

Budget and Schedule

We hesitate to mention it, but you're as bound to the available resources of our company as any other department. Managing data costs money. Someday someone will finally come up with a generic formula to quantify the cost of creating, managing, and storing data for those of you who have to weigh the choice of quick, cheap, and limited designs vs. more flexible and therefore more costly designs. In the meantime, data modelers are often on the front lines when it comes to recognizing a serious increase in complexity than the original scope took into account. You can create visual representations of scope creep on the model using color or version comparisons. This means it's your responsibility to help manage expectations and share risks with the project manager.

The data modeler is part of the team. It's part of your charter to make the project successful. Good data modeling streamlines the process and can save time and money in the long run.

Project Life Cycle

All projects, whether formal or informal, tend to go through certain stages. You'll find many different pictures of what project life cycles look like, one of the more common being the "waterfall" life cycle, which is a classic top-down analysis style. It provides you with a good set of steps, but the original waterfall design showed only the steps related in one direction (downward). Once a team (completely) finished one step, they went onto another (never to return to a previous step).

Over time we have come to the conclusion that this is a naive way of describing what actually happens in a project. Most life-cycle diagrams now attempt to show parallel processing and feedback loops that note the team can return to any step appropriate to iron out issues or respond to new understanding. This could be categorized as a *semistructured* life cycle. This is also known as an *iterative* approach. Extreme programming is one movement that stresses quick iterations through the life cycle in a sometimes unstructured (or semistructured) way.

In general, certain starting or planning tasks deal with strategy, analysis, and design, and certain execution tasks deal with building, testing, and deploying. They have a general flow from one task to the next. However, within a single project, each of these processes could be active concurrently, or they could be approached from steps traditionally considered a long way down the development path.

We tried to capture the idea of a general path and the whirlpool of swinging back around to any place along the life cycle if necessary in Figure 7-1. Notice that most of the steps don't simply move from one process to another. The overlaps will make it difficult to decide if you're in the strategize or analyze step or in the design or build step. Most of the time you're probably combining steps to move the project forward.

You can find more about project life cycles at www.yourdon.com, where Edward Yourdon calls this iterative, parallel, messy life-cycle activity a *radical* implementation of a structured project life cycle. At its most extreme, he states that the radical implementation would involve "all activities in the structured project life cycle . . . taking place simultaneously," while the opposite extreme would be a conservative sequential approach "finishing all of one activity before commencing the next." He rightly points out that you'll probably never work in either extreme but rather take a "middle-of-the-road" approach, blurring the boundaries of the steps between each other, as appropriate for the project in hand.

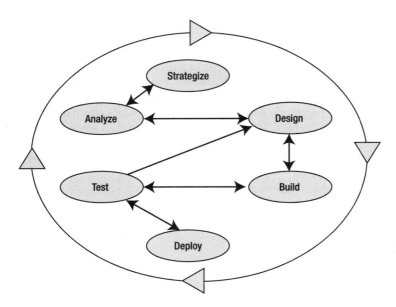

Figure 7-1. *Yourdon's radical implementation of a structured project life cycle*

The benefit of going over these steps isn't to compartmentalize and order them. It's to provide a list of steps that need to be accomplished, provide some concept of dependency, and acknowledge that you do what you have to do to get the job done. Needing to back up to earlier steps in the life cycle may be a sign of a part of the project that's misunderstood, mismanaged, or out of control. On the other hand, it may just mean that you need to iterate a bit more to have the whole thing understood. However, in doing so the team should be able to eventually weed out all "controllable" mistakes in order to improve the final product delivered at the end of the project. Such a life cycle can also help in performance appraisal in post-project analysis.

Let's now take a look at the different steps in the process with an emphasis on the modeling tasks.

Strategize

The strategy step in a project works through survey, feasibility, options, risk, and usually prioritization to see when the need should be satisfied. It was probably initiated by an outside organization requesting data management ingenuity to fix a problem or at the enterprise level identifying a need to come up with an innovative strategy for data management in a particular subject area. Having identified a need, this stage is a high-level identification of business clients, description of current deficiencies, and debate concerning the "should" and "ought" aspects of solving the problem as well as gathering options about "how" and guessing about time, budget, skills, resources, and enterprise return on investments.

Good strategy needs a lot of information. This is an intelligence-gathering step where quite a few educated guesses are made about impacts, costs, risks, and benefits. The modeler may be asked to provide anything from As-Is systems models to conceptual data flows or vendor application data scopes. This step should create something that could be called a *vision document* whose main purpose is to organize the thoughts of the key decision makers and get the project moving. It should be able to capture the objectives and the scope, priorities, and strategic goals, although alternatives and risks may still be on the table.

At the end of this step there is, at least, a list of decisions that need to be made, such as making the software vs. buying it, building it from scratch vs. enhancing your existing legacy systems, using in-house resources vs. hiring consultants, and producing it domestically or internationally, as well as the expected availability, security, and other administrative decisions. Alongside that list, a proposed budget, schedule, and team are generally organized.

■**Caution** If the manufacturing department has used the same multipart forms for the last 20 years to manage their data, they will be temporarily impacted by any change to their process. They may not recover in time to prevent a month or two of negative performance. Enterprise-critical tasks need to have special concern given to them before you can replace even an old, awkward legacy process with a cool new solution.

The following is a list of deliverables from this stage:

- Project proposal

- Business objectives and risk analysis

- Project charter

- Options, feasibility, and scope

- Enterprise development schedule

Analyze

This is the step where the detailed requirements gathering happens and is pivotal to any project. It's expected that at the end of it you should know everything you require in order to develop a solution for your customers that will solve the problem described in the project charter or vision statement. This part is probably the most important; you need the business strategy to be set here. This is where the data modeler has the most work to do.

At this stage the business team has one or more subject matter experts (SMEs) to represent them on the team. The SME explains, describes, and clarifies point after point until everyone is satisfied they have at least a general understanding (which will improve over time) of the data and functional needs. This is the foundation of the requirements documentation. (Unavailability of the SMEs at this point can seriously impact the schedule of a project. Their leadership and commitment is a critical success factor.)

During the gathering of information to create the requirements documentation, the team will gather documentation and samples representing the processes, screens, and reports they may need to support or replace. This exhausting process can take the form of joint application development (JAD) sessions, joint requirements workshops, interviews, prototyping, and observation, and it may involve the team delivering any of the following:

- A set of *use cases*, tracking data elements by processing them on paper and describing the nature of the management process.

- A *business process flow* diagram, using a modeling tool such as BPWin or Visio. This maps out the activity steps at a high level, sequentially noting dependencies and controls between them.

- A *work breakdown structure* (WBS) that divides the effort of the project into smaller and smaller details. This provides a hierarchical outline to help create a detailed project plan.

- A *state transition diagram*, which consists of circles to represent states and directed line segments to represent transitions between the states. One or more actions (outputs) may be associated with each transition.

- A set of *activity models*, which are decompositions of the business processes using a modeling style such as IDEF0.

There will be an infrastructure and hardware assessment. The team may even work up test cases to make sure they've gotten all the exceptions and failure points identified.

Sometimes all this documentation is overwhelming for the team, but even the smallest document could become important as understanding matures. The business analyst must work with the modelers during this phase to ensure that they share a common understanding of the requirements and the business realities. They can then communicate these requirements to the rest of the team. Each member of the development team needs to develop their own methods of controlling the information, or it may be necessary to acquire the help of a project librarian for this phase, especially in the case of large projects.

The modeler needs to keep a clear head and pick out the distinct data element usage and relationship rules. Develop a dictionary of data elements, data use, and concepts from the start. Capture the definitions and shape of the data as you go. The traditional requirements document may not call out this level of detail, but capturing it now will make every step after this one easier.

This stage generates a blueprint, a control document with a comprehensive set of requirements. However, you have to take responsibility at this stage to make sure you gather everything you need to know to build a fully attributed data model. Requirements or functional specification documents don't usually go down to the level of detail that members of the technical team need to do their jobs. From the modeler's perspective, the requirements document needs to have immense depth of detail at the logical data element level. So stay involved. Encourage mockups and hand-drawn concepts of screens and reports so that you can double-check your data elements.

By the time this stage is completed, you should have an almost complete paper system that can act as the instructions for the next stage. Not only that, but you should have determined any need to alter scope, budget, schedule, or resources because of critical issues that have been discovered during your analysis. The further along the path you go before noting a problem, the more troublesome it will be to fix. Trust me, no effort is wasted here, and you, as a modeler, may be called upon to create models at levels of analysis from conceptual through to logical fully attributed before the analysis stage is complete.

The following are the deliverables from this stage:

- Updates to previous documents

- Evaluation of the As-Is environment through the following:

    - Development of Conceptual, Logical, and Physical models

    - Assessment of hardware/infrastructure

    - Assessment of business rules, business process/flow diagrams, and/or use case scenarios

- Development of To-Be requirements through the following:

    - Development of Conceptual and Logical models

    - Draft business rules, business process/flow diagrams, and use case scenarios

    - Production of a detailed project plan outlining functional requirements, gap and impact analysis, proposed options and solutions, evaluation of vendor solutions, and mockup reports

Design

The design step (which may cover redesigning or optimizing existing tools) covers both the information technology architecture (technology, network, programming platform, and so on) and the application architecture (client front end, middle tier, database, and security). Choices made on one side may impact the other side. All the final detailed decisions have to happen now.

This stage covers absolutely everything that needs to be built to support the new tool. That includes training documentation, maintenance tools, audit functions, backup and recovery solutions, Internet use, client licensing issues, hardware enhancements, testing and release needs, and even customer feedback management. When you look at the list of tasks, designing the application is actually only one of a number of different concerns.

The data modeler at this point is focusing on data flow diagrams, state diagrams (especially when you have flows of data that you need to understand in order to determine what states the data will be in during different situations), and the Physical fully attributed model. However, the modeler is not usually alone, and can call on the help of DBAs, programmers, and business analysts in determining performance options and any operational objects required. You may need to create many small submodels to back up documentation for screens, procedures, and reports. Remember to keep them all in sync with each other. An understanding of the "application architecture" (with diagrams, if applicable) can also help here. The data modeler is often asked to help with the data portion of the solution design, which may require a fuller understanding the technical design in such areas as ETL and screen support.

The following are the deliverables from this stage:

- Updates to previous documents

- Development of To-Be environment through the production of the following:

  - Data flow and state diagrams

  - Physical models

  - Business rules, business process/flow diagrams, and use case scenarios

- Development of technical requirements in the form of the following:

  - System specifications (hardware and infrastructure)

  - Application distribution models

  - User interface, screen and report, and physical navigation designs

  - Installation and program specifications

  - Data conversion specifications

  - Security specifications

  - Archive/recovery specifications

  - Test strategies

Build and Test

As we told you at the beginning, many of these steps can be performed in parallel with each other, and the build stage is really coupled with the test and actual design stages. It's not until you've done some testing that you can confirm whether an aspect of your design works or is fully optimized. Many modelers spend a lot of time in the "design-build (proof of concept)-test" cycle. It almost appears to be a whirlpool for a while.

One thing the data modeler is often asked to help with is the generation of the Data Definition Language (DDL). The final fully attributed Physical model should be the template for the generation of the tables and constraints. The modeler is also needed to test the screens and reports to verify the design in terms of data definition and integrity between the data elements. You can use the model to double-check the precedence of record creation or deletion. As the modeler, you often know better than anyone what you expect to see in the fields and on the reports. You may also have test case documentation as a guide of expected results to check against.

The build and test phase can require the data modeler to help with data certification. A data analyst or quality assurance analyst can also perform this task, but the data modeler will at least be involved in validating the results. Data certification is the validation that the data data model has captured all the appropriate rules and associations needed to build a physical design that can be loaded and used appropriately. In certifying the data, you're checking the work of the ETL team and the development team.

The following are the deliverables from this stage:

- Updates to previous documents
- Finalization of documentation
    - Physical model
    - Final technical specification
    - Deployment strategy
    - Test case scenarios
    - Test statistics (change management)
    - Software
    - Training and help tools

Deploy

This is the goal. Finally, the team moves the code out of test and into production. You have a project completion party and move into system maintenance mode. We always judge an application's success on the basis of the number and scope of the enhancements suggested right away. When the business clients want to tie the new application to other systems, combine new data sources, or build new dashboard screens, you've truly done a good job. Here is our test for success: if you never hear from the client community once the application goes live, this should be interpreted as meaning no one is using the application.

At this stage, all the various models and analysis levels need to be revisited and examined against the final Physical model to make sure they're all in sync. Don't forget, the final data dictionary needs to be as production ready as the code.

The following are the deliverables from this stage:

- Updates of previous documents
- Post-project evaluation meeting notes
- List of expected next steps

Project Type

Many types of IT projects require data model support. In the following sections, you'll learn about three in particular, in terms of the types of models they will need. Remember that data models aren't *just* a pictorial representation of entities or tables. Every bit of analysis documented on that picture could be presented in text, and the diagram is only one product provided by the modeler to support a project. You'll focus here on enterprise, transactional, and data warehouse/enterprise reporting projects.

Metaphorically speaking:

- Enterprise project models are concerned with capturing the global dynamics of the storm

- Transactional project models are concerned with capturing the specific details in rain-drops, one at a time.

- Data warehouse/enterprise reporting projects' Dimensional models are concerned with gathering the raindrops and providing different ways of selecting and aggregating them simply and accurately.

Enterprise

An enterprise-level project generally documents business processes at a very high level. It's often a strategic project that's looking at the current data environment with an eye to enhancing or streamlining it in the future. It may be an ongoing project that creates an abstract view of the entire enterprise, or it may have a more restricted focus. Such projects allow an assessment of pedigree of the data being used and how it relates to other areas of the organization or to external suppliers or customers. Rarely will these projects aim to create a software product. Instead, the focus will generally be on giving an overview of the data used in business processes, through the development of a Conceptual model. Sometimes the goal is to determine definitions of data at the enterprise level, which can be used to drive enterprise-level data strategy.

These models often aggregate common ideas into one entity. For instance, if both the inventory and marketing applications keep a full-blown physical copy of the item records, then the enterprise model will show one conceptual reference to Item. These conceptual entities can then be mapped through Logical and Physical data models to actual implementations.

With enterprise project models the modeler needs to pay special attention to the names they choose, since these high-level concepts can be easily misinterpreted. For instance, *account* in the sales group may have a very different definition from *account* in the finance group. Definitions always help maintain clarity, but enterprise project models need to be especially careful because many different audiences review them.

Enterprise projects tend to use Conceptual models to document the following:

- General subject areas, which are entities

- Conceptual relationships, showing business process connections

- Notes, which document special circumstances

- Legends, explaining notations on the model

Transactional: OLTP

Transactional projects deal with building or enhancing software applications that create new enterprise data records (a single instance in a table that's a member of the data set). The main purpose of these projects is to provide a tool to collect new data or modify existing data in some structured way. These are traditional sales, inventory, human resources (HR), and accounting systems, to name just a few. Transactional projects can contribute to enterprise projects through the Conceptual models that are created to abstract the business. These Conceptual models are generally a more detailed view than an enterprise model because of the focused scope. Transactional systems are usually trying to solve one particular business problem or automate one business process; online transactional processing (OLTP) systems are directly tied to the business.

A transactional project doesn't always result in custom development of a new database, but the creation of a new piece of software is generally the goal. Transactional projects have a "make or buy?" step somewhere after detailed analysis. They need to be able to compare the data elements and business rules that are used in a company with an "off the shelf" solution. The model used here is generally a fully attributed Logical model. What good is buying an HR package if you need to be able to matrix people into different departments at a percentage of support, but the HR system will allow them to work for only one? Either you'll need to change the way you do business or you need to find a more flexible HR software solution.

Transactional projects tend to use all types of models to document the analysis needed to reach the goal.

- **Conceptual models**: Capture general/abstract concepts as entities, capture business process connections as conceptual relationships, include notes documenting special circumstances, and include legends explaining the notation used in the pictorial model.

- **Logical models**: Capture specific data sets as entities, capture data dependencies and usage as data relationships, include notes documenting special circumstances, and include legends explaining the notation used in the pictorial model.

- **Physical models**: Capture tables and views as data access/manipulation structures, and capture constraints as relationships.

Data Warehouse: Enterprise Reporting

Data warehouse or enterprise reporting projects provide quick, efficient, correct data reporting for the enterprise. Data warehouse projects focus on historical data to support trend analysis, data mining, and "what happened? and why?" reporting. Enterprise reports projects are concerned with "What's happening right now?" using operational data stores (ODS), collections of almost real-time data for operational reporting.

You may need to support this type of project with every type of data model we've discussed (Conceptual, Logical, and Physical). You may also need to use a specialized Physical modeling design called a *dimensional design*. (We already talked about normalization in Chapter 2). Dimensional modeling techniques intentionally denormalize (thereby being Physical-only models) the data model for query performance. They organize data to get it out of the database quickly, simply, and expediently. You'll consider this type of design in more detail in Chapter 12.

Quite often this style of model is used in the client-accessible portion of a data warehouse or an ODS. There may be other normalized layers involved to support the system. Dimensional models are often designed with simplicity and ease of use as their focus, resulting in fewer tables and therefore fewer required joins. This can increase query performance by orders of magnitude. Precalculated and preaggregated data is the rule, not the exception. These data structures can be built to be used by the general public with a drag-and-drop query tool, so the model is built to prevent user confusion and stress. Data organized dimensionally is data with training wheels on it. It has built-in safety nets such as full-named tables and columns for clarity, preaggregation to prevent mathematical errors, preformatting to speed the output and create consistency in reporting, and derivations based on enterprise-controlled formula rather than *ad hoc* answers. This data has been collected, reviewed, and blessed before publishing.

Data warehouse and data warehouse/enterprise reporting projects use every means available to ensure high-data quality, speed in data access, and ease of viewing. They tend to use all types of models to document the reported data, as outlined for transactional projects.

Project Style Comparison

Table 7-1 shows a short list of things that you could use to recognize what the models from each project will provide. Data warehouse projects will be focused on historic data, and enterprise reporting will focus on current data.

Table 7-1. *Project Goals and Deliverables Used to Determine Project Type*

Factors	Enterprise?	Transactional?	Data Warehouse/ Enterprise Reporting?
Build database objects	No	Yes	Yes
Maintain database objects	No	Yes	Yes
Document database objects	No	Yes	Yes
Manage relationship rules	Yes	Yes	Yes
Database inventory	No	Yes	Yes
Project deliverable	Yes	Yes	Yes
Data element definitions	Yes	Yes	Yes
Column definitions	No	Yes	Yes
Business interface analysis	Yes	No	No
Cross-application data element analysis	Yes	No	No

In transactional and data warehouse/enterprise reporting, the following is true:

- **The focus is almost always at the data object level**: You can follow all the data elements and see how they relate in one application.

- **Models are needed to create physical structures**: They iterate through abstraction, analysis, and physical design.

- **There are easy-to-recognize boundaries**: The scope of most transactional data models is one distinct application. The scope of a dimensional style data model and key reason for its creation is a fairly specific business reporting area focused on discovering the answer to a question such as "What product by geographic area is the most profitable?"

- **The scope is always based on the project**: This is true whether it's focusing on the invoice module of the sales application or looking to create an entirely new sales application.

- **Data model deliverables are more frequently kept up-to-date**: All the models keep their value by staying in sync with the database. They should be versioned and archived with every release and structure fix. Since these models are blueprints of a database, the programmers and DBAs may constantly refer to them.

In the case of an enterprise model, the following is true:

- **The focus is more generic,** providing an overview of all the data elements.

- **The model concentrates on the abstraction** of business concepts.

- **There are more loosely defined boundaries** because of the interconnectivity of business processes and external, as well as internal, data needs.

- **There's often a simple goal** of exploring a subject area/business process to determine what it includes.

- **Products may not be revisited** until a new project is launched to explore an adjacent business process.

Model Objective

As different types of projects need different types of analysis and design, data models need to be tailored to meet those needs. They're generally called out as formal deliverables on project plans. Therefore, you must build deliverables to satisfy a specific project need. They have a goal they're created to meet. You'll have many goals and milestones through the life of a project, and recognizing what these goals are will help you pick the analysis level of your model. In the following sections, you'll learn about three basic goals for building data models (Conceptual, Logical, and Physical), namely, high-level business abstraction, business process data element analysis, and database object physical design.

Abstraction Models

Abstraction is a process whereby you simplify or summarize a thing until it's representative of the main ideas or important points only. If your objective is to document complex business concepts in a fashion that's as simple to understand as possible, you're usually going to use a Conceptual model. For example, Figure 7-2 shows a business process abstract in the form of a Conceptual model of the shipping department for a startup company. It captures ideas referring to an entire warehouse full of products being sold and shipped in simple syntax. This could be the beginning of a custom development project.

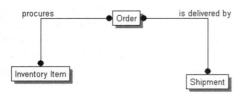

Figure 7-2. *Abstraction of shipping process concepts*

For the most part, if your goal is to look at the abstract, then you'll capture thoughts and ideas about how things are now, or how they could be in the future, in the Conceptual model. They often start as garbled scribbles on whiteboards or enthusiastic ramblings of someone who had a brilliant thought in the middle of the night. Conceptual models tidy up the chicken scratch into something that can be presented and talked about with customers who may or may not be database aware. At this level you're representing big data subject areas. Models such this become part of the decision-making process that begins a project. Conceptual models have to be understood by the users. They're documenting the clients' business fundamentals. Therefore, the business clients must be able to understand them and must agree with the rules and definitions of the concepts being presented.

Maybe the brilliant thought developed in the middle of the night is about legacy systems and how to increase functionality to reduce costs and service the customer better. You could have two Conceptual models that might look like Figure 7-3.

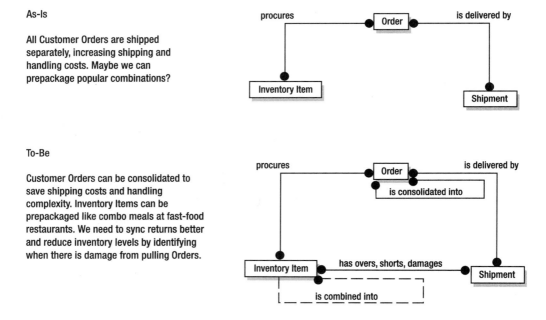

Figure 7-3. *Existing Conceptual model compared to possible future Conceptual model*

Both of these models look simple enough. However, consider the second one; it tells you that there's a possibility that the inventory item, order, and shipment data are currently all being managed in separate applications. Perhaps the data flows are currently flat files that are ported from one application to the next and batched at the end of the day, causing a timing issue. If the shipping manager and inventory manager both want to be able to track the impact of shipping companies on inventory levels and which companies are currently handling product, this may currently be almost impossible because it's all manual. As a result, this little model may represent a year's worth of project scope. It may even need to be pared down into smaller projects to improve handling the budget and resources. The model is just a tool to get data management discussions going.

Abstracting concepts is an important way to clear away the details and focus on the basics, providing a simple model with which to begin discussion of pros and cons, cost, and feasibility studies. Don't be afraid of getting things wrong at this stage as long as you're prepared to change them or even to remodel again from scratch.

Data Element Analysis Models

Analysis models are generally the ones built after a project is launched. They have all sorts of customers with all levels of expertise. You'll likely be using every analysis level, and level of definition, at your disposal to be able to capture and communicate back what you've discovered or are theorizing. You use the conceptual entity levels to set up and verify data scope, anticipated integration, and high-level business rules. Analysis models are working models. They may have lots of notes on them while everyone figures out how to move to the next step, as shown in Figure 7-4.

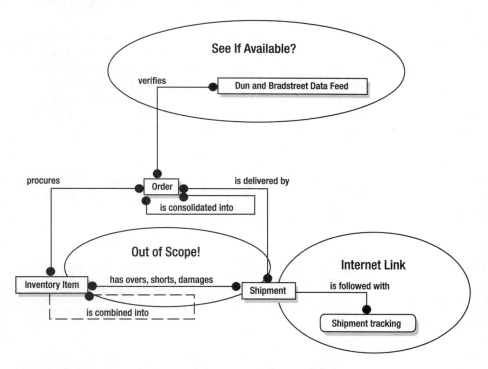

Figure 7-4. *In-progress scope model for new shipping department project*

You expand the Conceptual entity-level model into a Logical entity-level model and finally to a Logical fully attributed model. The analysis being captured on the model documents every stage of understanding, as the team figures out what needs to be done. In this case, if you need to impact multiple systems, you may need to perform a reverse-engineering effort to understand the As-Is of the systems themselves for comparison against your Logical fully attributed model. In doing this, you'll find the delta changes that need to occur.

Physical Design Models

Design models are at the database schema level. These are Physical models, although any new discovery should be reflected on the Logical model as well. So you may be impacting both models from time to time. The physical designs may be a series of options that are debated and argued over by the whole development team until all the processing, perform-ance, naming, structure, and sizing issues have been worked out. As an example, consider the model in Figure 7-5, which uses a class word abbreviation naming standard, Camel notation, and data types to support an Oracle platform.

The final Physical design model is the one that gets built, sometimes over many iterations, as it progresses from development, through testing, and finally onto production deployment. Once the database has been built from the model, you may be called upon to create submodels to support other efforts. The screen and report developers need to know the names of the tables and columns, as do the back-end procedure and initial load teams. Your models will be very popular at this point, and, since everyone wants the latest version, you'll be kept on your toes trying to keep them updated and distributed.

All iterations should be versioned. At this point in the game you don't know if you're going to have to loop back to an earlier version. Large teams can be difficult to keep up-to-date. You may need to keep a control log of the changes so that you can keep track of them. This is also the last time prior to production release that the clients can point out something that was missed. Any changes required at this point must be reviewed by the team as a whole, since what seems like a simple change to the model can impact screens, menu structures, reports, and even security. This is often a place where a team holds a late discovery for a "Phase 2"

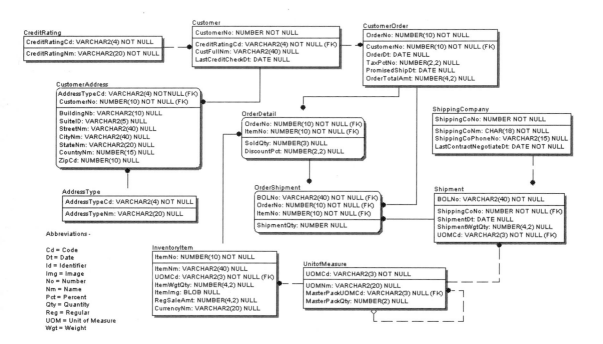

Figure 7-5. *Proposed Physical model of a small shipping system*

effort. One of the documents that's built to finish the project is this list of future enhancements that have been scoped out of this phase. You may have To-Be or delta models showing the changes that need to occur to support those enhancements. Physical models (and submodels) support building the tables, testing initial load processes, screen tests, report verification, and various other prerelease validation steps.

The Right Model

Over the course of this chapter you've seen how projects develop, what controls there are within them, and what model types you can use to aid the goals of the project. To round off the subject, you'll look at how all of these things come together to help you decide what model to choose. Data models go through similar maturing and iteration processes as a full project. At the height of a project you'll be moving rapidly between different models, from Conceptual to Logical to Physical and back to Logical, as you find out that there are exceptions to the business rules that the clients didn't mention earlier.

Project Type

The type of project will help you narrow down the analysis level of the models. Enterprise-level projects, for instance, almost never need Physical models, but transactional OLTP projects could use all three analysis levels (see Table 7-2).

Table 7-2. *Model Deliverables You Can Expect for Different Project Types*

Project Type	Analysis Level
Enterprise	Conceptual
Transactional	Conceptual, Logical, Physical
Dimensional or data warehouse	Conceptual, Physical

Model Goal

Your task helps you decide analysis level as well. If you want a high-level overview of the data system, or to play with new ideas or ways of organizing things, then you'll need to build a Conceptual model. On the other hand, if you want to analyze business rules and analyze data elements, then you'll need to build a Logical model. If you already know everything there is to know about the rules of the data elements and need to design tables, then you'll want to build a Physical model (see Table 7-3).

Table 7-3. *Model Deliverables Expected by Model Goal*

Model Goal	Analysis Level
Abstract	Conceptual
Analysis	Conceptual, Logical
Physical design	Physical

Customer Need

Now you need to determine who will be your customer in order to decide what level of definition you need. If your customer is someone who wants a general rundown of the data involved in the project, then you want an entity-level model. If you're working with someone who is concentrating on integration opportunities or key design choices, then you need a key-based view of the model. If the customer is someone who needs to see all the gory details, then you want a fully attributed model (see Table 7-4).

Table 7-4. *Model Level of Detail Deliverable Expectation by Customer Need*

Customer Need	Analysis Level
Overview	Entity
Focused identifier/uniqueness	Key based
All the details	Fully attributed

Choose one option from these three ways to narrow the definition of your product, and you'll see what model you need to build. Table 7-5 maps the combinations of ideas that focus the product definition of a model.

Table 7-5. *Deliverable Needs Combined to Focus on What Model Should Be Built*

Project Type	Model Goal	Customer View Need	Analysis Level	Level of Definition
Enterprise	Abstract	Overview	Conceptual	Entity level
Transactional	Abstract	Overview	Conceptual	Entity level
Transactional	Abstract	Overview	Conceptual	Fully attributed
Transactional	Analysis	Overview	Logical	Entity level
Transactional	Data element analysis	Focused identifier/uniqueness	Logical	Key based
Transactional	Data element analysis	All the details	Logical	Fully attributed
Transactional	Physical design	Focused identifier/uniqueness	Physical	Key based
Transactional	Physical design	All the details	Physical	Fully attributed
Data warehouse/enterprise reporting	Abstract	Overview	Conceptual	Entity level
Data warehouse/enterprise reporting	Data element analysis	All the details	Logical	Fully attributed
Data warehouse/enterprise reporting	Physical design: normalized or dimensional	Focused identifier/uniqueness	Physical	Key based
Data warehouse/enterprise reporting	Physical design: normalized or dimensional	All the details	Physical	Fully attributed

> **Note** Remember that if the model doesn't communicate what you're trying to get across to your audience, then it's useless.

These are still just high-level definitions of what's on a model and the details that show up. You have an almost unlimited set of choices, especially if you're using one of the modeling software packages. Making these choices just helps you narrow down what kind of model you're building and therefore what your checklist of information is. You still need to be aware of the level of understanding (rather than what they want to know) of your model customer, the needs of the project, and any methodology or external standard.

Model Tips

The following is a list of things you should keep in mind when modeling:

- Picking the level of analysis and detail of a model depends on many factors.

- Staying within scope is a challenge.

- Being wrong on a model can be a *good* thing. It stimulates discussion.

- There is no "one right" model. The models serve different purposes. Not all of them are schematics for databases.

- Sometimes the "correct" solution isn't the best solution for the enterprise.

- Models are products and have customers. Be customer oriented.

- Stay objective. Feedback for designs or analysis is meant to enhance, not criticize.

- Finding a way to keep the team in sync with each other at every model iteration requires a creative publish and deploy mechanism.

- Every model you build helps you build the next one.

- You'll need a second pair of eyes to look for your mistakes. You can be too close to see them.

The primary goal of your work is to create a model that your audience can understand. The "perfectly designed" model may not be consumable by your customers. Also, work with your audience to encourage them to think of better ways of doing things; sometimes resistance isn't because of a failure of design but because of the comfort level of your customers.

Summary

You looked at how you can use data models to document and communicate data rules, from the business data creators to the technical data tool machinists. You saw that all projects have scope, standards, budget, and schedule constraints to consider, and you saw detailed steps called out by most development life-cycle descriptions, in terms of strategizing, analyzing, designing, building and testing, and deploying. The data modeler is often involved from the first strategizing stage through to the building and testing stages. You also learned about the project types that help focus the data model needs:

- Enterprise

- Transactional

- Dimensional

You saw how the data model can be a flexible product to support many different goals. It's a critical factor to the success of a project, since without these models developers can't successfully move onto the design phase. Insufficient detail in the analysis stage of the project simply forces the team to revisit ground that the SMEs probably think they've already described in detail. You also looked at how data models grow and mature throughout the life of the project. Projects evolve and iterate in a radical, nonlinear fashion, very much like the projects and tasks they support. They can be used by the entire team to build, and verify, solutions to the challenges defined in the project scope.

Models in general should be constructed with an expectation that all the due diligence of definitions and accumulating project-specific "value added" knowledge will be included in the model. Data models certainly have to start someplace, but they should continue to mature throughout your project until you can hand one to a new team member and they can follow your analysis and design like a storybook.

CHAPTER 8

Building a Conceptual Model

This chapter begins a tutorial exercise that will allow you to follow the data analysis of a project from the Conceptual model to the Physical model. It will give you the opportunity to see how you can apply some of the principles you looked at in earlier chapters to discover and document the data area of a business process. We'll concentrate on the 20 percent of conceptual design tasks that return 80 percent of the value of creating a Conceptual model. Instead of analyzing a process unknown to you, we'll model the data and functions in the card game Solitaire. You're probably familiar with the game, which will help you concentrate on the process of modeling, rather than on the process of discovery. Many of you will have Solitaire on your computer; those without can simply get out the playing cards and work through the examples at your desk.

In the course of this chapter, you'll do the following:

- You'll review the top-down and bottom-up approaches to analysis.

- You'll gather the information for the Conceptual model using both approaches for comparison.

- You'll organize, refine, and scope the problem space.

- You'll use this information to define subject areas and objects of importance, as well as the relationships between them.

- You'll build a Conceptual entity-relationship (ER) data model.

Modeling the Business Rules

Solitaire may not seem like a typical example of a business process. In fact, it may seem more like a system or an application that has already been programmed, so why use it in this exercise?

The Solitaire application on your computer was built on rules gathered from a manual process. That manual process is a game to us, but it could just as easily have been something else, such as managing a checkbook or planning a party. It could even be a serious business process such as scheduling freight delivery or planning the next fiscal budget.

Many business processes now have automated tools to support them. Have you ever visited a trucking hub? It's a routing station for freight. To "win the game" at the hub, you try to use your trucking equipment as close to capacity as possible (measured by weight and volume), stop as few times as possible, and deliver with speed, safety, and care. Most processes can be viewed in terms of a game. They have rules you must pay attention to and a set of parameters against which to judge the results to determine if you've done a good job.

Data modeling works by first gathering the data elements that are required to support a process or activity. You need to be able to dive into a totally manual, partially automated, or fully automated process and find the underlying activity (rules of the game) in order to get an unobstructed and objective view of the data elements and their rules.

We want you to think beyond "Solitaire the application" for a moment and see the business process underneath. All processes have the following:

- Rules, controls, triggers, and check-and-balance requirements

- Equipment, tools, and forms

- People, players, staff, vendors, and customers

- Goals

- Durations, time, and dates

- The ability to win or lose

- The ability to get better over time

Solitaire is most likely on your machine, so you can test the rules as you go along. But we want you to concentrate on the process underneath rather than on "Solitaire the application." The way we'll approach it is that if a process doesn't involve a deck of cards, then it's out of the scope of this tutorial. We're focusing on the process and the data elements involved in the process. We chose to model this game because it will most likely already be on your computer and because we don't think this book will be marketed with a pack of cards included.

Some data modeling methodologies, like one offered by the company DACOM, would establish a step before creating a data model that creates an activity model. Activity models use completely different graphics and syntax like IDEF0. A good activity model goes into such a level of detail that you actually see each data element and how it supports the people or machines doing a job (along with a lot of other good information about controls/rules, process dependencies, teams, equipment, feedback loops, and timing constraints).

Unfortunately, you won't always have the opportunity to do that type of process analysis beforehand. And even if you do have an activity or process model, you often have to provide an overview that generalizes the organization and groupings of the hundreds of individual data elements for the team. This overview will provide an aggregation of the information as an easily understood and recognizable generalization of the data area of a business process.

But what you really need to build is a Conceptual model.

Defining the Objectives

What are you trying to accomplish in building a Conceptual model? In this example, you're going to draw a picture that portrays the data scope of a business process. You're also going to refine and clarify all the individual descriptions of a process until it's distilled into a single truth (or as close as you can get to it). To do that, you need to do the following:

- You should become informed enough to explain and defend the discoveries you make.

- You should learn the vocabulary of the process and its surroundings as the business sees it.

- You should identify the concepts or data elements, and determine the rules that govern them.

- You should validate the scope.

- You should build a Conceptual ER model.

Building the Conceptual model may be part of a project whose only objective is to explore a business process to find areas for potential improvement or purchased software support. On the other hand, creating this model may be part of a project that has already decided that a software tool would greatly enhance a business unit's ability to do a quality job in the most profitable way possible. Either way, the creation of the Conceptual model is generally the first task for the data modeler, right after the kickoff and charter sessions, or is sometimes part of a preliminary exploration to determine if a project is feasible.

■Note Data modeling isn't done in solitary confinement. You're always part of the larger team. So although you're going to work quietly from the platform of this book, you need to keep in mind that what you're analyzing would generally be part of the business team's daily activities. You need to meet with them and start to learn about their processes. Try to keep an open mind even if you're experienced in this business area. Making assumptions without validating them will cause you problems later. You may be responsible for the model, but you share the responsibility with the business process owners for getting the full scope of their concepts documented.

In learning about the client, try to pick up as many souvenirs as possible in the form of business documents. You can also find valuable information in physical reference manuals or on sticky notes posted in a long-time employee's cubicle. Get copies of anything that relates to the business process! Look for the following:

- Department charters or goal statements

- Samples of forms and/or reports

- Organizational charts

- Desktop procedures or workflow-related materials

- Training manuals

Looking at the current system's paperwork will not only give you an idea of the nature of the current data but also of the likely lifetime and evolution of the data that needs to be handled in the new system. Take a digital camera with you, and document how the physical world uses data elements. Simply getting a map of the company's site, with the names of buildings and departments, may help you remain clear in your discussions with the client, especially if your discussions are geographic in nature. Get, or make, a dictionary of common business terms. Find out if there's a professional dictionary that translates any technical terms into layperson's terms. In short, do everything you can do to get familiar with the world you're about to document.

Defining the Scope

Scope means the area covered or the limits that will govern your analysis. Analysts in general, and modelers specifically, are constantly fighting to get a better, solid definition and understanding of the boundaries around the scope. Scope is usually somewhat variable through an entire project. Documenting scope agreements with signatures can be helpful, but managing the scope is one of *the* most difficult tasks for most project managers. You're often caught in the conundrum of not knowing what needs to be done until you've traveled a certain distance into the project.

How are you going to discover and define the scope of your tutorial? You'll put the process Solitaire into an organizational framework and discover how it's going to be used. Just imagine you're the data modeler in an information services department on a college campus. Your boss tells you that the psychology department has decided to research the popular computer game Solitaire and its impact on office productivity by investigating the addiction level of employees to the game. The department has a theory that the positive feelings a player gets from winning a game outweigh the negative ones they get from losing, so the department needs to measure the ratio of wins vs. losses and analyze the details of a series of games played by a set of test subjects. In other words, the clients want to gather some data to validate their hypothesis. So, they want the data modeler to document the activity and design an application to collect the data they want to analyze.

Whether verbal or written, scope is defined through answers to questions. It's the first thing you have to discover. You ask your department manager, and then the psychology department's project lead, a series of questions, including the following. You need both viewpoints (sponsor and project lead) so you can manage the expectations of both groups.

Data modeler: "Who is the customer?"

Department manager: "Here's the name and phone number of a contact in the psychology department."

Project lead: "Our researchers are Matt, Jeff, and Stacy."

Data modeler: "Is this only about Solitaire?"

Department manager: "Yes."

Project lead: "Yes."

Data modeler: "Is it computer Solitaire or cards?"

Department manager: "It's the computer game, I think, rather than cards. It's the results (ratio of wins to losses) aspect they're concentrating on, not how they play it or rules of the game."

Project lead: "The phenomenon we're researching is the craze with the computer game. Why do people play it all the time? How often do they win vs. lose?"

Data modeler: "Why do they want to look at Solitaire data?"

Department manager: "To see if they can figure out why everyone wastes time playing it."

Project lead: "To determine if there's indeed a positive feedback to a person's ego that makes it worth playing."

Data modeler: "Do they want to capture all the details of all the games?"

Department manager: "They seem to, but you better validate it with them."

Project lead: "Possibly. It might give you more information to work with in the long run."

Data modeler: "Should we start with a Conceptual model?"

Department manager: "Yes. They want to see if it's feasible and within budget to build a little application and a data mart for statistical analysis."

Project lead: "If it will help us see what would be involved, that would be great."

Data modeler: "What is the timeline?"

Department manager: "As soon as possible."

Project lead: "We'd like to have an application available for researchers by next quarter. Basically we want the application available three months from now."

Data modeler: "Do you want to review my work?"

Department manager: "Yes. Let's review it before you deliver it to them."

Project lead: "We'd like to have a review with you when you've covered the full scope."

Many times defining a scope is more like this than actually having a scope document from which to work. This informal conversation set up the initial boundaries of the model for you. It gave you the following information with which to work:

- Your client is the psychology department, and you have specific contacts to speak with.

- The client is looking at Solitaire to determine why it proves to be so popular with people.

- Although they are using the computer version of this game, it seems to be the game of Solitaire, not the software application, that's important. The fact that you're analyzing the computer version of the game is of no consequence here. You could do the same conceptual analysis with a deck of playing cards, since the computer game is just an automation of all the activities of a manual game.

- The exact scope of your model isn't clear at this stage. You should therefore work with a larger scope than may actually end up being necessary.

- This has the potential for a continuation of the data analysis to a physical database design in the future. You need to keep that in mind when you gather information.

- The schedule is tight, so you need to be prepared to work with a programmer (really soon).

Of course, now that you have a basic idea of what the scope is, you should document it and start a project notebook to give you a place to return to and refresh your memory of what exactly was agreed to in the beginning.

Defining the Approach

Over the years we've found that, unlike an airplane (which has to choose one path), an analyst can mix approaches to get the best of multiple worlds. In fact, it'd be more of a chore to restrict your analysis to just one approach. The following sections highlight a couple of ways you'll approach gathering data concepts about Solitaire for this example.

Top-Down Approach

Using the *top-down* approach, you can discover and draft a description of the business process. That description supplies you with concepts that will be used as a starting place. This approach allows the process to tell the story about the data. This is a functional or process-driven analysis. You concentrate on how things *work*. You need to, as the name implies, start at the top and drill downward, increasing the level of detail in an iterative fashion. Without it you may miss the following:

- Assumptions everyone expects you to know

- Future developments that could change your direction

- Opportunities to increase the quality, usability, accessibility, and enterprise data

With it you gain the following:

- An understanding of the way things fit together, from high to low levels of detail

- A sense of the political environment that may surround the data

- An enhancement of your understanding of data importance

- The guide to the level of detail you need for different audiences

Knowing the Strategic Goals

Find out what the strategic objectives are for the process, group, department, and company. Strategic goals include all the plans to do the right thing at the right time to accomplish a long-term goal. Don't just concentrate on data management or the business area you're analyzing. Find out about the directions in which the business is moving. Are there mergers on the horizon? Is a new Web-based business being discussed? Is there a push for lowering the cost of operations? Almost any enterprise strategic goal can have some intrinsic impact on the world of data management.

Strategy is part of every process. You, as the data modeler, need to be able to clearly answer the following:

- What must the data be able to support?

- How will you know if it's right?

Interviewing People

In top-down analysis, people are the best source of your information. You need to discover the following:

- **Managers of the process**: How it should work

- **Process experts**: How it really works

- **Customers of the data**: What they need to get out of it

- **Suppliers of the data**: What do they think is needed, and what do they provide

- **Handlers of the data**: How it is it gathered, built, tested, and released

Bottom-Up Approach

The *bottom-up* approach focuses instead on the inventory of *things* in a process. It implies an in-depth understanding of as much of the process as can be known at this point. This is much easier to do at your desk, since you're probably quite used to dissecting screens, forms, and reports to get to data and data rules. Using this approach you discover and draft a list of potential elements without regard to how they're used. The list usually consists of a mixed set of very low-level, detailed notions and high-level concepts. The trick is to aggregate them to the same level of detail. This is a data-driven analysis. You concentrate on what things *are*. You concentrate on the parts rather than the process. You need to, as the name implies, start at the bottom and aggregate up while increasing your level of aggregation, again in an iterative fashion. Without it you may miss a real-world understanding of the data and how it fits together, as well as the following:

- Data areas that everyone expects you to know

- Relationships

- Fuzzy, currently undefined areas that need extra work to bring them to the same level of understanding

With it you gain the following:

- An understanding of the things involved

- A sense of the quality levels that may be inherent to the data

- An enhancement of your understanding of data definitions

Knowing the Tactical Goals

Tactical goals include all the activity to do the right thing at the right time to accomplish a short-term goal. Tactics is also part of every process. You need to be able to clearly answer the following:

- What is the data?

- How will you know if you have it all?

Interrogating Tools, Products, and Processes

In bottom-up analysis, the current environment is the best source of your information. It may not fit the strategic goals, but you need this information to be able to effect change. You need to obtain information about the following:

- **Tools**: What data they use, and how they use it

- **Processes**: How the data is created, used, moved, stored, and accessed

- **Data products**: What they provide

- **Data interfaces**: Who, what, where, when, and why they're currently in place

Documenting the Process: Top-Down Approach

For your first pass you'll concentrate on the steps that the process must go through to be successful. You may find these in process flows, training manuals, or other how-to documentation. You may also find that the only source of how things work is in the memories of the people doing the tasks. Top-down analysis often requires interviewing extensively, double-checking inconsistencies with descriptions, sequencing, and determining the criticality of the tasks. For this small process, you can play the game a while and note what you do.

You'll do the following to build the Conceptual model using the top-down approach of Solitaire. You will:

- Decide on your source(s) of information for interviewing.

- Create a list of activities and activity descriptions.

- Discover the most important elements in the activities.

- List and define the elements.

- Validate the activities with the business process community.

- Group the elements into concepts and validate the concepts against the scope statement.

- Define the concepts and relate them together.

- Validate the Conceptual model.

Deciding on Interview Sources

For this exercise, you'll mostly be working through the activity of Solitaire yourself—rather than doing the usual question-and-answer sessions. In most projects, however, it's a good idea to list interview targets and set up meetings with them. In fact, you may find it worthwhile to take the time to visit wherever the activity actually takes place. It may give you a great deal of insight to just get a feel for the environment. Even in the world of data modeling and software/application development, there's nothing like first-hand knowledge. The best efforts we've ever been a part of had highly experienced business representatives on the team who could guide us through the *normal* business processes and through the *unusual* way these processes worked.

Defining Solitaire Activities

Since you're doing most of this analysis solo, let's try to build a list of process steps by getting familiar with the process. Play the game if you're unsure about how it flows and the rules you must obey. So, what's going on with Solitaire? If it was a business process, you might refer to department documentation, training class materials, textbooks, or written procedures. You could refer to an application spec or users manual if you're looking at a process already supported by an automated tool. However, remember that these are the rules of the application, and they won't necessarily match the business process anymore. In the case of Solitaire, you could refer to a book about card game rules or discover the essence of the game by playing it yourself. Whichever way you do your discovery, you want to create a high-level description of what happens.

Defining the Solitaire Process Steps

By following the process outlined previously, you can outline these process steps:

- The player shuffles a deck of 52 playing cards.

- Lay seven cards face down to create piles in a line from left to right.

- Skip the card farthest on the left, and lay another card face down on top of each of the remaining six. Continue by skipping one more pile with each pass until you have seven piles of cards in quantities of one, two, three, four, five, six, and seven.

- Turn over the top card of each pile. (This is the status that the game begins in.)

- There's a pile of cards that's face down in the upper-left corner. (If you're playing by hand, you're probably holding it.) This is the draw pile. It has 24 cards.

- Including the draw pile, there are eight piles of cards on the playing area and empty spaces (where there are no cards currently) that indicate that four more piles are possible. That makes 12 piles of cards.

- In the playing area are seven playing piles. The first has one card. It's face up. All the other six have one card face up and an increasing number of hidden cards stacked underneath them. These are processing piles one through seven. The amount of cards needing to be processed is the number of the pile from left to right minus one. The total cards in the processing piles originally equaled twenty-eight in the quantity configuration of one, two, three, four, five, six, and seven.

- Above the seven playing piles are four discard piles (which are the final target piles for all cards to go to in order to win). Remove three cards from the draw pile in order. Turn them over so the third card down is visible and made available for processing at the beginning of each play.

- A move occurs when a card changes location from one playing pile to another, including the four discard piles.

- The end of each play occurs when no other moves are available and a new card must be drawn from the draw pile.

- Move the available card from the draw pile to an appropriate processing pile or to the discard pile. Move all other available cards from one pile to another.

- You can play until there are no more available moves.

- The player wins the game when all cards have been legally moved to the appropriate discard piles, which totals thirteen cards made up of one suit.

- Every game ends in a win or loss. A loss includes the abandonment of a game where moves are possible but the game is ended anyway.

Winning looks something like Figure 8-1 when played manually (though it is, of course, an electronic representation of the physical cards).

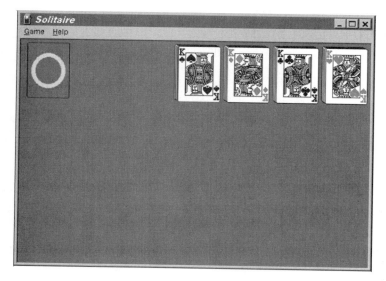

Figure 8-1. *Winning a manual game of Solitaire*

Winning looks like Figure 8-2 when played electronically.

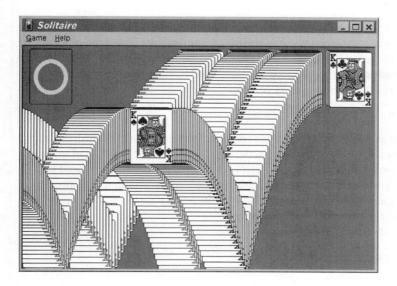

Figure 8-2. *Solitaire win using a software version*

Losing looks something like Figure 8-3. A lot of cards are left on the playing area that can't be moved.

Figure 8-3. *Solitaire lose, with no moves left*

Even if you get a good written description of the process, it's important to try it for yourself. Most procedures omit a wealth of assumed knowledge and experience. In this case, you can assume the player knows what an ace and a king look like, can distinguish between different suits, and understands that the game, when played with cards by hand, is slightly different from that played on a computer.

Building Activity Descriptions

You now have a small list of activities involved in the process of Solitaire. You need to have a complete description of the activities so there's no confusion over what's covered in the activity. You may get this through documentation, or you may need to write them yourself. You need this to validate your list with the business community. For example:

- The player shuffles a deck of 52 playing cards.

The player in a Solitaire game is completely in control of the movement of cards, within the rules of allowable movement. Shuffling is an activity that changes the position of one card to another. The deck is restricted to only suit cards. It excludes jokers, instructions, and any advertising cards. A Solitaire game always begins with the cards being shuffled. This process begins with a player rearranging the cards randomly without being able to see the new order. This process completes at the discretion of the player.

Activity descriptions should do the following:

- Define all the elements.

- Describe the beginning and end states of the process.

- Describe the trigger mechanism for the beginning activity.

- Describe any dependencies or feedback loops.

- Identify any controlling rules, mechanisms, or other activities.

Identifying the Important Elements

You now know what the activity of Solitaire looks and feels like. You'd probably consider yourself at least acquainted enough with the business process to begin modeling. You now need to determine the relevant concepts required for your model. In this case, you can review the rules with a highlighter and find just one of everything that seems to be a noun or important concept. In a real project, you may not have a list of rules yet, so brainstorm on a whiteboard or, better yet, with sticky notes that you can easily move and group. In this case, we'll go back over the bulleted list of rules and highlight the important words using italics.

- The *player* shuffles a *deck* of 52 playing *cards*.

- Lay seven cards face down to create *piles* in a line from left to right.

- Skip the card farthest on the left, and lay another card face down on top of each of the remaining six. Continue by skipping one more pile with each pass until you have seven piles of cards in quantities of one, two, three, four, five, six, and seven.

- Turn over the top card of each pile. (This is the *status* that the *game* begins in.)

- There's a pile of cards that's face down in the upper-left corner. (If you're playing by hand, you're probably holding it.) This is the *draw pile*. It has 24 cards.

- Including the draw pile, there are eight piles of cards on the *playing area* and *empty spaces* (where there are no cards currently) that indicate that four more piles are possible. That makes 12 piles of cards.

- In the playing area are seven playing piles. The first has one card. It's face up. All the other six have one card face up and an increasing number of *hidden cards* stacked underneath them. These are *processing piles* one through seven. The amount of cards needing to be processed is the number of the pile from left to right minus one. The total cards in the processing piles originally equaled twenty-eight in the quantity configuration of one, two, three, four, five, six, and seven.

- Above the seven playing piles are four *discard piles* (which are the final target piles for all cards to go to in order to win). Remove three cards from the draw pile in order. Turn them over so the third card down is visible and made available for processing at the beginning of each *play*.

- A *move* occurs when the card changes location from one playing pile to another, including the four discard piles.

- The end of each play occurs when no other moves are available and a new card must be drawn from the draw pile.

- Move the *available card* from the draw pile to an appropriate processing pile or to the discard pile. Move all other available cards from one pile to another.

- You can play until there are no more available moves.

- The player wins the game when all cards have been legally moved to the appropriate discard piles, which totals thirteen cards made up of one suit.

- Every game ends in a *win* or *loss*. A loss includes the abandonment of a game where moves are possible but the game is ended anyway.

■Note A basic naming standard is that entity names are always singular.

Next, write the possible entity names on sticky notes or something that will allow you the freedom to rearrange them. We'll tabulate them here for simplicity:

Player	Deck	Card
Card Pile	Status	Game
Playing Area	Empty Space	Draw Pile
Hidden Card	Processing Pile	Discard Pile
Play	Move	Available Card
Win	Loss	

Defining Your Elements

You need to be able to clearly define your discovered elements. Many times we're fooled by different names meaning the same thing (*synonyms*) and similar names for different things (*homonyms*). You have to be able to recognize them for what they are by whatever words, labels, slang, and technical terms are being used to identify them. You'll want to gather as much information as you can at this stage. It will help you with further analysis. For each element, you may want to add the following:

- **Definition**: A statement of precise meaning with detail that creates common understanding that *doesn't* use the name of the entity in the definition

- **Example**: An instance that illustrates the general concept

- **Includes**: A shortlist of common and recognizable examples that belong

- **Excludes**: A shortlist of common and recognizable examples that don't belong

You'll also find when you're defining things that some names just aren't complete enough and need to be changed for clarity sake. For instance, Pile would be better described here as a Card Pile. You may even want to further qualify it to Solitaire Card Pile if you need to deliver this model to an enterprise metadata customer later. If this were a game company you were supporting, it could be important to be able to differentiate the concepts.

■**Tip** Don't write sloppy definitions, such as "Card Pile = A pile of cards," or circular definitions, such as "Game = A contest" and "Contest = A game."

Remember that the more effort you put into your definitions, the greater chance you'll have of successfully communicating your discoveries to the project team and model reviewers. Use whatever dictionaries you can find printed in bound books, online references, or company standards. Dictionaries are available with any number of focuses—homegrown corporate dictionaries, highly focused technical and professional works, or a good, old, mainstream Webster's dictionary. Dictionary writers have already done the due diligence of making the definitions as clear as possible, so leverage their efforts. Using a dictionary (either online or printed) is a good way to write good definitions; in fact, when possible, use the unabridged dictionary!

Table 8-1 shows the potential entities and their definitions.

Table 8-1. *Defined Conceptual Entities*

Name	Definition
Available Card	A card, which is assessed to be able to be used in a play by satisfying many rules.
Card	One of 52 unique game pieces used in playing games that bear pictures of figures or numbers organized by suit. For example, the queen of clubs and the two of diamonds are cards.

Name	Definition
Card Pile	A collection of cards that behaves differently in the game of Solitaire. For example, the draw pile, discard pile, and processing pile are all collections.
Deck	A complete set of four suits of thirteen cards, making a collection of fifty-two individual cards. This doesn't include jokers, instructions, and extra vendor cards.
Discard Pile	A location of the activity in Solitaire where a card is removed completely from play. Only an ace can begin a discard pile.
Draw Pile	A location in Solitaire where a card is stored until such time as it's moved to the waste pile for processing.
Empty Space	A pile that has no cards.
Game	A contest played for sport or amusement (according to rules) made up of many small decisions that affect the outcome. In this instance, the game is Solitaire.
Hidden Card	A card with the back visible.
Lose	A point in the game where the inability to move all the cards to a discard pile becomes apparent.
Move	A change in position of a card from one pile to another.
Play	A play is a completed set of moves, finalized when the entire set of available cards are assessed and processed resulting in a move or pass.
Player	A participant in the game of Solitaire.
Playing Area	A physical location such as a table or a virtual location such as a computer screen where the game is being played.
Processing Pile	A location of the activity in Solitaire where cards are matched from the draw pile according to playing rules. All processing piles are originally set up through the layout of a game. If during the processing of the cards a pile is emptied, then a king may be moved to the pile position and used to process more cards.
Status	A state of concluding the game of Solitaire. For example, it could conclude with a win, lose, or quit.
Win	A completed movement of all the cards to a discard pile.

Validating Your Work

Now you should review your list with the business community to see if what you've documented is correct in their eyes. You may want to list your entities on a flip chart or on sticky notes and do a true/false session, where you describe the business rules very clearly to get a simple yes/no response from the business community (although it usually becomes a heated debate). Include absolutes such as "always" and "never" in the definitions and business rules to force recognition of business process anomalies. Jot down new discoveries. Make sure you take your definitions to the meeting with you. That way, even if you choose a name for the entity that isn't instantly recognized by the client, once they read your definition they'll see what you mean. In fact, at this point element names are really just handy shortcuts to the definitions. The definitions are the real knowledge.

You may need to iterate through this process if there's dissent between business process owners about what's correct. We've found sometimes that conflicting descriptions/definitions can be equally valid, even though they appear to be mutually exclusive or directly contradicting each other. This is because definitions reflect the audience's viewpoint. You need to add to your activity descriptions how apparent discrepancies or contradictions in process definitions can be true from different viewpoints and allow for these situations in the Conceptual model. You may find that your business processes have variations as well. Many people will describe what they think is the only way to do something without the knowledge of subtle variations that may exist even within an enterprise. The international community or even different departments supposedly using the same business process may have different rules as well. You need to make it part of your responsibility to know.

Aggregating into Concepts

Now you need to group like things together. You're looking to build aggregations that best cover the concepts in the process. Eventually, as you make these groupings, you can look for a generic label to describe them. This section covers how we'd group them and why.

The following concepts deal exclusively with the conceptual definition of one complete game:

- Game
- Win
- Lose

This is the only person we see:

- Player

Now list all the concepts relating to cards:

- Card
- Hidden Card
- Available Card

Hidden Card and Available Card have to do with the status of a card, not the card itself. However, at this level it's no problem to note that they're related to the same general topic. It's a judgment call as to whether to group them here or with Status.

The following concepts have to do with groupings of cards:

- Pile
- Empty Space
- Draw Pile
- Discard Pile
- Processing Pile
- Deck

This one has to do with location:

- Playing Area

These have to do with the details of allowed and specific moves of cards:

- Play

- Move

There is one concept left over:

- Status

This reminds you that in order to play a game you must be able to recognize the existing state. State of being in business processes may include the ability to recognize approval or availability states, versions, time durations, and maturing states such as part/assembly/product.

Now what? Look at the descriptions in the following tables to see why we combined certain entities under a common name. You get a much shorter list from these groupings than when you started. You're reducing and refining yet also increasing and simplifying. You're coming up with a way to express the activity of Solitaire in the simplest concepts possible in order to make Solitaire approachable to almost any audience. At this stage, the Conceptual model can be broken down as shown in Table 8-2, Table 8-3, Table 8-4, and Table 8-5.

Table 8-2. *"Who?" Entities*

Who	Description
Player	A person playing the game

Table 8-3. *"What?" Entities*

What	Description
Game	A process labeled Solitaire—the activity
Card	A playing piece for the game
Card Pile	A collection of playing pieces in the game

Table 8-4. *"Where?" Entities*

Where	Description
Playing Area	A location where the game is held
Card Pile	A location where the cards are moved to

Table 8-5. *"When?" Entities*

When	Description
Move	A single deployment of the rules of playing and the actual plays
Status	A state of a play, move, or game

All of these added together describe Solitaire from a very high but recognizable level. Did you leave anything out? Let's try doing this in a bottom-up style to see if the details match the aggregated names we've come up with to label the concepts. Remember, you're usually doing these top-down and bottom-up exercises concurrently.

Documenting the Process Rules: Bottom-Up Approach

This time you'll concentrate on the data elements that the process needs in order to function. You'll find the data elements and the rules they work by in Solitaire. Although much bottom-up analysis is done with some kind of documentation or visible sets of data examples, in this case you don't have Solitaire data reports. Since what you're concentrating on is actually the manual game, you'll write the rules to find the details. You'll be able to see the overlap with the top-down processing tasks you considered earlier. Remember, the top-down process concentrated on generalities, and now you're focusing on details. These are two different approaches for creating the full picture, resulting in the same, or a similar, result.

Documenting the Rules of the Activity

The activity list you created didn't deal at all with many vital concepts that are buried in the rules of Solitaire. Nothing in the activity steps describes the identification and description of a card suit, what role color plays, the importance of the ace and king, or even the way the game can be won or lost. These are the data elements and the rules that control Solitaire. Just write them out, and sort them a bit so they aren't so free-form. (Some of these rules are out of scope as defined by the clients, but doing a bottom-up approach may require you to delve into outlying areas to fully understand the details that are in scope.)

The following are the card rules:

- Fifty-two cards are played with in the game. These exclude jokers, instructions, and advertising cards found in the box.

- Suits are clubs, hearts, spades, and diamonds.

- Suits are red or black.

- Cards are face cards (jack, queen, and king), number cards (two through ten), or aces.

The following are the move rules:

- A play is completed when the entire set of available cards is assessed, resulting in a move or pass.

- Cards that are red move over black cards, and vice versa.

- Cards move from either the draw pile or another processing pile.

- Cards move over another card in decreasing order (king to two) in processing piles and the opposite (increasing order) in discard piles.

- The discard piles are populated in ascending order according to suit (two to king).

- Cards move to the discard pile from the draw pile or processing piles.

- Once a card has been placed on the discard pile, it can't be moved back to the pile from which it came.

- Once a card has left the draw pile, it can't be moved back to the draw pile.

- Only aces can move to empty discard piles.

- Only kings can move to empty processing piles.

The following are the pile rules:

- The first card in the discard pile is an ace.

- It doesn't matter which of the four piles to which a specific ace ultimately moves.

The following are the game rules:

- There is only one player for a game.

- You lose if you can't move all the cards to a discard pile.

- You win when all the discard piles show kings or when the draw pile and all the processing piles are empty.

Working with details like this allows you to identify relevant details to be flagged for review. You'll now look at them carefully and determine if they affect your conceptualization. It isn't a good thing to leave all the detailed analysis to the Logical and Physical model. At times it's the details that determine an aspect of a conceptual design. So you need to be aware of details that may affect the Conceptual model.

Describing the Rules

You also need to define the rules in order to document your understanding. Stating rules clearly can provide the means of validating an understanding of the problem. For example, the following are the Solitaire rules:

- Kings are special cards in the playing deck. Kings can move to empty processing piles. They're allowed to move from the available position of any pile (other than the discard pile) to any empty processing pile. This includes moving from one processing pile to another. This allows access to another card that was blocked by the king.

This rule is a little more complex than some. It isn't a simple statement. It requires several aspects of definition in order to fully understand it. You need to break business rules down into simple statements so you understand all the needs of the data. You should include not only all the applications of the rule but also all the exceptions to the rule, as well as any results from the application of the rule or any known exceptions. For example, you can write something like this as the special rules for kings:

- Kings can move to any empty (no cards in suit) processing piles.

- Kings can move from the available position of any pile (other than the discard pile) to any empty processing pile.

- This includes moving from one processing pile to another, allowing access to another card that was blocked by the king.

Identifying the Important Elements

This is the same process used when you discovered the nouns in the activities, but the list this time should include a different, wider range of nouns. Again, we'll review the bulleted list of rules and highlight the important words using italics.

The following are the **card** rules:

- Fifty-two cards are played with in the game. These exclude *jokers*, *instructions*, and *advertising* cards found in the *box*.

- *Suits* are *clubs*, *hearts*, *spades*, and *diamonds*.

- Suits are *red* or *black*.

- Cards are *face* cards (*jack*, *queen*, and *king*), *number* cards (two through ten), or *aces*.

The following are the **availability** rules:

- A card is *available* if it's *face up* and the *top card* of a pile that isn't the discard pile.

- A card is *blocked* if it's face up and *under* other cards of a pile that isn't the discard pile.

- A card is *unavailable* if it's *face down* or in the discard pile.

The following are the **move** rules:

- A *play* is completed when all *available cards* are assessed, resulting in a *move* or *pass*.

- Cards that are red move over black cards, and vice versa.

- Cards move from either the *draw pile* or another *processing pile*.

- Cards move over another card in *decreasing order* of face value, king to two.

- The *discard piles* are populated in *ascending order* according to suit, two to king.

- Cards move to the discard pile from the draw pile or processing piles.

- Once a card has been placed on the discard pile, it can't be removed from the discard pile.

- Once a card has left the draw pile, it can't be moved back to the draw pile.

- Only aces can move to empty discard piles.

- Only kings can move to empty processing piles.

The following are the **pile** rules:

- The first card in the discard pile must be an ace.

- It doesn't matter which of the four piles to which a specific ace ultimately moves.

The following are the **game** rules:

- There is only one *player* for a game.

- You *lose* if you can't move all the cards to a discard pile.

- You *win* when all the discard piles show kings or when the draw pile and all the processing piles are *empty*.

Again, write them on sticky notes, or use something else that will allow you to rearrange them. When using a bottom-up analysis method, you may have hundreds of elements, and there's much more danger of being fooled by two words that really mean the same thing. We'll tabulate them here for simplicity:

Card	Joker	Instruction Card
Advertising Card	Box	Suit
Heart	Club	Spade
Diamond	Red	Black
Jack	Queen	King
Ace	Face Card	Number Card
Availability	Face Up	Top Card
Blocked	Under	Unavailable
Available	Face Down	Play
Available Card	Move	Pass
Draw Pile	Process Pile	Discard Pile
Ascending Order	Descending Order	Player
Game	Win	Lose
Empty Space		

Defining Your Elements

You just did this with the top-down elements, so you may be able to reuse some of that work here. You still need to be able to clearly define your discovered elements. Even definitions become iterative through understanding. Make sure you update anything you enhance with more information. Table 8-6 shows the entities and definitions discovered using this method.

Table 8-6. *Potential Conceptual Entities and Definitions*

Name	Definition
Ace	One of four playing cards bearing a single pip, which is the first card in a discard pile in Solitaire.
Advertising Card	A card found in a deck that isn't used for playing purposes.
Ascending Order	An ordering of cards first with the ace, then the number cards two through ten, then the jack, queen, and king.

Continued

Table 8-6. *Continued*

Name	Definition
Availability	A checking process to determine whether a card is available to be used in a play.
Available	A status of a card allowing it to be used in a play.
Available Card	A card that's assessed to be able to be used in a play by satisfying many rules.
Black	A color traditionally associated with the suits of clubs and spades.
Blocked	A status denoting that a card can't be played. It's face up and under other cards of a pile that isn't the discard pile.
Box	A container of a deck of cards. Not all decks have boxes.
Card	One of 52 unique game pieces used in playing games bearing pictures of figures or numbers organized by suit. For example, the queen of clubs and two of diamonds are cards.
Club	One of four suits used in playing cards. The others are diamonds, hearts, and spades. Clubs are black.
Descending Order	An order of cards by king, queen, and jack and then by the number cards ten through two, finishing with the ace.
Diamond	One of four suits used in playing cards. The others are clubs, hearts, and spades. Diamonds are red.
Discard Pile	A location of the activity in Solitaire where a card is removed completely from play. Only an ace can begin a discard pile.
Draw Pile	A location in Solitaire where a card is stored until such time as it's moved to the waste pile for processing.
Empty Space	A pile that has no cards.
Face Card	A card in a deck that has a figure pictured on the face.
Face Down	A position of the card where the back is facing the player; cards are unavailable in this position.
Face Up	A position of the card where the suit and designator can be read. Not all face-up cards are available.
Game	A contest played for sport or amusement (according to rules) made up of many small decisions that affect the outcome, in this instance, Solitaire.
Hearts	One of four suits used in playing cards. The others are diamonds, clubs, and spades. Hearts are red.
Instruction Card	A card included in a deck that has the steps describing at least one game. This isn't a playing card.
Jack	A face card ordered between the ten and the queen.
Joker	A card included in a deck that has neither a suit nor a position in a suit. There are generally two provided and are used in some games but not Solitaire.
King	One of four playing cards bearing a figure representing the leader of a royal family that's allowed to change positions to an empty processing pile in Solitaire.
Lose	A game condition where there's an inability to move all the cards to a discard pile.
Move	A change in position of a card from one pile to another.

Name	Definition
Number Card	A card in a deck that doesn't have a figure pictured on the face. These are numbered two through ten.
Pass	A completion of a play that doesn't include a move of a card.
Play	A play is completed when the entire set of available cards is assessed, resulting in a move or pass.
Player	A participant in the game of Solitaire.
Processing Pile	A location of the activity in Solitaire where cards are matched from the draw pile according to playing rules. All processing piles are originally set up through the layout of a game. If during the processing of the card a pile is emptied, a king may be moved to the pile position and used to process more cards.
Queen	A card positioned between the jack and the king.
Red	A color traditionally associated with the suits of hearts and diamonds.
Spade	One of four suits used in playing cards. The others are diamonds, hearts, and clubs. Spades are black.
Suit	One of four divisions of cards: clubs, spades, hearts, and diamonds.
Top Card	A card positioned on a pile closest to the player.
Unavailable	A status of a card as not being able to be moved in a play.
Under	A position of a card beneath another card.
Win	A completed movement of all the cards to a discard pile.

Once again, you should review your list with the business community to see if what you've documented is correct in their eyes. Use a similar technique for review whenever possible so that the relationship between you and the business process owners strengthens over time. Familiarity in this case encourages a relaxed and comfortable working environment.

Comparing Methods

Since you're using the bottom-up method to verify that you captured the concepts correctly in your top-down approach, try to match all the lower-level elements to a higher-level element (see Table 8-7).

Table 8-7. *Comparison of Potential Entity List Using Both Methods*

Top-Down Concepts	Bottom-Up Elements
Player	Player
Game	Game
Card	Ace, Advertising Card, Available Card, Black, Box, Card, Club, Diamond, Face Card, Heart, Instruction Card, Jack, Joker, King, Number Card, Queen, Red, Spade, Suit
Card Pile	Discard Pile, Draw Pile, Empty Space, Processing Pile, Ascending Order, Descending Order
Playing Area	Playing Area

Continued

Table 8-7. *Continued*

Top-Down Concepts	Bottom-Up Elements
Move	Move, Pass, Play
Status	Availability, Available, Blocked, Face Down, Face Up, Lose, Top Card, Unavailable, Under, Win

We seem to have been able to match all the details with a more generic concept. So you have a good starting place for a Conceptual data model. You should do one more double-check before you accept that you've identified all the concepts. Review the definition of the top-down concepts and compare them with the bottom-up elements. The definition of the bottom-up elements should always be of narrower scope than the top-down concepts. For instance:

- **Move**: A change in position of a card from one pile to another.

- **Play**: A play is completed when the entire set of available cards is assessed, resulting in a move or pass.

Should we be using Move as our concept or Play? Play seems to incorporate the elements of Move and Pass. You should change your potential entity list to use Play.

This type of comparison is also a good gauge of analysis to come. Card looks to have a great deal of diverse aspects, but that doesn't mean it's more important. It just means that when you move onto the Logical design, it may explode into many more entities than Playing Area, which seems pretty isolated and self-contained.

Building the Conceptual Model

You now have a set of potential conceptual entities. You need to work with them a bit to finally create a Conceptual data model. In this section, you'll do the following:

- Expand the definitions.

- Review the potential entities and choose an appropriate set of entities.

- Relate the entities.

- Validate the business rules and publish the model.

You've defined seven potential entities for the Conceptual data model of Solitaire. Let's review them one by one (see Table 8-8). You'll further enhance the definitions and then see which ones you want to use.

Table 8-8. *Final Set of Conceptual Entities*

Name	Definition
Card	One of 52 unique game pieces used in playing games bearing pictures of figures or numbers organized by suit. For example, the queen of clubs and the two of diamonds are cards.
Card Pile	A collection of cards that behave differently in the game of Solitaire. For example, the draw pile, discard pile, and processing pile are all collections.
Game	A contest played for sport or amusement (according to rules) made up of many small decisions that affect the outcome, in this instance, Solitaire.
Play	A play is completed when the entire set of available cards is assessed, resulting in a move or pass.
Player	A participant in the game of Solitaire.
Playing Area	A physical location such as a table or a virtual location such as a computer screen where the game is being played.
Status	A state of activity noting a play, move, or game.

Enhancing Conceptual Definitions

At least half of the conceptual entities are difficult to define just because they're so common-place that we tend to define them in a circular fashion. However, at this point you need to have a list of crystal-clear definitions. This ensures you highlight any errors or inconsistencies before using the model in the physical design phase. As an example, you currently have this:

- **Card**: One of 52 unique game pieces used in playing games bearing pictures of figures or numbers organized by suit. For example, the queen of clubs and the two of diamonds are cards.

Fight to be as specific as possible. If you aren't specific enough in your definitions, you could end up spending hours creating a model based on a false assumption. So in this case, the phrase Game Pieces would be too easy to confuse with tokens or dice. You need to be more specific.

- **Card**: One of 52 specific combinations of suit and numbers (or face), usually displayed in rectangular form, that are used to play games. For example, the queen of clubs and the two of diamonds are cards.

You also need to add restrictions to your definition to remove any misunderstanding that you've analyzed every use of a card. You're concentrating on cards as they're used in Solitaire. You need to remove as many ways of misunderstanding the concept you're analyzing as possible.

- **Card**: One of 52 specific combinations of suit and numbers (or face), usually displayed in rectangular form, that are used to play games, in this instance, Solitaire. For example, the queen of clubs and the two of diamonds are cards.

It's also a good idea to explain that there are other cards and what they mean to your analysis, so you'll arrive at a definition like this:

- **Card**: One of 52 specific combinations of suit and numbers (or face), usually displayed in rectangular form, that are used to play games, in this instance, Solitaire. For example, the queen of clubs and the two of diamonds are cards. This excludes additional rectangular paper stock that's included in a sold pack, such as jokers or instruction cards.

With a definition like that it's pretty hard to misunderstand what we mean by Card in this Conceptual model.

You should feel free to specifically call out what isn't included in a definition of an entity. In some worlds, such as manufacturing, Card would have a larger meaning than you're using here. When you're targeting integration, those notes will be helpful. You should also document what isn't known so you can allow for further discussion. In this case, for example, it may be that no one knows what the function of the joker cards is. Table 8-9 shows more complete entity definitions.

Table 8-9. *More Complete Entity Definitions*

Name	Definition
Card	One of 52 specific combinations of suit and numbers (or face), usually displayed in rectangular form, that are used to play games, in this instance, Solitaire. For example, the queen of clubs and the two of diamonds are cards. This excludes additional rectangular paper stock that's included in a sold pack, such as jokers or instruction cards.
Card Pile	A temporary and changeable area used to process a collection of cards that behave differently in the game of Solitaire. A card pile doesn't have to have a card in it to exist. For example, the draw pile, discard pile, and processing pile are all collections.
Game	A contest played for sport or amusement (according to rules) made up of many small decisions that affect the outcome.
Play	A play is completed when the entire set of available cards is assessed, resulting in a move or pass during a game of Solitaire.
Player	A person who actively chooses a course of action to manipulate a game to its conclusion.
Playing Area	The location where a game of Solitaire is being carried out. For example, home, work, a park, a table, and a screen are all playing areas.
Status	A state of game activity such as a play, move, or game in the course of a game of Solitaire. For example, Complete, Win, Lose, and Pass are statuses.

Go through the list in Table 8-9 one more time. Does every concept seem to be at the same level of detail? Keep looking at Status. It doesn't quite seem to fit with the rest, in that Status is a workflow state that's possibly derivable from the game itself. Derivations such as this are often left off the Conceptual model unless the workflow state is used as a logic point for another business activity step. Our assessment is that it's a critical but more detailed aspect of a game of Solitaire. Let's remove it from the Conceptual model.

■Note Just because you move something off the Conceptual model doesn't mean you need to throw away the analysis you've done. Keep this information in your notes so you can use it in the Logical data model analysis.

If you're using a modeling software package, you might have a picture of conceptual entities at the definition level that looks something like Figure 8-4.

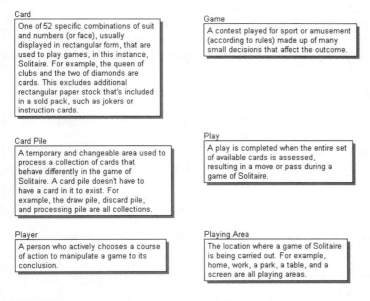

Card

> One of 52 specific combinations of suit and numbers (or face), usually displayed in rectangular form, that are used to play games, in this instance, Solitaire. For example, the queen of clubs and the two of diamonds are cards. This excludes additional rectangular paper stock that's included in a sold pack, such as jokers or instruction cards.

Game

> A contest played for sport or amusement (according to rules) made up of many small decisions that affect the outcome.

Card Pile

> A temporary and changeable area used to process a collection of cards that behave differently in the game of Solitaire. A card pile doesn't have to have a card in it to exist. For example, the draw pile, discard pile, and processing pile are all collections.

Play

> A play is completed when the entire set of available cards is assessed, resulting in a move or pass during a game of Solitaire.

Player

> A person who actively chooses a course of action to manipulate a game to its conclusion.

Playing Area

> The location where a game of Solitaire is being carried out. For example, home, work, a park, a table, and a screen are all playing areas.

Figure 8-4. *Solitaire entities, shown in definition form*

Adding Relationships

Now you need to figure out the relationships between the entities. This task is challenging since you need to be as specific, but as flexible, as possible with your naming. A relationship between two entities captures a business rule. The relationships shown in a Conceptual model are very high level. They aren't documenting relationships between data sets but rather between concept sets. Most Conceptual models have no concept of normalization. The attributes aren't filled in, there are no primary keys, and nothing is migrating. You're trying to identify connections or links between the concept entities. You want to note if it's conditional or restricted in some way.

Rules, when read in a statement from the symbols used in the data model, are represented by complete sentences. Entities are the nouns in the sentences, and relationships are the verbs. The restrictive nature of how they're built is a challenge to sentences that don't fit easily into this organizational structure.

- Each *<Entity A singular> <may or must> <have something to do with> <some quantity of> <Entity B plural>*.

In the following sections, you'll match every entity against every other entity to see if relationships exist between them. Then you'll review these relationships to see if they make sense together. Try to start with an entity that's key to tying everything together, such as Player or Game.

Analyzing Player Relationships

Let's start by trying to build complete sentences to and from Player with your other entities.

Player to Game

Try to build a complete sentence, taking what might be a rule between Player and Game in order to see if a conceptual relationship exists between these two entities. Remember, a relationship between entities consists of three parts: nullability (*may* or *must*), an active verb, and cardinality (how many). Consider these relationship aspects, which we've provided you between the brackets, as a fill-in-the-blank task:

- Each Player *<may or must> <do what? to> <how many?>* Games.

Fortunately, you're working on the Conceptual model of a small activity, so the verb phrases should be fairly simple to find. The key is to create as active a verb as possible between Player and Game. Our data modeling training has taught us to always consider *is* or *has* to be cheating, and *takes part in* is likely too passive. This is probably one of those horrible times when our language has created a noun based on a verb. Try *plays*, but *manipulates* may speak more to our psychology department. It's always a good idea to reread the definitions of your entities when you're relating them. Review these definitions:

- **Player**: A person who actively chooses a course of action to manipulate a game to its conclusion.

- **Game**: A contest played for sport or amusement (according to rules) made up of many small decisions that affect the outcome.

Is the following true?

- Each Player *<must>* play *<one or more>* Games.

It is if you assume a person can't be a player unless they play a game.
Is the following true?

- Each Game *<must> <be played by> <one and only one>* Players.

Yes! If that's true, it means you should be able to apply it to the definition you built earlier, and it would still be true, like so:

- A person who actively chooses a course of action to manipulate a game to its conclusion *must play one or more* contests . . . for sport or amusement (according to rules) made up of many small decisions that affect the outcome.

This is a good way of verifying your definitions, relationship verb phrases, and the proposed relationship. Figure 8-5 represents the relationship (refer to Chapter 2 to refresh your memory about which type of line and end symbol will best represent "one must have one or many").

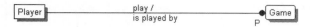

Figure 8-5. *Solitaire Conceptual model showing relationship between Player and Game*

Player to Card

A player does what to cards? It seems to us that a player shuffles, deals, chooses, moves, and discards cards. They all seem perfectly valid to us. See what we mean about these Conceptual model verb phrases? You need to find a generic, more aggregated (conceptual) verb to use in the Conceptual model. All of those clear, specific, real verbs suggest that a fairly complicated structure is going to be needed at the Logical model level to capture it all. Don't forget that you've discovered many specific relationships. Note it in the relationship definitions for the more detailed logical analysis phase.

- **Player**: A person who actively chooses a course of action to manipulate a game to its conclusion.

- **Card**: One of 52 specific combinations of suit and numbers (or face), usually displayed in rectangular form, that are used to play games, in this instance, Solitaire. For example, the queen of clubs and the two of diamonds are cards. This excludes additional rectangular paper stock that's included in a sold pack, such as jokers or instruction cards.

How about *manipulates*?

- Each Player must manipulate one or more Cards.

- Each Card must be manipulated by one or more Players.

That looks like Figure 8-6.

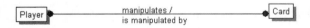

Figure 8-6. *Solitaire Conceptual model showing many-to-many relationship between Player and Card*

Player to Playing Area

These are the definitions:

- **Player**: A person who actively chooses a course of action to manipulate a game to its conclusion.

- **Playing Area**: The location where a game of Solitaire is being played. For example, home, work, a park, a table, and a screen are all playing areas.

This one is pretty easy and looks like Figure 8-7.

- Each Player must play in one or more Playing Areas.

- Each Playing Area may be played in by zero, one, or many Players.

Figure 8-7. *Solitaire Conceptual model showing many to-many relationship between Player and Playing Area*

Player to Play

These are the definitions:

- **Player**: A person who actively chooses a course of action to manipulate a game to its conclusion.

- **Play**: A play is completed when the entire set of available cards is assessed, resulting in a move or pass during a game of Solitaire.

So, does a player make a play? Maybe they direct a play? We vote for *direct*. It has a flavor of control and execution. You can see the *to* and *from* relationship verbs in Figure 8-8.

- Each Player must direct zero, one, or many Plays.

- Each Play must be directed by one and only one Player.

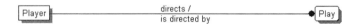

Figure 8-8. *Solitaire Conceptual model showing many-to-many relationship between Player and Play*

Player to Card Pile

These are the definitions:

- **Player**: A person who actively chooses a course of action to manipulate a game to its conclusion.

- **Card Pile**: A temporary and changeable area used to process a collection of cards that behave differently in the game of Solitaire. A card pile doesn't have to have a card in it to exist. For example, the draw pile, discard pile, and processing pile are all card piles.

Is there a direct connection between Player and Card Pile? Players are the ones who set up the game after the shuffle in the manual game. A card pile is then built by a player, as shown in Figure 8-9.

- Each Player must build zero, one, or many Card Piles.

- Each Card Pile must be built by one and only one Player.

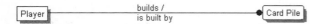

Figure 8-9. *Solitaire Conceptual model showing many-to-many relationship between Player and Card Pile*

Player to Player

Don't forget to check for recursive relationships. If the psychology department wanted to track how Solitaire spread from person to person through a teacher/student relationship, you'd need a recursive relationship here. Remember what a recursive relationship is? It connects an entity to itself. We don't remember anything in the scope about tracking this, so you'll assume for the moment that it isn't included.

You may find in the course of creating a Conceptual model that your instinct and experience of what could, should, or may be in scope (but hasn't actually been given to you) is very valuable. Share your thoughts with the clients and your team to see what they think.

Reviewing Player Relationships

Player is indeed a key to relating everything together. In fact, the model looks a bit like a spider at this point (see Figure 8-10).

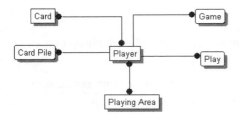

Figure 8-10. *Very simple view of the Solitaire Conceptual model at this point*

Not all of these relationships are going to make it through the iterative review process. You start with an assumption and then check and double-check it, changing your mind from one iteration to the next. Right now all the relationships you created make sense. Let's continue to connect the relationships.

Analyzing Game Relationships

Now let's go onto game relationships. Remember that you've already done Game to Player, since every relationship is two-way.

Game to Card

Again, review the definitions to keep the concept fresh in your mind:

- **Game**: A contest played for sport or amusement (according to rules) made up of many small decisions that affect the outcome.

- **Card**: One of 52 specific combinations of suit and numbers (or face), usually displayed in rectangular form, that are used to play games, in this instance, Solitaire. For example, the queen of clubs and the two of diamonds are cards. This excludes additional rectangular paper stock that's included in a sold pack, such as jokers or instruction cards.

Does Game directly relate to Card? A game of Solitaire couldn't happen without them.

- Each Game must be played with exactly 52 Cards.

- Each Card may be used in zero, one, or many Games.

This looks like Figure 8-11 when it's modeled.

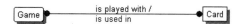

Figure 8-11. *Solitaire Conceptual model showing many-to-many relationship between Game and Card*

Game to Playing Area

These are the definitions:

- **Game**: A contest played for sport or amusement (according to rules) made up of many small decisions that affect the outcome.

- **Playing Area**: The location where a game of Solitaire is being carried out. For example, home, work, a park, a table, and a screen are all playing areas.

This relationship shows that although you're going through all the game relationships at one time, Playing Area is actually the parent entity. One game is located in one playing area. We don't think we've ever found anyone moving a game of Solitaire. They quit and start a new game if they want to change the location.

- Each Game must be located in one and only one Playing Area.

- Each Playing Area may house zero, one, or many Games.

This looks like Figure 8-12.

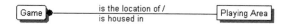

Figure 8-12. *Solitaire Conceptual model showing many-to-one relationship between Game and Playing Area*

Game to Play

These are the definitions:

- **Game**: A contest played for sport or amusement (according to rules) made up of many small decisions that affect the outcome.

- **Play**: A play is completed when the entire set of available cards is assessed, resulting in a move or pass during a game of Solitaire.

This one seems easy. Games consist of plays, which advance the Game to its conclusion, as shown in Figure 8-13.

- Each Game must be advanced with one or more Plays.

- Each Play must advance one and only one Game.

Figure 8-13. *Solitaire Conceptual model showing one-to-many relationship between Game and Play*

Game to Card Pile

These are the definitions:

- **Game**: A contest played for sport or amusement (according to rules) made up of many small decisions that affect the outcome.

- **Card Pile**: A temporary and changeable area used to process a collection of cards that behave differently in the game of Solitaire. A card pile doesn't have to have a card in it to exist. For example, the draw pile, discard pile, and processing pile are all card piles.

Is there a direct relationship between Game and Card Pile? Is it the same relationship that Game has with Card? Every game uses 52 cards. Every game uses the same set of card piles.

This is another place where you're going to have to make an educated assumption. Many relationships are so stable you might not even understand why you'd document them, such as Company to Department. Aren't all departments part of the company by default? Yes, but if you merge with another company, you may need to differentiate the two shipping departments. You're the modeler. You choose what relationships to note and which ones to leave as implied. We've chosen to leave Card Pile to Game as implied for the moment. We may choose to do the same thing with Card when we get to the final review.

Game to Game

Is there a relationship of Game to Game? One certainly could follow the other. Since the psychology department is looking at feedback statistics, let's assume the client will want to gather information about how many games in a row a person wins or loses. Figure 8-14 shows this recursive relationship.

- Each Game may precede zero or one Game.

- Each Game may be preceded by one and only one Game.

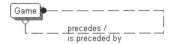

Figure 8-14. *Solitaire Conceptual model showing recursive relationship between Game and Game*

Reviewing Game Relationships

You can see the relationships are starting to tie the entities together. When you look at the business rules that are generated, you'll see the conceptualized story of the Solitaire process, as shown in Figure 8-15.

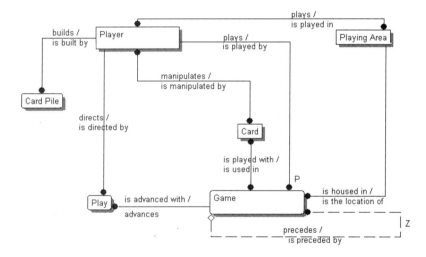

Figure 8-15. *More detailed view of the Solitaire Conceptual model at this point*

Analyzing Card Relationships

Now let's look at Card.

Card to Playing Area

- **Card:** One of 52 specific combinations of suit and numbers (or face), usually displayed in rectangular form, that are used to play games, in this instance, Solitaire. For example, the queen of clubs and the two of diamonds are cards. This excludes additional rectangular paper stock that's included in a sold pack, such as jokers or instruction cards.

- **Playing Area:** The location where a game of Solitaire is being played. For example, home, work, a park, a table, and a screen are all playing areas.

We don't see a relationship of Card to Playing Area. A game is played with cards, and a game is played in a playing area. This means that cards are in the playing area because they're a part of a game.

Card to Play

These are the definitions:

- **Card**: One of 52 specific combinations of suit and numbers (or face), usually displayed in rectangular form, that are used to play games, in this instance, Solitaire. For example, the queen of clubs and the two of diamonds are cards. This excludes additional rectangular paper stock that's included in a sold pack, such as jokers or instruction cards.

- **Play**: A play is completed when the entire set of available cards is assessed, resulting in a move or pass during a game of Solitaire.

On the other hand, Card is an integral element in Play. Cards are assessed, passed over, or moved during a play. How can you aggregate that into one verb? How about the generic verb *use* like in Figure 8-16?

- Each Card may be used in zero, one, or many Plays.

- Each Play may use zero, one, or many Cards.

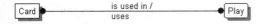

Figure 8-16. *Solitaire Conceptual model showing many-to-many relationship between Card and Play*

Card to Card Pile

These are the definitions:

- **Card**: One of 52 specific combinations of suit and numbers (or face), usually displayed in rectangular form, that are used to play games, in this instance, Solitaire. For example, the queen of clubs and the two of diamonds are cards. This excludes additional rectangular paper stock that's included in a sold pack, such as jokers or instruction cards.

- **Card Pile**: A temporary and changeable area used to process a collection of cards that behave differently in the game of Solitaire. A card pile doesn't have to have a card in it to exist. For example, the draw pile, discard pile, and processing pile are all card piles.

Cards are definitely located in and moved to card piles, as shown in Figure 8-17.

- Each Card must be part of one or more Card Piles.

- Each Card Pile may contain zero, one, or many Cards.

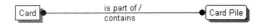

Figure 8-17. *Solitaire Conceptual model showing many-to-many relationship between Card and Card Pile*

Card to Card

Is there a relationship of Card to Card? Absolutely. Remember all the status types referring to cards under other cards? Figure 8-18 shows this relationship of Card to Card in the recursion.

- Each Card may cover zero or one Card.

- Each Card may be covered by zero or one Card.

Figure 8-18. *Solitaire Conceptual model showing recursive relationship between Card and Card*

Reviewing Card Relationships

You're starting to see relationships that may in fact be redundant. The Player to Card Pile, Player to Play, and Player to Card relationships are starting to look suspicious. Can you see why? There seem to be multiple ways to know the same information popping up in the model. If you know the player of the game, shouldn't you know the player of a card pile or card in a game as well? Similarly, if you know the player of the game, wouldn't you know the player of the play in a game? These relationships may be redundant. You really won't know until you get closer to finishing the model, but reviewing the relationships for these modeling issues is a good assessment as you go along. We've made a few notes on Figure 8-19.

We'll review all the suspicious relationships later in the validation of the completed bottom-up analysis, because right now they're only suspicious. You'll need a full view of the analysis to make sure they aren't needed. See if you can spot them as you go along, though.

Analyzing Playing Area Relationships

Let's now consider Playing Area.

Playing Area to Play

These are the definitions:

- **Playing Area**: The location where a game of Solitaire is being played. For example, home, work, a park, a table, and a screen are all playing areas.

- **Play**: A play is completed when the entire set of available cards is assessed, resulting in a move or pass during a game of Solitaire.

We don't think that a direct relationship exists between Playing Area and Play. Do you?

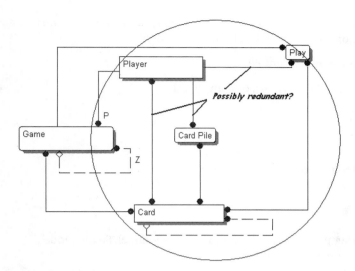

Figure 8-19. *Possible redundant relationships in the data model so far*

Playing Area to Card Pile

These are the definitions:

- **Playing Area**: The location where a game of Solitaire is being played. For example, home, work, a park, a table, and a screen are all playing areas.

- **Card Pile**: A temporary and changeable area used to process a collection of cards that behave differently in the game of Solitaire. A card pile doesn't have to have a card in it to exist. For example, the draw pile, discard pile, and processing pile are all card piles.

We don't think a relationship exists here either. And there doesn't seem to be a recursive relationship to Playing Area.

Analyzing Play Relationships

Now we'll consider Play.

Play to Card Pile

These are the definitions:

- **Play**: A play is completed when the entire set of available cards is assessed, resulting in a move or pass during a game of Solitaire.

- **Card Pile**: A temporary and changeable area used to process a collection of cards that behave differently in the game of Solitaire. A card pile doesn't have to have a card in it to exist. For example, the draw pile, discard pile, and processing pile are all card piles.

The problem here is that a play generally involves two card piles: the one the card moved from and the one to which it moved. However, since this is the Conceptual model, you can wrap the relationships together for the moment and let the detailed relationships show up in the Logical model's design. The Conceptual model looks like Figure 8-20.

- Each Play must occur in one or more Card Piles.

- Each Card Pile may be changed by zero, one, or many Plays.

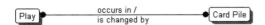

Figure 8-20. *Solitaire Conceptual model showing many-to-many relationship between Play and Card Pile*

Play to Play

Do plays have relationships to other plays? Certainly. They're also sequential. So the model needs the recursive relationship shown in Figure 8-21.

- Each Play may precede zero or one Play.

- Each Play may be preceded by zero or one Play.

Figure 8-21. *Solitaire Conceptual model showing recursive relationship between Play and Play*

Reviewing Play Relationships

You'll continue to add relationships. You can see that everything seems to be getting connected to everything. The relationships seem to be creating a maze or web. This may be an indication that you've modeled relationships that are redundant. You're just about ready to clear some of it up from the current view of the Conceptual model shown in Figure 8-22.

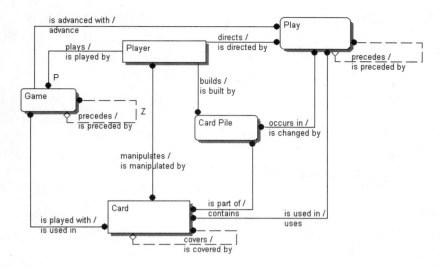

Figure 8-22. *Current view of the Solitaire Conceptual model at this point*

Analyzing Card Pile Relationships

What about Card Pile?

Card Pile to Card Pile

Rules govern the movement of cards from one type of card pile to another. The draw pile can provide cards only to the game. The discard pile can receive cards only from the game. Processing piles can do both. This is a structure you don't see very often. It's a many-to-many recursion, as shown in Figure 8-23. (As a reminder—the rules of Solitaire are out of scope—you're looking at them only to see if they help your understanding of the concepts needed in the model for your clients.)

- Each Card Pile may send to zero, one, or many Card Piles.

- Each Card Pile may receive from zero, one, or many Card Piles.

Figure 8-23. *Solitaire Conceptual model showing many-to-many recursive relationship between Card Pile and Card Pile*

That brings you to this model shown in Figure 8-24 as the final stage of this analysis.

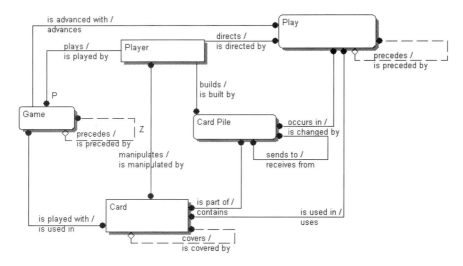

Figure 8-24. *View of this stage of analysis of the Solitaire Conceptual model*

Checking the Business Rules

Next, you need to take the list of business rules to the process experts and ask if you've captured what they were trying to tell you. Read them through once yourself to get a feel of the level of detail you're documenting. What's really amazing is that this is the high-level Conceptual model. Wait until you get to the fully attributed Logical model.

These are in forward (F) and then reverse (R) relationship sentence structure. Many modelers will remove the reverse sentences for simplicity (and to prevent the reviewers from being overwhelmed). This is your call. We prefer to show both.

- **F**: Each Player must play one or more Games.

- **R**: Each Game must be played by one and only one Player.

- **F**: Each Player must manipulate one or more Cards.

- **R**: Each Card must be manipulated by one or more Players.

- **F**: Each Player must play in one or more Playing Areas.

- **R**: Each Playing Area may be played in by zero, one, or many Players.

- **F**: Each Player must direct zero, one, or many Plays.

- **R**: Each Play must be directed by one and only one Player.

- **F**: Each Player must build zero, one, or many Card Piles.

- **R**: Each Card Pile must be built by one and only one Player.

- **F**: Each Game must be played with exactly 52 Cards.

- **R**: Each Card may be used in zero, one, or many Games.

- **F**: Each Game must be located in one and only one Playing Area.

- **R**: Each Playing Area may house zero, one, or many Games.

- **F**: Each Game must be advanced with one or more Plays.

- **R**: Each Play must advance one and only one Game.

- **F**: Each Game may precede zero or one Game.

- **R**: Each Game may be preceded by one and only one Game.

- **F**: Each Card may be used in zero, one, or many Plays.

- **R**: Each Play may use zero, one, or many Cards.

- **F**: Each Card must be part of one or more Card Piles.

- **R**: Each Card Pile may contain zero, one, or many Cards.

- **F**: Each Card may cover zero or one Card.

- **R**: Each Card may be covered by zero or one Card.

- **F**: Each Play must occur in one or more Card Piles.

- **R**: Each Card Pile may be changed by zero, one, or many Plays.

- **F**: Each Play may precede zero or one Play.

- **R**: Each Play may be preceded by zero or one Play.

- **F**: Each Card Pile may send to zero, one, or many Card Piles.

- **R**: Each Card Pile may receive from zero, one, or many Card Piles.

Note Every sentence must be true with no ifs, ands, or buts. Sometimes leading the clients through the maturing of the business rules helps them see problems early. You may even find business rules that your client overlooked or thought were unimportant. This serves to highlight that you've grasped the underlying process you've been asked to model.

Checking the Relationships

After you get feedback from the clients on the business rules, you'll want to review the relationships one more time. You need to both look for redundant relationships and review the identifying and nonidentifying nature of the relationships. Remember, identifying relationships (those that are needed to show a member of the parent entity is needed to identify member of a child entity) are shown with a solid line, and nonidentifying relationships (those where a member of the parent entity is used as a descriptor of a member of a child entity) are shown with a dashed line. For a more complete description of the types of relationships, you may want to revisit Chapter 3 and 4.

Adding relationships by comparing each entity to the others often leaves you with extra relationships in the Conceptual model. Relationships are a little more difficult to manage in the Conceptual model, since you aren't setting up primary keys or migrating them as foreign keys. This is documentation of concepts relating to each other. You don't have the rules of normalization to help you out here. It's time to make sure all the relationships are valid. Some of them may have fallen off in the business rule verification, but generally you'll find you still have some when you start to look at the model as a whole.

We've removed the second verb phrase in Figure 8-25 for simplicity. Now you can see why active verbs are always preferred in modeling. Take a moment to trace the lines, and see if you can read the model you've created.

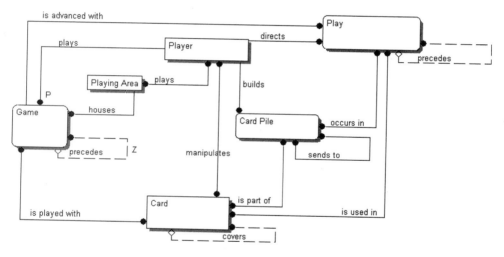

Figure 8-25. *Final view of this stage of analysis of the Solitaire Conceptual model*

Now let's focus on some of the relationships that may not be truly necessary to document this process. Let's start with Player again. We're removing the cardinality so you can concentrate on just the relationship for the moment.

- A Player plays in Playing Areas.

However, you also know these two facts:

- A Player plays Games.
- A Playing Area houses Games.

If you know the player participating in a game and you know a game is played in a playing area, then you already know what playing areas the player plays in. The scope emphasizes the desire to capture information about players and games. You're not expecting to need to know where Solitaire players might hang out if they aren't playing. You'll know where they play based on the games they play. Remove the relationship between Playing Area and Player, as shown in Figure 8-26. The relationship is true, but in this case it's derivable from other relationships. If your review finds that the relationship is derivable, then the relationship isn't necessarily true, valid, or necessary.

Now while you're here, let's review some of the other relationships. Let's review whether Playing Area to Game is identifying. Do you think that a playing area is descriptive or identifying for a game? It's probably descriptive, so change the relationship line to a nonidentifying relationship.

But how about Player to Game? Do you think that a player is nonidentifying or identifying of a game? Hmmm. Games don't really have a natural identifier that we can determine. They would probably be noted as the first, second, or third game of a player. We'll guess that this relationship is identifying, so leave the solid line between them. The clients told you they want to follow the game life of a player.

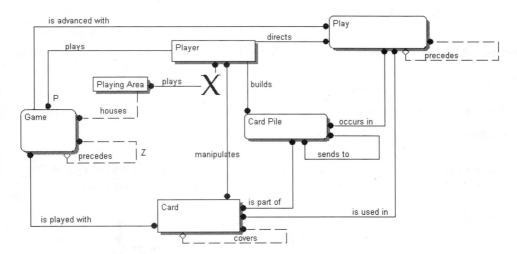

Figure 8-26. *Removing the many-to-many relationship from Playing Area to Player changes the relationship of Playing Area to Game to non-identifying.*

Let's try it again. You know the following:

- A Player directs Plays.

You also know the following:

- A Player plays Games.

- A Game advances with Plays.

Do you need the relationship of Player to Plays? Don't all the plays belong to one game? Don't you already know the player who played the game? Yes, you do. The relationship of Player to Play is redundant. Take it out, as noted in Figure 8-27. Now double-check for identification. Is the game descriptive or identifying for a play? It must be identifying, because the same play could happen in more than one game.

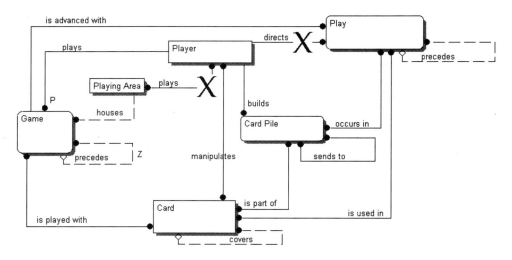

Figure 8-27. *Removing the one-to-many from Player to Play*

Follow down the relationship line to the next step.

- A Player builds Card Piles.

- A Play occurs in Card Piles.

You already know the player building the card piles because the play is part of a game. The Player to Card Pile relationship is redundant, so we've marked it for deletion in Figure 8-28.

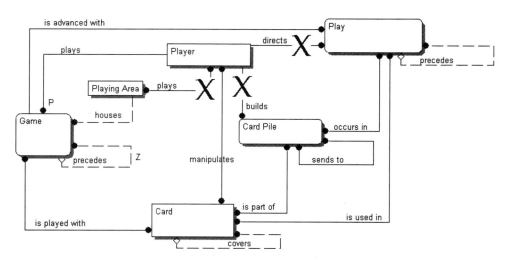

Figure 8-28. *Removing the one-to-many from Player to Card Pile*

Now look at the player of the game and the card.

- A Player manipulates Cards.

- A Game is played with Cards.

However, every game is played with the same 52 cards, and the player is moving the same 52 cards. What's important about the cards is what play they're used in, don't you think? If a player is playing a game, if the game itself is made up of players, and if the players use cards, then you need neither the relationship of Game to Card nor Player to Card, so Figure 8-29 shows them as being ready for removal.

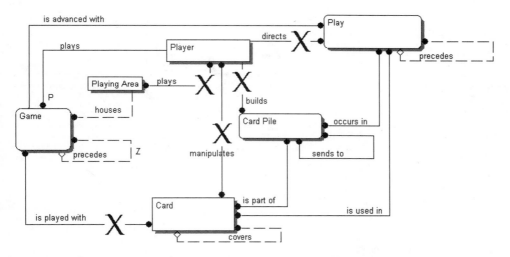

Figure 8-29. *Removing the many-to-many from Player to Card and Game to Card*

Finally, let's look at the relationships around Play, Card Pile, and Card. If every play occurs in card piles, and every play uses cards, is the relationship between Card and Card Pile necessary? Can you move a card to be a part of a card pile if the card isn't being moved in the context of a play? That depends on whether the original layout of the game is considered a play. When in doubt, go back to the definitions.

- **Play:** A play is completed when the entire set of available cards is assessed, resulting in a move or pass during a game of Solitaire.

That looks to us like the original layout isn't considered a play. At this point we'd call the clients and ask some questions about the original layout of the game. Since we know them well, we'll tell you that a game to them starts with the first play. The layout is out of scope. But wait. What about the rules that connect Card Pile to Card? What about the kings and aces that play special roles in special card piles? Perhaps there's a reason to keep the relationship in after all. But if that's the reason you're keeping the relationship, you need to rethink the verb to reflect this thought. You aren't using the relationship the way you had originally expected. You don't need to remember what card pile they're a part of; you can derive that through Play. You're using the relationship to note that kings can begin empty processing piles and aces can begin empty discard piles. Therefore, change the verb to *begins*.

You may want to add some titles and identification to the model itself as we've done in Figure 8-30. Rearrange the boxes and lines to suit your needs. Many people prefer to arrange the model so that the parents are above the children. We prefer to organize the model based on how we want to review the story. In this case, Game is the main focus, so it takes the far left positon to support reading the model from left to right. But you have to decide what works for you.

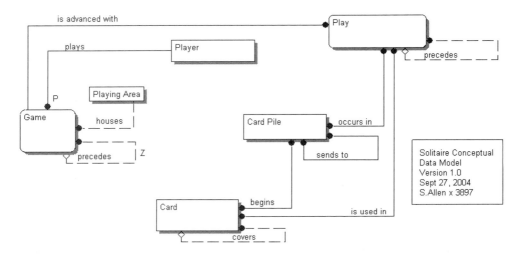

Figure 8-30. *Final Solitaire Conceptual model*

Publishing the Model

Now it's time to polish your model for printing. Check your spelling in the names, definitions, and relationships. Even good modeling software won't help you with that. Add notes, and make sure you can create and validate your true/false questions test from the model. Also add any points that need clarification. Publish your definitions (including the definitions of the relationships if you have generic details in the aggregated verb phrase). Remember, definitions at this point can't be too detailed. Make notations of items that aren't as well analyzed as you'd like. And put your name, e-mail, and phone number on everything so you can gather feedback.

The next step is validation in a model review with your peers, your manager, and the clients. That way, you'll cover all your bases. This step is important and sometimes quite a challenge for your people skills. You need to help people understand what they're reading. You need to practice patience, and try to teach them basics about modeling at the same time you're helping them to understand this particular model. You're often trying to show them a reality about their own business they either aren't aware of or don't want to acknowledge. Make sure you take notes in your meetings—better yet, assign someone to take notes during the meeting so you can concentrate on other things. You need to stay open to suggestions at this stage and may need to iterate new thoughts into the model.

■Note Sometimes it's helpful to ask your peers if you can do a model walk-through with them before anyone else, modeler to modeler. They may have some insight to offer before you report your findings to the outside world. They may help with entity names, definitions, and relationships from past experience. And sometimes they will see things you just missed by being too close to the problem. However, don't be afraid to defend your position. After all, you did the analysis.

Summary

In this chapter you began to apply the principles you learned about in the first half of the book. You looked at the game of Solitaire and broke down the processes of the game methodically to discover the concepts, which are the foundations of your model. You used two methods: top down, focusing on the actual process of the game itself, and bottom up, focusing on the data elements buried in the game rules.

You validated the analysis by comparing the results of those two methods and continued focusing until you determined the concepts you were going to document as entities. You defined them and began to build business rules between them by comparing each one with every other one, one at a time.

Then you took the relationships and built a list of business rules for the clients to validate in a true/false review. You then began the process of verifying from an overview perspective that all the potential business rules were actually necessary. You found several redundant relationships that could be deleted because the information could actually be deduced from other relationships. Finally, you cleaned up the model, created nice documentation, and went on the road with it doing model reviews with the team to verify your analysis and understanding of their business.

You've created a Conceptual data model of Solitaire. In the next chapter you'll push the analysis down to the detail level of a fully attributed Logical data model.

CHAPTER 9

■■■

Building a Logical Model

This chapter demonstrates the process of building a fully attributed Logical data model; it will be based on the Conceptual model you created in the previous chapter. That model contains Conceptual model entities and relationships that describe the activity of individuals playing one or more games of Solitaire.

Throughout this chapter, you'll discover and document the data elements and their relationships that are needed to support and describe the process of Solitaire. We'll cover each step along the way, and we'll sometimes loop back to change the model when making new discoveries.

To this end, we'll cover the following:

- We'll review the Conceptual model and show how to build logical subject areas.

- We'll propose entities for each subject area.

- We'll determine the attributes, note the candidate keys, and decide on a primary key.

- We'll outline the relationships between entities, which will provide the foreign keys.

- We'll apply several quality assurance (QA) checks, especially applying the rules of normalization.

We want to give you a real sense of the decisions you need to make when creating a Logical model, such as when to add elements or attributes, when to take them out, and how to work through to a finished product. Data modeling is an iterative process and involves a maturing of understanding. You may sometimes make changes to the model during the course of one exercise that you'll later undo. This will show the importance of allowing yourself the opportunity to change your mind while you're modeling.

In the previous chapter, you completed the Conceptual model for an activity called Solitaire. The model includes concepts for participants, location, materials, and rules, all of which are usually areas of interest for most business activities. However, you haven't yet identified any recognizable data elements. You've built a Conceptual model only, which is a handy exercise, but a Conceptual model is nowhere near a data map for the game of Solitaire. What you want to do next is develop the logical data elements using the entities on the Conceptual model as a scope definition or concept map. You'll test each of the Logical model entities by mapping back to the Conceptual model entities. The result of this mapping will be a fully attributed Logical data model.

Reviewing the Conceptual Model As a Guide

Remind yourself of the Conceptual model for Solitaire by looking at Figure 9-1.

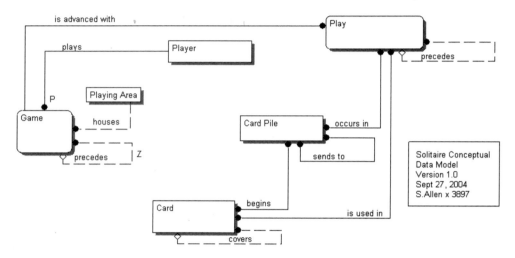

Figure 9-1. *Final version of the Conceptual model from Chapter 8*

The Conceptual model is to a data modeler what a rough draft is to an artist. It captures basic information about the elements that make up the whole, including how the elements interact. You'll use the Conceptual model as a guide for building the Logical model. But the Conceptual model can only take you so far. At some point you'll have to lay it aside and use other sources—such as interviews with subject matter experts (SMEs), more detailed process documentation, or experimentation—to document the process yourself. You do this to increase your understanding of the details needed for a fully attributed Logical model. You'll use the following techniques:

- Validate the scope of your understanding of the concepts involved in the clients' process.

- Group the concepts to form subject areas on which to focus.

- Find the Logical model's entities (via the concept definitions).

- Forge the first Logical model's relationships (using the concept relationships).

- Map the Logical model's elements to the Conceptual model's elements.

Each of the Conceptual model's documented entities shows you what you should explore next and therefore defines the *scope* of your analysis. Without a Conceptual model upon which to base the Logical model, the propensity for *data element scope creep* is high. You could easily find yourself analyzing entities and data that are irrelevant for this study (for example, those associated with the process of actually setting up the study for the psychology department). You could suddenly find yourself modeling historical aspects of the games or the nature of cards in general (such as the origin of playing card games or the relationship of modern cards to ancient Tarot or Kabala) or even expanding the playing area into a series of geographic entities and relationships (such as the city, state, country, building complex, surrounding architecture, furniture, or landscaping styles). Again, these aren't in the original description of the project, and they therefore don't appear in the Conceptual model. This type of scope creep is known as *top-down creep*, and the loss of focus in this manner has the effect of broadening the model's scope. Sometimes you may find it appropriate if you discover a larger abstraction or pattern in the problem space. The key is determining what your intended scope is and then making sure you stick to that scope.

As you continue with the Logical model analysis, you'll define relevant details of the entities in the Conceptual model. You have to be careful to avoid scope creep here as well. Think of Conceptual model entities as volumes in a set of encyclopedias. Each entity is a placeholder for detailed aspects about one concept. Some of those detailed aspects are also out of scope. For example, owned attributes about cards—such as tensile strength, combustion temperature, length, width, height, or weight—aren't relevant. However, you may not care about them, but someone else in the enterprise might. You need to be concerned that you get not only the right entities but the right attributes as well. This type of scope creep is known as *bottom-up creep*, and losing focus in this way deepens the scope of the model.

In summary, you have to stay focused on what you need for the project. Using the Conceptual model entities and their definitions as a guideline for your project's scope is one way of maintaining that focus.

■**Note** The better you capture the real-world logic of how the data elements naturally interact with each other, the better the chance the entities in the model will integrate into a larger enterprise view.

As you progress from the Conceptual model to the Logical model, bear in mind the following important points:

The process is highly iterative, and models are almost never right the first time. As you discover more detail in the Logical model analysis, you'll possibly make alterations to the Conceptual model.

Even the best initial analysis can yield only a partially correct or complete view, and it will always be skewed simply because it's a personal interpretation of the problem space. You probably can't get your model any better than 80 percent right on the first try. Don't be disappointed if you have to revisit your model a few times; this is a natural consequence of the process owners validating your model.

Logical models can document many "correct" solutions. You must ask yourself how abstract or how concrete you want the Logical model to be. Any concept that's abstract can have many interpretations and can yield different Logical models. Correctness may be only an interpretation of the client community; although you may disagree, ultimately you're modeling their process.

It's vital you keep the client community involved in your analysis. You need to stay in contact with SMEs, project sponsors, process owners, business partners, and those who will ultimately exercise your designs. Maintaining close contact through iterative model reviews is one of the ways to mitigate the risk of project failure.

Validating the Model

For the Conceptual model to act as a springboard into the next model, the process owners need to validate it. We mentioned this at the end of the last chapter, but it bears repeating. The business clients need an opportunity to review your understanding of the subject and agree or disagree with it. In fact, you may not have developed the Conceptual model with which you're working. Make time for a meeting to review it and expand your understanding. Even if you did author the Conceptual model, business processes can change quickly. Time lags between the completion of the Conceptual model and the start of the Logical model are dangerous.

Tip Keeping the business owners involved will help keep you from wasting time because of misunderstandings, uncommunicated changes, or model problems.

Therefore, take the time to review the entity names and definitions, the business rules, and the scope to ensure what you have still captures all the important information in an accurate manner.

Using the Feedback

Imagine you're back in your office at the university. You have the Conceptual model, now validated by your clients, hanging on the wall like a satellite picture of the campus. The following points came out of the clients' review of the model:

Playing Area isn't important to them. The study is restricted to work environments. This means you can either delete the entity or gray it out as a shadow entity. Shadow entities generally depict concepts that are out of scope (for any one of a number of reasons) but are still valid reference points. We'll leave Playing Area in the model to show you what a shadow looks like.

They missed the concept of Move. You explained it's one of the steps in a play. You read the definition to them. They decide that Move is a more detailed entity than the other Conceptual model's entities (but be aware that it could just as easily have gone the other way). You can make a note of the importance of this noun to the clients. You'll probably find that it's an appropriate entity in the completed Logical model.

They also disagreed with the definition of Player. They want to be able to have people in the player list who haven't necessarily played a game yet. They want you to change the name of the entity Player to Person to make it obvious when looking at the model. They also admit they haven't really decided yet what data they want to capture about the people who participate in the study. They're still working on it.

This means you're now working with the entities shown in Figure 9-2.

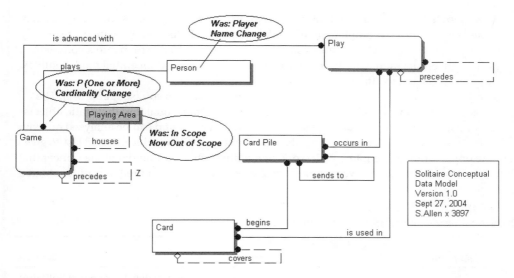

Figure 9-2. *Revisions to the Conceptual model*

Table 9-1 summarizes the remaining Conceptual model entities and their revised definitions.

Table 9-1. *Conceptual Entities*

Name	Definition
Card	One of 52 specific combinations of suit and numbers (or face), usually displayed in rectangular form, that are used to play games, in this instance, Solitaire. For example, the queen of clubs and the two of diamonds are cards. This excludes additional rectangular paper stock that's included in a sold pack, such as jokers or instruction cards.
Card Pile	A temporary and changeable area used to process a collection of cards that behave differently in the game of Solitaire. A card pile doesn't have to have a card in it to exist. For example, the draw pile, discard pile, and processing pile are all card piles.
Game	A contest played for sport or amusement (according to rules) made up of many small decisions that affect the outcome.
Play	A play is completed when the entire set of available cards is assessed, resulting in a move or pass during a game of Solitaire.
Person	A potential participant in a study being conducted by the psychology department.

Defining the Subject Areas

You're working with a really small Conceptual model, so it's going to be a little difficult not to simply use each Conceptual model entity as the basis for a subject area. A subject area is generally a set of data organized to reflect a specific area of business such as finance or sales. We use the term *subject area* to mean a set of data organized to increase the ability of a project team or team member to focus on an area of interest, to focus on data creation steps, or to improve readability and clarity.

Some people would say this definition overlaps with the concept of a submodel (which is a restricted view of the full complement of model members). It does. Subject areas are usually submodels of larger models. They're also stand-alone models that can map into a complete enterprise Conceptual model. In this case, you'll loosely group the Conceptual model entities into the areas you want to attack.

Start by grouping concepts into collections that make sense to you (see Table 9-2). The Card subject area seems well-defined and easy to analyze. Often you'll find that static objects such as forms, materials, and machines are already well-defined and can be analyzed quickly and easily. When possible, leave anything that the clients are still working on until last to give them the opportunity to complete their work. Remember, when you validated the Conceptual model, you learned the clients weren't too sure of exactly what they wanted to capture about a person.

Table 9-2. *Subject Areas from the Conceptual Model*

Subject Area Name	Conceptual Model Entity	Description
Card	Card	The materials needed to play the game of Solitaire
Card Movement	Card Pile Play	The movements of cards between card locations and the rules regarding allowed plays
Event	Game Person	The completed event of a single game of Solitaire including the person involved

If you refer to Figure 9-1, you'll notice some relationships that cross the boundaries between subject areas. You'll be building each subject area and then testing the relationships of the fully defined Logical model entities of each subject area to entities occurring in other subject areas. The relationships you see on the Conceptual model that link those entities together will help you find the relationships between the Logical model entities. Conceptual model relationships document process connections, and Logical model relationships are connections or overlaps between two distinct data sets (remember the mathematical set theory term *relation*).

Starting the Logical Data Modeling

You'll now exercise Dr. Codd's views on how to organize data into sets. A Conceptual model is too abstract a view for that, and the Physical model often has to take into account the target platform and programming language of implementation. The Logical data model is the true relational model. The other models you create contribute to the Logical model or are derived from it. So, you'll define each of the subject areas you're focusing on with the following:

- Entities

- Attributes

- Candidate and, eventually, primary keys

- Logical data types and domains

- Relationships, cardinality, and nullability

You'll perform another entity analysis, which will seem similar to the exhaustive process you did in Chapter 8 while building the Conceptual model. You'll review each of the Conceptual model entities and their relationships one by one to discover the more detailed logical entities/relationships hidden in the generality. When you did the bottom-up analysis in building the Conceptual model, you listed details and rolled them into concepts, which became the Conceptual model's entities. In Logical modeling, you'll be drilling down to the details.

You'll often get a feeling of déjà vu when it comes to the Logical model, especially when using an example of Conceptual modeling that's so detailed. You may feel like you've done this task before. And you have, but it was at a different level of detail. You should also note that you won't always do the modeling tasks in the serial fashion followed in this tutorial. Many times you'll know the default, or pattern, of logical entities that maps to an enterprise concept. Your tools will allow you to source them into new Logical models so that the entities Geography, Calendar Date, Employee, and Address, for example, are always modeled, named, defined, and related the same way from project to project. Then you can tweak the default slightly for business specifics.

This Conceptual to Logical to Physical model structure reuse allows you to leverage what you already know and plug sometimes even large areas into a model without having to completely re-analyze the business area. You have to validate the data elements and business rules each time, but you may not have to re-create them from scratch. You can learn from your manufacturing teammates and try to find parts of your own process that are repetitive in order to reuse sets of knowledge.

Modeling the Card Subject Area

The Card subject area was defined as the materials needed to play the game of Solitaire. It consists of one Conceptual model entity: Card. Figure 9-3 shows the Card component of the Conceptual model isolated into a submodel. Notice that when you isolate this subject area, the relationships to Card Pile and Play disappear from view. Remember that a subject area, or submodel, is just a focusing mechanism. Although they might not appear on the submodel diagram, the relationships still exist in the Conceptual model.

Figure 9-3. *The Card subject area from the Conceptual model*

As you'll recall from the previous chapter, you defined Card in the Conceptual model as follows:

- **Card**: One of 52 specific combinations of suit and numbers (or face), usually displayed in rectangular form, that are used to play games, in this instance, Solitaire. For example, the queen of clubs and the two of diamonds are cards. This excludes additional rectangular paper stock that's included in a sold pack, such as jokers or instruction cards.

Analyzing the Card Entity

We want to encourage you to pull out your deck of cards or launch Solitaire again. Picturing them in your head is a good way to start, but it's more helpful to have them in front of you as a reference. Without them, you'll forget things. List the single facts or nouns you find. Group them if it's obvious to you that they make a grouping. Pay special attention to synonyms, homonyms, and antonyms. The following are the important words for the Card subject area:

- Red/black

- Clubs, hearts, spades, diamonds

- Ace, king, queen, jack

- Numbers (10, 9, 8, 7, 6, 5, 4, 3, 2, and ace)

- 52 cards in a deck

- Single card

- Back design

- Card face or possibly card front (opposite of the back design)

Notice that you aren't sure at this point if an ace is a face or number card as it applies to the game of Solitaire; it might be both depending on the business rules. You'll need to clear this up at some point with the clients. Keep in mind that an ace might be either a face card or a number card, depending on the game being played. If your model is intended to be extended to other games, then this might be important. Remember that you're looking for simple grouping of things to put into sets (entities). For example, Red and Black are members of a set, since they're atomic in nature and would quite likely have similar information (attributes) available about them. Combined, they're members of the Color entity (set). Obviously, in this example the data set is small, having only two members, but it's still a valid set.

Sets (entities) can be singular or complex concepts. For example, members of the Ingredients set used in a bakery could be Water, Salt, or Baking Powder. It's just a simple list of every basic ingredient combined (using a recipe) to create a baked good. On the other hand, the Baked Good entity may be a compound concept, such as Recipe, Bake Event, and Package. You might need to know all those concepts to truly identify members of the Baked Good set because in your enterprise, donuts have a different pricing structure based on value of their ingredients, their freshness, and the quantity of donuts sold in the box.

Try to use entity names that are simple and easily understood. In this example, we see sets of Color, Suit, Face Card, Number Card, Card, Deck, and Card Side.

Are you wondering why Color and Suit are both entities when everyone knows that diamonds are always red and clubs are always black? We've separated these two sets to illustrate a point. Each of these things is a singular, definitive concept. They have a restricted set of members. They have the potential of owning attributes unique to describing members of their set; this is like color value in the world of painting, which has nothing to do with the color of a suit. Both Color and Suit have the potential of requiring business rules based on their membership like foreign key relationships to other data sets or intersection entities that rely on the set members of Color alone. Keeping the data sets as singular as possible to start with is the basis of relational theory.

Write these potential entities on a whiteboard, or start a new model in your software tool, putting Card, which is also the name of the subject area, in the center and the rest of the words in a circle around it, as shown in Figure 9-4. These are your first-draft Logical model entities based on the Conceptual model entity of Card, and it's time to pause and make sure you know what you mean by all of them. Again, as in the Conceptual model definitions, the names are just the shorthand label you choose for the concepts you're capturing. Table 9-3 shows how you could define the entities at this point.

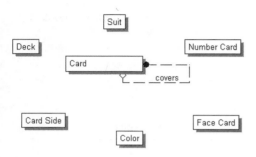

Figure 9-4. *Draft entity analysis of the Card subject area*

Table 9-3. *First-Draft Logical Entities*

Entity (Logical Element) Name	Definition
Card	One of 52 unique game pieces used in playing games bearing pictures of figures or numbers organized by suit. For example, the queen of clubs and the two of diamonds are cards.
Card Side	One of two faces of a card: the back and the front.
Color	One of two hues, red and black, used in the definition of the suit of a card.
Deck	A complete set of four suits of thirteen cards making a collection of fifty-two individual cards. This doesn't include jokers, instructions, and extra vendor cards.
Face Card	A card in a deck that has a figure pictured on the face.
Number Card	A card in a deck that doesn't have a figure pictured on the face.
Suit	One of four groups of cards: clubs, spades, hearts, and diamonds.

Analyzing the Card Category

Category relationships, as discussed in Chapter 3, simplify the list of entities by noting that some sets are simply subsets. A category always has a master (also described as a *supertype*) entity that contains the full conceptual set, with branches off it to further define individual members (known as *subtypes*) in the set. Sometimes the members of the supertype entity can belong to only one of the subtypes (an exclusive membership) or can have membership in many (an inclusive membership). These subtypes can have their own unique attributes. To distinguish between category entities on the Logical model, you can use a discriminator (a hollow circle in IDEF1X notation) at the intersection point; all the branches come from it.

Finding the categories is sometimes a good place to start enhancing your entity list, because they almost always show up in documentation and processes as a part of a list and are generally pretty easy to recognize by the clients. Some modelers prefer to leave them until later in the process. Our preference is to gather them early so we can recognize their innate, unique requirements, which causes them to share or isolate attributes and relationships from each other. Recognizing them as a family unit can be helpful in simplifying the model. If you find they confuse your team, then you can build a submodel with the subtype category structures omitted.

What clues do you have that a category structure is buried in the list of entities? Look at the definitions in Table 9-4.

Table 9-4. *Definitions of Two Data Sets*

Data Set	Definition
Face Card	*A card in a deck* that has a figure pictured on the face
Number Card	*A card in a deck* that doesn't have a figure pictured on the face

We recognize that you have entities (data sets) that sound similar, both being described as "a card in a deck." They're potential subtypes in a category, which is a collection of restrictive groupings for its members, which are similar in nature: notice the repetitive fragment of the definition "a card in a deck." Categories are recognizable because of the following points:

- They behave only slightly differently. For example, the category Property Insurance needs assessed value of property, the category Life Insurance needs medical condition of person covered, and the category Travel Insurance needs duration and destination.

- The clients expect to see them grouped together. They think of these as *types* of policies no matter how different they are from each other.

■Note Don't underestimate the need to pay attention to what the client expects to see. As mentioned in the previous chapter, you should, wherever possible, use existing terminology and relationships familiar to the client, rather than inventing your own or using more generic terms.

On the other hand, use your best judgment and experience. Before taking the clients' word on the existence of categories, get more information. Sometimes the clients use or report on items in the same manner when those items are really completely different entities (not subsets of a supertype). It's important to try to keep the presentation or process requirements separate from the data design.

You know there are number and face cards in the deck. Do you need to note that cards are divided into these subsets? Let's test it.

- **Do they share attributes?** Yes, they share the attributes Name and Suit (so they have shared attributes).

- **Do the clients expect to see them grouped together?** They think of these as *types* of cards? Yes.

A further point you need to test here is whether the categorization of Card into Face Card and Number Card is a complete or incomplete category? Since we decided that the jokers, instructions, and advertising cards are out of scope, no other card types exist that you haven't discovered, making it a complete category. Figure 9-5 shows the complete Card category.

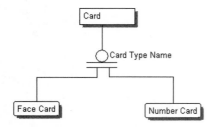

Figure 9-5. *Card category structure*

Categories are usually decision points for procedural processing, so they're important to the logic or application processing that uses the Physical design. A programmer will assume that all the records can be treated in the same way unless you document a distinct "type" differentiation with a category. For example, the entity Account at a bank is often categorized into many different types. This allows the programmer to note that many different rules will apply to an account based upon the type of account it is. For example, it could be that a customer will not need to order checks if they have only a savings account.

Analyzing the Card Relationships

Your next task is to tie all the new Logical model entities together with relationships. Remember that a relationship has an optionality notation (optional or mandatory) and a degree of cardinality ("how many?"), as you saw in the previous chapter. You'll draft the relationships using the identifying solid line. You'll revisit that as you put in attributes and can test with foreign keys. Let's start with the relationships to and from Card.

Card to Suit

Start by reviewing the definitions.

- **Card**: One of 52 unique game pieces used in playing games bearing pictures of figures or numbers organized by suit. For example, the queen of clubs and the two of diamonds are cards.

- **Suit**: One of four groups of cards: clubs, spades, hearts, and diamonds.

When you write the business rules from both directions, you get the following:

- Each Suit must differentiate zero, one, or many Cards.

- Each Card must belong to one (and only one) Suit.

This means you change the relationship verbs into *differentiates/belongs to* for the model to keep "active voice." So Card to Suit has a one-to-many relationship. Draw a line between them, and put a dot at the many end, near Card. Add the verb phrase, as shown in Figure 9-6.

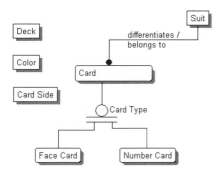

Figure 9-6. *Card to Suit relationship*

Card to Color

What about Card to Color?

- **Card**: One of 52 unique game pieces used in playing games bearing pictures of figures or numbers organized by suit. For example, the queen of clubs and the two of diamonds are cards.

- **Color**: One of two hues, red and black, used in the definition of the suit of a card.

Cards have colors. That seems pretty obvious. But wait, all the diamonds and hearts are red, and all the clubs and spades are black. If you know the suit, then you already know the color on the card, right? Therefore, the relationship isn't from Color to Card; it's from Color to Suit.

Card to Card

We talked about this in the Conceptual model design. Does the relationship of Card to itself still hold true?

- **Card**: One of 52 unique game pieces used in playing games bearing pictures of figures or numbers organized by suit. For example, the queen of clubs and the two of diamonds are cards.

Cards have relationships to each other when it comes to being able to place them in sequential order. We're not sure if you'll need this relationship by the time you finish the Logical model, but adding it now is a good way to remind you that you want to take a closer look at it before you finish. This is a recursive relationship, which is sometimes harder to read because the entity name on both ends of the verb phrase is the same.

- Each Card may cover zero, one, or many Cards.

- Each Card may be covered by one (and only one) Card.

Figure 9-7 shows the Card to Card relationship.

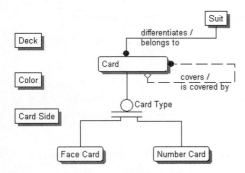

Figure 9-7. *Card to Card relationship*

Color to Suit

The following are the definitions:

- **Color**: One of two hues, red and black, used in the definition of the suit of a card.

- **Suit**: One of four groups of cards: clubs, spades, hearts, and diamonds.

    - Each Color must illuminate two Suits.

    - Each Suit must be illuminated by one (and only one) Color.

The change to active voice gives you *illuminates/is illuminated by*. These Card relationships are very stable. They're probably stable enough that you might want to document them using the restriction of two. There aren't many times you'll ever use the ability to call out the number of relationships that exist. The only reason you might hesitate here is if you think other types of cards might be added into this set in the future. Draw a line from Color to Suit with a dot by Suit. Add the number 2 by the dot, and add the verb phrase, as shown in Figure 9-8.

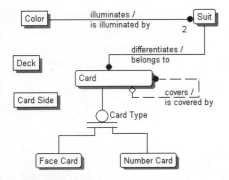

Figure 9-8. *Color to Suit relationship*

■**Tip** Use strong, detailed verbs. Bring as much life to the model as you can.

Card to Deck

Where does Deck fit in?

- **Card**: One of 52 unique game pieces used in playing games bearing pictures of figures or numbers organized by suit. For example, the queen of clubs and the two of diamonds are cards.

- **Deck**: A complete set of four suits of thirteen cards making a collection of fifty-two individual cards. This doesn't include jokers, instructions, and extra vendor cards.

    - Each Deck includes exactly 52 Cards.

    - Each Card belongs to one (and only one) Deck.

This gives you a draft model that looks like Figure 9-9.

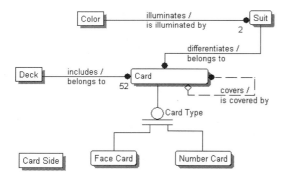

Figure 9-9. *Adding the Card to Deck relationship*

Again, this could be a very stable relationship. You may want to note that the model has 52 cards. However, in an environment where you might want to use this model in future projects, you may want to keep the model more generic to allow for using the jokers, using two decks, or losing some of the cards, in which case a relationship of "exactly 52" will be too restrictive.

Card to Card Side

Here are the definitions:

- **Card**: One of 52 unique game pieces used in playing games bearing pictures of figures or numbers organized by suit. For example, the queen of clubs and the two of diamonds are cards.

- **Card Side**: One of two faces of a card: the back and the front.

Now let's look at Card Side. The members of the set are Back and Front, which is actually an important thought in a game where turning the card from face down to face up is important. The simple rule is to attach Card Side to Card. After all, every Card has a back and a front. Therefore, every Card is related to two Card Sides. That's pretty simple. In fact, it's almost too simple. So ask yourself if there's anything about the members of the set that will restrict their behavior in following the business rules of Solitaire.

How about the member of the set Back? Isn't there a business rule that the whole deck must share a back design (to prevent someone from cheating by knowing which card has which design)? Some game software even has the back card design as an option you can set. So although every card has a back, it may be the design, shared by the deck, which is interesting and important. These thoughts have led you away from relating Card Side to Card and toward relating Back Design to Deck. Notice how similar the concepts and entities are and how subtle the differences can be.

Let's add Back Design as an entity to the model, and write down a relationship between Back Design and Deck. If you were modeling the virtual world of the computer game of Solitaire, the definition of and the business rules related to Back Design would be as follows:

- **Definition**: Back design is the pattern or color used to decorate one side of every card in a deck.

- **Business rule**: Each deck may be decorated with one or many back designs.

So with a virtual deck, which can be redecorated by choosing a preference at will, you could write the rules as follows:

- Each Deck must be decorated by zero, one, or many Back Designs.

- Each Back Design must decorate zero or one Deck.

But if you're looking at Solitaire in terms of the game being played with a physical pack of cards you'd actually have the following relationships:

- Each Deck must be decorated with one and only one Back Design.

- Each Back Design may decorate zero, or one, or many Decks.

As you can see, you could have different relationships depending on characteristics of the process. One uses physical playing pieces where the other is using virtual ones. You'll often find yourself analyzing a process that can happen in two completely different environments (teller deposits and ATM deposits, for example), so carefully look at the details of the activity from both worlds. Don't assume that the business rules for the data are the same because the final product is the same.

However, when you find yourself undecided about the details of a relationship, you should return to the project's scope. Remember the following from Chapter 8 where you were interviewing the clients?

Data modeler: "Is it computer Solitaire or cards?"

Department manager: "It's the computer game, I think, rather than cards. They want to focus on the results (ratio of wins to losses), not how they play it or the rules of the game."

Project lead: "The phenomenon we're researching is the craze with the computer game. Why do people play it all the time? How often do they win vs. lose?"

By reminding yourself of the project's true scope, you can resolve the choice with the details of the relationship.

Well, it seems to us that the discovery of Back Design changes the understanding of Card Side. Back isn't a side of a card anymore but rather a picture, or a Back Design. So following that logic, do you need a Front Design? Front Design could be interesting, since the following is true:

- Each Card must have exactly one Front Design.

- Each Front Design defines exactly one Card.

This is a one-to-one relationship. In the world of Logical modeling, this is extremely suspect, though one-to-one relationships do occur from time to time. However, in this case, the front design of a card pretty much is the card. So let's remove Card Side from the model. Make a note to yourself that you've considered Card Side to be unnecessary. You may need to come back to these notes when you review the model with the client. Figure 9-10 shows what the model currently looks like.

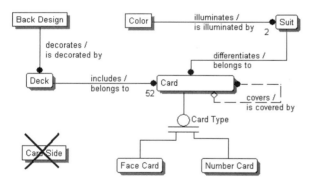

Figure 9-10. *Adding the Back Design relationships*

So now Card has all the relationships you found. Now you need to refresh the entity definition documentation and to start adding some attributes.

▓**Note** Every time you perform a task that adds value to the model, you may impact the results of a previous analysis step. Don't forget to update your model at each stage.

Analyzing the Card Entity Details

At this stage you have a list of the potential entities used in the Card subject area. Now you need to flesh out these entities by determining the appropriate attributes for each one. To begin adding the attributes, let's consider the complete list of the entities and their definitions you've drawn up for the Card subject area, as listed in Table 9-5.

Table 9-5. *Entities in the Card Subject Area with Definitions*

Object Name	Definition
Back Design	A pattern used to decorate one side of every card in the deck.
Card	One of 52 unique game pieces used in playing games bearing pictures of figures or numbers organized by suit. For example, the queen of clubs and the two of diamonds are cards.
Color	One of two hues, red and black, used in the definition of the suit of a card.
Deck	A complete set of four suits of thirteen cards, making a collection of fifty-two individual cards. This doesn't include jokers, instructions, and extra vendor cards.
Face Card	A card in a deck that has a figure pictured on the face.
Number Card	A card in a deck that doesn't have a figure pictured on the face.
Suit	One of four groups of cards: clubs, spades, hearts, and diamonds.

Try to start with an independent entity (one that has no parents), which are entities represented in IDEF1X by a graphic element of a box with square corners and no solid-line relationships connected to them. They contain records that can be created completely on their own (without dependencies on other data sets existing first), and they share their attributes only with the entities that are related to them. These are the simplest, most atomic lists of things in your model. Let's start with Color.

Color Analysis

At this point, you need to refer to the list of attribute types (classes) in Chapter 3 to give you the flavor of any given attribute and help you determine what the attributes are in this case. Remember, you need a high-level classification of data meaning, considering an attribute's use and definition. The list of attribute types can help you identify what attributes an entity might need or use. You can look over the list we're using in Table 9-6.

Table 9-6. *Class Word List*

Type Word	Meaning	Logical Data Domain
Amount	A monetary number.	Number
Code	An alphanumeric meaningful abbreviation.	Text
Date	A calendar date—month, day, year.	Date
Description	A textual account or portrayal.	Text
Flag	A one letter or number Boolean set.	Text
Identifier	A unique recognition tag in the form of a character and/or number, system-generated ID, or a globally unique identifier (GUID). This may be process driven or nonsensical and insignificant to the data user.	Text

Continued

Table 9-6. *Continued*

Type Word	Meaning	Logical Data Domain
Image	A nonlanguage visual object.	Blob
Name	A textual label.	Text
Number	A place in a sequence.	Number
Quantity	A number totaling a measurement by a unit.	Number
Sound	An aural resonating object.	Blob
Text	An unformatted language segment.	Text
Time	A moment such as hour, minute, second, and so on.	Time

Color Attributes

You've already identified the members of the set represented by the entity Color; they're Red and Black. You can see by reviewing the class words that the relevant attribute class is Name. Red and Black are valid values of the Color Name attribute. Put Color Name in the box signifying the Color entity, and add the data domain, which is Text or String with this modeling tool.

You need to keep in mind two important points when you begin to develop attributes for an entity. Attributes should be both single-valued and nonderivable. The best way to explain this is to show an instance table of something that breaks this rule.

Test for Single Values The best way to test your ideas about attributes is to gather a sample set of data from the field and review it to see if your understanding of the way the individual values combine is correct. Figure 9-11 shows an example of having too many values in an attribute. Modeling the first draft of the attributes of Back Design seems simple enough. You might be tempted to just start adding the basic attributes without really thinking about the reality of the values contained in those elements. This figure shows a basic rough draft of Back Design. Everything seems fine at the first review of the elements—at least nothing probably jumps out at us as being wrong.

Figure 9-11. *Rough draft of the entity Back Design*

It isn't until we review the instances of the records that are a part of this entity data set that we begin to see a potential problem. Review the instances in Table 9-7, and pay special attention to any cells containing commas, which generally note multiple values.

Table 9-7. *Sample Instance Table for the Draft of Back Design*

Back Design Name	Back Design Color Name	Back Design Description
Plain	Red	Solid color with no design background
Plaid	Blue, Green, Yellow	A geometric line design of overlapping bars of color
Country Scene	Blue, Green, Red, Brown	Hills and lake with a country road

We'd say that many back designs have a single color combined with a design that makes them more interesting. But the reality is that cards are often printed with a photograph or complicated scene to help market them. Back Design Color Name therefore can't be an owned attribute of Back Design. Back Design Color Name is quite likely owned by a separate entity that deals with the allowed multiplicity of Color to Back Design, as shown in Figure 9-12.

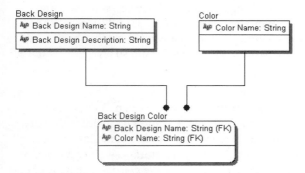

Figure 9-12. *Change to draft Back Design entity to allow for multiple colors*

Test for Derivability The second thing to watch out for in attributes is the derivable values. For instance, you may be tempted to model Card like Figure 9-13.

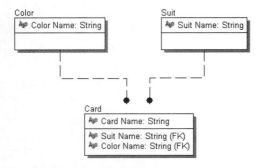

Figure 9-13. *Rough draft of the Card entity*

Again, this looks fine at first glance. What would be wrong with this? An instance table may help again, but you probably need many more records to recognize the patterns, dependencies, or formulas that denote a derived attribute. So let's just think about this one.

Look at Suit Name and Color Name. What are the rules regarding the type of cards used in Solitaire? Do you know the color name of the card if you know the suit? Of course you do. Hearts and diamonds are always red, and clubs and spades are always black. The Color Name attribute is owned by the entity Suit, not Card, as shown in Figure 9-14.

Figure 9-14. *Reworked draft of Card entity*

Derivable attributes have no real function in a Logical model. However, your team may choose to implement a physical column and maintain it with procedures and triggers. Attributes are the most basic things known about an entity; columns are locations for physicalized data values managed for performance, security issues, quality needs, and so on.

Color Key

The entity Color is pretty simple. You have only one attribute to work with, namely, Color Name. Since you can always determine the difference between Red and Black with the name, Color Name automatically becomes a candidate key. What would another candidate key be? You could create Color ID if it seems appropriate. Color Name is a natural key, since it exists as a real-world data element, but Color ID could be a surrogate key where you'd assign a number to a color to identify it. In the Logical model, try to avoid surrogate keys if you can; they're more often a change made specifically for the Physical model. Try to approach each entity list of candidate keys with an open mind. Neither choice (natural or surrogate) of key is always the answer. Allow yourself the flexibility to choose a key style based on your needs.

Let's promote Color Name from the candidate key to the primary key for the Logical model, moving Color Name above the line in the entity box of your software model, as shown in Figure 9-15.

Figure 9-15. *Color entity with the primary key in place*

■**Note** For a reminder of what constitutes candidate and primary keys, refer to Chapter 3. Remember, a candidate key is an attribute, or a combination of attributes, that can uniquely identify an instance of an entity. A primary key is the modeler's choice of which candidate key will uniquely identify an instance of an entity.

Color Definition

Now add your definition.

- **Color Name:** The textual label identifying one of two hues, red and black, used in the creation of the suit of a card.

Let's break this down to see what it tells you. The part of the definition that states "textual label" tells you that you need an attribute of type Name. "Identifying" tells you that Color Name is the primary key, and the rest of the sentence provides the definition of the entity Color as "one of two hues, red and black, used in the creation of the suit of a card."

Color Foreign Key

Having identified Color Name as the primary key of Color, and checking the relationships you defined for this subject area, the relationship between Color and Suit with the Color primary key in place now looks like Figure 9-16.

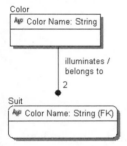

Figure 9-16. *Attributed Color entity related to Suit*

As you can see, you now have the first migrating attribute, since Color Name appears in the Suit entity too. The "FK" following Color Name indicates that Color Name is a foreign key in the Suit entity and will be automatically flagged with this tag by most modeling software.

Color Relationship Check

You need to determine whether the relationship between Color and Suit is an *identifying* or *nonidentifying* relationship. Deciding between these options means deciding whether you need the source data element to identify a member of the target set. In this case, the question is whether you need to know what color a suit is to identify it. Since clubs, hearts, diamonds, and spades are completely recognizable by the shape of the image or by the name text without specifying their color, the answer is no, and the relationship between Color and Suit is therefore nonidentifying. You can denote this relationship with a dashed line and move Color Name below the line in the Suit entity, as shown in Figure 9-17.

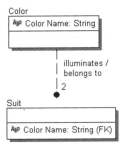

Figure 9-17. *Changing the relationship from identifying to nonidentifying*

Notice that when we changed the relationship from identifying to nonidentifying, the corners of the Suit entity changed. Suit is now an independent entity. It doesn't require a color to exist. Color Name isn't needed in order to find a member of the Suit set.

That concludes what you need to do for this entity. Each entity needs to follow the same steps:

- Determine the attributes.

- Determine the candidate keys.

- Determine the primary key.

- Write a definition for each attribute.

- Follow all the foreign keys to their destinations and check for identifying or nonidentifying status. (You may need to revisit this as you learn more about the related entities.)

Suit Analysis

Now let's consider Suit, and begin by looking at what attributes you have.

Suit Attributes

The set has four members: hearts, clubs, spades, and diamonds. These are the suit names (Suit Name), and each suit has a color (Color Name), which is the foreign key from Color. Is there anything else? How about that each suit has a special symbol? Let's add Suit Symbol Image as an attribute.

■**Note** You may be thinking that the attribute type Image is a bit redundant here, since Suit Symbol seems pretty self-explanatory. However, remember that Suit Symbol could be a description rather than an image, or it could be an ID in a symbol set. It could even be a text block where the history of the symbol is noted. Include the class word in the name you choose to reflect the type of data that will be represented here.

Suit Key

Now you have some choices. Suit Name identifies Suit, although Suit Symbol Image is unique and completely recognizable as well. You could also consider a Suit ID as a candidate, but we don't think it's necessary in this instance; Suit Name or Suit Symbol Image satisfies the test for natural keys in terms of existence and stability. Let's use Suit Name as the primary key (PK) and Suit Symbol Image as an alternate key (AK), as shown in Figure 9-18.

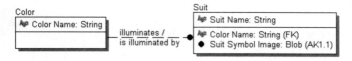

Figure 9-18. *Suit attributed with a primary key, foreign key, and alternate key*

Suit Definition

Make sure you have the data type domain from the attribute type list correctly documented, and write up the two new attribute definitions.

- **Suit Name:** The textual label identifying one of four groups of cards. They're clubs, spades, hearts, and diamonds.

- **Suit Symbol Image:** The nonlanguage visual object representing a suit in a deck of cards.

Suit Foreign Key

Having identified Suit Name as the primary key of Suit, and checking the relationships you've defined for Suit in this subject area, the relationship between Suit and Card now looks like Figure 9-19.

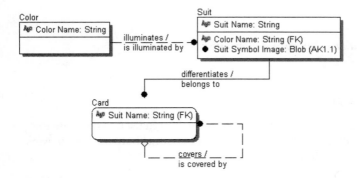

Figure 9-19. *Suit related by foreign key to Card*

Suit Relationship Check

Now you need to look at the relation from Suit to Card and whether that relationship seems to be identifying or nonidentifying.

Do you think you need to know a card's suit to identify the card? Is a queen or a nine enough to identify a card? No. Suit is definitely an identifying relationship, so note the relationship as identifying. The model stands as is.

Back Design Analysis

The next independent entity that's in the subject area is Back Design.

Back Design Attributes

Now let's look at the attributes for Back Design. Keep the clients in mind, and check with them about the necessity for this entity. They think they might want to see if the colors or images on the backs of the cards are of interest in their study. So they'll want to know what back design was chosen for the cards during a given game. (We suppose the palm trees might be viewed as an escapist image from work.) As far as attributes go, we can think only of a name and an image for Back Design. Let's name them and define them.

Back Design Key

What identifies a back design? You have two attributes and two candidate keys, because both will uniquely identify the back design. Back Design Name is one attribute that will work as a primary key. You can make the second attribute, Back Design Image, an alternate key. See the (AK1.1) notation in Figure 9-20? Alternate candidate keys can use multiple attributes in combination to create a unique key. The (AK1.1) notation designates that Back Design Image is the first attribute in the first defined alternate key.

Figure 9-20. *Back Design entity with a primary and alternate key*

Back Design Definition

Write up the two new attribute definitions.

- **Back Design Name:** The textual label identifying a single pattern used to decorate the reverse side of a deck of cards. For example, solid blue with a white border, exotic flowers, plaid, and a logo are all back design names.

- **Back Design Image:** The nonwritten visual pattern used to decorate the reverse side of a deck of cards.

Back Design Foreign Key

Having identified Back Design Name as the primary key of Back Design, and checking the relationships you defined for Back Design in this subject area, the relationship between Back Design and Deck looks like Figure 9-21.

Figure 9-21. *Relating Back Design to Deck*

Back Design Relationship Check

Now you need to look at the relation between Back Design and Deck and see whether that relationship seems to be identifying or nonidentifying. This is a tough one. You're working with a virtual deck of cards to begin with, so one could say there really aren't multiple members of the entity Deck. The only way to differentiate between the virtual decks seems to be through the choice of Back Design. Let's leave the Back Design to Deck relationship as identifying for now and check it again when you get to Deck.

Card Analysis

You can move on to look at Card, the first of the dependent entities (it's dependent because Suit Name is part of the key) and the first category with two subtype entities. Let's start by finding appropriate attributes for Card and its subtypes.

Card Attributes

You'll now look at Card, Number Card, and Face Card in a group because they're a special set of entities. They act like a family of entities with close ties to each other and are generally analyzed as a set.

You previously pulled out Face Card and Number Card as types, since they look different and act differently. As you begin to list the attributes, try to keep in mind that any attribute that applies to all members of the entity Card should be placed in the supertype entity. Any attributes that apply only to a specific type of card are placed in the subtype Face Card or Number Card. Look at the entity-level model of this category in Figure 9-22 to remind yourself of what you're working with.

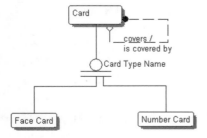

Figure 9-22. *Entity-level view of the Card category*

What attributes of the entity Card would you need to identify and describe? You already know that Suit Name will be an attribute. Card Name should probably be there as well, along with Card Type Name.

Ordering, or *precedence*, seems to be an important aspect of cards in the context of Solitaire: only certain cards are allowed to move, based on ascending or descending order. In the case of number cards, you know that their number value works to sort them in an order; 2-3-4 is very intuitive. Face cards are a little trickier, because unless you're familiar with the cards, you have no idea if a king is followed by a queen or a jack; K-Q-J is certainly not alphabetical or intuitive. So how do you set up the order? You need to know the name of each card's preceding card. What would examples of that look like? Let's make sure you understand the data (before you model it) by looking at another instance table in Table 9-8.

Table 9-8. *Instance Table Showing Relationship of Card to Card*

Card Type	Card Name	Preceding Card
Face	King	Queen
Face	Queen	Jack
Face	Jack	Ten
Number	Ten	Nine
Number	Nine	Eight
Number	Eight	Seven
Number	Seven	Six
Number	Six	Five
Number	Five	Four
Number	Four	Three
Number	Three	Two
Number	Two	Ace
Number	Ace	Precedes no other cards
Face	Ace	King

It looks like ace, when it's defined as a number card, has no preceding card. Face and number cards precede both face and number cards. So, sequencing isn't so simple after all, but there's definitely a sequential relationship between cards you need to model. This relationship between the cards is a recursive one, since one member of Card, as an entity, is related to another member of Card. This may mean you need a Before Card Name.

■**Note** You can read more about recursive relationships in Chapter 3.

So, if you place these attributes into the category structure, it might look like Figure 9-23.

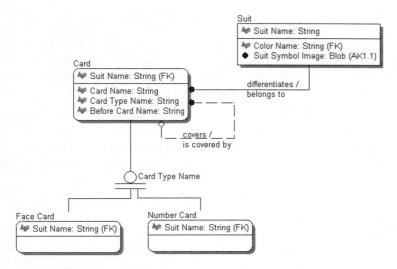

Figure 9-23. *Card category with new attributes*

Card Key

You've already decided that Suit Name is part of the Card entity's key. It does seem as though Card Name is also part of the key needed to make up a unique card. Do you also need Card Type? No. The cards are unique with a composite key of a Card Name and a Suit Name, as shown in Figure 9-24.

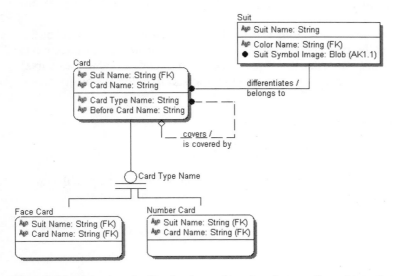

Figure 9-24. *Changing the Card primary key also changes the primary key of the subtype entities.*

See why entity definitions are so important? If you had defined Card as having 52 different names and used, as an example, the queen of hearts (which is truly a legitimate name even if it does combine data elements), you could have considered Card Name as a candidate key. As it is, you need both the Card Name and the Suit Name attributes to create a unique composite key. In other words, you need both pieces of information to identify one of the fifty-two members of the set Cards.

Caution Take special note of how every decision you're making impacts other places in the model other than just the single entity where you're making the changes. Changing one primary key can create large ripple effects in your model.

Card Relationship Foreign Key

The only foreign key relationship that Card has right now is a foreign key to itself. This is called a *recursive relationship*, and it requires some special handling of the migrating columns using a process called *role naming*.

Card Recursive Relationship When you drafted the subject area for Card, you included a relationship that connected Card to itself. You said that one card covered another to explain that cards can be ordered. Those of us who have played with this type of card take for granted that the ordering of cards is as follows: ace, king, queen, jack, ten, nine, eight, seven, six, five, four, three, and then two. But this may not be intuitive—not every card name in the set is based on a number. The game of Solitaire uses this ordering pattern (with one minor exception, the ace) to determine legal moves.

As we began to contemplate this ordering relationship, we thought *precedes* would be a much more descriptive verb for this recursion than *covers* (which came from the Conceptual model). The verb *covers* sounds more like what happens when you move a card in the course of a game, rather than describing the general rules pertaining to card order. The business rule will now read as follows:

- Each Card may precede one and only one Card.

- Each Card may be preceded by one and only one Card.

Not only is this a single parent hierarchy, but it's also a single child hierarchy, so the dot will have a *Z* next to it to qualify the daisy chain of cards, as shown in Figure 9-25.

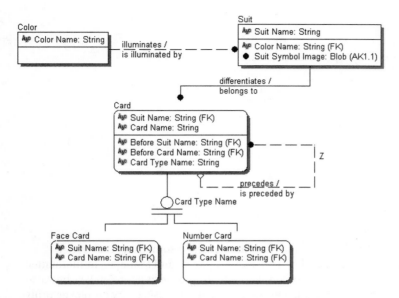

Figure 9-25. *Finalizing the recursive relationship of Card to Card*

Card Attribute Role Naming Role naming is the task you need to do in recursive relationships to allow the same attribute to reside multiple times in the same entity. The name is generally based on the business rule that requires the attribute to be included more than once.

When you added the recursive relationship to Card, you did it to be able to find the preceding card. You do this through attributes in the Card entity that link one Card to another. Now that you've defined the primary key of Card, you should end up with duplicate attributes named Card Name and Suit Name in the entity Card (because of the rules of migrating a key). If you were using a modeling tool (like us), you probably wondered why the duplicate set of attributes from the recursive relationship (Card Name and Suit Name) didn't show up. In most modeling tools, it's illegal for the same attribute to appear twice in the same entity. If an attribute has the same name as another in the same entity, the software assumes the reference to the second attribute is really referring to the first attribute. This isn't by accident or the result of a software feature; it's an IDEF1X rule that two attributes in the same entity can't have the same name. To support this recursive relationship, you role-name the second set of attributes, changing the attributes' names to Before Card Name and Before Suit Name. Because Before Suit Name and Before Card Name are attributes in this entity based on a relationship, they're now shown with the "FK" notation after them to mark them as migrating keys, as shown in Figure 9-26.

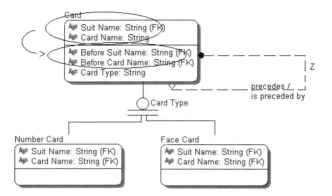

Figure 9-26. *The role-named attributes of the Card recursive relationship*

Role naming is actually a renaming of the attribute names to something that better describes the data element. For instance, let's consider Employee and Manager, implemented as a recursive relationship. Employee ID would migrate to Employee as a foreign key, because a manager is also an employee. Every employee has a manager ID. Also, every employee probably has an annual reviewer, the person who hired them, and possibly an administrative assistant (who are employees, too). So the entity Employee has recursive relationships resulting in role-named foreign keys of Manager Identifier, Hiring Manager Identifier, Annual Reviewer Identifier, and Administrative Assistant Identifier. They all link back to Employee ID, as shown in Figure 9-27.

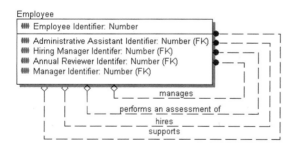

Figure 9-27. *An extreme example of recursion*

In this case, the second Card Name and Suit Name are there only to show the order of the cards. You need to change the names of the attributes to note their roles. A good verb phrase for the relationship can help make this clear. With some software tools you can even make the renamed attribute visible, as shown in Figure 9-28. This can come in handy when the role name isn't intuitive.

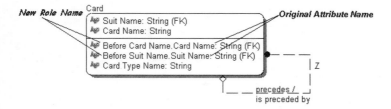

Figure 9-28. *Role names showing original name for reference*

Card Definition

The following are the definitions for Card:

- **Suit Name**: The textual label identifying one of four groups of cards. They're clubs, spades, hearts, and diamonds.

- **Card Name**: A textual label identifying one of thirteen cards. For example, the king, queen, eight, and ace are all card names.

- **Before Card Name**: The textual label noting the name of the card that a card comes after in a sequence of cards. This is the name of the card that precedes it.

- **Before Suit Name**: The textual label noting the suit of the card that a card comes after in a sequence of cards. This is the suit of the card that precedes it.

- **Card Type Name:** A textual label identifying cards as being either a number or a face card.

If you're using modeling software, the data domain will migrate to the new attribute of all foreign keys. If you're working this model by hand, you need to make *absolutely* sure that the data domain is the same as the source attribute.

Card Relationship Check

Did you find any attributes unique to Face Card or Number Card during the attribute discovery step? No? Then you may want to remove the categorization, since it doesn't seem useful at this point. The categories have neither owned attributes nor relationships that are unique to themselves. But you'll keep Card Type Name in the remaining Card entity so you can still differentiate between face and number cards, as shown in Figure 9-29 on the following page.

Now you need to look at that recursive relationship and the migrating key one last time. Answer honestly—do you really need to know the suit of a card to know the sequencing of the cards? Is the card order business rule that the king of hearts comes before the queen of hearts? Or just that kings come before queens? In reality, it's just the card face designator that determines card ordering, isn't it? And to really drive the point home, look at Card Type Name. Does the suit matter when determining whether a king is a face or number card? Of course not. If that's the case, you'd be breaking First Normal Form (1NF) to leave Card Type Name in the Card entity, because the Card Type Name attribute doesn't depend on the whole key. So, since the ordering of the cards during play is always the same regardless of suit, and the type code is always the same regardless of suit, you can connect the members of the entity Card in a sequence *without* regard to Suit.

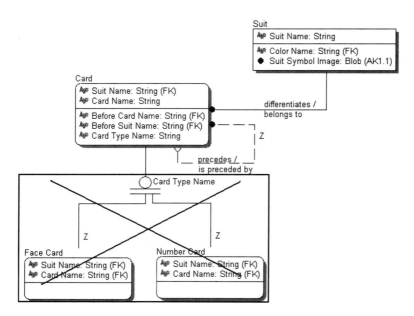

Figure 9-29. *Removing the subtype entities from the Card category*

You can see the entire Logical model as it now stands in Figure 9-30.

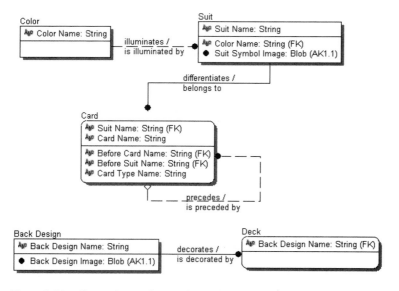

Figure 9-30. *All entities in the Card subject area on which you've worked*

If the notion of sequencing and differentiating number cards from face cards is really decided by the card name alone, then there must be an entity on the Logical model whose definition describes the members of a set, which is identified by the face designation of a card alone (without any suit relationship). This may be a difficult notion to absorb. Many entities you model "logically" seem completely illogical. It's entirely possibly you can't even separate the ideas of a card face and suit from each other because they don't exist in the real world. But the Logical model captures business rules that manage sets that don't exist in the real world. The sets are real. You discovered a partial key dependency and business rules that pertain to playing cards regardless of their suit affiliation. You have a new entity.

■Note This is how data modeling works. You suggest an attribute and the rules that apply. Then you start trying everything you know (or think you know) about the set members to see if it fits. When something doesn't totally pass the test, you back up and recheck the assumptions.

Let's now see what you need to do to create an entity dealing with the set of unique face values that, when combined with Suit, makes a card as we generally see it. In fact, let's call it Card Face, as that's part of what we differentiate on the face of the card. It needs a definition like this:

- **Card Face**: One of thirteen card designations. For example, the king, queen, eight, and ace are all card faces. Together they make the full complement of cards defined as a suit of cards.

And it needs a relationship to Card.

- A Card Face must identify one or more Cards.

- A Card must be identified by one and only one Card Face.

Card is now actually the intersection (association) between Card Face and Suit. So the model now looks like Figure 9-31.

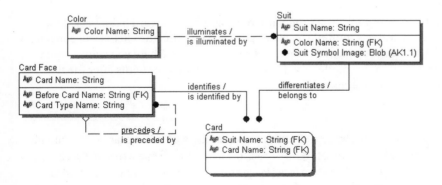

Figure 9-31. *Creating new entity Card Face and changing ownership of Card Type Name*

Deck Analysis

You have one final entity in the Card subject area. Let's look at Deck.

Deck Attributes

Now what are the attributes of Deck? The software version of Solitaire has only one Deck, and it doesn't have names, dates, numbers, or IDs. The only attribute that we can think of is Back Design Name.

Deck Key

What identifies a deck of cards? Even in real life, we can't think of anything that makes one deck of cards unique from another one. If the back design on multiple decks of cards is the same, you can combine them without an issue. Afterward, you'd probably be unable to separate them into their deck of origin. At least you wouldn't be sure what deck each card came from without coffee stains, age differences, or torn corners. When in doubt, you may want to put a placeholder in an entity just to say there must be something that identifies it and see to where the foreign key migrates. Let's add a Deck Key Identifier for that reason.

Deck Definition

Here are the definitions for the attributes of Deck:

- **Deck Identifier**: A unique recognition symbol for a complete set of four suits of thirteen cards, making a collection of fifty-two individual cards. This doesn't include jokers, instructions, and extra vendor cards.

- **Back Design Name**: The textual label identifying a single pattern used to decorate the reverse side of a deck of cards. For example, solid blue with a white border, exotic flowers, plaid, and a logo are all back design names.

Deck Foreign Key

Review the model. Is Deck important? It's the path to recognize that a card has a back design. We said the software version has multiple back designs. Do you think the clients will consider Back Design important? Maybe yes, maybe no. This could be a case where you want to note Deck as not being relevant to this model. You have to validate with the clients after the first pass at getting the attributes together anyway.

■**Note** You'll find logical entities that have no attributes or don't make sense as a managed set of records. These entities may be important for future data development, but they often are removed from the Logical model; they're interesting but unused. If they're needed in the next phase, then the clients may need to review their business processes to create new data for this section of the model.

So, at this stage, let's say there's no data of interest about a deck, with the exception that there has to be a deck to play a game, and cards are part of a deck. You'll denote this on the model with a shadow entity.

- A Deck must include one or more Cards.

- A Card must be included in one and only one Deck.

Shadow Entities A *shadow entity* is an entity included in a model but isn't fully analyzed. Shadow entities are often placeholders or interface points with other systems or entities that may become important in future. The details of their structure are out of scope for the model in question. Shadow entities serve a couple of purposes. When you're creating your Logical model and you're suddenly faced with a seemingly important entity that you can't seem to find anything specific to document, then you may have a shadow entity. For instance, a Logical model of a hotel booking service may include shadow entities for transportation-type entities such as airlines, trains, buses, or taxis. This might be done in order to later explore the relationships of scheduled arrival/departure times to guest check-in/check-out schedules. Having the shadow entities on the model reminds everyone of this potential future link. An entity could be a shadow entity if it's easily recognizable as being owned by a different project team. In that case, you'd just need to put a placeholder in your model until the other project team is through with its analysis.

■**Note** You'll even find shadow tables on the Physical model. They're tables that are integrated in some fashion but aren't built or owned by the project. You may need to document relationships to them and ultimately build physical constraints in your model to support them, but you'll never create them from the Data Definition Language (DDL) generated from your model.

Don't be afraid to document shadow entities in your model. Seeing them documented gives the clients a comfortable feeling that you haven't left something out and that you know about things that are beyond the project's current scope.

Deck Relationship Check

You've added a shadow entity for Deck to document that it's a valid concept for the Card subject area. Now that you've defined Deck Identifier as the key of Deck, Back Design Name no longer seems a good choice as an identifying attribute of Deck. Change the Back Design to Deck relationship to nonidentifying.

Figure 9-32 shows the Card subject area after all your hard work.

In reality, you'd hardly ever have entities float down from the Conceptual model to a subject area like Card did in this case. However, using the Conceptual model from the previous chapter has helped you focus enough to complete one portion of the Solitaire Logical model.

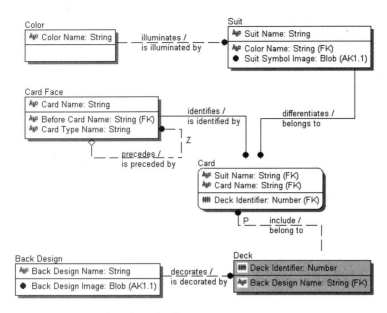

Figure 9-32. *Completed Card subject area*

Card Subject Area Review

When you've completed the first draft of a subject area, you may want to set up another couple of reviews to validate your work. Subject areas often align themselves to experts in that portion of the model. Subject matter experts (SME) often have limited time and appreciate not having to review everything. Before the review, check everything one last time.

- Does every entity and attribute have a good name? A class word? A definition?

- Does every relationship have a strong verb phrase?

- Have you really thought about relationship cardinality? Optionality? Identifying relationships vs. nonidentifying relationships?

- Does every entity have a primary key defined? Have you identified the alternate keys?

- Did you specify role names for every attribute appearing in an entity multiple times? Did you change the definitions of these attributes to clarify their roles?

- Do you have a title for the subject area? Date? Notes?

- Is the diagram as clear, clean, and easy to follow as you can make it?

You can answer these questions for Card, so you can move onto the Card Movement subject area.

Modeling Card Movement Subject Area

The Card Movement subject area addresses the movements of cards between card locations and the rules regarding allowed plays. Review the subject area scope by reading the definitions in Table 9-9 of the two Conceptual model entities and referring to the relationships currently modeled.

Table 9-9. *Card Movement Subject Area Entity Definitions*

Entity Name	Definition
Play	A play is completed when the entire set of available cards is assessed, resulting in a move or pass during a game of Solitaire.
Card Pile	A temporary and changeable area used to process a collection of cards that behave differently in the game of Solitaire. A card pile doesn't have to have a card in it to exist. For example, the draw pile, discard pile, and processing pile are all card piles.

This time you have two Conceptual model entities to analyze (Card Pile and Play), which together will form the Card Movement subject area.

Analyzing Card Pile

Figure 9-33 is a picture of card piles for you to review. Make a list of the things (nouns and concepts) you find.

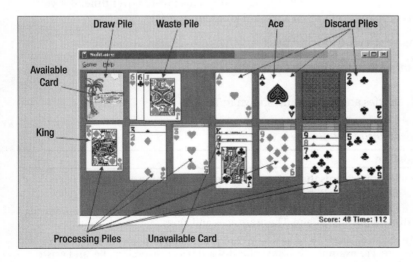

Figure 9-33. *Things of interest in a game of Solitaire*

From Figure 9-33, you might find the following items of interest:

- Discard pile
- Draw pile
- Waste pile
- Processing pile

- Available card
- Unavailable card
- King
- Ace

Note Note that you need to get used to the jargon of your clients while you're modeling for a larger audience. In this list we've used the general term *discard pile*, also described as a *foundation pile* in the book *Official Rules of Card Games*, 74th edition (International Playing Card Company, 1991). You need to balance client jargon against the wider readability of your model.

You'll see a lot of repetition in these titles. Pile is there four times. Card is there twice but only in the context of the valid moves within a game, and because you aren't capturing all the rules of Solitaire, you can ignore it. Kings and aces seem to be there only because they're special cards that begin a processing pile and a discard pile, respectively. We listed them because we discovered they were special when we looked at the rules of the game and because the clients may want to gather statistics about events that occur within those areas. Not all rules are discovered at the beginning of your analysis; they're often discovered over time. But you know from the list you compiled earlier that aces and kings are special.

- Only aces can move to empty discard piles.
- Only kings can move to empty processing piles.

So, let's begin with entities and definitions, shown in Table 9-10.

Table 9-10. *Card Movement Entity Definitions*

Entity Name	Definition
Card Pile	A collection of cards that behave differently in the game of Solitaire. For example, the draw pile, discard pile, and processing pile are all card piles.
Pile Start Card	One of two styles of cards, allowed to change positions to an empty processing or discard pile in Solitaire. These are aces and kings.
Card Pile Type	One of several activity areas where card processing happens in the game of Solitaire. For example, the draw pile, discard pile, processing pile, and waste pile are all card pile types.

Card Movement Category Analysis

Now let's look to see if there are any categories (subtype and supertype groupings) in this list of potential entities by reviewing their names and definitions. See the clue word *type* in Card Pile Type? That should be a signal you might need to split an entity into discrete subsets. You even have the list of subsets in the definition of Card Pile Type: discard, draw, waste, and processing. Do they follow the rules for needing a category?

- They behave similarly.

- They behave only slightly differently.

- They share some attributes.

- They have some different attributes.

- The clients expect to see them grouped together.

Based on this criteria, they seem to meet all the requirements to be members of a category (subtypes of a supertype called Card Pile). Consider these pile types to be a potential category as you continue the analysis. If they're going to become entities in their own right, you need to define them so you know what they are (especially since we changed their technical names).

- **Draw Pile**: The location in Solitaire where a card is stored until such time as it's moved to the waste pile for processing.

- **Waste Pile**: The location of activity in Solitaire where a card is made available for play in a cyclic manner until they've all been processed. A card may return to the draw pile when the draw pile has been completely moved to the waste pile but not all the waste pile cards have been processed.

- **Discard Pile**: The location of the activity in Solitaire where a card is removed completely from play. Only an ace can begin a discard pile.

- **Processing Pile**: The location of the activity in Solitaire where cards are matched from the draw pile according to the playing rules. All processing piles are originally set up through the layout of a game. If during the processing of the card a pile is emptied, then a king may be moved to the pile position and used to process more cards.

From what you know at the moment, there are no other pile types, so the category is complete. The entities and category relationship leave you without a need for the Card Pile Type entity, since it has been replaced by the category structure discriminator for Card Pile, (namely, Card Pile Type Name). You can delete Card Pile Type from the entity list. This leaves you with the entities shown in Table 9-11 within the subject area.

Table 9-11. *Expanded Entity Set for Card Movement Subject Area*

Entity Name	Definition
Pile Start Card	One of two styles of cards, allowed to change positions to an empty processing or discard pile in Solitaire. These are aces and kings.
Card Pile	One of several activity areas where card processing happens in the game of Solitaire. For example, the draw pile, discard pile, and processing pile are all card piles.
Draw Pile	The location in Solitaire where a card is stored until such time as it's moved to the waste pile for processing.

Continued

Table 9-11. *Continued*

Entity Name	Definition
Waste Pile	The location of the activity in Solitaire where a Card is made available for play in a cyclic manner until they have all been processed. A card may return from the Waste pile to the Draw pile when the Draw pile has been completely moved to the Waste pile, but not all the Waste pile cards have been processed.
Discard Pile	The location of the activity in Solitaire where a card is removed completely from play. Only an ace can begin a discard pile.
Processing Pile	The location of the activity in Solitaire where cards are matched from the draw pile according to playing rules. All processing piles are originally set up through the layout of a game. If during the processing of the card a pile is emptied, then a king may be moved to the pile position and used to process more cards.

Card Pile Relationships

Now let's analyze how these entities might relate to each other.

Card Pile to Pile Start Card

Let's review the definitions.

- **Card Pile**: One of several activity areas where card processing happens in the game of Solitaire. For example, the draw pile, discard pile, and processing pile are all card piles.

- **Pile Start Card**: One of two styles of cards, allowed to change positions to an empty processing or discard pile in Solitaire. These are aces and kings.

It seems that some of the card piles have specific rules about what card can be used to start the pile, so there must be some kind of relationship between the piles and a specific start card. Review the rules if you need to refresh your memory. Pile Start Cards are kings and aces. Do they always relate to Card Pile in exactly the same manner? (In other words, is the relationship from the Card Pile entity or from one of the subtypes?) No, there's a difference; aces begin discard piles, and kings sometimes begin processing piles. Since these members of the Pile Start Card set behave slightly differently in the business world, this makes them another category.

We know these look like single values. But if you need to show detailed relationships like this to your audience, then you have to break them out. Sometimes you have to go all the way down to this level of detail in the Logical model design. You need only one member, one record, or one instance to create a mathematical set. Create a category out of Ace and King, with Pile Start Card as the supertype. Now set up the relationships.

- Each Ace may begin zero, one, or more Discard Piles.

- Each Discard Pile must be started by one and only one Ace.

- Each King may begin zero, one, or more Processing Piles.

- Each Processing Pile may be started by zero or one Kings.

Each of these relationships are to a category subtype and are therefore nonidentifying. A member of a true subset can't be identified in a different manner from the set to which it belongs. Figure 9-34 shows the first draft of the new category and its relationships.

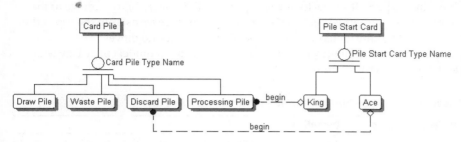

Figure 9-34. *Draft of two categories with relationships at the subtype level*

Card Relationship Optionality

Let's pause to consider the "may" portion of the sentence in the King to Processing Pile business rule. Optionality is described by the "may" or "must" part of the business rule. Optionality rules are always concerned with the parent side of the relationship (where the foreign key originates) and notes the mandatory or nonmandatory rule for the migration of the source data. The optionality rules are as follows:

Identifying relationship: This is always mandatory. The primary key from the parent entity migrates as a foreign key to the primary key area of the child entity. The foreign key is NOT NULL, and the child is dependent upon the parent for both its identification and existence.

Nonidentifying/mandatory relationship: The primary key of the parent entity migrates as a foreign key to the nonkey area of the child entity. The foreign key is NOT NULL, and the child is dependent upon the parent for its existence only.

Nonidentifying/optional relationship: The primary key of the parent entity migrates as a foreign key to the nonkey area of the child entity. The foreign key can be defined as NULL, in which case there's no dependency from the child to parent entity at all. There's no relationship when the foreign key value isn't specified, but when the key value *is* specified, it must reference a valid parent.

Most modeling software will default to either mandatory or nonmandatory relationships from the source. Be wary of defaulting. If you're aren't careful, you'll forget to change the default value to what you mean it to be.

Analyzing Play

Now you have to do the same thing for Play. Here's the definition:

- **Play**: A play is a sequence of moves ending with a single pass, which results in the entire set of available cards being assessed.

Let's consider the concepts of Play, Move, and Pass. You might also consider things involved in creating the setup of the cards such as Shuffle, Layout, and Deal. A play seems to stand on its own as a collection of moves, and a move stands on its own as an event of card movement, but what's a pass? It seems to us that a pass is either the inability to move or the choice not to move any more cards and to select the next card three cards from the top of the draw pile. A pass could be considered a special type of play that has no moves.

Let's start the Logical model entity list based on the Conceptual model entity Play with the entities and definitions shown in Table 9-12.

Table 9-12. *Entities and Their Definitions for the Conceptual Entity Play*

Entity (Logical Element) Name	Definition
Play	A move or series of moves beginning with a play shuffle and completed when the entire set of available cards is assessed. Not all available cards must be moved, even if there's a legal move available before the player begins a new play by choosing to refresh the waste pile with a new set of cards provided from a deal of the draw pile.
Move	The change in location of a single card from one card pile to another one.
Deal	The movement of three new cards from the draw pile to the waste pile.

Play Relationships

Let's see how these entities are related.

Play to Move

First, review the definitions.

- **Play**: A move or series of moves beginning with a play shuffle and completed when the entire set of available cards is assessed. Not all available cards must be moved, even if there's a legal move available before the player begins a new play by choosing to refresh the waste pile with a new set of cards provided from a deal of the draw pile.

- **Move**: The change in location of a single card from one card pile to another one.

This relationship almost writes itself from the definitions:

- Each Play may include zero, one, or many Moves.

- Each Move must be part of one and only one Play.

Play to Deal

The following are the definitions:

- **Play**: A move or series of moves beginning with a play shuffle and completed when the entire set of available cards is assessed. Not all available cards must be moved, even if there's a legal move available before the player begins a new play by choosing to refresh the waste pile with a new set of cards provided from a deal of the draw pile.

- **Deal**: The movement of three new cards from the draw pile to the waste pile.

Again, you can see the relationship clearly defined in the definition of Play. Good definitions are invaluable.

- Each Play must begin with one and only one Deal.

- Each Deal must begin one and only one Play.

Oops, this is a one-to-one relationship! You need to check whether this means both entities are really representing the same thing with different names. Look at the definitions again. Are they the same? If you have 32 plays in a Solitaire game, how many deals will you have gone through? Thirty-two, right? The really important question is, are you actually interested in capturing information about a deal? Think back to the scope. The psychology department wants to capture information about each game but to what degree? Do they need every move of every card captured?

Sometimes you can get so caught up in an analysis that you'll forget to step back and remind yourself what the objectives are. The scope has been defined such that you want to model the game with an emphasis on its relationship to a player, so you don't need to worry about Deal, or indeed Shuffle or Layout. If you were modeling the process of Solitaire to create a Solitaire application, then that would be a different matter; all of these would become important again. In the scope, plays and the moves they're made up of are important but only from the perspective of what card moved and to where. The clients don't expect to be able to capture options prior to moves. They don't really care if a person is a good Solitaire player. They just want to know what cards are being played, how many moves were made in the game, and whether the player won or lost.

Combining Card Movement

We had to cover more than one Conceptual model entity in this section because both of them were included in this subject area, so you have to look at whether there are relationships between the two sets of entities discovered. (Let's also reduce the detail a little and begin by using just the parent-to-child verb phrase on the relationship line, as shown in Figure 9-35.)

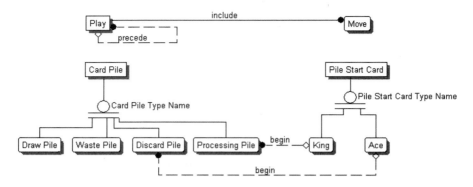

Figure 9-35. *Movement subject area entities*

What would the relationships between these entities be? It looks to us as though we need to relate Move to the Card Pile entities. What do you know from the analysis? Moves happen as an impact within and between all card piles. Any relationship between them will be at the Card Pile level rather than at the level of any of the subtypes. Therefore, two relationships exist. You might come up with something like this:

- Each Move must start at one and only one Card Pile.
- Each Card Pile must begin zero, one, or many Moves.
- Each Move must complete in one and only one Card Pile.
- Each Card Pile must complete zero, one, or many Moves.

A move also needs a card, doesn't it? Let's go ahead and relate the Card subject area and the Movement subject area right now before we forget.

- Each Card must be used in zero, one, or many Moves.
- Each Move must move one and only one Card.

That brings you to Figure 9-36, as shown on the following page.

Now before you add all the details, let's review the model again. Can you simplify it? Is anything out of scope? Are all these sets important to the process of Solitaire as it applies to the needs of the clients? The clients don't seem to want to capture or test whether a player is making correct moves or if the potential moves are legal. In that case, you don't need any logical structures relating to the rules of play—just the entities about the events in a game. As a result, Pile Start Card, King, and Ace can be shadowed out, or even deleted, as shown in Figure 9-37.

You're going to hear us say this repeatedly: modeling is an iterative process. You put things in your model, and you take them back out of your model. When you're going to remove several entities from your design, you may want to save a prior version in order to capture your analysis. You never know when you might want or need to bring those structures back.

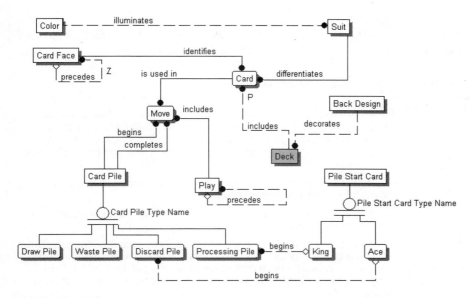

Figure 9-36. *Adding the Card subject area to the Card Movement subject area*

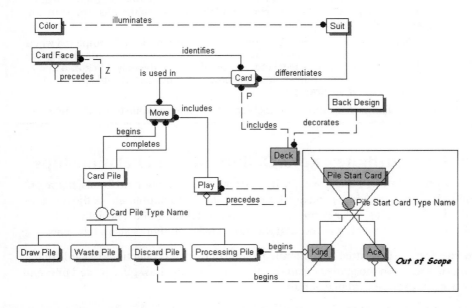

Figure 9-37. *Reducing the entities on the Logical model to match the original scope*

Card Movement Entity Details

Now let's define the Movement Subject area in more detail. Table 9-13 shows what the glossary looks like now. You need to find the attributes for each of the entities.

Table 9-13. *Card Movement Subject Area Entity Definitions*

Object Name	Definition
Card Pile	A temporary and changeable area used to process a collection of cards that behave differently in the game of Solitaire. A card pile doesn't have to have a card in it to exist. For example, the draw pile, discard pile, and processing pile are all card piles.
Discard Pile	The location of the activity in Solitaire where a card is removed completely from play. Only an ace can begin a discard pile.
Draw Pile	The location in Solitaire where a card is stored until such time as it's moved to the waste pile for processing.
Processing Pile	The location of the activity in Solitaire where cards are matched from the draw pile according to the playing rules. All processing piles are originally set up through the layout of a game. If during the processing of the card a pile is emptied, then a king may be moved to the pile position and used to process more cards.
Waste Pile	The location of activity in Solitaire where a card is made available for play in a cyclic manner until they've all been processed. A card may return to the draw pile when the draw pile has been completely moved to the waste pile but not all the waste pile cards have been processed.
Play	A move or series of moves beginning with a play shuffle and completed when the entire set of available cards is assessed. Not all available cards must be moved, even if there's a legal move available before the player begins a new play by choosing to refresh the waste pile with a new set of cards provided from a deal of the draw pile.
Move	The change in location of a single card from one card pile to another one.

Looking at the Attributes, Keys, Definitions, and Relationships

This time let's try to go through the process a little faster. Decide on your attributes, figure out what identifies the instances, write good attribute definitions, and double-check the relationships to and from the entities. Refer to the list of class words for Card Pile. The definition example tells you there's certainly a name, and the model tells you there's also a type name.

- **Card Pile Name**: The textual label identifying one of thirteen collections of cards that behave differently in the game of Solitaire. For example, the draw pile, discard pile, and processing pile are all card pile names.

- **Card Pile Type Name**: The textual label identifying a collection of cards that behave differently in the game of Solitaire. For example, the draw pile, discard pile, and processing pile are all card pile type names.

Now you have a problem, since these two attribute definitions are almost the same. This is a case where some of the constituents of the set are actually named by the type label. This category structure is defined at such a level of detail that the type is the same as the name. Of course, when dealing with pretty small sets, such problems do arise in real life. For example, take the list of states and territories in the United States. The District of Columbia has different business rules about legal matters than Oregon does. Also, differences exist between the states and territories such as the Virgin Islands, Guam, American Samoa, and the trust territories of the Pacific Islands (Palau Islands). If your clients are interested in specific legalities in these areas, you may need to note territories as a separate category, differentiating them from the rest of the 50 states. However, in this example there isn't an overall name you can give to the type. Each one is a type unto itself. Although you can divide normal States category from US Territories as a first differentiation, you may need to subdivide the US Territory category further, which may leave you with each set having a single member.

There doesn't seem to be much to know about card piles since you aren't concerned with the rules of Solitaire. It seems to be pretty obvious that the card pile name is the primary key in this case. At this point, you're probably wondering why we're leaving Card Pile as a category at all. Since this is a Logical model, we're still convinced that leaving the category in the model will be useful and that you should document and share it with the clients during the reviews. You'll explore options on how to design a Physical model table for this category in the next chapter.

Note We keep telling you to simplify your model, but there's also another consideration. You must leave details in your model that you think are going to be important. This is part of the art of data modeling.

Now let's look at Play and Move. What do you know about a play? Plays are a sequence of events in a game, so there's quite likely a means of ordering them. You can do this by capturing the time of a move, or, in this case, since you're in manual mode, you'll just order them by number. You really aren't interested in the specific times when the moves have been made; you just care about the order of the moves within a game.

Is there anything else? You could count the moves to find out how many were part of a given play. Unless the client is using a stopwatch, it's hard to imagine capturing any time duration. A play's sequence number should be unique within one game, but looking at the design it becomes apparent you'll need a combination of Game and the sequence to create a completely unique key over time. The key *must* include Game in order to be able to store more than one game's worth of information. But the sequence is still part of the key, so put Play Sequence Number in the key position.

Make sure you role-name the two card piles involved in Move to Begin Card Pile Name and End Card Pile Name so that you can see them nonunified by the software. Then review the key.

- **Play Sequence Number**: The order in which a play occurs in a game

Figure 9-38 shows where you are right now.

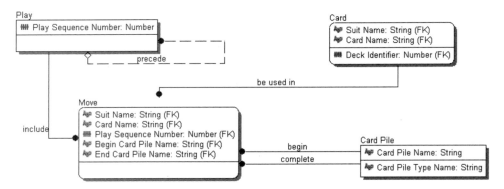

Figure 9-38. *Attribution of Move and Play*

If you now consider the Move entity, you already have quite a collection of attributes. You've gathered the play, the card, and the two card piles with which Move interacts. Plays come in order in a game. Moves come in order in a play. Let's add Move Sequence Number. Figure 9-39 shows the resultant diagram.

- **Move Sequence Number**: The order in which a move occurs in a play

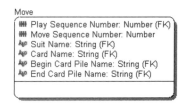

Figure 9-39. *Proposed key for the Move entity*

If you know the play sequence number and the move sequence number, do you need to also know the card piles or card involved to make an instance of a move unique? Let's check and see (refer to Table 9-14).

Table 9-14. *Sample Instance Table for the Move Entity*

Play Sequence Number	Move Sequence Number	Card Name	Suit Name	Begin Card Pile Name	End Card Pile Name
1	1	Queen	Heart	Processing	Processing
1	2	Ace	Club	Waste	Discard
1	3	9	Diamond	Processing	Processing
2	1	5	Club	Processing	Processing
2	2	5	Club	Processing	Processing

If you look at the data here, it seems you need only Play Sequence Number and Move Sequence Number to make a record unique, even in the last example where the player moved the five of clubs twice in a row from the processing pile to processing pile.

By the way, from the data in Table 9-14, you probably noticed that you can't tell which of the processing piles a move affects. You need to add the processing pile number to Move to document exactly which processing piles are the beginning and ending card piles of a move. But these attributes need to allow NULL values since the concept of a pile number applies only to processing piles.

- **Begin Card Pile Name**: The textual label identifying one of thirteen collections of cards that behave differently in the game of Solitaire. For example, the draw pile, discard pile, and processing pile are all the beginning places of the card being moved.

- **Begin Card Pile Number**: The number differentiating a processing pile that's the beginning place of the card being moved.

- **End Card Pile Name**: The textual label identifying one of thirteen collections of cards that behave differently in the game of Solitaire. For example, the draw pile, discard pile, and processing pile are all the ending places of the card being moved.

- **End Card Pile Number**: The number differentiating a processing pile that's the ending place of the card being moved.

Looking at these definitions, this means you need to change the relationships of Card Pile and Card to Move from identifying to nonidentifying ones.

Card Movement Subject Area Review

You've knocked off another subject area. Review all the points you looked at before. Double-check the following:

- **Names of the entities**: Are they all singular?

- **Names of the attributes**: Are they descriptive, even when standing alone? Do they all have class words? Did you specify role names?

- **Definitions for both entities and attributes**: Are they complete?

- **The relationships**: Is it identifying or nonidentifying? Are cardinality and optionality specified? Do the verb phrases use active voice?

Figure 9-40 shows what the model looks like now.

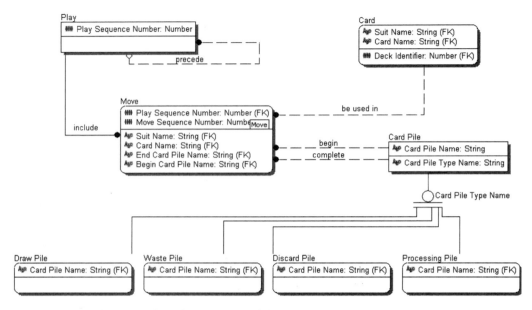

Figure 9-40. *Final version of Card Movement subject area*

Modeling the Event Subject Area

The Event subject area was determined to be a completed event of a single game of Solitaire, including the person involved. You can begin by reviewing the Conceptual model entities in the subject area in Table 9-15. Remember that you scoped out Playing Area, so it's just here as a reference.

Table 9-15. *The Conceptual Entities and Definitions for the Event Subject Area*

Object Name	Definition
Game	A contest played for sport or amusement (according to rules) made up of many small decisions that affect the outcome.
Person	A potential participant in a study being conducted by the psychology department.
Playing Area	A physical location such as a table or a virtual location such as a computer screen where the game is being played.

Analyzing the Event Entity

The Conceptual model's entities in this subject area—Game and Person—should be a breeze. As you iterate through an analysis, your job should become easier and easier. You learn so many things early on in an analysis that continue to be true with each iteration. You now have experience with Solitaire, so you should feel comfortable drawing on your memories about the games as distinct events. What important words come to mind? We're thinking about Game, Win, Lose, and Quit, which probably could be grouped together like so:

- Game

- Ending Game State

Person is a little more difficult. You know that Solitaire doesn't seem to care about the person. There's no login and no score keeping. There's no data of interest captured about a person—only that there has to be a person to play a game. Data about the person will have to come from outside the business process you're analyzing. This means you'll have to ask the clients if they have any specific need for information. They may have forgotten to get back to you about what they're going to need. Make sure to send them a reminder that you still need that information.

Note Don't be surprised if you even have to find data elements outside the walls of your company. Internet data use is becoming more and more popular, and departments buy many data sets from outside vendors such as the U.S. Post Office.

So, shadow out Person for the moment; you'll review this with the clients at the model review. Table 9-16 shows the entity definitions (we're leaving the shadows in for the moment).

Table 9-16. *Entity Definitions for Event Subject Area*

Object Name	Definition
Game	A contest played for sport or amusement (according to rules) made up of many small decisions that affect the outcome.
Ending Game State	The state of concluding a game of Solitaire. For example, win, lose, and quit are all ending game states.
Person	A participant or potential participant in a study being conducted by the psychology department.
Playing Area	A physical location such as a table or a virtual location such as a computer screen where the game is being played.

Analyzing the Event Relationships

You may have noted that you still have some relationships left over from the Conceptual model. That's because the Conceptual model entities don't break down much further. You don't have to reinvent anything you already know.

Game to Person

What are the business rules between Game and Person?

- Each Person may play zero, one, or many Games.

- Each Game must be played by one, and only one, Person.

Game to Ending Game State

Let's now look at Game to Ending Game State.

- Each Ending Game State may document zero, one, or many Games.

- Each Game must conclude with one and only one Ending Game State.

The only games being captured are completed ones, so every game must have an ending game state, as shown in Figure 9-41.

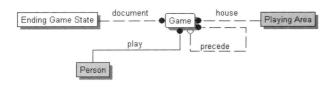

Figure 9-41. *Entity-level diagram for Event subject area*

Attributes, Keys, Definitions, and Relationships

You don't know about Person or Playing Area right at the moment. So those entities could be empty until the clients tell you otherwise. We have a tendency to show an ID primary key in grayed-out entities just to be able to speak to the foreign key relationships that are there logically and to test them for identification status.

- **Person ID**: A nonsignificant value uniquely identifying a person who is a participant or potential participant in a study being conducted by the psychology department.

- **Playing Area ID**: A nonsignificant value uniquely identifying a playing area, which is a physical location such as a table or a virtual location such as a computer screen where the game is being played.

As these IDs are the only attributes in their entities, let's make them the primary keys. Game seems really important to me, but it sure doesn't seem to have an identifier. Perhaps there are interesting things to know concerning the date/time?

- **Game Start Date**: The month, day, and year when the game began

- **Game Start Time**: The 24-hour clock for the hour, minute, and second of the day when the game began

- **Game End Date**: The month, day, and year when the game completed

- **Game End Time**: The 24-hour clock for the hour, minute, and second of the day when the game completed

Out of these attributes, what could act as the identifier? The Start attributes might work. But we're beginning to think you might want Person to help identify the Game. What about Person ID and Start Date/Time? We can't imagine being able to begin two games of Solitaire at exactly the same time. Leave the relationship of Person to Game as an identifying one (a solid line).

Many times you'll see date and time noted as a single attribute. This is perfectly valid, but we usually don't do this anymore when we're Logically modeling, as it hides the data element of time. So why not just keep them separate until you transform your Logical model to a Physical model? During the Physical model creation process, you'll think about the physical design options. On the other hand, you may want to simplify the attributes as much as possible for your clients. Like we said before, this is a judgment call.

Ending Game State should have at least a name. States or statuses in general should also always have a description to document the meaning of the status.

- **Ending Game State Name**: A textual label uniquely identifying the concluding state of a game

- **Ending Game State Description**: A nonstructured textual account of the concluding state of a game

Event Subject Area Review

Double-check everything. We would have reminded you that you need a role name here for the recursive Game to Game relationship, but we think we've just made it redundant. If the person, date, and time identify a game, then you can derive which game preceded another without a recursive relationship. This recursive relationship is still valid for the Conceptual model, but let's remove it for the Logical model, as shown in Figure 9-42.

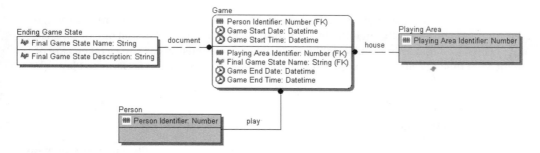

Figure 9-42. *Fully attributed Event subject area*

Putting It All Together: The Full Picture

Let's look at the three subject areas (Card, Movement, and Event) on one model (see Figure 9-43). Card, Movement, and Event are floating loosely together in space like subassemblies in manufacturing. But it's really beginning to look like a Logical data model.

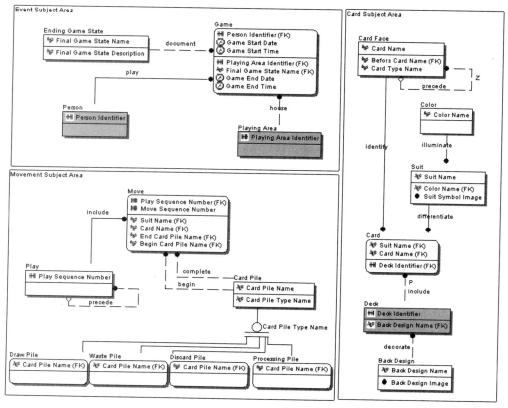

Figure 9-43. *All subject areas together in the Logical model*

Return to the Conceptual model for a moment to remind yourself of where you thought the connections lay. Go through the relationships on the Conceptual model one by one. We think you'll find that either you've deliberately deleted relationships or you've taken care of them all in the Logical model except one. The only one left to work out is Game to Play.

Relating Game to Play

What are the definitions of the entities?

- **Game:** A contest played for sport or amusement (according to rules) made up of many small decisions that affect the outcome.

- **Play:** A move or series of moves beginning with a play shuffle and completed when the entire set of available cards is assessed. Not all available cards may be moved even if there's a legal move available before the player begins a new play by choosing to refresh the waste pile with a new set of cards provided from a deal of the draw pile.

It seems to be as simple as this:

- Each Game must be made up of zero, one, or more Plays.

- Each Play must be part of one and only one Game.

Adding that relationship connects all the entities into a cohesive story about the entities and their respective data elements in regard to Solitaire. Figure 9-44 shows the Logical model.

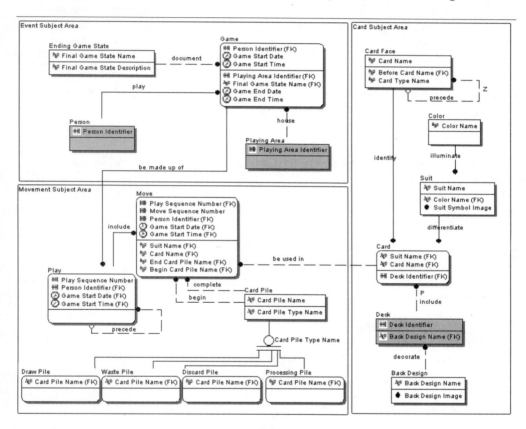

Figure 9-44. *Putting all the subject areas together and connecting Event to Movement*

Performing Quality Assurance Checks

Before you can deliver the model to your clients and do a model walk-through, you need to do some quality checking. You should consider the model as a prototype, which you need to subject to further review over time.

Checking for 1NF

You may be wondering how we could have gotten this far without really talking about the normal forms as they apply to the structure. It seems to us that if you can conceptualize every entity as a set of things, then as a natural outcome of the process, you'll generally be able to fulfill the requirements of normal forms as you work on your model. Remember, however, that normal forms are the cornerstone of what we do. You're gathering the data and grouping it into sets that meet these rules of conduct. Review the model once more to see if you're on target. You built the Logical model without explicitly using the normal form yardstick. Now let's try to break our model by comparing it to the business rules, which in this case are the rules of the game. And, trust us; if you stick to them, you'll stay out of so much trouble in the physicalization stage.

▪Note If you need to refresh your memory, then refer to Chapter 2 for a more detailed discussion about normal forms.

Let's review the normal forms against the Game entity in Figure 9-45 and see how it stands up.

Figure 9-45. *Broken Game entity*

First Normal Form (1NF) demands that every member of the set is the following:

- Depends on the *key*

- Is unique and uniquely identified

- Can be identified forever by the same values of the same sets of attributes

- Has no repeaters of anything either internally to an attribute or by having multiple attribute groups

It also means that if you choose to use a surrogate key (which you did for Person and Playing Area), you must revisit this decision in the physicalization phase. We admit that using a surrogate key in a Logical model is a bit strange. We do it when we want to be able to follow the foreign key migrations from entity to entity. However, if no data element actually exists that identifies a member of a set, or if the data elements are too complex to model (like DNA tags or other biorecognition identifiers—which are about as close to a natural key as you can get for living beings), it may be appropriate to leave the key undefined. Any entity with no defined primary key on the Logical model is a natural candidate for a surrogate key on the Physical model.

If you choose to use a surrogate key in the Logical model, you should define the surrogate key carefully. You want to prevent your model from representing the jack of spades 15 times in the Card entity because of an inability to recognize and enforce uniqueness in the set. The goal is to recognize a member of the set and be a member one time and one time only, not to make the row in a table unique.

When checking for adherence to 1NF, it's also important to look for repeating groups. Text blocks that allow "value A, value B, value C" are just as illegal in Logical modeling as attributes named Pile Position 1, Pile Position 2, Pile Position 3, and so on, would have been in the Card Pile entity. Looking over Game, it seems that you've satisfied 1NF, but we'd probably include Person ID, Game End Date, and Game End Time as alternate keys, as shown in Figure 9-46.

Figure 9-46. *Alternate key definition for Game*

Review every entity. Can you find a single attribute or group of attributes of each entity that can act as a unique identifier? Well, since you added a few logical placeholders, the answer is "yes." Remember, the normal forms are cumulative. Second Normal Form (2NF) depends on 1NF being true as well.

Checking for 2NF

2NF demands that every aspect of every member of the set depends on the *whole key*. All the extra information (attributes) in an entity must be dependent on the entire key. Again, surrogate keys are a problem here unless you identified the natural key against which to check. For example, if you had left the relationships shown in Figure 9-47 in place, you'd have broken 2NF.

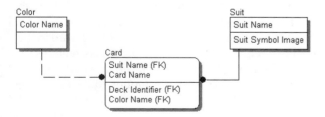

Figure 9-47. *Broken entity/partial dependency on the key (Color dependent only on Suit)*

Although cards do have color, Card is dependent on Suit Name only, not on Card Name. All spades are black, and all hearts are red. The "ownership" of the attribute belongs to Suit.

Checking for 3NF

Third Normal Form (3NF) demands that every attribute of every member of the set depends on nothing but the key. Here again we'll break the rule by adding Color Name into the Move entity, as shown in Figure 9-48.

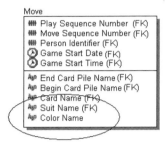

Figure 9-48. *Transitive dependency (not dependent on the key at all)*

These types of checks are simple enough to do when you're pounding away at a large model. That's one of the reasons we tried to get you to think about designing the model the way we did. Sometimes you're working with a list of attributes and just trying to find the right entity to take ownership of them. In this case, we moved Color Name back into the Move entity just to show you an example. The entity breaks 3NF if any of its attributes depend not on an attribute in the key but on an attribute in a nonkey position.

Checking for BCNF

Boyce-Codd Normal Form (BCNF) demands the following:

- Every attribute must be a fact about a key.

- All keys are identified.

BCNF tells you what to do when you find issues in 2NF and 3NF. Dependencies between attributes in an entity require another entity to solve the problem. The nondependent attributes in question either become foreign keys from their own base entity or are derived from the primary key migration of the new entities. In this case, you can solve the dilemma by changing the ownership of Color Name to the correct entity (Suit). You still know the color of card in the move, but you have to find it by following the foreign keys back to Suit. BCNF also requires that all attributes be an "entity-owned fact." This is the reason you broke Color into its own entity. Color in this model is a very small set. But Color has its own definition that had nothing to do with Suit. Suit isn't the correct origin for Color Name; Color is.

Checking for Too Many/Too Few Attributes

If you're seeing one really huge entity, with more than 15 attributes (and we've seen some with as many as several hundred), you quite likely haven't satisfied all the normal form rules yet. Look at the entity again! On the other hand, if you have entities without any attributes of their own, double-check to make sure the entity is really necessary. You may need to look at a few in the example model.

Too many entities may indicate you've strayed out of scope or overabstracted the solution. If your model is bulging at the seams with boxes, and you thought you had a small project, you should carefully review the entities again. You may need to review what you discovered with your project lead. Too few entities may indicate that you have a hole somewhere in your analysis. (The Solitaire model is supposed to be small, and look how long it took to get to this point!) If you have too few entities, the project deals with very few data elements in a complicated fashion, or you're missing something. Again, review the scope, and check with your project lead.

Checking for Accurate Role Names

It's so easy to lose track of role names in a working model. The modeling tools don't help you much, and there isn't a good way to see the role names (although some software has an option that allows you to turn on role naming in order to see what attributes have been renamed). You should trace every relationship in the model and verify that the primary key from the parent entity is in the child entity. If multiple relationships exist between two entities, then you should have as many foreign keys as there are relationships, unless you're unifying the keys on purpose. Having two card pile names in Move requires role naming, as shown in Figure 9-49.

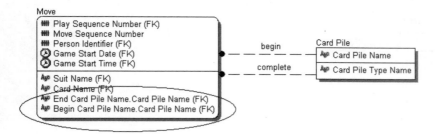

Figure 9-49. *Example of role naming*

Remember that two relationships exist from Card Pile to Move. Therefore, you need two attributes in Move that can be traced back to Card Pile.

Checking Quality with Instance Tables

In trying to quality check your design, don't rule out just taking a good look at the data. We keep saying that entities are sets of things. We generally describe this as *spreadsheet analysis* for the clients. Write some values out, and play with the data. See what becomes visible.

Color

Table 9-17 shows the Color instance table.

Table 9-17. *Color Instance Table*

Color Name PK
Red
Black

Suit

Table 9-18 shows the Suit instance table.

Table 9-18. *Suit Instance Table*

Suit Name PK	Color Name	Suit Symbol Image AK
Hearts	Red	♥
Diamonds	Red	♦
Clubs	Black	♣
Spades	Black	♠

Card

Table 9-19 shows the Card instance table.

Table 9-19. *Card Instance Table*

Suit Name PK	Card Name PK
Hearts	Ace
Hearts	Two
Hearts	Three
Diamonds	Ace
Diamonds	Two
Diamonds	Three
Clubs	Ace
Clubs	Two
Clubs	Three
Spades	Ace
Spades	Two
Spades	Three

Can you see how easy it is to double-check your key designations? In the case of Card, for instance, you could easily have missed that Suit Name should be part of the key. Look how simple it is to see the repeating values with an instance table. With more complicated data, a Microsoft Excel spreadsheet can help you sort through for QA checking using its powerful built-in functions (such as pivot tables). For serious data analysis of really large data sets, you may need to set up test tables and check your design using SQL SELECT statements. Or you can try to generate a default physicalization in a simple relational database management system (RDBMS), such as Microsoft Access, and sample load some data to make sure it passes the reasonability test.

Don't deliver your model until you're pretty sure you have it right. We worked with a team once that had to de-scope an entire subject area of the project because it took several months to figure out that it took a combination of seven attributes to make every member of the set unique!

Performing a Peer Model Walk-Through

This is another way to make sure the Logical model is quality work. Let another modeler look it over and give you feedback. This is the most valuable method of gaining experience. We don't do it, or offer to do it, for each other nearly enough. Your group will probably have lots of wonderful suggestions that will make your model look more standard to the department charter. They should help you to keep your spirits up. And we hope they will also truthfully tell you when your entity and attribute names are dreadful, before you expose them to the clients.

Applying Finishing Touches

The following are some finishing touches you can implement:

- Make sure you add your name and the extension, date, and time to all your documentation.

- Version numbers are also nice, such as 1.0.0, or 1.0.1, and so on. We find that when there are several iterations of a model, a version numbering scheme similar to that used in software design is helpful.

- Page numbers are nice on the longer documents (we always seem to forget to add them).

- File path addresses are great if you're handing out hard copies of documents that are being stored on a shared server.

- Add the project name and stage of development, especially if this is going to be a long project (more than three months).

- Always add a glossary to documentation that's full of acronyms or words that might be beyond the realm of the readers.

- Print a copy, and put it on the wall; looking at it daily will help (and it will be a good reference for when you need to talk about the model).

If you need to create iterations of your documents and models, use some kind of versioning technique. Numbers and dates are great, but try to help out with visual clues, such as stickers or a color band, if you can. It's so much easier to see the blue stripe, or the panda sticker, on your desk than it is to see "v2.15" in the footer of a document. Use some color in the model and documentation to highlight important parts. You may, for example, want to change the background color of certain entities to show the difference between the fairly quiet and stable entities, such as Color, as opposed to the volatile entities, such as Game Move. But if you do use color on your model, be sure to add a color key to the model so you never forget what the notation means.

At this point, you're ready for a model walk-through with your project team and then with the clients. Get a business rules report ready, and do the true/false test. Polish your glossary for delivery. Do a spell check on everything. And be prepared to come back to the model with changes.

Figure 9-50 shows the Logical model you developed in this chapter.

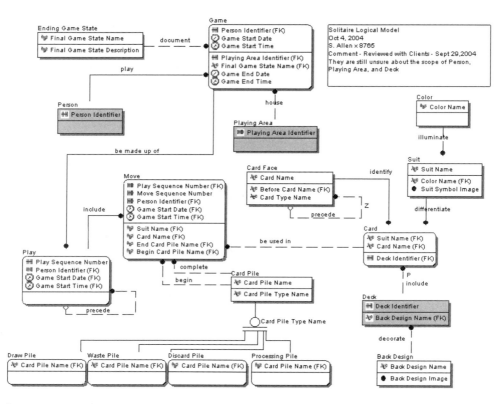

Figure 9-50. *Final Solitaire Logical model*

Summary

In this chapter, you saw the iterative nature of the process by which you've drawn up this model. You poured over each entity and its attributes to ensure that the definitions and relationships you have are accurate and make sense. The key steps in the creation of a Logical model are as follows:

1. Reinforce the scope of your analysis often.

2. Determine the logical entities from your conceptual entities.

3. Define attributes for your entities.

4. Discover primary keys.

5. Verify the relationships between entities.

6. Double-check all you've done in light of your business rules and normal forms.

7. Validate your work against as many sources as possible, such as instance tables, SMEs, and model reviews.

■ ■ ■

CHAPTER 10

Transforming a Logical Model into a Physical Model

This chapter covers the process of transforming a Logical model into a Physical model. Fortunately, the process is pretty straightforward (provided you have a good Logical model from which to work). When you're finished with this chapter, you'll have a solid design that you could either deploy or enhance by continued tuning by working with the database administrator (DBA).

In this chapter, you'll look at these topics:

- Creating shorter names for tables and columns to avoid database management system (DBMS) naming issues

- Deciding on the category structures

- Checking the status of any shadow entities

- Choosing the primary keys for the tables

- Reviewing and possibly role-naming the foreign key names

- Reviewing the defined data type and size information

- Estimating volumetrics

- Adding software application management (operational) structures

- Performing quality tests for the following:

  - Data form, fit, and function

  - Naming standards

  - Requirements satisfaction

  - Stewardship

  - Integration and interfaces

- Creating Data Definition Language (DDL) scripts for the tables

Checking the Project Status

Data modeling generally takes place in parallel with all sorts of other project tasks. If all is going well, then by the time you're ready to transform your Logical model into the initial Physical model design, the team will have signed off on the following:

- Business requirements and scope

- Process analysis (often flow diagrams and use cases) and definitions

- The Logical model, including the following:

  - Definitions

  - Entities

  - Attributes

  - Relationships

  - Planned extraction, transformation, and loading (ETL) architecture (data movement)

  - Data management strategy (quality checks, stewardship, error handling, and so on)

This isn't to say that some outstanding items aren't still being worked on, but it's important to have as stable and comprehensive an understanding of the data, the business processes, and the business policies as possible *before* beginning the Physical model's design.

Taking the Next Steps

What's the rest of the team doing while you're beginning the Physical model design? They're starting to explore the technical implementation issues—the front-end application needs, system architecture choices, and transaction process management options. In fact, one of the first decisions that's probably going to be made is whether the proposed solution is still cost justified based on what the team now knows. They will look at identified improvements (such as timesaving and decision-making abilities) and genuine process improvements to determine if they're significant enough to justify further expenditures on a custom software solution. All of the team's efforts, including the creation of the Logical model, are part of that decision-making process. Those efforts will bring you to this point.

In some companies, the process of going from a Logical to Physical model involves a complete change in task owner. The skill sets involved in Logical and Physical modeling are very different. It may be that the Logical modeler simply hands over the signed-off Logical model to a DBA for physicalization. On the other hand, employee roles vary between companies, and sometimes the Logical modeler is also the DBA!

The decisions that have to be made about the design at this point are based on an intimate working knowledge of the target DBMSs, screens/forms, interfaces, processing, security, and other hardware/software/infrastructure issues. We'll take you through the Solitaire example to a first-draft physical design using Oracle as the target RDBMS. But we don't claim to be DBAs or database-tuning wizards. If you'd really like to pursue this aspect of transforming a Logical model to Physical model, you can read more about it in *Pro SQL Server 2000 Database Design* (Apress, 2004).

Beginning the Process

Transforming the Logical model to the Physical model is another period of discovery; but this time the focus is on how to build the data repository. This task is a critical juncture for an application development project team. This is where, as they say, the rubber hits the road. A poor physical design can result in poor performance, in an overly complex design, in a design that results in poor quality data, or in all of these. Changes to the Physical data model structures impact all code that uses them. Changes to the physical database design become broader, more difficult, and more expensive to implement the further you are into a project. Granted, you're only going to take a first pass at physicalizing the model, but you must be extremely diligent even at this stage. It's the starting place for the DBA and programmers to tune and enhance the design to support the application. Once the DBA builds the database, the repercussions of changing something as seemingly insignificant as a misspelled column name can be extremely costly. We refer to the cascading impact as a *ripple*, but sometimes it feels like a tidal wave.

Physicalizing Names

When you finished the Logical model design in the previous chapter, it included the entities and attributes named in full-word descriptive titles. The first task in this chapter is to shorten those names for simplicity so you don't run into any table and column name length issues when implementing the Physical model. Always remember that DBMSs have table and column name length restrictions as well as reserved words that you need to be aware of and avoid.

Our target for transforming the Logical model from Chapter 9 (as shown in Figure 10-1) is Oracle 8, which allows only 30 characters for table and column names.

Consistency is more important than almost anything else when naming database columns, especially in the art of abbreviation. Remember the attribute type (class word) list from Chapter 3, as shown in Table 10-1? Each type (data class) should have a standard abbreviation. Your DBA or data management group might already have a standard abbreviation list for you to use. Ensure that the abbreviations you use are documented in the model so nobody will be confused in situations where different projects use different abbreviations.

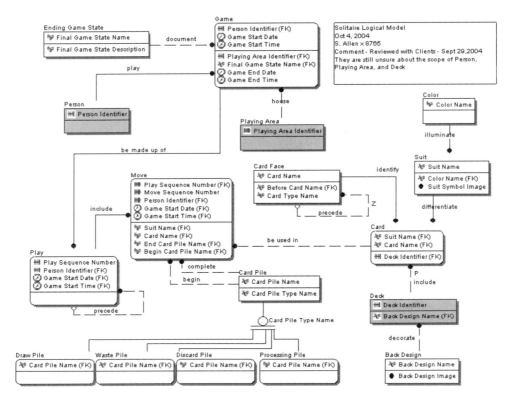

Figure 10-1. *Finalized Solitaire Logical model*

Table 10-1. *Class Word List and Definitions*

Class Word	Abbreviation	Meaning	Data Domain
Amount	Amt	A monetary number.	Number
Code	Cd	An alphanumeric meaningful abbreviation.	Text
Date	Dt	A calendar date—month, day, year.	Date
Description	Dsc	A textual account or portrayal.	Text
Flag	Flg	A one letter or number Boolean set.	Text
Identifier	Id	A unique recognition tag in the form of a character and/or number, system-generated ID, or a globally unique identifier (GUID). This may be process driven or nonsensical and insignificant to the data user.	Text
Image	Img	A nonlanguage visual object.	Blob
Name	Nm	A textual label.	Text
Number	Nb	A place in a sequence.	Number
Quantity	Qty	A number totaling a measurement by a unit.	Number
Sound	Snd	A nonlanguage aural object.	Blob

Class Word	Abbreviation	Meaning	Data Domain
Text	Txt	An unformatted language segment.	Text
Time	Tm	A moment—hour, minute, second, and so on.	Time

Note that most DBMSs can't create objects with embedded spaces in the object name because it becomes problematic for the code parser to recognize where the names end. So you need to remove them either using underscores or using Pascal notation (having a capitalized letter note the next word in the name). Either method results in all names being a single text string label that identifies the correct table or column in the table. We'll use Pascal notation in this example. Table 10-2 shows the entities in Pascal notation.

Table 10-2. *Removing Spaces from Entity Names*

Entity Name	Table Name
Back Design	BackDesign
Card	Card
Card Face	CardFace
Card Pile	CardPile
Color	Color
Discard	DiscardPile
Draw	DrawPile
Ending Game State	EndGameState
Game	Game
Move	Move
Person	Person
Play	Play
Playing Area	PlayArea
Processing	ProcessPile
Suit	Suit
Waste	WastePile

Notice that we removed the *ing* from some of the names and added the word *Pile* to the subtype category tables (at least until we decide how to deal with them). We tend to use names for tables that are as simple as possible while still making them recognizable. In some companies, you'll have standards in place for table names, such as prefixing each table with a project tag to group application tables (such as *Sol_* for the Solitaire project) or using a generic numbering system to restrict the length of table names. Older versions of DB2 have a maximum of table name length of eight characters (which may explain highly restrictive naming standards still enforced in your company) that prevent you from using recognizable names. Remember that the consistency created by standards compliance is important to the enterprise. You should also store the table definition in your enterprise metadata management system, which could be as simple as a spreadsheet or as robust as a metadata repository software solution such as Computer Associates' AllFusion Repository for z/OS.

Table 10-3 shows an attempt at renaming the attribute names to draft column names. Double-check the names to remove any plural forms. All tables and columns should be named in singular form to represent their set membership. Now change the attribute names into proposed column names by applying the class word abbreviations, and check the consistency in the names.

Table 10-3. *Changing Attribute Names to Column Names*

Table Name	Attribute Name	Column Name
BackDesign	Back Design Name	BackDesignNm
BackDesign	Back Design Image	BackDesignImg
Card	Card Name	CardNm
Card	Deck Identifier	DeckId
Card	Suit Name	SuitNm
CardFace	Before Card Name	BeforeCardNm
CardFace	Card Name	CardNm
CardFace	Card Type Name	CardTypeNm
CardPile	Card Pile Name	CardPileNm
CardPile	Card Pile Type Name	CardPileTypeNm
Color	Color Name	ColorNm
DiscardPile	Card Pile Name	CardPileNm
DrawPile	Card Pile Name	CardPileNm
EndGameState	Final Game State Description	EndGameStateDsc
EndGameState	Final Game State Name	EndGameStateNm
Game	Final Game State Name	EndGameStateNm
Game	Game End Date	GameEndDt
Game	Game End Time	GameEndTm
Game	Game Start Date	GameStartDt
Game	Game Start Time	GameStartTm
Game	Person Identifier	PersonId
Game	Playing Area Identifier	PlayAreaId
Move	Begin Card Pile Name	BeginCardPileNm
Move	Card Name	CardNm
Move	End Card Pile Name	EndCardPileNm
Move	Move Sequence Number	MoveSeqNb
Move	Suit Name	SuitNm
Move	Play Sequence Number	PlaySeqNb
Move	Game Start Time	GameStartTm
Move	Person Identifier	PersonId
Move	Game Start Date	GameStartDt
Person	Person Identifier	PersonId

Table Name	Attribute Name	Column Name
Play	Game Start Time	GameStartTm
Play	Play Sequence Number	PlaySeqNb
Play	Game Start Date	GameStartDt
Play	Person Identifier	PersonId
PlayArea	Playing Area Identifier	PlayAreaId
ProcessPile	Card Pile Name	CardPileNm
Suit	Suit Name	SuitNm
Suit	Color Name	ColorNm
Suit	Suit Symbol Image	SuitSymbolImg
WastePile	Card Pile Name	CardPileNm

We used the standard abbreviations for all the class words, we had to abbreviate one that wasn't a class word (*Sequence* turned into *Seq*), and we changed the ending state attributes from *Final* to *End*. All these little changes add up to a higher-quality final result. Now the attributes for the ending state have names that make their origin more apparent, and we've applied a name transformation standard consistently so the team can read any cryptic names of the table columns with confidence.

You'll want to maintain an abbreviation key on the Physical model so anyone unfamiliar with the project standards can still feel fairly confident that they're looking at a company name rather than a component name when they're looking at CoNm in a Parts table, for example.

■**Note** Try to use the same abbreviation for a word throughout the entire model. Some companies manage abbreviations at the enterprise level and have a standard abbreviation list for projects.

Figure 10-2 shows the updated model. We know this renaming process seems like a simple step, but it's fundamentally important—so take special care when doing this.

Now you have a good list of potential tables. You need to use this list to see if you have data structures already in place that will allow for reuse to integrate with your system, rather than having to spend time designing a custom table to allow for that functionality. You don't want to cause the clients to spend time and money building and maintaining a data set they could have shared with someone else.

Ask around. You know what you have. Now check other tables and columns in other applications, including those that are part of an enterprise's central data store. You wouldn't believe how many duplicate Calendar tables exist in some mainframe environments. Besides, if you can find a source to share and get the appropriate authorization to use it, then you can shadow out those tables and reduce the number of programming and ETL tasks. You could be a hero to the whole team.

Unfortunately, in this case, you don't have any outside sources. You have to work with the whole scope.

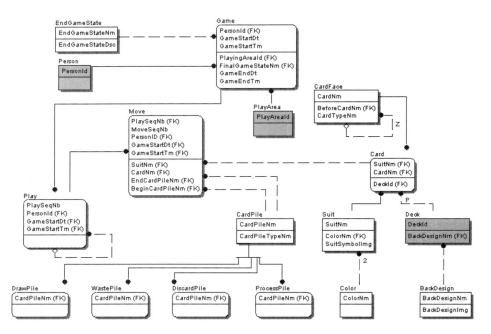

Figure 10-2. *First-draft Physical model with new name changes*

Creating Tables from Logical Categories

One of the next steps in transforming the Logical model to a Physical model involves determining the physical deployment structure of categories. Remember, a category is a large group of things that can be divided into types or smaller groupings of the larger data set. Each group has a supertype and one or more subtypes. All the members of the supertype should be included in one or more of the subtypes. And this duality of meaning can be challenging in how to create the correct structure for table storage.

The only category you have to work with in the Solitaire example is the Card Pile category, and because it's too simple to really give you a feel for the thought process of choosing a category implementation, let's look at another category introduced in Chapter 3. This example will allow you to look at the different data storage designs for categories.

Remember the car order system from Chapter 3? You had a Vehicle category in the Logical model that looked like Figure 10-3.

This category separates vehicles into three subtypes: Car, Truck, and Van. All vehicles should be able to be identified as one of these Vehicle subtypes. However, we've added a new entity called Camper. Only trucks can be sold with different camper options. We added this to show you how subtype relationships are important when you start to choose a physicalization option for this category.

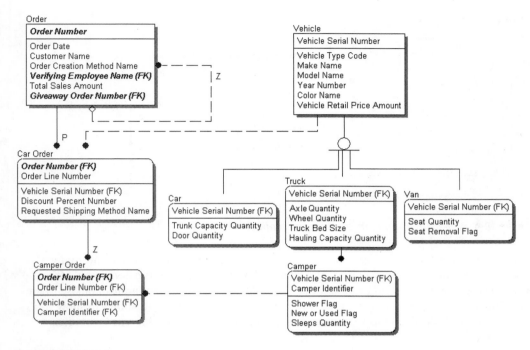

Figure 10-3. *Vehicle category structure*

You have three basic options when transforming Logical model categories into Physical model table structures, and we'll cover each in turn.

- Rolled-up categories

- Rolled-down categories

- Expanded categories

In the following examples, we've pointed out the special features of each choice. Decide what's most important by reviewing the Logical model and thinking about your team/application/client needs.

Introducing Rolled-up Categories

The first approach takes all the extra attributes of the children (subtypes) and rolls them into the category supertype. This results in these attributes being merged, with the union of all the attributes of the supertype and the subtypes contained in one table. It will transform the category into a table that looks like Figure 10-4.

Rolling All Attributes Up to One Table

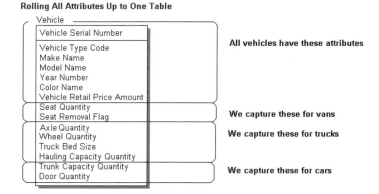

Figure 10-4. *Rolled-up option for category physicalization*

This would create a storage area for data that looks like Table 10-4. Notice how many columns need to allow NULL values. This is required because each column is valid only for certain category subtypes. Many data validation rules need to be coded in the database to prevent incorrect data from being entered. Table 10-4 uses a few of these attributes to show you the necessity of allowing empty columns for each row of data when using this technique.

Table 10-4. *Instance Table of the Rolled-up Category Example*

Vehicle Serial Number	Vehicle Type Code	Seat Quantity	Seat Removal Flag	Axel Quantity	Wheel Quantity	Truck Bed Size	Hauling Capacity Quantity	Trunk Capacity Quantity	Door Quantity
72	Car							16	2
241	Truck			2	4	73	1485		
821	Car							14	4
309	Van	5	Y						
81	Truck			3	10	216	6000		
56	Van	8	N						

If you were to use the rolled-up category method to implement the database, the Physical model for the car order system would look like Figure 10-5.

Notice that every time you need to see if a camper can be included in a car order, the set of Vehicle records relating to that Car Order must be programmatically tested using the Vehicle Type Code field to see if the vehicle is a truck. By merging the attributes into a single table, you've lost the ability to enforce the data integrity rules that relate specifically to cars, trucks, or vans using database relationships.

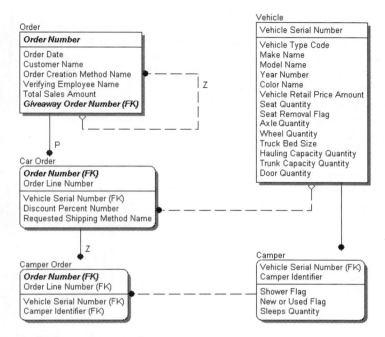

Figure 10-5. *Rolled-up Vehicle category*

When considering using this category implementation mechanism, you need to remember the following:

- This approach results in the least number of tables.

- Foreign key migrations that appear in the master category are represented only once.

- Business rules/relationships based on the subtype will need to enforce these rules by means other than database foreign key constraints; in other words, explicit data relationships have been traded for ease of access to the subtypes' data.

- All the attributes in the master category table that belong to the subtypes need to be null allowed.

In this choice, supertype and subtype category members have no independence from each other whatsoever. We generally use this structure when the subtypes look and behave similarly. Try to avoid this choice if there are relationships unique to the subtypes, but you can override this general rule if other considerations (such as ease of data access) are more important and you take the proper care to ensure data integrity.

Choosing a rolled-up design for your categories is generally the solution with which development teams will be the most comfortable. This approach simplifies data access and pushes the complexity of working with the individual subtypes into another system layer (usually the application or ETL). This approach has drawbacks, but if the development team is dependable and if the architecture supports a single point for application database access, then it can be a workable solution.

Introducing Rolled-down Categories

The rolled-down method of physicalizing category structures takes all the attributes of the supertype and transfers them to each of the subtypes. In doing this, the type code attribute in the Vehicle entity becomes obsolete (as it would in any category structures that use this technique for physicalization), since each subcategory is distinctly identified by its own table. Figure 10-6 shows the physical design for rolled-down categories for the car order example. Notice that each subtype table has the same structure except for a few special columns that are distinct to individual subtypes.

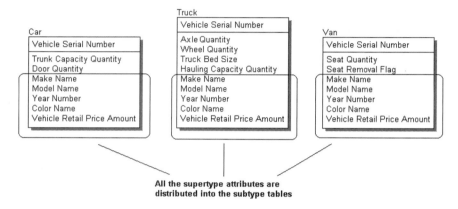

Figure 10-6. *Rolled-down option for category physicalization*

Table 10-5, Table 10-6, and Table 10-7 show examples of data for each of the tables from Figure 10-6.

Table 10-5. *Instance Table of the Rolled-down Category Example for* Car

Vehicle Serial Number	Trunk Capacity Quantity	Door Quantity	Make Name	Model Name	Year Number	Color Name	Vehicle Retail Price Amount
72	16	2	Toyota	Avalon	2005	Silver	30K
821	14	4	VW	Beetle	2004	Pink	18K

Table 10-6. *Instance Table of the Rolled-down Category Example for* Truck

Vehicle Serial Number	Axel Quantity	Wheel Quantity	Truck Bed Size	Hauling Capacity Quantity	Make Name	Model Name	Year Number	Color Name	Vehicle Retail Price Amount
81	3	10	216	6000	Chevrolet	Tandem Grain	1973	Yellow	6K
241	2	4	73	1485	Toyota	Tacoma	2003	Red	18K

Table 10-7. *Instance Table of the Rolled-down Category Example for* Van

Vehicle Serial Number	Seat Quantity	Seat Removal Flag	Make Name	Model Name	Year Number	Color Name	Vehicle Retail Price Amount
309	5	Y	Toyota	RAV4	2005	Blue	18K
56	8	N	VW	Van	1999	Green	8K

Choosing this style of category physicalization affects the relationships in the model. The separate relationships for subtypes found in the Logical model can now be supported directly by the physical design. By choosing this design, you can now restrict the vehicles that can have camper options to trucks only, using database level constraints.

However, making this design choice has other implications. You may have to create a unification column to implement the foreign key relationship between Car Order and Vehicle from the original Logical model. Since all the vehicle types can be purchased during a car order, the primary key of the Vehicle table, Vehicle Identifier, must migrate to that table from each of the three subtype tables. The records must then be differentiated by the Vehicle Type Code field in the Car Order table to determine in which subtype table each record is stored. If...Then...Else logic must then be used to determine which table to query for extra information about a given vehicle. From a programmatic standpoint, the unification process may be unwieldy, complex, or both. Figure 10-7 shows how the keys from the separate subtype tables can be unified in the Car Order table.

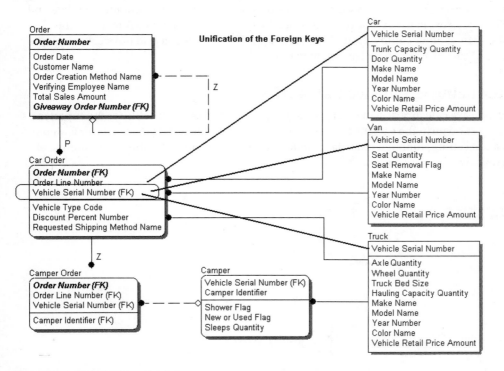

Figure 10-7. *Rolled-down* Vehicle *category*

When considering using this design method, you need to remember the following:

You lose a single source for foreign key migrations of the master category and may have to use a unification process to note the multiple sources.

You have to expend extra effort in order to report on the common attributes of the sub-types. Good examples of this are the Vehicle fields Make Name and Vehicle Retail Price Amount, which are now in three tables. Recombining these data elements can have a large performance impact, but you can address this by using reporting tables, hand-coded SQL, or special views.

Most subtype attributes should be created as NOT NULL in the physical design, unless the attribute is actually optional. Remember that when using rolled-up categories, the attributes had to be null allowed because the table needed to support multiple subtypes (which had some mutually exclusive attributes). In this case, the normal rules of attribute nullability apply.

If you want the combined sets of primary keys of all the subtypes to be united, you'll need to add programming rules to check for uniqueness when each subtype record is created.

With this design choice, subtype tables are independent, and no master or supertype table combines the smaller sets of records into one. We tend to use this structure when the supertype is considered to be abstract and has little reason to exist on its own. You can also use it if the clients consider the subtypes to really be substantially different things. This design is also quite appropriate if each subtype needs different processes to maintain their data and if differences exist in data security, ownership, the need for maintenance screens, or the requirement of other complex interfaces. It may just make more sense to physically deploy the logical category as completely separate physical tables.

Introducing Expansive Categories

The expansive category design involves choosing to create a separate table for the supertype and each subtype in the category. This is the design you'll likely get if you use the default phys-icalization settings found in most data modeling software. Figure 10-8 shows an example of the expansive category design.

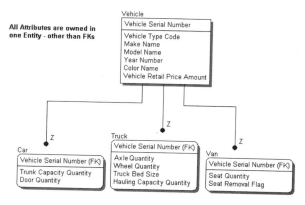

Figure 10-8. *Vehicle category in expansive category design*

Table 10-8, Table 10-9, Table 10-10, and Table 10-11 show sample data for the physical design in Figure 10-8.

Table 10-8. *Instance Table of the Expanded Category Example for* Vehicle

Vehicle Serial Number	Vehicle Type Code	Make Name	Model Name	Year Number	Color Name	Vehicle Retail Price Amount
72	Car	Toyota	Avalon	2005	Silver	30K
821	Car	VW	Beetle	2004	Pink	18K
81	Truck	Chevrolet	Tandem Grain	1973	Yellow	6K
241	Truck	Toyota	Tacoma	2003	Red	18K
309	Van	Toyota	RAV4	2005	Blue	18K
56	Van	VW	Van	1999	Green	8K

Table 10-9. *Instance Table of the Expanded Category Example for* Car

Vehicle Serial Number	Trunk Capacity Quantity	Door Quantity
72	16	2
821	14	4

Table 10-10. *Instance Table of the Expanded Category Example for* Truck

Vehicle Serial Number	Axel Quantity	Wheel Quantity	Truck Bed Size	Hauling Capacity Quantity
81	3	10	216	6000
241	2	4	73	1485

Table 10-11. *Instance Table of the Expanded Category Example for* Van

Vehicle Serial Number	Seat Quantity	Seat Removal Flag
309	5	Y
821	N	4

This physical category design involves building tables for the supertype and each subtype. The tables maintain connectivity to each other through an identifying relationship. Now each column and relationship can be maintained wherever it's most appropriate (in either the supertype or subtype tables), as shown in Figure 10-9.

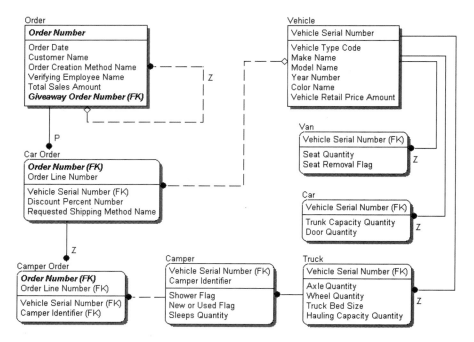

Figure 10-9. *Expanded category option*

When considering using this design, you need to remember the following:

- This design generally results in the largest number of database tables.

- The supertype acts as a single source for all foreign key migrations, except specialized ones for the subtypes.

- Almost any request for reporting data about a subtype will require a join to the super-type table.

- Any process or query interacting with the supertype and subtype tables will involve extra joins and more complex SQL.

This choice offers the most structural flexibility and growth potential but is generally the most complicated. This design also keeps as many of the rules of integrity at the database level as possible. We generally use this structure design when we have a fairly complex category with several attributes and relationships unique to the supertype or the subtypes.

Returning to the Solitaire Example

Let's return to the Logical model for Solitaire, as shown (at the entity level only) in Figure 10-10, and pick a Physical model design for the Card Pile category. You'll start by reviewing the relationships between Card Pile and the other entities. Right now, all the relationships are at the supertype level, connecting to the Card Pile entity rather than the Discard Pile, Waste Pile, Processing Pile, and Draw Pile entities.

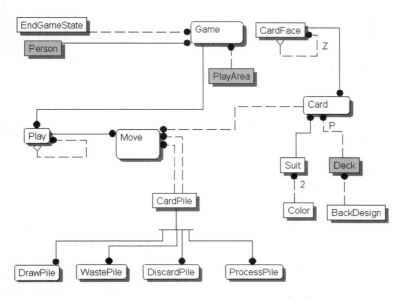

Figure 10-10. *Logical model for Solitaire at the entity level*

Now review the attributes using Figure 10-11. This is a pretty dull category. The subtypes have no specific attributes. Remember that the clients told you the project's scope didn't include the rules pertaining to the game of Solitaire. They're interested only in capturing a player's moves, not the permitted moves. So, the Logical model loses some of the special relationships and owned attributes of the Card Pile category.

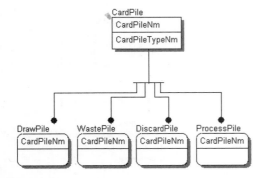

Figure 10-11. *Logical model for Solitaire at the attribute level*

Under these circumstances we'd propose using a rolled-up design and would actually drop the Card Pile Type Name attribute, which is unnecessary at this point. As you can see by looking at Table 10-12, the card pile type code really just repeats the card pile name, with the exception of the discard and processing piles. Since you're not interested in the available moves, or in which card piles can participate in which moves, the card piles differ only by their names. Since they differ only by their names, they're now *instances*, instead of classes or types.

Table 10-12. *Instance Table of Card Pile Category*

CardPileNm	CardPileTypeNm
Draw Pile	Draw Pile
Waste Pile	Waste Pile
Discard Pile Diamonds	Discard Pile
Discard Pile Hearts	Discard Pile
Discard Pile Clubs	Discard Pile
Discard Pile Spades	Discard Pile
Processing Pile Position 1	Processing Pile
Processing Pile Position 2	Processing Pile
Processing Pile Position 3	Processing Pile
Processing Pile Position 4	Processing Pile
Processing Pile Position 5	Processing Pile
Processing Pile Position 6	Processing Pile
Processing Pile Position 7	Processing Pile

This changes the evolving Physical model design to look like Figure 10-12.

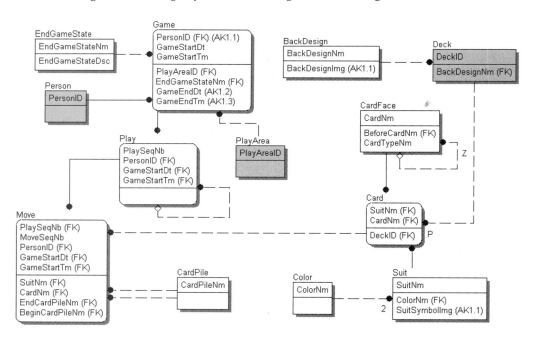

Figure 10-12. *The model after adjusting the Card Pile category*

Examining Shadow Entities

The fact that Person, Deck, and PlayArea are still shadowed should glare out at you at this stage of your transformation. These tables are integrated into the solution in some fashion but aren't built or owned by the project. You may need to document relationships to them and build physical constraints relating to them in a future iteration, but you'll never create them from this model. At this point what you need is to have another discussion with the clients. They tell you they've decided PlayArea and Deck are out of scope, and they're still working on a survey form with the information they want to capture about Person. You'll need to remind them that the risk is increasing of being unable to deliver the software if they don't get you the specifications about Person soon.

When you examine shadow entities on a Physical model design, you'll want to document exactly why they're still there. You may document shadow entities to show that relationships or some source data come from these entities, despite that the physical tables or files may not be in the design's scope. Generally, this is noted on the model or explained in the entity definitions. You may note the system where the database table actually exists, the directory path and name of a flat file on the mainframe, or, as in this case, the status of the ongoing analysis in this area, as shown in Figure 10-13.

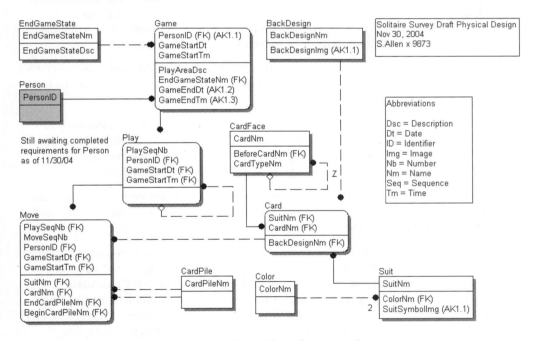

Figure 10-13. *Removing most shadow entities with explanation of exception*

Deciding the Primary Keys

Now that you've chosen a structure for the categories and determined what to do with the shadow entities, it's time to look at the choices for the physical primary key. Remember that we're now talking about table designs rather than information designs. The analysis you did to build the Logical model design was an attempt to document as much as possible about pure data and the rules that govern its behavior, including what made each member unique and identifiable. The knowledge you discovered is still applicable, but you have several options in generating the physical database keys. In addition, when choosing a primary key for a table, you have several parameters to consider. These parameters are prioritized according to your information management charter, project requirements, DBMS strengths and weaknesses, and future needs. The considerations for the choices are as follows:

Integrity: Integrity emphasizes the necessary uniqueness of a data set. You need to ensure quality data by preventing duplicate data records. Having two or more records that seem to be the same leaves a user wondering which one to pick. (We've seen programmers having to code for this problem by just picking the one that occurs first.) Duplicate data can cause anomalies when relating data from different tables. Duplication often occurs because of inconsistencies in the business keys that have created duplicate entries for things that are the same but need to be treated differently.

Performance: You also choose a key to support inserting, updating, deleting, and selecting the correct data as quickly as possible. Designs may impact performance when keys are multicolumn, use slower-to-match data types such as large textual strings or date/times, or involve any column that might need to be updated. The key to performance is that *data access* is important. Performance is one aspect of data access. Avoid keys that make your design more difficult to navigate or maintain.

Integration: You should try to be sensitive that other systems might want to use the tables you're building. Sometimes we review the choices of primary key with an eye to the enterprise's needs, rather than just the system.

Data readability: Since primary keys are the bit of data that migrates, sometimes you might consider migrating simple/stable names rather than having to join back to get a piece of information. For instance, migrating a state name or abbreviation field can remove quite a few joins because enough of the data is there for simple use.

Maintainability: Someone has to take care of the system after you deploy it. Try to think about how difficult it will be to add new structures, audit and fix anomalies, or deal with bulk load increases in data scope from time to time.

Security: Sometimes instead of worrying about making the foreign keys understandable, you can try to do just the opposite. Using pseudokeys can mask significant information. Using ID numbers for sensitive lists such as bank accounts or personal information can allow foreign key data migration without storing sensitive information in the target table. To decode the foreign key into the real attribute, users must be granted privileges to select from the parent table. Nonbusiness keys can serve as a simple form of encryption.

Data element ownership: Sometimes you can review what actually owns, manages, and issues the data elements you're considering for a primary key. Data elements whose size, content, or type can be altered by an influence outside your enterprise—such as the government, a phone company, or the U.S. Post Office—are a risky choice for a primary key. What would you do if U.S. Social Security numbers, ZIP codes, and phone numbers change their size and content in the future? We foresee another Y2K impact. An extreme position taken by some is that you should *never* have a business intelligent key as part of your primary key of any table. The rationale is that if you make your design dependent on business processes and practices, you run the risk of having your entire design destabilized by arbitrary changes in business policies or by business management decisions.

The DBA: Also, the DBA may have knowledge and experience that leads them to favor one primary key choice over others. They know the environment on which the application will be running. The DBA should be involved in the discussions about primary key choices.

Reviewing the Primary Keys

You should review each table *individually* before you commit to choosing its primary key. The default choice made by the modeling software is to use the primary key you chose during the Logical model development as the physical table's primary key. Just because it was your logical key, though, doesn't necessarily make it the best choice for a physical key. However, it's good practice to use the candidate keys you discovered as unique alternate keys, even if you don't choose to use any of them as a primary key.

Remember that primary keys are chosen because they do two things.

- They provide an identifier for the DBMS to find the record quickly.

- They provide a uniqueness constraint to avoid duplicate entries.

Using natural information for a primary key may end up violating the second principle if the business arbitrarily changes. It's much easier in the long run to use a system-assigned key for the record locator component of the primary key and apply separate "unique" constraints to enforce business uniqueness and prevent data duplication.

Natural Key

Let's return to the Logical model. What primary key for the Color table would be more appropriate than ColorNm in this Physical model design? What's the advantage of using a Color ID or Color Code in its place? In this case, there's no advantage. There are only two short color name values; you aren't going to get any discernable performance increase by making a nonsignificant number the primary key. You have no other systems on the horizon with which you anticipate integrating (although checking with the users is always a good idea). Using the Color Name values of Red and Black is much more useful in the Suit table than the system-generated ColorId values of 1 and 2. ColorNm is already simple and understandable. And, finally, no one has mentioned a need to encode this data for security's sake.

You can treat the Suit, Card, CardFace, EndGameState, BackDesign, and CardPile tables the same way as Color. Figure 10-14 highlights these tables on the Physical model. Each of these tables has a simple, solid, useable primary key already defined. It makes sense to use these existing keys. That leaves you with having to make a primary key decision about the Game, Play, and Move tables. Their primary keys have some aspects that make it important to take a little extra time and care with them.

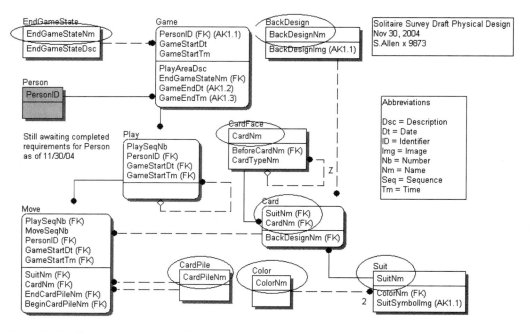

Figure 10-14. *Choosing the natural key for some tables*

Each of the current primary keys on these tables does the following:

- Includes more than two columns

- Has date and time data types in some columns

- Are found on the model's primary tables (measured by potential record quantity and highest usage)

What are the alternatives if you don't use a natural (primary or alternate) key? We know of three. Let's look at them now.

Surrogate Keys

Surrogate keys are almost never defined in the Logical model. They either don't map to real data elements or are derivable, both of which are reasons why you avoided these keys in the Logical model. Until the Physical model transformation stage, you never considered these as another type of candidate key. Three types of surrogate keys exist.

- **Concatenated surrogate keys**: These are compressed, multicolumn data strings.

- **Semisurrogate keys**: These replace a portion of a multicolumn key with a system-generated number.

- **Surrogate keys**: These are completely system generated.

Let's look at Game in Figure 10-15 to review the choices.

Game
```
PersonID (FK) (AK1.1)
GameStartDt
GameStartTm

PlayAreaDsc
EndGameStateNm (FK)
GameEndDt (AK1.2)
GameEndTm (AK1.3)
```

Figure 10-15. *Choosing the primary key of* Game

Let's look at the instance for Game, as shown in Table 10-13.

Table 10-13. *Instance Table for* Game

Person Id	GameStartDt	GameStartTm	PlayAreaDesc	EndGame StateNm	GameEndDt	GameEndTm
1	1/6/02	1824	Palm Trees	Win	1/06/02	1852
1	1/6/02	1853	Palm Trees	Lose	1/06/02	1910

These rows tell you that Person 1 has played two games; they won one and lost one. Sometimes looking at sample data helps make the primary key choices clearer than the Logical modeling did. But in this case, we still don't see any natural keys, other than the one we already found. However, our experience has told us that you should avoid having dates and times in a primary key if possible. This is mostly because of the way DBMSs want to format date and time data for you. Using dates and times in a primary key can become extremely complicated and can make using the key programmatically awkward. So let's decisively rule out making the natural key the primary key in this case.

Concatenated

What about a concatenated surrogate key? Concatenating your values compresses the three columns (GameStartDt, GameStartTm, and PersonId) into a single value (for example, 01060218241, 01060218531, and 01060219121). This is called a *smart key*, although it's *not* always a smart choice. This type of key is used quite frequently in manufacturing systems for part numbers. The clients can read this kind of key the way librarians read Dewey Decimal numbers for a book to get an overview about the book's subject matter (000 is the Computers, Information, and General Reference category, 500 is the Science category, 600 is the Technology category, and so on). In fact, clients love these kinds of keys because they're human readable. But note that you can always build a derivable column to store this kind of smart key without also using it as the primary key.

If you choose to use a concatenated surrogate key, then you move the Logical model primary key attributes below the line, identify them as an alternate unique key, and create a new GameID attribute to serve as the primary key. Don't forget to note the natural key when you move these attributes below the line. Also remember that one of the characteristics of a primary key is that it mustn't be updated. For this reason, concatenated keys can cause a bit of trouble; they have to follow the same rule as other primary keys and therefore can't be updated, but the side effect is that you can't update the alternate key either, since your alternate natural key is the foundation for the derived, concatenated primary key.

The table and data now look like Figure 10-16.

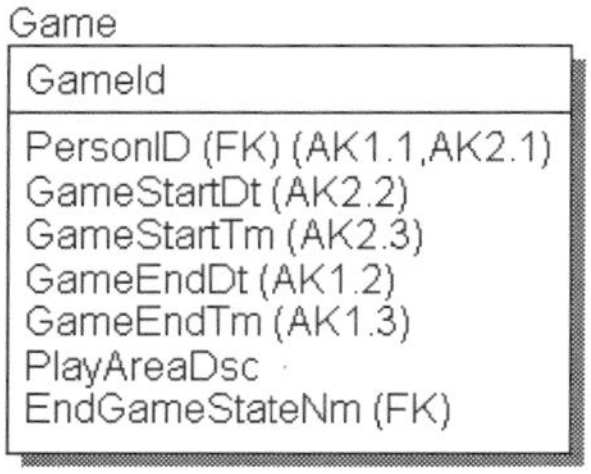

Game

GameId
PersonID (FK) (AK1.1,AK2.1) GameStartDt (AK2.2) GameStartTm (AK2.3) GameEndDt (AK1.2) GameEndTm (AK1.3) PlayAreaDsc EndGameStateNm (FK)

Figure 10-16. *Choosing to use a concatenated key as the primary key of* Game

And the instance table looks like Table 10-14.

Table 10-14. *Instance Table for* Game *After Creating a Concatenated Key*

GameID	Person Id	Game StartDt	Game StartTm	PlayAreaDsc	EndGame StateNm	Game EndDt	Game EndTm
01060218241	1	1/6/02	1824	Palm Trees	Win	1/06/02	1852
01060218531	1	1/6/02	1853	Palm Trees	Lose	1/06/02	1910

The biggest risk for this type of key actually comes from clients (especially power clients who are doing some of their own ad hoc reporting) who request adding a certain special code to the key to make reporting easier. Try to make their lives easier, but don't ever allow a portion of a concatenated key to be anything other than the immortal, never-changing, natural key attributes. A primary key must be stable; otherwise, you have the challenge of cascading a primary key change, which isn't a good thing.

■**Note** A concatenated key should only ever consist of the elements that are part of a natural key in order to preserve the mapping to the significant data elements that are being referenced.

Semisurrogate

Semisurrogate keys have the interesting aspect of preserving parts of the natural key while replacing other parts with an assigned key. In the case of Game, migrating PersonId from Game to Move may make a lot of sense, but migrating Game Start Date and Game Start Time from Game to Move probably isn't all that important. When the game started isn't relevant information when looking at a given move, except as a way of differentiating between games. But you may actually want to do a great deal of analysis of the Move records based on who played the game. Having the PlayerId data element readily available in the Move table may provide an advantage, as the clients can then easily select the records they want from the Move table based upon the PlayerId.

Remember, primary keys have several roles to play, with uniqueness being the most important, but not the only, role. Your choice impacts more than the table you're looking at; your decision impacts all the tables to which the foreign key migrates. You could replace Start Date and Start Time of Game with a number identifying one of the games a player has played. (You may be tempted to call it a sequence number. Don't. If you ever had a problem with data being loaded into the table out of order, your sequence generator would be out of step and could cause errors.) Most surrogate keys need to be simple, nonsignificant identifiers.

To apply semisurrogate keys to the Game table, you need to have a resultant key of Person 1–Game 1, Person 1–Game 2, and so on. To achieve this, you need to remove GameStartDate and GameStartTime from the key, dropping them under the line, as shown in Figure 10-17.

Game

| Personid (FK) (AK1.1,AK2.1) |
PersonGameid
GameEndTm (AK1.3)
GameEndDt (AK1.2)
GameStartDt (AK2.2)
GameStartTm (AK2.3)
PlayAreaDsc
EndGameStateNm (FK)

Figure 10-17. *Choosing to use a semisurrogate key as the primary key of* Game

Note that we didn't call the new game identifier GameID, because it isn't the whole identifier of the Game. It's an identifier of only one of a single player's games. The data now looks like Table 10-15.

Table 10-15. *Instance Table for* Game *After Creating a Semisurrogate Key*

Person GameId	PersonId	Game StartDt	Game StartTm	PlayAreaDsc	EndGame StateNm	Game EndDt	GameEnd Tm
1	1	1/6/02	1824	Palm Trees	Win	1/06/02	1852
2	1	1/6/02	1853	Palm Trees	Lose	1/06/02	1910

You must manage semisurrogate keys with an eye to both natural data element issues and system-generated identifier issues. The primary key of Person can't change. The relationship of a specific Person record to Game can't be changed. And finally there has to be a test for the uniqueness of PersonGameId for each Person.

Surrogate

Finally, we'll cover the tried-and-true surrogate key. Surrogate keys are also known as *system-assigned keys* (or SAKs). To implement these, you need the system to generate a unique number each time a record is inserted into the table and use that as the primary key. Remember to put a unique index on any natural keys to prevent inadvertently duplicating any rows. Surrogate keys are a great addition to your physical design arsenal. In fact, they're a good choice if you need to set up a large table that might have performance issues, since DBMSs generally find numeric keys much easier to sort and locate than text. But you should never apply surrogate keys as a default key design.

■**Note** Surrogate keys are often defaulted as the primary key of everything, without a single thought about what other choices might be made. This can promote a kind of narrow view of the design and lack of concern about the data's quality.

Using surrogate keys requires that certain issues be addressed, just like using concatenated and semisurrogate keys. None of these primary keys *means anything* to anybody. To fulfill all the roles of a primary key, you must give at least one natural key a unique index to maintain data set member uniqueness. When you're using surrogate keys, you may also have to deal with the issue of concurrency (handling concurrent requests for new keys) and the reusability of key values. Oracle and DB2 UDB deal with this problem by using "sequence generator" structures, which are independent of tables. In SQL Server, you specify a column as being an *identity* column. This makes reusability of the surrogate key in SQL Server difficult between different tables. Before deciding on surrogate keys, make sure the RDBMS handles them in a way that will be helpful.

The good news with using surrogate keys is that they're generally fast, simple, and small. The design looks exactly like the concatenated choice, as shown in Figure 10-18.

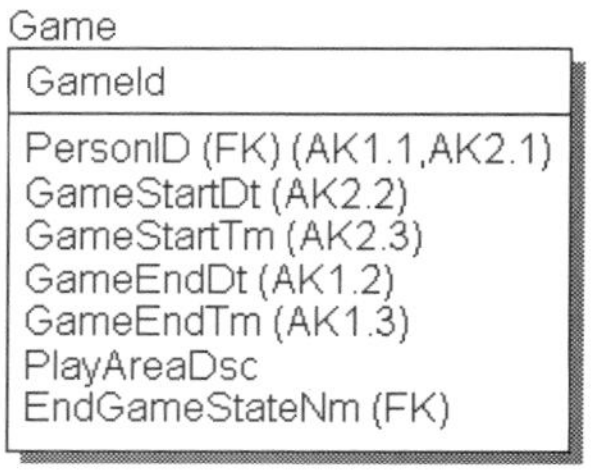

Game

Gameld
PersonID (FK) (AK1.1,AK2.1)
GameStartDt (AK2.2)
GameStartTm (AK2.3)
GameEndDt (AK1.2)
GameEndTm (AK1.3)
PlayAreaDsc
EndGameStateNm (FK)

Figure 10-18. *Choosing to use a surrogate key as the primary key of* Game

However, the data looks a little different, as shown in Table 10-16.

Table 10-16. *Instance Table for* Game *After Creating a Surrogate Key*

Game ID	Person Id	Game StartDt	Game StartTm	PlayAreaDsc	EndGame StateNm	Game EndDt	Game EndTm
15	1	1/6/02	1824	Palm Trees	Win	1/06/02	1852
49	1	1/6/02	1853	Palm Trees	Lose	1/06/02	1910

How to Choose

All these options have pros and cons. Table 10-17 provides a checklist of the necessary functions and characteristics of the primary key.

Table 10-17. *Checklist of Primary Key Choice Considerations for Game Table*

Factor	Natural?	Concatenated?	Semisurrogate?	Surrogate?
Integrity maintained	Yes	Yes	Yes	Yes
Performance	Not good Date and time data types and three columns	Better: but still a long number	Better still: small numbers in two columns	Best: one small number
Access complexity	Difficult: multiple business-oriented fields	Easy: one business-oriented field	Moderate: two non-business-oriented system-generated values	Easy: one non-business-oriented numeric value
Integration	None on the horizon	None on the horizon	None on the horizon	None on the horizon
Data readability	The best: readable elements with the exception of PersonId	OK: those familiar with the data will be able to recognize it	Compromise: distinctive person and game differentiation but no real data	None
Maintainability	Dates and times can be awkward to join to	Won't be able to use this for individual data elements. The join will have to be to individual columns.	Fairly simple for future use; will have to join to get real data elements	Fairly simple for future use; will have to join to get real data elements.
Security	Almost none: all the data is right there to read	Almost none: all the data is right there to read	Better: game dates and times have been substituted for an ID	Best: can't read any Person or Game columns without a join.
Data element ownership	Client owns all data elements	Client owns all data elements	Client owns all data elements	Client owns all data elements
DBA	Might want to use a single ID: will check	Might want to use a single ID: will check	Might want to use a single ID: will check	Might want to use a single ID: will check

So, you can see the following:

- The natural key from the Logical model is three columns long and has Date and Time elements. However, it's true to the world and will be well understood in a drop-down list of choices.

- The concatenated key is awkward if you're looking for the moves of Player 1 and you don't want to join back to Game to find the game IDs for Player 1, but it's informational from a shortcut perspective.

- The semisurrogate key has problems with a potential misunderstanding of the number (it's nonsignificant by itself and not necessarily a sequence of the games), and yet it has some information that may be valuable to the client.

- Finally, GameID migrates only nonsense numbers with no information value at all, but it does the job simply. This choice has the highest performance potential.

What would you pick? Remember, you have to consider the needs of not only the client but also the programmers and DBAs. In this case, we'd probably lean toward the semisurrogate key. We like being able to have PlayerID in the Move table. But this decision would definitely require some discussion. Figure 10-19 shows how changing the primary key of Game changed Play and Move.

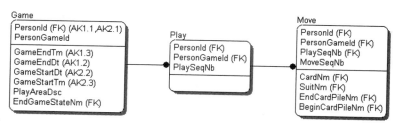

Figure 10-19. *Choosing to use a surrogate key as the primary key of* Game

What does an instance table for Play look like? Let's review it in Table 10-18.

Table 10-18. *Instance Table of Play*

PersonId	PersonGameId	PlaySeqNb
1	1	1
1	1	2
1	1	3
1	2	1
1	2	2
1	2	3
1	2	4

In Table 10-18 you can see that Person 1 had a quantity of three plays in Game 1 and a quantity of four plays in Game 2. Go through the following short survey of the key design:

- **Data integrity**: Yes, it was maintained.

- **Performance**: Number data types are easy to join, but the primary key consists of three columns.

- **Data accessibility**: This is moderate because of database joins across two columns, but at least the columns are non-business-oriented numeric values.

- **Integration**: None are on the horizon.

- **Data usefulness**: None of these columns is useful, except for PlaySeqNb.

- **Maintainability**: We don't foresee any problems.

- **Security**: The identity of the player and the game are masked with surrogate keys.

- **Data element ownership**: This is the client who owns these data elements.

- The **DBA**: The DBA might want to use a single ID; you'll check this.

Now look at an instance table for Move in Table 10-19.

Table 10-19. *Instance Table of* Move

PersonId	Person GameId	PlaySeqNb	MoveSeqNb	SuitNm	CardNm	EndCard PileName	BeginCard PileName
1	1	1	1	Clubs	King	Waste	Draw
1	1	2	1	Hearts	Two	Processing	Draw
1	1	2	2	Clubs	Jack	Processing	Processing

In Table 10-19, you can see that, on the first move of Game 1, Player 1 put the king of clubs on the waste pile, which ended Play 1. On Play 2, Person 1 was able to move the two of hearts out of the draw pile to a processing pile and the jack of clubs from one processing pile to another.

So, is there any reason to not choose the current key for Move, which is PersonId-PersonGameId-PlaySeqNb-MoveSeqNb, now that you've taken the date and time elements out of it? The primary key data elements are all short number columns, but there *are* four of them. This key doesn't migrate to anywhere in this application. There's no security issue suggesting you'd be better served with a surrogate key. Based on this information, we'd leave it as is and expect to have a discussion about it with the DBA later.

Now let's review each of the foreign keys for name appropriateness and definitions.

Foreign Key Naming/Definitions

First list foreign keys and their sources. When a primary key migrates from one table to the next, it often means something subtly different in its new location. This is one case where having software migrate the definition along with the foreign key column for you may actually contribute to a poorer-quality product in the long run. Modeling software generally takes all the values (names, definitions, and data types) from the parent table and applies them to the child tables. If you're building your model manually, you may think about what's happening a bit more. Remember to review those automatically generated or migrated default definitions one last time before you commit the names and definitions to the database design.

How does the data migrate now? Table 10-20 shows the foreign key data elements. We added the verb phrases to remind you of *why* the elements migrate to the child table. Pay special attention to the role names in bold in Table 10-20. Even if none of the other attribute definitions change when the keys migrate, these role-named attributes should have different definitions reflecting their roles.

Table 10-20. *Parent-to-Child Entity Review with Relationship Names and Primary Keys*

Parent Table	Verb Phrase	Child Table	Parent Primary Key	Child Foreign Key
BackDesign	*decorates*	Card	BackDesignNm	BackDesignNm
Card	*is_used_in*	Move	CardNm	CardNm
Card	*is_used_in*	Move	SuitNm	SuitNm
CardFace	*precedes*	CardFace	CardNm	BeforeCardNm
CardPile	*ends*	Move	CardPileNm	**EndCardPileNm**
CardPile	*begins*	Move	CardPileNm	**BeginCardPileNm**
Color	*illuminates*	Suit	ColorNm	SuitNm
EndGameState	*documents*	Game	EndGameStateNm	EndGameStateNm
Game	*contains*	Play	PersonGameId	PersonGameId
Game	*contains*	Play	PersonId	PersonId
Person	*plays*	Game	PersonId	PersonId
Play	*includes*	Move	PersonGameId	PersonGameId
Play	*includes*	Move	PlaySeqNb	PlaySeqNb
Play	*includes*	Move	PersonId	PersonId
Suit	*differentiates*	Card	SuitNm	SuitNm

    Remind yourself of the original source tables (independent tables where the data originates before it becomes a foreign key), their columns, and their definitions. (The source table is listed together with the source column, separated with a forward slash.) Table 10-21 shows the source tables, key columns, and definitions.

Table 10-21. *Source Tables and Definitions*

Source Table and Column	Definition
BackDesign/BackDesignNm	A textual label identifying a single pattern used to decorate the reverse side of a deck of cards (for example, exotic flowers, plaid, and a logo).
CardFace/CardNm	A textual label identifying one of thirteen cards (for example, king, queen, eight, and ace).
CardPile/CardPileNm	A textual label identifying a collection of cards, which is the location of a play in the game of Solitaire (for example, draw pile, discard pile, and processing pile).
Color/ColorNm	A textual label identifying one of two hues, red and black, used in creating the suit of a card.
EndGameState/EndGameStateNm	A textual label identifying the outcome of a completed game (for example, win, lose, and quit).
Person/PersonId	A nonsignificant value uniquely identifying a person who is a participant, or potential participant, in a study being conducted by the psychology department.
Game/PersonGameId	A nonsignificant number uniquely identifying a single game played by a person.

Source Table and Column	Definition
Play/PlaySeqNb	An ordered number identifying a single play in a single game and noting the order in which it happened.
Move/MoveSeqNb	An ordered number identifying a single move in a single play in a single game and noting the order in which it happened.
Suit/SuitNm	A textual label identifying one of four divisions of cards: clubs, spades, hearts, and diamonds.

Now let's consider the target tables, their foreign key column names, and their definitions (listed in the same order as the source tables and columns). We've listed these and italicized the suggested changes in Table 10-22.

Table 10-22. *Suggested Changes to Definitions*

Target Table and Column	Definition
Game/BackDesignNm	A textual label identifying a single pattern used to decorate the reverse side of a deck of cards (for example, exotic flowers, plaid, and a logo).
CardFace/BeforeCardNm	A textual label identifying one of thirteen cards *(for example, king, queen, eight, and ace).*
Move/CardNm	A textual label identifying one of thirteen cards *that's being used in a move during a play of a game of Solitaire* (for example, king, queen, eight, and ace).
Move/SuitNm	A textual label identifying one of four divisions of cards *that's being used in a move during a play of a game of Solitaire.* They are clubs, spades, hearts, and diamonds.
Move/BeginCardPileNm	A textual label identifying *the originating* collection of cards, which is a location of a play in the game of Solitaire (for example, draw pile, discard pile, and processing pile).
Move/EndCardPileNm	A textual label identifying *the concluding* collection of cards, which is a location of a play in the game of Solitaire. (for example, draw pile, discard pile, and processing pile).
Suit/ColorNm	A textual label identifying one of two hues, red and black, used in creating the suit of a card.
Game/EndGameStateNm	A textual label identifying the outcome of a completed game (for example, win, lose, and quit).
Game/PersonId	A nonsignificant value uniquely identifying a person who is a participant in *<removed* potential—*now they're playing>* a study being conducted by the psychology department and *who is the player of the game.*
Play/PersonId	A nonsignificant value uniquely identifying a person who is a participant in a study being conducted by the psychology department and *who is the player of the game conducting the play.*
Move/PersonId	A nonsignificant value uniquely identifying a person who is a participant in a study being conducted by the psychology department and *who is the player of the game conducting the play and determining the move.*

Continued

Table 10-22. *Continued*

Target Table and Column	Definition
Play/PersonGameId	A nonsignificant number uniquely identifying a single game played by a person and *of which this play is an event.*
Move/PersonGameId	A nonsignificant number uniquely identifying a single game played by a person and *of which this move as part of the play is an occurrence.*
Move/PlaySeqNb	A ordered number identifying a single play in a single game and noting the order in which it happened and *of which this move is an occurrence.*
Card/SuitNm	A textual label identifying one of four divisions of cards: clubs, spades, hearts, and diamonds.

Now let's review the data dictionary to double-check it. Do you think when ColorNm migrated from Color to Suit that the definition of the column remained *exactly* the same? Does the color name represent the same set of values (without exceptions)? It looks that way, and therefore both the names and definitions remain the same in both locations.

What about SuitNm for Suit and Card? That seems OK, too. How about CardNm in CardFace? We already had to put a role name of BeforeCardNm on the foreign key. However, we missed changing the definition to reflect this role, didn't we? Now is the time to clear that up. Usually all you need is a modifying clause to explain why this role-named foreign key column is different from its source column.

- **Was**: A textual label identifying one of thirteen cards (for example, king, queen, eight, and ace)

- **Should be**: A textual label identifying *the card preceding* one of thirteen cards (for example, *null before king, king before queen, nine before eight, and two before ace*)

Note If you have a definition that reads the same for two differently named attributes, then either your name or your definition is wrong. The meanings of the attributes are either different or identical; they can't be both. You should always review columns that have the same names in different tables for complete consistency.

Review the changes you made to see if they help build a clearer definition of not only the data element in that table but also the role it plays once it gets there. It can be confusing to find a column that has migrated to 20 different tables but always has the same definition. For instance, PersonId in the Game table is the person who played the game, but in the Move table, PersonId is the person who made the move.

Have you ever looked at different reports that all have Date on them somewhere and no label explaining exactly what that date is? And reports aren't the worst offenders. We've reviewed database designs consisting of hundreds of tables and tried to find specific data elements only to be completely frustrated by the lack of specifics in the column names.

> **Note** Make sure you create the Physical model design with future analysts in mind. Help them out. Be as specific and descriptive as possible in your column names, and make sure they have good definitions. Only use the same column name for exactly the same data elements.

Adding Data Types and Sizing

Now you need to review your maturing Physical data model. This time let's concentrate on the physical details of the columns. When you first decided on the class word for each of your columns, you determined the general definition of that column's data type. Unfortunately, physical data types completely depend on the DBMS you're targeting, so you need to know what data types are specific to the database you're working with in order to go much further with the design.

You can, however, document a preliminary choice for the DBA and programmer from your analysis. These columns will ultimately be the clients' concern. They will know better than anyone how big they think things need things to be. You do want to make sure you challenge the clients to make sure they really understand the necessary content and that their assumptions aren't compromising the design.

Having sample data and conducting a review with the clients can be a big help. Some data types such as images, dates, binary, and integers have built-in or default sizes. Text and numbers are your biggest concern. Remember that textual data types allow numbers, but numeric data types don't allow alphabetical or special characters (except for a few specific numeric notations, such as the minus sign and decimal point).

Clients often give you really generic requirements for text field sizes. We've listed our suggestions for column size classifications. Note that these aren't platform-specific data types yet; they're just estimated sizes.

- **Tiny**: Flags or a single character for small codes

- **Small**: Three to six for abbreviations

- **Medium**: 20–40 for names

- **Large**: 40–2,000 for descriptions and paragraph text blocks

- **Really large**: 2,000+, sometimes called Long, for almost unlimited text space

Numbers generally come in the following, called *scale*:

- **Tiny**: 1–9

- **Monetary**: Will generally need at least two decimal places

- **ID**: Whole numbers with lots of space for growth (usually a system-generated number)

- **Hundreds**: 3–999 spaces

- **Thousands**: 4–9,999 spaces

You must also specify the precision of the number if you're working with decimals and percentages.

- **Amount**: Two after the decimal

- **Percent**: Two after the decimal (or all whole numbers depending)

- **Scientific notations**: As many as the clients want after the decimal

You may also need to refer to a data management sizing standard. Use the previous generalities, and apply the first cut. Varchar2 is the most flexible text type in Oracle. We're using it as an example for textual values, as shown in Table 10-23.

Remember that all the foreign key data types and sizes must match their source column exactly.

Table 10-23. *Columns with Draft Data Types, Sizes, and Nullability*

Table Name	Table Column Name	Table Column Data Type	Table Column Null Option
BackDesign	BackDesignNm	VARCHAR2(20)	NOT NULL
BackDesign	BackDesignImg	BLOB	NULL
Card	CardNm	VARCHAR2(10)	NOT NULL
Card	SuitNm	VARCHAR2(10)	NOT NULL
Card	BackDesignNm	VARCHAR2(20)	NULL
CardFace	CardNm	VARCHAR2(10)	NOT NULL
CardFace	CardTypeNm	VARCHAR2(10)	NOT NULL
CardFace	BeforeCardNm	VARCHAR2(10)	NULL
CardPile	CardPileNm	VARCHAR2(15)	NOT NULL
Color	ColorNm	VARCHAR2(10)	NOT NULL
EndGameState	EndGameStateNm	VARCHAR2(20)	NOT NULL
EndGameState	EndGameStateDesc	VARCHAR2(60)	NOT NULL
Game	EndGameStateNm	VARCHAR2(20)	NULL
Game	GameEndDt	DATE	NULL
Game	GameEndTm	NUMBER(5)	NULL
Game	PersonGameId	INTEGER	NOT NULL
Game	GameStartDt	DATE	NOT NULL
Game	PersonId	INTEGER	NOT NULL
Game	GameStartTm	NUMBER(5)	NOT NULL
Game	PlayAreaDsc	VARCHAR2(60)	NULL
Move	CardNm	VARCHAR2(10)	NOT NULL
Move	SuitNm	VARCHAR2(10)	NOT NULL
Move	BeginCardPileNm	VARCHAR2(15)	NOT NULL
Move	EndCardPileNm	VARCHAR2(15)	NOT NULL

Table Name	Table Column Name	Table Column Data Type	Table Column Null Option
Move	PersonId	INTEGER	NOT NULL
Move	MoveSeqNb	NUMBER(3)	NOT NULL
Move	PersonGameId	INTEGER	NOT NULL
Move	PlaySeqNb	NUMBER(3)	NOT NULL
Person	PersonId	INTEGER	NOT NULL
Play	PersonId	INTEGER	NOT NULL
Play	PersonGameId	INTEGER	NOT NULL
Play	PlaySeqNb	NUMBER(3)	NOT NULL
Suit	SuitNm	VARCHAR2(10)	NOT NULL
Suit	ColorNm	VARCHAR2(10)	NOT NULL
Suit	SuitSymbolImg	BLOB	NULL

Double-check the attribute nullability one more time. Figure 10-20 shows the resultant model.

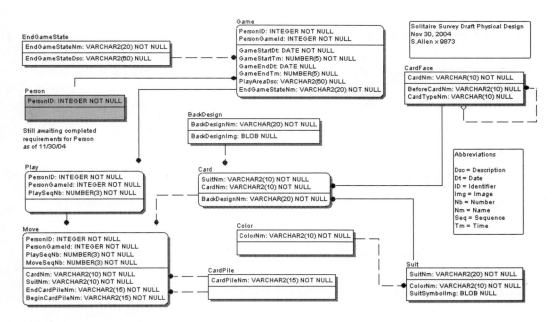

Figure 10-20. *Draft Physical model with data types and nulls defined*

Now you have something that's really looking like a Physical model design. Remember that even though it looks good enough to deploy, this is only a first pass. You still need to involve the DBA and the programming team in a review process. You should consider this current model to be the 1.0 version to use for the review cycles.

Performing Quality Checks and Getting Extra Value

You've worked through the simplified steps to take a Logical model design to a Physical one. Is there anything else you can do to make sure it's right before you deliver it? Yes, you can still perform a number of other checks to verify the correctness of the design.

- You can create instance tables with sample data and review them against the model.

- You can review the names and definitions for tables and columns with the whole team.

- You can verify the completeness of scope by mapping the model to the stated requirements.

- You can try to break the model with "what if?" analysis.

- You can identify the owners (stewards) of each table and data element.

- You can build and deploy the Data Definition Language (DDL) in a test environment and then load data into your test database.

Building Instance Tables

Build an instance table of each of the tables, and try to walk through all the screen and report requirements. Try to deliberately break what you've designed by putting strain on the data sizes and nullability constraints. Then set the instance tables side by side to try to answer a series of questions. In the case of this Solitaire model, you can ask these questions:

- What are the suits with a color value of Red?

- How many games have an ending game state of Won?

- How many games have an ending game state of Lost?

- What's the ratio of games with an ending game state of Won to the total number of games played?

Get the clients to help you make up questions they'll want answers to as they use the data.

Double-checking Names and Definitions

Double-check the names and definitions of the tables and columns one more time. We can't emphasize enough how dreadful it is to find out after three weeks of programming effort that you modeled and implemented a table or column name incorrectly. And we can't tell you how many times we've had to let an incorrect name go onto production because it would have been too costly to fix. Although imperfections will always appear at some stage, try to minimize your naming errors as much as possible.

Reviewing the Requirements

A functionality review of the data requirements is another good check. Your development team should have a good version of the development requirements by now. They will also be aware of the screen and report designs, which will help them test the model. Compare your model with them, and carefully document any extraneous or missing data elements. Spotting any missing data elements is the harder, but crucial, task.

Telling the Story

Sit down and verbalize the activity being captured by the data elements. The psychology department is collecting data about people playing Solitaire.

- **Can they differentiate between players?** Yes (although you still don't know anything about the individuals).

- **Can they differentiate between games?** Yes.

- **Can they differentiate between moves in a game for a player?** Yes.

- **Can they determine the possible moves a player had to choose from in order to evaluate which choice the player made?** No. (But they told you they didn't want to know this information.)

These are just a few of the questions you need to ask in order to test the scope boundaries one last time for appropriateness.

Identifying the Data Stewards

Data stewardship means that someone has taken responsibility for the correctness of a data set. It doesn't necessarily mean they "own" the data or the physical structure that houses the data. Who could own ColorNm, after all? However, you should be able to find someone willing to look at the data set from time to time to verify the correctness of the records. Consider this a red flag if you can't find anyone to do this; it may suggest that the data no one wants to monitor is out of scope or needs to be integrated from a different system where data stewardship is already established.

After all the care and concern you've put into the models and designs, many people may think *you're* the data steward. It's hard to explain that although you may be considered the steward of the data structures, you don't watch over or validate the data on a day-to-day basis. Someday we hope to see random selections of data records periodically sent to the data stewards for verification (such as inventory control cycle counting). This activity should be incorporated into applications, along with the application administration and help functions.

Building Test DDL

Let's look at some sample DDL generated from the model. This is a great data model validation; if you can't build and load the database, then you've missed something. Figure 10-21 contains a subset of the Solitaire model, showing Color, Suit, and Card.

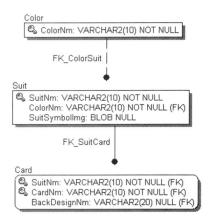

Figure 10-21. *Fully attributed Physical model showing relationship names replaced by database constraint names*

You should be able to follow every detail of the DDL from the model. These are the names you chose for table and columns, plus the sizes and whether they were `Null`:

```
CREATE TABLE Color (
    ColorNm      VARCHAR2(10) NOT NULL
);
```

Here are the definitions you slaved over to add to the DBMS library files where they'll never get lost (Oracle lets you do this but not all DBMSs do):

```
COMMENT ON TABLE Color IS 'One of two hues, red and black, used
in the creation of the suit of a Card.';

COMMENT ON COLUMN
Color.ColorNm IS 'A textual label identifying one of two hues,
red and black, used in creating the suit of a Card.
They are Red and Black.';
```

Here's the primary key you chose, after much thought, to identify a record in the `Color` table:

```
ALTER TABLE Color
    ADD ( PRIMARY KEY (ColorNm) ) ;
```

Let's now consider `Suit`. You can follow every choice you made here too.

```
CREATE TABLE Suit (
    SuitNm       VARCHAR2(10) NOT NULL,
    ColorNm      VARCHAR2(10) NOT NULL,
    SuitSymbolImg   BLOB NULL
);

COMMENT ON TABLE Suit IS 'One of four divisions of cards:
clubs, spades, hearts, and diamonds.';
```

```
COMMENT ON COLUMN Suit.SuitNm IS 'A textual label identifying
one of four divisions of cards: clubs, spades, hearts, and diamonds.';
COMMENT ON COLUMN Suit.ColorNm IS 'The textual label identifying one of
two hues, red and black, used in creating the suit of a Card.';
COMMENT ON COLUMN Suit.SuitSymbolImg IS 'A nonlanguage visual object
representing a suit in a deck of cards.';

ALTER TABLE Suit
    ADD ( PRIMARY KEY (SuitNm) ) ;
```

And finally let's consider Card.

```
CREATE TABLE Card (
    SuitNm          VARCHAR2(20) NOT NULL,
    CardNm          VARCHAR2(20) NOT NULL,
    BackDesignNm        VARCHAR2(20) NULL
);

COMMENT ON TABLE Card IS 'One of 52 unique game pieces used
in playing games bearing pictures of figures or numbers organized
by suit (for example, the queen of clubs and two of diamonds are cards.';
COMMENT ON COLUMN Card.SuitNm IS 'A textual label identifying one
of four divisions of cards: clubs, spades, hearts, and diamonds.';
COMMENT ON COLUMN Card.CardNm IS 'A textual label identifying one of
13 cards that precedes the card noted in the record ordered from king
to ace (for example, king for the queen, eight for the seven, and two
for the ace).';

ALTER TABLE Card
    ADD ( PRIMARY KEY (SuitNm, CardNm) ) ;
```

If you now consider the relationship between the Color and Suit tables, you can see the relational integrity constraint requires that a color name exists in the Color table before it can be inserted into the Suit table.

```
ALTER TABLE Suit
    ADD ( FOREIGN KEY (ColorNm)
            REFERENCES Color ) ;
```

As for the relationship between Suit and Card, you can see the foreign key constraint that makes sure all Suit names appear in the Suit set before it can be used in the definition of Card.

```
ALTER TABLE Card
    ADD ( FOREIGN KEY (SuitNm)
            REFERENCES Suit) ;
```

Every graphical symbol and nitpicky little detail from the model ends up in the DDL. Every choice you made from the beginning of the tutorial has become part of the foundation for the Physical model of your clients' Solitaire survey application.

Reviewing Other Potential Issues

Now that you have a Physical model in your hands, you can consider a number of further modifications.

Adding Operational Columns

You may be asked to add columns to the tables that have nothing to do with the clients' data needs. The DBA may have a set of physical columns that they usually add to the model for table/data/process/error handling management. We call these *operational columns*, referring to the process of managing the operations involved in creating and managing the data itself. These come in handy when someone is trying to troubleshoot or audit the database. The ETL team may also need to add attributes or tables to facilitate their data migration procedures.

For the Solitaire example, a DBA would usually add columns such as these:

- `CreateID`: The user or process creating the record

- `CreateTimeDt`: The date and time stamp identifying when the record was inserted

- `CreateTerminalID` (or `UserId` or `SourceId`): Other information identifying the individual who inserted the record

- `LastModifiedByID`: The user or process that last updated the record

- `LastModifiedDt`: The date and time stamp identifying when the record was last updated

- `LastModifiedByTerminalID` (or `UserId` or `SourceId`): Other information identifying the individual who last updated the record

These column additions are generally the last modifications made to the Physical model before the test environment is built, only because they make the model so much bigger. In this model, the added operational columns would outnumber the actual data columns and make it harder to concentrate on the actual data. Sometimes you'll even need to add extra tables that have to do with operational management of the application (such as sequence number management). It's all part of the Physical model.

■**Note** These tables and columns will generally not show up on the Logical model. They won't be elements that map from the Logical model to the Physical model. In fact, sometimes these elements aren't even put in place by the data modeler. The model may be given to other members of the team who will hone and polish the Physical model design.

Documenting Population

One of the things the DBA needs in order to continue the process of physicalizing is an estimate of the number of table rows and the table's growth rate (this is technically referred to as *volumetrics*). The clients are going to have to help you with growth rate, but from your analysis you should be able to come up with some insights about the number of rows. If similar data stores are already in existence, you may even be able to estimate some growth statistics from them. However, keep any estimation formulas simple, and use a rule of thumb in your analysis (which you and the team will decide on), such as the following:

- **Small**: Fewer than 100 records

- **Medium**: Fewer than 100,000 records

- **Large**: More than 100,000 records

    Color-code the model, and add notes next to the table name. Be aware that you may still have to guess on an actual quantity. For example, in Figure 10-22, we've used shading to highlight the largest tables for the DBA.

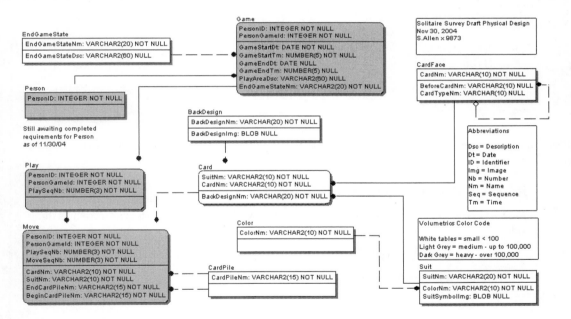

Figure 10-22. *Using shading on the Physical model to show volumetrics*

Documenting Volatility

Another thing that could be useful to the DBA is an overview of how much SELECT, INSERT, UPDATE, and DELETE activity is expected on each table, using a scale such as Static, Mildly Active, and Very Active. This would obviously need to be a different view of the model, as shown in Figure 10-23.

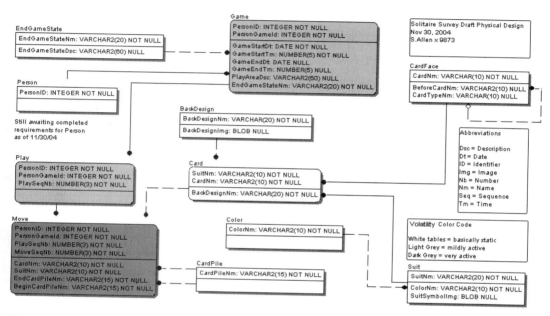

Figure 10-23. *Using shading on the Physical model to show* SELECT, INSERT, UPDATE, *and* DELETE *activity*

Recognizing the Model's Power

You can use the model to now show other important physical database aspects, such as the following:

- Frequent query paths

- Targeted integration points

- Special security sensitivities

- Criticality of quality

- Known required speed requirements

- Expected data use statistics in screens and reports

- Pedigree information for data sources

- Stewardship of data elements

You usually need to address several issues while the model matures toward a final design. Keep the model up-to-date and useable for everyone. Adding other information to the Physical model helps with the next set of decisions to be made and performance enhancements such as indexing and denormalization. The more the team knows about the use of the data at this point, then the more informed their next decision will be. For example, it's riskier to denormalize data into a table when that table has a large number of records, is more active, or is volatile.

It's important that the model communicates your understanding of the subject area clearly. Ideally, your model will confirm concepts, highlight inconsistencies between requirements documents, prompt discussion about the physical database, and ensure everyone understands the data, the data relationships, and the business problem.

Now you're ready for a data model walk-through with the rest of the team. You have some marvelous documentation to help move the team onto the next steps. Don't expect it to be perfect, however; there are always further changes to these models as they're reviewed.

Summary

In this chapter you took your Logical model and transformed it into a transactional, fully attributed Physical model. In creating this Physical model, you followed these basic steps:

1. You broke down the categories in the Logical model in terms of tables in the Physical model.

2. You identified suitable primary keys for each table.

3. You defined and named the physical foreign keys.

4. You tested the accuracy of the Physical model.

You also saw how reviewing and enhancing the data model happens over several iterations, and you double-checked that the model makes sense. It's crucial that this Physical model is as accurate as possible—it's the foundation for both programmers and DBAs. Mistakes made at this stage can prove to be costly, and all team members should be involved in developing and verifying the Physical model's accuracy.

Although the Physical model, in its completed state, should be ready to implement, it's also important to realize that each system will require a trade-off between the processes of physicalization and denormalization.

And remember, although you've gotten through transforming the Logical model to the Physical model, your clients have left the details of Person outstanding. You'll have to deal with this missing information in the next chapter.

■ ■ ■

CHAPTER 11

Designing a Physical Model Only

This chapter covers the process of building a Physical data model without first going through the steps of creating a Conceptual model to guide the analysis and then building a Logical model. This method is usually used only when the alternative is no data modeling involvement in the design at all. It usually arises out of an emergency or a need for expediency and is normally used when you're assigned to maintenance projects or when you're trying to accommodate new requirements that aren't part of the original analysis.

We'll continue our tutorial of Solitaire and flesh out the player portion of the Physical model design; we'll also show how to add the new requirement of tracking new player information. This covers a "bottom-up" approach to data modeling, where the design starts with specific data needs rather than a conceptual understanding of the subject area.

Real-World Constraints

Why would you create a Physical model design without going through the traditional, disciplined, industry-approved approach of the Conceptual, Logical, and Physical model design stages? In an ideal scenario, the development and review of each of the models we've discussed throughout this book would get sufficient time in the project. However, in the real world of business, projects fall behind schedule, grow short of resources, and go over budget. On smaller projects, the business may not be able to afford the time and effort it takes to carry out the full analysis cycle. Team members often have to accomplish project goals without the ideal skills, the analytical tools, the proper time, or the correct access to resources. Teams also often find themselves sideswiped with unexpected requirements that need to be incorporated long after the Conceptual and Logical models have been completed. Many types of real-world constraints in your organization may force you to start your design at the Physical model design.

For "quick fixes" to existing systems, this kind of modeling is frequently the chosen methodology, with no thought given to Logical or Conceptual models at all. It takes a highly developed and strategically aligned data management group to be able to funnel software change requests through the full data modeling process without being perceived as a bottleneck.

In these scenarios, you have to be pragmatic and do the best you can with regard to the constraints. These are times when some analysis is better than no data management of the solution at all. Although speed is important in these situations, this doesn't mean you can't apply standardization, normalization, and quality in order to develop a solution that will support future growth. With no data management oversight, this kind of project will generate suboptimal table structures compared with those carefully chosen under calmer circumstances.

▇**Caution** The key point here is that this isn't recommended as the normal choice, but as an exception it's better than no modeling at all.

Despite the need for expediency, sometimes you really need to strongly protest this approach. This approach is a particularly bad idea when you're working with the following:

- **Mission-critical data elements**: When the whole enterprise is going to need the data

- **Systems with long life expectancies**: When the system has to last in order to be a cost-effective solution

- **Shared-environment impacts**: When bad table design and poor performance could seriously impact other users on the same servers

Sometimes it's worth putting up a fight. However, in the case of the Solitaire example, you know this is intended to be a stand-alone, single-semester project, running on a single department machine. So it shouldn't impact anyone else.

Where to Start

The only good thing about modeling this way is that you usually have a very defined set of data elements that need to be physically implemented. These data elements are usually part of a new form or report that needs to be supported by an existing table design. The key points at the outset of this work are as follows:

Read as much documentation about the existing system as you can, including documents such as enhancement requests or system design documentation, so that you know as much as possible about the existing system.

Identify a complete set of data element requirements, if possible. Get copies of all the forms or reports relevant to the task. Talk to the clients to establish exactly what they want.

Begin with the existing Physical model table design. Capture every data element as-is from the sources. You may be working from a complicated set of Microsoft Excel files, forms, or documents, which may not be normalized at all. Try to start with a simple table design for each source. For now, show no relationships to other data sets, and list the data elements in these simple tables.

Look for opportunities to normalize your data by testing these simple tables against the rules of normalization or by looking for natural restricted values and repeating groups.

Rework your table and column names. The original column names will have more to do
with the preexisting labels and source column names than any deep understanding of the

data. This means that the definitions of the names will be much narrower and in danger of being misunderstood in the future. Good, solid definitions are an absolute must here.

Review each data element, and consider whether it can be further divided into sub-elements. Focus particularly on text information in forms and reports. Reexamine the clients' requirements, and consider what information they really need immediately. Remember that you'll use this Physical model design in actually implementing the application, so you'll need to consider reporting requirements.

Consider what elements could be sourced as a foreign key from existing data sets or tables.

Consider what elements lend themselves to being used as primary and alternate keys. Determine and verify relationships between data elements, and apply the requirements of the various normal forms.

Reexamine the clients' requirements, and try to plan for the system's future growth.

With this checklist in mind, let's look at the new requirements for the Solitaire system as the first example in this chapter.

The Solitaire System

In the case of the Solitaire model, the clients have finally given you a copy of the form they intend to use to register the Solitaire players who have volunteered to allow their games to be analyzed. It's late in the project, and the budget doesn't allow the team to keep the programmer much longer. You're asked to add the new requirements to the existing table design in as short a time as possible.

At this point, you'll want as complete a set of data element requirements as you can get. You'll want examples of completed forms as well as blank ones to help you understand the data rules. Figure 11-1 shows the form.

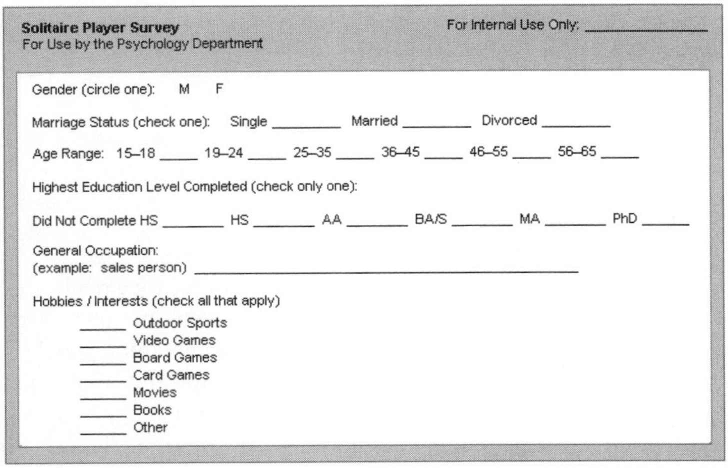

Solitaire Player Survey
For Use by the Psychology Department

For Internal Use Only: ____________

Gender (circle one): M F

Marriage Status (check one): Single ________ Married ________ Divorced ________

Age Range: 15–18 ____ 19–24 ____ 25–35 ____ 36–45 ____ 46–55 ____ 56–65 ____

Highest Education Level Completed (check only one):

Did Not Complete HS ______ HS ______ AA ______ BA/S ______ MA ______ PhD ______

General Occupation:
(example: sales person) ________________________________

Hobbies / Interests (check all that apply)

_____ Outdoor Sports
_____ Video Games
_____ Board Games
_____ Card Games
_____ Movies
_____ Books
_____ Other

Figure 11-1. *The Solitaire player registration screen*

Model Exactly What You See

The table you're building to begin with is Player, using a definition that looks something like this:

- **Player**: Information about a Solitaire player as captured by the psychology department registration form

Start with Labels

One of the best ways to begin is to make a list of all the labels you find on the form. You have so much flexibility today in handling data with dynamic screen creation and looping queries that it's hard to remember the old days of simple, fill-in-the-blank data gathering. This form doesn't offer much flexibility, so go with the notion that the data elements are singular, stable columns that support the form. Your design doesn't have to be any more sophisticated than the form itself.

Reports can be a little more complicated in that they often have headings, subheadings, and detailed data in the display. When working with either forms or reports, don't force all the data into one table if it doesn't make sense. Start with what's easy to understand, and begin designing there.

Generally, a single form can begin as a single table. Simply using the headings from the form shown in Figure 11-1 as data elements will give you a good start; it results in a flat table that looks like the one on the left of Figure 11-2. You'll find many tables in production-deployed applications that look like this; forms have simply been made into database tables, without any thought to future expansion or maintainability.

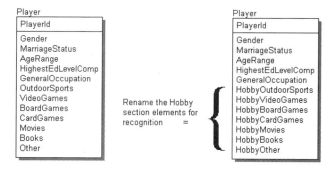

Figure 11-2. *A starting point for supporting the form*

At this point you need to review these names and consider how descriptive they really are. The last seven columns are concerned with hobbies, so you should alter the column names to reflect this. The resulting table appears on the right side of Figure 11-2. The next thing you'll look for are the columns that seem to repeat. Without naming the columns appropriately, you can easily miss repeating groups of attributes.

Apply Naming Standards

No matter what your table structures look like, don't let the design stay like this first draft. Even when you're pressed for time, it's important to set up the column names properly. At least then, when you revisit this table in the future, you'll have meaningful and helpful column names. In other words, get your attribute types in place using class words. Every column name must use class words (these are usually defined by your data management group) and should reflect the attribute type at the end of the column name no matter what naming convention was used in the source. Refer to the previous chapter if you need a reminder of what class words are available to you.

While you're looking at the column names, make sure they're complete enough to be meaningful on their own. Add modifiers if you think there may be confusion in the future.

■**Note** Table and column names are almost always permanent once they're built. Even if you get the chance to enhance the design in the future, you'll rarely get the opportunity to change table and column names. Choose carefully.

Whatever you do, make sure you aren't responsible for the existence of a table that's filled with columns named Column1, Column2, Date, Name, Description, and so on. Table 11-1 shows the column names for the Player table based on the example form.

Table 11-1. Player *Table's Column Names*

First Version Column Name	New Column Name
PlayerId	PlayerId
Gender	GenderFlg
MarriageStatus	MarriageStatusNm
AgeRange	AgeRangeNm
HighestEdLevelComp	HighestEdLevelCompCd
GeneralOccupation	GeneralOccupationTxt
HobbyOutdoorSports	HobbyOutdoorSportsFlg
HobbyVideoGames	HobbyVideoGamesFlg
HobbyBoardGames	HobbyBoardGamesFlg
HobbyCardGames	HobbyCardGamesFlg
HobbyMovies	HobbyMoviesFlg
HobbyBooks	HobbyBooksFlg
HobbyOther	HobbyOtherFlg

Introducing class words to the original table structure gives you the table design shown in Figure 11-3.

Figure 11-3. *The* Player *table with naming standards applied*

Note that this design isn't in Third Normal Form (3NF), and it's not flexible. You'd need to alter the table to be able to track a new type of hobby. This design also doesn't ensure quality data. The HighestEdLevelCompCd field stores free-form codes, and any record whose value deviates from the list of approved codes could cause reporting anomalies. Also, the GeneralOccupationTxt field could be named Stuff because there's no way to add any data integrity checks to validate the data it contains. Clearly, this isn't an ideal design.

Although it's not pretty, it works. At least you've standardized the names and entered definitions for each field. You could take this table design and add it to the model you finished in the previous chapter since it supports the current data requirements of the clients.

But with requirements that are as simple as these, you should be able to do a quick-and-dirty Logical model design first (especially since a Logical model already exists for this subject). Please consider modeling a Physical model design directly only as an emergency contingency measure. Most modelers consider creating only a Physical model design to be a cop-out. Again, it may break your heart to do this, but it happens. So let's take this example one step further. You can do certain things to give it just a bit more quality and flexibility.

Create Lookup Tables

You know that the form, as it was given to you, has a restricted list of values for three columns: MarriageStatusNm, AgeRangeNm, and HighestEdLevelCompCd. Assume that you're probably dealing with the *first* version of the form and also assume that someone is, at some later point, going to realize they left off "Widow/er" from the list of valid marriage statuses, "12–14" from the list of valid age ranges, and the "GED" from the list of valid education levels. If each of these lists of values lives in its own table, a new value can be added without a database design or programming change. The following is an Oracle example of how you could implement these integrity checks *without* creating any new tables:

```
CREATE TABLE Player (
   GenderFlg Varchar2(1) NULL
      CHECK (GenderFlg IN ('M', 'F'),
   MarriageStatusNm Varchar2(10) NULL
      CHECK (MarriageStatusNm IN
      ('Single','Married','Divorced')
   AgeRangeNm Varchar2(5) NULL
```

```
CHECK (Age IN ('15-18', '19-24', '25-35',
'36-45', '46-55', '56-65'))
```
...

Hard-coded (or *nailed-up*) is the term used to describe data values explicitly stored in screens, procedures, triggers, views, Hypertext Markup Language (HTML), and so on. Hard-coded values aren't dynamically selected from a set. Frequently, values are hard-coded without any thought given to the effort and cost of data maintenance that has to be shouldered every time a list of values changes. For example, if the set of values is kept in a drop-down object on a screen, every time the list changes, you need to deploy a new version of the screen code. If code used in a screen, trigger, procedure, or view uses hard-coded filters, makes reference to literal values, or uses IF...THEN case logic, then you must know what programming code needs revising and change *all* affected code *appropriately* when a business rule changes.

■**Tip** As a rule of thumb, all data values should be stored in database tables. All business restrictions of data values should be stored in database tables.

Give the list of data values some room to grow. See if you can move some of the columns in the current table design into new tables of their own so you have a single place to maintain and update these values. In this case, you can create new tables for the data stored in the MarriageStatusNm, HighestEdLevelCompCd, and AgeRangeNm columns. The relationships between these new tables and the main table are nonidentifying. At this stage, you'll use a cardinality from the new tables to the main table of zero, one, or many. The table design now looks like Figure 11-4.

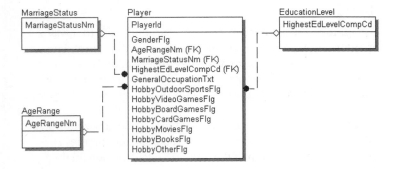

Figure 11-4. *Adding lookup tables to the* Player *table design*

Look Again for Important Data Sets

At this point you need to look at the model again to determine whether you really have the data sets you need. Let's look at the form. The reason you have a pile of hobby flags is that the form presented the data set as a set of check boxes, which allows for multiple optional selections. Currently, each option results in a true/false or yes/no data value. If you analyze the data without the business rules, you might think yes/no is the data set you're looking at here.

> ■**Note** Not all the data sets consist of the values captured on a form. Sometimes the form labels them-
> selves are values in a data set.

What you really want to capture here is Hobby. Right now it has seven members of the set defined. Pull Hobby out as a separate table. Can more than one player enjoy a hobby? Yes, that's why you have all those flags on the form. It's also obvious that one player can enjoy more than one hobby. So, you have a many-to-many relationship between the set of hobbies and the set of players. At this point, you need to create an intersection (associative) table and remove all the hobby flags from the Player table. Figure 11-5 shows the Player model that allows multiple hobby values.

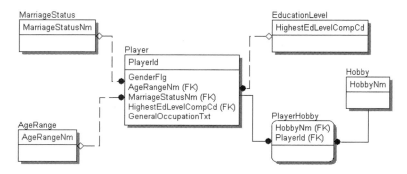

Figure 11-5. *The* Player *model allowing multiple hobby values*

Check Out the Text Fields

The next review should be the columns you classified as Txt. You classified them that way because they seem to contain unformatted, multivalued, multielement, or free-form data. Text fields are basically just "stuff" fields, and, we assure you, they do legitimately exist. In their current form, these data elements can't be automatically validated. You can't check for illegitimate values or prevent the clients from violating the original intention of the data element stored in the column.

The only . . .Txt column in the Player table is GeneralOccupationTxt. Review your notes from the initial discussion with the clients, and consider what sort of information they're expecting to capture about each player's occupation. If they want to allow the person filling out the form to note multiple occupations, then break out the column into a one-to-many relationship. The clients may think they will never want to report or search on that field, but you need to assume they will.

We've seen text blocks take on such a life force that you'd be stunned. Suddenly, a poor programmer is parsing a text string for dates, asterisks, and pound signs to identify different data elements and then forcing an application to interpret and respond to the results. At best, if you build a Physical model design that encourages a single entry in each field, you'll have built a structure that supports future development. It will provide you the capability to expand and extend the model as requirements change. At worst, you'll have designed an extra table. Figure 11-6 shows the Player model allowing multiple occupations.

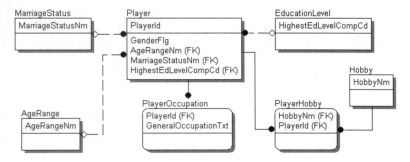

Figure 11-6. *The* Player *model allowing multiple occupations*

Look at Keys and Data Types

You need to apply all the regular polishing techniques here, too. As a reminder, you need to do the following:

- Select the appropriate primary keys.

- Review the foreign keys for correct definitions and names.

- Provide some generic data type and size information.

- Double-check naming conventions, and reevaluate the model.

- Add other details that may be pertinent to the rest of the team.

Primary Key Choice

Look closely at the current key choices. Every column that's a longish text field should be reviewed, since Txt data elements are almost never good choices for primary keys. They're just too undisciplined. Let's look at the PlayerOccupation table. Since GeneralOccupationTxt is going to be far too general to use in the primary key, let's move it below the line in the PlayerOccupation table and create an ID column called PlayerOccupationID as the primary key instead. Although it's possible at this stage to move PlayerId out of the PlayerOccupation primary key (since the new PlayerOccupationID field is, by definition, unique), we'll keep it in for now. We like to keep as much of the natural key intact as possible.

Now look at the name columns. Most name-type data elements that end up in a primary key position can easily be replaced by a code to shorten the migrating value. The only issue here is that you'd need to ask the clients if they want to take responsibility for creating and maintaining a new data element. Right now all the data elements they want are on the form, and you're proposing a new one. Make sure you discuss this with the clients at your design review meeting. It's important you ensure the clients are fully aware of any effect your design may have on their system and on its maintenance.

Most clients seem to like codes when they have to type in values from the keyboard. They want to use *S* instead of *Single* or *VG* instead of *Video Games* when inputting data on screens. But they generally want the full name on reports. The important point here is to help them do both. Give them long names on their reports if they have only codes, and use existing long names to build short codes that are as intuitive as possible for screen input. Document your coding scheme alongside your model to ensure a minimum of confusion. If the clients agree your coding convention is acceptable, then, in this example, the new model would look like Figure 11-7.

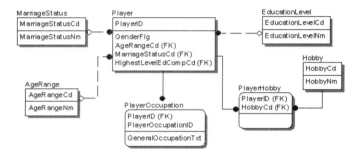

Figure 11-7. *The* Player *model with code fields substituted for name fields*

Physical Model Design Detail Characteristics

Next, you need to make your best guess on other physical characteristics of the model before you can deliver it to the database administrator (DBA). Other physical characteristics you need to consider include the following:

Choose appropriate data types (including size and precision) for your columns: Using any information you have about the sample values that appear on the form, choose the most restrictive data type that allows for actual and anticipated sample values. Pay particular attention to the current and anticipated size of textual code or description values and the number of decimal places required for numeric values.

Choose appropriate nullability for the columns: Based on the information you've gathered, determine if the columns are optional or required, and then set column nullability.

Determine anticipated data population statistics: Your DBA will want to know how much data is being stored for each record, the anticipated number of records, and the growth rate.

Highlight your assumptions regarding the model's level of precision, and, in particular, note areas where background detail is lacking. This will help your DBA assess the system's physical requirements. You may need to add default operational data columns to the tables as well. Return to the design standards, and make sure this hurried analysis activity has followed as many of the rules as possible. Figure 11-8 shows the Physical model design with data types.

Often you'll permit less restrictive data rules (such as allowing columns to be null allowed) in this type of modeling than in situations where a more thorough analysis of the data elements is possible. You may want to give text columns a little larger maximum size, or you may use more inclusive data types to store the data than what's strictly necessary. You may, for example, choose not to specify the number of places after the decimal for columns where the

source data suggests that one is sufficient. You need to assign Physical model design characteristics that will support a broad spectrum of data values in the future without having much
of a clue as to what those values will be.

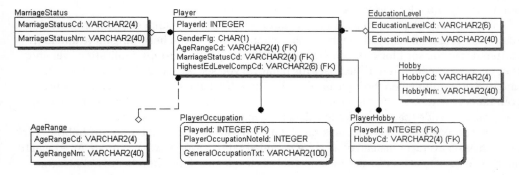

Figure 11-8. *The Physical model design with data types*

■**Tip** Most nonkey columns should be null allowed unless it states otherwise on the form.

Quality and Compromise

What now? You're probably going to cut out some of your walk-throughs, but you do need to
reevaluate and justify your design before it goes to the DBA to be built in the test environment.
In the same way that you went straight to a Physical model design in this chapter without
doing a Logical model design first, you'll probably let the technical team look at the design
first, rather than the business team. In these situations, the design has to meet the technical
team's requirements and development schedule as much as the business team's requirements.

In the current design, you have eighteen data elements in seven tables, compared to the
thirteen data elements in the single table with which you started. This isn't a huge difference
in terms of the number of database objects, but it's a huge difference in the quality, integrity,
and expandability of the data elements themselves. Are seven tables harder to code for than
one? Oh, yes. So why in the world is this a better design than the nice single table you had at
the beginning? It certainly isn't quicker to implement, and the new design increases the risk of
not being able to meet your deadlines (which weren't changed when the new requirements
came in).

The key question to ask yourself is, what do you do if, next week, you're asked to put a
new field in the database describing the probability for game success based on a player's hobbies? How would this fit in the nice single table? It would be implemented as seven separate
new columns. Each one of the hobby-related columns would have to have a corresponding
probability factor column. If there were three or four more interesting pieces of information
having to do with hobbies, then the quantity of new table columns skyrockets, making the
impact on the application bigger and bigger.

You can frequently find that kind of column growth in applications that didn't recognize and remove buried value lists or that chose to denormalize these value lists on purpose. These designs have repeating groups that go on and on. Not only that, but having implemented that design, it becomes extremely difficult to revise the design and physical implementation without incurring considerable cost (and application downtime).

When you do implement a flat table column solution, what happens to the front-end screens and reports? Can you see the initially simple input screen becoming more and more cluttered? Do you see blocks of code managing those repeating groups, replicating over and over in every screen or report that uses the data? Do you see the danger of missing a code maintenance point when the logic needs to be altered? A flat table design encourages programmers to write code that interprets the design. Any time the data requirements change, every piece of code that interprets this data is affected, wherever it's located.

Now think about querying that kind of data. How do you find out how many hobbies each player lists on average? Instead of a nice SQL-coded SELECT AVG(COUNT)...GROUP BY PlayerId query, you have to use a procedural loop analysis to get an average number of hobbies for each player. The same goes for any hobby-related column that shows up in the future. Reporting becomes increasingly difficult, since it has to include procedural code that determines how to combine large numbers of disparate values. The bottom line is that adding new data elements in the future will be a much more complicated task if you leave normalization activities until later. It's important to recognize that this type of approach doesn't result in a smart design. A simple, quick, and easy solution that meets your current requirements may quickly become a maintenance nightmare.

On the other hand, it's best to acknowledge right away that project teams have to pick and choose between Physical model designs in the same way a family has to pick between houses they want to buy. How much analysis can you afford to do initially when compared against the project's available budget and prioritized requirements? When you're under pressure to complete your design quickly, remind everyone that whatever design is chosen today is likely to be around for a long, long time. In fact, a poor design will often be around longer than the person doing the choosing.

The structure you have now for the example lends itself to enhancement and is relatively accommodating with respect to potential future needs. What have you gained by taking a little time to refine the design?

- You've isolated as many of the data sets as you could find.

- You can now easily expand data elements owned by those data sets over time.

- You can now set up new relationships to simple data sets.

- You've simplified future integration with other systems because you've simplified the definition of the data content and the effort needed to understand it.

The new model presents a fertile environment for growth. It's a good idea to build (and/or design) for the foreseeable future if you can afford it. If you have to go forward with a simple flat table design, at least apply existing naming standards and document what the business rules are.

That's as far you can go for now. You've taken a tiny little form and designed a fairly normalized set of data structures for it. Test the model against the normal forms to prove it to yourself.

At this stage you could continue with a further backward step and create a Logical model design, though we won't cover that exercise here. The design you've created so far addresses the needs of the player form. You could create a Logical model for the `Player` table in the context of this project if you wanted to get a higher level of understanding of the player data and how it relates to the analysis of game activity. It's possible to add this new model into the larger Solitaire project model by hooking it into the shadow entity called `Person` in the existing Logical model. You'd have to change the name of the table to `Person` or modify the foreign keys to be valid for relationships with `Player`.

This amounts to about six to eight hours of work when you include the definitions, quality checks, and report generation. Almost any team should give you a day to do this, as it will later be worth the time to both the application and the clients. Again, this time spent up front developing and documenting a normalized design could be worth hundreds of hours of maintenance in the future. Creating a Logical model will allow you to understand and document the way the data really exists, rather than just the way it might be used on one form or report.

Now let's try an exercise that has a more complicated set of data rules embedded in it.

Something a Bit More Challenging

The psychology department has decided it also wants to keep track of the students who help with the research project. It needs to keep certain information about the students for tax purposes and wants to add this information to the project database.

We hope your project manager would argue that such a huge addition to the requirements at such a late date is an unreasonable imposition. In fact, sometimes your ability to provide a quick-and-dirty Physical model design for your project manager can give them the ammunition they need to explain how significant a proposed change actually is. However, we'll show the worst-case scenario here; we'll assume you were unable to defer these requirements and that you're still up against an unchanged hard deadline. Once again, you're performing emergency data modeling. Let's begin by taking a look at the registration form (see Figure 11-9).

Applying the general principles outlined earlier in the chapter, you can begin by noting exactly what you see and create one large preliminary list of data elements that could be implemented as a flat table. You do this so you don't lose anything during your analysis; without this long list, it would be easy to lose something along the way. Figure 11-10 shows the form as a flat table.

We repeated section labels in names if the field name applied to multiple fields in multiple sections, such as `NameLast`, `NameFirst`, and `NameMiddle`. This prevents duplication of column names in the model after the first pass, when the form labels have been simplified.

This table doesn't currently have a primary key, because you have no idea what's going to make the record unique at this stage. But you need something to use as a bookmark for a key. Some would elevate the Social Security number as a unique identifier to the primary key; however, only a certain set of the student body will have these numbers. Resist the temptation to use Social Security numbers for much of anything. This is sensitive information, sometimes protected by law, which in many cases may need to be encrypted to meet data protection act requirements.

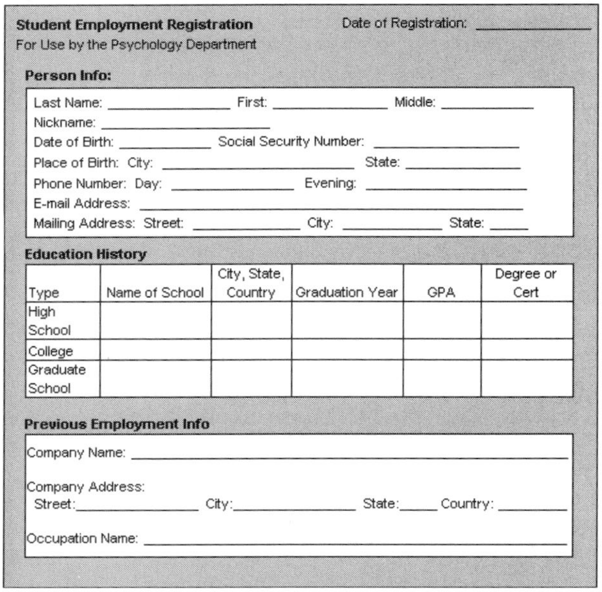

Student Employment Registration Date of Registration: ____________
For Use by the Psychology Department

Person Info:

Last Name: ____________ First: ____________ Middle: __________
Nickname: ________________
Date of Birth: __________ Social Security Number: ______________
Place of Birth: City: ____________________ State: ____________
Phone Number: Day: ____________ Evening: ________________
E-mail Address: ____
Mailing Address: Street: ___________ City: __________ State: ____

Education History

Type	Name of School	City, State, Country	Graduation Year	GPA	Degree or Cert
High School					
College					
Graduate School					

Previous Employment Info

Company Name: ____

Company Address:
Street:____________ City:____________ State:____ Country: ________

Occupation Name: ____

Figure 11-9. *The student employment registration form*

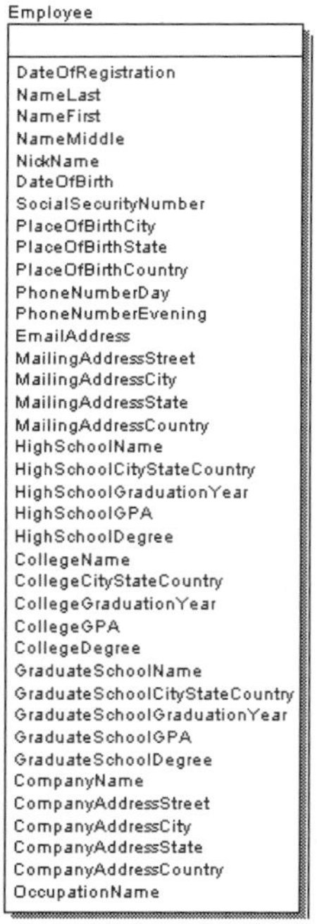

Figure 11-10. *The student employment registration form as a flat table*

Tip It's usually a bad idea to use codes (so-called smart codes, or otherwise) as members of a primary key unless your project controls the process by which these codes are created. You don't want your primary key to be invalidated because an external entity decided to change the way they construct, issue, or format special codes.

When in doubt and in a hurry, create a surrogate key ID field to act as the primary key.

Classifying the Data Elements

Organize and rename the data elements by class word. Table 11-2 lists the original and revised column names.

Table 11-2. Employee *Table's Column Names, Original and Revised*

First Version Column Name	New Column Name
CollegeCityStateCountry	CollegeCityStateCountryTxt
CollegeDegree	CollegeDegreeCd
CollegeGPA	CollegeGPANb
CollegeGraduationYear	CollegeGraduationYearNb
CollegeName	CollegeNm
CompanyAddressCity	CompanyAddressCityNm
CompanyAddressCountry	CompanyAddressCountryCd
CompanyAddressState	CompanyAddressStateCd
CompanyAddressStreet	CompanyAddressStreetTxt
CompanyName	CompanyNm
DateOfBirth	EmpBirthDt
DateOfRegistration	EmpRegistrationDt
EmailAddress	EmpEmailAddressTxt
GraduateSchoolCityStateCountry	GraduateSchoolCityStateCountryTxt
GraduateSchoolDegree	GraduateSchoolDegreeCd
GraduateSchoolGPA	GraduateSchoolGPANb
GraduateSchoolGraduationYear	GraduateSchoolGraduationYearNb
GraduateSchoolName	GraduateSchoolNm
HighSchoolCityStateCountry	HighSchoolCityStateCountryTxt
HighSchoolDegree	HighSchoolDegreeCd
HighSchoolGPA	HighSchoolGPANb
HighSchoolGraduationYear	HighSchoolGraduationYearNb
HighSchoolName	HighSchoolNm
MailingAddressCity	EmpMailingAddressCityNm

Continued

Table 11-2. *Continued*

First Version Column Name	New Column Name
MailingAddressCountry	EmpMailingAddressCountryCd
MailingAddressState	EmpMailingAddressStateCd
MailingAddressStreet	EmpMailingAddressStreetTxt
NameFirst	EmpFirstNm
NameLast	EmpLastNm
NameMiddle	EmpMiddleNm
Nickname	EmpNicknameTxt
OccupationName	EmpOccupationNm
PhoneNumberDay	EmpDayPhoneNb
PhoneNumberEvening	EmpEveningPhoneNb
PlaceOfBirthCity	EmpPlaceOfBirthCityNm
PlaceOfBirthCountry	EmpPlaceOfBirthCountryCd
PlaceOfBirthState	EmpPlaceOfBirthStateCd
SocialSecurityNumber	SocialSecurityNb

■**Note** If this is as far as you can go with the Physical model table design, you need to abbreviate some of the more lengthy names.

This will leave the flat table structure shown in Figure 11-11.

Now you need to look over the text data again to look for any opportunity to include more detail in the design.

Text Fields

You need to examine the text data fields in the model to determine any important data elements that are currently obscured within them. In this case, the relevant fields are as follows:

- CollegeCityStateCountryTxt

- GradSchoolCityStateCountryTxt

- HighSchoolCityStateCountryTxt

- CompanyAddressStreetTxt

- EmpEmailAddressTxt

- EmpMailingAddressStreetTxt

- EmpNicknameTxt

- EmpOccupationTxt

Employee

EmpId
EmpRegistrationDt
EmpLastNm
EmpFirstNm
EmpMiddleNm
EmpNickNameTxt
EmpBirthDt
SocialSecurityNb
EmpPlaceOfBirthCityNm
EmpPlaceOfBirthStateCd
EmpPlaceOfBirthCountryCd
EmpDayPhoneNb
EmpEveningPhoneNb
EmpEmailAddressTxt
EmpMailingAddressStreetTxt
EmpMailingAddressCityNm
EmpMailingAddressStateCd
EmpMailingAddressCountryCd
HighSchoolNm
HighSchoolCityStateCountryTxt
HighSchoolGraduationYearNb
HighSchoolGPANb
HighSchoolDegreeCd
CollegeNm
CollegeCityStateCountryTxt
CollegeGraduationYearNb
CollegeGPANb
CollegeDegreeCd
GraduateSchoolNm
GraduateSchoolCityStateCountryTxt
GraduateSchoolGraduationYearNb
GraduateSchoolGPANb
GraduateSchoolDegreeCd
CompanyNm
CompanyAddressStreetTxt
CompanyAddressCityNm
CompanyAddressStateCd
CompanyAddressCountryCd
EmpOccupationNm

Figure 11-11. *The student employment registration (*Employee*) table with renamed columns*

To aid you in this task, you should speak to the clients to determine any expected patterns or rules regarding the data collected in these text fields. Get the clients to give you sample data. If they've already received some completed paper forms, look at them to help you understand the data that has been collected. You need to know what *your clients* are expecting (not what *you're* expecting) before you can analyze them with any confidence. If, for instance, the clients are expecting values such as William Cody, Buffalo Bill in the EmpNicknameTxt column, you should consider this as a field containing multiple values for the purposes of normal form rule analysis. You won't know until you ask.

Street addresses are usually left as text, since there's generally little value (except to the U.S. Post Office) in splitting the number of the building, the street or route name, the P.O. box number, or apartment number from the remainder of the address text. Remember, though, many real and distinct data elements are buried in address text fields. If it became important, for example, to find everyone living on the 1000 block of Main Street, a programmer would have a hard time parsing for the values when the data is contained as a single block of text.

You probably already wondered why we left the ...CityStateCountry... multielement columns together. Generally, you'd pull apart such fields. However, our rule of thumb is that your first pass through the model should document what you're given as closely as possible. The form designer didn't create separate fields for different data elements, so maybe you shouldn't either. Starting with what you see gives you a starting place for data element discussions while referring to things that should be familiar to the clients.

There may be reasons unknown to you regarding why the form was created that way. If the clients don't care about the distinct data elements that make up an address, then they may not care (other than for information) about what is being put in the combined ...CityStateCountryTxt columns either, especially as those data elements are treated differently in different parts of the form. Just make sure you classify them as Txt so you and the programmers will know in the future that the data here is extremely undisciplined.

Note It's easy to assume a level of detail that isn't necessary. If you hadn't looked at the ...CityStateCountry... form fields as a modeler, it's likely that no one else would have thought to pull apart those data elements. A lot of form data is modeled and loaded into databases using the "One Form Blank = One Database Column" rule.

When you encounter no desire for true data integrity, you may want to compress several fields on the form and simplify the data. Why not offer a FullAddressBlockTxt of VARCHAR(2000) instead of calling each address component separately? The clients probably have separate lines for addresses because the addresses don't otherwise fit on paper. On checking with the clients, they tell you that in this case, all the addresses are basically informational. They don't expect to use the addresses in any reports.

Tip Try to not add details to your model just because you know they exist in the real world. Unless you're building with corporate standards in mind, then the customer knows best, and you should implement according to their requirements.

Send any fields you think are unclear, or whose data is uncontrolled, to the clients for clarification, and then change the model appropriately.

Normalization

Now let's continue to refine the model. You'll use normalization tests in the following sections to see if you can identify some of the simple data sets that are buried in this flat table.

First Normal Form (1NF)

Look at the list of columns in the table. Remember, First Normal Form (1NF) requires every column of the table to depend on the *key* exclusively. What do you make of the columns shown in Figure 11-12?

Figure 11-12. *Some repeating groups in the* Employee *table*

One of the industry standard phrases we use when talking about 1NF is "remove repeating groups." Data elements that repeat can't possibly depend entirely on the key. Fields that store phone number information occur twice. A phone number for an employee depends on two pieces of information (namely, the employee and the phone number's type). There's a one-to-two relationship between employees and employee phone numbers at the moment.

When you look for repeating groups, concentrate on the back part of the column name and clumps of columns that seem to be grouped in repeating patterns. In this case, Name (Nm), Text (Txt), Number (Nb), Number (Nb), and Code (Cd) occur three times in a row for school information that's part of an employee's education history. This school information consists of another set of repeating columns, and the repetition in these cases is more dramatic than the single repeating columns for phone numbers. Each type of education history for an employee has a collection of informative columns. The data about one level of education for an employee depends on the employee and the level of education involved. At the moment you'll find a one-to-three relationship. These columns are easily broken out from the current flat table to be made more relational, as shown in Figure 11-13.

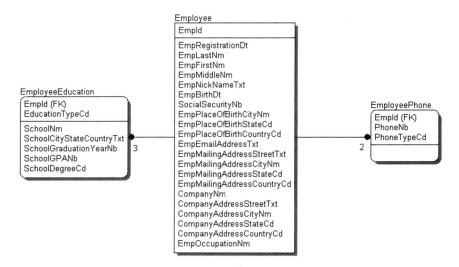

Figure 11-13. *The* Employee *table with some repeating groups removed*

Let's now consider the address elements with regard to repeating groups (see Figure 11-14).

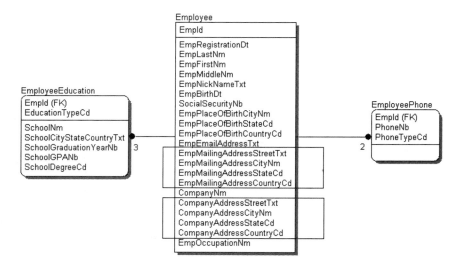

Figure 11-14. *Address repeating groups in the* Employee *table*

Repeating groups of values are multiple instances of the same data elements allowed for a member of a set, such as the three education information instances you just removed. So you need to be careful here. These addresses aren't both about an employee, are they?

CompanyAddress doesn't depend on Employee but rather on Company. Create a new table for Company, and relate it to Employee. Make the company name and address information into attributes of the Company table, as shown in Figure 11-15.

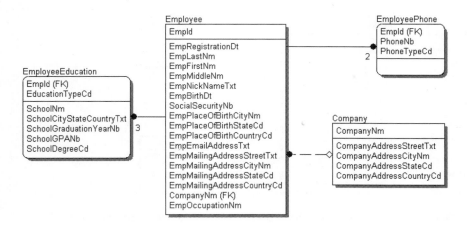

Figure 11-15. *The* Employee *model with a new* Company *table*

Note that company information in the Employee table is really a violation of 3NF, because the company information doesn't depend on the key of Employee. Even though you're resolving 1NF violations, you've suddenly resolved a 3NF violation. Resolving normal form violations isn't always a sequential process.

Do you see how far you've come—and rather quickly at that? Don't think that because you're being pressed to complete a solution quickly that you can't bring value to the design. Granted, even repeating groups aren't always easy to recognize, but there's always the notion of going for "low-hanging fruit."

Your clients may not want you to go any further than this. Believe it or not, sometimes data integrity rules get in their way. It's quite likely that they will appreciate the new expanded flexibility of EmployeePhone and EmployeeEducation. The new Company table provides them with the means to analyze the company an employee worked for, which wasn't possible using the previous design. However, remember that you should always be sensitive to the clients' needs. You need to consider questions such as whether this is an enterprise-critical development project, where the structure may need to integrate with other applications, or a department-specific project. Keep in mind that even the department-level development projects (especially if they're successful) have the potential of becoming enterprise-critical in the future. If the checks for these student employees ever need to be cut by the payroll department, then you may need to be much more sensitive to what's happening here and maybe even suggest a different business solution rather than expanding this application.

You're probably beginning to see a more relational design growing from the single-employee registration form. During the evolution of a model such as this, periodically test your model against the normal forms to ensure your design conforms to them. Look, for example, at EmployeeEducation, which you just created. What does SchoolCityStateCountry have to do with EmpID or EducationTypeCd? School location information actually depends on the school, rather than the employee or the degree, so you should create a School table to comply with 1NF. Figure 11-16 shows school information separated from EmployeeEducation in the Employee model.

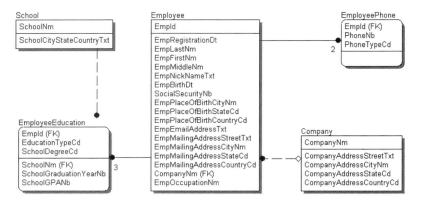

Figure 11-16. *School information separated from* EmployeeEducation *in the* Employee *model*

Second Normal Form (2NF)

Second Normal Form (2NF) requires that every column of a table depends on the whole key. Look at EmployeeEducation. How dependent is SchoolDegreeCd on both EmpID and EducationTypeCd? Can a player get a high school diploma in graduate school? No. Choices of degree are restricted to the level of education, so the relationship needs to be managed in a different table. Not only that, but no matter what the registration form tells you, you can get both your master's and your doctorate degree in graduate school. SchoolDegreeCd has to be part of the key of EmployeeEducation.

When you discover something that would change the rules of the paper form, such as the ability to get two degrees from the same school, you must review your findings with your clients. They will usually tell you they forgot about the exception or they've allowed people to write on the back of the paper form when the form doesn't allow the correct education history information to be captured, for example. If they do allow this kind of data capture method, then press them slightly and find out what else people write on the backs of forms. Figure 11-17 shows degree information separated from EmployeeEducation on the Employee model.

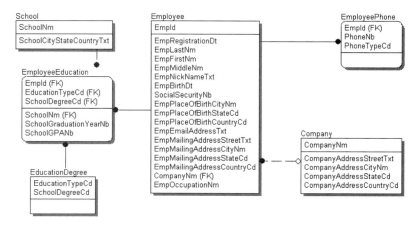

Figure 11-17. *Degree information separated from* EmployeeEducation *on the* Employee *model*

Third Normal Form (3NF)

Adhering to 3NF means you ensure every attribute of every member of every set depends on *nothing but the key.* How about all the geographical data elements in this model? What do you make of the City, State, and Country attributes? Can the state Idaho be a state in the country Mexico? Should you look at the state and country data sets and try to find the relationships between them in this kind of data modeling?

Well, the nice thing about doing the analysis this way is that you can save all the data sets for the clients/team/DBA/programmer to check. In effect, you'd have a set of denormalization options that can easily be integrated into the model. If you don't get as much of the analysis documented as possible, nobody will know what the options are.

Let's look at the geography sets and consider the relationships between them. For example, if you pull out an atlas, you'll find a city named Newport in the states of Washington, Oregon, Arizona, Nebraska, Minnesota, Missouri, Indiana, Ohio, Kentucky, Tennessee, North Carolina, Virginia, Pennsylvania, New York, New Jersey, Vermont, Maine, Rhode Island, and New Hampshire. (Wow!) As a result, the entities City and State will have a many-to-many relationship that needs to be resolved with an intersection table of the type you've seen in the previous three chapters. Double-check the role names for the two relationships from StateCity to Employee. A modeling tool will just migrate one set of keys unless you role-name them. The resultant model would look like Figure 11-18.

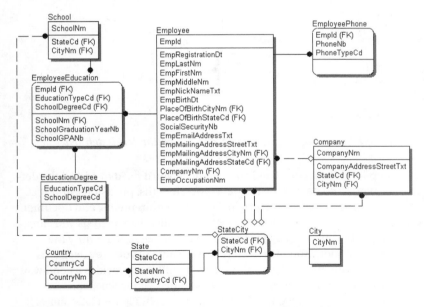

Figure 11-18. *The* Employee *model with geography tables added*

Boyce-Codd Normal Form (BCNF)

Here's where the restricted lists are born. Adhering to Boyce-Codd Normal Form (BCNF) means creating separate tables to control what are often tiny sets of reused data in the form of drop-down or pick lists. BCNF says that every attribute must be identified by a key. The unique list of valid attribute values must be part of an identified set.

Is the list of `EducationTypeCd` values managed anywhere? No. Is it a unique data set? Yes, certainly. How about `PhoneTypeCd` values? We can easily see them as lists being managed by the clients. Let's separate them, giving the clients the option of allowing the codes full names if required. Now the model looks like Figure 11-19.

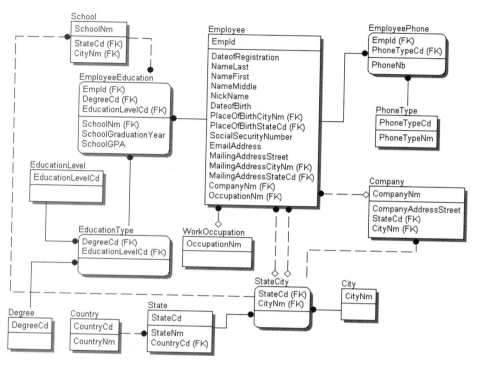

Figure 11-19. *The* `Employee` *model with degree, phone type, and education levels defined*

This is where you'll stop for this model. To polish the model, you'd need to add all the definitions, revisit the primary keys, and determine the data types, lengths, precisions, and NULL rules. Review your design again, look back at the original clients' requirements, and document your analysis to ensure you present the team with the highest-quality data analysis you can under the existing constraints. Take time to scan for known weaknesses, and identify the things you perceive to be trouble spots. You may need to justify some of your key decisions. You may want to document your analysis in layers the way you built it. It provides a good way of walking through your analysis, reminding you of what was gained with each step.

Figure 11-20 shows the model in 1NF, Figure 11-21 shows it in 2NF, Figure 11-22 shows it in 3NF, and Figure 11-23 shows it in BCNF.

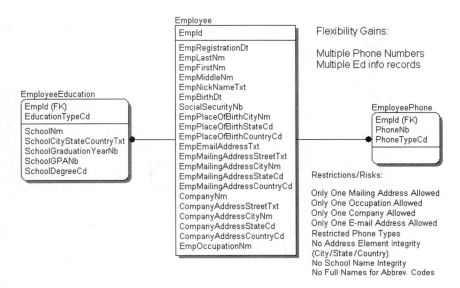

Figure 11-20. *The* Employee *model after the application of 1NF*

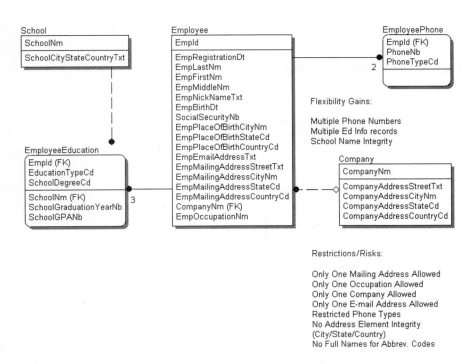

Figure 11-21. *The* Employee *model after the application of 2NF*

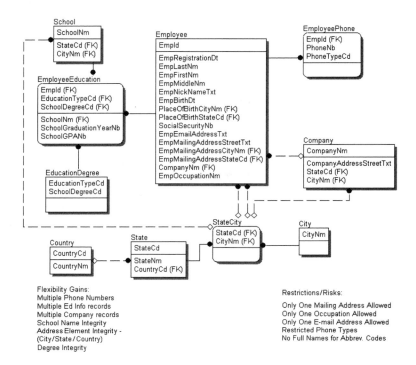

Figure 11-22. *The* Employee *model after the application of 3NF*

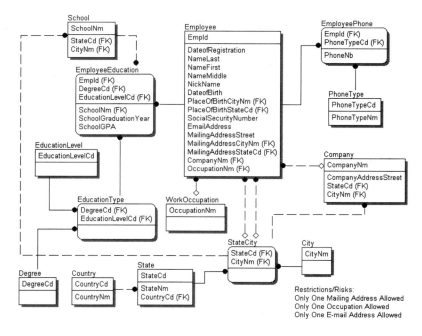

Figure 11-23. *The* Employee *model after the application of BCNF*

It would be a small task to upgrade this to a Logical model design. If the team chooses to take this scope forward to development, then you may want to bring the data elements all the way back to the Logical data model at your leisure.

Remember that if you integrate models that were designed separately (such as the Player and Employee models), then you need to look for integration points. Find the data sets that are really the same even if they're treated or named slightly differently. For example, there's a similarity between the WorkOccupation table in this model and the GeneralOccupation text in the Player model. You'd want to find out what, if any, difference there was between the set of employees and players. Do they share any attributes because they're both types of people? What difference is there between HighestEdLevelCompCd and Degrees?

If your clients require that the model you've developed should be integrated with the Player model and Solitaire, then you could list this as a design requirement in your initial scope development phase. This would ensure you avoid building a similar structure twice.

Other Physical Model–Only Designs

You may run across other kinds of tables from time to time that are 100 percent physical. These are tables used to manage the working application and will not be found in a Logical model design (except maybe in a metadata model). DBAs and programmers generally design them for database maintenance, but if you manage the models, then they may become part of your documentation. They aren't modeled in the purest form of the word in that they don't support the clients' business process and never go from Conceptual to Logical to Physical model designs. However, it's worth being aware of them.

They generally fall into three categories:

- *Operational tables* are physical structures that store information related to the technical operation of the application.

- *Staging tables* are physical structures that support data migration—or extraction, transformation, and loading (ETL)—activities.

- *Archive tables* are physical structures that store historical data not required for day-to-day activity.

These types of tables have nothing to do with the business subject area. You can put these tables in your Physical model design, but they don't make a lot of sense in the context of Conceptual or Logical models, since they're physical constructs that help with the physical management of data.

Operational Tables

Sometimes, at the application management level, data that you would never have modeled needs to be stored. You might find tables that hold filenames, dates, and status from downloads that synchronize the data in one table with another. You might see operational tables that manage partitioning of data by value for certain login names. For instance, Login X is able to see Florida employee data. All the employee data is in one table, but a view is dynamically built that partitions it based on an operational security table. Operational tables can do the following:

- They can store authorization, authentication, and security audit information.

- They can support data migration (ETL) efforts by tracking ETL processes and their completion.

- They can store user session or display preference information.

Operational data doesn't have to be in separate tables, and it's quite frequently tacked onto the end of your data tables in the form of creation dates, user IDs, or security flags at the record level. In some databases, tables manage sequence number generation. They include `LastNumberAssigned`. You may see operational tables managing statistics on the activity of the application. There are lots of reasons for them to be part of your implementation. Figure 11-24 shows an operational table that's supporting an ETL process by tracking the date and time of the data load, the number of records loaded, and the final completion status.

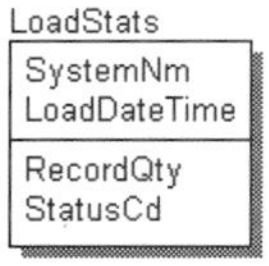

Figure 11-24. *A sample operational table supporting an ETL process*

You'll often see operational tables floating around the edges of Physical model designs with no relationships to anything else. They're there to hold bits of information that the application needs to remember in order to perform some of its functions correctly. They deal with timing, security, and business rules based on value. The DBA adds these tables to the database, and you end up adding the tables to the model as you get deeper in the project development and closer to full-scale system testing.

Staging Tables

Staging tables are usually completely segregated from the application data. They're used for the conversion of data from one system to another in a one-time or periodic load process. For the most part, staging table design will be handed to you by the programmers who design the conversion technical requirements.

You can see in Figure 11-25 that the employee data is coming in from an outside source. The programmers are going to have to find a way to parse out the last/first/middle name because the data coming in is concatenated together. They also have to try to figure out the address data elements and translate the Dun and Bradstreet number into a company name.

The staging table also includes a source name, load date, and error code, probably for feedback to the source system that a record was unloadable for some reason.

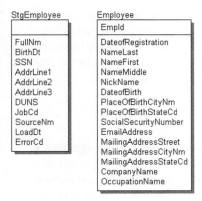

Figure 11-25. *Employee data staging table and the* Employee *table it supports*

Staging tables are notorious for not having primary keys. They need to be large and flexible in order to accept data that may not have the same stringent quality rules embedded in it that the target system has. Programmers need a "sandbox" working area to catch and clean the data before it can move to its new home. This is often called *ETL effort.* A transactional system may only need these types of table to support the initial load. Data warehouse applications may need them to permanently support this type of data loading.

Archive Tables

The last kind of Physical model design–only table you may see is the archive table. Generally, these look almost exactly like another table in the database; they're almost identical in structure and in name. They're used as a form of "nearest line storage" for large active data tables, such as in Figure 11-26, for inactive employees who are removed from the Employee table following specific business rules.

Employee	InteractiveEmployeeHistory
Empld	**Empld**
	ArchiveDateTime
DateofRegistration	
NameLast	DateofRegistration
NameFirst	NameLast
NameMiddle	NameFirst
NickName	NameMiddle
DateofBirth	NickName
PlaceOfBirthCityNm	DateofBirth
PlaceOfBirthStateCd	PlaceOfBirthCityNm
SocialSecurityNumber	PlaceOfBirthStateCd
EmailAddress	SocialSecurityNumber
MailingAddressStreet	EmailAddress
MailingAddressCityNm	MailingAddressStreet
MailingAddressStateCd	MailingAddressCityNm
CompanyName	MailingAddressStateCd
OccupationName	CompanyName
	OccupationName

Figure 11-26. *The* Employee *table and an* Employee *archive table*

Also, a kind of history table exists for audit purposes. You may want to keep only the most current version of a record in a data table. But you may need to be able to see the history of all the updates and "whodunits" for research purposes. Again, you almost never model these kinds of requirements; the DBA simply adds a Physical model design table to take the primary key of each record and adds a time stamp to separate versions by creation time.

Summary

This chapter covered the best practices you'll need in case you have to leap straight into a Physical model–only design. This is often the case when you have insufficient project time or money to follow a rigorous Conceptual/Logical/Physical model designing methodology. You looked at what you can do to improve upon existing Physical model designs, prior to their implementation, in order to ensure that the application being developed not only runs smoothly but also has some room for expansion to meet future requirements. In particular, this chapter noted the need to do the following:

- Document the clients' requirements accurately.

- Review as much data as possible to aid your design.

- Meet the requirements of normal form in your design.

- Verify overlap with existing models and projects to avoid unnecessary repetition of analysis.

It bears repeating that these steps are to be taken only when time or budget constraints don't allow for a more rigorous analysis. To thoroughly understand the full set of options for Physical model design implementation, you should always carry out the Conceptual/Logical/Physical model design methodology outlined earlier in this book. Don't rush straight to the Physical model design; this approach is always to be a "make-do" approach to data modeling.

CHAPTER 12

■■■

Introducing Dimensional Data Modeling

In the previous two chapters, you created Physical model designs that adhere to the relational normal forms. You created a disciplined table design that manages single, atomic data sets. These normalized database designs are often most appropriate for online transaction process (OLTP) applications, since the separation of data into related atomic sets supports a large number of transactions from a large and disparate set of users. In interacting with this kind of database, the focus is on the continual manipulation of data at the level of a single row.

Problems in performance generally arise when attempting to use highly normalized databases for online analytical processing (OLAP) systems. OLAP systems address issues of business analysis, business intelligence, and decision support. They focus on analyzing large amounts of data, generating aggregate statistics, creating ad hoc queries to investigate the details behind these statistics, and identifying historical data trends over time.

What makes normalization good for OLTP systems (separating data into different sets and the ability to operate effectively on a single record) contributes to performance problems when normalized data designs are used for OLAP systems. Analytical databases often need to perform operations on hundreds, thousands, or millions of rows at a time. Although strictly normalized structures ensure absolute data integrity, attempting to quickly retrieve and process large quantities of data from multiple tables within a normalized database design requires query complexity that can often overwhelm your hardware. The result is unacceptable query performance.

To address these query performance issues, an alternative method for creating Physical table designs was created. Dimensional modeling is a technique that, through a systematic approach to denormalization, optimizes the Physical model's design to support analytical and ad hoc query operations on large quantities of data.

In this chapter, we'll show you how to create Dimensional modeling designs using the Solitaire example and how to build two data marts. In the course of creating these two designs, you'll learn about the following:

- The nature of OLAP databases (data warehouses and data marts)

- What Dimensional modeling is, and why you need it

- The structures in a Dimensional model, such as star schemas, fact tables, and dimension tables

Understanding OLAP Database Basics

The two most common types of databases that support OLAP activity are data marts and data warehouses. Both of these types of structures are designed to hold data collected from a business's day-to-day operations. They generally integrate data from a variety of sources and source systems (which are generally OLTP applications), and they organize this data with analytical processing needs in mind. The data found in OLAP databases is stored as a "read-only snapshot" of a given point in time and is therefore not subject to updates.

The main difference between a data mart and a data warehouse is this: a data mart is intended to store a single snapshot of the business data, and the data warehouse will contain more than just a single point-in-time snapshot. A data mart is usually intended to be exposed to query tools or decision support applications and therefore usually follows a Dimensional model design. A data warehouse may have a Third Normal Form (3NF) design or a Dimensional model design, depending on its purpose within the enterprise. If a data warehouse has a 3NF design, it's likely to feed dependent data marts and therefore is infrequently accessed. If the data warehouse has a Dimensional model design, it may be supporting an OLAP query tool or application directly. It's important to note that the terms *data mart* and *data warehouse* generally describe a database's use rather than imply a Physical model design.

Data marts generally have the following characteristics:

- They have a Dimensional model design.

- They're accessed by OLAP (business intelligence) tools or an OLAP application.

- They contain a single point-in-time snapshot of data.

- They're periodically refreshed from a source system (usually a data warehouse).

- They don't have other dependent OLAP databases.

Data warehouses generally have the following characteristics:

- They have either a Dimensional model design or a normalized design.

- They're infrequently accessed by any process that isn't an extraction, transformation, and loading (ETL) process, unless they have a Dimensional model design.

- They contain a time variant and historical view of the data.

- They're periodically refreshed from a source system (usually source OLTP systems).

- They have dependent data marts.

The similarity of data warehouses and data marts has led to a difference of opinion of how these different databases can and should be used. Some enterprises perceive data marts to be the building blocks of their data warehouse. *The Data Warehouse Lifecycle Toolkit: Expert Methods for Designing, Developing, and Deploying Data Warehouses* (John Wiley & Sons, 1998) defines a data mart and data warehouse as the queryable source of data in the enterprise. It also says, "The data warehouse is nothing more than the union of all the constituent data marts."

Other enterprises use data marts as a presentation layer for OLAP tools; the source data is stored in a normalized data warehouse, and the data marts have Dimensional model designs. In this case, a data warehouse is created using a variety of table designs (possibly a combination of normalized and Dimensional model designs) and may have several different layers (including staging, core, and presentation layers) that support all the processes involved in managing enterprise data.

No matter which position your enterprise has taken, Dimensional modeling is an integral part of designing your OLAP database (whether it's a data mart or a data warehouse).

So, what is Dimensional modeling? It's a methodology for modeling data that starts from a set of base measurement events and constructs a table called the *fact table*, generally with one record for each discrete measurement. This fact table is then surrounded by a set of dimension tables, describing precisely what's known in the context of each measurement record. Because of the characteristic structure of a Dimensional model, it's often called a *star schema*. Dimensional models are the logical foundation of all OLAP systems.

The key to a Dimensional model is in determining the relevant context (or *fact*). A Dimensional model that's designed to find trends in sales information will likely treat each sale as a fact. Any supporting information important to that analysis, such as the country of sale or the month of the year, will be a *dimension*. Don't worry too much about the definitions of *fact* and *dimension* at this point; we'll cover several examples of how to identify facts and dimensions throughout this chapter.

Asking Analytical Questions for Dimensional Models

Like all modeling techniques, Dimensional modeling requires you to know and understand the business requirements of the clients. A Dimensional model is particularly good at answering questions such as the following:

- What are the quarterly net sales for the company by department, region, and product?

- What are the costs of transportation by product, service level, vendor, region, and time of year?

- What are the combinations of products being purchased together by store, time of day, purchase threshold, and advertising campaign?

Sometimes it's not clear which questions are really important to the user, but the goal of the analysis may be clear. An interview with the clients will help determine what analytical questions they may ask. Such interviews help determine the information objectives (as highlighted in bold in the following list). They may say the following to you:

- **"I want to know what products to cut from the inventory because they aren't performing."**

    - Q: "How do you know they aren't performing?"

    - A: "I compare the quarterly net sales for the company by department, region, and product."

- **"I want to know if I need to renegotiate the contracts with the transportation companies."**

  - Q: "What triggers you to renegotiate the contracts?"

  - A: "When the contracts are within three months of expiring, I start looking at the costs of transportation by product, service level, vendor, region, and time of year."

- **"I want to know what products to put together in the aisles to encourage people to buy more."**

  - Q: "What research do you do to decide product location?"

  - A: "I do market research by looking at the combinations of products being purchased together by store, time of day, purchase threshold, and advertising campaigns."

You start a Dimensional model with the knowledge of the sorts of question the clients want to answer, what data they want to analyze, and how they want to be able to sort, restrict, and aggregate the answers to their questions. This analysis is usually captured in a document called a *dimensionality matrix*; this is a matrix that shows the facts along one axis, shows dimensions along the other axis, and shows the relevant data at the intersections. Note that when you're talking with the clients, you may not find out exactly what questions they will ask—they may not know the questions, only the *types* of questions they will ask. For a Dimensional model, that's enough.

Introducing Dimensional Model Terminology

The components of a Dimensional model are as follows:

- **Fact**: A measurement, typically numeric and additive, that's stored in a fact table. This is also known as a *measure, key performance measure*, or *key business measure*.

- **Fact table**: The central table in a Dimensional model (star join schema), characterized by a composite key, that represents a business fact and contains several foreign keys to dimension tables.

- **Dimension**: An independent entity in the model of an organization that serves to aggregate, group, or filter facts from the fact table. Dimensions usually represent fundamental ways of accessing and presenting business information.

- **Dimension table**: A table in a Dimensional model representing a dimension.

- **ETL**: This stands for *extraction, transformation*, and *loading*, which is the movement of data from one place to another involving from/to source(s) and target(s) as well as rules for any changes that are built into the movement. This process uses tools from simple SQL transactions to batch processing to sophisticated automations tools such as Informatica.

Introducing the Benefits of Dimensional Design

It's pretty obvious that you already have all the data stored in your normalized structures to answer the questions your clients might like to ask. Why not just write reports off those structures and be done with it?

Well, some business questions are simple, and some are complex. Part of the reason why a query is simple or complex is because of the design of the underlying data storage structures. Data sets in their most normalized form are disciplined compilations. They're so atomic that they have the feel of an extremely narrow, highly specialized collection of objects, such as single containers of shoelaces, radishes, and paper clips. 3NF data is isolated into tables that box up and control each member of a set. This is the most appropriate way to collect, remove, and modify a single instance. The problem with this design comes when you want to aggregate these sets in order to answer a question. To use a 3NF database to answer some business questions, you need to trace and gather data elements from five, ten, twenty, or more tables, which probably involves an unwieldy number of table joins in your SQL query. Performing table joins is a slow process, since the contents of each table is read before the correct and aggregated data required is returned. Larger numbers of joins will inevitably lead to the database engine spending a longer time processing the given query. Frequently, these queries are also too complex for an unsophisticated data user to build correctly.

Most denormalization is an attempt to help solve this problem. Denormalization breaks normalization rules so that you can store information differently, reducing the need for a large number of joins. Look, for example, at how the Physical model design for the Solitaire exercise is organized. Often, normalization doesn't cause you any problems. See how easy it is, for example, to determine the color of the queen of diamonds? It's a single join from Card to Suit (see Figure 12-1).

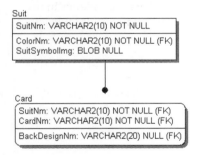

Figure 12-1. *The* Suit *to* Card *relationship in the Solitaire application*

Things get more complicated, though, if you want to know how many cards of each color have been played for all documented games, subtotaled by age, player occupation, and player hobbies. To return these aggregate counts, the database first needs to join the Suit, Card, Move, Play, Game, Player, PlayerHobby, PlayerOccupation, AgeRange, and Hobby tables to gather the appropriate information. Figure 12-2 shows this information (we've italicized the matching columns for you).

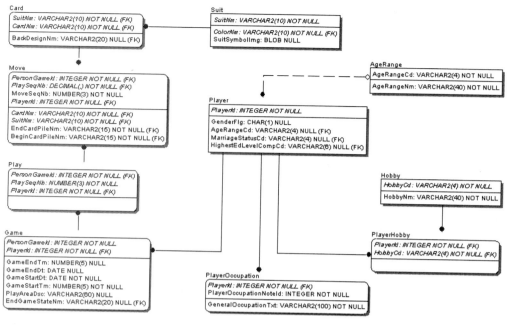

Figure 12-2. *Tables used in a complicated analytical query*

You must perform nine joins to get to all the information you need from the normalized model. If you need to answer this question often, you might want to create new data structures that reorganize this data. A dimensional star schema, which allows redundancy in the table, brings all the pertinent data elements into one simple structure and avoids table joins.

Introducing Star Schemas

A *star schema* is so called because its general design pattern, once modeled in a Physical model, appears to be a star (see Figure 12-3).

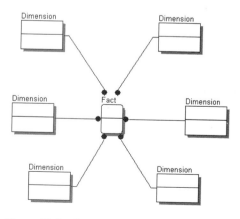

Figure 12-3. *The star schema*

> **■Note** It's traditional (although not required) for the relationship lines in star schemas to be diagonal rather than orthogonal (straight with bends). The relationships here usually read from the outside toward the inside, following the normal one-to-many relationship. One dimension is related to many facts.

Understanding Facts and Dimensions

As you can see, star schemas center on a single *fact* table. This fact table is linked to a number of *dimension* tables. *Base facts* are those that are simple replications of data in the source system(s), and numeric facts generated from other data in the source system are termed *derived facts*. You generally build those in a series of processes collectively known as ETL.

You need to understand the business requirements to build fact tables that contain the correct *measures* of interest (such as sales amount). These measures come in the following forms:

Perfectly additive numeric measures (a.k.a. additive facts): These are the basic numeric facts in a fact table. They can always be handled correctly in a mathematical process (addition, subtraction, average, and so on) and can be grouped by any dimension. An example would be `RetailPriceAmt` of the `InvoiceLine` fact table. They offer enormous possibility for aggregation and trend determination.

Semiadditive and nonadditive numeric measures: These measures aren't quite as flexible. These measures generally occur in the form of prederived values (such as percentages or pregenerated averages) or measures of intensity (such as account balances, temperatures, or inventory levels) that don't behave correctly in additive mathematical formulas. Totaling these measures may not make sense when you're adding, subtracting, or averaging data. For example, adding temperatures, even if they're documented as numbers, probably doesn't make sense.

Textual facts: These aren't useful for anything other than counting. Most of the textual information about a fact should be found in a dimension. An insurance company may add `CarColorName` to the `Accident` fact. It may not make sense to have a whole dimension table to track this color information, but it may not make sense to add `CarColorName` to the `Vehicle Dimension` fact either. It could be added to the fact table for reference.

Degenerate fact dimensions: Degenerate facts are usually bits of data used to reference a higher-level form or aggregation, such as a `BillOfLadingNumber` on a `ShippedMaterial` fact table, for example. They're generally part of the identifying set of attributes of the fact table, but they're used for very little else. Research being done about a single bill of lading would generally happen in the operations system, not in the analysis reports. These are referred to as *degenerate dimensions* (although there's no dimension table to reference back to).

Factless fact: This is a fact table without a numeric measure. It's usually an event-type table where a row exists only to say something happened. For example, you may not have additive fact information for a customer phone call. You may put a default quantity field of 1 in your `Customer Phone Call` table in order to make summation easy, but there may be no operational measures.

The following sections contain a few advisory warnings about keys in Dimensional models.

Avoiding Source System Keys

When we say "avoiding source system keys," we mean to avoid using the key from your data's system of origin. You might expect that source system primary keys would be a good choice almost by default. Unfortunately, this isn't always true. You may want to avoid using system primary keys for a number of reasons:

New sources: You may need to add source data from other systems to your database later, and the new source will most likely use a different primary key.

Data duplication: The IDs or natural keys from a given source system lock you into using not only existing data sizes and data types but also existing *values* from the source system. You may be forced to deal with addressing the issue of nonunique IDs if you're adding new data from sources that have similar constructs and generation functions. This is especially true if the source application is installed in multiple locations and if the data is expected to be compiled into one data mart.

Structure synchronization: Source systems change. Having a primary key that's specific to the data mart keeps you from having to address changes in the source systems feeding your database. The rule of thumb is to not use keys that you can't control.

History: It may be part of your requirements to save changes to data from source systems. If you need to record both the old and new versions of the record using the source system primary key, then you're now faced with the problem of adding a time dimension and having a primary key that won't support this need.

Avoiding Smart Keys

A *smart key* is a key that's constructed according to a particular coding scheme or formula. In a Dimensional model design, using natural data elements as keys, or using elements based on a formulaic composition of natural data elements as keys, may cause you problems. Keep the source system data in nonkey positions.

Avoiding Multicolumn Keys

One of the primary goals of a Dimensional model design is speed through a reduced number of joins. The best database performance for those necessary joins will come from using single, numeric keys.

Understanding Fact Granularity

The term *granularity* describes the level of detail contained within a fact table. A table may contain data that's highly detailed (such as the separate product lines on an order), or it may contain data that has been summarized (such as one record for one store for one year's worth of aggregated sales facts). The word *grain* brings to mind different kinds of wood. Softwood has broader, looser grain, and hardwood has narrower, tighter grain. Just like a builder uses different woods to fulfill different needs, your choice of the granularity of the fact table should be made with an understanding of the different functionality that may be required in the future.

Think of fact tables that refer to aggregated types of data, such as the invoice rather than the invoice line, as being more like the softwood. It's less able to support detailed analysis. Think of fact tables that refer to the most granular data available as being more like the hardwood. They have a better chance of supporting refined data analysis and ad hoc data mining needs to get to the root cause of a trend in the future.

Introducing Snowflake Schemas

The star schema is the simplest representation of the business entities and their relationships in the Dimensional model. However, sometimes you apply some level of normalization to the star schema's dimension tables and create a variation known as a *snowflake schema*. A snowflake schema decomposes one dimension into separate, related dimension tables. In this way, you can define one-to-many relationships among members of the original dimension table.

The classic snowflake removes low cardinality attributes from one dimension table. Look at the simple design in Figure 12-4 for customer service calls for an international company. Consider GeographyDim. The columns that refer to Country will have only a fifty-state-to-one-country cardinality in the case of U.S. records. Pulling out the Country columns into CountryDim reduces the redundancy of CountryNm, CountryAbbrNm, and GrossNtlProductAmt by a factor of 49. This may make sense to your team in the case of certain dimensions.

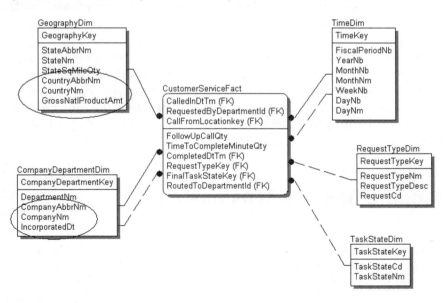

Figure 12-4. *The customer service fact star schema*

So, for example, Figure 12-5 shows a star schema transformed into a snowflake schema. In performing this transformation, you've removed the Country columns from GeographyDim and have removed the Company columns from CompanyDepartmentDim.

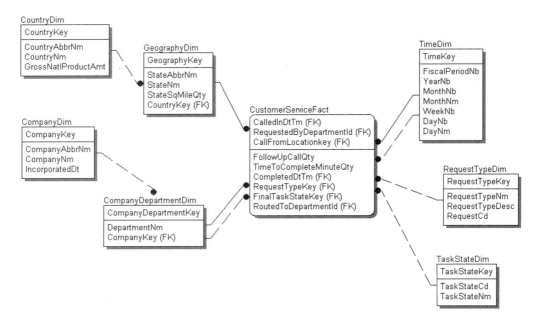

Figure 12-5. *The customer service fact snowflake schema*

Many practitioners suggest that Dimensional models should be snowflaked only if there's an excellent reason for doing so. Ralph Kimball in his "A Trio of Interesting Snowflakes" article for *Intelligent Enterprise* on June 29, 2001, had this to say about snowflakes:

> *A classic physical snowflake design may be useful in the backroom staging area [of a data warehouse] as a way to enforce the many-to-one relationships in a dimensional table. But in the front room presentation part of your data warehouse, you have to demonstrate to me that the end users find the snowflake easier to understand and, moreover, that queries and reports run faster with the snowflake, before I am comfortable with the snowflake design.*

Understanding Base Dimensions and Subdimensions

In cases where you're working with unevenly distributed descriptive columns in the subtypes of a category, it may make more sense to design a base dimension to hold shared columns, rather than rolling up the columns of all the subtypes into one dimension. Separate subdimensions would then contain the columns that aren't common.

As an example of this, Kimball suggests that Web shoppers be broken into groups of Web site visitors (of which you know very little) and actual customers (of which you know quite a bit). Instead of rolling all the attributes of the logical entity Shopper up to one dimension, he suggests breaking the dimension in two. The Shopper dimension becomes the base dimension, with a one-to-zero-or-one relationship to the Customer dimension, which in turn contains information about a shopper who actually purchased something (see Figure 12-6).

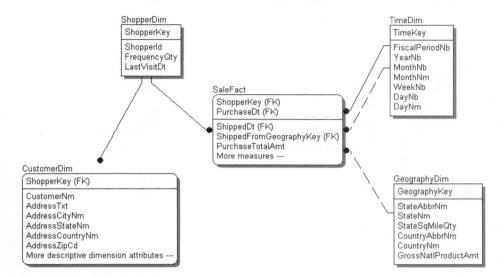

Figure 12-6. *The Web shopper example of base dimensions and subdimensions*

Another example is that of financial product data. Different types of financial accounts have a great variety of attributes. Combining all the different account types in one dimension may cause you to end up with a dimension containing hundreds of columns, most of which are empty for every given record. Again, you may decide to build a base dimension that isolates the core attributes and a set of "context-dependent" subdimensions—much like a logical category structure shown in Chapter 9. The key in the base Account dimension points to the proper extended account subdimensions. This example would look a lot like the Web shopper model, but it would have multiple relationships from ShopperDim to other child dimensions.

A final example, shown in Figure 12-7, deals with many-to-many relationships in a multi-enterprise calendar dimension. In this case, you're working with many idiosyncratic divisions of dates into various fiscal, manufacturing, and planning calendars with parochial views of seasons and holidays. Kimball says the following, "Although you should make a heroic effort to reduce incompatible calendar labels, many times you want to look at the overall multi-enterprise data through the eyes of just one of the organizations."

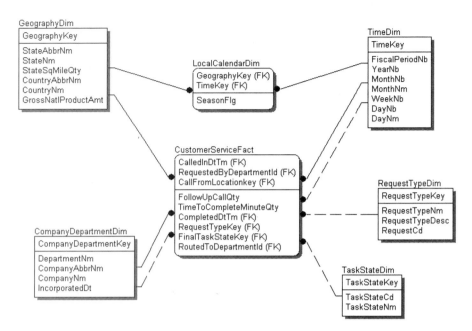

Figure 12-7. *The Web shopper star schema with a local calendar*

This time the figure shows the base table as a generic calendar table. Each subdimension will have pretty much the same set of columns with different values. Australia may denote November 1 as being part of Spring, but Canada may have November 1 in Fall. This type of subdimension snowflake structure includes both the key of the base dimension and the organization dimension.

Revisiting the Solitaire Model

Let's now take a look at the existing Solitaire model (see Figure 12-8). (Note that this is still the Physical model—we turned off the data types to simplify the figure.) The shading separates the tables into groups according to whether the table's activity is high, medium, or low.

Using this copy of the model is particularly helpful, since it highlights the expected transaction activity. Facts have a tendency to be found where the transactional activity is the greatest. Game, Play, and Move are the tables with the highest expected volume of records and the largest number of transactions. These three tables will see the highest level of activity as new games are played and the moves are recorded, and they therefore seem to be prime candidates for fact tables.

■**Note** The attributes chosen to be stored in fact tables are generally found where the data activity in an enterprise is the highest.

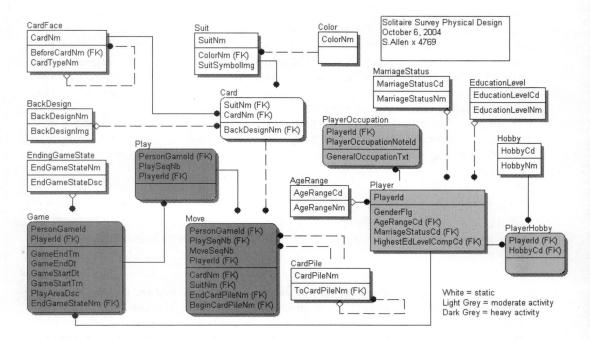

Figure 12-8. *The Solitaire model*

Targeting the Facts

Just as you did when you created the initial Logical and Physical models, the first task is to discover and document your clients' requirements. What do your clients back at the psychology department want to learn from the data they've collected? Their latest information need (or objective) is "to analyze the moves and wins or losses in Solitaire games and to see if any game play trends are based on the time of day, day of the week, back design choice, player age, player marital status, player hobbies, or education level of a player." When you question the clients further, you find they're actually interested in discovering trends having just about anything to do with how moves are grouped into plays. They're targeting game and move information only.

In general, to create a data mart (the fact and dimension tables for this schema), you need to learn the following:

- Where does the data come from?

- What type of questions are usually asked?

- What answers are needed in the future?

- What grouping, filtering, or data restrictions are needed?

Find out how your clients do this kind of analysis now. In this case, the clients probably have no current method of performing this analysis, but you'll often find that your real-world clients have tried-and-true processes on which they count. In fact, you may have to remind them that their new application, processes, data sources, and designs may allow them to analyze their data in a new way. Let them brainstorm a little, comparing their past and future abilities, to see if they can envision new analyses. It's quite likely they'll be able to show you values on existing reports that are meaningful to them or show you screens or spreadsheets where they build aggregations. You need to incorporate all of these things into their data mart. You want to bring as many analysis requirements together as possible and build a "one-stop shop" for them to perform their analysis.

Don't restrict your research to just their current goal, however. Today, for example, they may be looking only for monthly data, but you should try to anticipate their future needs and consider allowing them to "drill down" to a lower level of detail (a weekly view, for example) in the future.

Note When possible, capture the next lower level of detailed data in fact tables, even if it expands the scope of your requirements. Try to anticipate your clients' needs whenever it's feasible to do so.

It also never hurts to do a little reconnaissance to see if their fact and dimension tables might already exist or be useful from an enterprise perspective. Departments in a business don't stand alone. If there's a requirement for a particular fact or dimension in one department, chances are that some other department may benefit from having it as well. A fact or dimension may already exist in another department, and if this is so, it could substantially reduce the time needed to create your model. What do you need to provide your clients with in your data mart? In your discussion with them, their stated aim was to be able to do the following: to analyze the moves and wins or losses in Solitaire games to see if any game play trends are based on the time of day, day of the week, back design choice, player age, player marital status, player hobbies, or education level of a player.

If you dissect this requirement into clauses, then you start to see the entity sets the way you did in the Logical modeling exercise. In this case, you have to analyze the following:

- The moves

- The choice of back design

- Wins or losses in Solitaire games

This is to find out if there are any trends within the following:

- Time of day

- Day of the week

- Player age

- Player marital status

- Player hobbies

- Education level of a player

Dimensional modeling still revolves around the organization of the data sets. This time you're looking to organize the sets into the structure of a data mart, so you need one central fact table with a series of dimension tables linked to it. Looking at the list, you'll find you seem to be working with two significant concepts, namely, games and players. Now if you read the requirements, you can surmise that the clients want to focus on, or measure, the facts about games. They have also told you they want to be able to look for trends about those facts by various aspects of the players and time concepts. This gives you your first indicator that you'll be looking for discrete measurable facts about games, which will be the basis for the fact table of this data mart. Meanwhile, the more textual, informational data referring to players and time will become the dimensions.

So how do you focus on the facts?

Choosing the Granularity

What grain choice do you have in this case? Review the tables that contain the Game data elements, as shown in Figure 12-9.

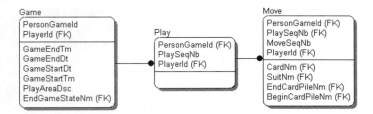

Figure 12-9. *The Solitaire* Game *data elements*

Since the clients told you they aren't interested in plays, you'll ignore the Play table and look at the other two levels of detail:

- Details of single games

- Details of single moves

You can provide the data at the level of Move, or you can aggregate it up one level to that of Game. If you wanted to show this data at the Game level, you'd have to summarize the Move information and store it with the Game information. You could satisfy the requirement as it's currently stated by creating the fact table out of games or moves. However, the rule of thumb says you should always provide the lowest level of granularity that satisfies the requirements. The requirements suggest you need to focus on Game and Move.

The choice of granularity defines the fact table. If you expect a single record for each game, the granularity is at the level of Game. If you expect a record for each move in a game, the granularity will be at the level of Game+Move. You could also specify your granularity to record a single record for all games that happened over a day for a player. The granularity in that case would be at the level of Day+Game+Player.

Choosing the right grain to support your clients' requirements is important. Given the requirements, you'll design two data marts. One will be at the Game level and meets the clients' requirements. The other will be at the Game+Move level to show an option for future flexibility.

This additional design option would still allow the clients to analyze games but would also provide them with the added ability to "drill down" to the details of a game (to the game moves).

Choosing the Measures

Measures, as mentioned earlier, are the data elements used to do data mining or analysis. As the name suggests, they're often things you can weigh, count, time, price, or get the length, width, or height of.

Designing stores of information at a defined granularity organizes measures in an easy-to-manipulate form (simple numbers are best, but textual measures are allowable) and are the foundation of a data mart. Measures are answers to the questions about duration such as "When *does something* happen?" or "How *much/many/long/high/wide*?" Or they're the answers to calculation questions such as "What is the *average/minimum/mean/max/delta from/growth rate*?" We covered the types of measures earlier in this chapter.

You also need to be able to recognize whether this fact is an original base fact or if it has been derived by combining two or more facts together. For example, if you note that TotalBilledAmt from a source system data record is a base fact, this will be important if you're providing a SummedChargeAmt fact in your fact design (which consists of all the charges in the details of the invoice). TotalBilledAmt is a static fact based on an event that has occurred. SummedChargeAmt is a derived fact based on preexisting details. The clients may consider this to be an important aspect of the data. They may be looking for salespeople who consistently give large discounts to certain accounts. Whether a fact is a base fact or a derived fact is important to the ETL team as well, because loading the first is a simple transfer, and loading the other may involve a complicated post-process formula that needs to be maintained.

In this situation, start with a submodel of Solitaire focusing on the identified facts, Game and Move, as shown in Figure 12-10. Take special note of the attributes you can count, measure, or add. We've removed Play by denormalizing PlaySeqNb into Move. Also, we've suppressed the data types on the Physical model again so that you can concentrate on the column names.

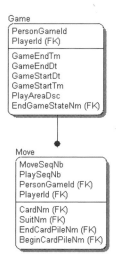

Figure 12-10. *The Solitaire* Game-Move *submodel*

You can list the things that are simply base facts from these original tables.

- Who played the game?

- When did the game start?

- When did the game end?

- Was the game won or lost?

- What back design was used?

And you can also begin to identify questions about these facts that can be answered with the information provided.

- How long was the game in minutes and seconds?

- How many moves were there?

- How many red moves were there?

- How many black moves were there?

- How many hearts moves were there?

- How many clubs moves were there?

- How many diamonds moves were there?

- How many spades moves were there?

- How many moves were made from the draw pile?

- How many moves were made to the discard piles?

- How many moves were made to the processing piles?

- How many moves were made to the waste pile?

- How many moves were made from the waste pile?

This list will do for now. Double-check your sample list of questions against the clients' requirements to remind yourself of what they want to know. These quantities will be the basis for their analysis. They may ask you to add precalculated averages or other measures when they review the list.

What about measures for `Move`? The movement of a card from place to place in a game is an event. This event has no measure, other than that it happened. You could store this as a value of 1 (noting that one event happened), but you don't need to do so (although you may choose to do so anyway so it can be added easily using a `SUM` function rather than a `COUNT` function). The event is stored in a factless fact table.

You'll want to carefully document the measures, their definitions, expected values, quality checks, and formulas. It's extremely important to the ETL team, since they will be loading the fact table.

Fact Definitions

Table 12-1 shows the fact definitions.

Table 12-1. *Fact Definitions*

Question	Mapped To...	Base? Derived?	Additive Factor
Who played the game?	Game.PlayerId	Base	Textual
When did the game start?	Game.GameStartTm, Game.GameStartDt	Base	Textual
When did the game end?	Game.GameEndTm, Game.GameEndDt	Base	Textual
Was the game won or lost?	Game.GameEndStateNm	Base	Textual
What back design was used?	GameBackDesignNm	Base	Textual
How long was the game in minutes and seconds?	Game.GameStartTm, Game.GameStartDt, Game.GameEndTm, Game.GameEndDt	Derived	Fully additive
How many moves were there?	Game.PlayerGameId, Move.PlayerGameId	Derived	Fully additive
How many red moves?	Game.PlayerGameId, Move.PlayerGameId, Move.SuitNm, Suit, ColorNm	Derived	Fully additive
How many black moves?	Game.PlayerGameId, Move.PlayerGameId, Move.SuitNm, Suit, ColorNm	Derived	Fully additive
How many hearts moves?	Game.PlayerGameId, Move.PlayerGameId, Move.SuitNm	Derived	Fully additive
How many clubs moves?	Game.PlayerGameId, Move.PlayerGameId, Move.SuitNm	Derived	Fully additive
How many diamonds moves?	Game.PlayerGameId, Move.PlayerGameId, Move.SuitNm	Derived	Fully additive
How many spades moves?	Game.PlayerGameId, Move.PlayerGameId, Move.SuitNm	Derived	Fully additive
How many moves were made from the draw pile?	Game.PlayerGameId, Move.PlayerGameId, Move.BeginCardPileNm	Derived	Fully additive
How many moves were made to the discard piles?	Game.PlayerGameId, Move.PlayerGameId, Move.EndCardPileNm	Derived	Fully additive
How many moves were made to the processing piles?	Game.PlayerGameId, Move.PlayerGameId, Move.EndCardPileNm	Derived	Fully additive

Question	Mapped To...	Base? Derived?	Additive Factor
How many moves were made to the waste pile?	`Game.PlayerGameId,` `Move.PlayerGameId,` `Move.EndCardPileNm`	Derived	Fully additive
How many moves were made from the waste pile?	`Game.PlayerGameId,` `Move.PlayerGameId,` `Move.BeginCardPileNm`	Derived	Fully additive

Having considered the nature of the facts or measures and the level of granularity for the data mart, let's now begin to construct a data mart for Game.

Creating the Game Data Mart

Let's design the data mart at the granularity of Game. In doing so, we'll start with a discussion of the GameFact table.

The GameFact Table

Begin by noting the granularity of the fact table. How do you identify a single game? In this case, you know the primary key of the source table Game. Remember that a game was an event for a player in the Solitaire solution, so it took two pieces of information to uniquely identify it. The composite primary key (pair of IDs) represents a row that will have data values looking something like this: PlayerGameId = 15, PlayerId = 127 (which when joined back to the Player table means you're working with the 15th game of a 36-to-45-year-old male who is married and is a BA/S-level librarian), as shown in Figure 12-11.

Figure 12-11. *The* GameFact *table with primary key*

Now you add the measures following the same naming conventions you used in the Physical modeling process, as shown in Figure 12-12. Remember that every column name must contain a class word, every column name must be in Pascal notation (which we chose from several options of physical naming conventions), and you must be consistent when it comes to using abbreviations. As in every stage of modeling, make sure you have clear names; the clients may actually be using a software tool to query these tables and will probably be able to create some SQL queries themselves. Clear column names are therefore helpful. (If your physical naming standard makes the column names too obscure for client use, you may want to consider using a database view to make the names more recognizable.)

GameFact

| PlayerId |
GamePlayerId
GameEndTm
GameEndDt
GameStartDt
GameStartTm
PlayAreaDsc
EndGameStateNm
GameDurationMinQty
MoveQty
RedMoveQty
BlackMoveQty
HeartMoveQty
ClubMoveQty
DiamondMoveQty
SpadeMoveQty
FromDrawPileMoveQty
ToDiscardPileMoveQty
ToProcessPileMoveQty
ToWastePileMoveQty
FromWastePileMoveQty

Figure 12-12. *The attributed* GameFact *table*

Review the key for the GameFact table against the guidelines for keys in Dimensional models. Since you're concerned with performance, and we've already discussed how compound keys aren't efficiently queried, you need to reexamine the choice of PlayerId and GamePlayerId as the GameFact table's primary key.

You could remove PlayerId from the key and still have a unique primary key, but remember that you also want to remove any dependence on the keys that are used in your source system (the Solitaire application). To do this, you need to move both GamePlayerId and PlayerId out of the primary key and replace this key with a surrogate key that's entirely contained within the data mart. As you can see in Figure 12-13, a GameKey attribute, created for this model and specific to this data mart, is the best choice for a primary key for the GameFact table.

GameFact

GameKey
PlayerId
GamePlayerId
GameEndTm
GameEndDt
GameStartDt
GameStartTm
PlayAreaDsc
EndGameStateNm
GameDurationMinQty
MoveQty
RedMoveQty
BlackMoveQty
HeartMoveQty
ClubMoveQty
DiamondMoveQty
SpadeMoveQty
FromDrawPileMoveQty
ToDiscardPileMoveQty
ToProcessPileMoveQty
ToWastePileMoveQty
FromWastePileMoveQty

Figure 12-13. *The* GameFact *table with a surrogate primary key*

Game Dimensions

Remember that dimensions usually represent a fundamental way of accessing and presenting business information. In this way, dimensions are sometimes described in terms of "roll-up" points or pivotal aspects of the facts. So the next step is to look at the ways the clients wanted to "slice and dice" the game data, or, in other words, how they want the data presented for their analysis. Those are the dimensions you need to identify. What were the requirements? Remember, they want to investigate the following:

- The *moves* of a game
- The *age of a player* in a game
- The *marriage status of a player* in a game
- The *hobby of a player* in a game
- The *education level of a player* in a game
- The *time of day* of a game
- The *day of week* of a game
- The win or lose *status* of a game
- The choice of *back design*

The items in italics in the previous list are the game-related items the clients identified as being important to their analysis. Group these items by concepts or nouns by looking for similarities. From the same list, player-related attributes make up a large share of the required reporting points.

The Player Dimension

Make a subject area (a submodel including just the tables pertinent to the discussion) from the source system model of Player and review it (see Figure 12-14).

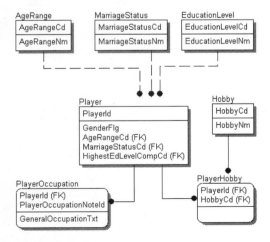

Figure 12-14. *The* Player *subject area from the Solitaire model*

To build the player dimension, you need to denormalize the data elements you broke out for normalization earlier. By denormalizing these attributes, you'll reduce the joins needed to query the player information. This is relatively simple to do when relationships in the model treat `Player` as a child entity. As shown in Figure 12-15, all the nonidentifying relationships on the model (denoted by the dashed lines) are relationships where `Player` is the child. Bring all the player-related data elements from the earlier list of potential dimensions into the `Player` table. This includes attributes from the `EducationLevel`, `MarriageStatus`, and `AgeRange` tables.

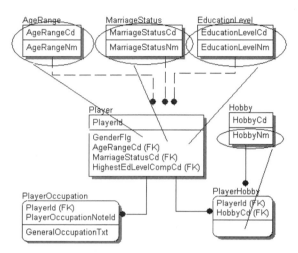

Figure 12-15. *Denormalizing player-related attributes into the player dimension*

The purpose of creating a Dimensional model design is to provide the fastest response time for analytical queries. Since joins slow a database query down, getting rid of as many joins as possible can significantly reduce this response time. However, removing those tables reduces the design's ability to enforce data integrity, because now there's no database constraint to prevent invalid values from being stored in the denormalized fields, as shown in Figure 12-16. To make query response time a priority, it's generally expected that the burden of data quality has been placed on the source systems or the ETL process.

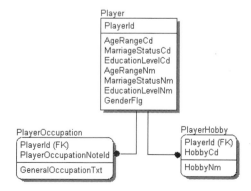

Figure 12-16. *The player dimension containing denormalized values*

PlayerHobby and PlayerOccupation have a one-to-many relationship with Player. Each row in these tables may refer to multiple Player entries. You must choose whether to use a snowflake design to represent this or try to denormalize the data. You must choose between a restrictive, more simplistic structure that will exhibit better performance and a completely flexible, more complex structure with a potential performance impact. Here we've chosen the more complex choice. We changed the name of the table to include the string "Dim" (in compliance with a local data warehouse naming standard), moved the source system ID fields out of the primary key, and created a new surrogate key column to act as the primary key for Player. Figure 12-17 shows the dimensional snowflake scenario for PlayerOccupation.

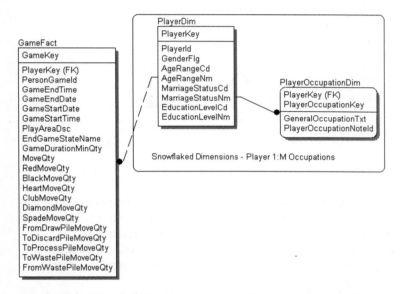

Figure 12-17. PlayerOccupation *snowflake design option for the player dimension*

Continuing the denormalization activity for the player dimension, you can optionally bring all the Hobby value options into Player as flag fields. You should make this type of decision (which constitutes a fairly significant denormalization) after considering the requirements of the clients and the quantity and stability of the Hobby list of values. The requirements don't seem to include any discussion or consideration of the simplicity of the Dimensional model design with respect to client navigation. You may need to return to the clients to discuss the importance of the ease of navigating this design. You'll also want to verify the current list of hobbies for completeness and how stable the clients think they are. You'll go forward with the belief that the forms are printed with a predetermined list of hobby choices, that there will be no write-ins allowed, and that the clients think the list is extremely stable. Based on these assumptions, you'll end up with a simple PlayerDim design, as shown in Figure 12-18.

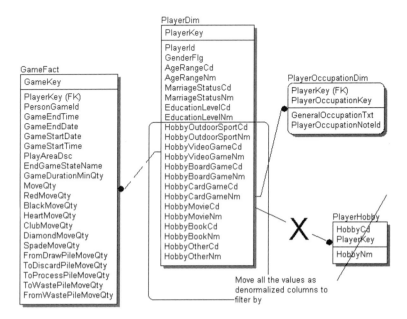

Figure 12-18. *Player hobbies denormalized into the player dimension*

What do you do to denormalize the applicable Hobby attributes? We suggest making a column that has the actual name and code of the hobby rather than creating a flag field for each hobby, since the values stored in these columns will show on the physical reports.

You must also remember to follow the data mart design standards. We've renamed the dimension table PlayerDim, given it a new surrogate primary key, and removed the migrated PlayerId foreign key field from the GameFact table.

The Player source system key (the PlayerId attribute) should be kept as part of the player dimension table for reference and for updating. Some teams may choose to keep the mapping of PlayerKey to PlayerId in a staging area; this type of data isn't usually a useful attribute from the clients' perspective, but the ETL team will find it useful for auditing or occasional updates.

Now, relate the PlayerDim dimension table to the GameFact fact table. Several options are available to you for doing this. The GameKey attribute will ensure that the record is unique, so you can use a nonidentifying relationship. Some modelers prefer to make the granularity of the GameFact table more apparent by creating a multipart key. You could also use an identifying relationship, if you want, to note that this fact table is at the Game/Player granularity level.

In Figure 12-19, we've chosen the first option: to remove PlayerId from the GameFact table and use a nonidentifying relationship to connect PlayerDim to GameFact.

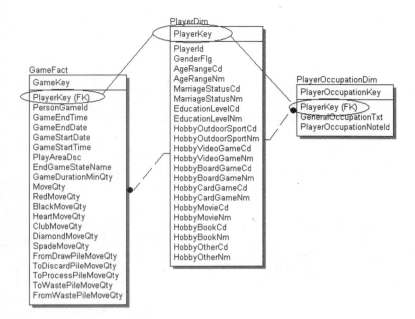

Figure 12-19. *The* GameFact *data mart with completed player dimension*

The Time Dimension

Continuing the review of the requirements, you can now review the time dimension. The clients have indicated they're interested in the following time-related information:

- Time of day of a game

- Day of week of a game

- Win or lose status of a game

Time information is stored twice for every Game fact (the game's start date/time and the game's end date/time). In the Dimensional model, you'll relate this dimension to GameFact twice using role names. Note that the Solitaire system isn't the source for the data in this dimension. Fortunately, most relational database management systems (RDBMSs) have well-developed abilities to handle date and time values. Any format or date/time data element that isn't supported by your relational database will require a programmer to write a process to populate these fields. Find out from the clients how they'd like to see hours and minutes displayed. You have lots of options when it comes to displaying dates and times.

- Local time in 24-hour format

- Local time in 12-hour format

- Time names (midnight, noon)

- Greenwich mean time in 24 hours (for comparison of events globally)

- Greenwich mean time in 12 hours

- Local a.m./p.m. notation

- The "o'clock" name

- 00:00 notation

- Running minute number starting from 1 at midnight (helps sequencing)

- Day period name (late night, early morning, late afternoon, early evening)

■**Note** Sometimes you have to enhance dimensions from data sources outside your targeted sources.

In Figure 12-20 you can see how to relate the new TimeDim dimension to the GameFact table. Each nonidentifying relationship was role-named so that the fields in the GameFact table clearly identify what data they contain. Make sure you replace the original time attributes in the GameFact table with the foreign keys from the TimeDim table.

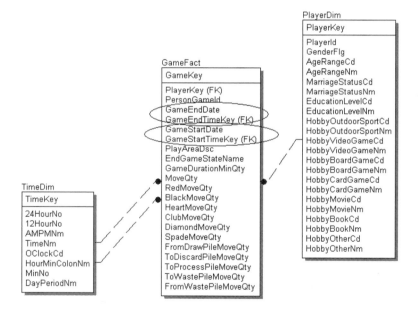

Figure 12-20. *Adding the time dimension to the* GameFact *data mart*

Note that the TimeDim table stores many attributes about the time dimension (hour number, 24-hour number, minute number, a.m./p.m. designator, and so on) and that some of these are different formats for the same basic data. In this case, this technique allows different views or display formats for the same time dimension value.

The Day Dimension

The day dimension is used similarly to the time dimension. The GameFact table stores the dates the games started and ended. Time, at the day level of granularity, has a number of interesting and descriptive attributes and formats. Items to consider when constructing the day dimension are as follows:

- Day in month number

- Day in week name

- Day in week number

- Day in week abbreviation

- Week number Sunday–Saturday

- Month number

- Month name

- Month abbreviation

- Century year

- Standard holiday name (although holidays are usually snowflaked with lots of added attributes)

- DDMMYY

- MMDDYYYY

- Number of day in the year

- Season name

- Quarter number

- Half-year number

- Leap-year flag

At this point, you may ask why we didn't consider this information when we addressed the time dimension. After all, the day is just a higher-level view of the time, isn't it? Although we could have defined the time dimension to include calendar days as well as the time of day, here we implemented the day and time as separate dimensions. The main advantage to separating these two dimensions is that you can more easily perform analysis based upon the time of day a game was played without having to consider the days on which these games were played. This design allows for a somewhat easier separation of the time of day information from date information. But this is a judgment call. You could just as well have combined the date and time into one dimension and replaced each pair of date and time attributes in the original GameFact table with a single reference to a time dimension table.

Now that you've created the day dimension, let's relate it to the GameFact table twice, remembering to role-name the relationships and remove the original source system columns, as shown in Figure 12-21.

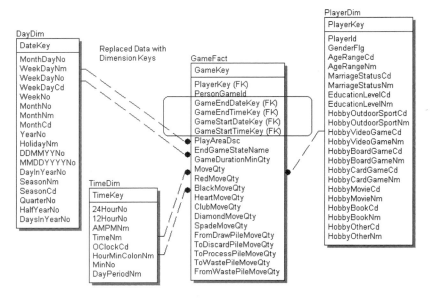

Figure 12-21. *Adding the day dimension to the* GameFact *data mart*

At the end of the first pass, the GameFact data mart looks like Figure 12-22.

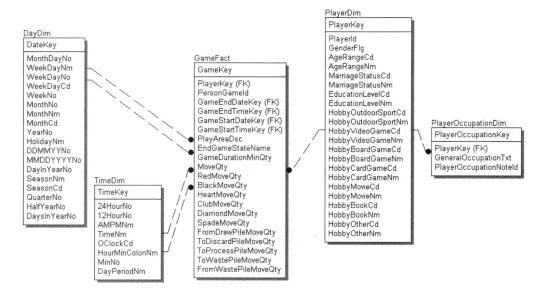

Figure 12-22. *The* GameFact *data mart with time, day, player, and player occupation dimensions*

The Back Design and Win/Lose Status Dimension

Just two requirements are left. You still need to address the clients' requirements to track the following:

- The back design choice

- Win or lose status of a game

Return to the source system to see what data elements exist for them (see Figure 12-23).

Figure 12-23. *The original* BackDesign *and* EndingGameState *tables*

Each of these tables has a name and a description. Quite frequently in Dimensional modeling you'll want to avoid storing anything that would be too large or awkward to display easily on a report or online screen. Check with the clients first, of course, but it's a good bet you can safely remove GameStatusDesc and BackDesignImg from the dimensions. It's particularly hard to imagine how the clients would use the back design image in creating aggregated statistics. What's important here is to keep the names of the back design and game state. Move the source system keys (the BackDesignNm and EndGameStateNm fields) out of each of the primary keys, and add data warehouse–specific surrogate keys. Relate each of these dimensions to GameFact. In draft form, the model now looks like Figure 12-24.

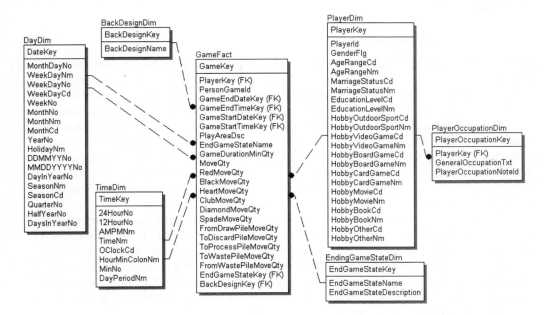

Figure 12-24. *Adding* EndingGameState *and* BackDesign *to the* GameFact *data mart*

Finishing the Game Data Mart

Now that you've completed the first draft of the Dimensional design, you need to polish it by addressing the following issues:

- Adding data types and database NULLs
- Creating conformed dimensions
- Handling slowly changing dimensions

Adding Data Types and Database NULLs

You now need to add your data sizing and data types to the model, as well as determine which fields can contain NULL values. Normally, all the relationships between the fact and dimension tables are required. In cases where there may not be valid or known data for a dimension relationship, a record is often inserted into the dimension table to represent the "unknown" value, rather than using a database NULL. Avoiding database NULL values in your fact table simplifies the query structure (eliminating the need for costly outer joins) and may prevent varying results when executing summarization queries.

Your requirements may cause you to make different choices when it comes to representing source data in your fact table. In some cases, incomplete data records may be permitted in the fact table in order to match fact records to the original source data. Or you may implement a transformation as the data is loaded that changes empty spaces in certain numeric fields into a zero value. (If you do this, beware of accidentally changing the meaning of a query that calculates averages.) Or you may transform empty text into the literal string "Not in Source" to provide the clients with a way of reporting on the records in the fact table that are missing certain values.

Creating Conformed Dimensions

We've already talked about the process of how you join data sets. Fact tables are also data sets, containing unique members of enormous sets of data. Clients often want to be able to combine the results of queries from different fact tables into a single summary report or view. This is more easily accomplished when the dimensions related to these multiple fact tables use the same keys.

If you can ensure that the dimension tables in multiple star schemas use the same values and the same keys, then your dimensions are said to be *conformed*. If you don't use the same structure and content in your dimension tables across different star schemas, you can get a bad case of *stove piping*, or data and data structures that have been built to be used in one system only. Dimension tables referring to the same concept but whose data values (and keys) are different are *unconformed*.

Creating a Dimensional model with unconformed dimensions results in your new fact table being isolated, and it will be more difficult to integrate with other Dimensional models that use some of the same concepts. This will result in an enormous amount of data redundancy. Think about how many date/calendar tables might be created to support different Dimensional models, when all the enterprise really needed was one. And think about how much effort needs to be expended to change the data values in all the affected sources, should there be a need for the source data to change.

■Tip Share dimensional tables with as many projects as you can. This is the best way to prevent your data mart from becoming a stovepipe.

In this example, you'd need to look outside the Solitaire application to find out if someone else has been doing Dimensional modeling and creating related data marts. If related data marts exist, you may want to review their dimension tables and see if it makes sense to conform to them. If you can conform your time and day dimensions, for instance, then the research and design you're doing may be combined with other related data gathered elsewhere.

Handling Slowly Changing Dimensions

Now that you've created a Dimensional model, you need to review the dimensions again with the clients to determine any historical requirements. Data changes. Source system data changes because errors are fixed. Predefined hierarchies are reorganized (possibly introducing a requirement to see As-Is roll-ups as well as As-Was), dates are classified into different fiscal reporting periods, and even addresses change when a road gets a different name to honor a local hero. Data is cleaned, matured, mutated, and enhanced in source systems. And your data mart may need to stay in sync.

You need to ask the clients the following questions:

- Will the data records be loaded once or updated?

- Do you care about knowing that records changed?

- If you care, do you want to know what the previous values were?

- How many changes do you want to be able to see?

The game data mart has no concept of history. The data gathered about the players was based on a one-time registration that won't be updated. However, all the attributes could contain incorrect data and could be fixed.

You need to review each column in each dimension table to see how you want to manage data value changes. Do you want to overwrite original values with the updated values, keep both the original and updated values, or keep the most recent original value and the updated value? The dimensions need to be structured correctly to support these changes. Is it OK to overwrite MarriageStatusCd, or do you need to know it was updated? How about AgeRangeCd or HighestEdLevelCompCd? Each field may need to be treated differently. For some columns, a simple overwrite is fine, but in others it's critical to keep a full history of all changes. What we're trying to emphasize is that change control isn't only at the table level; it's at the column and row levels, and the choices made concerning historical data may change the table's design.

Types of Data Changes

Let's look at what change value types are available to you (as found in *The Data Warehouse Lifecycle Toolkit: Expert Methods for Designing, Developing, and Deploying Data Warehouses* (John Wiley & Sons, 1998).

Type 1

According to *The Data Warehouse Lifecycle Toolkit*, Type 1 changes involve a simple overwrite. There's no record of the old data value remaining in the data mart. In fact, you have no way to know that anything has actually changed. This is the simplest type of change, but it gives the least ability to track changes. You can only do As-Is analysis with this type of history management.

A Type 1 change does the following:

- It can easily fix incorrect data.

- It doesn't track any prior data values.

- It doesn't require changes to the dimension table structure.

- It doesn't insert any new records.

Type 2

Type 2 data updates add a whole new record every time something you want to track changes. So, for example, if a company with `CompanyNumber` = 123 changed its `CompanyName` from "Jones Ltd." to "Jones & Harry," you'd end up with two records for this company in your dimension table. A query that selects sales for `CompanyNumber` = 123 would give you all of 123's sales, and a query that selects sales for `CompanyName` = Jones & Harry, would return only those sales that occurred after the database recorded the name change. This allows you to "perfectly partition history" (or provide As-Was analysis) and uses records that were valid for only a given point in time.

A Type 2 change does the following:

- It tracks all changes of interest, providing a "permanent memory."

- It perfectly partitions history.

- It requires the dimension table to include a date span noting when the data on the record was valid.

- It adds a new record to the dimension table every time something of interest changes.

Type 3

Type 3 changes take two subtly different forms, depending on historical data requirements. Either a Type 3 change does the following:

- It compares the existing dimension table record to the new record to be stored.

- It requires the dimension table structure to include an `Original<ColumnName>` attribute.

- It modifies the existing dimension table record when a value changes by moving an attribute value to the `Original<ColumnName>` column if it's the original data value. The new value is stored in the `<ColumnName>` field. After the initial update, every subsequent change simply updates the `<ColumnName>` column.

or it does the following:

- It keeps track of two values (the current value and the previous value).

- It requires the dimension table structure to include a Used to be<ColumnName> attribute.

- It modifies the existing dimension table record when a value changes by moving the existing attribute value to the Used to be<ColumnName> column while updating the <ColumnName> column with the new value.

Type 3 changes add an addendum to the record of either the original or the previous value. This type of change doesn't allow for the ability to perfectly partition history, but it can provide some visibility to change.

Note Every dimension table could have attributes managed by Type 1, 2, or 3 for history management. You'll generally have a combination of rules for different attributes within the dimension.

Dimension Table Structures Supporting the Change Types

As an example, let's review the PlayerDim table and how the structure would look after implementing each of these options (see Figure 12-25). We've added the new columns needed to support the change control at the bottom of the tables and italicized them.

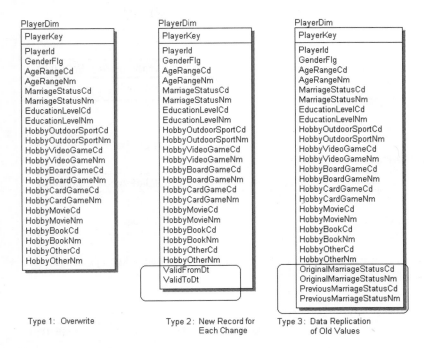

Figure 12-25. *Type 1, 2, and 3 changes applied to the* PlayerDim *table*

We added an example of each of the two options of Type 3 changes. In practice you'd probably pick only one of these (although there's no reason why you couldn't keep the original status name, which is set only once, as well as a previous status name value, which would be updated as many times as `MarriageCd` was updated).

Examples of Actual Data Entries Subject to the Change Types

Let's assume the only data element where you're concerned about changes is the player's marriage status. In the case of Type 1 data, yesterday's entry looked like Table 12-2.

Table 12-2. Player *Table Before a Type 1 Change*

PlayerKey	PlayerId	...	MarriageStatusCd	MarriageStatusNm
1875	398	...	S	Single

While today, after a simple update to `MarriageStatusCd` and `MarriageStatusNm`, it looks like Table 12-3.

Table 12-3. Player *Table After a Type 1 Change*

PlayerKey	PlayerId	...	MarriageStatusCd	MarriageStatusNm
1875	398	...	M	Married

In the case of Type 2 data, yesterday the example looked like Table 12-4.

Table 12-4. Player *Table Before a Type 2 Change*

PlayerKey	PlayerId	...	MarriageStatusCd	MarriageStatusNm	ValidFromDt	ValidToDt
1875	398	...	S	Single	1/1/04	

And today it looks like Table 12-5.

Table 12-5. Player *Table After a Type 2 Change*

PlayerKey	PlayerId	...	MarriageStatusCd	MarriageStatusNm	ValidFromDt	ValidToDt
1875	398	...	S	Single	1/1/04	6/1/04
8769	398	...	M	Married	6/1/04	

And finally, using an example of a Type 3 change where you choose to keep just the original data value, yesterday the data looked like Table 12-6.

Table 12-6. Player *Table Before a Type 3 Change*

PlayerKey	PlayerId	...	MarriageStatusCd	MarriageStatusNm	OriginalCd	OriginalNm
1875	398	...	S	Single		

And today it looks like Table 12-7.

Table 12-7. `Player` *Table After a Type 3 Change*

PlayerKey	PlayerId	...	MarriageStatusCd	MarriageStatusNm	OriginalCd	OriginalNm
1875	398	...	M	Married	S	Single

Note This type of data value management is really important to the clients. Frequently the data mart or data warehouse is the only place where they can see this type of history.

Data Element Definitions

We hope by this point you understand the importance of data definitions; by having a record of your analysis, you have a basis for quality data management. These items are even more important here. You need to document much more than the data element descriptions when you're creating a Dimensional model. Table 12-8 shows some ideas of what you'll probably document.

Table 12-8. *Things You May Want to Document in a Dimensional Model*

What You Might Need to Capture	Definition
Server location	Test, quality control, or production location if you know it.
Server database name	For the source data (if you know it).
Data mart name	What do you refer to this collection of tables as?
Table name	Table name.
Table type	Fact or dimension.
Table description	A complete sentence or paragraph describing what this fact or dimension covers. The granularity would be good to note.
Column name	Column name.
Column data type	Number or text; make it specific to the deployed structure.
Column size	The allowed size of a data value.
Column definition	A complete sentence or paragraph describing what the clients mean by all their data elements (such as profitability increase percent, for example).
Column type	Base or derived.
Staging steps	A brief textual description of your understanding of the expected steps needed to acquire the data from the source system and transform it into the target value. You'll need the following: Source system location Source table name(s) Source column name(s) Derivation/formula/transformation requirements

Continued

Table 12-8. *Continued*

What You Might Need to Capture	Definition
Formula	Need to document the clients' formula to create this data value.
Value change management	Type 1, 2, 3.
Additive rules	Additive, semi-, non-.
Business owner	The clients to whom feedback is sent and communication is due.
IT owner	Programmer or team in charge of maintenance.
Accuracy need	Are there "sanity" checks for data quality checks?
Criticality need	Is this data element mission-critical to the enterprise?
Security or sensitivity requirements	Who can or can't see it? Why?

Reviewing the GameFact Data Mart: What Have You Done?

You've now concluded the first exercise of building a Dimensional model. You designed a fairly typical star schema at the granularity of a single game. You should now have a good idea of how to approach Dimensional modeling. As a review, what did you do?

In this exercise, you did the following:

- Gathered requirements and determined the goal of the fact table

- Chose the granularity and measures

- Determined the dimensions and chose whether to use a snowflake design for them

- Related the dimensions to the fact and determined the history requirements of all dimensional data elements

- Validated general design decisions with actual data

- Detailed all Physical model design needs for table creation

- Documented all data analysis definitions for team reference

Like relational modeling, Dimensional modeling takes practice. If you can, solicit feedback from someone who has experience creating this kind of model. If you have access to experienced ETL people, get some idea of how different choices in the star schema affect the ETL design. Also, lots of Web sites and newsgroups exist; use them.

Creating the GameMove Data Mart

Let's try one more exercise and build a data mart for Move. Now that you've already constructed a Game data mart, this will be much easier. Let's review the requirements. You need to analyze the following:

- The moves

- Wins or losses in Solitaire games

You do this to find out if there are any trends within the following:

• Time of day

• Day of week

• Age

• Marriage status

• Hobby

• Education level of a player

Grain and Measures for GameMove

Just like before, you begin with choosing the granularity for your data mart. This time, the granularity is at the level of each move for one play for one game for one player (see Figure 12-26).

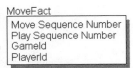

MoveFact

| Move Sequence Number |
| Play Sequence Number |
| GameId |
| PlayerId |

Figure 12-26. *The* MoveFact *table*

Next you try to determine which measures are important. Game moves are events. Look at the current columns in the source system table shown in Figure 12-27. Is there anything here you can measure or count in any way?

MoveFact

| Move Sequence Number |
| Play Sequence Number |
| GameId |
| PlayerId |
| |
| Suit Name |
| Card Name |
| End Card Pile Name |
| Begin Card Pile Name |

Figure 12-27. *The* MoveFact *table with primary key and attributes*

As an event, Move doesn't do much other than occur. There's an implied numeric measure MoveQty, but it's always of quantity 1. How many moves does each Move represent? One. You create this little measure to give the clients a number to sum and average rather than count in code. Creating this attribute also provides a column to select against and apply SUM functionality to, rather than requiring the report designer to create a derived column in the report. Add the measure to the design, as shown in Figure 12-28.

Figure 12-28. *The* MoveFact *table with implied measure* MoveQty

Dimensions for GameMove

Now let's determine which dimensions you need. You know that a GameMove consists of one card moving from one card pile to another. So you need to include cards and card piles as dimensions. Make a subject area for Card, and review the available attributes (see Figure 12-29).

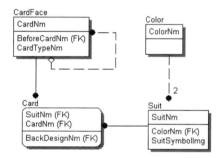

Figure 12-29. *The Solitaire* Card *submodel*

You'll now review the Card submodel's data elements and use as much as you can. The suit symbol images are probably not very useful as part of the analytical reports created in Dimensional modeling, but all the rest of the attributes probably are. Denormalize these attributes into Card to create a CardDim table.

Create a new data mart key to reduce the risks of using current system keys, as shown in Figure 12-30.

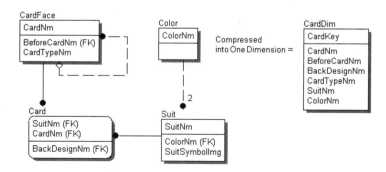

Figure 12-30. *Creating the denormalized card dimension with a surrogate key*

Add all the descriptive attributes you need, and then relate it to the MoveFact fact table, as shown in Figure 12-31.

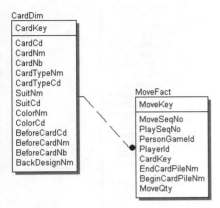

Figure 12-31. *The* MoveFact *data mart, including the card dimension*

Now let's follow the same process for CardPile (see Figure 12-32).

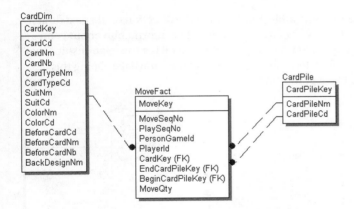

Figure 12-32. *The* MoveFact *data mart with* CardDim *and* CardPile *dimensions*

Now look at the MoveFact table shown in Figure 12-33. PlayerId will be replaced when you relate PlayerDim with the fact table. In including the PlayerDim table from the GameFact data mart, you get to exercise the concept of conforming the dimensions. Conforming to this dimension means that any analysis based on Player will be able to bridge the GameFact and MoveFact fact tables.

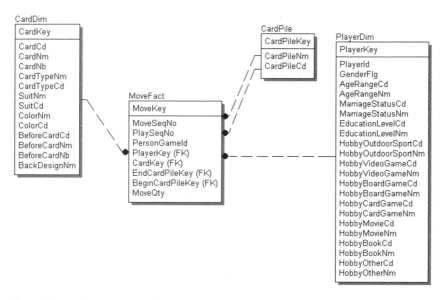

Figure 12-33. *The* `MoveFact` *data mart with a conformed player dimension*

The `PersonGameId` field in the `MoveFact` table points you in the direction of the next dimension. In this case, you can actually build a dimension of descriptive information about games and build a `GameDim` table. You'd implement a snowflake design involving the relationships that make sense and denormalize those that don't need to be part of the snowflake. Doing this would create a schema that looks like Figure 12-34.

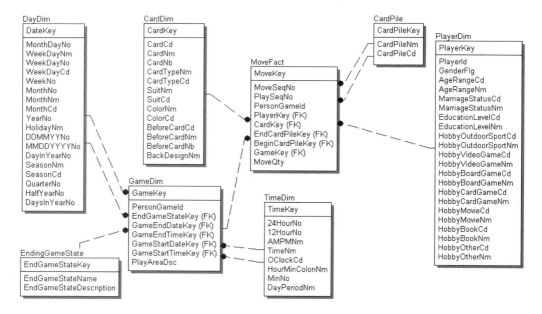

Figure 12-34. *The* `MoveFact` *data mart with a snowflake design for the game dimension*

But could you also take the descriptive attributes of Game and locate them in the GameMoveFact table? This is called putting the facts "at the wrong level of granularity." This can be dangerous when dealing with otherwise additive facts. Measures and descriptive facts are "at the wrong level of granularity" if they refer to data stored at a different level of detail. When you move data elements that solely describe a game into Move, you end up duplicating these values as many times as there are moves for that game. This deliberate duplication can lead to incorrect reporting if not managed carefully.

Note Clients will want to put facts into tables at the wrong level of granularity. They will want to be able to report on summary or master record values at the same time they're reporting on detail values.

For example, clients may push to have a measure called InvoiceTotalAmt, belonging to an Invoice, be put into the InvoiceLineFact. The danger here is that InvoiceTotalAmt may look like it's an additive fact, but it's not. Since it's replicated numerous times across multiple invoice rows, it isn't additive. Descriptive information such as what's in GameDim, however, is fairly safe. The move did happen between the start and end time of the game. The move was a part of a game that was won or lost. You may choose for simplicity to design the star schema like Figure 12-35.

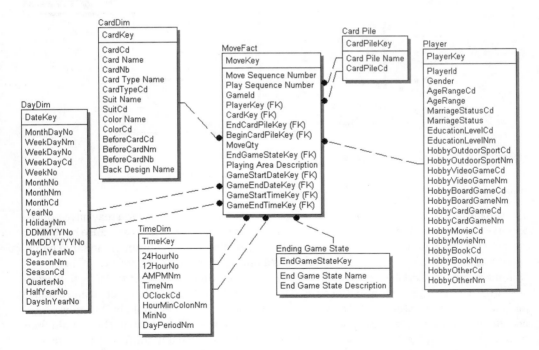

Figure 12-35. *The* MoveFact *data mart with game data at the wrong level of granularity*

Notice you haven't added any of the potentially additive measures from GameFact into MoveFact. And look at how many of the dimensions you were able to conform! With this many conforming measures, you could actually make a good case to the clients that they don't need all the GameFact descriptive attributes in the MoveFact table. They should be able to select the correct set of Game records based on the Player records, for instance, and combine GameFact and MoveFact through the PlayerDim table. But for this example, you'll leave the design like this, because this is how the clients want to be able to perform their analysis. You should document that several columns in the MoveFact table are at the wrong level of granularity, however, so they can be removed at a future date if it becomes appropriate. Figure 12-36 shows the GameFact data mart.

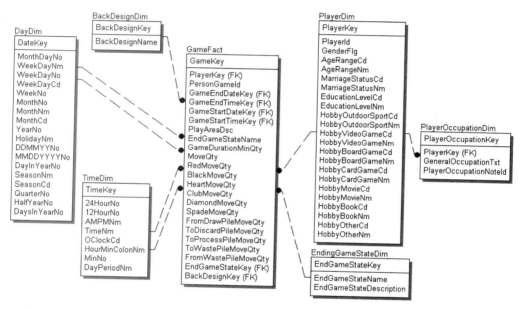

Figure 12-36. *The* GameFact *data mart*

Role-Named Dimensions

You can perform one more task to make navigation easier for your clients. You may have noticed you have two dimensions that play multiple roles in the fact table. These can cause havoc if your clients use a query tool. It can be difficult to remember which column of the same name in a given table is the one they wanted to use as a filter. For example, suppose your clients wanted to sum the MoveQty field from the GameFact table, where the GameStartTmKey field was later than 12 p.m. but the GameEndTmKey field was earlier than 1 p.m. If they were using a drag-and-drop query tool, showing them a picture of the tables, then they could build a query by clicking MoveQty, GameStartTmKey, and GameEndTmKey from the GameFact table. They would then need to go twice to TimeDim to restrict the selection. This can be really confusing and forces the user to do a lot of labeling work that you could do for them.

The way to get around this is to build role-based views and hide the physical table from the clients (and their query tool), as shown in Figure 12-37.

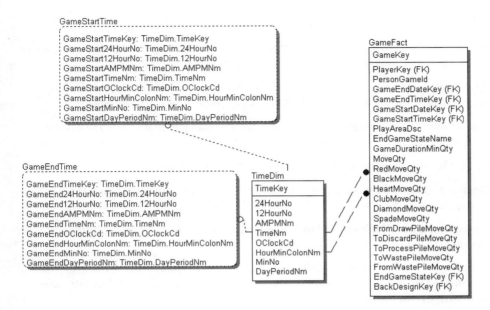

Figure 12-37. *The* GameFact *data mart with role-based views for the time dimension*

You should name the columns in the role-based views to match the role-named columns in the table, since most of the query tools will recognize this similarity and automatically create the join clause for the clients. You should do this for any dimension that has to play more than one role. You can see that, along with conforming dimensions, you may want to conform column role names between fact tables to be able to conform the role-based views as well. Using views for a presentation layer can be a powerful technique and can add to the usability of the new data mart.

Finishing Up

And there you have it. As soon as you polish the entire design with the role-based views, add data types and sizes, determine what to do with NULL values, and add definitions, your second star schema is finished.

Don't forget these designs need to be reviewed by the team and your clients. Polish all your deliverables by using colors, pictures, labels, and a little bit of imagination to make them easily comprehensible. Once you're in the review meeting, remember to verify both the clients and the database administrator (DBA) needs, since the DBA is physically implementing the Dimensional model.

In the grand scheme of things, these examples have resulted in small data mart designs. If this were a data warehouse design project, you would have barely started. All we can do in these exercises is to show you how to bring your design to a point where you can review and verify your work with other experts. Remember, you don't have to be completely finished with the whole model to begin that effort.

Make sure you keep up with any alterations in the definitions and that your documentation, including graphics, is up-to-date. Don't forget to communicate changes to the team.

Summary

Dimensional modeling has just as many special terms as the other modeling techniques we've covered. The key definitions to remember in this case are as follows:

- **Data mart**: A data design primarily intended to address specific analytical or departmental needs, storing a single snapshot of data, optimized for performance.

- **Star schema**: A data design comprised of a central fact table that's linked to a number of dimension tables.

- **Fact table**: A table containing all the required measures of interest.

- **Measures**: Quantities by which attributes are assessed. For example, time, data, length, and so on are measures.

- **Dimension tables**: Tables linked to the fact table containing the fact attributes and appropriate details.

- **Granularity**: The level of detail held in the fact table. This relates to the hierarchy of information stored (for example, in terms of a given time period, store location, sales representative, and so on).

- **Snowflake schemas**: A variation of the star schema design in which dimension tables are broken down into multiple dimension tables with a hierarchy.

In this chapter, you built two separate data marts. The first data mart (Game) involved the design of a fact table with several additive measures, and the second example (GameMove) designed a factless fact table with descriptive attributes at the wrong level of granularity. You looked at the options for designing dimensions and the power of using conformed dimensions. You also looked at the different techniques of storing changing values using a change policy. Finally, you learned about role-playing views to help the clients use their query tools.

In the next chapter, you'll try to retroactively model (reverse engineer) a system that's already designed and in use.

CHAPTER 13

■■■

Reverse-Engineering a Data Model

Although the majority of this book has focused on designing new systems and designing Conceptual, Logical and Physical data models, you'll sometimes need to use your modeling skills to document preexisting database objects and elements. This process is known as *reverse engineering* since you're working back from the existing system to develop a Physical model. You can also use this analysis to create a Logical model. In working backward, you need to compile solid documentation about the data elements, relationships, structure, rules, processes, and quirks of an application. Although we can't provide a complete guide to reverse engineering in a single chapter, we'll cover various techniques you can use to unearth the data map from an existing database. In this chapter, you'll consider a sample database and work backward from it to devise both a Physical model and a Logical model. In the course of the example, you'll do the following:

- You'll look at all the resources available to you: the relational database management system (RDBMS) library data, database creation scripts, user manuals and training documentation, and front-end application screens.

- You'll see how modeling tools can help you capture a Physical model of the existing data.

- You'll see how to develop a model without using modeling software tools.

- You'll work with the Physical model to reverse engineer a Logical model.

You can document the As-Is process to create an inventory of data structures that details exactly what's in the database. Using the Physical model, you could continue with this technique to get a handle on the logical definitions and data relationships. The Physical model you create could generate Data Definition Language (DDL) code to re-create the data structures in another environment, or the extraction, transformation, and loading (ETL) team might use it to determine how to map and load data elements from source systems. You can also use this model as a tool to compare basic data elements, business rules/relationships, general data types, and definitions in the case of system merges or software replacement.

It's not as easy to come up with a common database as it was to come up with a common game to analyze. Solitaire is as close to a universal game as we could find, but databases aren't nearly as universally deployed. Therefore, we've decided to use the Microsoft Access example database Northwind, but we'll also throw in some small samples of other types of systems for comparison. We assume that most of you can access the Northwind database. Although using this database as the example may make the exercise seem specific to the tool, the techniques used to pull out the tables, columns, definitions, relationships, and indexes are standard, no matter what the platform.

Getting Started

Reverse engineering starts by concentrating on building a Physical data model, but it doesn't end there. To fully document an existing system, you need to know more than just what data objects the system owns. You also need to know what the data elements really are, what other objects the system uses, what functionality the system provides and supports, and any known system shortcomings or problems.

You need to answer several questions: Where does the data come from? Where does it go? Who uses it and for what? Plus, you want to know not just what data the application was originally designed to store and process but what it has been forced or tricked into managing. You need to concern yourself with what the system does today, as well as understand where it originated. It's also important to gain an understanding of the applications that use or update this data in order to gauge how critical the database is. You need to find out how many users would shout if you switched off a particular database!

Determining the Project's Needs

Most reverse-engineering tasks occur in response to a project need. You can prioritize needed information in a similar fashion to the analysis you did when working on the physical-only exercise. This prioritization will help you decide when to conclude your analysis.

In starting a reverse-engineering effort, you'll do the following:

Determine the goal of the reverse-engineering effort: Are you trying to replace, rebuild, restore, or document a system? Talk to the clients to establish exactly what they want. This conversation will tell you if the product of this task will support another effort or if it's the goal itself.

Start with the data storage structures: Start with database tables/columns, linked documents and spreadsheets, file systems, or any other type of data collection. You need to document the design exactly the way it currently exists.

Find all the unique identifiers: This includes surrogate, natural, and concatenated identifiers. Find any documented rules that govern their creation, updates, or deletions. Talk to subject matter experts, and check your findings against actual data in the database.

Find relationships between data sets: Try to find relationships between separately stored data sets and between data elements internal to a data set.

Profile the data to find or create data definitions: In a reverse-engineering effort, definitions are an absolute *must*. Some of them could be pretty complicated since you may discover that a data element is "sometimes this and sometimes that."

Identify the rules: Try to identify all the rules of the system incorporated into screens, back-end code, and reports. You may find logical data rules that are deployed outside the data storage structure or database.

Gathering all this information about an existing system will allow you to create a model of the physical data structures and, sometimes more important, definitions and descriptions of data element management rules in a Logical data model.

Obtaining Resources

In starting a reverse-engineering effort, you should try to obtain the following resources:

Access to the production system or a copy of the production system you're reverse engineering: Directly interacting with screens and reports will help you understand the scope, behavior, and data found in the system. Access to a nonproduction copy of the system that has a good selection of current production data is best. Working without this may limit your understanding of the data or the system's behavior.

Access to the RDBMS metadata library or catalog data: This will provide you with useful information regarding tables, columns, views, triggers, indexes, integrity constraints, relationships, and synonyms. (The data you capture will vary depending on the RDBMS.)

Access to the system's program code: If you've only compiled code, you'll find your ability to make assessments fairly restricted. You need to see how the application uses database tables, columns, and relationship definitions. You should look particularly for items such as DDL scripts; stored procedure and database trigger definitions; data access maps, including Enterprise Application Interchange (EAI) mappings, Extensible Markup Language (XML), and Unified Modeling Language (UML) definition files; data move scripts such as load routines, Data Transformation Services (DTS) scripts; ETL files; and report generation code.

Access to production data: You need to know if your assessment of table/column names and definitions is accurate. Look for sample data from production databases to help determine the nature and diversity of the data contained in the system. You need to gather information about the records and investigate data element values. You'll determine what data is contained within the data set. We've reverse engineered empty tables (those containing no records) hundreds of times. Once you see what your database tables contain, you can restrict your efforts to focus on what's being used. You need to review the distinct data values that exist in table columns. Do you find what you expect? Check the validity of the data values. Does it seem as though the end users are being creative and working around any nullability or data integrity rules by manipulating data values?

Copies of historical or descriptive data: Look for user guides/manuals, help files, and project notebooks to help you in documenting the system's local features. Conduct interviews with project team members, and chat informally with programmers or DBAs. You may want to attend any pertinent training classes and read any training materials you can find.

All systems are comprised of data and programs that manipulate that data. You're looking to capture any information that will help you understand the structure of the data and how it's manipulated. You also want to find out how it's used at the enterprise level. You'll certainly want to bring any system shortcomings, anomalies, or defects to the team's attention. If you have enough time and resources, you should be able to create a credible Physical, Logical, or even Conceptual data model by working backward from the original reverse-engineered Physical model. You may even be able to assist with creating a business process model based on the functionality you discover in your system analysis.

Analyzing the Data Structure

The first and probably most important task of a reverse-engineering project is to identify the data elements, their definitions, and how they're organized. You can do this in a couple of ways. Automated modeling tools can help by documenting database structures from a database connection or the database creation scripts. When the modeling tool can't help you, you must perform these tasks manually.

Modeling Tool Support

Many of the modeling software tools available to you, such as ERwin or DataArchitect, will connect straight to a database or will read DDL scripts. If you can connect to the database, you can capture critical database metadata from the database structures or RDBMS library/catalog tables on the system.

RDBMS Connection

In Chapter 2 we discussed Dr. Codd's rules of relational databases. The fourth rule is as follows: The description of the database structures is represented at the logical level in the same way as ordinary data so that authorized users can apply the same relational language to database structure interrogation as they apply to regular data.

Therefore, all RDBMSs have a library or catalog where details about the data management/storage/access/manipulation of database objects is kept. This information will be the foundation of your reverse-engineering modeling efforts. Bear in mind that building a Physical data model of the current database structures will provide only a point-in-time snapshot of the system. Databases change often, and although the library or catalog will always be current, your model will not be automatically updated when the production system changes. Still, a snapshot of the database structures will be useful to you in your reverse-engineering work and will serve as a starting point for determining table and column names and definitions.

As an example, we used ERwin 4.1 to reverse engineer the physical database shown in Figure 13-1 from the `Northwind.mdb` Access file.

Although this model is useful, you need to be aware of a number of caveats:

The model the software automatically provides wasn't in an easily printable format. It took us 15 minutes to rearrange the boxes and lines to fit the page.

Some empty boxes on the model represent database views. Some database views have columns that are visible in the view box, and others don't. Modeling software can't always make sense of the SQL code that defines a view. However, in this case, ERwin brings the code into the model for you and creates an empty placeholder.

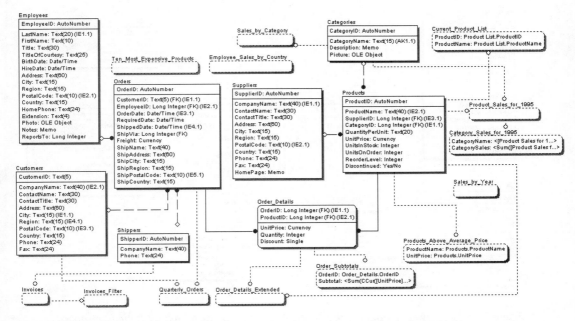

Figure 13-1. *The reverse-engineered Physical model of the Access 97 Northwind database*

You'll normally get a log report to help you when the software has problems interpreting the data from the database. Your log file may look something like this:

View 'Employee Sales by Country' has been imported as user-defined SQL since ERwin was not able to parse it.

You can use your modeling software's view editor to look at the view definition code. If you take the example of the Order Details Extended view, then the code looks like this:

```
create view "Quarterly Orders" AS
SELECT DISTINCT
   Customers.CustomerID,
   Customers.CompanyName,
   Customers.City,
    Customers.Country
FROM Customers
RIGHT JOIN
Orders ON Customers.CustomerID = Orders.CustomerID
WHERE Orders.OrderDate BETWEEN '19970101' And '19971231'
```

Stop for a moment to appreciate the richness of the information you can capture with such tools. If you remove the views from the model, the model looks like Figure 13-2.

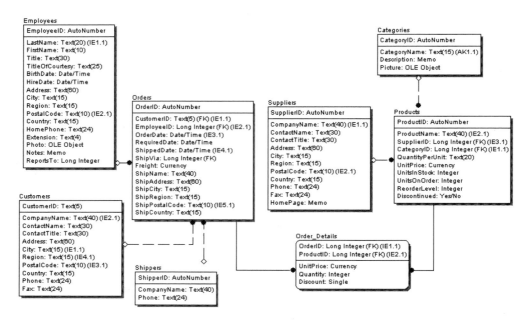

Figure 13-2. *The Physical model of the Access 97 Northwind database with views removed*

In this model, you can see that we've identified primary keys, alternate keys, foreign keys, relationships, data types, sizes, and even some database object definitions (if the database has place for them in the libraries)—all captured nearly instantly.

■**Note** To use a modeling tool to capture details about your database, you must be able to log into the database, and you must have been granted SELECT permission on all the database objects by the database administrator (DBA).

Let's reverse engineer Northwind one more time, only this time using the example of the Northwind database provided with SQL Server 2000 (see Figure 13-3).

Notice the differences between this model and the one generated earlier from Figure 13-2. Obviously, the Northwind database has a different structure in Access as opposed to SQL Server. The data types are different between these two versions. More tables and views appear in the SQL Server version (the views aren't in Figure 13-3). The SQL Server 2000 version also has a new recursive relationship at the database level, which relates Employee to itself. The Employee table is the same in both versions other than a new column in the SQL Server version called PhotoPath. However, now the column ReportsTo is a role-named foreign key with an integrity constraint managed in the database. In the Access version, that relationship is managed in the front end.

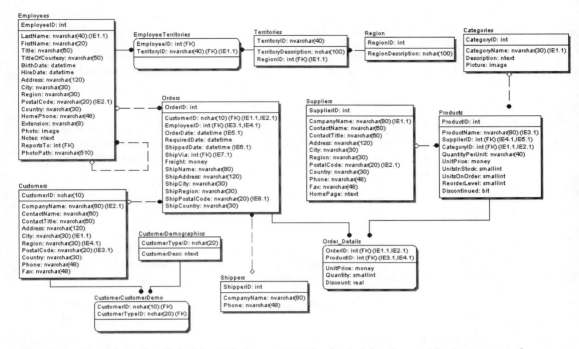

Figure 13-3. *The Physical model of the SQL Server 2000 Northwind database with views removed*

The source system you use for your initial reverse-engineering effort matters. You might have to reverse engineer copies of the "same" system several times in a data consolidation project because these databases aren't really the same. You need to be aware of a database's version number and which service packs have been applied. We've also come across systems that were initially implemented from the same model but over the years have been subtly modified in their respective local environments to support different needs.

■Note When reverse engineering data models, it's critical to document the exact location and version of the system you analyzed.

With a software tool such as ERwin, you can quickly generate a complete list of tables, columns, views, indexes, and integrity constraints known to the RDBMS. If your task is to provide a list of database constructs such as this, the majority of your work (other than compiling the data you captured into some readable reports) is probably done. Some reverse-engineering jobs are about an hour long and result in some object lists and a data model diagram.

Unfortunately, querying the RDBMS may not always provide you with what you want. This may be for any of the following reasons:

The business constraints (relationships) weren't built into the database design, the front-end application controls some or all the integrity, or database triggers were used to implement business rules that didn't fit easily into the database as constraints. In these cases, your model will come back without a single relationship line.

The table and column definitions are blank. In this case you'll have a great list of table and column names but no comments or definitions. This can make some reverse-engineered structures almost useless. If columns aren't named intuitively, you'll have no idea what tables or columns mean or where a data element is stored.

Data elements are stored in files outside the RDBMS, in the front end, or in directory structures that are accessed directly by the application.

Even if your database has been completely documented and deployed with comments and definitions, sometimes you still won't be able to use modeling software to help you create a reverse-engineered model. You might run into any of the following problems:

- You can't get the security or communication link set up between the modeling software and your database.

- The RDBMS isn't compatible with your software.

- The data structures used by the existing system aren't part of an RDBMS. Sometimes you're trying to model data elements that occur in files such as Microsoft Excel or Word documents. Other times you might be working with nonrelational hierarchical or network databases, which normally aren't interpreted very well by relational modeling tools.

If you can't use your modeling software to automatically generate a Physical data model, you can still use alternative methods, such as importing the create scripts or resorting to sketchpad and a pencil.

Data Definition Language Imports

In cases where you simply can't get sufficient information from the source system, you'll need to look at the system source code to create a database. Your DBA is generally the best point of contact in finding a code library or providing you with the file they used to create the tables. This file is generally referred to as the DDL of a system, or a *create script*.

If you choose to work with DDL files, be careful. The create scripts may no longer be accurate, and they may be cryptic, especially if you're working with a vendor-supplied software package. You also have no way to know if the DDL you're using refers to tables that are being used and in existence. This is especially true if the DDL is old, but even if the DDL is generated from existing tables, you can't be certain that the tables actually contain any data. DDL is definitely not the method of choice when it comes to database reverse-engineering techniques. If you can, it's much better to use the database's metadata tables.

■**Caution** Create scripts are usually not kept up-to-date. Even if they're accurate, a series of scripts implemented after the fact may alter the database structure.

From an updated DDL script, you'll have access to all the table names, column names, data types, sizes, precision, and nullability. The script may also contain default column values, data object definitions, and comments left behind by those who have maintained the system over the years. To be able to import DDL text, your modeling software must be able to read scripts written for that RDBMS. If the modeling tool can't read DDL scripts for your database platform, you'll have to resort to entering the data by hand.

The following code shows a typical DDL script that creates two tables named Employees and Orders for an Oracle database:

```
CREATE TABLE Employees (
    EmployeeID          ROWID NULL,
    LastName            VARCHAR2(20) NOT NULL,
    FirstName           VARCHAR2(10) NOT NULL,
    Title               VARCHAR2(30) NULL,
    TitleOfCourtesy     VARCHAR2(25) NULL,
    BirthDate           DATE NULL,
    HireDate            DATE NULL,
    Address             VARCHAR2(60) NULL,
    City                VARCHAR2(15) NULL,
    Region              VARCHAR2(15) NULL,
    PostalCode          VARCHAR2(10) NULL,
    Country             VARCHAR2(15) NULL,
    HomePhone           VARCHAR2(24) NULL,
    Extension           VARCHAR2(4) NULL,
    Photo               CLOB NULL,
    Notes               LONG VARCHAR NULL,
    ReportsTo           INTEGER NULL);

CREATE UNIQUE INDEX PrimaryKey ON Employees
(   EmployeeID          ASC);
CREATE INDEX LastName ON Employees
(   LastName            ASC);
CREATE INDEX PostalCode ON Employees
(   PostalCode          ASC);
ALTER TABLE Employees
   ADD ( PRIMARY KEY (EmployeeID) ) ;
```

```
CREATE TABLE Orders (
    OrderID          ROWID NULL,
    CustomerID       VARCHAR2(5) NULL,
    EmployeeID       INTEGER NULL,
    OrderDate        DATE NULL,
    RequiredDate     DATE NULL,
    ShippedDate      DATE NULL,
    ShipVia          INTEGER NULL,
    Freight          NUMBER DEFAULT 0 NULL,
    ShipName         VARCHAR2(40) NULL,
    ShipAddress      VARCHAR2(60) NULL,
    ShipCity         VARCHAR2(15) NULL,
    ShipRegion       VARCHAR2(15) NULL,
    ShipPostalCode   VARCHAR2(10) NULL,
    ShipCountry      VARCHAR2(15) NULL);

CREATE UNIQUE INDEX PrimaryKey ON Orders
(   OrderID          ASC);
CREATE INDEX CustomerID ON Orders
(   CustomerID       ASC);
CREATE INDEX EmployeeID ON Orders
(   EmployeeID       ASC);
CREATE INDEX OrderDate ON Orders
(   OrderDate        ASC);
CREATE INDEX ShippedDate ON Orders
(   ShippedDate      ASC);
CREATE INDEX ShipPostalCode ON Orders
(   ShipPostalCode   ASC);
ALTER TABLE Orders
   ADD ( PRIMARY KEY (OrderID) ) ;
ALTER TABLE Orders
   ADD ( FOREIGN KEY (CustomerID)
            REFERENCES Customers ) ;
ALTER TABLE Orders
   ADD ( FOREIGN KEY (EmployeeID)
            REFERENCES Employees ) ;
ALTER TABLE Orders
   ADD ( FOREIGN KEY (ShipVia)
            REFERENCES Shippers ) ;
```

Figure 13-4 shows a Physical model created by importing this DDL into a modeling tool.

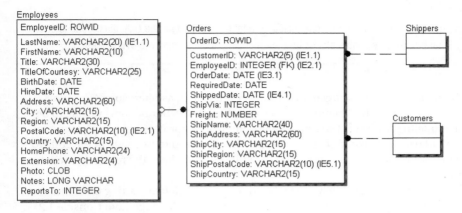

Figure 13-4. *A Physical model of Northwind created by importing a DDL script*

As you can see, we extracted much of the same information we got from the RDBMS library catalog. The column names, data types, data size, and nullability came directly from interpreting the CREATE TABLE command statement. You can also determine the primary keys of each table by looking at the following lines within the script:

```
CREATE UNIQUE INDEX PrimaryKey ON Employees
(   EmployeeID          ASC);
CREATE UNIQUE INDEX PrimaryKey ON Orders
(   OrderID         ASC);
ALTER TABLE Employees
   ADD ( PRIMARY KEY (EmployeeID) )
ALTER TABLE Orders
   ADD ( PRIMARY KEY (OrderID) ) ;
```

You can determine the foreign key definitions from the following lines:

```
ALTER TABLE Orders
   ADD ( FOREIGN KEY (CustomerID)
            REFERENCES Customers ) ;
ALTER TABLE Orders
   ADD ( FOREIGN KEY (EmployeeID)
            REFERENCES Employees ) ;
ALTER TABLE Orders
   ADD ( FOREIGN KEY (ShipVia)
            REFERENCES Shippers ) ;
```

This explains the empty boxes on the diagram. You have foreign keys that reference the tables Customers, EmployeeID, and ShipVia. However, the create script creates only the Employees and Orders tables, so the modeling software can't determine a structure for the Shippers and Customers tables and leaves them empty. The DBA can help you determine any synonyms that have been set up in the existing database to reference a table in a different system.

> **■Caution** We haven't had much luck getting a clean model from importing the DDL files. Code is often full of so many legal but obscure syntax blocks that the modeling tool can become overwhelmed.

Be aware that even scripts autogenerated from sources such as Microsoft SQL Server Enterprise Manager seem to build code that's legal in the RDBMS but not always able to be parsed by the modeling software. The errors can result in an incorrect or incomplete model. It may take a bit of trial and error to figure out what changes need to be made in the code to provide a clean import. Review the errors, and carefully double-check the resulting model with the script itself.

For instance, we created the following SQL script using the default setting from the Generate SQL Script option in Enterprise Manager for Microsoft Management Console 1.2 (version 5.0, Service Pack 2) on SQL Server 2000. ERwin 4.1 can't parse the COLLATE clauses. They need to be removed in order to do an autoimport.

```
if exists (select * from dbo.sysobjects where id = object_id(N'[dbo].[userinfo]')
and OBJECTPROPERTY(id, N'IsUserTable') = 1)
drop table [dbo].[tbcinfo]
GO

CREATE TABLE [dbo].[userinfo] (
    [login_id] [varchar] (255) COLLATE SQL_Latin1_General_CP1_CI_AS NULL ,
    [Name] [varchar] (255) COLLATE SQL_Latin1_General_CP1_CI_AS NULL ,
    [extra] [varchar] (255) COLLATE SQL_Latin1_General_CP1_CI_AS NULL ,
    [location] [varchar] (255) COLLATE SQL_Latin1_General_CP1_CI_AS NULL
) ON [PRIMARY]
GO
```

The exact error given by the software is "Unable to parse 'COLLATE' of line 6." Figure 13-5 shows the only part that was successfully imported.

Figure 13-5. *Results from the unsuccessful import of the* UserInfo *table DDL script*

Using an automated tool can be helpful, but you must carefully check the results. The DBAs or programmers who create and manage the DDL may be able to help by determining what options to use in creating DDL without the bits that can't be parsed.

Manual Processing

When the software tool can't help, the only alternative is to build the model yourself. Start with any code that could have been used to create the original structures. If the code doesn't exist, you'll have to create the model using whatever documentation is available to you. You could use the system's technical documentation, training materials, and reference manuals. You may have to browse existing data sets to see how they're structured. You may need to get hold of a developer copy of a software tool to see what table and file structures are used. Or it may be as simple as opening a Microsoft Excel file and exploring the data structures contained in it.

Code

In those cases where you can't use the RDBMS library/catalog or the database's DDL with your modeling software, you can at least use whatever DDL you have to cut and paste the table and column names into your model to prevent typos. Even if you can't write code, you can see that it isn't all that hard to read the create scripts. The name following the word *Table* is of course the table name. The other names found in the DDL are the column names, and each column has its data type, size, and nullability specified. Well-developed code, which you'll want to get your hands on, is nicely organized with a new line for every object and tabs to help you see what's happening.

Sometimes you'll find odd things when you look at code. Note that CategoryID in the following example is null allowed in the Access version of Northwind.mdb. (This column is required in the version found with SQL Server 2000.) That's extremely interesting, as CategoryID is called out later in the script as the primary key. But primary key values aren't supposed to contain NULLs!

We were shocked when we first saw this. When we researched it, we discovered that it's considered to be a "feature" that could be used to handle the processing of records that were only partially complete. Nevertheless, this is still a bad idea. Avoid NULL values in your primary keys!

```
CREATE TABLE Categories (
    CategoryID          AutoNumber NULL,
    CategoryName         Text(15) NOT NULL,
    Description         Memo NULL,
    Picture           OLE Object NULL
);


COMMENT ON TABLE Categories IS     'Categories of Northwind products.';
COMMENT ON COLUMN Categories.CategoryID IS
'Number automatically assigned to a new category.';
COMMENT ON COLUMN Categories.CategoryName IS     'Name of food category.';
COMMENT ON COLUMN Categories.Picture IS 'A picture representing the food category.';


CREATE UNIQUE INDEX CategoryName ON Categories
(
    CategoryName          ASC
);



ALTER TABLE Categories
    ADD ( PRIMARY KEY (CategoryID) ) ;
```

In addition, you may have to learn to read other types of code. Look at code written for a network-style database. You should know that it's pretty challenging to reverse engineer databases and generate a relational data model when the databases in question aren't relational to start. In a relational model, you can expect data sets to be connected by primary key migration. Many nonrelational database platforms don't work that way.

Notice that the DDL syntax is quite different but that the required data elements are still there. Instead of a *table*, you'll find code referring to a *record*. The data type is in front of the *field name* (what you're used to calling *columns*), and the size comes after the field name. A definition note is set immediately after the name (this is probably optional) and is helpful when trying to reverse engineer this DDL.

Network and hierarchical systems also don't use primary and foreign key concepts. You won't find keys to help you determine how the data fits together. The connectivity, or relationships, is called out in set structures like the one at the bottom of the following script that connects updte_rec to bus_date_rec. The script shows data linkages by pointer rather than showing migrating data values.

The following code contains unique indexes, such as cstmr_code in custmr_rec:

```
record custmr_rec{
unique key
char  cstmr_code[9];        /* Customer Code */
char  cstmr_name[31];       /* Customer name */
char  cstmr_taxable_ind[2];/* Y=Customer is taxable */
char  cstmr_active[2];      /* N=Inactive */
char  cstmr_reserve_1[4];   /* Reserved for future use */
char  cstmr_reserve_2[4];   /* Reserved for future use */
char  cstmr_reserve_3[8];   /* Reserved for future use */
}


record updte_rec {              /* Update log record */
long  upd_bdate;            /* Business Date of update */
long  upd_sysdate;          /* Date of update */
long  upd_systime;          /* Time of Update */
long  upd_fld;              /* Field ID of updated field
char  upd_code[4];  /* Type of update (HIRE, PROM) */
char  upd_userid[9];  /*LoginID of user making change */
long  upd_rec_no;           /* Record number updated */
long  upd_fld_no;           /* Field number updated */
long  upd_old_val;          /* Old value */

long  upd_new_val;              /* New value */


/* To retrieve records busdate chronologically */
        compound key updbdate_key {
                upd_bdate      ascending;
                upd_sysdate    ascending;
                upd_systime    ascending;
}
```

```
compound key updsystime_key {
                upd_sysdate    ascending;
                upd_systime    ascending;
}

set bdate_updte_set{
        order   last;
        owner   bus_date_rec;
        member  updte_rec;
}
```

This code looks different from the relational database DDL, but you can still find the column names, sizes, and data connections for documentation purposes (see Figure 13-6).

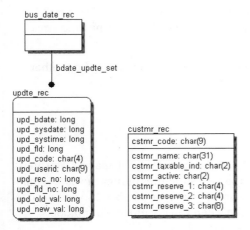

Figure 13-6. *A Physical model from network database DDL*

■**Note** A data modeler should learn to read code they work with often, even if they don't, or can't, write it.

General Data Structures

Sometimes you don't even have code to help you document your data structures. You may be analyzing data structures that have no concept of create scripts, such as Microsoft Excel spreadsheets. In these cases, you're looking for a file type construct with data elements ideally labeled at the top of the spreadsheet columns. The further away you get from data stored in relational database products, the more difficult it will be for you to reverse engineer a Physical data model. The lines start to blur between reverse engineering and business process/data analysis.

Structure Assessment

Many people seem to think reverse engineering is only about documenting the existing database structures. But you can gather more information during this first pass by learning about what's really going on in the application. You can learn a lot about an application if you ask questions such as the following:

- Do the structures and names suggest a fairly normalized or denormalized structure?

- Are there large numbers of columns with obvious repeating groups?

- Can you see dependencies that are internal to the tables (breaking Second and Third Normal Forms)?

- Does it look like the same data element is repeated in multiple tables?

- Do the columns seem to be defined differently compared with what you'd expect? Are NULLs allowed where you don't think they should be? Do the data types and sizes make sense?

- Can you see business rule inconsistencies (based on your understanding from other models) in the data structures and relationships?

- Are there too many indexes? Or none at all?

- Do all the tables have a primary key?

These questions represent information gathered at the highest level of analysis. You aren't yet able to make judgments about the suitability of the data structures or how the data is managed. All you can see are the data structures actually occurring in the database, so you need to capture and analyze all the physical attributes you can when you document your models.

Figure 13-7 shows just that little category table found in Access.

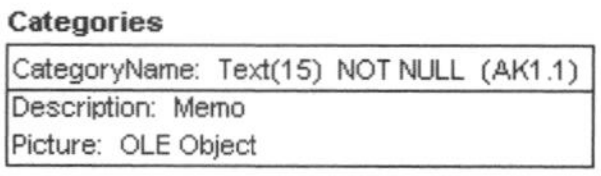

```
Categories
CategoryName:  Text(15)  NOT NULL  (AK1.1)
Description:  Memo
Picture:  OLE Object
```

Figure 13-7. *The Northwind* Categories *table*

Table 13-1 shows the information captured about this table, and Table 13-2 shows the information captured about the columns in the table.

Table 13-1. *Table Information Captured About the* Categories *Table*

Table Name	Comment on Table	Primary Key	Index
Categories	Categories of Northwind products	CategoryID	CategoryName

Table 13-2. *Column Information Captured About the* Categories *Table*

Table Columns	Comment on Column	Data Type and Size	NULL/NOT NULL
CategoryID	Number automatically assigned to a new category	AutoNumber	NULL
CategoryName	Name of food category	Text(15)	NOT NULL
Description		Memo	NULL
Picture	A picture representing the food category	OLE object	NULL

Remember that the definitions you captured are what the original programmer *thought* was going to be stored in those columns. The actual data found in these columns may be more complex than the description suggests; you'll need to verify how up-to-date the column descriptions actually are. From the information you've captured, what can you conclude about the Northwind.mdb database, based upon the Physical model shown in Figure 13-8?

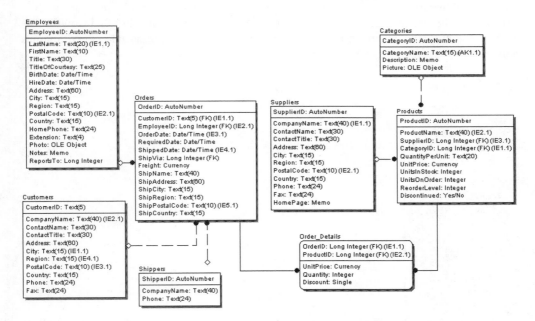

Figure 13-8. *The Physical model of the SQL Server 2000 Northwind database*

You know the following information:

- The Northwind database looks fairly normalized.

- There aren't any glaring repeating groups of columns.

- Other than some geographical dependencies in addresses, there don't seem to be any glaring normal form violations.

- Each data element generally seems to exist only once in the database, but some of the columns don't support that conclusion (there are three `Region` columns in this database). We're assuming that there simply isn't a modifier in the name to distinguish `Employee Address Region` from `Supplies Region`.

- There seems to be some nullability in the business rules that doesn't make much sense. Products don't seem to require a supplier and aren't required to be in a category; orders don't seem to need to have a customer or employee overseeing the process.

- A few `NOT NULL` rules and some null-allowed columns are in primary key positions. (Remember this is Access, where null primary keys are permitted.)

- The database appears to be lightly indexed.

- All tables have a primary key.

What if your reverse-engineered model looked like the one in Figure 13-9? Just having a copy of the table structures may not be that useful in identifying the data elements. We wish we could tell you that we hardly ever come across tables such as this one, but that wouldn't be true. Tables such as the one in Figure 13-9 appear on a pretty regular basis at larger companies where there has been at least 10–15 years of custom development.

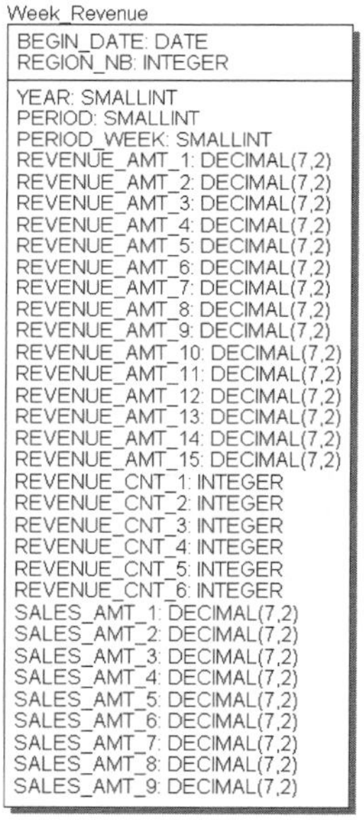

```
Week_Revenue
BEGIN_DATE: DATE
REGION_NB: INTEGER

YEAR: SMALLINT
PERIOD: SMALLINT
PERIOD_WEEK: SMALLINT
REVENUE_AMT_1: DECIMAL(7,2)
REVENUE_AMT_2: DECIMAL(7,2)
REVENUE_AMT_3: DECIMAL(7,2)
REVENUE_AMT_4: DECIMAL(7,2)
REVENUE_AMT_5: DECIMAL(7,2)
REVENUE_AMT_6: DECIMAL(7,2)
REVENUE_AMT_7: DECIMAL(7,2)
REVENUE_AMT_8: DECIMAL(7,2)
REVENUE_AMT_9: DECIMAL(7,2)
REVENUE_AMT_10: DECIMAL(7,2)
REVENUE_AMT_11: DECIMAL(7,2)
REVENUE_AMT_12: DECIMAL(7,2)
REVENUE_AMT_13: DECIMAL(7,2)
REVENUE_AMT_14: DECIMAL(7,2)
REVENUE_AMT_15: DECIMAL(7,2)
REVENUE_CNT_1: INTEGER
REVENUE_CNT_2: INTEGER
REVENUE_CNT_3: INTEGER
REVENUE_CNT_4: INTEGER
REVENUE_CNT_5: INTEGER
REVENUE_CNT_6: INTEGER
SALES_AMT_1: DECIMAL(7,2)
SALES_AMT_2: DECIMAL(7,2)
SALES_AMT_3: DECIMAL(7,2)
SALES_AMT_4: DECIMAL(7,2)
SALES_AMT_5: DECIMAL(7,2)
SALES_AMT_6: DECIMAL(7,2)
SALES_AMT_7: DECIMAL(7,2)
SALES_AMT_8: DECIMAL(7,2)
SALES_AMT_9: DECIMAL(7,2)
```

Figure 13-9. *An unhelpful table structure*

What can you conclude about this table?

- It isn't normalized.

- It's unknown if there are repeating groups in the structure; you can't tell what the data elements are by looking at the column names.

- The table looks like it might be part of a data mart of weekly sales information for each region in the enterprise. It might be a reporting table, but you don't know what the measures might be.

- It looks like it's a reasonably efficient structure; it's just nonintuitive.

- There's a primary key, which makes a Region Week of sales data unique.

It's hard to get any useful business information from studying this table's physical structure. The structure appears to be so dependent on related programs or the data presentation that there's little you can learn from studying the diagram.

But we wouldn't stop there in analyzing this structure. There must be more information about this table. It's quite possible that if you look hard enough, you'll find a view, report, or load routine that will help you figure out what the real data elements are. The table was obviously designed to be flexible. In this case, a view holds the key to understanding these data elements. Once you see the view definition, the table starts to make a bit more sense, as shown in Figure 13-10.

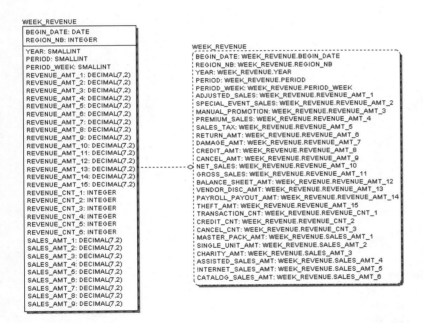

Figure 13-10. *The* Week_Revenue *table and view*

If possible, you need to check the view code to see if any restrictions in the view's WHERE clause could help you with your definitions. In this case, the view code is simple. Every row in the Week_Revenue table is available in the Week_Revenue view, but some columns have been excluded.

```
CREATE VIEW WEEK_REVENUE
   BEGIN_DATE,
   REGION_NB,
```

```
        YEAR,
        PERIOD,
        PERIOD_WEEK,
        ADJUSTED_SALES,
        SPECIAL_EVENT_SALE,
        MANUAL_PROMOTION,
        PREMIUM_SALES,
        SALES_TAX,
        RETURN_AMT,
        DAMAGE_AMT,
        CREDIT_AMT,
        CANCEL_AMT,
        NET_SALES,
        GROSS_SALES,
        BALANCE_SHEET_AMT,
        VENDOR_DISCOUNT_AMT,
        PAYROLL_PAYOUT,
        THEFT_AMT,
        TRANSACTION_CNT,
        CREDIT_CNT,
        CANCEL_CNT,
        MASTER_PACK_AMT,
        SINGLE_UNIT_SALES,
        CHARITY_DONATION,
        ASSISTED_SALES,
        INTERNET_SALES,
        CATALOG_SALES)
   AS SELECT
        WEEK_REVENUE.BEGIN_DATE,
        WEEK_REVENUE.REGION_NB,
        WEEK_REVENUE.YEAR,
        WEEK_REVENUE.PERIOD,
        WEEK_REVENUE.PERIOD_WEEK,
        WEEK_REVENUE.REVENUE_AMT_1,
        WEEK_REVENUE.REVENUE_AMT_2,
        WEEK_REVENUE.REVENUE_AMT_3,
        WEEK_REVENUE.REVENUE_AMT_4,
        WEEK_REVENUE.REVENUE_AMT_5,
        WEEK_REVENUE.REVENUE_AMT_6,
        WEEK_REVENUE.REVENUE_AMT_7,
        WEEK_REVENUE.REVENUE_AMT_8,
        WEEK_REVENUE.REVENUE_AMT_9,
        WEEK_REVENUE.REVENUE_AMT_10,
        WEEK_REVENUE.REVENUE_AMT_11,
        WEEK_REVENUE.REVENUE_AMT_12,
        WEEK_REVENUE.REVENUE_AMT_13,
        WEEK_REVENUE.REVENUE_AMT_14,
```

```
   WEEK_REVENUE.REVENUE_AMT_15,
   WEEK_REVENUE.REVENUE_CNT_1,
   WEEK_REVENUE.REVENUE_CNT_2,
   WEEK_REVENUE.REVENUE_CNT_3,
   WEEK_REVENUE.SALES_AMT_1,
   WEEK_REVENUE.SALES_AMT_2,
   WEEK_REVENUE.SALES_AMT_3,
   WEEK_REVENUE.SALES_AMT_5,
   WEEK_REVENUE.SALES_AMT_6,
   WEEK_REVENUE.SALES_AMT_7
FROM WEEK_REVENUE
```

Finding this view code allows you to see how the table columns are used in the view. Now that you know the names of the data elements as they're described in the view, you have a better chance of coming up with a definition for each column in the table, as shown in Table 13-3.

Table 13-3. *The* Week_Revenue *Table Column Names and Their Names in the View*

Column Name	View Label
BEGIN_DATE	BEGIN_DATE
REGION_NB	REGION_NB
YEAR	YEAR
PERIOD	PERIOD
PERIOD_WEEK	PERIOD_WEEK
REVENUE_AMT_1	ADJUSTED_SALES
REVENUE_AMT_2	SPECIAL_EVENT_SALE
REVENUE_AMT_3	MANUAL_PROMOTION
REVENUE_AMT_4	PREMIUM_SALES
REVENUE_AMT_5	SALES_TAX
REVENUE_AMT_6	RETURN_AMT
REVENUE_AMT_7	DAMAGE_AMT
REVENUE_AMT_8	CREDIT_AMT
REVENUE_AMT_9	CANCEL_AMT
REVENUE_AMT_10	NET_SALES
REVENUE_AMT_11	GROSS_SALES
REVENUE_AMT_12	BALANCE_SHEET_AMT
REVENUE_AMT_13	VENDOR_DISCOUNT_AMT
REVENUE_AMT_14	PAYROLL_PAYOUT
REVENUE_AMT_15	THEFT_AMT
REVENUE_CNT_1	TRANSACTION_CNT
REVENUE_CNT_2	CREDIT_CNT

Continued

Table 13-3. *Continued*

Column Name	View Label
REVENUE_CNT_3	CANCEL_CNT
SALES_AMT_1	MASTER_PACK_AMT
SALES_AMT_2	SINGLE_UNIT_SALES
SALES_AMT_3	CHARITY_DONATION
SALES_AMT_5	ASSISTED_SALES
SALES_AMT_6	INTERNET_SALES
SALES_AMT_7	CATALOG_SALES

Remember that you're just trying to document the system as is. Don't try to figure out why a table structure such as this was deployed (although it may seem like the right thing to do at this time). Sometimes things were done for many good reasons. The design might be part of a security plan, or it could be that another part of the system required this strange structure. Document it objectively and with as much detail as you can.

Analyzing the Data

The next step in the process of reverse engineering is to profile the data to verify that it conforms with what you think the definition of the column/table is. Unfortunately, Northwind was never a production database, so the data values its tables contain are polished test values. In true production systems, three things occur with startling regularity.

- Simple data columns suddenly begin to store multiple instances of unusual values that the columns weren't designed to store.

- A data column is generally used to store the data it was intended to store, but if a certain special character is inserted into the column, then the column has a different meaning.

- The data source has dried up, and there are no longer any instances of this data occurring in the business. As a result, the column "just isn't used anymore."

When you're profiling data in production systems, several common validations can provide valuable insight into your data. The following sections cover some techniques you might employ to query and report on the data in your relational database.

SELECT COUNT

How many states are there in the United States? The answer is 50, unless you're including U.S. territories. But if you do business only in 12 states, the answer might be 12. If you get an answer of 72, there's a problem either with the name or definition of the column or with the quality of the data.

How many months do you expect to find in a year? Twelve seems to be the obvious answer, but we once worked with a system that had an eighteen-month growing year for agriculture. Every other year had two occurrences of January records. That came as a bit of a surprise.

SELECT COUNT/GROUP BY

Ratios are also a good tool for profiling your data. Select the count of the records in the table, and then select the count of specific values in the target column. If you have 100 records in the Employee table and 99 of them have N/A in the LastReviewedByEmpId column, you can question the business rule that everyone is the subject of an annual review. Group the employee records by their month of hire. If all the employees seem to be hired in January, you can question whether that makes sense. Ratios can help you identify patterns in the data that don't make sense.

SELECT COUNT DISTINCT

How many distinct values for a calendar month would you expect to find in a database? If there are more than twelve, or if they aren't the twelve you expect to see (for example, three of them are February misspelled twice, and the months of August and November are missing), then you need to find out why; this may be a data quality issue or just an unusual data definition.

When we're profiling data sources, we like to find out how many ways creative clients have gotten around NOT NULL rules. Clients can be creative; they could enter N/A, Unknown, or a series of spaces or zeros. When you look at the distinct values, you may see values that cause you to question the column definitions.

SELECT MIN

What's the oldest date you'd expect to see in your database? If, for example, you're profiling a payroll system and the minimum date in the HireDate field is in the 1500s, then you have a problem. In a case such as this, someone likely came up with some quirky date to flag certain employees. For example, we came across a date that was a flag used years ago during a data migration project to denote the lack of a valid data value. If you come across instances like this, you'll need to document them because the values obviously represent important enterprise data and represent data differently than the original intent.

SELECT MAX

What's the largest LibraryFineAmt value you'd expect to see in your database? You'd probably not expect a value more than $100. If you find something that far exceeds your determined reasonability factor, you need to find out why. The column might contain dollar values that mean something different than intended. It may be that in extreme cases the cost of replacing the book is added to the fine amount. If that's the case, it would change the definition of that column.

What would you think if you looked for the greatest CreateDate, and it was more than three years ago? You'd probably realize that no one has inserted any data into this data set in a long time. This might also mean that no one uses this data, but check with your DBA before you assume—they may have to look at database logs to see if that's true.

SELECT

Sometimes you need to browse the data to see what you notice. What does it mean if you find names in address lines? It could be that these names are on an "Attention to…" address line or that the address is found on George Washington Boulevard.

What about values that look like <#name%date&text*number> that are stored in a text field? In these cases, you've probably discovered a column that's being used as a junk pile. Instead of adding new columns, a lot of different data elements were crammed into one database field. All those special characters are probably parsed by some application code that separates all the data elements.

Select columns from a table you think should make sense together, and put them side by side. State and Country. BirthDate and GraduationDate. Look for things such as the state of Quebec in India or student graduation dates that occur before birth dates.

Assessing the Data

You should be able to take the results of your data profiling and provide some statistical report summarizing the quality of the data you found. You can also use this analysis to update the definitions of some of the tables and columns. You'd be able to provide commentary like that shown in Table 13-4 and Table 13-5 for the small Categories table in Northwind.mdb.

Table 13-4. *Table Assessment for the* Categories *Table*

Table Name	Data Quality	Row Count
Categories	Good: even better than database rules allow	8

Table 13-5. *Column Assessment for the* Categories *Table*

Column Name	Definition in Code	Data Type	Null?	Data Review Found
CategoryID	Number automatically assigned to a new category	AutoNumber	NULL	All rows have a unique number—no nulls.
CategoryName	Name of food category	Text(15)	NOT NULL	All names are intrinsically different—no duplication by misspelling.
Description		Memo	NULL	All categories have descriptions—no nulls; seem appropriate to the name.
Picture	A picture representing the food category	OLE object	NULL	All categories have OLE objects. We didn't open them to review for appropriateness.

Reviewing Data Rules in Code

Once you've captured as much as you can from examining the structures and the data, you'll want to review any other code that may have business rules embedded in it.

Data Manipulation Language (DML)

Data Manipulation Language (DML) can be a prime source for business rules. Reviewing the IF...THEN...ELSE structure of procedural code lends itself to easily picking up some of the rules not found in the database structures.

DML consists of procedures and triggers (stored procedures that are fired by events in the database such as INSERT or DELETE statements). This code will help you to verify that the data elements behave just the way you thought they did. You may find some clues to denormalization decisions in triggers that fire after INSERTs or UPDATEs, which may point to extra places the data is stored. This will help you determine what the base data elements are and what data elements are derived.

Look at the interesting macro we found in Northwind.mdb, as shown in Table 13-6. If you look at Validate Postal Code section, you can see that there's definitely a series of true/false statements suggesting a relationship between the country and ZIP code to prevent incorrect values being inserted into the database. You'll need to note this in the Logical model. You can't document this effectively in the Physical model because no physical relationships support these business rules.

Table 13-6. *Macro Code for* Validate Postal Code *Subroutine*

Formula	Action	Description
IsNull ([Country])	StopMacro	If Country is NULL, postal code can't be validated.
[Country] In ("France", "Italy", "Spain") And Len([PostalCode])<>5	MsgBox	If postal code isn't five characters, display message...
...	CancelEvent	...and cancel event.
...	GoToControl	
[Country] In ("Australia","Singapore") And Len([PostalCode])<>4	MsgBox	If postal code isn't four characters, display message...
...	CancelEvent	...and cancel event.
...	GoToControl	
([Country]="Canada") And ([PostalCode] Not Like "[A-Z][0-9][A-Z] [0-9][A-Z][0-9]")	MsgBox	If postal code isn't correct for Canada, display message...
...	CancelEvent	...and cancel event.
...	GoToControl	

Reports

You may find that your data elements are manipulated in some of the strangest ways when they occur in reports. Look at the following expression that inserts data into a block of text on an invoice. It's actually fairly simple to decipher.

```
IIf([Region] Is Null,[ShipCity] & "  " & [ShipPostalCode],[ShipCity] & " " &
[ShipRegion] & "  " & [ShipPostalCode])
```

If there's no Region, find ShipCity, add a space, and add ShipPostalCode; otherwise, use ShipCity, add a space, add ShipRegion, add a space, and then add ShipPostalCode.

Look at the sales figure in the report shown in Figure 13-11. Do you think the cents were truncated or rounded? You can't tell until you check out the code from the report.

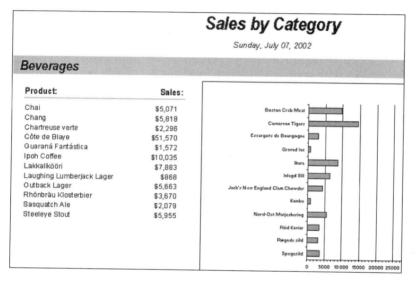

Figure 13-11. *A sales report from the Northwind database*

The following is the procedure that creates a Sales by Category report from the SQL Server 2000 Northwind database. Look at how many functions are being applied to TotalPurchase. You'll discover that the sales amounts were rounded, among other things. We start to get nervous when we find currency values being rounded. We realize it's necessary in some cases, but seeing this makes us want to check the data definitions again to make sure we've correctly noted that they aren't straight summations. The other thing to notice here is that many data elements are used in creating this value.

```
CREATE PROCEDURE SalesByCategory
    @CategoryName nvarchar(15), @OrdYear nvarchar(4) = '1998'
AS
IF @OrdYear != '1996' AND @OrdYear != '1997' AND @OrdYear != '1998'
BEGIN
    SELECT @OrdYear = '1998'
END
```

```
SELECT ProductName,
   TotalPurchase=ROUND(SUM(CONVERT(decimal(14,2), OD.Quantity *
                           (1-OD.Discount) * OD.UnitPrice)), 0)
FROM [Order Details] OD, Orders O, Products P, Categories C
WHERE OD.OrderID = O.OrderID
   AND OD.ProductID = P.ProductID
   AND P.CategoryID = C.CategoryID
   AND C.CategoryName = @CategoryName
   AND SUBSTRING(CONVERT(nvarchar(22), O.OrderDate, 111), 1, 4) = @OrdYear
GROUP BY ProductName
ORDER BY ProductName

GO
```

You may find your data elements sliced, diced, rearranged, and merged with data elements that don't even exist on your model. The only pointer to the existence of such extra data element ingredients is in the report code itself.

External Code

Don't forget to look for other systems and processes that use the data from the system you're reverse engineering. You may find that even a small, seemingly unimportant application can be a cornerstone of data integration. Keep an eye out for the following:

Data access maps: EAI mappings, XML files, and UML files. These show how the data has been migrated to other systems. More and more tools can help you connect systems; take advantage of the analysis that has already been done.

Data move scripts: Load routines, DTS packages, and ETL routines. These can also help determine how the data has been migrated to other systems. They're a wonderful source of information, since they document links to other systems. You may even find that a data element is coming from a source system that you've already thoroughly modeled. If so, you'll be able to use your prior analysis to document a definition and other pedigree information.

Analyzing the Front End

Once you have a foundation of understanding based on the analysis of the back end, you can enhance it by exploring the front end (if one exists) and any reports that are available. You'll want to verify what you learned about the data sets and their relationships to each other. Even simply using the application yourself will help you understand what the data elements are and what they're being used for. You're now going to verify the assessment of the data elements by mapping a label on a screen or a report to the identified data elements. In the following sections, you'll double-check relationships by looking at the configuration of screens and noting how a system user manages the data.

Screen Labels

Screen labels can be very enlightening about the nature of the data element. Sometimes the names and design of the database aren't helpful in knowing what's really there. Screen labels and report headings are designed to be read and understood by a much larger audience than the tables. As an example, refer to Figure 13-12, which is a screen from the Access system.

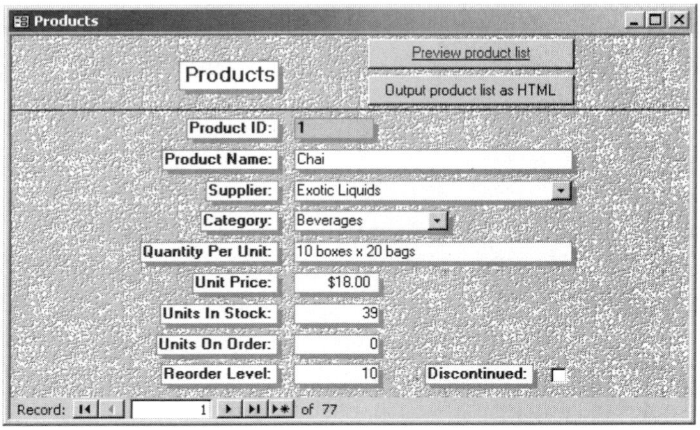

Figure 13-12. *The Northwind Products screen*

This is a typical screen. The screen name is Products. You can guess that this maps to the Products table. Just because the names match doesn't mean this is true, but it's a good place to start. If there's no Products table, try to match the screen labels to the table housing most of the product information. In this case, the data elements map one for one, and they even occur in the same order (see Figure 13-13). The two foreign key IDs are being represented on the screen by the longer names from their parent tables. We italicized the data element for you.

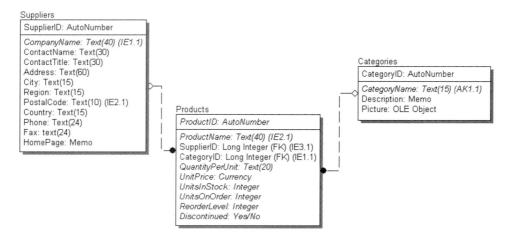

Figure 13-13. *The Physical model of the Northwind* Products *subject area*

Check off the data elements you've accounted for in some way. Be aware that the screen labels may be vague or may have significantly renamed the database attribute for presentation purposes. This is a good way to double-check your analysis. You could actually create a screen-to-table map by comparing the data elements to your model. This often gives a more understandable logical name vs. physical name, which might be hard to decipher. Screen-to-table mappings are handy for documentation assisting maintenance tasks and impact analysis studies. Sometimes these mappings already exist, and sometimes you need to create them by hand. A sample screen-to-table map looks like Table 13-7.

Table 13-7. *Sample Screen-to-Table Map*

Screen Name	Screen Label	Table Name	Column Name	Type/Size
Products	Product ID	Products	ProductID	AutoNumber
Products	Product Name	Products	ProductName	Text(40)
Products	*Supplier*	*Suppliers*	*CompanyName*	*Text(40)*
Products	Category	Category	CategoryName	Text(15)
Products	Quantity per Unit	Products	QuantityPerUnit	Text(20)
Products	Unit Price	Products	UnitPrice	Currency
Products	Units in Stock	Products	UnitsInStock	Integer
Products	Units on Order	Products	UnitsOnOrder	Integer
Products	Reorder Level	Products	ReorderLevel	Integer
Products	Discontinued	Products	Discontinued	Yes/No

This is a simple mapping, so we'll just point out the cases where it isn't so intuitive. Notice that the Supplier field on the form comes from the database column CompanyName, not Supplier. It can actually be quite challenging to figure out what screen fields map to what database columns, or even what tables are used on the screen. Not all screen mappings are as neat and intuitive as this one. Sometimes the mainframe system screens can be easier to work with when creating a screen-to-table map, since mainframe screens often have a one-to-one relationship with physical tables. When a web screen design displays information from several tables simultaneously, creating this kind of a map can be tough.

You may want to take a snapshot of each screen and map it to its underlying table structure. If you need to dig *really* deep to figure out where the screen data originates from, you'll probably need to ask for a programmer's help. You may need to pull apart the screen code and determine exactly which tables and columns are being used. This work can be tedious and will probably need to be justified for cost and time in the context of the requirements of your project.

Now let's review the one part of the Orders screen that isn't quite as simple a mapping (see Figure 13-14). Consider the Ship Via fields circled on the form.

Can you map the Ship Via field on the screen to a table column? Look at the Orders table. Notice that this table has a foreign key named ShippedVia. You're fortunate that the constraints for these tables actually exist in the database. Quite frequently you'll begin your reverse-engineering analysis with a pile of disconnected boxes and try to figure out how they fit together.

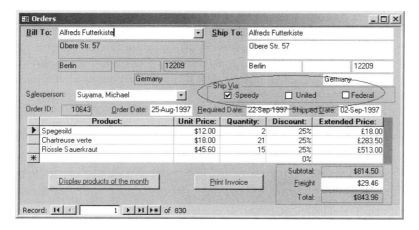

Figure 13-14. *The Northwind Orders screen*

`ShipperID` changes names as it migrates to `Orders`, and it becomes `ShipVia`; it has been role-named. But something else happened as well. Generally, data types, sizes, and names are your first clues that a column is a foreign key, since these attributes usually remain the same as the key migrates from table to table. The exceptions to this rule can be hard to spot. When columns have different names, data types, and sizes in different tables and they just don't match, finding these foreign key relationships becomes tougher, and verifying them is more difficult. In this case, while the data type in the `Orders` table is still a `Long` integer, it no longer has an AutoNumber data type (as it did in the `Shippers` table). The data type as well as the column name has changed (see Figure 13-15).

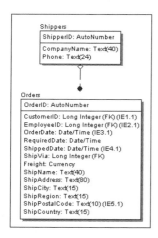

Figure 13-15. *The Northwind database* `Orders` *subject area*

Double-check the values in `Shippers` compared to `Orders`, as shown in Figure 13-16.

Order ID	Customer	Employee	Order I	Require	Shippe	Ship Via	Fre
10248	Vins et alco	Buchanan	Jul-1996	Aug-1996	Jul-1996	Federal Shipp	$32
10249	Toms Spez	Suyama,	Jul-1996	Aug-1996	Jul-1996	Speedy Expre	$11
10250	Hanari Carr	Peacock,	Jul-1996	Aug-1996	Jul-1996	United Packa	$65
10251	Victuailles	Leverling,	Jul-1996	Aug-1996	Jul-1996	Speedy Expre	$41
10252	Suprêmes	Peacock,	Jul-1996	Aug-1996	Jul-1996	United Packa	$51
10253	Hanari Carr	Leverling,	Jul-1996	Jul-1996	Jul-1996	United Packa	$58
10254	Chop-suey	Buchanan	Jul-1996	Aug-1996	Jul-1996	United Packa	$22
10255	Richter Sup	Dodswortl	Jul-1996	Aug-1996	Jul-1996	Federal Shipp	148
10256	Wellington	Leverling,	Jul-1996	Aug-1996	Jul-1996	United Packa	$13
10257	HILARIÓN-/	Peacock,	Jul-1996	Aug-1996	Jul-1996	Federal Shipp	$81
10258	Ernst Hand	Davolio, N	Jul-1996	Aug-1996	Jul-1996	Speedy Expre	140
10259	Centro com	Peacock,	Jul-1996	Aug-1996	Jul-1996	Federal Shipp	$3
10260	Ottilies Käs	Peacock,	Jul-1996	Aug-1996	Jul-1996	Speedy Expre	$55
10261	Que Delícia	Peacock,	Jul-1996	Aug-1996	Jul-1996	United Packa	$3
10262	Rattlesnake	Callahan,	Jul-1996	Aug-1996	Jul-1996	Federal Shipp	$48

Shipper ID	Company Name	Phone
1	Speedy Express	(503) 555-9831
2	United Package	(503) 555-3199
3	Federal Shipping	(503) 555-9931
(AutoNumber)		

Figure 13-16. *Sample data from the Northwind database* Orders *table (left) and* Shippers *table (right)*

Well, we have to say that this table has some unexpected data. Instead of the ShipVia column storing a numeric value, you can see the name of the company instead. What you didn't know is that Access 2000 has a function that translates all foreign keys into user-friendly names derived using the tables from which they originate. If you hadn't double-checked the data type, you might have thought that the ShipVia column contained text rather than a Long integer. This example illustrates why you shouldn't make assumptions when you're doing this kind of analysis. You have to diligently work through the quirks of every new database platform.

You won't always find tables and columns for all the data elements on the screen. Data can also be stored in small hard-coded lists managed by screen objects such as drop-down lists or as "88 levels" in old COBOL programs. It's important to note these data structures on the model diagram or as part of the table definitions since the data values are probably important to know.

Data Relationship Screen Rules

The other way an analysis of the front end can help you is in identifying relationships and business rules, especially those that don't show up in back-end analysis. Frequently you'll find that a simple column in the database is really a fairly complicated concept in the user interface. On the screen, look for labels that have similar names to columns or tables, and investigate drop-down boxes or checklists to give you an idea of the relationships between the various data elements. Take, for example, the Categories screen in Northwind using Access (see Figure 13-17).

You can easily verify (or derive) the one-to-many relationship of a category to a product based on what you can see here on the screen. There's only one category name listed at a time on the screen with a scrolling list of products, so you'd deduce that one category has many products. You can double-check this by looking again at the Products screen and verifying that each product can be in only one category at a time. Reviewing the table definitions again verifies that this one-to-many relationship looks right.

If the database doesn't have the integrity constraints, you may have to figure out how the data elements are related. Column names, data types, and sizes are a good first clue. The second is how the screen seems to treat them (see Figure 13-18).

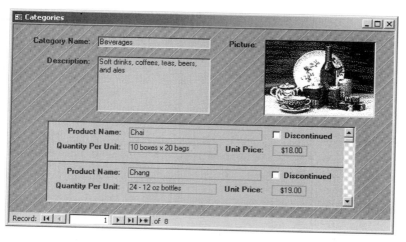

Figure 13-17. *The Northwind Categories screen*

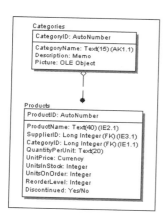

Figure 13-18. *The Northwind Database* Categories *subject area*

Finding and verifying relationships is another place where you may need to ask for a programmer's support to get to the code that manages the screen, as shown in Figure 13-19.

Notice that the design mode view of the detail portion of the screen links the child field CategoryID to the master field CategoryID. This proves the foreign key relationship that created the list of products based on which category is being displayed. The assumption based upon what you saw on the screen was a good one, and seeing the screen design confirms this.

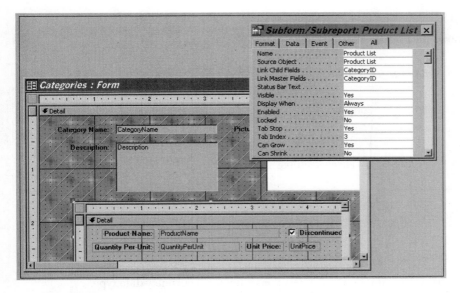

Figure 13-19. *The Northwind Categories screen in design mode*

Derived Values

The Northwind database doesn't seem to store derived values at the table level, which makes the task of reverse engineering the model a lot easier. However, that isn't always the case. If derived values exist in the database tables, you need to figure out what the derivation is and from where the inputs come. Examples of derivations include totals, discounts, averages, and other useful math operations.

Derived values are especially important to clients. They rarely look at the tiny bits of detail data needed to create the answers, but when they're concerned that a subtotal is incorrect, the Physical data model needs to be able to explain how the subtotal was calculated. Figure 13-20 shows a formula from one of the screens in the Northwind database. Each formula should be mapped for ease of use.

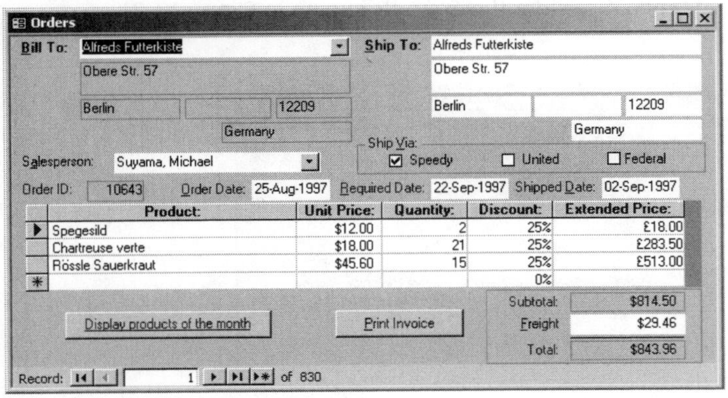

Figure 13-20. *The Northwind database Orders form showing derived values*

Formula Map

Table 13-8 shows the formula map.

Table 13-8. *A Sample Formula Map for the Northwind Database*

Screen/Report Name	Value Label	Formula	Table Name	Column Name
Orders	Extended Price	`CCur([Order Details].` `[UnitPrice]*[Quantity]*` `(1-[Discount])/100)*100` `AS ExtendedPrice`	`Order_Details`	`OrderID` `ProductID` `UnitPrice` `Quantity` `Discount`

In this case, the formula creates the `ExtendedPrice` value by performing the following calculation:

```
Unit Price * Quantity * PercentageDiscount
```

It then uses the `CCur` function to convert this value into a currency data type.

Using Historic/Descriptive Information

Use whatever existing historical data and documentation you can acquire to extend your knowledge about the database. This can involve some, or all, of the following:

User guides/manuals: Get a personal copy of anything you can. You'll probably be book-marking, highlighting, and scribbling notes in the margins before you're done. If you can find an old copy of a document that has already been "enhanced" by clients with their comments, then so much the better. An even better situation would be to find an older and a newer version of the user guide, since you'll then be able to compare the two to find out what features have been added to the system over time and when. This will point you in the direction of any properties peculiar to the system.

Help files and comments in code: Look at what the programmers thought was important enough to comment in their code. Consider the example shown in Figure 13-21.

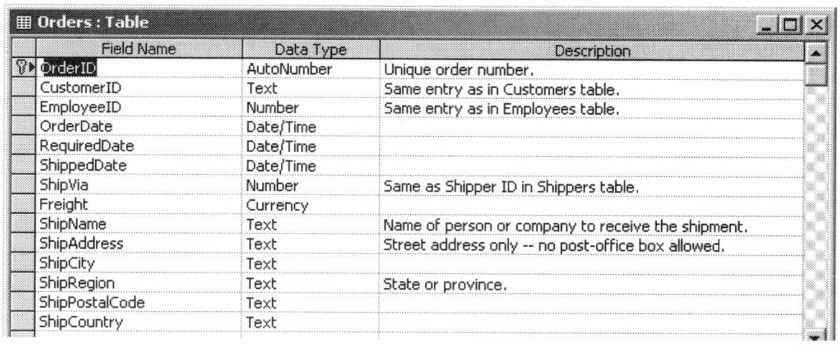

Figure 13-21. *The Northwind database* Orders *table in design mode*

Notice that the `ShipAddress` field isn't supposed to have any Post Office box numbers allowed. We don't know how they planned on preventing this, but it's at least noted here. After you confirm that the rule is still valid, you should add this information to your column definition. Similarly, note that `ShipRegion` is defined in broad terms as being a state or province. The original client representative on the development team may be able to help review and critique the help files. Go through them to get a perspective of how they thought the screens, sections, functionality, and reports were supposed to work, since the actual programmer probably never read the help text. Compare that description with what else you find.

Project notebooks: Any notebooks used by the development team can be useful. These are generally really hard reading, but sometimes the system you're working with is so old that this is the only thing that's helpful. Try to find someone to help you go through the documentation, unless you're familiar enough with the system to map the filenames to screens or processes. Otherwise, you'll just get lost.

Training classes: Take the time to audit any application training classes or just spend time with the teacher. Get any tutorials that exist and follow them. The more you know about how the data in the system is meant to be, the easier it will be to notice any exceptions.

Interviews/informal conversation: Find the people who are using the system, and train with them if you can. Listen closely to things that bother them about the system and how they work around it. People have the most ingenious ability to come up with solutions that don't involve asking information technology (IT) for application changes. A typical solution is to use multiple abbreviated terms in text fields to denote attributes that weren't properly modeled.

- Find the people who use the data from this system. They will be able to document, point by point, all the shortcomings of the data. They will expound on data quality issues; it's important to document these quality issues since they may cripple future projects.

- Find the people who maintain the system, such as the DBA and chief programmer. They will have stories to tell about the system that will probably cause you to wonder how it could have stayed in production so long without being replaced.

Applying Finishing Touches

Make sure you put the finishing touches on your model. Make it easy to read by adding notes and comments. Pay particular attention to noting items you think will be lost if you don't write them down (see Figure 13-22).

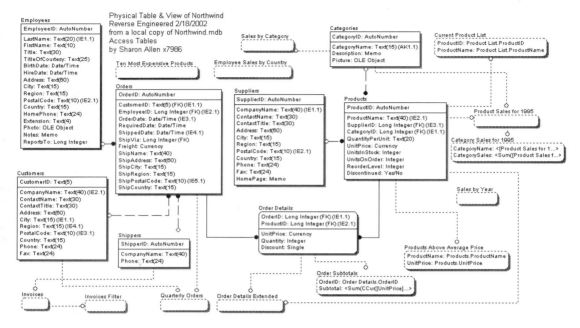

Figure 13-22. *The completed, reverse-engineered Northwind database physical model*

Building a Logical Model

At this point, it may seem counterintuitive to talk about creating a Logical model for the Northwind database. After all, the database is already in production, and you've just created a Physical model of that production database. The primary goal of creating a Logical model is to use that model to develop a good Physical model. Why would you want to spend the time and effort to create a Logical model?

Remember that Logical models and Physical models serve two different purposes. The Logical model is intended to document an understanding of data sets and business rules. A Physical model is used as a blueprint for a database that will be physically deployed. You've spent some effort reverse engineering a Physical data model for the Northwind database. Although this model provides you with a view of the way the data sets and business rules were implemented, it doesn't necessarily provide you with an implementation-independent view of how the data is truly related. A Logical model will document how the data is used by the business, rather than how the physical structures have been implemented to support the business. The Logical model will provide you with a business perspective and business understanding of the concepts that are deployed according to the Physical model.

If you suggest creating a Logical model at this stage, you'll likely run into resistance. You may not be given the opportunity to create one, but you should make the case for doing this extra level of analysis. An implementation-independent data model is a useful communication and educational tool.

You need to build as complete an understanding as possible of your physical solution before you can try to derive any logical relationships. Deriving a logical model from a physical one is a matter of finding the business rules in the application, whether or not they exist in the Physical model design. You must capture what's allowed and what isn't allowed. What data sets own an attribute? What identifiers are available, and can they be used as keys? Can an employee have multiple titles over time? Can an order contain multiple lines of the same product? Can a customer be related to other customers? Do customers have multiple shipping addresses? The answers to these questions will help to enhance the existing system or compare it to a potential off-the-shelf replacement.

Names

In the Northwind example, you start with the Physical model you built in the previous sections, as shown in Figure 13-23.

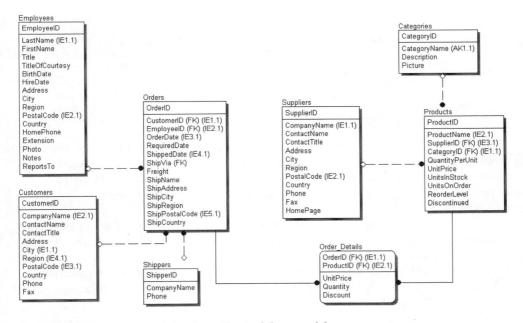

Figure 13-23. *The Northwind database Physical data model*

Build a report showing a list of the physical tables and build logical entities based on this list. Remember that entity names are always singular and descriptive of the data set. Review the definitions you found in the physical RDBMS, and look for logical data sets. Look for similarities in the data, and remember to apply the skills you learned in the chapter on Logical modeling. To help you, we've italicized a few things in Table 13-9 that should jump right out at you from the start.

Table 13-9. *Proposed Entities for the Northwind Database Logical Model*

Table Name	Table Comment	Proposed Logical Name	Notes
Categories	*Categories* of Northwind products	Product Category	Category of product?
Customers	Customers' *names, addresses, and phone numbers*	Customer	This may be a subcategory of Company to include shipping companies.
Employees	Employees' names, titles, and personal information	Employee	
Order_Details	Details on products, quantities, and prices for each order in the Orders table	Order Line	
Orders	Customer name, order date, and freight charge for each order	Order	
Products	Product names, suppliers, prices, and units in stock	Product	
Shippers	Shippers' *names and phone numbers*	Shipping Company	May be a subcategory of Company to include shipping companies.
Suppliers	Suppliers' *names, addresses, phone numbers, and hyperlinks to home pages*	Supplier	May be a subcategory of Company to include shipping companies.

From their definitions, Customers, Shippers, and Suppliers look like they have quite a bit in common at this point. We italicized some of the common elements, which suggest the presence of a category, but you need to look closer at the primary definitions and the unique identifiers to determine whether you've found enough commonality to group these entities into a category.

Next, you can do the same thing for the columns. You're going to make the names singular and descriptive, and you'll ensure that each name contains a class word to remind you of the nature of the data element (see Figure 13-24).

So far, it doesn't look much different from the Physical model you reverse engineered earlier. But you still have work to do. You'll now try to find the natural or candidate keys.

Keys

It's clear that the programmer used surrogate primary keys but didn't define many alternate (unique) keys. So you may have to perform some data validation to determine which other data elements uniquely identify a row.

Note This model was created using ERwin 4.1. The IE.1 notes are inversion entries that denote nonunique indexes in the database. They aren't alternate keys. "AK" stands for *alternate keys* in this tool, and they're unique indexes.

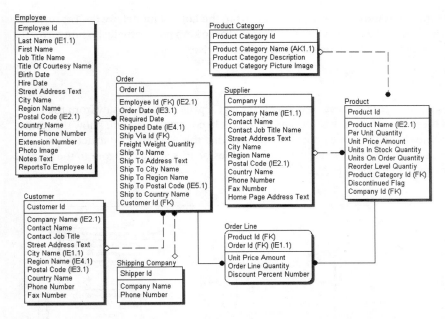

Figure 13-24. *The first draft of the Northwind database Logical model*

See if you can find the natural keys by looking at the data, and choose one to be the primary key position. Change the model to reflect this. Surrogate keys are rare in Logical models, so remove them from the model to help you narrow down the data elements that could be natural keys, as shown in Figure 13-25.

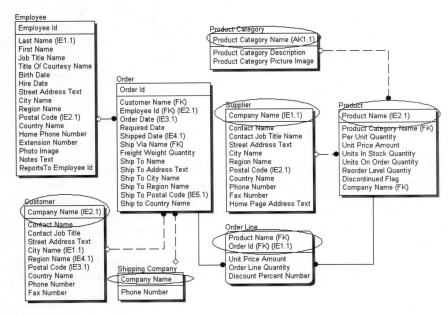

Figure 13-25. *Identifying keys in the Northwind database Logical model*

Despite wanting to remove the surrogate keys from the Logical model, we left `EmployeeID` and `OrderID` as keys of the `Employee` and `Order` tables. These keys may actually be nonsurrogate keys that are used to manage those sets in the enterprise.

Categories

Now let's examine the `Supplier`, `Customer`, and `ShippingCompany` tables. You saw from the descriptions of these three tables that the sets have a lot in common, and you know that quite a few of the columns have the same names. We believe that this is a category structure the programmer chose to implement as three separate tables, so let's add a category to the Logical model to reflect this, as shown in Figure 13-26.

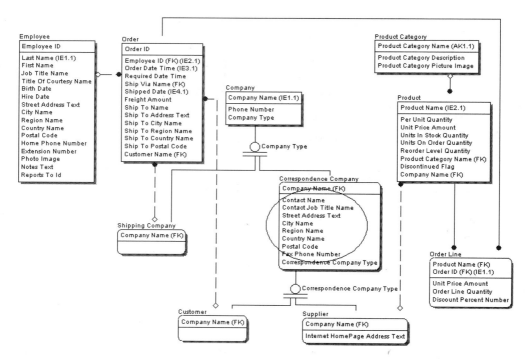

Figure 13-26. *Creating a category in the Northwind database Logical model*

You certainly could have cheated here and reduced the category structure to one layer. However, the business rules built into the physical design don't allow for shippers to have the attributes that are circled in Figure 13-26. You need to create a two-layer category that allows Company to own the Phone attribute (which is the only completely shared attribute). To build the second categorization, we created the Correspondence Company supertype entity (the set of companies to which we send mail) to own all the attributes shared by both Customer and Supplier. It's important, if you're backing into a Logical model, that you properly represent the business rules, even if they don't always make sense. Sometimes the point of deriving a Logical model from an existing Physical model is to show inconsistencies in the business rules. The model now makes it clear that the application doesn't treat shipping companies the same as other companies.

In Figure 13-27, you can see a category structure that probably shows how the enterprise really works. In reality, the attributes dealing with contacts and correspondence also apply to shippers. After all, someone has to be able to pay them, negotiate fees, and look up lost shipments. But right now, that data must be managed outside the Northwind.mdb application.

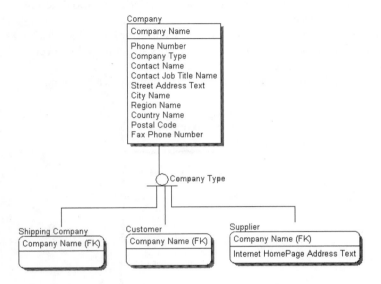

Figure 13-27. *An alternative category structure for companies*

Now let's look at the Product Category entity (see Figure 13-28) and the actual data occurring in the table.

	Category ID	Category Name	Description	Picture
	1	Beverages	Soft drinks, coffees, teas, beers, and ales	Bitmap Image
	2	Condiments	Sweet and savory sauces, relishes, spreads, and seasonings	Bitmap Image
	3	Confections	Desserts, candies, and sweet breads	Bitmap Image
	4	Dairy Products	Cheeses	Bitmap Image
	5	Grains/Cereals	Breads, crackers, pasta, and cereal	Bitmap Image
	6	Meat/Poultry	Prepared meats	Bitmap Image
	7	Produce	Dried fruit and bean curd	Bitmap Image
	8	Seafood	Seaweed and fish	Bitmap Image
*	(AutoNumber)			

Record: 14 ◀ | 1 | ▶ ▶I ▶* of 8

Figure 13-28. *Data from the* Categories *table in the Northwind database*

The first thing you should notice is that all the entries are very much alike. Each one has a name with which to identify it, a description that expands the understanding of the name, and a picture. We generally don't show a category structure on a Logical model unless it's of value to show the hierarchy. For instance, some of the subtypes might own their own attributes, such as the temperature needed for refrigeration of cold products or the shelf life of perishables. They may also need to be considered separately in order to support detailed business rules such as a special relationship for special equipment needs of refrigerated products. You could represent this data in a category structure since products are divided into different groups, but in this case we don't think it's necessary.

You need to make a decision about how you want to show this on your Logical model. We'd tend to say that there's a potential enterprise need for a category structure. Whichever structure you choose here is a question of modeler preference.

Figure 13-29 shows how it'd look if you chose to treat Product Category as a category.

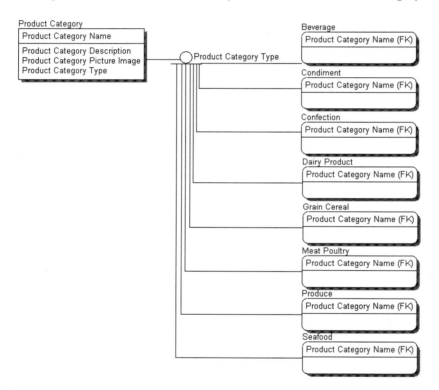

Figure 13-29. *Product Category as a logical category*

You need to review each of the entities to see if categorization is valid and desirable. Review Employees and Orders to see if you think they would benefit from a category design.

Other Rules

Look at the last attribute in Employee, as shown in Figure 13-30. Reports To Employee Id certainly implies a recursion to Employee. You may want to check the data to verify that the rules are being managed, even though we didn't find a constraint at the database level. Add the relationship, and make sure you role-name the new column.

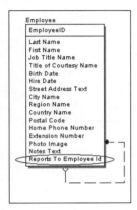

Figure 13-30. *Adding the recursive "reports to" relationship to Employee*

You also want to apply normalization rules to your model since this is a logical view of a system with its own business rules. Look for repeating groups and data value interdependencies. Remember that you discovered a dependency between a country and ZIP codes in a macro? You may want to dig deeper into how the application maintains that rule and model it. You want to model this rule even if it hasn't been physically implemented in the database (see Figure 13-31).

	Macro Name	Condition	Action	Comment
				Attached to the BeforeUpdate property of the Suppliers form.
	Validate Postal Cod	IsNull([Country])	StopMacro	If Country is Null, postal code can't be validated.
		[Country] In ("Frar	MsgBox	If postal code is not 5 characters, display message...
		...	CancelEvent	...and cancel event.
		...	GoToControl	
		[Country] In ("Aust	MsgBox	If postal code is not 4 characters, display message...
		...	CancelEvent	...and cancel event.
		...	GoToControl	
		([Country]="Canac	MsgBox	If postal code not correct for Canada, display message and...
		...	CancelEvent	...and cancel event.
		...	GoToControl	

Figure 13-31. *The suppliers macro in the Northwind database*

Physical implementations often pull data sets and rules out of the Logical model and manage them in places other than the RDBMS. Don't forget to model rules that are managed in front-end code, triggers, and procedures. Figure 13-32 shows the normalized Northwind database Logical model.

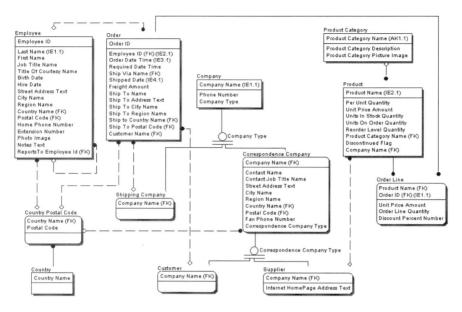

Figure 13-32. *The Northwind database Logical model*

Relationship Names

Finally, you'll want to add relationship verbs to the model to document the business rules, as shown in Figure 13-33. Since this is a reverse-engineered model, you'll want to interview the clients to make sure you choose appropriate verbs.

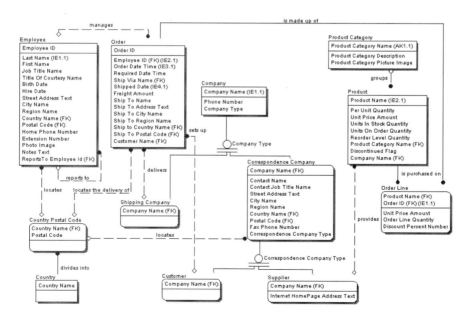

Figure 13-33. *The Northwind database Logical model with verb phrases*

At this point you should revisit the cardinality and nullability and verify that this is how they were implemented in the system. They may not be the true enterprise business rules, but you're documenting the As-Is model.

Finishing It Up

Every step you took in creating the Logical model adds more value and increases your ability to communicate the purpose of a system and how it uses data elements. Document every insight for posterity. As always, you need to annotate the model. Make it clear what this model is documenting. Give it a title. Verify that any documentation derived from it clearly identifies from where the source data came. Always add dates to your document, including when the model was last modified. In the case of reverse-engineered models, you'll want to add the physical locations and names of the databases being analyzed.

Add whatever information you need to make the model a valid reference document. In the Northwind example, we added some extra notes in case we work on the Northwind.mdb again. We noted that Ship to Recipient is probably a reusable set of Ship to values based on the customer, not the order. Country Postal Code can probably be expanded to take on relationships to City and Region. And we think there's a potential problem with verifying Order Unit Price Amount against the product information. (This is an assumption on our part. It seems that Unit Price Amount in Product can change. The unit price stored in Order Line is a point-in-time value. But if the customer complains, there's no way to verify that the correct amount was used if there's no history of Unit Price Amount changes at the product level. You might want to discuss that with the business team.) Figure 13-34 shows the annotated Northwind database Logical model, and Figure 13-35 shows the annotated Northwind database Physical model.

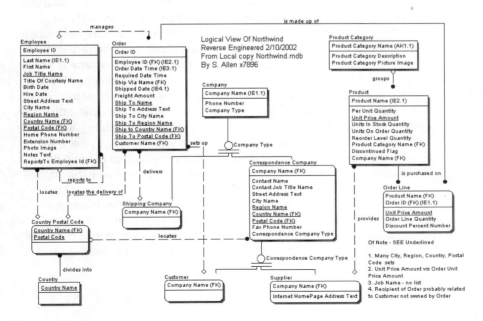

Figure 13-34. *The annotated Northwind database Logical model*

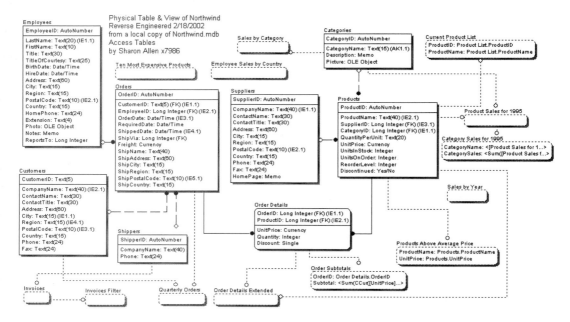

Figure 13-35. *The annotated Northwind database Physical model*

Summary

In this chapter you considered the nature of reverse engineering. It's the process by which you extract information from existing systems in order to work backward and derive a Physical model and work further back to a Logical model, if possible. The nuances of different database systems and development platforms often make this process a difficult task. You've seen how modeling tools such as ERwin can help in taking snapshots of existing databases and in producing Physical models from which you can begin to verify table and column names. While you can generally document table and column names through using such tools, or by reviewing database creation scripts, it's the relationships between tables that are the most difficult to verify. This is where screen analysis, documentation, employee know-how, training, and other "soft" skills can prove invaluable in figuring out exactly how data is being used by the system in question. Only by learning as much as possible about using the application can you determine how the existing data structures are being used and how this compares with the original design.

Reverse engineering has an important role to play in helping improve the efficiency of enterprise applications (by determining faults in the design), aiding integration of existing systems (by pinpointing table and column definitions and relationships between such tables), and allowing comparisons of existing systems with potential new system solutions.

■ ■ ■

CHAPTER 14

Communicating with the Model

This chapter covers the various techniques you can utilize on an optional basis to increase the usability of your data model and the amount of information you can provide within it. Having been through the process of creating the data model, you'll want to make it a sought-after deliverable and optimize its abilities to help solve problems. The techniques covered in this chapter will allow you to highlight salient points of interest and preserve information with the model that tends to become disconnected and lost over time. Not only that, but using a detailed publication format can streamline the deployment of new data analysis.

In the course of this chapter, we'll cover the following:

- **Element arrangement**: Ordering tables/columns or entities/attributes to illustrate rules of precedence that may exist

- **Textual additions**: Using items such as titles, versioning numbering, and legends to aid swift understanding of the model and how it's being used

- **Visual enhancements**: Using color, images, or font styles to emphasize important information

- **Publication formats**: Producing information for local file storage, for a file library, or for distribution on the Web

Why Add More?

Why, indeed? You've completed the modeling tasks. All the entities/tables/views, attributes/columns, and relationships/constraints have been polished, detailed, and honed until they meet your quality standard. What more is there to data modeling than that? Well, you can find the answer in any customer relationship management (CRM) book. You, as the preferred vendor of data models, have a responsibility to the customers of this analysis to make it as simple as possible for them to comprehend your document, recognize what they're looking for, and make the best use of it.

Data models are syntactically complex documents that amalgamate graphics and text to describe conclusions based on analysis. Modeling uses notations and standards that are known to only a select few in the enterprise, and yet the model may need to be available to audiences that you aren't even aware of, such as the facilities team members (who are looking for People-Soft data elements to help them collect and manage parking assignments) or finance employees (who are auditing the sources of the annual report). As a result, you need to make sure the model can be read without you having to act as the guide.

When you make additions to the model for communication's sake, you need to stay sensitive to any given requirements since different enterprise environments may restrict the use of some of the techniques we'll cover in this chapter. Some departments or organizations have requirements for delivered documentation that will cause you to tailor your standard formats to their needs, adding specific elements such as colorization or unique sign-off notations. On the other hand, if they intend to fax the model to various parties, for example, then they may lose any colorization you've used in the document. In that case, you'd need to suggest some other method of highlighting the pertinent information, such as different font styles. In other cases, you may need to stay within strict parameters for text additions, perhaps along the lines of released drawings in manufacturing.

You'll also have soft requirements that occur during a project. Developing a team relationship and making yourself, and your models, a welcome addition to the effort may also be a deciding factor of how you choose to enhance the model. Sometimes what's required is a slightly more personable and lighthearted technique. Other times you'll choose an extremely serious approach to emphasize the seriousness of your documentation. You should conduct both methods with professionalism and utilize them appropriately for your clients.

Note Remember that you're developing models for clients, not just to suit your own needs.

Arranging Elements

Arranging elements is a basic technique that may make reading your model simpler by implying precedence in the creation and deletion of data sets from the position of the entities/tables. (Here's a sample rule of existence: B can't exist without A; in other words, the order of data creation A must be created before B.) This may not mean the order of the table creation, because the database administrators (DBAs) may first create the tables and then apply the constraints in ALTER statements. What this refers to is loading and creating the data—a topic that's of great importance to the extraction, transformation, and loading (ETL) team.

Up until now, the arrangement of the entities and tables in our examples have concentrated more on keeping the box elements (entities, tables, and views) as close to each other as possible, with as short a line element (relationships and constraints) as possible, while making sure nothing disappeared behind anything else. (Relationship lines are especially vulnerable to this in large models, so it can become hard to recognize their actual connectivity.) This is a compressed style that keeps the model as small as possible and is used frequently when printing or when incorporating model images in a document. However, let's consider the object arrangement in the model from the end of Chapter 10; Figure 14-1 shows the deliverable document you sent to your clients, the psychology department.

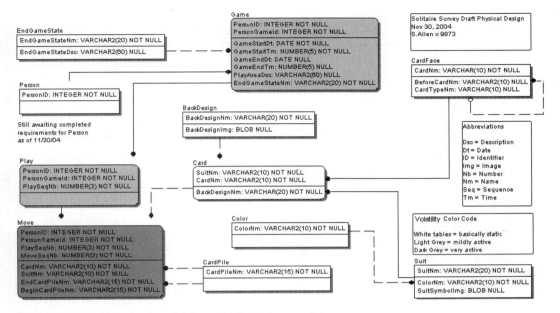

Figure 14-1. *Final Physical model from the Solitaire tutorial*

The arrangement of the objects on this model doesn't make it easy to know the order in which the tables need to be loaded. Notice the hard-cornered tables (independent tables) and how they're spread throughout the model. Remember that the square, or hard-cornered, boxes tell you that their data sets have to depend on others for identification. Therefore, they should be in the first set of tables loaded. You still need to look at the nonidentifying columns to check for foreign keys that would order them differently—but checking for independence is a good place to start.

Precedence for adding and deleting data can be important to both DBAs and programmers as they implement Physical models and develop production-ready applications. The screens have to flow logically based on data that must be created in a certain order. The ETL team must load historic data for the test, quality, and production releases in a certain order. The DBAs must enable and disable referential integrity (RI)—constraints—in a special order too. Knowing the precedence is an important aspect of managing the data, and you can organize the model to help make that clear.

If you rearrange the model to note precedence, you need to move every table that's a parent above its child or children. In Figure 14-2 you can see that it's now much easier to find the order in which data values must be created to enable support of the integrity constraints. For instance, notice that Color must be loaded before Suit.

Rearranging your model and highlighting the parent tables like this may also simplify and enhance your ability to "tell the story" during a model walk-through. You'll notice that in this case the independent (hard-cornered) tables—namely, EndGameState, Person, CardFace, BackDesign, Color, and CardPile—appear in the top portion of the model. These are the simple List of Values (LOV) tables that are often a useful starting point for the team's programming tasks.

Game and Suit are next in line. Suit, although it's independent, has a foreign key to Color, whose data needs to be in place if RI has already been turned on. Game needs to be next because of a dependence on Person.

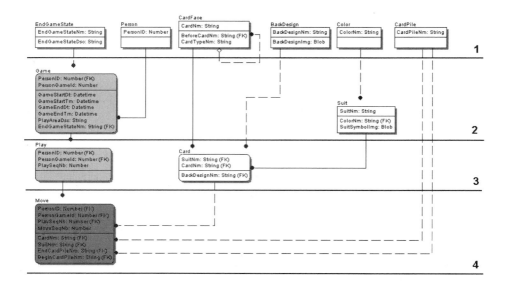

Figure 14-2. *Physical model rearranged to show load order*

Such element arrangement is often requested for submodels that support the technical team since, as we've outlined, it makes the task of identifying core tables and constraints much easier. This is a useful and powerful technique, but it becomes hard to implement in complicated designs without making the model so large that it becomes unreadable.

Adding Text

What we mean by "adding text" to your model is the simple addition of headings, notes, and legends that can increase your clients' ability to read and depend on the model you present to them. These extras, when used appropriately and judiciously, help capture knowledge that has a tendency to disappear after a project has been completed. This is often information that different members of the project team have in their own heads but overlook as not being important or useful enough to document.

Adding Titles and Headings

To illustrate how text can aid understanding of models, let's consider a situation where you're looking through your department's model archive for any work that has been done with the Conceptual entity Order in the past. You find a small Physical model named ShippingOrderTest, as shown in Figure 14-3.

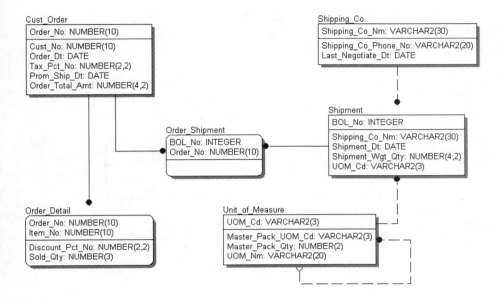

Figure 14-3. `ShippingOrderTest` *Physical model*

Figure 14-3 is a six-table subset of something having to do with shipping and orders. Unfortunately, you have no way of knowing anything else about it. You're left wondering the following:

- Has it been deployed?
- Who is responsible for it?
- What system is it a part of?
- Where are the structures it designed?
- When was it last updated?
- Is it part of a larger model?

Models aren't just stand-alone documents. They fit into the processes governing the management of data. You need to add some information to make that link easy to recognize. How much easier would it be in this case if, instead of the model shown in Figure 14-3, you came across the model shown in Figure 14-4?

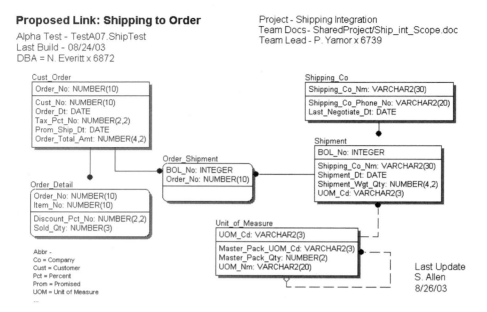

Figure 14-4. *Annotated* ShippingOrderTest *Physical model*

Now you can tell so much more than in Figure 14-3. Specifically, you now know the following:

- The title of the model, ShippingOrderTest, has a different connotation to the title of the document, "Proposed Link: Shipping to Order," which describes an attempt to integrate two departments rather than checking something about shipping orders.

- This was once a proposed solution (as stated in the model title) and may be still.

- The name of the project ("Shipping Integration").

- Where the project documentation is stored (in SharedProject/Shp_int_Scope.doc).

- Who the team lead is (P. Yamor).

- How to contact the team lead (the telephone extension is 6739).

Perhaps more important, you know that this model has been deployed on a server. Specifically, you know the following:

- The stage of testing at the time this model was created (alpha test)

- The server name (TestA07)

- The schema or database name (ShipTest)

- The DBA who is in charge of it (N. Everitt)

- How to find the DBA (on extension 6872)

You also have a feel for the following:

- The age of the model/project

- The name of the author or updater (S. Allen)

- The last date it was touched (the model was last updated 8/26/03)

This second model, with all the extra information, leaves the client with a much higher expectation of the information quality being presented in comparison to the model with all this information omitted.

You may want to come up with a standard set of title elements that are included with every data model for your department. This will add consistency and professionalism to your product. The following is a list of elements we've found to be important to know about any model with which we work. Not all of these items are applicable all the time. Again, you need to use your judgment to know what's important for your use.

- Project/application/subject area name

- Model or submodel name

- Last worked on date

- Name of modeler

- Contact details for more information

- Brief description of model purpose

- Unusual, project-specific or confusing (multimeaning) abbreviations (with the regular ones being referenced in the standards document)

- Brief description of method to create model (in other words, whether it has been reverse engineered)

- Source of analysis information

You can group this information into a block on one side of the model, as shown in Figure 14-5.

Although this looks polished and professional, it can make it difficult to relate specific text to specific model objects. See the note in the organized text. Just think how hard it might be to find the table this was referring to if the model was very large.

Therefore, you may want to separate and emphasize some parts of the text by using positioning and extra characteristics such as bubble boxes, colored text, or lines, as shown in Figure 14-6. Here we positioned the note about the Cust_Order table right next to the table.

It's a good idea to standardize a location on the model for this information for the sake of consistency. One of the corners of the model is generally appropriate.

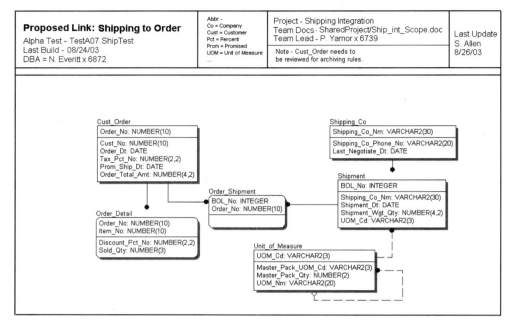

Figure 14-5. *Header block for extra model text*

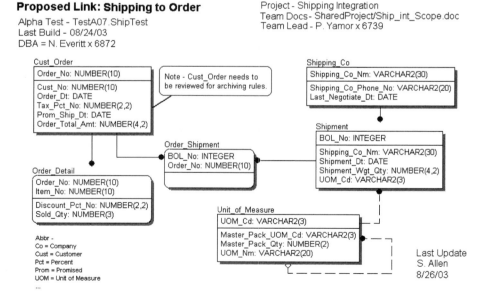

Figure 14-6. *Positioning text to indicate relationship to specific model objects*

Versioning Notation

Change control, or versioning, of the model can be a serious, disciplined corporate procedure requiring check-out and check-in, review boards, and environment (development, test, quality assurance, and production) release controls. It may also be a more casual project process created to keep everyone informed of what version of the model is current. Whatever processes are put in place, it's crucial that the project documentation is managed so as to ensure the entire team is always working with the latest design.

The model may include status notification that it represents a level of analysis (Conceptual, Logical, or Physical), or it could note which of the physical environments (design, alpha, beta, or production release) it's documenting. We often add elements to the model to note the changes in status and use numbering schemes to note new releases. You can also include notes to document the precise changes (or delta) from the previous model. To make the version clear to the team, you may need to provide the following elements in addition to the normal title/heading information:

- Version number
- Brief description of version impact
- Release/environment name
- Team lead to contact about the release
- Information for contacting team lead
- Location of other supporting documents
- Release database information
- DBA in charge of release
- Information on how to contact the DBA

Let's look at an example of how to notate versioning of a data model to support a change to a database. Assume that Figure 14-7 represents a part of a database that was recently released to production, and number it 1.0 since it's the first release.

■Note Numbering releases is a standard you need to determine. We've seen standards ranging from X.Y.Z (where *X* is a major release, *Y* is an enhancement, and *Z* is a bug fix) to the simple 1, 2, and 3.

Now that this model has been implemented in a production environment (as noted on the left side of the model), the clients have discovered that this first release had a few shortcomings. While these are small issues, they still need to be cleared up, and the following requests for corrections (we'll term them *problem corrections* here) have been sent to the team:

- `Shipping_Co.Shipping_Co_Nm` should be `Varchar2(20)`.
- `Shipment.Shipping_Co_Nm` should be `Varchar2(20)` also, as it's the foreign key.

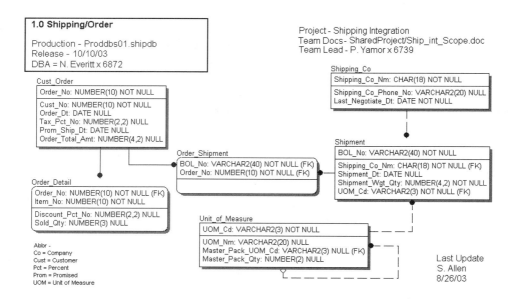

Figure 14-7. *Version 1.0 of a Physical data model*

The clients have also taken this as an opportunity to request new data elements and to point out that this system is already evolving. Their requested changes (we'll term them *change requests*) are as follows:

- Add `Taken_By_Emp_ID` to `Cust_Order`.

- Add `Back_Order_Qty` to `Order_Detail`. Populate by checking quantity on hand in inventory at time of order creation.

The modeler may be asked to review any change to the design to find the best solution to data elements or rule additions, deletions, and modifications. This provides you with an opportunity to change the model before the database changes. On the other hand, depending on how your organization manages data structure changes, you may be told of the changes after they occur, in which case you're merely updating the model to reflect the database's current state.

In this example, we'll create two submodels so that the problem correction and the change request can be reviewed and implemented separately from each other. The problem correction model will require text to document the modifications that have been carried out in fixing the bugs identified by the clients. We sometimes change the font or color of the changed values so that they're easily recognizable to the maintenance team, as shown in Figure 14-8.

As you can see, in this case we've used bold type to highlight the attributes that have been modified, and we've added a note at the top of the model to explain what changes have been made.

1.0.1 Shipping/Order

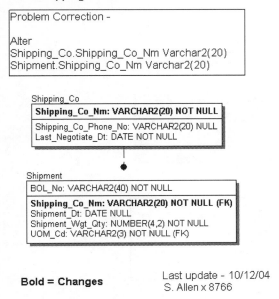

Problem Correction -

Alter
Shipping_Co.Shipping_Co_Nm Varchar2(20)
Shipment.Shipping_Co_Nm Varchar2(20)

Bold = Changes   Last update - 10/12/04
                            S. Allen x 8766

Figure 14-8. *Proposed problem correction data model*

We'll do something a little different with the change request. Notice that even this "simple" enhancement of integrating the HR_Employee table into the model, adding a requested field, and discovering a need to add a (not requested) field to Order_Detail may require something rather involved. Integration always requires extra sensitivity. You need to be aware of not just the structures but also the quality of the data and the processes in place to maintain it. Your database needs may not be easily satisfied by what looks at first glance to be an easy integration solution. The modeler is often involved in reviewing the many optional enterprise sources for data. For instance, if the human resources system doesn't include contractor and temporary employee records but those people can create orders, then you may need to suggest integrating to a more comprehensive company resource system.

Figure 14-9 shows the submodel for the change request. Notice the text block outlining some impacts and proposed methods (such as using a live database link rather than replicating the table) of satisfying the request. You may want to put the proposed methods here, or you may need a fairly extensive document that explains the techniques for satisfying the request. You may be proposing a solution that will even have a ripple effect on another system.

This series of notations on the model can support the technical team by providing a good blueprint of what's about to be impacted. The DBAs and programmers may know of aspects that will cause other issues by being able to see at a glance what's being targeted for change. Providing documentation that can easily be reviewed like this can prevent one change control

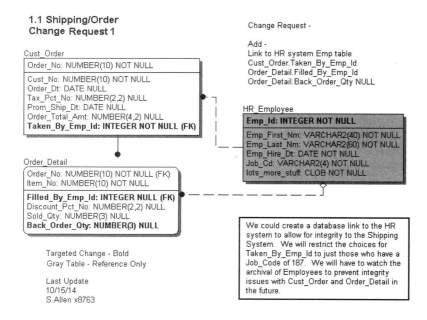

Figure 14-9. *Data model supporting analysis for Change Request 1*

from causing other problems. Use the model to note expected impacts to other uses of the data structures, including the following:

- Reports and screens, which now need to accommodate the new, larger sizes

- Application impacts stemming from adding functionality, such as new flexibility in the data

- ETL impacts stemming from changed data source availability

- Backup and recovery processes, which may need to be reworked

Trying to note the expected impacts and jog everyone's memory to look over their areas of expertise can save a great deal of time, money, and frustration.

Changes like this one are almost always multifaceted mini-projects that need analysis and planning of more than simply the database structure to ensure that they don't disrupt, or impede, the success of the project. Your model may need to be matched with other documents to create a "database change control package" that details all the implications of the proposed change.

After all the analysis has been done, you may decide to roll several problem fixes and change requests into one production release. Some modeling software (such as ERwin 4.1) allows you to consolidate changes into a single version using a merge function.

Sometimes the data model isn't used to update the database but instead is compared with it, and refreshed accordingly, on a periodic basis. In these situations, the data model becomes a snapshot of a moment in time for the database, generally the original creation. The data model may then be notated with a "Last checked against *<environment/database name>*" date as a versioning element.

Creative Versioning Techniques

We all know that modeling and managing models is serious work. In this context, the next set of enhancements can be seen as gimmicks. They need to be used sparingly to continue to be powerful and to avoid the perception that you don't take the subject matter seriously. However, we've used these techniques to great advantage. (In fact, we've won awards and kudos for them.) Don't underestimate the power of laughter in relieving stress and binding a team together.

■**Note** Whatever you choose to use in your presentation should be to support the content, not hide it, and to support your team members, not patronize or antagonize them.

Versioning data models so that people recognize there's a new copy on their desk can be tough. Many desks have paper piled all over them. The paper printouts generally come in a restricted set of sizes, so the paper doesn't help much with recognizing the newest version. In addition, the boxes and lines on the new version may be in the same places as the last model you delivered. Finding the newest model when there are six on your desk may be like trying to find a needle in a haystack.

How can others easily pick out the latest version? Even with extra text and numbering, the differences are often so subtle that they're virtually invisible to anyone other than the person who cares very much about the latest change. People don't read data models like a book. They refer to them when necessary.

We've used many methods of making it easy to recognize that a new version of a model has just been delivered. This is especially important during the first weeks after completing the Physical model design. You may have changes to the model every two hours, especially if the development team has been divided up to work on different aspects of the project in parallel. Everyone needs to keep up-to-date on the shared objects, and this can prove increasingly difficult if numerous model versions are piling up on desks.

This is our suggestion: add something to the model that will make it easy to recognize a change. We've added the following to models with surprising results. The team members generally like it, and they can easily find the latest version on their desks. These enhancements don't replace dates and numbers, but they often get to be what the team looks for when finding the new model.

- Stickers

- Stamps

- Vocabulary words

- Quotes

- Facts: sports, weird topics, space, and so on

We left a meeting once where the developers were referring to the "pre-frog" model. We furiously wracked our brains to figure out what acronym they were using until they pointed to the model where the latest sticker (a bright-green frog wearing roller skates) was dancing on their packets of model changes. As our understanding became apparent, the ensuing laughter cleared some of the tension that had been building during the review. Obviously, there's no significance or ability to order the version by using a frog sticker. It was just a dramatic visual that differed from the basketball sticker on the last version. We tend to keep a drawer full of colorful stickers to use to visually emphasize a new version of a model.

You're probably going to say that your third-grade teacher used to do this stuff. You're right, and it worked! Just be careful not to overdo it; it can cost your credibility if you pay too much attention to doing cute stuff and too little to getting the job done right.

■**Tip** Documentation real estate is prime, so don't let informality get out of hand.

Adding Notes

Notes can be invaluable to those wanting to know more about the model in the future. You can always resynchronize the Physical data model with the database in order to determine structure names, or you can reverse engineer a Logical model from a production database. However, what you can't always do is find some basic information about the model or the project that sponsored it.

While this type of enhancement to a model can clutter the graphic, bear in mind that separate documentation you provide along with the graphic has a tendency to get lost. Again, it's a question of using whatever means you feel comfortable with in order to convey the necessary information effectively. We've taken to adding a "text-only" page of the model, which isn't always printed, noting facts we don't want to forget. Don't automatically put a note on the printable graphic portion of the model. Instead, in each case, determine if you have a special need to couple this piece of information tightly with the model.

■**Note** Data model documentation requires advanced skills in technical editing to decide what's important and what's extraneous in the context of the objective. You must justify including information on the basis of its value in helping to understand the subject matter. You'll never have enough space for everything.

You can add anything to the model in a note. As we mentioned earlier, a large amount of information gets lost to the enterprise since it only ever spends time in the minds of the project team and isn't recorded. We can't tell you how many times we wished we had the diary of the person who left a model behind for us to maintain. We've contacted a few over the years to try to get information, but in most cases they had already erased that part of their temporary memory. We've used notes on models to create that diary for those who have to follow us; it includes the following:

- Unsolved issues/questions

- Suggestions

- Final choices

- Disclaimers

- Risks

- Warnings

- Policies

- Team communiqués

- Schedule, including milestone dates and critical meetings

- Parallel task status

- Particularly complicated business or processing rules

Once again, you need to judge your audience before you send out a model that looks messy or unprofessional. It may have too much unnecessary information for people to be able to focus on their task. Some of these comments may not be of interest even though they may all be interesting to you. Keep the "noise" level down by including only what's important to support the task being accomplished by the delivery of a data model. You can always add documentation in other places than the visible background of a data model.

Adding Legends

Legends are the translation devices in documentation used to explain the meaning of the various model elements you might use, such as the following:

- Abbreviations

- Formatted text

- Shading

- Graphics/images/icons

A legend doesn't have to be a multivalued list. It can simply be a statement such as "Changes in Red" or "FKs in Italics." Highlighted features (in any fashion) need to have their meaning documented; otherwise, the client will be none the wiser as to what you're trying to convey.

Tip Don't assume what you meant to highlight using an emphasis technique is obvious. Build a legend on the model to document it.

Abbreviation Legend

You've seen us use an abbreviated legend on many of the examples in this book (including Figure 14-7). It's generally found more often on Physical data models since Conceptual and Logical models try to use full names whenever possible. But any time you have to abbreviate words, you should keep an abbreviation legend handy. Make sure this text block can be printed along with the graphic. Having it separate from the model isn't helpful.

It's also advisable to build a standardized set of abbreviations for the model, if not for the enterprise. Try to keep them intuitive. Some abbreviations or acronyms are so obscure that no one would recognize them without a key. We had to use "LTLG" and "GTHG" on one model recently to denote "Less than lowest level of processing goal" and "Greater than highest level of processing goal" for targeted percent variance allowances in process grading. If the abbreviations or acronyms we used got lost somehow, then no one would ever figure out (short of reading the code or the definitions) what those letters were meant to convey.

You also need to be careful to watch for abbreviations used for multiple definitions. For example, we've seen *pt* used to mean "part," "participant," "percentage," and "partial." At the other extreme, you need to avoid using more than one abbreviation to mean the same thing. For instance, you could use *no*, *nb*, and *nbr* to mean "number." Standardizing can help, but we almost all have legacy issues to contend with, and it's important to stay consistent with what's already in place.

Finally, we all like simple things, and short names make coding quicker and easier. However, we find system names tend to be overabbreviated rather than vice versa. Avoid the possibility of confusion in your data element names by using full names wherever possible.

■**Note** Have some sympathy for the maintenance team in your naming and your documentation of naming conventions. Sponsor and advocate a standard abbreviations list for the department.

Formatted Text and Shading Legend

It's easy to forget the power that you have available to you in the form of italics, underlining, and bolding to bring an aspect of the model to the forefront. Using shading on the model is often a powerful way to single out elements for scrutiny. All of these can help in telling people why you want particular elements to be noticed. We often mirror the formatting used on the model in the legend to make it even simpler to understand. For an example of this, refer to Figure 14-8.

As you can see, the legend states not only what we've highlighted using bold type but also why we've shaded one of the tables. Documentation is important in enabling effective communication with the person viewing the model.

Adding Graphics/Images/Icons

Don't ignore the wealth of small graphics, images, and icons you can use. They can be helpful in reviewing a design. In Figure 14-10, do you recognize this little part of the Solitaire modeling project?

The data domains are noted here with little symbols rather than text. This enables you to review the different data types at a glance, and it makes the model more compact than if you display the domains in ordinary text format. For example, the little clock means a date/time, ABC is a name field, and the dollar sign is a cost.

You may be able to increase the provided set of icons by importing ones that are meaningful to your team. You'll need to create a legend for these as well to ensure that the meaning is clear to the reader. These tiny pictures may be especially useful to you when you're working at the Conceptual and Logical levels since they portray concepts well.

Entity icons are also powerful for providing a simple definition of the sets you're documenting, as shown in Figure 14-11. You'd probably back this model up with additional layering of details, which allows everyone to gain understanding of your analysis in an iterative fashion.

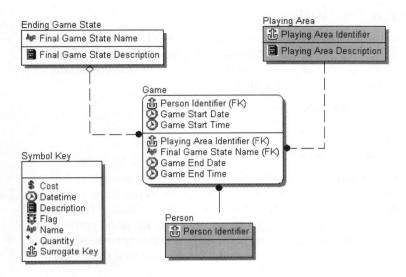

Figure 14-10. *Data model enhanced with iconic information*

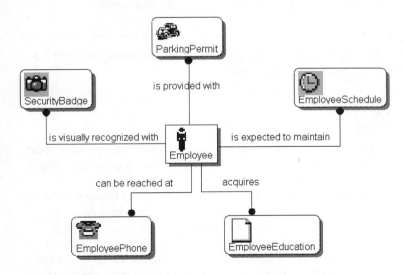

Figure 14-11. *Entity-level Logical model using iconic enhancements*

Publishing Data Models

Publishing data models is one of the procedural issues that should be discussed when you have your initial meeting with the clients. You generally have several options, but it's up to the modeler to present the model in the format that's acceptable to the clients. You can present the pictorial and backup documentation in the following formats:

- Paper (the most widely used form of a data model, big or small)

- Electronic files in a shared environment

- Database (model management software)

Each situation will generally require some form of security policy regarding access to the models and data management documentation. Clearly, models developed using company-sensitive information should be accessible only to those with sufficient authority. However, balancing security with reasonable access is a tough call. The names of the tables and columns in your company can be worth quite a bit to anyone working in serious corporate espionage. On the other hand, ad hoc query tool support is creating a valid need for your customers to know this information. Like we said, this one is tough.

Electronic document files are usually not accessible without using a licensed copy of the software used to generate them, so direct access to them is rare. Commonly these files will then be generated in report formats for wider distribution, tailored appropriately for the clients. The graphics may go out as .pdf files, but the reports will be produced in whatever format is standard for your company, such as Microsoft Word or Excel documents, for example.

▪Note You, and your department, must find a way to establish and maintain a publication policy that provides your documentation consistently and appropriately to your customers.

Publishing on the Web

So many companies aren't housed in the same facilities anymore, and the challenges of supporting a team spread temporally and geographically are huge. Many companies are now starting to leverage the Web for internal affairs as well as external ones.

Some modeling tools are really getting serious about providing reports in Hypertext Markup Language (HTML) format. For example, ERwin 4.1 has several Web-friendly template-style reporting options for you. They allow you to extract information from the main file you're working on and link this information to a Web page. Since you can provide login controls to such pages, this is a means to distribute selected information to end users. The graphics from your model are stored in a .gif or .pdf file, and the model elements are provided in searchable, linked documents. For companies with intranets and enough technical support for rapid content changes, distributing documentation this way can be ideal. Figure 14-12 illustrates this facility using the conceptual view of the Solitaire model.

Entity	
Name	**Definition**
Card	One of 52 specific combinations of suit and numbers (or face), usually displayed in rectangular form, that are used to play games. In this instance Solitaire. Example: Queen of Clubs, 2 of Diamonds Excludes - additional rectangular paper stock that is included in a sold pack, such as Jokers or Instruction cards
Card Pile	A temporary and changeable area used to process a collection of cards, which behave differently in the game of Solitaire. A Card Pile does not have to have a Card in it to exist. Example: Draw Pile, Discard Pile, Processing Pile
Game	A contest played for sport or amusement (according to rules) made up of many small decisions, which affect the outcome.

Figure 14-12. *HTML model definition report*

Sharing the Files

Some of your customers may actually be partners in adding to, and maintaining, the electronic documentation in a project. DBAs and data modelers often share the model. The data modeler takes the model to a certain point in the design, and then the DBA takes over, generally after the first draft of the physicalization. Programmers may also share Physical models as they work on the code necessary to implement the design and take advantage of data modeling software (such as Visio Professional, ERwin, and DataArchitect) that includes functionality for creating triggers and procedures attached to the design.

It can get to be quite a challenge with so many people needing to actually update the model. It's fortunate that some software will merge model changes into a single file. Otherwise, you need to be careful not to lose the value you've added to the model by overwriting the wrong file.

Archiving the Files

Have we convinced you yet that any company could have hundreds of data models? You may have production, test, development, vendor, legacy, enterprise, Conceptual, entity-relationship (ER), and fully attributed (FA) models covering any subject and supporting any department. Managing all these models efficiently may require the creation of a *data model library* (also referred to as a *model repository*).

Creating such a repository could be as simple as collating all the models on a shared server somewhere. On the other hand, software such as Computer Associates' ModelMart enables you to store your models in a database, broken down into their own data elements.

You'll want to figure out your own naming, indexing, card catalog, and identification system for locating your models and knowing what they cover. You may want to create an overview document (index) so that someone could use search criteria to look for a particular model by department or model type, for example.

Having models in a repository also supports enterprise-standard object reuse between models. This is a great boon to your process. We waste way too much time reinventing Address,

Employee, Item, and a hundred other entities/tables and attributes/columns that are completely static once the enterprise has determined what it wants for a universal template of that data.

■**Note** Modelers, DBAs, programmers, and analysts need to be able to reuse model structures the way we reuse code, in other words, simply, easily, and with complete confidence that they'll work.

Summary

Data models form the foundation documentation for many types of enterprise analysis, such as database development, reverse engineering, or application integration projects. Such models can be enhanced through judicious use of text, images, color, and formatting in order to help customers focus more easily on important features. This makes impact analysis, data element usage, and changes to the model, through the various iterations that will inevitably take place, more immediately obvious. Without a simple means of keeping the whole development team, as well as the clients, aware of the current version of the model or any modifications that are required, confusion will reign.

Models also have to have a reliable publication method tailored to any security and access requirements. This may involve models being published on a company intranet or the creation of a central model repository. Creating a repository makes for improved reuse of existing models and, as a result, more efficient management of data elements (and their subsequent growth) within a given enterprise.

CHAPTER 15

■ ■ ■

Improving Data Quality and Managing Documentation

Until we became data modelers, we never realized that data spent so much time wandering in and out of systems. Managing a data element may seem like a simple task, but chances are it's not. People often overlook that data goes on to become information. Data tends to begin life in a relatively simple online transactional processing (OLTP) system and is then summed, truncated, rolled up or down, averaged, factored, apportioned, parsed, and basically chewed up and pressed into a mold by the time it's displayed on reports for upper management. Data may move from the mainframe to midrange systems or to desktops. It is subject to manual Microsoft Excel processes, is filtered, is manipulated, and at some point is finally delivered on printed or Web page reports.

All of this activity can make it difficult to keep track of where the data came from, where it was sent, and what it really means. Data and information are central to an organization's management, so a data modeler has an important role to play. This chapter covers some techniques that may help you keep track of your data's meaning, sources, and targets. These techniques usually don't affect the Logical model, but you can use the analysis results from applying these techniques when you have to make physical database decisions about denormalization options or other deployment issues.

The more you know about the nature of a data element and its relationship with individuals, with the business, and with the larger world, the better prepared you are to design a solid, forward-looking Physical model design. You can also use your model as a framework for locating and leveraging other information about and within the enterprise. Using the model as a reference point for providing information can help everyone see the data connections in your company.

In this chapter, we'll cover the following:

- Improving data quality

  - Fidelity analysis (measuring the integrity, accuracy, and completeness of a data element)

  - Criticality (determining the importance of individual data elements being correct)

  - Sensitivity and privacy (understanding your moral and legal responsibility to secure data elements)

- Stewardship (understanding the assigned responsibility for ensuring data quality)

- Cross-footing (checking the validity of data by comparing multiple sources of information)

- Process validation (ensuring data is used appropriately and as intended)

- Risk and mitigation (knowing about the problems in your data and lessening their impact)

- Using data mappings to trace and audit the validity of data elements

  - Mapping to the Conceptual model

  - Mapping to the Logical model

  - Mapping to the Physical model

Introducing Data Quality

In modeling efforts, it's easy to overlook the need to gather information about what data is valid for a given data element. Data modelers are generally concerned with the structural aspects of the data, including an element's data type, size, and precision. Yet it's the content of the data itself that makes the enterprise function and tells you the story of rules, relationships, and exceptions of the business processes. Just because a given set of data adheres to the structure of a data model doesn't mean the data represents what the model says it does.

Data quality needs a champion in the information technology (IT) department. The data modeler, by using the normal forms to build Logical and Physical models, helps to provide a framework that promotes quality data. But creating a design that can effectively organize the data isn't enough. Just because a table design is built to provide a Third Normal Form (3NF) schema doesn't mean the data will stay that way once the design is implemented. Developers and database administrators (DBAs) have to respond quickly to rapidly changing business rules and the need for new data elements. They solve problems creatively and may short-circuit your design by overloading database fields (putting data into a field that will permit it but isn't designed for the purpose) or by squatting (finding an obsolete, unused database field in which to store new data elements). So, the more you find out, document, and share with the development and DBA teams, the better informed everyone is. You can then help these teams anticipate problems and add flexibility and safeguards to keep the quality of your enterprise data high.

Don't think that our discussion of data quality in this chapter is comprehensive. Every enterprise, by its nature, seems to focus on its own particular view of the data it owns. It continually fascinates us to see that what's important to one enterprise is completely irrelevant to another. Government agencies, private companies, service-oriented businesses, manufacturers, media, and banking industries all care about different data elements differently.

Data analysis is important. It doesn't contribute directly to your work in the form of adding entities or attributes to your model, but it does allow you to add details to your definitions and notes and can give you tremendous insight into your model's accuracy. If a data model is an engine, the data applied to the Physical model design is the fuel. Knowing the details of your data can help you tune your model so it's most effective.

Fidelity Analysis (Data Quality Analysis)

Fidelity is a word we don't see too often. In the world of engineering, this term refers to how close something adheres to a standard. When discussing fidelity in the context of data, it refers to data quality as a degree of consistency. Data quality is a composite measure of the following:

- **Data structure quality**: How well does the data conform to its expected structure, including size, precision, and data type?

- **Data syntax and format quality**: How consistently and correctly does the data content adhere to its expected format?

- **Data value validity**: How consistently does the data content use values that are considered reasonable and expected?

- **Data value accuracy**: How well does the data content represent the real world?

- **Data value completeness**: How well does the presence of data content meet the scope of the data demanded by the business?

Data quality is a measure of the structure, format, validity, accuracy, and completeness of a given set of data. When data corresponds to all its expectations in these areas, you know it's in an expected structure, has an understood format, is valid, is accurate, and is complete. When you can say with certainty that a piece of data meets all these criteria, you can be confident of your data content and your understanding of what it means.

Performing a data quality analysis, however, is tough work. While certain tools can help with some of this analysis by offering automated and systematic data profiling and analysis features, we have yet to find a tool that evaluates all the structural and content aspects of data that are helpful in a data quality analysis. If you're tasked with performing a data quality analysis, you'll likely have to do some of the data profiling work yourself. But by automating some of the labor-intensive processes of profiling the data in enterprise systems, data profiling software can help in highlighting any basic data anomalies and incompatibilities. If you're diligent about following up on these issues, you can deal with them before the database is built and before problems are discovered during the extraction, transformation, and loading (ETL) processes.

In the context of modeling, a data quality analysis is most helpful in determining where the actual data may differ from the assumptions provided to you during your discussions with the business or technical teams. By knowing what the real data looks like, you can more easily and more quickly determine where requirements may be incorrect and how you can adapt your design to accommodate the data that will actually be stored in the database. This type of analysis can produce eye-opening statistics that tend to challenge interview answers, written requirements, and even system documentation.

Data Profiling

Before you can analyze your data, you need to profile it. *Data profiling* is a process of compiling statistics and information about a set of actual data. Because business users and the technical team may not be aware of all the anomalies found in a data set, data profiling allows you to quickly scan a large amount of data, make some general observations about the entire set, and review these observations with your clients. You'll often find that your clients have forgotten that a data set contains exceptions to the business rules. Identifying these exceptions early in the data design process can save you a lot of rework later.

To create a data set profile, you should start by gathering details about each data set (or table) and flat file field (or table column).

For each data set (or table), you should capture the number of rows in the data set.

For each field (or table column) in the data set, you should capture the following:

- The minimum field value

- The maximum field value

- The number of instances of NULL, 0, N/A, spaces, or other special field values

- The number of distinct field values

- Each distinct value and the number of occurrences of each unique value

You should use any information you've obtained from your client interviews or existing system documentation to make some decisions about the expected values or range of values for each column. Document what you think is a reasonable set of values for each column.

When you've captured your data, consider putting it into the format shown in Table 15-1 and Table 15-2. Table 15-1 shows general information about the column definition and specifications. Table 15-2 summarizes the data occurring in that column and the results of the profiling activity.

Table 15-1. *Employee Hire Date Column Specifications*

General Column Information	Data Value
Table name	Employee
Column name	Hire_Date
Column specification	DATE and NOT NULL allowed
Row count	1,500
Expected range	3/17/1998 (company established) to current day

Table 15-2. *Summary Results from Profiling the Employee Hire Date Column*

Data Field Information	Data Value	Record Count
Minimum value	09/09/1099	276
Maximum value	01/01/3999	36
Number of values containing NULL, 0, N/A, spaces, and so on		0
Number of unique values		216
Values with frequencies	09/09/1099	104
	03/17/1998	15
	03/18/1998	1
	...<there would be 216 distinct dates here— we're not showing them for brevity>	

What new information does this data profile provide? It shows that even a physical database field designated as NOT NULL with a relatively strict data type of DATE can be manipulated to hold values that mean something other than what you'd expect. Note from the example in

Table 15-2 that you've discovered two nonsensical employment dates (09/09/1099 and 01/01/3999) that appear to be used to record something other than a hire date. After some investigation, you might find that all employee records where the Hire_Date = 09/09/1099 were loaded from another system, and a special value of 09/09/1099 was used when an employee's hire date was missing. In this case, the date was chosen to be absurd on purpose, so this value identifies records that were converted from the other system. Program code can remove these records from certain reports based on the absurd date. But don't be surprised if no one even remembers why this weird date was used in the first place.

You may find that the other absurd date, 01/01/3999, is being used only on employee records that represent independent contractors. The system may force the clients to enter a hire date, even though it doesn't apply to contractors. Why are contractors in the Employee table? Perhaps the human resources department discovered that the Employee table has been integrated into several other systems, such as the e-mail system, and that e-mail accounts can't be set up without an employee's record. In this case, a quick workaround was discovered; by inserting this nonsensical date to bypass the data rules built into the tables, the contractors can now have e-mail accounts.

In these cases, you've identified data that's structurally valid (these are dates, after all), formatted correctly, and complete, but it fails the test of validity and accuracy when compared with the original data requirements. You may or may not be able to fix the data, but at least you've spotted the problem and can communicate it to the team, as well as make well-informed decisions when discussing database constraints for these fields.

These hypothetical situations aren't uncommon or ridiculous. They happen every day, even to models that were carefully constructed. Although a modeling effort may have been complete and accurate at the time, almost nothing (including data rules) stays stable forever. Sometimes the only way you can find out what data is really present in a system is to profile it.

In this example, the client faced system constraints that required the entire enterprise workforce to be represented in the Employee data structures. The system owners quickly concluded that contractors and temporary help had to be included in the Employee table just to get them e-mail accounts. Forcing those non-Employee records into the Employee table then caused the Hire_Date column to do double-duty as both the employee's hire date and their employment status.

Data profiling can help you identify problems such as the following:

- Whether natural keys are actually unique

- Whether identified data types are truly accurate

- Whether nullability has been correctly specified (watch for values such as whitespace, N/A, and other absurdities)

- Whether fields have embedded multivalues, such as comma-separated lists of values

- Whether the definition for a field actually matches the data stored within that field

Criticality Analysis

When performing a data quality analysis, you must also determine how important it is to have quality data. In a perfect world, you'd always want your data to be of the highest quality. In practice, however, you'll have limited resources to address data quality issues. A criticality analysis will help you classify your data elements on the basis of the importance of their data quality.

The quality of some data will be important, and the quality of other data will not be so important. For example, the data quality of your middle initial may not be important, but the data quality of your Social Security number is likely to be critical. Critical data often has extra validations and an audit process to try to prevent data corruption and ensure accuracy.

Remember that what's important to one company may not be important to another. You need to find out which data elements are critical from your clients' perspective and respond accordingly. If the data is worth collecting, someone is probably depending on it being right, but the reality is that not every data element is maintained at the same level of quality. A criticality analysis tells you what the impact will be to the enterprise and the clients if it's wrong.

■**Note** Criticality classification isn't an excuse to allow bad data into your design. It simply allows you to focus on those data elements that will have a severe impact on the system if they aren't stored and maintained appropriately.

The real trick here is to identify effective and appropriate methodologies of maintaining compliance by preventing data from falling below the fidelity level required. You can use some of the statistics you generate from your fidelity analysis to test whether "highly critical" data elements are more than 95 percent accurate (use whatever benchmark is appropriate). If you can create a fidelity test that provides you with the ability to monitor your critical data, you can participate in helping to identify potential problems.

Although some organizations have status, risk, and criticality catalogs, a single industry standard doesn't seem to exist. Instead, in the following sections, we've included the data criticality scale that we've developed. It uses a simple ranking on a scale of one to four, with level one being the most critical. Classifying your data elements in this way allows you to focus on ensuring the data quality of the elements that are the most important to you. Tailor a criticality scale of your own that will work for you in your enterprise.

Level One: Absolutely Necessary

This data *must* be correct, or you won't be able to complete vital business functions. This data probably doesn't permit NULL values. Validation should include a list of valid values, a format mask, or the ability to check individual values against alternative sources. Data values that fall into this category must be corrected when there's an identified problem, even if it requires extensive manual intervention. These data elements can't be wrong, and life-threatening situations, serious public safety issues, or corporate security breaches may result if they are.

Examples of this classification of data include the following:

- The Global Positioning System's values for longitude, latitude, and altitude readings of a plane in flight for air-traffic control systems

- The drug name, dosage, and patient ID of a prescription in a pharmacy

- Routing control values such as the current state of traffic lights (to prevent both directions from being green at the same time) or the current usage of railway tracks to prevent one track from being used by two trains traveling in opposite directions

Level Two: Important

This data is expected to be correct. If it's wrong, it will cause significant problems within the enterprise. When this data isn't correct, it represents a serious risk to existing business processes. Incorrect data *will* cause summation-reporting anomalies, require special process handling, create annoying duplication of effort, or leave a final process unable to complete because of inaccuracy.

Data values that fall into this category will be fixed when there's an identified problem but generally not as quickly as data classified as level one. Since data elements at level two aren't as critical, you usually have time to carefully fix problems when you discover them.

Examples include the following:

- A sales total on an invoice for a retail firm

- An address on a delivery for a freight company

- Beneficiary information for processing death benefits

Level Three: Good to Have

This data should be correct. If errors occur, some reports may be incorrect, but the impact of the incorrect data isn't far-reaching. This data will be corrected only if it requires minimal effort. As a rule, these data values are informational and generally result in few repercussions if they're wrong. Incorrect data *may* cause reporting anomalies, require special handling, create annoying duplication of effort, or leave a final process unable to complete because of inaccuracy. However, generally these errors are ignored or explained. This type of data is seldom "cleaned up" (but can cause the data warehouse team problems later).

Examples include the following:

- The ZIP codes for addresses used in bulk mailings for an advertising firm

- The reprint date for books in a library

- The car color for rental firms

Level Four: Noncritical

This data may be correct, but if it isn't correct or present, there's little to no impact. Very little concern is shown over the accuracy of this data. This data is usually null allowed in the physical database and may be generic text. This data can't ever be used to trace or substantiate any conclusion and will probably never be fixed if found to be incorrect.

Examples include the following:

- The age of pet on an application for a dog or cat license

- The "visiting from" location gathered in the guest book at an antique store

- Hair color for the Department of Motor Vehicles

Sensitivity and Privacy Analysis

We're all becoming more aware of the need to protect the privacy of people's data. A company can now be sued for privacy breaches if someone's identity is stolen and it's due to a company's negligence. This is as much an issue of awareness as it is an issue of data security. People give others access to data that they don't recognize as being sensitive. They behave as though their access privileges extend to creating and publishing data that should have been noted as being "for your eyes only." The theft of information is often not a breakdown of security but a breakdown of awareness of responsibility.

Tip Data is an asset; it's a resource just like inventory, money, and energy. Protect data as you would any of your enterprise's assets!

Publication of or access to some data elements has to be restricted. Noting these security restrictions is another component of data analysis. You can apply pretty much the same type of scale to data sensitivity and privacy as you did to data criticality. We suggest the classification mechanism in the following sections to help you categorize the sensitivity of your data elements. You need to document your data elements' security requirements and make them available to your entire team.

First Degree: Legally Protected Private

This data *must* be protected. This data could be damaging to the livelihood, security, or reputation of the company or individual if stolen or published. In fact, exposing this data may have legal ramifications. Data elements meeting this security classification may be encrypted or stored separately from less-sensitive data in a secure area, such as a server in a walk-in safe. Access to this data probably requires manager approval.

This data may involve company financial records, personal information (pay rate, reviews, and complaints), research and development (R&D) concepts, political contributions, contract negotiations, staffing-level scenarios, medical issues, or security monitoring. Examples include the following:

- Tax identification (Social Security) numbers

- Personal financial information

- Medical test results

Second Degree: Enterprise-Defined Private

This data is expected to be protected. You can probably base this level of privacy on what you expect to be able to keep private from your co-workers. Item names for products currently being sold are public, but the names of the products currently in R&D should be restricted. Data elements meeting this security classification have less potential for legal damage than those of the first degree, but serious damage to the enterprise can still occur if this information becomes widely distributed. (Note that some of our examples may be considered first-degree data elements in your enterprise.) Examples include the following:

- Next season's marketing plans

- Test results for research before publication

- Product formula and processes

Third Degree: Morally Defined Private

This data should be private. For example, you may communicate employees' birth dates and months, but their years of birth are private because some people prefer it that way. Although disclosing employee city names may help promote the car-pooling program, you may want to keep employee street and address numbers private so no one gets an unexpected visit from a co-worker. Examples include the following:

- The age of any children living at home, unless volunteered

- The names of people who checked out a book at a library

- Any family connections to famous/infamous people (politicos, criminals, or celebrities), unless volunteered

Fourth Degree: Public

This data is public. You can fully expect everyone to know or have access to this information. Examples include your company's current product line and hours of business. In fact, if this information wasn't public, you'd have other problems. If the dates and times that a consultant is available to meet clients isn't public, then arranging appointments with that person will be problematic. You may also have certain legal requirements to make some information public, such as data elements that need to be published in the company prospectus or disclosed to a government regulatory agency. Depriving public access to some data can be as legally detrimental to the enterprise as disclosing private data that should be protected.

Stewardship

Stewardship is the responsibility for the validity of certain data elements in an enterprise. For example, you can assume that the human resources department is ultimately responsible for the list of current employees, and therefore the department must have tools to be able to audit the list or be involved in any decisions about the intended use of the list. You usually won't know exactly who owns all the data in your systems. For many years we established data stewardship by following existing application boundaries. For example, if your department owned an application, it owned the data content and the quality of the data elements. Unfortunately, in a world of integrated databases, dividing data responsibility in that way doesn't work.

■**Note** Stewardship should at least be assigned at the entity or table level. (Sometimes it may be even more specific.) Sometimes this responsibility may even be set at a partition within the data set itself (such as region or pay level).

To document the proposed ownership of data, you may want to create a list that looks like Table 15-3.

Table 15-3. *Table Ownership and Access, Showing Stewardship Responsibilities*

Table	Table Definition	Owner: Department or Specific	Access Available To . . .
Color	Stores the list of valid values for color type (for example, Black & White, Colorized, and Color)	Manufacturing	DBA
Contract Text	Stores reusable riders, clauses, footnotes, and terms and conditions	Legal	Application owner
Geo	Stores the valid list of geographic areas or territories (for example, Western Europe, France, and Lyon)	Shipping	Application owner
Grade	Stores the valid list of grades used to qualify a product (for example, A++, B, and C)	M. Martin	End client
Language	Stores the valid list of languages (for example, German, Spanish, and English)	Legal	Application owner

Alternatively, you may want to create typed lists within tables, as in Table 15-4, where all the status lists are implemented in one table, called Status, using a type code to differentiate them.

Table 15-4. *Sample Status Codes Values and Their Owners/Stewards*

Status Lists	Status Definition	Current Known Values	Owner
Activity status	The status of an activity remark as it's routed for review	Open and Resolved	Unknown
Company status	The status of a company record	Active and Inactive	Finance
Geo status	The status of a geographic area record	Active and Inactive	Shipping
Product status	The status of an existing product	Active and Inactive	Marketing
Proposal sales order status	The status of a proposal sales order through its life cycle	Pending, Signed, Unsigned, Clean, and Unclean	Sales

Don't confuse stewardship with security. Having sufficient privileges to change data values is different from whether you're responsible for ensuring they're correct. The person with the security privilege to add records to a table may be a different person than the table's assigned data steward (although in that case these people will likely be working closely together).

Cross-Footing

Cross-footing is the action of using different data sources or methods to reproduce the same result set. It's a truth test for your data. The more ways you have to verify the quality of your data, the more power and value the data wields.

Derivations

You probably have many data elements that are stored repeatedly in different systems without the checks and balances needed to keep everything in sync. For example, some reports contain derived values. Sometimes you might store these derived values in tables, probably most often in data warehouse tables. One way to mitigate the risk of inconsistent derived values is to provide cross-footing validation from other sources. You may want to create a cross-footing analysis as shown in Table 15-5.

Table 15-5. *Cross-Footing Information for Monthly Gross Sales Amount*

Data Value	Formula	Cross-Foot Formula
Monthly gross sales amount	Sum (Daily Gross Sales Amount) for all sales falling within one calendar month as defined in the daily sales summary procedure	Sum (Transaction level: Sale Amount + Tax Amount – Discount Amount) for all sales falling within one calendar month for all departments

Look at the formula and cross-foot formula in Table 15-5. You may find that the validation consistently arrives at a larger number than the formula currently being used. When you do more research, you may find that the daily sales summary procedure doesn't remove "return" transactions from the summation. Creating the two aggregated figures and tracking down the differences can help uncover existing anomalies.

■**Note** You can prevent serious data audit problems by double-checking your figures against different sources of the same data. Your team will have to determine which alternate sources are appropriate and what the correct frequency of this validation should be.

Reasonability Checks

You may be able to set up data quality reasonability checks. These checks focus on identifying gross errors in data by setting maximum and minimum limits on the individual values. You might set a reasonability check that the weight of a patient is always between 1 and 1,000 kilos or that any equivalent weight measured in pounds will always be a larger number than a weight measured in kilos, for example. Although you can implement these kinds of reasonability validations as relational database constraints, often you'll be analyzing data whose source isn't relational and where no equivalent validation is available or where your relational data source had few check constraints implemented. Table 15-6 shows sample reasonability checks you might consider for columns found in the hypothetical Employee, Item, and Shipment tables.

Table 15-6. *Examples of Reasonability Checks*

Table	Column	Reasonability Rules
Employee	Hire Date	Never earlier than company origin date Never later than today
Item	Master Pack Quantity	Always greater than one
Shipment	Bill of Lading Total Weight	Never greater than equipment weight rating

Process Validation

As the modeler, you probably know the business rules in the model better than anyone; therefore, you'll probably be the one to do any process validation. You can test for the business rules by exercising the front-end screens and reports and by querying the tables to watch for appropriate data behavior. You may want to take the business activity descriptions (sometimes called *use cases*) and follow a record from creation to deletion to verify the data is being handled as intended. Sometimes there's a slip-up in the deployment of the plan. Catching it before it goes to production can save a lot of analysis later.

Make a checklist of your relationship and cardinality statements. Open the application tool, and test it by exercising the functionality that has been provided. Review the screens and reports, and check for the ability to create and report multivalued relationships even when normally only one exists (such as an e-mail address in the following example). You may even need to try the screens and then analyze the database tables to verify that what you think should be happening is indeed happening.

Make sure you validate the business rules you documented in your model, such as the following:

- Every employee may be contacted at zero, one, or many e-mail addresses.

- Every item must have one or more item versions.

- Every organization must be staffed with one or more employees.

- Every department may be located in zero, one, or many staffed sites.

- Every site may be the location of zero, one, or many staffed sites.

Tip You analyzed the processes that helped build the software. Sometimes that makes you a valuable resource to the test team that's verifying the design requirements made it to implementation.

Risk and Mitigation Analysis

As a data modeler, you also need to document anything you find that makes you nervous about a proposed data management technique. Most data management risks threaten non-compliance with one of the data quality checks we've already discussed. You must document and communicate any data issues dealing with the following (currently or in the future):

- Table/columns not being used as designed
- Data not being recognized as being mission-critical
- Data not being recognized as being enterprise-sensitive
- No one being responsible for data quality
- No checking of data values for reasonability
- No double-checking of calculated values
- No ongoing verification of growing enterprise data concepts being handled correctly
- Data being collected without any understood business need or projected future use (the "let's record everything" syndrome)

A risk and mitigation analysis combines what you found in the previous analysis with the following:

- Categorizes each issue as high, medium, or low risk
- Justifies the categorization with a potential impact statement
- Documents the actual solution to remove the risk
- Suggests methods of mitigating or reducing the risk by means other than the current solution

Risk mitigation doesn't eliminate the risk; it makes the risk less severe. You may want to encourage a suggestion box or add an online problem-reporting application to gather intelligence from around the company about data shortcomings stemming from inadequate functionality, rule shortcomings, or changed business processes. Gathering and reviewing the options can help the IT department manage responses by providing possible solutions and mitigation plans.

You may want to provide something like the examples in the following tables. This type of analysis can help build strong communication ties between the business clients and the data management team. The brainstorming that has to occur between the groups to solve the issues is an opportunity to stay in touch with the evolution of the data elements, in terms of both definition and usage. Table 15-7 shows potential data management risks.

Table 15-7. *Potential Data Management Issues*

Description	Potential Impact	Impact Analysis	Solution	Mitigation Options
Customers with an Unsatisfactory credit rating are still available in the pull-down list on the Order screen. New orders are allowed to be created for them.	High	There could be an increase in severely past due billing and/or eventual bad debt that the company will need to absorb. (The cost is to be determined.)	Remove customer name from the pull-down list until credit rating is Satisfactory or better.	Allow *x* worth of orders while still in Unsatisfactory credit rating. Will need to check rating and billing amount and status of open orders. Allow manager overrides to system rules. Allow the accounts receivable group to suspend and reinstate customer order privileges.
Regional managers have only one contact phone and an e-mail address in the system.	Medium	There's often an urgent requirement to communicate with the regional managers. One phone number and one e-mail address aren't enough ways to contact them.	Add a "many" table for both phone numbers and e-mail addresses for employees.	Manage extra contact information data outside the current system and enforce that it's to be secured and accessed by rules within the operations department. Expand the current field lengths, and change the definition of the fields to Phone Contact Information and E-mail Contact Information. This will allow the clients to add however much information they want. Get all the regional managers 24/7 pagers, and use the pager number in the Phone Contact Information field.

Description	Potential Impact	Impact Analysis	Solution	Mitigation Options
Order system is susceptible to being offline on weekends and evenings. IT doesn't provide 24/7 help support.	Medium	The order department has to revert to a manual system when this happens and then input the orders later. There's always a potential for "lost" orders and bad data written on the forms without the access to the system's data integrity.	Add a 24/7 help desk to the IT charter. Fix whatever is impacting the order system.	Have a floating primary support assignment for the IT department. Person on "primary duty" to carry a pager for the duration of the assignment. Develop rollover application support that allows the clients to use a backup system to be merged invisibly when the system problem has been diagnosed and returned to online status.

Using the Data Model As a Knowledge Framework

We're biased about the value an enterprise will get from a high-quality data model. At the onset of each modeling effort, we can envision how each high-level entity connects to other entities in other models or to business functions. Each conceptual entity can result in many logical entities, and each logical entity can be deployed either as a single table or as multiple physical tables, which in turn can be deployed in multiple locations. These tables can be the foundation for many applications, code blocks, screens, reports, and Web sites. In an ideal world, each of the concepts, entities, and tables has an owner and a steward. Highly skilled people maintain the concepts and physical implementations. Business processes would grind to a halt without them.

Documenting the connectivity between elements, as well as the ability to trace these connections and audit them, is critical to managing an enterprise's information. As an activity, *mapping* is a term used to describe the indexing and tracking of these interrelationships. As a document, a *mapping* describes how these elements interrelate.

At the beginning of this book we discussed how data elements can be conceptual, logical, and physical. We followed the transition of data elements from high-level concepts to actual physical table columns. You can easily create a mapping to show how these concepts relate. What may not be quite so obvious is how you can map your models and data elements to other concepts.

You can map your data or data model entities to the following:

- Physical hardware (showing how the data is used with development, test, production, and backup servers or individual desktop computers, routers, and printers)

- Program code (showing how the data supports screens, reports, and procedures)

- Other documents (showing how the entities figure in project plans, in standards, and in change control processes)

- Locations (showing where data is physically or virtually located)

- Other models (showing sources of data, versions, and subject areas)

- Organizations (showing how the data relates to the project sponsor, other interested parties, and your data security organization)

- Pathways (showing the data's flow through the network, ETL processes, and load routines)

- People (showing individuals responsible for data authorship, stewardship, and support)

- Processes (showing how data supports system processes)

Since mappings document interrelationships, this discussion will highlight how you can use the data models as a starting place for discovering connections between data and other things. If you've built and maintained mappings prior to starting a project, you can save a lot of time not having to research known business processes, validate data element definitions, and discover data relationship rules. Mappings may also reduce the amount of time you have to spend on determining the impact of a given change by being able to quickly show you which hardware, software, networks, code, screens, and clients are affected. You may be able to justify additional budget or staff by being able to provide an overview of the complexity of your data management environment. Using mappings can help ensure the smooth loading of data in the event of system upgrades or the introduction of new applications.

■**Note** Data mappings help you quickly see the interdependencies between your data structures, data definitions, data owners, business concepts, physical hardware, and software applications.

If mappings are stored in a central repository, you can create a "Where Used" report to help you determine the impact of a potential change. You'll now review a sample "Where Used" report for the EmployeeID column of the Employee table.

This sample report first shows the data element's basic definition captured during a prior modeling effort (see Table 15-8).

Table 15-8. *A Basic Definition for* EmployeeID

Data Element	Definition
EMPLOYEE.EMPLOYEE ID	The nonsignificant, system-generated, surrogate key that uniquely identifies an employee

The next section shows which servers currently house this data element (see Table 15-9). Note the existence of a different server for each phase of the development life cycle.

Table 15-9. *The Servers Housing the* `EmployeeID` *Data Element*

General Purpose of Element in Main Computing System	General Hardware Use Description	Hardware Name
Original creation on	Production box	STDHP001
Three-year backup on	Backup box	STDHP006
Final archive	To disk	Off-site disk storage location 2
Release test area	QA: beta test box	STDHP003
Development test area	Integration: alpha test box	STDHP010
Development area	Programmer development box	STDHP015
Development area	Programmer development box	SQLSERV008
Development area	Programmer development box	SQLSERV010

The following section shows how program code uses the `EmployeeID` data element (see Table 15-10).

Table 15-10. *The References to* `EmployeeID` *in Program Code*

General Purpose of Element in Programming Code	Code Type	Code Name
Production creation	Screen	`EmpStartInput`
Production query	Screen	`EmpFind`
Production report restriction	Screen	`EmpHistoryReportParam`
Employee history identification	Report	`EmpHistoryRpt`
Payroll check identification	Report	`SalaryCheckCreationRep`
Security privilege allocation	Procedure	`AssignPriv.sql`

The following section of the report shows the existing documents where this data element is referenced (see Table 15-11).

Table 15-11. *Documents Containing References to* `EmployeeID`

General Purpose of Element in Document	Document Type	Document Name
HR application description	Training manual	People Manager 2.5 Training Guide
Integration review for merging international and domestic applications	Project proposal	Human Resource Consolidation in 2009
Company standards	Data format standard	IT Data Element Development Standard 1.9
Change to format from number to text to allow for more characters in company acquisition (legacy data)	Change control	CC 2345345.5

The last section of the report shows which data models contain the data element (see Table 15-12).

Table 15-12. *Data Models Containing the Attribute* EmployeeID

General Purpose of Model	Model Type	Model Name
Human resources consolidation analysis	Conceptual	HRConsolidation Preview
Reverse engineer of People Manager 2.5	Physical	PeopleManager25
As-Is and To-Be analysis for change control CC 2345345.5	Physical	CC2345345AsIsToBe

We've simplified this example; in most enterprises, a complete EmployeeID report would show pages and pages of mappings. Creating a complete repository of all the relationships between your data elements and other items in your enterprise requires a significant effort. But the panic and confusion felt during the Y2K crisis would likely have been reduced if we could have relied on dependable documentation of this type.

Relationships to the Conceptual Model

Since Conceptual models are generally at a high level, they map to high-level visions within the enterprise. You can document relationships to the Conceptual model or to the entities the model contains. Depending on the purpose of your mapping, you might choose to document the relationships between the following:

- The Conceptual model and its scope, purpose, or sponsor

- The conceptual entities and the high-level concepts and definitions

- The relationships documented on the Conceptual model and the business's rules and policies

- The general notes found on the Conceptual model and any outstanding policy, regulatory, or other issues

Your Conceptual model can map to the following:

- New company initiatives such as a data warehouse project or a customer relationship management (CRM) system. Your Conceptual model could document the expected data foundation (scope) that the project would cover.

- Subject area models that add a certain level of detail to the highest conceptual thoughts. Remember that subject areas often overlap; you may need to note more than one.

- Documentation from projects that were spawned by it, vendor documentation (if that data is being managed by a purchased software package), or even whitepapers and analysis documents about the conceptual subject area.

■**Note** The hardest thing about this type of documentation is knowing when to begin, when to stop, and how to keep it accurate.

You'll now look at an example of a Conceptual model and what mappings might exist. Refer to the Conceptual model of a marketing department, as shown in Figure 15-1.

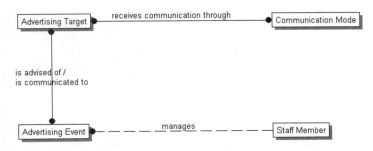

Figure 15-1. *The marketing department's Conceptual model*

Given the Conceptual model shown in Figure 15-1, what other objects within the enterprise might be related to it? In this example, say you discover that a CRM initiative exists that affects the marketing department. Table 15-13 shows the mapping.

Table 15-13. *Enterprise Initiatives Related to the Conceptual Model*

Model Name	Enterprise Initiative	Status	Reason
Marketing Conceptual	CRM	In review	Possible enhancement to the marketing application giving more visibility to the planned and actual advertising targets by event

This mapping is at a high level; it maps the entire conceptual subject of the marketing department to the CRM initiative. If you had more information, you might be able to create a more detailed mapping, such as Table 15-14, which maps the Conceptual model to the Logical model.

Table 15-14. *A Mapping of the Conceptual Model Entities to the Logical Model Entities*

Model Name	Entity Name	Entity Definition	Logical Entity
Marketing Conceptual	Advertising Event	An advertising event is a communication activity, which is sponsored by an enterprise and carried out by an enterprise, that announces opportunities to an advertising target through one or more communication modes.	Communications Logical–Communication Advertising Logical–Advertising Message
Marketing Conceptual	Advertising Target	An advertising target may be a person, family, or audience. Each target receives communications about advertised events through an advertising model.	Marketing Logical–Client Advertising Logical–Household Communications Logical–Person Communications Logical–Company Communications Logical–Contact
Marketing Conceptual	Communication Mode	A communication mode is a method of deploying and disseminating information either with a specific receiver (such as mail and phone call) or to an intended audience via a billboard, a radio, or a television.	Advertising Logical–Address Advertising Logical–E-mail Advertising Logical–Phone
Marketing Conceptual	Staff Member	A staff member is an employee or contractor who is working with the enterprise to plan, deploy, manage, and review advertising events.	HR Logical–Employee Enterprise Logical–Work Force

These examples may make it seem easy to create mappings, but it's quite exacting and tedious work. It is, however, a wonderful tool to use when you just want to do something such as clarify the Communication Mode concept, for example. It's sometimes hard to justify the effort needed to create this kind of mapping until you're under pressure to research something like this. The Y2K problem wouldn't have caused so much concern if we had just known how big the problem was. Without this kind of documentation, the impact of change is unknown and requires research. If you have this kind of documentation, you should be able to refer to it and at least get a general answer, even if it isn't a complete answer.

Relationships to the Logical Model

The Logical model documents data in a way that's a little closer to what we recognize in the physical world. As documentation, the Logical model is the hub connecting Logical, Conceptual, and Physical models together. It also serves as the document that connects people, processes, departments, budgets, justifications, and schedules to the data. Figure 15-2 shows the critical positioning of the Logical model.

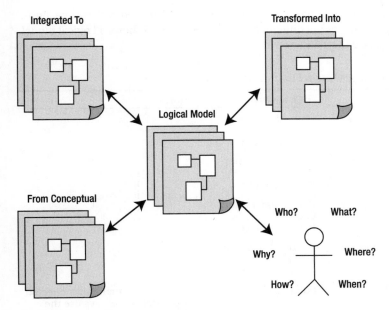

Figure 15-2. *Relationships to and from the Logical model*

Again, you have to choose what connections you want to document. Are you documenting a relationship between something and the model, or are you documenting relationships to the Logical model entities? Let's look at an example of a logical mapping by examining a single entity from the marketing department's Logical model. Figure 15-3 shows the Address entity from that model.

Figure 15-3. *The* Address *entity from the marketing department's Logical model*

For this logical Address entity, you may want to document the expected data source. Entities without well-defined data sources are difficult to deploy. Table 15-15 shows a Logical model mapping between attributes and their data sources.

Table 15-15. *A Mapping of the Logical Model to Its Data Sources*

Entity Name	Attribute Name	Data Source	Note
Address	City Name	Phone Solicitation Web Site Purchased List	
Address	Street Name	Phone Solicitation Web Site Purchased List	
Address	State Name	Phone Solicitation Web Site Purchased List	
Address	Country Name	Phone Solicitation Web Site Purchased List	
Address	Postal Code	Purchased List	We don't use manually collected zip codes. We always use the latest vendor file.
Address	Communication Address ID	System	
Address	Room Number	Phone Solicitation Web Site Purchased List	
Address	Building Number	Phone Solicitation Web Site Purchased List	
Address	Room Type Name	Phone Solicitation Web Site	

This type of mapping is helpful when trying to determine which data sources you need to represent all the required data elements in your model.

Relationships to the Physical Model

The Physical model represents physical data structures as they're to be deployed. As such, the Physical model relates to many other physical items used in deploying and supporting an application. Physical models are related to the physical hardware upon which they're deployed, the users who access them, the data the databases store, and the other systems that push or pull physical data to or from the deployed database. Figure 15-4 shows how the Physical model relates to other physical objects that are part of the solution.

Physical object mappings are the most commonly found mappings in use in enterprises today. They're found in many IT groups; DBAs have mappings of applications to servers, programmers have mappings of code blocks to database names, and both groups have mappings showing which databases are on which servers. The infrastructure team also has mappings showing virtual addresses related to the various computing locations throughout the enterprise.

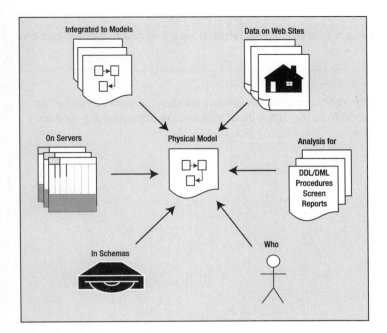

Figure 15-4. *Relationships to the Physical model*

Unfortunately, we don't always share the mappings we create; therefore, you'll find that effort is often duplicated between groups. For example, the DBAs want to know what data elements are on what server. The programmers want to know what data elements are referenced in what code. The network team wants to know what servers are moving data across the T1 lines from the Web. The security team wants to know which data elements are being shared between which groups. Everyone has a slightly different need for knowing about these interrelationships, but all groups basically want to understand where certain data elements are, where they're going to be in the future, and the means by which they move between the physical servers.

Using the Physical data model as a starting place for all physical mappings is a good idea. But if you use the model in this way, it's absolutely necessary to keep the model valid at all times and synchronized with the physical environments. Fortunately, many modeling software tools offer the ability to compare physical databases with a model and to highlight the differences. If you have this kind of tool, your work in keeping your model up-to-date will be easier; if you don't have this capability, you'll need to spend time manually comparing the database against its model.

Admittedly, a freshly reverse-engineered Physical model is more often used as the source data for physical mappings than documented models. However, sometimes you may not have the access to reverse engineer certain tables. The model, however, is usually public, and the team that manages these models is usually accessible (unlike some DBA groups). The challenge in creating Physical model maps is in how all this mapping information can be stored in a repository that simultaneously provides flexible reporting and the correct security. A product called MetaCenter (`www.dataag.com`) allows you to use named ERwin objects (entities, attributes, and so on) to set up mappings to database objects, documents, or in fact pretty much anything you'd like.

■**Note** New data management software is constantly being released. You should be aware of new tools that might help you do your job.

The example of physical data model mappings will use a small subject area model of the Employees table reverse engineered from the SQL Server 2000 version of Northwind, as shown in Figure 15-5.

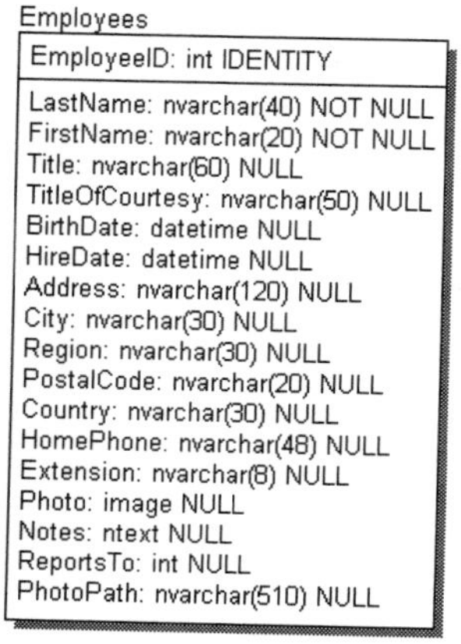

Employees
EmployeeID: int IDENTITY

LastName: nvarchar(40) NOT NULL
FirstName: nvarchar(20) NOT NULL
Title: nvarchar(60) NULL
TitleOfCourtesy: nvarchar(50) NULL
BirthDate: datetime NULL
HireDate: datetime NULL
Address: nvarchar(120) NULL
City: nvarchar(30) NULL
Region: nvarchar(30) NULL
PostalCode: nvarchar(20) NULL
Country: nvarchar(30) NULL
HomePhone: nvarchar(48) NULL
Extension: nvarchar(8) NULL
Photo: image NULL
Notes: ntext NULL
ReportsTo: int NULL
PhotoPath: nvarchar(510) NULL

Figure 15-5. *The physical* Employees *table from the Northwind model*

Table 15-16 shows a mapping of each physical column to its corresponding logical attribute name, as well as the stored procedures where it's referenced in code.

Table 15-16. *A Mapping of the Physical Model Columns to Their Logical Model Attributes and Existing Stored Procedures*

Table Name	Column Name	Data Type	Attribute Name	Stored Procedure Name
Employees	EmployeeID	Identity	Employee Identifier	EmployeeIns.sql EmployeeUpd.sql EmployeeDel.sql JobChangeUpd.sql BadgeUpd.sql
Employees	LastName	nvarchar(40)	Employee Last Name	EmployeeIns.sql EmployeeUpd.sql
Employees	FirstName	nvarchar(20)	Employee First Name	EmployeeIns.sql EmployeeUpd.sql
Employees	Title	nvarchar(60)	Employee Job Title Name	EmployeeIns.sql EmployeeUpd.sql JobChangeUpd.sql

Table Name	Column Name	Data Type	Attribute Name	Stored Procedure Name
Employees	TitleOfCourtesy	nvarchar(50)	Employee Title of Courtesy Name	EmployeeIns.sql EmployeeUpd.sql
Employees	BirthDate	datetime	Employee Birth Date	EmployeeIns.sql EmployeeUpd.sql
Employees	HireDate	datetime	Employee Hire Date	EmployeeIns.sql EmployeeUpd.sql
Employees	Extension	nvarchar(8)	Employee Phone Number Phone Type=Company	EmployeeIns.sql EmployeeUpd.sql
Employees	Photo	image	Employee Photo Image	EmployeeIns.sql EmployeeUpd.sql BadgeUpd.sql
Employees	Notes	ntext	Employee Note Text	EmployeeIns.sql EmployeeUpd.sql
Employees	ReportsTo	int	Manager Employee ID	EmployeeIns.sql EmployeeUpd.sql JobChangeUpd.sql
Employees	PhotoPath	nvarchar(510)	Employee Photo Access Path Text	EmployeeIns.sql EmployeeUpd.sql BadgeUpd.sql

■**Note** In a real-world application, you'd expect many more stored procedures to be listed in the Stored Procedure Name column.

Note that all the columns are referenced in the INSERT and UPDATE procedures, but only EmployeeID is referenced in the DELETE procedure. There's also a process to update the EmployeeID badge image (BadgeUpd.sql) that uses EmployeeID, Photo, and PhotoPath. And finally there's a procedure to change an employee's job classification (JobChangeUpd.sql) that also uses the EmployeeID, Title, and ReportsTo columns.

This type of mapping allows you to see the potential impact of table structure changes. You can see at a glance which columns will have the largest impact on the stored procedures.

Pedigree Mappings

Ever wonder where a report's data originated? An old story is that a chief financial officer (CFO) separately asked four different vice presidents the same question: "What was the total gross sales from the western region last quarter?" And he gets four different answers! What's disconcerting is that each of them brought him an *IT- produced report*!

You may find yourself in requirements meetings where hours are spent trying to decide *which* net sales figure to use or *which* data source is the most appropriate place to find that data. Now, we don't mind that there's a need to build three different summations of a sales total, but it does bother us when we publish them with identical labels and no way to determine which method was used to calculate the total. A simple report label change or a note in the report footer would correct this problem.

After all, how important is it to know how a derived value was calculated? Ask anyone on the data warehouse team. They deal with many disparate figures sourced from different systems all over the enterprise. The only way to manage these derived figures is to trace the data pedigree to its source and determine why the figures are different.

■**Note** We spent part of our careers with a highly successful data warehousing team. It's sad to say that after implementation the business analysts spent a lot of time proving that the figures in the reports were indeed correct. Each customer had reports showing summations, averages, and totals that disagreed with ours. We knew where we had sourced the data; the real challenge was to figure out what data they had used and then to explain the discrepancies in formulas, sources, or timing.

Table 15-17 shows a pedigree mapping.

Table 15-17. *Pedigree for Total Quarter Manufacturing Hours on the Finance Budget Quarter Report*

System	Process Step	Note
Payroll database and manufacturing database	Add the worked hours for each shift in the work month.	
Payroll database and manufacturing database	Calculate the overtime hours and multiply by 1.5. Add the inflated overtime hour quantity.	Finance wants to see hours in terms of pay rate.
Rework database	Minus hours used for setup, maintenance, and rework.	
MRP database	Add 20 percent management hours.	For overhead adjustment.

Table 15-17 is a sample of what a pedigree would look like, but you may want to supplement the example by documenting the procedure or report code block that eventually placed it on the report.

Role Name Mappings

This is one of the most useful mappings you can create. Everyone wants to be able to follow database relationships. They want to know where to find the most common keys. But sometimes these keys aren't easily recognizable because they've changed their names through role naming.

A role name mapping follows the path of a key as it migrates between entities or tables. A key may migrate to its owning entity, as in the example of an employee's supervisor also being an employee. That same employee key may migrate to the Item table with the role name of Inspected by. It may even migrate to another system or application through an integration process. When that happens, it's easy to lose sight of what it is and where it originated.

▩**Note** Keep track of where data elements have migrated and what they're called in the other entity. This will save you a lot of time when you need to do an impact analysis of making changes to that column.

For an example, let's look at a portion of the marketing department's Logical model, as shown in Figure 15-6.

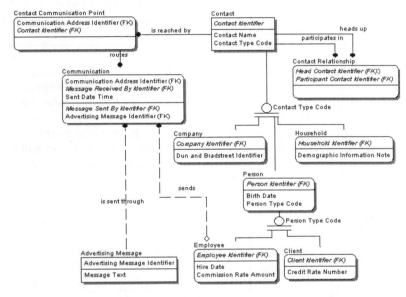

Figure 15-6. *A portion of the marketing department's Logical model*

Note the italicized attributes, which all represent Contact Id, even though they may have different attribute names because of role naming. Table 15-18 shows a role name mapping for this model.

Table 15-18. *A Role Name Mapping for the Marketing Logical Model*

Entity Name	Entity Base Name	Attribute Base Name	Role Name
Person	Contact	Contact Identifier	Person Identifier
Client	Contact	Contact Identifier	Client Identifier
Company	Contact	Contact Identifier	Company Identifier
Contact Communication Point	Contact	Contact Identifier	Contact Identifier

Continued

Table 15-18. *Continued*

Entity Name	Entity Base Name	Attribute Base Name	Role Name
Household	Contact	Contact Identifier	Household Identifier
Employee	Contact	Contact Identifier	Employee Identifier
Contact Relationship	Contact	Contact Identifier	Head Contact Identifier
Communication	Contact	Contact Identifier	Message Received by Identifier
Communication	Contact	Contact Identifier	Message Sent By Identifier
Contact Relationship	Contact	Contact Identifier	Participant Contact Identifier

It's now quite easy to recognize all the Contact Id references in this system. Role naming can be a valid part of designing data structures, but if the name just seems to change without much thought, it can be confusing. With this type of mapping, you can see exactly to where the data element has migrated and its new name, if any.

Although the previous example discussed the Logical model, you can also create a role name mapping for the physical design. This mapping can also be helpful in following key values from table to table. Figure 15-7 shows the Physical model for the marketing department example.

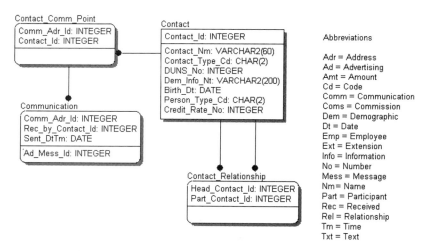

Figure 15-7. *The Physical model for the marketing department*

Table 15-19 shows a role name mapping for this Physical model.

Table 15-19. *A Role Name Mapping for the Physical Model*

Table Name	Column Base Name	Foreign Key Column Name
Contact_Comm_Point	Contact.Contact_Id	Contact_Id
Communication	Contact_Comm_Point.Contact_Id	Rec_by_Contact_Id
Contact_Relationship	Contact.Contact_Id	Head_Contact_Id
Contact_Relationship	Contact.Contact_Id	Part_Contact_Id

Summary

In this chapter, you looked at data quality issues and the analysis that can help identify and address them. We discussed suggestions for analysis that should be addressed up front in the Logical modeling process. Unfortunately, in our experience modeling software doesn't store this information (although some gives you options of creating user-defined elements to deal with these issues). When creating mapping, documentation becomes more common; the tools will probably adapt to store this information and provide the capability to track what you've discovered for each entity, table, attribute, and column. We discussed documenting the following:

- Data fidelity

- Data criticality

- Data sensitivity and privacy

- Data stewardship

- Cross-footing as a method of validating data

- Data process validation

- Risk identification and mitigation

You also looked at creating mappings, which are documents that help you manage the relationships between your models and other documentation, organizations, and requirements. Keeping this type of information in mapping documents is a stopgap measure that you'll have to continue until metadata management becomes an integral part of your enterprise. In discussing mapping documents, you looked at many different examples, including the following:

- Conceptual mappings

- Logical mappings

- Physical mappings

- Pedigree traces

- Data element roles

CHAPTER 16

Introducing Metadata Modeling

In this chapter, we'll cover *metadata*, a topic that has grown over the past few years and has gained an independent body of knowledge of its own in data management. It's data about data—information that gives you an overview *about* software/business process solutions rather than the data values organized *in* such solutions. Having a repository that contains information about known data quality problems, for example, is helpful in identifying potential issues with extraction, transformation, and loading (ETL) or even the database design. Descriptions of the data contained in your systems (from the perspective of both form and function) and how the data is used can be instrumental in enabling you to manage the full scope of tasks, goals, and strategies taking place in data management teams.

From a data modeler's perspective, metadata is another data modeling project with another set of clients and another set of data. But because you use the metadata in modeling, managing, and maintaining your documentation, you're also part of the client group and must contribute your own requirements and business processes to the project.

In this chapter, you'll examine the following:

- Metadata definitions

- Metadata uses

- Metadata data models

- Metadata research

Defining Metadata

The definition of metadata you'll hear most often is that it's "data about data," but metadata could be defined just as easily as "knowledge about knowledge" or "information about information."

These definitions have a certain appeal in their simplicity. Think of all the resources in your public library that exist only to help you find the resources that can provide answers to your questions. Those tools are the starting place for most research. For example, you use the *Guide to Periodicals* to find articles by subject or by author. You also use encyclopedias, bibliographies, card catalogs, computer search tools, dictionaries, and anthologies; these are tools that contain collections of prebuilt sets of "knowledge about knowledge" organized in such a way that they help reduce the time it takes you to find an answer.

In a library setting, metadata exists at many different levels. Individual books have indexes and tables of contents that help you find what you're looking for more specifically than a card catalog does. Even chapters within a book often have a bulleted summary of their contents. These are all metadata elements. They aren't always aggregated into a single repository, but they all perform the same function, which is to provide pointers to locations of more information or to present summarized statistics. You'll actually hear people refer to meta-metadata or, in other words, information regarding information about data.

■Note A *metadata repository* is a "card catalog" for enterprise data.

In David Marco's *Building and Managing the Meta Data Repository: A Full Lifecycle Guide* (Wiley, 2000), Marco gives a more comprehensive definition of metadata.

> *Meta data is all physical data (contained in software and other media) and knowledge (contained in employees and various media) from inside and outside an organization, including information about the physical data, technical and business processes, rules and constraints of the data, and structures of the data used by a corporation.*

From this definition you can see that everything we've discussed with regard to analyzing, developing, or modeling data in this book can be enterprise metadata. If you can't search an existing collection of metadata about your enterprise's physical data, business processes, data rules and constraints, or data structure organization, then you'll waste time rediscovering and capturing this information. You may even increase waste in your enterprise by duplicating processes, data stores, and functionality that's thriving in some isolated corner of the company only because you have no way of knowing it exists or finding out whether it meets your needs.

■Note Reinventing anything that exists (without adding any additional value) is a waste of time, money, and resources. Data duplication is sometimes intentional (for performance reasons), but it needs to be managed and planned, not accidental.

You could look at metadata as the information by-product of everything you do. You can glean information from your plans, designs, implementations, and post-implementation experience. We all have a disparate set of media and environments from which to gather data. Furthermore, you can store this data in a wide variety of formats, such as the following:

- On desktop computers
- On paper
- On visual, aural, and animated media

- On a mainframe

- On a server

- In models, mappings, and definitions

- On Web sites

- In people's memories

Metadata management is the means by which you fit this "data puzzle" together. Although you'll always have a need for solutions to problems that use the diversity and uniqueness of each data platform and tool, you need to maintain virtual connections to all the enterprise data sources so that your understanding of the puzzle stays valid and up-to-date. Figure 16-1 shows a few of the many potential sources of metadata.

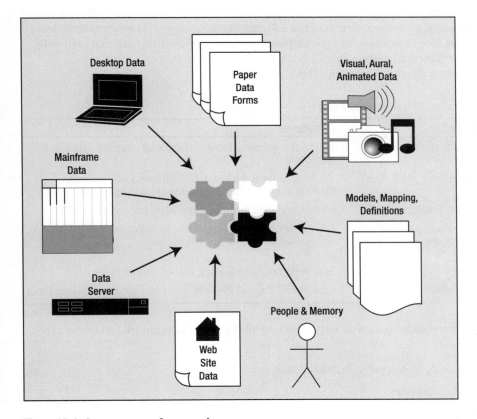

Figure 16-1. *Some sources for metadata*

In Figure 16-1, the puzzle pieces represent an *enterprise metadata repository*. This repository stores and manages all the metadata captured from various sources in various formats from across the company.

An example of a metadata repository is a library's information asset catalog. If you start every project with a trip to a repository, you may find that a great deal of what you've been tasked to provide already exists. You may need to modify some structures to meet your specific needs, but the basic information will be there.

You can collect metadata about every process and procedure; this involves more than just capturing facts about tables and columns. Metadata can be information based on lessons learned from experience or trial projects and is generally divided into two major groupings: technical metadata and business metadata.

Technical Metadata

Technical metadata refers to information about applications, tools, and systems supporting the enterprise data management solutions. It includes information about database structures, front-end objects, networks, hardware, software, and the relationships between them.

This information supports designers, developers, and administrators during the development, maintenance, and management of the information technology (IT) environment. Metadata documents the connections of tools, applications, and systems that combine to provide answers to your information questions.

Table 16-1 lists examples of technical metadata.

Table 16-1. *Technical Metadata Examples*

Technical Metadata	Description
Infrastructure information	Hardware, software, connectivity, and capacity (used and available)
Deployed data storage structures	Table/column names, data definitions, keys, indexes, domain values, archiving strategy, and purge rules
Programs/code information	Names and descriptions, dependencies, and schedules
Integration: data load process information of internal and external data sources	Data elements, mapping source to target, frequency, conversion rules, and encoding rules
Report and query	Access patterns, frequency, and execution time
Data model information	Conceptual, Logical, Physical, and the mappings between them

Technical metadata also involves connecting all the items in Table 16-1 in terms of the following:

- Relationships or mappings between them

- Version information

- Security information

- Audit controls and balancing

- Project and team relationships

You can see that this metadata encompasses machines, networks, and software. You can use this information to be able to generate your own statistics, trends, and overviews of how the IT world works. You can also use it to streamline the processing of data requests by being able to easily locate and target solution requirements.

Business Metadata

Business metadata focuses on making technical metadata understandable and usable by the business community. It provides explanations, mappings, road maps, and translations of the technical solutions and the business needs. This type of metadata is built with the help of the business community and helps businesses know how to tap into the rich data resources available to them. Table 16-2 lists some examples of business metadata.

Table 16-2. *Business Metadata Examples*

Business Metadata	Description
Dictionary of names, term translations, and definitions	Physical structure to business terms, technical terminology, and business terminology
Subject areas information	Definitions, content, and location
Data quality information	Rules and statistics, pedigree mappings in terms of relative values of particular data sets, and data restriction/domain rules
Rules for preprocessed data elements	Description of exact rules for summations, derivations, formulations, and the justification of which data sets are included in aggregations and which are excluded
Data element business parameters	Stewardship assignments, criticality assessment, and sensitivity assessment
General data-processing information	Refresh dates, error handling, archive strategy, and purge rules

You may sense a bit of overlap between technical metadata and business metadata. Business metadata generally supports clients who need to understand the business implications of data rather than the details of collecting and storing it. These are often data miners doing ad hoc querying from the decision support structures, or they may be power users who need to identify and locate the correct sources to use to answer their questions.

Live Metadata

Other things that aren't created as reference collections of facts about data are sometimes referred to as metadata. These metadata values serve as critical variables inside actual code and tools.

One of the challenges of any metadata repository is that once the metadata is collected, it's disconnected from the processes it describes. A danger exists that your metadata may fall out of step with reality. It takes serious discipline to maintain metadata outside of automated processes. Some metadata repository applications try to resolve these issues by maintaining connectivity, or simply providing visibility, to these sources rather than building a separate, static collection of metadata information.

Document management tools that can maintain lists and hierarchies of their contents exist. For example, data model management software such as Computer Associates' Model-Mart keeps the models and their contents in a database.

■**Note** Gathering and reporting metadata from live sources guarantees a certain level of validity with reality, preventing separate lists of metadata from getting out of sync.

.NET and XML

In .NET and Extensible Markup Language (XML), metadata is defined as self-describing data that's built in such a way that you don't need to refer to another document to understand what the data represents. In other words, the metadata tells you what it's about. The most common examples of this kind of metadata are XML code files and .NET assemblies. For example, a .NET assembly contains its own metadata and can provide information about itself to the Windows operating system so that the operating system no longer has to look in the Windows Registry (or catalog) for this information. This isn't the case with Component Object Model (COM) objects, which have no metadata and aren't self-describing. Their information is held or registered separately in the Windows Registry under HKEY_LOCAL_MACHINE.

Self-describing structures are often used in Electronic Data Interchange (EDI) tasks where the source and target need cooperative data standardization for two parties to be able to interact. The definition of what the data elements *represent* in the metadata is as important as the values themselves. However, even self-describing data needs to be accessible to centralized research, or it too becomes isolated and disconnected from the business world that it supports. You still need a central repository where this data is collected.

ETL and EAI Tool Catalogs

ETL software creates maps and processes that move data from sources to targets. Each mapping includes any rules for error handling and conversion that are needed to move and consolidate records. These tools are frequently used to supply operational data stores (ODS), decision support systems (DSS), and data warehouses with their data.

These files—or *mappings,* as they're called—are considered metadata sources and are often tapped into directly to provide business views of data pedigrees (see Chapter 15) and graphical views of ETL process flows. This type of software stores that information in its own repository; again, metadata is best used if it's available to everyone.

DBMS Library Catalog Tables

When we make references here to *library catalog tables,* we mean database management systems in the most generic sense. Any type of data storage system, whether it's a relational, hierarchical, or network database, includes a structure to manage its own content (known as a *data dictionary*). Most of us are familiar with gathering information about tables and columns from these structures. Depending on the individual database catalog, other information may also be available. Some database systems carry statistics of use, definitions of tables and columns, create script information, or even metadata about the database management system (DBMS) itself, such as version, build, and license date information.

Collecting Metadata

Why do indexes, bibliographies, outlines, tables of contents, and concordances exist? They exist because it's too difficult to remember all the things you might ever want to know about a subject. In fact, it's impossible to tell what subjects are going to be the most important ones to even narrow down the scope of the information. You have the challenge of determining what metadata elements you're going to make available to a wide customer base; different elements are important to different customers.

Tables 16-3, 16-4, 16-5, and 16-6 show some of the perspectives used to determine what to gather, organize, and provide for the enterprise.

Specifically, data miners, decision support analysts, and ad hoc report writers who read the base data are usually interested in the metadata shown in Table 16-3.

Table 16-3. *Types of Metadata Useful to Those Who Read Metadata*

Data Use Customers See Importance in...	Metadata May Provide...
Empowerment to help themselves as much as possible	An enterprise card catalog for research
Targeted, quality information	Location of targeted data elements Definitions of subtle differences if the same data element occurs multiple times The people to contact if the data values don't seem to be what the customer expects
Speed: to reach their goal faster	Complete location information The people to contact for access support
Backup details: explanation of what was used to create the data that their decisions are based on	Descriptions of pedigree, stewards, and processes creating data Detailed descriptions of formula Schedule information of when data was created

Input operators and application administrators who create data are usually interested in the metadata shown in Table 16-4.

Table 16-4. *Types of Metadata Useful to Those Who Create Metadata*

Data Creation Customers See Importance in...	Metadata May Provide...
Inventory of data elements they're responsible for	A list of data elements stewardship assignments to be reviewed periodically for accuracy
Domain descriptions and business rules regarding their processes	Visibility to definitions Visibility to constraints Visibility of data element to data element business rules
Archive schedules	Schedule information and the people to contact if retrieval is necessary
Knowing interface/integration details to help troubleshoot data values	Description of ETL, Enterprise Application Interchange (EAI), and data movement processes and the people who manage them Mapping of source and targets

DBAs, programmers, and data modelers who manage the data environment are usually interested in the metadata shown in Table 16-5.

Table 16-5. *Types of Metadata Useful to Those Who Manage the Data Environment*

Data Environment Management Customers See Importance in. . .	Metadata May Provide. . .
Research into addition/modification/ deletion of structures	Visibility to missing, duplicated, or unnecessary data elements both by name and definition
Analysis documentation providing design specifications	The Conceptual, Logical, and Physical model element mappings
Inventory of data objects/elements in systems, applications, and so on, that they support	A list of tables, procedures, and so on, mapped to applications and environments
Domain descriptions and business rules regarding their processes	Visibility to definitions Visibility to constraints Visibility of data element to data element business rules
Archive schedules	Schedule information and the person to contact if retrieval is necessary
Knowing interface/integration details to help troubleshoot process problems	Description of ETL, EAI, and data movement processes and the people who manage them Mapping of source and targets Schedule of interfaces and error handling
Upcoming changes	Visibility to both As-Is and To-Be

Senior management is usually interested in the metadata shown in Table 16-6.

Table 16-6. *Types of Metadata Useful to Senior Management*

Enterprise Organization Sees Importance in. . .	Metadata May Provide. . .
Corporate knowledge	Better knowledge survival in the event of loss, relocation, or promotion of staff
Empowerment to help themselves as much as possible	An enterprise card catalog for research, especially things such as the location of reports
Profitability	Visibility to missing, duplicated, or unnecessary data elements both by name and definition

You have a vast amount of information at your fingertips. You need to figure out how to organize it and use it to your advantage to save time, resources, and money.

Building a Metadata Repository

Considering the scope and charter of metadata, how do you get your arms around it? Metadata obviously isn't new. As corporate organizers, researchers, and managers of data, we build and keep metadata in documents, charts, spreadsheets, and databases to help us get our jobs done. We've personally retained huge spreadsheets of metadata about tables, columns, data sizes, definitions, and locations of data we've used. It gives us a starting point for familiar structures, a place to look for integration points, and a sanity check for standard names and sizes.

However, these documents aren't usually user-friendly. Business customers want more ad hoc access to their data and now have user-friendly data access/manipulation tools that use simple point, drag, and click functionality (such as products provided by Hyperion, Business Objects, and MicroStrategy). The business clients created the data, and they want to use it.

This is where the metadata repository comes into play as a comprehensive enterprise library of what you know about your data environments. Building such a repository is similar to the way you'd address any other business process. You start with a clear understanding of what you want to accomplish, how you'll know if you're successful, and where you intend to draw the boundaries. You document the processes, analyze the needs, and provide solutions. From that you build the scope and requirements for your metadata repository. Then, the data modeler can begin to document the data elements and business rules.

Conceptual Metadata Model

We've talked about how you can use the Conceptual model as a tool to help the wonderful problem-solving, brainstorming, creative-questioning activities that happen at the onset of any project. A metadata repository project should also start this way. The absolute first question that needs to be answered is, who will use the repository? Every department or team mentioned needs to have a representative on the project starting at that moment.

The biggest problem with modeling metadata is that the business process of gathering and storing metadata is fairly complicated. It's a mix of accessing sophisticated stores of metadata (such as the system catalog in SQL Server or an Informatica repository), finding and referencing manual data stores (such as spreadsheets, files, and documents), and gathering currently nonexisting data elements and relationships.

The who, when, why, and wherefore of gathering and managing metadata are still nebulous. What metadata means to your organization should be discussed and agreed upon. As covered in Chapter 15, the following metadata may be useful to your enterprise:

- Physical hardware (showing how the data is used with development, test, production, and backup servers or with individual desktop computers, routers, and printers)

- Program code (showing how the data supports screens, reports, and procedures)

- Other documents (showing how the entities figure in project plans, adhere to standards, and change control processes)

- Locations (showing where data is physically or virtually located)

- Other models (showing sources of data, versions, and subject areas)

- Organizations (showing how the data relates to the project sponsor, other interested parties, and your data security organization)

- Pathways (showing the data's flow through the network, Data Transformation Services [DTS] processes, or load routines)

- People (showing individuals responsible for data authorship, stewardship, and support)

- Processes (showing how data supports system processes)

Starting at that high level helps everyone define the direction at the outset. Begin metadata Conceptual modeling with questions such as the following:

- What data is involved?

- What will some of the reports be?

Determine if the goal of collecting the metadata is to do one of the following:

- To follow the development cycle of data for the enterprise

- To find integration opportunities

- To increase the level of data quality in existing systems

- To manage data redundancy

- To catalog the systems, applications, tables, columns, triggers, procedures, indexes, and so on

- To create a feedback loop so that data sources can be acted upon

- To provide an entry point for non-IT clients to find data support objects (reports, data elements, and formulas)

You may want to start your metadata model with a Conceptual model, such as the one in Figure 16-2. Note the main entities of Requirement, Person, Process, and Information Asset. These relatively abstract concepts provide you with a framework that will help you think about and organize your metadata.

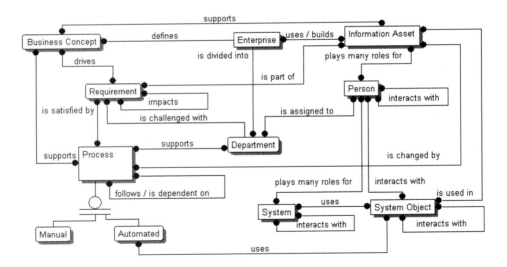

Figure 16-2. *A sample Conceptual metadata model*

As always, you need good definitions in order to understand a Conceptual model. Table 16-7 shows the definitions of the entities in the Conceptual metadata model from Figure 16-2.

Table 16-7. *Conceptual Entity Definitions*

Entity Name	Definition
Business Concept	A thought, idea, or definition used by your enterprise. This may be your definition of gross, net, profitability, or security, for example.
Department	A business unit that's a permanent or temporary grouping of people in the enterprise. Generally this requires a budgeting aspect.
Enterprise	The aggregation of business units required to satisfy your customers. This may include vendors linked to you by process as in your supply chain management star vendors, for example.
Information Asset	Data or a collection of data used to provide knowledge or information to the enterprise.
Person	An individual connected in some way to your enterprise. These may be employees, contacts, contractors, temporary help, and customers.
Process	An act or series of acts proceeding from one to the next accomplishing a goal. These are either manual or automated.
Requirement	A goal or necessary action to accomplish a goal.
System	An orderly, interconnected, complex arrangement of parts, principles, and procedures. A system may be as simple as the filing cabinets in your legal department or as complex as the new bar code task management system.
System Object	An element used by a system. These are filing cabinets, cash registers, procedures, tables, databases, routers, networks, and so on.

If this model and these definitions seem terribly high-level, remember that the Conceptual model is just a starting point. The more you work with the definitions, the more detailed and better they will get. Remember that this model isn't a generic one but is simply one we've developed based on the mapping concepts we've found to be important to data modelers over time. You need to go through the process with your team and listen to their needs in order to build your own model.

Even if your team stops metadata modeling at the Conceptual model, you'll have a significant amount of information to use in comparing various vendor metadata tool packages.

Logical Metadata Model

You can use the Conceptual model from the previous section to work toward a Logical model in the same way in which you converted the Solitaire Conceptual model into a Logical one. During this process, you can begin to drive the metadata repository requirements toward a greater level of detail. You go through all the steps to create a Logical model based on all the requirements and data integrity rules that can be determined from the customers.

From the modeler's perspective, this is just another analysis of data sets important to the enterprise. A metadata modeling project will probably be run like any other modeling project. But we're also going to warn you that this model can become very large; your model may consist of several hundred entities if you take it all the way to the logical, fully attributed level of analysis. Your Logical model can stop at enterprise analysis detail, with some attribute definition, if you're working with a vendor's product, but it will have to be more detailed if you're developing an entirely custom-built solution.

One of the complaints we hear about relational modeling is how complicated it can be. Remember, creating a Logical model is just a way of organizing sets of data. It's not a way to store them physically. The only data element model we've found you can really verify with customers is the Logical, fully attributed model. But don't try to present a complex model all at once; model deliverables need to be scoped into subject areas to include only what's necessary for the person or task at hand.

Figure 16-3 contains an example of a Logical metadata model. It covers only one tiny corner of metadata, in this case information regarding the places, operating systems, and upgrade installations for a set of SQL Server instances on a number of different servers. These logical entities represent the System, Hardware, and System Object entities from the Conceptual model.

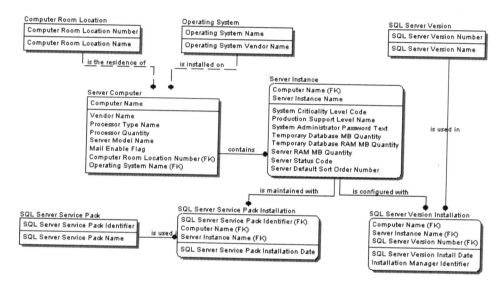

Figure 16-3. *A sample Logical metadata model*

This model serves as the basis for a physical repository that would help DBAs track which servers have had which versions of SQL installed on them, for example.

Physical Metadata Model

You may use the Logical metadata model as a basis for building your own Physical metadata database, or you might use it only to evaluate whether a metadata repository tool is a good match for your organization. Creating a Physical metadata model from your Logical metadata model will be necessary only if your team decides to build your repository. If your team decides to build its own repository, you'll need every scrap of your determination, creativity, perseverance, and sense of humor. You'll design a database that will not only satisfy the need for data integrity but will also address issues of usability, complexity, expandability, and maintainability. Having said that, the process steps you need to take are the same as those you looked at in transforming a Logical model into a Physical model in Chapter 10. It's important to also bear in mind that many other groups also use metadata, so check if any work is taking place that you could leverage.

Understanding a Data Modeler's Metadata

Up until this chapter on metadata, we've been talking about data modeling in terms of supporting business client needs. Once you move into the subject of data about data, you'll discover that you are your own client. Metadata is data describing data, and a modeler models the data. A natural overlap occurs between modeling data and collecting metadata, and you end up being both the steward and the customer of these data elements.

Data Modeling Tools and Metadata

Throughout this book we've talked in general terms about modeling tools that can assist you. Using these tools results in creating electronic documentation that behaves as a mini-database of metadata information elements. The elements either own information or share information through relationships. Entities relate to attributes in a one-to-many relationship. Data types relate to columns in a one-to-many relationship. Each attribute owns its definition. Each model owns its notes. All that information you used to create your model is metadata. Some modeling tools work with model management applications that are databases unto themselves and store metadata about the models you create with the tool.

A good portion of your analysis and design products contributes to enterprise metadata. What would a Conceptual model that's particular to your view of metadata look like? It'll probably look something like the model in Figure 16-4.

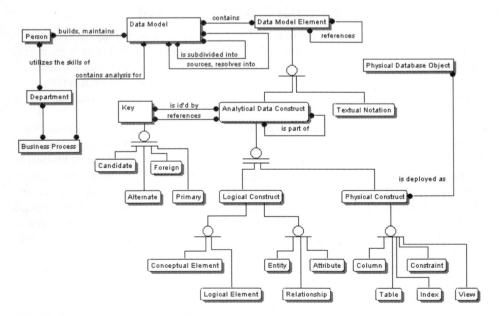

Figure 16-4. *A Conceptual model of a data modeler's metadata*

We wanted to highlight the names of things we've been talking about all along, so we broke out Data Model Elements into a level where you can recognize the elements' names. This is one part of the metadata that a data modeler contributes to the enterprise.

This is just the model of the metadata at the conceptual level. Imagine what the fully analyzed and attributed Logical model would look like!

Data Modeler: A Customer of Metadata

You could take the model shown in Figure 16-4 and use it to help build a data model metadata repository. Once it was built, your data modelers would become one of its best customers. In every new project, the interview and analysis phase includes the step of searching the metadata repository for subject areas and implementation information that already exists.

You could use metadata about any business process you're trying to support. Past project documentation would be available, searchable, and gain new importance as a historical record. You wouldn't want to retry old solutions that didn't work, and equally, during your analysis you'd need to get a feel for the strengths and weaknesses of existing business processes. You could reuse portions of other models to drive enterprise standard structures and definitions. Reusing those structures would reduce the time to market for any project, even if the existing model is used only as a starting point for verification and/or modification as the need arises. You could even load models produced by others with whom you've networked, or you could load "common" designs, templates, and patterns you've purchased. You could use existing table designs to help steer your own designs by looking at both the similar and the unique to inspire new solutions.

This data collection could become a key source of information about the state of the data foundation of the enterprise. It can provide the ability to just see what has happened, not only at the level of the data values but also how the data has been managed.

Understanding the Future of Metadata

The future of metadata management is firmly tied to the future of data management in general. Although we currently see disconnected islands of data, separated by storage type, application boundaries, data style, and disjointed data management vision, the future promises to include a much more connected and integrated world of data. Data management is taking on more and more importance, and metadata is an integral part of managing, controlling, and leveraging data.

Certain organizations are striving to bring some commonality and standards to the chaos. The recently merged Meta Data Coalition (MDC) and Object Management Group (OMG) are attempting to define an industry-standard version of the metadata models. Anyone interested in learning about common metadata models will find a growing set of open-information models, now referred to as *model-driven architecture*, and the Common Warehouse Meta model. These are platform-independent models that are trying to document the commonality of data elements and determine a standard set of names. This should serve to help you leverage work already completed and make you more productive. You can find more information on this subject on the Web at www.corba.org.

Summary

In this chapter you considered the nature of metadata, which is becoming ever more crucial. If you take the example of an order entry system, you now know that metadata isn't the orders in the order entry system but rather the following:

- Statistics about the orders

- Information regarding an order's makeup

- The manner in which orders are organized and stored

- Who can access the order data

- What users can do with orders

- Where the order data flows to and from

- How the order data gets there

- What the origins of the structure of an order are

- Who created the order entry system

- What project created the order entry system

- What problem the order entry system solves

The importance of metadata is its ability to help you manage staff, clients, and resources. You need to serve everyone better by providing cost-effective, high-quality tools and the faster delivery of your results to your customers. To do that, you need to be able to use the knowledge of your enterprise's successes, failures, existing solutions, and abandoned efforts to make intelligent decisions. In short, you need to recognize the importance of your ability to manage your data's shared environment.

CHAPTER 17

Exploring Data Modeling Working Practices

In this last chapter, we'll share some of the lessons we've learned from our 30 years of data modeling. In that time, we've mainly been relational database modelers, and we've had the opportunity to work as employees and consultants in government agencies, in the entertainment and trucking industries, and in international and domestic companies, both large and small. That gives us a potpourri of experiences in data modeling challenges.

We'll break the chapter into two parts. The first half will cover the nature of a data modeler's work practices, including good and bad habits. Although it isn't possible to give you an absolute formula for success, we can highlight a best-practices checklist that you can adhere to in your modeling work. Equally, the list of bad practices should act as a warning signal should you find some of them familiar during the course of your work.

In the second half of the chapter, we'll share some of our thoughts regarding planning and developing your own modeling projects based on the lessons we've learned over the years. We'll cover the following:

- Custom solutions

- Purchased solutions

- Legacy and forensic work

Introducing Work Practices

Let's start by examining the working practices of a data modeler, starting with worst practices and moving on to consider some best practices.

Worst Practices

We gathered the information in the following sections by surveying several teams. Managers, project leads, and programmers shared with us their observations of data modeler behavior that can lead to perceiving the inclusion of a modeler as being a handicap rather than an asset. Such behavior can cause so many negative results that having any modeler assigned to a project becomes an unwelcome addition. The following practices will result in poor team cooperation, broken schedules, and model mismanagement.

Team-Blocking Behavior

A data modeler always works with other people; it's one role that can't work completely independently. Relationships with clients, development and maintenance programmers, database administrators, managers, and data management staff are all vital and ones that a modeler needs to cultivate.

Maybe we're wrong, but our experience is that quality data modeling depends more upon the person modeling than some other skills. If a programmer can't deliver a good program, they're replaced with someone who can. If a modeler can't deliver good analysis and design, then the modeling step tends to be removed along with the modeler. All of the following ways of behaving will ultimately silence the voices around you. Keep this bad behavior up for a while, and no one will ever visit your office or invite you to participate in a project again. The teams surveyed said that they are impacted negatively when the data modeler acts in any of the ways discussed in the following sections.

Is Arrogant

The number-one behavior that can break up a partnership is just not listening to or respecting anyone. *Arrogance* in this case leads to the assumption that you, the modeler, don't need to do the following:

- Pay attention to the needs of a client because you modeled something like it before

- Listen to the project manager because you've been on a development project before

- Spend time with the database administrator (DBA) because you've designed for this platform before

- Work with the programmers because you don't care how they implement it anyway

- Go to conferences, read articles, or network because you "know it all"

- Learn anything new because the old way works just fine

Is Uncompromising

Another behavior that can cause teamwork problems is being *uncompromising*. Individuals who won't back down, even in the face of legitimate needs by the team, will protect their design at all costs (which can be costly indeed). Their general stance is the following:

- "My way or the highway."

- "I'm the data modeler and always know best."

- "There's only one right answer, namely, mine."

- "Normal forms must be protected at all costs."

- "Standards are the law."

- "I want all or nothing."

- "All shortcuts and denormalizations are bad."

An example of being uncompromising is being a perfectionist when making a delivery that's the crucial deliverable. People who are uncompromising become objectionable by blocking every suggestion and generally being inflexible. It can also mean the modeler knows there's a problem but is ignoring or obfuscating the expected outcome.

Is Obstructive

We've heard repeatedly about modelers who didn't want to let anyone see their formative work, like a touchy portrait artist. They're *obstructive* by not communicating the analysis until they're ready to publish a completed work. An obstructive modeler hides the model because they believe the following:

- It isn't fully detailed.

- It doesn't have all the definitions.

- It hasn't been reviewed.

- It doesn't contain all the subject areas.

- It has crossing relationship lines.

- It isn't pretty yet.

They're unresponsive to questions regarding the model and avoid confronting any difficult issues they may have uncovered in their analysis. They might even wait until the last minute to provide the answer, which they've known about for weeks.

This type of modeler could be not sharing for a lot of reasons. Lack of trust is the most common reason. But if you don't trust your team, then how are they going to trust you?

Is Defensive

Defensive behavior has to be one of the hardest to avoid. We data modelers wouldn't commit a solution to paper if we didn't think it had some merit. Pride of ownership can get in the way of being a team player, though. It can be extremely difficult not to interpret as criticism all suggestions and responses to your analysis. Don't get *defensive*. It isn't personal; it's business. A defensive data modeler can sometimes do the following:

- Be hostile about nonmodelers' observations

- Interpret all suggestions as criticism

- Protect the design because it's theirs

- Treat all suggestions as threats to the design

- Make the team questioning your design uncomfortable

This can lead the modeler to push everyone around with threats and dire predictions, subtly defeating other people's suggestions by making jokes of them or being condescending.

Uses Avoidance Techniques

Modelers are usually part of the core team of custom software or corporate data analysis projects, but they don't always make "just being there" a priority. Examples of avoidance techniques are delaying scheduling and being "the last to arrive and first to leave" for meetings (or just not showing up at all after agreeing to attend). This can stall the analysis for so long that it may even force a reduction in scope. In doing so, the modeler may say things such as the following:

- "Mañana . . . tomorrow."

- " . . . I promise."

- "I'm getting to it as fast as I can."

- "Just as soon as *x* does *y*."

- "I'm still thinking about it."

- "You got it!" (aloud). "Not in your lifetime, buddy!" (in their head).

Being obstinately slow, or overcommitting the schedules so that they can't find any time to satisfy anyone, will impact both the project schedule and the team. Equally, the modeler can slow progress by refusing to review their work until the model is "just right," avoiding asking for help until it's too late, taking more pride in nursing an issue than in fixing it, or stalling until the requirements are done, the review has happened, it's signed, and so on.

Bluffs the Team

You know bluffing has its place in poker, but it's a form of deceit in business since it means you aren't telling the whole truth. It's a little like paying on credit; you get the cash now, but you had better make good on it really soon or the penalties could be more than you want to pay.

Bluffing about the completeness of your tasks or your ability to meet deadlines can make the schedule look better (for a little while) and involves communicating to the team with the following:

- **Little white lies**: By announcing things such as "the model is 90 percent complete" when you haven't started definitions yet.

- **Half the story**: By saying you've consulted the clients, when you've consulted clients from only one business discipline during the process of modeling a business area that spans more than one.

- **Impractical recommendations**: By making black-and-white statements such as "never denormalize—it's bad" when you know you must be sensitive to performance and application requirement needs.

- **Techno-babble jargon**: Saying things such as "doing this breaks Boyce-Codd Normal Form" rather than "it's easier to maintain a simple list of values and migrate a key where they're needed" just to keep people from questioning you.

- **Silence when you should speak up**: By knowing there are other projects doing work in the same subject areas that could potentially be an opportunity for integration but keeping quiet about it because it could increase the complexity of your analysis.

- **Irrational suggestions when you should be quiet**: By taking up a project team's time with enterprise-level solutions when they have neither the authority nor opportunity to even consider them. Save those suggestions for an audience who could consider doing that.

This leaves you being perceived as a hypocrite (by misrepresenting the facts), two-faced (by sending ambiguous messages on purpose), or a troublemaker (by causing trouble when your real opinions are acted on by outside forces). It's possible you'll be perceived as all of these.

Is Thoughtless

This is a matter of *disrespect*. A modeler can show disrespect by doing the following:

- Interrupting constantly
- Being patronizing
- Making unconfirmed assumptions
- Making personal comments
- Generalizing with *always*, *never*, *all*, and *none* statements
- Being unwilling to share in the "grunt" work

Is Critical

The modeler is in a unique position of being in contact with pretty much every group, skill, position, and client involved with the team. This means they have the power to *criticize* everyone if they want.

This is a great technique to use if one needs to shift the spotlight off themselves to someone else's issues (we're being sarcastic here). This involves constantly doing the following:

- Blaming instead of solving
- Keeping score like it's a contest
- Spouting sarcasm at every opportunity
- Being overly sensitive and using it as an excuse to launch an attack

Is Incomprehensible

This one came up quite a lot in our survey. Unfortunately, we do have a pretty large body of "reserved" words. Some of them sound so familiar to people that they get confused when we seem to be using them to mean something completely different in conversation. Other terms are as alien as a whole different language. This technique renders the model and the analysis *incomprehensible* whether you mean to do that or not. What use is it then? It fails at its most basic need.

Talking fast and using data modeling terms without explaining them can reduce any audience to complete silence. Spraying words such as *entity*, *attribute*, *relationship*, *primary key*, *category*, and *foreign key* without regard for your audience's level of understanding will leave everyone nonplussed and frustrated. For instance, which of the following would you rather hear the data modeler say?

- "When choosing the physicalization option for the category Vehicle, we need to take into account that logically the subtype Truck has relationships unique to it that the supertype and other subtypes don't support in the form of an identifying foreign key to the Camper entity."
- "Only the truck type of vehicles can have campers. Should we break it out to its own table?"

These both pretty much say the same thing. The first sentence is perfectly valid when talking with other modelers—but most of us would use the second option when speaking with anyone else on the team.

Is Passive

Refusing to take the initiative and portraying an attitude of *passivity* can be intentional in a "passive-aggressive" rebellion, or it can just be a lack of drive or confidence in what to do next. The modeler can frustrate everyone around them if they have to have clear directions for everything they do. In this respect, the modeler can drive everyone crazy by doing the following:

- Following the project plan like stereo instructions without recognizing the need to be flexible or provide realistic feedback

- Speaking only when spoken to

- Never offering to help, to learn, or to participate

- Never introducing new concepts, clients, and techniques

- Never sharing their experience and intuition to provide better options than the ones already suggested

How to Stall a Schedule

Having a team member who contributes to stalling the schedule is one of the worst nightmares for a project manager. The data model has exactly the same function on a project as the foundation of a building. *Everything* is based on the rules, names, and definitions captured in the model.

DBAs often can't decide on a platform, estimate size, or brainstorm support until at least the Logical model is done. Programmers can draft screens, but they need the Physical model design to be complete before they can do much in the way of true design for the data manipulation. Even the network team needs to know the size, shape, and frequency of the data movements in order to know if they have enough bandwidth. This places the data modeler right in the critical path for a project. Ignoring that for very long can have devastating results.

Fall Into Analysis Paralysis

Ever try to paint a sunrise while it's happening? It changes so quickly that it's almost impossible to paint. You can capture it with a camera, but enterprise data rule cameras don't exist yet. So you're left with returning each morning at dark and attempting to catch a little more day by day.

You're probably thinking that enterprise processes are more long-lived than sunrises and should be easier. We used to think so too, but we've seen process changes increase in frequency so much that almost every new project is hard-pressed to deliver anything before it becomes partially obsolete. We try to build in expandability, but even that's based on just the gut impressions about future needs when a nicely defined and dependable five-year plan (that doesn't change every quarter) would give us a much more concrete guide. We have to succumb to delivering "throw-away" applications, reports, and data collections in order to keep up with the flood of needs around us and the time/money/resource constraints of a company.

So, the impression the customers have of data modelers is that we get stuck analyzing. From their perspective, we get 80 percent complete, realize we missed something, go back and analyze it, find out it impacts what we thought we had captured, alter it, and start all over again. They get the most frustrated when it's the Logical model. We can't tell you how many times we've heard the question, "When can we start coding?" But if you don't know yet how the data fits together logically, you're really guessing what the best design is for the physical tables.

Endless analysis will leave your team stuck in the mud going nowhere. It can be a result of scope creep, an overabundance of options, or an uncompromising viewpoint that the team has to provide an all-or-nothing solution.

Don't Communicate

One thing about data models is that they look great on paper. There's no way from glancing at them to know how good they are. Your team takes for granted that you have it right just because they have a wonderful graphic in their hand. They make assumptions about what they need to do from conversations with clients, so if the modeler doesn't take them back to the actual data elements and relationships from time to time, they may be misleading themselves as to the complexity coming.

A great way to blow a schedule is by not communicating constantly with the people who need to know. The modeler needs to revisit not only the clients who gave them the data rules but also the extraction, transformation, and load (ETL) team and programmers as their code matures. All of a sudden someone is going to realize they didn't make room for something, didn't realize that an option had to be multiple (rather than single), or didn't modularize their tasks enough to prevent a huge ripple from occurring when a change needs to be made.

Perform One Task at a Time

This may be pretty simple, but we've known people who just can't multitask. Unfortunately, the tasks in modeling often take place in parallel. But there are ways to take shortcuts in the event of a schedule issue. It's easy to slow a project simply by forcing clients to tell you one more time what an address, e-mail, or name looks like, rather than using your own experience to develop the details yourself. It's true that clients have to be stewards of the data elements for which they ask you to provide storage and manipulation tools. They need to take responsibility for the definition, size, and rules surrounding their data elements. However, they're busy generally doing their "real" jobs and have trouble fitting tasks such as creating definitions for 300 data elements into their schedules. The modeler can easily stall a team because they can't quite get the clients to commit to something and aren't willing to make some best guesses for them to review and fix.

Never Admit You're Wrong (or Ask for Help)

We all get things wrong from time to time. The worst thing for a schedule is having someone know something is wrong and being afraid to admit it. Generally, the further you get, the worse it's going to be to fix. Models aren't good places to leave an error. Someone will trip over it eventually. Refusing to ask for help if you need it will inevitably lead to problems in the long run. What, for example, will happen if the modeler assumes that modeling for a financial application can't be any different than modeling for a manufacturing application, despite that they've never modeled one before?

Equally, you as a modeler won't be truly effective in your workplace if you never consider the possibility of using new tools or taking training classes. Not spending any time with the clients, DBA, and developer(s) means you won't grasp the finer details of the system you're trying to model.

Mismanage the Model

What else impacts a project? Eighty percent of our models are simply used to document and communicate information about enterprise data. They're information repositories and storyboards living in our department but published to customers who count on them. The following is a list of frustrations provided by our project customers; these are the things they find the most annoying about working with a data modeler (in no particular order):

The model objects are constantly reorganized: It can be disorienting to the customers if you move the boxes (entities, tables, and views) with every model revision. They think you do it on purpose so that they can't find anything, when you're really just trying to make it all fit. However, from the model customers' perspective, inconsistent placement of entities or tables on your diagrams, in combination with poor documentation of the changes, will lead to confusion and frustration.

You don't make sure the model is legible: Sometimes shrinking models drastically to fit them on a single print page, forcing it into tiny font sizes, will make the model illegible to the client. They'd rather have bigger paper or multiple pages. Remember to use submodels to focus on a small area. Or consider getting a big plotter for the department to print really big models.

You're inconsistent with the level of model information: Keep in mind that if the model, which is complicated already, is too filled with extras, the customer may be frustrated trying to read it. WTMI (which stands for *way too much information*) can turn the model into busy wallpaper.

If too much information is bad, then so is too little. We've changed jobs enough to know how frustrating it is to come into a department and not be able to discover anything about a model we found. Model customers have this problem too, mostly with versions of the same model. It can be incredibly frustrating to have six versions of the model in your In basket and not be able to tell which one is the current release.

You take the time to make all these models but don't have a data element library to show the latest version: Making it someone's responsibility to manage a collection of information about any aspect of the models, applications, or data elements for the client is a good idea. However, it will quickly become a useless resource if it isn't kept up-to-date.

Not knowing the rules for appropriate denormalization: Denormalization without appropriate thought to the rules of normalization will lead to data integrity problems. Working with the attitude of "never denormalize" or "always denormalize" will lead to problems. Be smart in your choices.

You can be so inflexible about your standards that it's hard to work with you: This is a suggestion that the letter of the law isn't always the best choice. A company standard just means that it's normal and has been agreed upon by some group of people. So use standards under normal circumstances. You'll always trip over *unusual* circumstances where you'll need to be flexible with these standards in order to provide a tailor-made solution. Sticking rigidly to your tried-and-trusted procedures can result in a poor design. However, bear in mind that you'll also damage the model if you don't apply any naming standards whatsoever. Five different tables containing the quantity of OrderProduct will probably lead to data integrity problems sooner or later.

Preaching to be careful with the data but not backing up your own work: Backing up is something that nobody forgets to do, right? After all, we work in the information technology (IT) department. Well, let's just say it's something that's easy to forget. Your client isn't going to be happy if you turn up for a review meeting without a model to present because your hard drive crashed and you lost all your work.

Best Practices

Having considered the worst practices that you can bring to the modeling world, the following sections cover the best practices. They directly parallel the worst practices, guiding you as to how to avoid the pitfalls we've already outlined. The project team works best when the data modeler has the qualities listed in the following sections.

Is Willing to Listen to Colleagues

Listen everywhere—in the lunchroom, over walls, in one-on-one meetings, in chartering sessions, in brainstorming sessions, on the Internet, in articles, and on bulletin boards. As a modeler, you need to keep finding ways to tailor your skills to meet the changing data world around you; you never know where a good idea is going to come from, so keep your ears open.

Is Able to Compromise

Obviously, some issues are difficult to compromise on. Security, quality, integrity, project-critical objectives, and even standards are tough to make flexible if there are opposing sides. Sometimes you're right to stand up for your cause, but sometimes you have to be a little flexible. Find a way forward. This doesn't mean you have to give up on what's important to your department or you personally, but you can almost always find a solution to make both sides comfortable.

Is Accessible

Note your thoughts, reservations, difficulties, and stages of development on the model. Create a disclaimer, stating the stages of evolution, and then publish them. Even formative models are the property of the team. Letting the team see the model helps everyone get a feel for how big, complicated, and far along the model is. It also allows everyone to see how the model has evolved and what decisions have been made along the way. This can reduce tension and provide a visual status of the analysis.

Is Receptive

Let go of ownership. The data modeler may have done the analysis, but it's always an enterprise-owned solution. Make sure someone in the enterprise is brought in along the way to support the design afterward. Sometimes you have to take a step back to let go. We find that providing more than one solution up front helps reduce the "it's my model" emotions.

Is Punctual

Modelers should probably be optional invitees to almost every meeting in a development project. However, they should find a way to attend at least 75 percent of them (and be on time). The small, unnoticed comments, frowns, politics, and hesitations are critical indicators of the completeness of the analysis and the soundness of the model. Make it a point to hang out with the team as much as possible, and try to be the first to get there and the last to leave if you can. Even being able to document areas where you can tell there's a problem can be valuable when making a decision later.

Is Transparent

Be as truthful to your team as possible. Sometimes you'll need to choose the correct moment to break bad news. But keeping everyone updated on how things are going is the best way to prevent nasty surprises. The earlier the team knows about potential stumbling blocks and pitfalls, the more time they have to find a practical solution to overcome them.

Is Respectful

A great teammate is blind to everything other than the talent of the person next to them. You need to simply respect everyone on the team for lending you their unique perspective and talents. You need to help create a comfortable and safe environment for everyone. Utilize all the talent available to the team. If a colleague can perform a task faster and more efficiently than you, then let them do it, or ask them to help you gain proficiency in that skill.

Reserve judgment, and do your research before you criticize any team members. Always offer a compromise, alternative, or suggestion to fix what you think is a problem. Blaming individuals won't fix whatever problem you perceive there to be.

Communicates Effectively

You have to be able to communicate with your team, or they will eventually assume they can't communicate with you and back off. Clients are worse. They will dread having to talk to you and avoid you if you aren't able to connect with them, even at the cost of a less-successful project. Put together a five-minute "what I mean when I say . . ." presentation, and begin your model sessions with it to ground everyone in vocabulary you tend to use frequently as their data modeler. Even those who heard it before will probably appreciate the refresher.

Is Self-Motivated

You need to be self-managed in many ways. No one, not even us, can tell you what directions to work first. The thing we like best about modeling is that each analysis is an adventure. Imagine what the early explorers would have done if they had to wait until someone told them what to do next. You need to be willing to act like a sponge, soaking up ideas and thoughts from within the organization or department in which you're working. Be dynamic, and get out front. Hang out with the clients and allow your curiosity to help you absorb information to aid you in your modeling.

Is Schedule-Oriented

Impacting a project schedule is something to avoid whenever possible. Having said that, sometimes you have to accept that your schedule will be delayed. We've spent most of our modeling careers helping data customers tell us requirements. The frustrating thing is that they want to concentrate on their suggested solutions instead. We've had to gently turn them around again and again to focus on the problem at hand, cataloging and documenting them to the fullest and, finally when that's completed, look at alternative methods for satisfying them.

Change requests, application suggestions, and purchase proposals are almost always given to you with a solution in mind. They usually go through review committees and get approved before the technical team is ever approached. Then the team is obliged to try to work with that solution and the assumed schedule to deploy it.

Most necessary schedule hits happen when you figure out that you've been given a solution, rather than requirements, and the solution isn't going to work for any number of reasons. You have to find out what the solution is trying to solve. Then you have to take those obstacles one by one to the clients and find a solution that will work.

Other delays happen when you find that the requirement to upgrade, change, modify, integrate, or enhance existing systems has a huge impact on satellite systems. Take, for example, a company that's going international but still needs to use the existing human resources (HR) system. The requirement is to change the Social Security number to be null allowed, which means that not all employees will have them now. The project team gets started, only to find that Social Security numbers are integrated with the payroll system, the quality control department for inspectors, the security team for ID numbers, and the Internet team for primary key of accounts. Each of the new discoveries expands the analysis to unexpected realms. Taking a hit on the analysis portion of this schedule is important. The team could have gone forward with the simple solution to make Social Security numbers null allowed and caused impacts on other systems.

Note You can't be so focused on the scope provided by a project team that you refuse to notice or point out that you're sawing off the limb you're sitting on. In other words, try to avoid making very shortsighted decisions if you can.

Obeys Pareto's Rule

Pareto's rule states that a small number of causes are responsible for a large percentage of the effect—in a ratio of about 20:80. In other words, 80 percent of the benefit will come from 20 percent of the effort. Modelers can't generally act independently in applying this principle, but in helping the team to keep on schedule you may be called on to partition some of the scope and offer options that can be safely set aside in order to call the analysis complete, just to stay on schedule.

The best thing to do is to find the appropriate 20 percent (according to Pareto) and call it a day. The biggest trick is finding the *right* 20 percent on which to concentrate. A "Where Used" analysis finding every screen, procedure, table, report, and code block where a data element is used or a "Criticality" matrix that focuses on the necessity of having a data element "correct" at all times sometimes helps. You can consider the rule in terms of the following:

- Approximately 20 percent of requirements generate 80 percent of the functionality.

- Approximately 20 percent of one's functionality will absorb 80 percent of the resources.

Or you can say the following:

- Approximately 80 percent of the requirements will be satisfied with 20 percent of the model.

- The remaining 80 percent of the model will only support 20 percent of the requirements.

■Note Avoid getting stuck on some small return issue that will impact the schedule. Isolate it and phase it into a follow-up release if you can.

Respects the Law of Diminishing Returns

This is the other thing that's good to keep in mind. It's also called the Law of Decreasing Returns and the Law of Variable Proportions. This law says, if one factor of production is increased while the others remain constant, the overall returns will relatively decrease after a certain point. This is mathematically represented in a sort of "lazy S," which shows you have to exert more and more effort to achieve incrementally less and less. In fact, after a certain point, you can work as hard as you want and basically get nowhere; but in the initial stages, a small amount of effort results in a disproportionate amount of benefit, as shown in Figure 17-1.

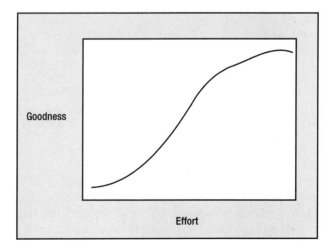

Figure 17-1. *A diminishing returns graph*

When the modeler finds the Logical modeling including hundreds of entities, it may be time to consider phasing in an approach to avoid getting trapped in this type of "less for more" scenario. You can break your modeling effort up into subject areas (banking vs. sales) or functionality (assigning a cashier to a register vs. creating a deposit). Only you will know that the working model is getting too big to handle or how to partition it so you can focus better.

Manages Expectations

You have to help everyone know where you think things might change, might need extra analysis, or might be wrong (when the issue interfaces with another group). The team can often work around those areas until you have a better feel for them. It's your product, and you need to take responsibility as if you were solving problems of your own making and keep everyone informed about your progress. Share as much as you can, not only about the model but your gut feelings about the analysis in order to help keep people out of minefields as long as possible.

Uses Initiative

Sometimes a draft solution based on previous experience can give you a real head start since it makes the process go faster. People generally find it easier to tell you that you have it wrong than to be able to tell you what's right. Remember that waiting around for clients to give you enough time for all your questions is sometimes impossible. Just finding compatible meeting times could impede the pace of the project.

Your clients probably have other applications, so look up how their Address table is designed. Even if you think it's not the best design, it will have the advantage of being able to be totally integrated in the future. Check out the vendor package data structures, and look at what the particular SAP, PeopleSoft, or Oracle solution for data design is.

What about previous models and how you solved the security requirements there? Were those solutions similar? Can you reuse not only the structure design but the documentation as well?

Do you ever make friends with other modelers? Network with them to see if they have a solution you can adapt to your needs. None of us knows everything, and it can be a pretty lonely place without networking. We've worked in companies where we were the ones on staff who knew what relational theory was. You can send a virtual call for help if you get stuck to bulletin boards and associations; refer to some of the resources in Appendix A.

Try to find a way to patchwork structures together to help shorten the creation cycle. Build a "best of . . ." solutions document for your enterprise and use it. Some great books cover patterns of data that crop up repeatedly; again, refer to Appendix A for resources. Use existing professional terminology listings and industry dictionaries to give "best-guess" definitions. Don't force the clients to tell you what a city name is, for example. Again, give them a target solution. Do some of the work for them, and put notes in the model if you have to, explaining that this is still waiting for approval from the clients.

Start a collection of data dictionaries from every source imaginable. Pull definitions from every model you can, and build yourself a metadata definitions document. Use it whenever you can to help build a common understanding of what those data elements are to the enterprise.

Note Add a task to every project to build common lists of definitions for you and the team to use in the future.

Asks for Assistance

Asking for help or explaining a difficulty isn't a sign of weakness. It takes some strength to admit to needing training, extra time, or a helper. The funny thing is that you'd probably never let a co-worker drown in tasks if you knew they were struggling. So let someone help you out once in a while. We spend our lives trying to make tools that will help other people get their jobs done faster. Why don't we ask once in a while for a tool for ourselves? Even the DBAs and programmers are good at automating their routine tasks by utilizing drag-and-drop or point-and-click tools to reduce typing errors. You can really gain some time in simple, and sometimes even cheap, solutions if you just work up the courage to ask management.

■**Note** What saves time generally saves money. You can model by using a pencil and drawing a design on paper, but you can increase your productivity enormously with a modeling tool to help.

There's also the type of gain you make by being more educated. A few days learning how the client does their job can be invaluable. Finding out the methods a DBA has to performance-tune one of the platforms can help you understand what they're facing in the Physical model design world. Take a basic class in one of the programming languages. It will help you know when to push back when a programmer says something can't be done. Even knowing the wonders of Unified Modeling Language (UML), object-oriented design, and data warehousing techniques makes you a much more valuable asset to your enterprise.

■**Note** Knowledge (about nearly anything) is power in modeling.

Try to get a budget for one or two books a year, and build a department library, picking up modeling texts, software books, and specialist dictionaries. That way, you'll have a good chance of building your definitions with due regard for specific industry standards.

Keep project documentation in soft as well as hard copy, especially if there are handwritten notes involved. You'd be surprised how often an application needs to be altered but no one knows anything about who/what/where/when/why it was created in the first place. Manual artifacts from your analysis exploration may help trigger a memory of more than just the content of the notes. They can help you recall a more complete string of reasoning that led you to a design choice.

Manages Model Effectively

The following are best practices directly related to the bulleted list of model mismanagement provided in Chapter 14, which focused on communicating with the model:

Be consistent in model versions: You know that from your perspective, a graphic symbol's position means nothing. Having an entity in the top-left, center, or right-bottom area has no meaning. However, to avoid confusing the customer, be as consistent as possible in the position of entities on your diagrams, and document any changes so they're clear to the client. If you use submodels for most of your publication, you may be able to keep most elements in their usual place. On the big model, you may need to use color or text formatting to help people see where a box went. Finally, you can add a note to provide directions to the new location if need be.

Create readable models: We all struggle with models that have far too many objects for the paper size on which we have to put them. But in your quest to fit everything on the page, take pity on everyone and keep the font size of your model easily readable. If you're shrinking to fit a paper size, never go lower than 70 percent. Anything less than that leads to the customer thinking that you're unaware, or uncaring, of their inability to use your document.

Add appropriate information: We provided you with all kinds of suggestions for things you might want to put on a model. Now we'll retreat backward a bit. Some of the modeling software will actually allow you to create a reusable library of notes so you can create and store all those things but manage what shows up on one print of the model. Add the extras judiciously. Consider the visual presentation since you don't want people to get tense just by looking at your model.

At the other end of the scale, don't omit important levels of detail. No matter how much of a draft you think the model is, at least add the following information before you publish it anywhere:

- The name of the project/application

- What it's a model of: enterprise Logical model, production Physical model, or test data mart

- Your name and extension

- The date the model was last updated (not printed)

- A version number so that someone can find the right one at a glance

Create a data element library: One of the most powerful tools you can provide your department and perhaps others customers is a data element library. If you decide to provide a collection of information about any aspect of the models, applications, or data elements, you need some way to keep them accurate. You may need to audit them from time to time, wipe out and refresh the information, or simply add methods for the library customers to check for themselves. You should never publish this type of information and allow it to get stale. We know that can be difficult. It's better sometimes to force a new request for this type of data if you aren't confident in its upkeep. Creating a tool and not maintaining it can be as dangerous as giving your teenager a car and not providing either training or maintenance of the brakes. You never know when someone is going to make an enterprise-critical decision based on your library.

Be judicious in denormalization: Just because you can denormalize doesn't mean that it's always the answer. Every time it seems important to break one of the rules of normalization, especially one of the first three forms, you should question whether there's another way to approach the problem. What risks are involved in denormalizing, and what benefits will you gain? Is there a way to mitigate any risk you'll incur by doing this? This is where discussions with the DBA and developers will help in determining what's best for the system with which you're currently working. Denormalization should be a last resort to a relational modeler, except in the case of Dimensional modeling. Try to use common sense to make the decisions, and have a good reason for doing so.

Be flexible: When unusual circumstances crop up, create a standard "bypass the standard" technique. You don't want to lose total control; you just need to bend it a little. You may even have written the standard in the first place. Make following standards a process with people in mind—one that can evolve as the need arises. And realize that some of your standards need to be more open to flexibility than others. The laws of normalization aren't very flexible in creating a Logical model design, but the options available for performance tuning that requires some amount of denormalization in your Physical model designs are pretty boundless.

■**Note** Be prepared to bend your own rules.

At the opposite extreme, ensure you never deliver your products without any naming standard whatsoever. We've all had to work with physical names that made us wonder if someone came up with them by using Scrabble letters. Even the most common abbreviations are used multiple ways to mean the same thing, and sometimes the same abbreviation is used to mean multiple things. Not every enterprise has a "common abbreviations" list. Or not all the abbreviations in it may suit your needs. A rule of thumb is to at least be consistent within the confines of a project.

Back up your work: Do what you recommend to everyone else and protect your most valuable assets in at least two ways. Store a version off your system in a department-shared environment and the other in a disaster recovery mode, possibly off-site. And a helpful hint—save the model often while you're working on it.

Having considered an overview of what constitutes best working practices for a data modeler, let's look in more detail at some factors that will help you plan and develop your own modeling projects.

Understanding Data and Design

We've tried through this book to help you become aware that the task of analyzing and designing repositories for data isn't just a formulaic process. The data itself—what's captured in spreadsheets, forms, and documents—is *only* the physical manifestation of what you're trying to manage. If you're modeling a distribution warehouse and have never seen one, stop what you're doing and check out the reality, go kick a few tires, and then start modeling. The more you're familiar with the messy, dirty, human business processes, the better. As modelers, we need to "have vision" and be able to understand the details, the exceptions, and the mechanisms by which the customer gets around systems. By understanding data problems, you can often find flexible and simple ways to solve them.

Logical-to-Physical Transformations

One of the greatest mysteries in our professional careers is the relationship (or sometimes lack thereof) of the Logical model to the Physical model. We find ourselves baffled by what's implemented in comparison to what we thought we documented in the Logical model. The departure of one from the other is sometimes astonishing. Our advice to you is to stay in touch with the development and maintenance teams as much as you can. Do your best to determine what's actually happening with the data, rather than what the team or clients either *perceive* or think *ought* to be happening. Don't assume your designs are being used the way you planned them to be used. People often use tools to fix problems extremely creatively. Toasters make great paperweights, and buckets make good stools. If someone can force data into a field, they might do it regardless of the intent of the field—especially if it's just too difficult to get approval to make a database change to include new understanding.

Keep the model updated, create and maintain risk-assessment documentation, and try to maintain the mapping of the Logical model to the Physical model along with a list of design decisions. And make sure you stay in touch with not only the design team but the clients as well. The key is to minimize the opportunity for a data element to be used in a way that isn't part of the game plan. Point out that a new data element may need to be created rather than using the old one. The two data elements may describe facts that aren't in sync with each other.

The Physical model can take on a life far beyond your ability to manage. It depends on the organization, change control, custom development processes, qualifications for a successful project, and the enterprise disbursement of data architecture authority. In other words, if your company has separated the Logical modelers from the Physical modelers to the extent that you're working with a "throw-it-over-the-wall" process, you may have great difficulty finding a method of reviewing and noting denormalization choices that you'd consider bad designs.

If "on time" and "on budget" are the highest criteria for success, then the database design may be more subject to changes to support fast, inexpensive solutions than if customer satisfaction, enterprise architecture standard, or sustainable data quality are the criteria. However, the mark of a good data modeler is being able to spot false economy and pointing out and convincing decision makers that short-term savings could result in a long-term cost. We admit that we end up breaking more of our data standards to support fast and cheap solutions than we do to support actual performance gains.

Fallacies About Physical Data

It took us years of working in IT to see the following fallacies. Maybe we're just not that bright, but these shook the very foundation of our world. We thought certain rules were simply understood to be set in stone. We didn't realize what they implied.

Application owners *own* their data: We hear members of the computer services group constantly say they take care of the machines and software but that the users own the data. They wash their hands of all bad data events the way that auto manufacturers and the highway builders often try to lay 100 percent of the blame for accidents on the drivers. Data is an enterprise asset owned by the entire company, not just one portion of it. If something is occurring systematically at the data creation stage, the whole company often suffers in the long run. You're all in this together. If "bad" data happens, it should be up to IT to try to find out the cause and fix it if it's in their power or bring the problem to someone else's attention if it isn't.

Application owners control all their data: There are just too many data values that act as logic points in applications for the application owners to be able to claim they control all the data. If the value for affirmative changes from *Y* for "yes" to *J* for "ja," many applications lose their ability to process IF...THEN...ELSE statements that depend on finding a *Y*. Lots of code depends on finding certain values. Most of these types of data values lie in the List of Values (LOV) type of data (although even procedures that are counting on finding dates can give incorrect results when faced with text or numbers). The application owners have to follow certain laws in their own tool, or it will cease to function correctly. This means they don't control all the data. The tool they're using has control responsibility as well.

Designs can be flexible: Designs can be flexible to a point. You can make the list of "type" codes flexible enough to include new ones or create client-controlled lists so that Vehicle_Type can grow to anything the client wants to add. We've run across the following two problems:

> There's generally a great deal of logic surrounding the values of these types of lists. Even innocuous things such as lists of countries, colors, or departments can cause breakage. You have to verify that there's *no* logic based on the values of these data entities for them to be truly flexible. It can't matter whether a product is red, green, or white, unless you can capture the rule for color logic and describe it as a relationship on the model. Otherwise, a programming change has to happen for a new color, such as silver, to be treated the same as white.

> You have to choose a design sometime, and all designs have some restrictions associated with them. Some have less than others, but we've never run into a completely flexible design.

Approach the concept of flexibility as shades of gray. Review your choices, and decide what can't be done if you design it that way. We often add a note to the models of each Physical model design to point out implied restrictions using that structure. Being as normalized as possible or using object-oriented database design helps, but nothing is truly flexible. This simply illustrates that data modeling provides a snapshot of ever-changing business requirements.

Primary keys never change: We started data modeling living under the incorrect assumption that primary keys can't be updated. They *can* be in many RDBMSs. Not only that, but some designers expect to be able to modify them. Countries, rock bands, and Web sites change their names (which we always thought of as their natural key). An acre of land once identified by a lot number is divided up into development lots. The thing, person, or event is still what it was when it started, but now it has a new natural primary key. This is one of the best arguments for surrogate keys. Coding gets tricky when the programmers have to deal with the change of a migrating key. They have to change all foreign keys to match, or you lose the links during the update. Some tools provide a CASCADE UPDATE function, or they have to write triggers and stored procedures to fire automatically to take care of this event. Again, you have to watch for logic points. If reports have been programmed to look for *USSR*, but the business now needs to look for *Russia*, there will be problems when the update happens. We've been left wondering if there's a real *natural* key that isn't not subject to change.

Primary keys are *never* null: We don't think they're logical, but some RDBMSs (mostly older versions) allow a single NULL to exist in the primary key. A primary key has been implemented to simply mean unique. A single instance of NULL *is* unique. We've also come across interesting uses of nonsignificant identification in what we thought was supposed to be a natural primary key. Creative clients uses words such as "N/A-1, N/A-2, . . ." to make up uniqueness when you meant for them to put in a Contract_Number, for example. This probably means there isn't enough validation in the design, but it can be hard to prevent creative people from doing creative things.

Understanding Project Lessons

We've probably been involved in more than 100 projects over the course of 30 years. Some ran as long as two years, and others were as short as a week. The following sections include some of our best guesses about how to estimate the time and resource support that the various stages of a project can take. These are only guides to give you an idea of what sort of ballpark you're playing in; it isn't possible to give you absolute numbers, and you shouldn't take these formulas as such. We'll break the lessons up into custom development, purchased solutions, and forensic work.

Custom Solution Projects

In these kinds of projects, you get to start from scratch and find a solution. You draw from everything you know, everything you learn, and everything you want to be in order to come up with a series of products that helps the project team build an application. You'll be asked to provide an estimate of duration for most project plans.

Remember that the modeler should stay with the project from start to finish if that's possible. This means being present when the initial project prescoping and chartering sessions take place, as well as attending the post-deployment assessment and evaluation meeting and all the work in between. We're assuming a high level of support to the team here, not a casual "over-the-wall" type of data model delivery. Ongoing and sustaining effort isn't easy to estimate, but as a rough rule of thumb our modeler support formula is as follows:

- It takes eight hours per programmer per week prior to the test build.

- It takes four hours per programmer per week for the duration of the project.

So, if the project plan calls for twenty weeks of planning and developing and another ten for testing and implementation using four programmers, the modeler could estimate the following:

```
(8 hours 3 20 weeks 3 4 programmers)
+
(4 hours 3 10 weeks 3 4 programmers)
or 640 + 160 = 800 hours
```

This comes out to 20 weeks full-time for a 30-week project.

Our simplest estimation is that the data modeler is on a custom development project from start to finish for 75 percent of the time (although they will move to full-time during some phases and into half-time in others). A small project such as Web page development will need only half a day a week. Some of that will just be meeting to touch base; some will be to respond to action items. Sustaining support requires you to stay in touch.

- Update the model as necessary.

- Maintain the documentation appropriately.

- Publish and deliver new documentation.

- Stay abreast of new discovery in development and testing.

Table 17-1 summarizes what we consider to be reasonable definitions of small, medium, and large projects. The durations given are in terms of achieving a first reviewable draft. Remember that all models are iterative, so we've included the time spent updating them to a final version.

Table 17-1. *Definition of Project Characteristic Terms*

Quantity	Small	Medium	Large
Duration	Anything less than three months	More than three months but less than six months	More than six months
Number of Third Normal Form (3NF) entities	Less than twenty entities	More than twenty to fifty entities	More than fifty entities
Size of team	Any size team less than five	A team of between five and seven	A team of more than seven
Conceptual modeling time	Ten hours per business process	Twenty hours per business process	Forty hours per business process

Quantity	Small	Medium	Large
Logical modeling time	Ten hours per subject area	Twenty hours per subject area	Forty hours per subject area
Physical modeling time	One hour per nonoperational attribute	One hour per nonoperational attribute	One hour per nonoperational attribute

Phrases to Watch Out For

The following sections cover the warning signs in a custom development project. If you see any of these, it means you need to heighten your sensitivity to the team and the customers. You may need to manage expectations, speed up your response, spend some time explaining what you're doing, or prevent your work from being pushed aside.

"When Can We Have the Database Design?"

This will generally come from the programmers on the team who are impatient for tables to be built so they can begin coding. Don't think you have to have the whole design done in order to give them some of the design. Programmers want to get started and need to be supported. What you should be leery of is letting them start coding without the team approving the part of the Physical model design with which they'd like to start.

Once programmers start using names and structures, it's difficult to change their code. You have to use some level of reasonability about the maturity of the design and manage expectations that some things will be likely to change all the way until you get out of the testing phase.

The best answer to this question is "when the team approves of it."

"Why Do You Need to Do a Logical Design?"

The answer to this question is threefold:

- So that the data elements can be stored in the most appropriate structures

- So that the enterprise has a view of what data elements are in this project

- So that you can identify the correct source of all the data elements

The problem has always been that Logical modeling takes time. If these things aren't important to the person asking the question, or they think they already know the answers to these concerns, you won't be able to defend it. Unfortunately, a Logical model isn't universally regarded as a value-added process.

"What's So important About Third Normal Form?"

Be careful with this one. This is usually questioning data modeling in general, rather than whether 3NF is the appropriate level of modeling. In fact, nine times out of ten, others don't know what 3NF is. Try to find out the person's level of understanding before you answer. Never go on the defensive. People only believe something is true if they find out for themselves. You can give them information, but they have to make up their own mind.

"What Development Needs Are You Designing For?"

During the course of a project, we've heard clients state the following:

- "We'll never need to share this data with anyone."

- "We'll never need to store that much data."

- "We'll never have that many users."

- "We'll never have to support international access."

- "We'll never have to provide 24/7 support."

- "We'll never need to modify that."

- "We'll never need to report that way."

- "We'll never need to capture data to that level."

And they're almost always shortsighted about their needs (sorry about that, guys!)

Try to provide structures that your feelings tell you will support additional needs in the future. If you're overruled on something you feel passionate about, then make sure your alternative design stays with the program documentation somehow along with a risk assessment. That way, a future team will have a head start. On many occasions when clients utter these sentences, the opposite is true!

"We Always . . ."

In a similar vein, we've heard clients state the following:

- "We always have that information when we create this record."

- "We always report that way."

- "We always take the weekend off."

- "We always need to have a person on call."

- "We always provide this information on this report."

- "We always send this data to that department."

- "We always ship U.S. domestically."

- "We always have only one phone number."

- "We always buy in U.S. dollars."

- "We always have a manager for a department."

The words *always* and *never* are to be suspect at all times. You're allowed to not believe them and provide extra functionality in the form of flexibility, such as allowing for many products per order vs. one, space for international addresses (even if they don't think they will ever use it), and so on. Your goal as a modeler is often to turn these *always* and *never* statements into "Until we had this new application, we always/never used to . . .". Help your clients recognize that they used to do it that way because their system restricted them to those choices. You're helping them design a brave new world of data rule possibilities.

Purchased Solution Projects

Logical and Physical data models for commercial applications are interesting concepts. The vendor generally tells you these models don't exist, often for proprietary reasons. If we thought they really didn't exist, we'd be questioning the database design from the start.

Sometimes a data modeler will be asked to support a team deploying a commercial, off-the-shelf solution (COTS) such as Oracle Financials, Lawsen, SAP, PeopleSoft, or smaller packages. Sometimes they'd like you to look at the structures with an eye to helping with the first data load, custom report building, or indeed data conversion issues. While it can sometimes be hard to work with such commercial packages, since you may not be able to readily access the definitions of the tables and columns that the enterprise data resides in, you can use all your reverse-engineering skills. Granted, some systems are so complicated that you'd be foolish to manipulate data using anything other than the means provided by the software tools. However, that doesn't mean you can't work to integrate purchased solutions with existing systems or create a way for users to develop their own ad hoc queries of a data warehouse, for example.

Estimating Support

Find out what the team wants. Sometimes it's just a simple reverse engineer of the tables or screens to aid reporting on the database objects. You have to manage expectations of what a model will be able to do for them. We've worked with vendor packages that have no constraints created at the database level. This means the reverse-engineered data model is just a collection of boxes. Sometimes the naming convention is totally alien to what they're used to; SAP, for example, abbreviates *German*. A data model such as this provides little to the general metadata of the company. It's difficult (at least for us) to offer a model without definitions, relationships, and a key to naming conventions, but we try to help where we can.

No Model Available

Always ask the vendor for a model. Even if the Physical model design is proprietary, the Logical model design shouldn't be. The business rules of what the system is providing should be in the Logical model. We fully admit to being almost constantly turned down by vendors. But if enough of us ask, maybe someday it will be provided without having to nag for it.

Logical

The only way to build a Logical model (which documents the data elements, definitions, and business rules without any physical denormalization to cloud the fundamentals) from most vendor packages is from the front end. You have no access to the code, and the database design isn't usually much help because of proprietary issues. This is reverse-engineering analysis with a lot of shortcomings. Our estimate is something like this:

- Two hours per setup screen (application configurables)

- Four hours per LOV screen

- Eight hours per transaction screen

So, if the application has two screens to set up security and application management configurables, with nine different lists to be set up and twenty transaction screens, the modeler could estimate the following:

```
(2 hours 3 2 set up screens)
+
(4 3 9 LOVs)
+
(8 3 20 OLTP screens)
or 4 + 36 + 160 = 200 hours
```

This turns out to be five weeks full-time for the vendor application.

Physical

Building a Physical data model is a pretty straightforward task, unless you're being asked to document constraints that are being managed in the front end or through stored procedures. You can generate a Physical model quickly based on your software tool's ability to connect to the RDBMS the application is installed on, whether it's designed to be read from that platform, and what's actually available for it to read in the RDBMS catalogs. The following are our suggestions for producing just a Physical model:

- **Manual creation type**: One hour per table

- **Automatic reverse engineer**: Four hours to clean up the graphic

- **With relationships that aren't in the DBMS**: Two hours per table

So, if the application has twenty tables and your software can access it, it'd take about four hours to produce a picture. If you're typing it out (assuming tables of an average of 15 columns), it'd take about a week (40 hours).

Definitions

Definitions (*comments*) may or may not be provided at the database level. If they are, then your software will bring them in from the dictionary tables of the RDBMS. Or you may be able to find them in a Data Definition Language (DDL) file as comments. If not, then a half hour per column is a good benchmark, with a caveat that you'll probably not be able to provide all of them (some will be a mystery forever). If this application had twenty tables averaging fifteen columns each, you might need about four weeks to get all the definitions together based on data profiling and testing your ideas by exercising the screens and reports to verify your analysis.

Non-normalized Designs

Don't expect to understand the Physical model design of a commercial application. We've been overwhelmed by what's provided as the table designs of really respected software companies. Some of them are aggregations of older, previously independent applications, possibly modified from previous hierarchical or network designs, that are patched together with a new front end for backward compatibility. Sometimes the database is deliberately designed to be a total mystery as part of the security measures of the vendor.

So, unlike other types of data element analysis, don't expect to come out of a vendor-supplied product analysis understanding the underlying structure of the data.

No Naming Legend

Generally, vendor structures don't come with a list of abbreviations or terms used in the data structures. This means the only way to create a data dictionary or set of table/column definitions will be a full database data profiling. The tables and columns will not necessarily be named to help you search for something. We find columns named just NAME or just DATE without any clue as to which name or date is meant. But by far the worst recognition has to do with abbreviations and surrogate keys. Without constraints at the database level, nonsignificant numbers representing foreign keys to somewhere are useless. And without some naming standard to work with, figuring out abbreviations is nothing more than an educated guess.

Questions to Ask

Sometimes the DBA or data modeler is invited to preview vendor software before the decision is made to buy it. If you're asked to review it, then try to bring up these issues before the purchase has been made:

Can you integrate? You need to know if there will be enough understanding of the data structures to allow other enterprise system integration. If this is a new HR system, then can you use the employee data for other systems directly, or do you need to build an intermediary system that's basically duplicated data just to be able to access and use it correctly? Depending on the criticality of the enterprise data to be managed in a vendor application, we give low marks to an application that can't be integrated into the enterprise data concepts.

Can you bulk load? Most vendors provide some start-off functionality that assists in launching a newly deployed system. Ask if you can do it more than once without bothering the existing data. Will it check for duplicates of the members of the set, rather than surrogate key uniqueness (which is pretty rare)? We generally feel pretty comfortable bulk loading custom-designed systems (even if we have to truncate and reload part of the system more than once) because we understand all the nuances of the data design. This isn't usually the case in vendor designs. At least make people aware that after the initial load, there's a potential that even large quantities of data will need to be entered manually in order to use the data integrity checks that are only at the screen level.

Can you write your own reports? This is generally a crucial question for us. Don't let the vendor say, "Yes, if you use our report writer." Many provided report writers are slimmed down for client usage and can't support the more complicated queries, formatting, security, merging of other system data, or logic tree analysis that many companies require. You want to know if you can write reports, query the data, and basically access the data through a programmatic method by using the tools currently standard in IT. This means you can capitalize the reporting tricks already in use in the database without having to translate them all into another tool.

Legacy and Forensic Analysis

Sometimes this type of analysis reminds us of those deep-sea submarine exploration shows. You're totally in the dark, and funny-looking objects keep swimming into your meager spotlight. The time it takes to unearth and document a legacy system depends on how long it has been used and modified, how integrated to the enterprise it is, and how large is it.

Table 17-2 shows an extremely general estimate (just to give you a starting place) for most analyses; it contains our size definitions for a large, medium, and small legacy system.

Table 17-2. *Definition of Data Model Characteristic Terms*

Quantity	Small	Medium	Large
Number of tables	Less than twenty tables	Twenty to fifty tables	More than fifty tables
Number of integration source/targets	Zero to one live integration source/targets	More than two live integration source/targets	More than five live integration source/targets
Number of database code objects	Less than ten database code objects (triggers, procedures, and so on)	More than ten database code objects (triggers, procedures, and so on)	More than twenty database code objects (triggers, procedures, and so on)
Conceptual modeling time	Four hours	Four hours per ten tables	Eight hours per ten tables
Logical modeling time	One hour per nonoperational attribute	One hour per nonoperational attribute	May be impossible/two hours per non-operational attribute
Physical modeling time	One hour per nonoperational column	One hour per nonoperational column	One hour per non-operational column

Note You may totally disagree with any or all of these estimate factors, but we always think it's easier to take someone else's estimate and say that it's wrong than to invent one in the first place. So leverage these thoughts to come up with your own formulas.

Questions to Ask

All knowledge is valuable to the enterprise. Some of it is just more valuable than others. Take the task of documenting a legacy system, for instance. You need to ask these questions:

Is it worth analyzing? Why this system? Why not another one? Is it because it's being replaced? Are you trying to find the data scope? What's the desired knowledge goal in dissecting this application or suite of applications? Just how complicated would this analysis be? What's the cost benefit from knowing this information?

When was it last used? Some applications die natural deaths. The last customer gets transferred, or the business process changes. Monitor the activity of the database, and see whether it's being used by a significant number of users or whether you're actually wasting time reviewing a data desert. How important is this system to the enterprise? Who can you talk to who was employed here when the system was first deployed?

Is there any documentation? Search code libraries. Ask for training documentation and programmers manuals; even the code itself may have notes in it. Try to find the original project documentation. Sometimes (although not often) you'll find an original Physical data model from which you only need to create delta documentation. Do be careful, though, since any documentation you find will need to be validated before you can rely on it to make any decisions.

Expectations from Data Profiling

The best way to get definitions for a legacy system is simply to match table/column name assumptions with the data actually in the column. Then you can say with certainty that although the column says `Employee_First_Name`, you don't think that Mr., Mrs., and Dr. are really first names. Most legacy systems have been performing their jobs for a long time, and having odd data values (such as titles in the first name column) doesn't always cause serious problems. Many data anomalies have been accepted by the enterprise because nothing stopped on account of it.

Tracing Surrogate Key Values to Their Source

Surrogate keys have been around for a long time. They're almost the rule rather than the exception. Unfortunately for a data modeler trying to trace data, they add a level of complexity to your task. You need a skilled programmer at your elbow for a while, or you need to learn how to query that RDBMS. We've had helpful DBAs port the data and data structures into a neutral environment (such as Access) where we could work without screwing up the live data, only to find that we still couldn't figure out what was happening. It's unfortunate, but sometimes the data alone can't tell the story.

The problem especially lies in the areas where the referential integrity (RI) constraints at the database level haven't been created to let you know where the data originated. That, along with less than helpful column naming, can leave you with only the front end or the application management code to help find how the data is built and to where it migrates. When you have natural keys to work with, you at least have some chance of finding values that are codes or names. But when you're working with generic sequence numbers created on each and every table for primary keys, you lose almost all ability to narrow down the possible sources for parent-to-child relationships.

Human Intervention

Have you ever looked at a report from an application and been confused because the things being reported don't seem to exist in the system you're analyzing? We've had to take a lot of reports apart to figure out that there has been some translation or aggregation code added to change values into what the customer wanted to report, rather than change the original data values at source.

You may find instances where the data values in the legacy system never seem to be reported, caught, or fixed when they caused problems. There's some human intervention going on that causes dissimilar values to be grouped, dramatic changes to occur from one value to another, and even masking and filtering that seems to change critical enterprise totals. Your data profiling results will probably only confuse you in these circumstances.

If you're doing a legacy analysis, you need to be aware that the whole data story doesn't lie in the database design. Suggest that someone needs to pull apart the reports, screens, and interfaces as well to get a whole picture. We've tried to follow data values as they move through the enterprise. They're created in one system, transferred to another, and report out to a desktop. On the desktop they're sifted, sorted, rounded, truncated, mutated, and modified. From there they're moved into an aggregated view in Focus, Lotus 1-2-3, or Excel. Then they're loaded back into other systems, which move them again. Finally, they end up in the data warehouse or operational data store (ODS) with no history of how they came to be.

Legacy systems have been around long enough to become an intrinsic part of what can be termed the *great data dance*. You'll need to pay special attention to the interfaces that take place, when, using what logic, from what source, and to what target. Without that view of the life cycle of the data elements, you have an incomplete picture of the data structure.

Closing Thoughts

Finally, let's look at the few things that will make the most difference to your ability to data model.

Model Reviews

Model reviews are critical. This is where you get buy-in, validation, and approval of your discoveries. Incorrect models can be fixed in a moment, but lack of model reviews will take a toll on your credibility that may take years to repair. Model reviews where you encourage participation, feedback, and brainstorming by the rest of the team can open doors, build strong relationships, and help your career goals. Take them seriously. Realize that model reviews have goals and objectives as much as the models themselves do. Focus on what you want to accomplish. Then do everything you can to help make it a success.

Make sure everyone with an interest in the project is invited and that they all receive whatever documentation you need them to read prior to the meeting. This is your time to explain what you've discovered. You need to present with confidence and at a technical level appropriate for your audience. Don't bore the project manager with table definitions or the DBA with definitions of entities and attributes.

Remember to ensure that notes are taken of the meeting, paying particular attention to any issues, points of contention, or action items that arise. Writing these issues down will convince the audience that these are important enough to spend more time on than you have in the model review. It also allows you to follow up on any points raised.

Experience Counts

Data modeling, project management, programming, and database administration are all skills that mature over time. They aren't simple classroom knowledge skill sets. They benefit from time in real problem-solving situations. We don't expect this book to do anything more than provide a framework for someone who wants to build, read, or review a data model. You have to do it a few times to get comfortable with the language, the choices, and when to make them.

Don't get frustrated if it doesn't seem to be easy. It isn't always easy. But it's simple. Remember learning soccer? The rules are simple enough. The ball movement is simple enough. Winning a game isn't necessarily easy, but it's based on simplicity. The more you play, then the more comfortable you will be with the challenges and the more confident you will be about your choices.

■Note Be passionate about gaining experience; model everything you can lay your hands on; review what you did with the programmers, DBAs, clients, project managers; and soak up everything they tell you. But keep returning to the concepts of normalization to check the results.

Responsibility vs. Authority

Unfortunately, we're frequently asked to be responsible for things that we have no authority to control. Data modelers are generally given the responsibility to analyze, document, and provide documentation about the enterprise data. They're generally relied on to provide a beginning database design.

However, they're rarely given the authority to enforce that any of their designs, suggestions, or analysis conclusions are acted on. Therefore, they aren't independently authorized to build an integrated, safe, secure, well-managed data environment. Instead, data modelers are simply part of the chain of authority. The DBAs may have the authority to approve or disapprove a database design, and the programmers may have the authority to change the design in order to meet schedule or budget. The data modeler may only have the authority to suggest, encourage, and promote relational designs.

We've seen authority for the database designs lay in many places, and we've also seen no authority framework provided at all, in a sort of data management free-for-all. Perhaps worst of all have been the times we've witnessed a data management group given authority for the data structures of the company that have created a bottleneck, brick wall, legalistic, ivory-tower department that's avoided at all costs. We've watched departments literally buy their own servers to avoid having to deal with data management authority. How sad. Instead of bringing about a better data world they've created a world that includes data sharing resistance, revolution, and civil war.

You need to find out what your authority is, what the authority of the team members you work with is, and how to provide the best product you can within that framework. Talk with your manager about it. Draft a process model of how data analysis and modeling fits into the processes of data management in your world. You may even find ways to improve what's currently happening to the betterment of everyone's common data.

Summary

Team building, maintenance, and support are crucial to the success of any project. You saw in the first half of this chapter how bringing attributes such as arrogance, defensiveness, obstruction, and an inability to compromise to the team will impair its ability to function efficiently. You should instead aim to be open minded, willing to listen to other inputs, and exacting in the production of definitions and concepts so you can draw up the highest quality data models.

Don't negatively impact the schedule if you can help it. Recognize and deal with "analysis paralysis" by knowing if you've hit something that really needs extra time or if you're just stuck. Try to find the right mix of perfectionism, communication levels, educated guessing, requesting assistance, tools, training, and research material to get the job done.

And, finally, treat your models as the best product in your line. Deliver it with quality and aplomb. Make sure the customers are comfortable with the following:

- Placement of the objects

- Readability of the text

- Amount of information available

- Quality of information

- Denormalization choices

- Standards

- Security measures for protecting the model

In the second half of the chapter, we attempted to provide a distilled version of some of our experience with data and design. We told you about the surprises we've had about data, especially in our expectations of how it behaves. You looked at some "best-guess" formulas for determining how long projects involving custom design or modeling the purchased systems might take you. Of course, we can't add anything that's unique to your world, so you may want to take our numbers and double them! We finished off by covering some of the "softer" issues around your modeling work, including model reviews and authority for data management.

Data modeling is something that will provide you with constant challenges and opportunities to learn. It's a great job and is a position full of opportunities to explore new business processes, try out new technical tools, and potentially make a lasting difference in managing data assets. It's a job that not enough people take seriously, which can result in badly designed, inefficient databases that are full of data anomalies; this can cost companies time, money, credibility, and losses of opportunity in a fast-moving world. As a data modeler, it's your mission to eradicate these misuses of data and lead your colleagues to a world where well-behaved, predictable, and usable data becomes the norm.

With a grasp of basic relational theory and practice in creating definitions for entities, attributes, tables, columns, and relationships, you, as a data modeler, can become a powerful and valuable asset in helping deliver well-designed, robust, high-performing applications within any organization.

Data Modeling: Resources

John Donne wrote, "No man is an island, entire of himself," and neither are information technology (IT) professionals. Even if you're the only person in your company who knows what data modeling is and how to read a data model, you don't have to feel alone.

You have dozens of ways to keep the communications lines open between you and the outside data modeling/management world. This appendix covers just a few.

Organizations

Many companies will actually pay for your annual dues to belong to a professional organization. But even if yours won't, the fees are usually small enough that you'll still benefit from being a member.

Dozens of organizations exist that are dedicated to data management. The following are two that are interesting. Organizations can be local or international; specific to one skill set or more generic; and small, encouraging person-to-person meetings, or large, offering more virtual connections. Look for one or more organizations that suit your needs.

DAMA International

Data Management Association (DAMA) International is *the* professional organization of data modelers (http://www.dama.org/). DAMA has the international group as well as local chapters. It's a good place to swap war stories and find out what's happening in the data modeling world.

AITP

The Association of Information Technology Professionals (AITP) offers opportunities for IT leadership and education through partnerships with industry, government, and academia (http://www.aitp.org/). AITP provides quality IT-related education, information on relevant IT issues, and forums for networking with experienced peers and other IT professionals.

Books

We could spend a lot of time talking about other resources you might find helpful. You need to keep reading. The following are some suggestions of other materials you can use to improve your understanding of data modeling:

Bobak, Angelo. *Data Modeling and Design for Today's Architectures*. Norwood, MA: Artech House Publishers, 1997.

Brackett, Michael H. *Practical Data Design*. Englewood Cliffs, New Jersey: Prentice-Hall, 1990.

Bruce, Thomas A. *Designing Quality Databases with IDEF1X Information Models*. New York: Dorset House, 1992.

Carlis, John, and Joseph Maguire. *Mastering Data Modeling: A User-Driven Approach*. Boston, MA: Addison-Wesley, 2001.

Chiantico Press. *CASE: The Potential and the Pitfalls*. Hoboken, NJ: John Wiley & Sons, 1989.

DAMA International. *Implementing Data Resource Management*, Third Edition. New York: DAMA International, 2000.

Date, C. J. *An Introduction to Database Systems*, Eighth Edition. Boston, MA: Addison-Wesley, 2003.

Date, C. J. *The Database Relational Model: A Retrospective Review and Analysis*. Boston, MA: Addison-Wesley, 2000.

Davidson, Louis. *Professional SQL Server 2000 Database Design*. Hoboken, NJ: Wrox, 2001.

DeAngelis, Carla. *Data Modeling with ERwin*. Indianapolis, IN: Sams, 2000.

Durell, William. *The Complete Guide to Data Modeling*. Princeton, NJ: Data Administration, 1993.

English, Larry P. *Improving Data Warehouse and Business Information Quality: Methods for Reducing Costs and Increasing Profits*. Hoboken, NJ: John Wiley & Sons, 1999.

Flavin, Matt. *Fundamental Concepts of Information Modeling*. New York, NY: Prentice-Hall, 1981.

Fleming, Candace C., and Barbara von Halle. *Handbook of Relational Database Design*. Boston, MA: Addison-Wesley, 1989.

Fowler, Martin. *Patterns of Enterprise Application Architecture*. Boston, MA: Addison-Wesley, 2002.

Fowler, Martin. *Analysis Patterns: Reusable Object Models*. Boston, MA: Addison-Wesley, 1996.

Halpin, Terry. *Information Modeling and Relational Databases: From Conceptual Analysis to Logical Design*. San Francisco, CA: Morgan Kaufmann, 2001.

Halpin, Terry. *Conceptual Schema and Relational Database Design*. New York, NY: Prentice-Hall, 1995.

Hawryszkiewycz, I. T. *Database Analysis and Design*, Second Edition. New York, NY: Prentice Hall, 1991.

Hay, David C. *Data Model Patterns: Conventions of Thought*. New York, NY: Dorset House, 1995.

Hernandez, Michael J. *Database Design for Mere Mortals: A Hands-On Guide to Relational Database Design*, Second Edition. Boston, MA: Addison-Wesley, 2003.

Hoberman, Steve. *Data Modeler's Workbench: Tools and Techniques for Analysis and Design*, First Edition. Hoboken, NJ: John Wiley & Sons, 2001.

Hudson, Debra L. *Practical Model Management Using CASE Tools*. Hoboken, NJ: John Wiley & Sons, 1993.

Inmon, William H. *Data Architecture: The Information Paradigm*. Hoboken, NJ: John Wiley & Sons, 1992.

Jones, Paul E., and Robert M. Curtis. *Logical Database Design*, Second Edition. Hoboken, NJ: John Wiley & Sons, 1988.

Kimball, Ralph. *The Data Warehouse Toolkit: The Complete Guide to Dimensional Modeling*, Second Edition. Hoboken, NJ: John Wiley & Sons, 2002.

Purba, Sanjiv (Editor). *Data Management Handbook*, Third Edition. New York, NY: Auerbach, 1999.

Redman, Thomas C. *Data Quality: The Field Guide*, Newton, MA: Digital Press, 2001.

Reingruber, Michael C., and William W. Gregory. *The Data Modeling Handbook: A Best Practice Approach to Building Quality Data*. Hoboken, NJ: John Wiley & Sons, 1994.

Rishe, Naphtali. *Database Design: The Semantic Modeling Approach*. New York, NY: McGraw-Hill, 1992.

Ross, Ronald G., and Wanda I. Michaels. *Resource Life Cycle Analysis: A Business Modeling Technique for IS Planning*. Houston, TX: Business Rules Solutions, 1992.

Ross, Ronald G. *Entity Modeling: Techniques and Application*. Houston, TX: Business Rules Solutions, 1987.

Sanders, G. Lawrence. *Data Modeling*. Danvers, MA: Course Technology, 1995.

Silverston, Len. *The Data Model Resource Book, Vol. 1: A Library of Universal Data Models for All Enterprises*, Revised Edition. Hoboken, NJ: John Wiley & Sons, 2001.

Silverston, Len. *The Data Model Resource Book, Vol. 2: A Library of Universal Data Models for Industry Types*, Revised Edition. Hoboken, NJ: John Wiley & Sons, 2001.

Simsion, Graeme, and Graham Witt. *Data Modeling Essentials: Comprehensive Guide to Data Analysis, Design, and Innovation*, Third Edition. San Francisco, CA: Morgan Kaufmann, 2004.

Tannenbaum, Adrienne. *Metadata Solutions: Using Metamodels Repositories, XML, and Enterprise Portals to Generate Information on Demand*. Boston, MA: Addison-Wesley, 2001.

Teorey, Toby J. *Database Modeling and Design*, Third Edition. San Francisco, CA: Morgan Kaufman, 1999.

Thalheim, Bernhard. *Entity Relationship Modeling: Foundations of Database Technology*. New York, NY: Springer-Verlag, 2000.

Yourdon. *Yourdon Systems Method: Model-Driven Systems Development*. New York, NY: Prentice-Hall, 1993.

Internet Resources

The following is a sampling of our favorite Internet resources to get you started.

Newsletters

These are newsletters you can read regularly:

- **The Data Administration Newsletter**: http://www.tdan.com/
- **Enterprise Warehouse Solutions**: http://www.ewsolutions.com/

Online Magazines

The following are all online magazines:

- **Business 2.0**: http://www.business2.com/
- **Intelligent Enterprise**: http://www.intelligententerprise.com/
- **DM Review**: http://www.dmreview.com/
- **Darwin Magazine**: http://www.darwinmag.com/
- **New Architect**: http://www.newarchitectmag.com/
- **DB2 Magazine**: http://www.db2mag.com/
- **KM (Knowledge Management) World**: http://www.kmworld.com/
- **Data Warehousing**: http://www.datawarehousing.com/
- **Data Warehouse**: http://www.datawarehouse.com/

Training

Any training helps you to be a better data modeler. But you especially need training in how to run meetings, give presentations, facilitate analysis sessions, and support software development life-cycle methodologies.

You also need training in the basics of the data world. But don't stop there. If you want to specialize in data modeling for banks, for example, take accounting classes. Keep learning until you drop.

Courses

Almost every country in the world offers college-level courses in data modeling. Most of them are called something other than data modeling, though. The subject of data modeling is usually covered in courses leading to a designation or degree in the following:

- Data management

- Database design

- Decision sciences

- Information management

- Information organization

- Information resource management

- Information science

- Information studies

- Knowledge management

- Knowledge organization

The following companies offer classes:

- **A.D. Experts**: http://www.adexperts.com

- **Anubis**: http://www.anubisinc.com

- **Aonix**: http:// www.aonix.com

- **Computer Associates**: http://www.ca.com

- **Datanamic**: http://www.datanamic.com

- **Embarcadero**: http://www.embarcadero.com

- **IBM**: http://www.ibm.com

- **Microsoft**: http://www.microsoft.com

- **Oracle**: http://www.oracle.com

- **Popkin**: http://www.popkin.com

- **Rational**: http://www.rational.com

- **Silverrun Technologies**: http://www.silverrun.com

- **Sybase**: http://www.sybase.com

- **Visible Systems**: http://www.visible.com

Conferences

Whatever you do in your career, stay in touch with the world. Network with others, trade stories on the Internet, and attend conferences. Conferences are rich learning experiences that can't be easily replaced.

Annual

The following are annual conferences:

- **DAMA International Symposium**: http://www.wilshireconferences.com/
- **TWDI World Conference (The Data Warehouse Institute)**: http://www.dw-institute.com/
- **Software Development Conference (SDI)**: http://www.sdexpo.com/
- **Information Quality Conference (by Larry English)**: http://www.infoimpact.com/
- **Committee on Data for Science and Technology (CODATA)**: http://www.codata.org/
- **Business Rules Forum**: http://www.businessrulesforum.com/
- **KM World**: http://www.kmworld.com/

Various Sponsored Events

The following are sponsored events:

- **Digital Consulting Institute (DCI)**: http://www.dci.com/
- **The Brainstorm Group**: http://www.brainstorm-group.com/bsgweb/index.asp

APPENDIX B

■ ■ ■

Glossary

This appendix defines a fairly comprehensive set of terms used in relational data modeling.

1NF: Acronym for *First Normal Form*. A relation is said to be in 1NF if and only if each attribute of the relation is atomic. More simply, for an entity to be in 1NF, each column must contain only a single data value, and each row must contain exactly the same columns. All repeating groups must be eliminated.

24/7: A term referring to the availability of a system. This is generally interpreted as "no scheduled downtime." Within some technical support teams, this can be interpreted as meaning "no unscheduled downtime."

2NF: Acronym for *Second Normal Form*. To be in 2NF, an entity must first fulfill the requirements to be in First Normal Form (1NF). Additionally, each nonkey attribute in the entity must be functionally dependent upon the primary key. All redundant data is eliminated.

3NF: Acronym for *Third Normal Form*. To be in 3NF, an entity must first fulfill the requirements of Second Normal Form (2NF). Additionally, all attributes that aren't dependent upon the primary key must be eliminated.

4NF: Acronym for *Fourth Normal Form*. To be in 4NF, an entity must first fulfill the requirements of Third Normal Form (3NF). Additionally, all attributes are single valued for a member of the set.

5NF: Acronym for *Fifth Normal Form*. To be in 5NF, an entity must first fulfill the requirements of Fourth Normal Form (4NF). Additionally, it must be verified that if the constituent parts of an entity were divided, they couldn't be reconstructed.

abstract class: In object-oriented modeling, a class, generally a supertype, that isn't intended to exist on its own but serves to define a base of common attributes and operations for one or more subtypes.

abstraction: The process of ignoring or suppressing levels of detail to provide a simpler, more generalized view.

access: 1. The operation of reading or writing data on a storage device. 2. A security privilege. 3. A Microsoft relational database management system (RDBMS).

access transparency: The masking of differences in data representation and access mechanisms to simplify the view of processes and objects to anyone using them.

ad hoc query: Any query that can't be determined (isn't stored and reused) prior to the moment the query is issued. It's usually dynamically constructed Structured Query Language (SQL), often by desktop-resident query tools.

aggregate: In Unified Modeling Language (UML), a class that's the "whole" part of a whole-part relationship.

aggregation (data): Data that's the result of applying a process to combine data elements. This is data that's taken collectively or in summary form. Usually, this is a sum, count, or average of underlying detail data.

aggregation (UML): A form of Unified Modeling Language (UML) association that denotes the grouping of multiple instances of one class into a composite entity.

a.k.a.: Acronym for *also known as*.

alias: An alternative label used to refer to a data element or table. This is sometimes called a *synonym* by database systems.

alphanumeric: Physical data that's represented by numbers, letters, or special characters.

alternate key: Column or combination of columns, not the primary key columns, whose values uniquely identify a row in a table.

analysis paralysis: The fear of moving forward until your analysis or product is perfect.

ANSI: Acronym for the *American National Standards Institute*, which is an organization that offers up-to-date resources on national and international standards activities.

API: Acronym for *application programming interface*, which is the reference built into computer applications to facilitate communication among applications.

application: A group of algorithms and data linked together to support specific computer processing.

architecture: The science or art of building. This includes the designing and planning process that occurs in problem solving. The rules that define the structure of the solution and the relationships and dependencies within or outside of it are the final result—be it a network, system, application, database, or business function.

archival database: A collection of data organized to support a specific application as a backup removed from the original set.

arity: The characteristic defining the quantity allowed in a relationship. For example, unary = 1, binary = 2, and ternary = 3.

artificial key: A system-generated, nonsignificant, surrogate identifier or globally unique identifier (GUID) used to uniquely identify a row in a table. This is also known as a *surrogate key*.

ASCII: Acronym for *American Standard Code for Information Interchange*, which is an eight-bit code for character representation; it includes seven bits plus parity. This format for data storage and transmission is commonly referred to as *text format*.

As-Is: The current state of being. This is a term used in analysis to note the design of existing structures or processes.

association: The Unified Modeling Language (UML) term denoting a connection of a class to itself or others. This is the rough UML equivalent of a relationship.

association class: A Unified Modeling Language (UML) class that resolves an intersection between two other classes but requires that there be only one intersection for any two class instances.

associative entity: An entity created to resolve a many-to-many relationship. This is also known as an *intersection entity*.

ATM: Acronym for *asynchronous transfer mode*, a packet-based, switched, point-to-point data transmission protocol capable of transmitting data, voice, video, and audio simultaneously at high speeds.

atomic-level data: Data elements that represent the lowest level of detail. For example, in a daily sales report, the individual items sold would be atomic data, and roll-ups such as invoice and summary totals from invoices are aggregate data.

attribute: A data item that has been "attached" to an entity. By doing this, a distinction can be made between the generic characteristics of the data item itself (for instance, data type and default documentation) and the entity-specific characteristics (for example, identifying and entity-specific documentation). It's a distinct characteristic of an entity for which data is maintained. An attribute is a value that describes or identifies an entity, and an entity contains one or more attributes that characterize the entity as a whole. An entity example is Employee, and an attribute example is Employee Last Name.

audit trail: Data that supports tracing system activity (inserts, updates, and deletes) occurring on a physical database or application. Some operational columns in tables contain audit trail information about each record.

availability: 1. The amount of time a system is functioning and is accessible to its clients. 2. A measurement of computer system reliability; the amount of time a system is accessible to the clients is divided by the amount of time that it isn't accessible to the clients.

Bachman diagrams: Named for Charles Bachman, this is a single-to-double arrow notation to create a data structure diagram (DSD) to build a Logical model design.

backbone: Part of a communications network that usually links nodes or local area networks (LANs) in a diverse arrangement of communication facilities that support multiple clients inside a building, across a city, or between countries. The backbone provides a central support system and is generally one of the most permanent parts of a communications network.

backup: 1. A table or file that stores a copy of the database tables used for an application, 2. The process of copying a file or files to another storage device (disk or tape) to ensure that the data can be restored if the primary copy is accidentally or intentionally destroyed or damaged.

base tables: The normalized data structures maintained in the target warehousing database. Also known as the *detail data*.

baseline: A tested and certified version of a deliverable representing a conceptual milestone that thereafter serves as the basis for further development and that can be modified only through formal change control procedures. A particular version becomes a baseline when a responsible group decides to designate it as such.

batch: A computer application that runs in a sequential series of processing steps.

BCNF: Acronym for *Boyce-Codd Normal Form*. To be in BCNF, an entity must first fulfill the requirements of Third Normal Form (3NF). Additionally, all data sets must be identified and segregated. All attributes must be identified by a primary key.

binary element: A base element of data that either exists as two values or the states true or false or exists as one or zero.

Boolean operation: Any operation of which each of the operands and the result take one of two values.

bottom-up analysis: An analysis technique that focuses on finding the most granular details and building up incrementally to a comprehensive overview.

business case (or business driver): A business problem, situation, or opportunity that justifies the pursuit of a technology project.

business rule: An operating principle or policy that your software must satisfy utilizing logic to calculate or otherwise derive a business-related result.

call: To invoke the execution of a program or process.

candidate key: Any attribute or group of attributes that uniquely identifies each instance of an entity and that's a possible choice for the primary key.

cardinality: The cardinality of a relationship represents the number of occurrences between entities. An entity with a cardinality of one is called a *parent entity*, and an entity with a cardinality of one or more is called a *child entity*.

CASE: Acronym for *computer-aided system/software engineering*, which is a computer application that facilitates through automated functions the process of designing databases, developing applications, and implementing software.

catalog: The directory of all files available to a computer.

category: A logical design structure with a supertype parent and subtype children that divides a master concept into smaller concepts. An example is a supertype of Vehicle and subtypes of Car, Truck, and Van. This is also known as a *generalization hierarchy*.

CGI: Acronym for *Common Gateway Interface*, which is the industry-standard specification for communication between a Web server and a database server.

Chen diagrams: Named for Peter Chen in 1976, this is one of the original semantic data model languages. This is recognized by the use of a chicken-foot graphic to denote "many" on the relationship lines.

CISC: Acronym for the *Complex Instruction Set Computer*. The central processing unit designed to support the direct execution of complex operations in one (or few) processor cycle.

class: The basic component used to create Unified Modeling Language (UML) class diagrams. A class is a combination of the data attributes and common methods representing an object in the real world. This is the rough UML equivalent of an entity.

class diagram: A Unified Modeling Language (UML) design artifact that shows the object classes and associations that exist between them. This is the rough UML equivalent of a data model.

class hierarchy: A Unified Modeling Language (UML) structure with a supertype parent and subtype children that divides a master concept into smaller concepts. This is the UML equivalent of a category.

class words: Simple words used to categorize attributes and columns. Examples are ID, Text, Number, and Date.

client-server system: A software application in which application processing is jointly performed by components that are physically separate (the client and the server). For example, a client computer may communicate over a network to exchange data with a server computer that stores a database.

COBOL: Acronym for *Common Business-Oriented Language*, which is a high-level, third-generation programming language that's used primarily for business applications.

column: 1. Data structure that contains an individual data item within a row (record); the model equivalent of a database field. 2. The name for a field in a relational database management system (RDBMS). A column is a physical implementation of an attribute.

complete category: A category that notes all the subtypes allowed.

composite key: A candidate key made up of more than one attribute or column.

composition: A form of Unified Modeling Language (UML) association that denotes the containment of one class within another.

concatenate: To link more than one atomic data element into a single string of characters and use the result as a single value.

conceptual: An analysis level describing data requirements from a business point of view without the burden of technical details. It's a collection of data structures that expresses the data needs of an organization. It's a high-level logical representation of data concepts.

Conceptual data model: Represents the overall logical structure of a database, which is independent of any software or data storage structure. A Conceptual model often contains data objects not yet implemented in the physical databases. It gives a formal representation of the data needed to run an enterprise or a business activity.

concurrent: Things being executed simultaneously. An example of this is analysis happening in parallel with prototyping.

conformed dimension: A dimension whose data is reused by more than one dimensional design. When modeling multiple data marts, standards across marts with respect to dimensions are useful. Warehouse users may be confused when a dimension has the similar meaning but different names, structures, levels, or characteristics among multiple marts. Using standard dimensions throughout the warehousing environment can be referred to as "conformed" dimensions.

conformed fact: A fact (measurement) that's used in more than one dimensional design. When developing multiple data marts, it's useful to maintain some standard for fact tables. Data warehouse or data mart users may be confused when a fact has the same meaning but different names or when the same name is used with inconsistent meaning across data marts. The practice of consistently using common facts throughout the warehousing environment can be referred to as "conformed" facts.

constraint: 1. In general, a restriction of possibilities. 2. In a database, a programming object that restricts the behavior of data within or between tables in a database.

COTS: Acronym for *commercial, off-the-shelf software*, which is a vendor-provided software solution that usually comes in a box. Most of these have little if any custom work needed to provide a solution. This is the "buy" decision of a make/buy analysis.

CPU: Acronym for *central processing unit*, which is the processor that contains the sequencing and processing facilities for instruction execution, interruption action, timing functions, initial program loading, and other machine-related functions.

CRC card: Acronym for *class responsibility collaborator card*, which is a custom development business architecture design document consisting of a large index card that's used to document the responsibilities and collaborators of a type while architecting the business model, the requirements analysis of the application domain model, the class during software design, and the programming class comments.

DA: Acronym for *data analyst*, *data administrator*, or *data architect*, which is a skill set or job title chartered with direct responsibility of the analysis, identification, understanding, design, and management of data element specifications and business rules as they pertain to the enterprise.

DASD: Acronym for *direct access storage device*, which is a mainframe disk drive that stores information.

data: Information documented by a language system representing facts, text, graphics, bitmapped images, sound, and analog or digital live-video segments. Data is the raw material of a system supplied by data producers and is used by information consumers to create information.

data cleansing: The process of correcting errors or omissions in data. This is often part of the extraction, transformation, and loading (ETL) process of extracting data from a source system, usually before attempting to load it into a target system. This is also known as *data scrubbing*.

data cube: Proprietary data structure used to store data for an online analytical processing (OLAP) end user data access and analysis tool.

data definition: Specification of data entities, including their attributes and relationships, in a coherent database structure to create a schema.

data dictionary: The cross-reference of definitions and specifications for data categories and their relationships.

data element: The most atomic, pure, and simple fact that either describes or identifies an entity. This is also known as an *attribute*. It can be deployed as a column in a table in a physical structure.

data integrity: The condition that exists when there's no accidental or intentional destruction, alteration, or loss of data.

data mapping: The process of noting the relationship of a data element to something or somebody.

data mart: A database, generally following a dimensional design, that's optimized for data access and retrieval and contains a single point-in-time snapshot of data. It's usually designed to facilitate end user analysis of data or reporting. It typically supports a single analytic application used by a distinct set of workers.

data mining: An information extraction activity whose goal is to discover hidden facts contained in databases. Using a combination of machine learning, statistical analysis, modeling techniques, and database technology, data mining finds patterns and subtle relationships in data and infers rules that allow the prediction of future results. Typical applications include market segmentation, customer profiling, fraud detection, evaluation of retail promotions, and credit risk analysis.

data model: A method of visualizing the informational needs of a system that typically takes the form of an entity relationship diagram (ERD). A graphic representation that identifies the structure, content, and relationships of the information used by an organization's business systems (manual, automated, or both). A data model is the specification of data structures and business rules to represent business requirements. This is an abstraction that describes one or more aspects of a problem or a potential solution addressing a problem. Traditionally, models are thought of as one or more diagrams plus any corresponding documentation. However, nonvisual artifacts such as collections of class responsibility collaborator (CRC) cards, a textual description of one or more business rules, or the structured English description of a business process are also considered to be models.

data modeling: A structured approach used to identify major components of an information system's specifications. Data modeling enables you to promote data as a corporate asset to share across the enterprise, provide business professionals with a graphical display of their business rules and requirements, bridge the gap between business experts and technical experts, establish consensus/agreement, and build a stable data foundation.

data-oriented design: Also known as *information engineering* (IE), a system design philosophy that focuses the analysis of software requirements on the system's data requirements.

data profiling: The process of compiling statistics and information about a data set's content, usually in the context of a data quality assessment.

data propagation/replication: The process of transmitting a copy of the data inside tables in one database to another, remotely connected database. This process often involves keeping the two databases synchronized for data changes.

data quality assessment: An analysis of a data source that focuses on how well the data structure, syntax, format, values, accuracy, and completeness meet expectations.

data record: Identifiable set of data values or fields treated as a unit. This is an instance of an entity. It's a member of a data set. It's a tuple in a mathematical set.

data warehouse: A database that can follow a Third Normal Form (3NF) or dimensional design and that houses a time-variant collection of data from multiple sources. It's generally used to collect and store integrated sets of historical data from multiple operational systems and then feed one or more dependent data marts. In some cases, a data warehouse may also provide end user access to support enterprise views of data.

database: A collection of interrelated fact instances (data) stored together with controlled redundancy according to a schema to serve one or more applications. Also, it's a tool/ product or uniquely defined and segregated instance driven by a tool/product designed to manage a collected variable set of related fact instances.

DBA: Acronym for *database administrator*, which is a skill set or job title chartered with direct responsibility of the contents and functioning of a database. This may include some or all the following: design, development, operation, safeguarding, maintenance, and access to or the use of a database and by extension the server on which it resides.

DBMS: Acronym for a *database management system*, which contains and controls information in some structured form so that it can be accessed in an efficient manner. Most DBMSs support some form of Structured Query Language (SQL) as the primary access method. A DBMS may or may not be relational. If it is, it's referred to as an RDBMS.

DDL: Acronym for *Data Definition Language*. The syntactical language used to define a database and its schema to a database management system (DBMS) or relational database management system (RDBMS). In other words, this is the syntax that a given DBMS understands and is used to manipulate the structure of the database, from initial database creation to additions, modifications, and deletions of all database objects (tables, columns, indexes, and so on) to the eventual removal of the database. Another term used for DDL is *schema*. Because each DBMS is slightly different, the DDL statements that each use are also different—sometimes completely alien to each other.

definition: A formal statement of the meaning describing the significance of a thing. This may use examples of correct and incorrect meaning to enhance clarity for the reader.

delimiter: A flag, symbol, or convention used to mark the boundaries of a record, field, or other unit of storage. Many data transfer processes include a translation process of creating a tab- or comma-delimited file from the source, which is interpreted to load to a target.

delta: The difference between two similar structures. You can have a delta between values, documents, or structures.

denormalization: An intentional violation of the rules of normalization done to increase performance of a database. It typically occurs in varying degrees during all phases of physically implementing a database. Database designs are often denormalized to accomplish a specific performance-related goal. Denormalization can't be done without a thorough understanding of the data and the needs of the customer.

dependent entity: An entity that's always a child entity. This is an entity that has one or more foreign keys included in its owned attributes.

derived data: Data that's the result of a computational step applied to reference or event data. Derived data is the result either of relating two or more elements of a single transaction (such as an aggregation) or of relating one or more elements of a transaction to an external algorithm or rule.

descriptive data: The data that records the nonmetric or nonmeasurement properties of something. Data that isn't additive or for which mathematical operations don't make sense is descriptive data; for example, a customer name or Social Security number is descriptive data. This term describes the content of the data. The alternative to descriptive data is *metric data.*

dimension: An independent entity in the model of an organization that serves to aggregate, group, or filter facts from the fact table. Dimensions usually represent a fundamental way of accessing and presenting business information.

dimension table: A table in a Dimensional model representing a dimension.

Dimensional model: A data model influenced by performance considerations and optimized for data access and retrieval. This is a form of entity-relationship (ER) modeling that's limited to working with "measurement" types of subjects and has a prescribed set of allowable structures.

DKNF: Acronym for *Domain Key Normal Form.* To be in DKNF, an entity must first fulfill the requirements of Fifth Normal Form (5NF). Additionally, all constraints must be the logical consequence of the definition of the keys and the domains (data value rules). In other words, all foreign keys must match the attributes/columns and basic data type and length definition of the primary key to which it refers.

DML: Acronym for *Data Manipulation Language,* which is a syntactical programming language supported by a database management system (DMBS) or relational database management system (RDBMS) used to access a database schema in order to insert, update, delete, or select records from/to a table.

DNS: Acronym for *Domain Name System,* which is the mapping of an Internet address such as 123.45.6.789 to the more easily remembered Internet domain name.

domain: The defined restriction/allowable rules applied to a data element or attribute in an entity.

drill down: The process of exposing progressively more detail by making selections of items in a dynamic report or further enhancing a query.

DSS: Acronym for a *decision support system.* This generally consists of a suite of software/hardware that supports exception reporting, stoplight reporting, standard repository, data analysis, and rule-based analysis. It generally includes a database designed and created for end user ad hoc query processing using dimensional database designs.

EDI: Acronym for *Electronic Data Interchange,* which is a standard for electronically exchanging information among computer systems. This is commonly used to pass order, billing, and shipping information between companies.

encryption: The transformation of data from a recognizable form to a form that's unrecognizable without the algorithm used for the encryption. This is commonly used to safeguard data in a database (such as by using passwords) or during transmission.

enterprise data model: A high-level, enterprise-wide framework that describes the subject areas, sources, business dimensions, business rules, and semantics of an enterprise.

entity: The abstraction of a person, place, thing, or concept. An entity comes under scrutiny when it has characteristics of interest to an enterprise and there's a defined need to store information about it.

ERD: Acronym for *entity relationship diagram*, which is a document that visually identifies the relationships between data elements and describes them in varying levels of detail.

ETL: Acronym for *extraction, transformation, and loading*, which is the movement of data from one place to another involving from/to source(s) and target(s) and rules for any changes that are built into the movement. This process uses tools from simple Structured Query Language (SQL) transactions to batch processing to sophisticated automation tools such as Informatica.

exclusive category: The rule in a category structure requiring all members of the supertype to be a member of one and only one of the subtypes.

external data: Data not collected by the organization, such as data available from a reference book, a government source, or a proprietary database.

fact: A measurement, typically numeric and additive, that's stored in a fact table, such as a measure, key performance measure, or key business measure. Facts are typed as descriptive or metric.

fact table: A physical table storing a discrete item of business information. In fact/qualifier modeling, this term describes a role in which business data may be used. The alternative is to be used as a qualifier.

federation: The process of creating a community of separate objects.

flag: An indicator or character that signals the occurrence of some condition. Flags tend to be binary in nature, allowing only a True or False type of fact.

flat file: A collection of records that are related to one another that haven't been organized to meet relational normal forms. Originally a file was stored only outside a database. Now you can refer to a table structured this way as a flat file.

foreign key: 1. Column or combination of columns whose values are required to match a primary key in some other table. 2. Primary key of a parent entity that's contributed to a child entity across a relationship. The parent primary key migrates through the relationship to become an attribute of the child entity.

frequency of update: The time period between updates of records (hourly, daily, weekly, and so on). This could describe the expected amount of activity in a table or a scheduled process, such as loading a data warehouse or data mart.

FTP: Acronym for *File Transfer Protocol*, which is a process commonly used to transfer data files across Transmission Control Protocol/Internet Protocol (TCP/IP) networks, including the Internet and intranets.

fully attributed: A level of definition on a data model making all attributes or columns visible.

function-oriented design: Also known as *structured analysis*, a design philosophy that uses process decomposition to break the requirements of the functionality of the system down into a procedural hierarchy.

generalization: The process of forming a more comprehensive or less restrictive class (a superclass) from one or more entities (or classes, in Unified Modeling Language [UML]).

generalization hierarchy: A grouping of entities that share common attributes. A hierarchy has two types of entities: a supertype is a generic parent entity that contains generalized attributes, and key subtypes are category entities that inherit the attributes and key through the relationships of the supertype entity. Each subtype entity will contain the migrated foreign key and only those attributes that pertain to the category type. There are two reasons to build a generalization hierarchy: First, an entity can be partitioned into "type" ranges, and subtypes have distinct attributes. Second, a subtype requires relationships that shouldn't be generalized at the subtype level.

granularity: A classification of data based upon the level of detail at which data is recorded. Atomic, base, and summary are all classifications of data granularity.

group attributes (composite attributes): An attribute consisting of more atomic attributes. For example, Address consists of Street Number, Street Name, City Name, State Name, Country Name, and Zip Code. Creating a group attribute allows you to reuse the definitions and specifications consistently.

GUI: Acronym for *graphical user interface*, which is the computer system interface that uses visual elements, including icons and graphical controls, to facilitate interaction with end users.

heuristic: A type of analysis in which the next step is determined by the results of the current step of analysis.

hierarchical database: A database management system based on a tree structure allowing a child object to have only one parent object it's related to using record pointers rather than migrating data elements (foreign keys).

history table: A table used to capture the existing values and data/time of modification for a record prior to the update in the original table. This table can keep multiple copies of the same record over time, saving the changes for analysis.

hit: An occurrence of data that satisfies a defined search criteria.

householding: A methodology of consolidating names and addresses.

HTML: Acronym for *Hypertext Markup Language*, which is a syntactical programming language that uses a tagging protocol to provide uniform displays of fonts, tables, and other World Wide Web (WWW) page elements on most browser applications.

HTTP: Acronym for *Hypertext Transfer Protocol*, which is the standard for transmitting and exchanging Hypertext Markup Language (HTML) pages.

IDEF1X: Acronym for *Integration DEFinition*, which is one of a group of modeling methods (this one focusing on data modeling) that can be used to describe operations and processing in an enterprise. IDEF was created by the U.S. Air Force. It was originally developed for the manufacturing environment; IDEF methods have been adapted for wider use and for software development in general.

identifying relationship: A type of relationship where the primary key of the parent migrates to a position in the primary key of the child.

IE methodology: Acronym for *information engineering methodology*, which is a data modeling syntax developed by Clive Finkelstein and James Martin in 1976.

impedence mismatch: A term meaning incompatibilities between modeling philosophies, such as between Unified Modeling Language (UML) and Integration DEFinition (IDEF1X). A concept that suffers from the impedence mismatch of two modeling philosophies can't be effectively represented in both.

inclusive category: The rule in a category structure allowing all members of the supertype to be a member of one or more of the subtypes.

incomplete category: A category that doesn't display all the subtypes allowed.

independent entity: An entity that has no foreign keys included in its owned attributes.

index: A data structure associated with a table that's logically ordered by the values of a key. It improves database performance and access speed. You normally create indexes for columns that you access regularly and where response time is important. Indexes are most effective when they're used on columns that contain mostly unique values.

information: Data that has been processed in such a way that it can increase the knowledge of the person who receives it. Information is the output, or "finished goods," of information systems. Information is also what individuals assimilate and evaluate to solve problems or make decisions.

instance: Each entity represents a set or collection of like individual objects called *instances*. Each instance must be uniquely identifiable and distinct from all other instances.

integration: As a role and responsibility of one or more warehousing data stores, this term refers to structuring and storing data to serve as a single source of information organized by subjects of business interest. Data integration includes all activities and structural adjustments needed to provide a scopewide single source of consistent data.

integrity: The concept that data will be available, will be consistent, will produce accurate results, and will not be changed unintentionally.

interface: The common boundary of separate things. This is the point of mediation.

internal data: Data collected by an organization such as operating and customer data.

Internet: The worldwide system of interconnected computer networks. The Internet is built on a series of low-level protocols such as Hypertext Markup Language (HTML), Hypertext Transfer Protocol (HTTP), and File Transfer Protocol (FTP); it provides easy and powerful exchange of information.

intersection entity: An entity created to resolve a many-to-many relationship. This is also known as an *associative entity*.

intranet: An organization's internal system of connected networks built on Internet-standard protocols and usually connected to the Internet via a firewall.

ISDN: Acronym for *Integrated Services Digital Network*, which is a nonleased digital phone line. ISDN is a digital standard that allows data transmission and is the most common means for delivering high-speed data services to remote locations.

ISO: Abbreviation for *International Standards Organization*, which derives from the Greek word *iso*, meaning "equal." This international organization, founded in 1946 and composed of national standards bodies from more than 75 countries, has defined a number of important computer standards. The most significant of these is Open Systems Interconnection (OSI), which is a standardized architecture for designing networks.

JAD: Acronym for *joint application development*, which is an analysis process facilitating both the business and technical teams to explore and develop an understanding of a business activity, which could lead to the launch of a software tool development project by defining system requirements. The JAD focuses on documenting the As-Is and proposing one or several To-Be business improvements that could impact current procedure as well as tools.

JCL: Acronym for *Job Control Language*, which is the syntactical mainframe programming language used to control the execution of applications.

join: The operation that takes two relations (sets or tables) and produces one new relation (query result: set or view) by collecting the combined rows and matching the corresponding columns with a stated condition to test between the two.

key: A data element (attribute or column) or the combination of several used to identify a member of a set, instance of an entity, or record in a table.

key-based: A display level of a data model that focuses the attention on the primary keys of the entities and the relationships between them.

LAN: Acronym for *local area network*, which is the short-distance data communications network used to link computers and peripheral devices, usually limited to communication within a building or campus.

legacy system: An existing data creation, management, and reporting system in a company generally still in use.

Logical model: A specification of what data elements and business rules are required to support a business activity. The Logical data model represents a view of an organization's data from a business perspective.

mainframe: The large-capacity computer that provides high levels of processing power, security, and stability.

mandatory relationship: A business rule that requires the existence of a relationship between two different entities.

many-to-many: A relationship cardinality that describes neither entity as being the parent of the other. Each member of the set described by an entity may relate to many of the members of the set of the other entity. For example, an employee may work on many projects. A project may be supported by many employees.

measure: In Dimensional modeling, a specific data item that describes a fact or aggregation of facts. Measures are implemented as metric facts.

metadata: Literally, data about data. Metadata includes data associated with either an information system or an information object for description, administration, legal requirements, technical functionality, use, and preservation. Business metadata includes business names and unambiguous definitions of the data including examples and business rules for the data. Technical metadata is information about column width, data types, and other technical information that would be useful to a programmer or database administrator (DBA).

metadata repository: A centralized database containing metadata captured from around the enterprise.

methodology: A disciplined set of processes/procedures whose intent is to increase the success factor of analysis, design, implementation, and maintenance of a business solution.

migrating key: 1. The intentional duplication of attributes or columns (foreign key) between entities or tables to identify (refer back to) the link. 2. Instances or records being linked by a relationship between them.

migration: The process by which data is moved to or from one data storage device to another.

mission-critical: Something that's considered essential and vital to a successful operation. If these systems, functions, hardware, applications, or data elements fail to perform to the standard needed, the enterprise is jeopardized.

MOLAP: Acronym for *multidimensional online analytical processing*, which is a type of OLAP analysis provided by a system relying on dedicated, precalculated data sets.

MPP: Acronym for *massive parallel processing*, which is the interconnected group of processors with processing functions divided among the individual processors using automated algorithms for optimized work load distribution.

network: A system of interconnected computing resources (computers, servers, printers, and so on).

network database: A database management system based on a tree structure allowing a child object to have more than one parent object it's related to using record pointers rather than migrating data elements (foreign keys).

nonidentifying: A type of relationship where the primary key of the parent doesn't migrate to the primary key of the child. The foreign key isn't used to provide unique identification.

normalization: A formal approach in data modeling that examines and validates attributes and their entities in the Logical data model. The purpose of data normalization is to ensure that each attribute belongs to the entity to which it has been assigned, that redundant storage of information is minimized, and that storage anomalies are eliminated. The ultimate goal is to organize data elements in such a way that they're stored in one place and one place only.

null: A database value indicating that the information is missing, unknown, not yet known, or inapplicable. Placing a zero in the row, for example, wouldn't reflect the accurate state of the concept of null because zero is a value.

nullability: The data element characteristic of noting that some members of the set can exist with no value for a data element. Nulls aren't the same as spaces, N/A (not applicable), or the word *null*. Nulls are truly valid occurrences of nothing.

object-oriented design: A design philosophy methodology that breaks a system down into objects, embodying both data characteristics in the form of attributes and process characteristics in the form of methods.

ODS: Acronym for an *operational data store*, which is an integrated database of operational data. Its sources include legacy systems, and it contains current or near-term data. An ODS is similar to a data warehouse but contains a limited amount of information (perhaps 30 to 60 days); a data warehouse typically contains more data spanning a longer time frame.

OLAP: Acronym for *online analytical processing*, which is a type of analysis supported by software that transforms data into multidimensional views and that supports multidimensional data interaction, exploration, and analysis. SAS is an example of an OLAP tool.

OLAP database: A database that supports online analytical processing (OLAP). Generally, OLAP databases are supported by data warehouses and data marts.

OLTP: Acronym for *online transactional processing*, which is a database with read and write access where transactions are actually entered, modified, and/or deleted. Because of performance considerations, read-only requests on the database may be routed to an operational data store (ODS). Typically, an OLTP is a fairly "normalized" database.

one-to-many: A relationship cardinality noting that each member of the set in the child entity is related to only one member of the set of the parent entity at a time.

OOA: Acronym for *object-oriented analysis*, which is a software engineering requirements and specification approach that's expressed as a systems object model, which is composed of a population of interacting objects—as opposed to the traditional data or functional views of the systems.

OOD: Acronym for *object-oriented design*, which is a design method in which a system is modeled as a collection of cooperating objects, and individual objects are treated as instances of a class within a class hierarchy.

OODB(MS): The acronym for *object-oriented database (management system)*, which is a database that allows the storage and retrieval of multiple data types, such as text, video, audio, and tabular data.

OOSE: The acronym for *object-oriented software engineering*, which is the process of solving customers' problems by the systematic development and evolution of high-quality software systems within cost, time, and other constraints using an object-oriented approach.

operational data: The data that's maintained by day-to-day operational systems. This data typically represents a "point-in-time" view of the business and is typically both redundant and highly volatile. Operational data is the most common source of data for a data warehouse.

optional relationship: The opposite of a *mandatory relationship*.

ORM: Acronym for *object role modeling*, which is a Conceptual modeling approach that pictures the application world as a set of objects that play roles (parts in relationships with a cardinality of one, two, or more). ORM is a modeling language made up of graphic and textual notations that can capture the rules regarding management of enterprise data and processes.

parameter: A data value that's used to trigger, filter, or restrict a process or program.

parent: The source entity or table of columns that's shared with another entity or table that it's related to through the migration of its primary key to a foreign key in the child.

Physical model: The Physical data model supports the needs of the database administrator and application developers, who focus on the physical implementation of the model in a database.

pointer: A physical address of a data record or other groupings of data that are contained in another record.

primary key: Column or combination of columns whose values uniquely identify a row in a table, or the attribute or group of attributes selected from the candidate keys as the most suitable to uniquely identify each instance of an entity. The primary key should be efficient, it must not contain any null parts, its values must remain static, and it should be a data element under your control.

program: A sequence of instructions that tell the computer what processing to do.

protocol: A set of semantic and syntactic rules that determines the behavior of functions in achieving communication.

query: A clearly specified request for data that returns records that satisfy the specifications.

rack and stack: A colloquial phrase recognizing the ability to analyze data and order the results into sequential order across many subsets. This generally refers to ordering by a summation or aggregation numeric value such as volume and sales during a period of time.

RDBMS: Acronym for *relational database management system*, which stores data in tables (relations) that are two dimensional. The tables have rows and columns. Data items at an intersection of a row and column are attribute or data values. RDBMSs can use a primary key to identify a row in a table. Rows can reference each other with a specialized use of the primary key as a foreign key constraint that links the two together.

record: In relational databases, a single instance in a table. In the context of hierarchical and network databases, a record is a data structure.

recursion: A relationship that connects an entity or table to itself.

redundancy: The storage of multiple copies of identical instances of a thing (database, table, record, or value).

referential integrity: A feature of some database systems that ensures that any record stored in the database is supported by accurate primary and foreign keys.

regression analysis: A set of statistical operations that helps to predict the value of the dependent variable from the values of one or more independent variables.

relational: A database in which data is stored in multiple tables. These tables then "relate" to one another to make up the entire database. Queries can be run to "join" these related tables together.

relationship: A logical link between two entities that represents a business rule or constraint.

repeating groups: A collection of data elements that occurs several times within a given record instance. This is generally observed as multiples of similar data elements, such as multiple phone numbers, addresses, or time period columns.

ROLAP: Acronym for *relational online analytical processing*, which is a type of OLAP analysis supported by a relational database.

role name: A deliberate name change of the attribute or column migrating as a foreign key to note a different or special purpose in the collection of data elements.

roll-up: The act of summarizing or aggregating data to a level higher than the previous level of detail.

row: A single instance in a table. This is also called a *record*.

scalability: The capacity of a thing to expand to accommodate future requirements.

schema: 1. Another term for Data Definition Language (DDL). The distinction between the terms is that DDL is usually reserved to the structure of the database, and schemas might include scripts to load data into the structures or assign security permissions to users. 2. The logical and physical definition of a database structure often represented as a graphic or data model.

shadow entity/table: A table or entity that the modeler has noted as being important but is out of scope for some reason. This could be because of it representing an integration to a database/table/subject area/entity external to the subject area—one that's outside the bounds of the analysis but necessary to note for some reason or being problematic in some way. On a Physical model, this generally denotes a table that will not be built.

shared aggregation: In Unified Modeling Language (UML), the ability of a class to belong to more than one supertype in a class hierarchy.

slice and dice: A colloquial phrase recognizing the ability to analyze data along many dimensions and across many subsets, including analyzing a data warehouse from the perspective of fact tables and related dimensions.

slowly changing dimension: In Dimensional modeling, a dimension whose structure and values change infrequently.

smart key: A key that's constructed according to a particular coding scheme or formula. For example, 0202200516 = the 16th trouble call received on February 2, 2005.

snowflake schema: A set of tables comprised of a single, central fact table surrounded by normalized dimension hierarchies. Each dimension level is represented in a table. Snowflake schemas implement dimensional data structures with fully normalized dimensions. Star schemas are an alternative to snowflake schemas.

source code: A sequence of instructions, including comments describing those instructions, for a computer system. This is also known as *program code*, as *program source code*, or simply as *code*.

SQL: Acronym for *Structured Query Language* (pronounced "see-kwill"), which is a language used to communicate with a relational database management system (RDBMS) and that provides a fairly common syntax for applications to use when submitting queries. It allows users to define the structure and organization of stored data, verify and maintain data integrity, control access to the data, and define relationships among the stored data items. Data retrieval by a user or an application program from the database is also a major function of SQL. SQL is a fourth-generation language, enabling the user to tell the computer what data they want without telling the computer how to get it.

staging area: A database design used to preprocess data before loading it into a different structure.

star schema: A star schema is a set of tables comprised of a single, central fact table surrounded by dimension tables. Each dimension is represented by a single dimension table. Star schemas implement dimensional data structures with denormalized dimensions. Snowflake schemas are an alternative to a star schema design.

state: The values of an entity's attributes at a point in time.

subject area: A set of entities or tables organized to reflect a specific area of business such as sales, finance, or manufacturing.

subtype: A subset of the membership of a category entity.

supertype: The master grouping that can be broken into multiple sets of members of a category entity.

surrogate key: A single-part, artificially established identifier for an entity. Surrogate key assignment is a special case of derived data—one where the primary key is derived. A common way of deriving surrogate key values is to assign integer values sequentially.

synonym: An alternative label used to refer to a data element or table. This is also called an *alias* in some database systems.

table: Collection of rows (records) that have associated columns (fields), or data arranged in rows and columns. In a relational database management system (RDBMS), all information is stored in the form of tables. Each table in a database stores information. Tables have unique names, usually identifying the logical entity whose data is stored within. Table names should be singular. Each row in the table describes one occurrence of an entity. Each column, or field, in a table describes an attribute of that entity. Rows and columns can be in any order in a table. A row applies only to a table, but it's part of a complete record.

TCP/IP: Acronym for *Transmission Control Protocol/Internet Protocol*. The networking protocol that supports communication across interconnected networks, between computers with diverse hardware architectures and various operating systems. This is generally regarded as the industry standard for computer and Internet connections.

time stamping: The technique of tagging each record with a value that represents the time that the data was accessed, processed, or stored.

time-variant data: Data whose accuracy is relevant to some moment in time.

To-Be: A planned change to an existing structure or process. This is a term used in analysis to note possible future design of structures or processes.

top-down analysis: An analysis technique in which the general rules and concepts are gathered first and used as guidelines to explore and document more and more details.

trend analysis: The process of looking at homogeneous data over a duration of time to find recurring and predictable behavior.

tuple: A single member of a set. In the set Color, Red, Yellow, and Blue are each a single tuple.

UML: Acronym for *Unified Modeling Language*, which is a nonproprietary, third-generation modeling language. It's an open method used to specify, visualize, construct, and document the development artifacts of an object-oriented software-intensive system.

unconformed dimension: A dimension that has not been designed or populated in a manner that can be counted on for consistency between different data marts.

unique key: 1. Defines the attributes and relationships that uniquely identify the entity. 2. A column or columns that contain unique values for the rows of a table. A column in a unique key may contain a *null*. Therefore, a unique key defined for an entity may not make a suitable primary for a table.

URL: Acronym for *uniform resource locator*, which is the address for a resource on the World Wide Web (WWW). All public Web sites have URLs. The first part of the URL, prior to the colon, specifies the access method. The part after is interpreted according to the access method (for instance, two slashes indicate a machine name), and the part after the period indicates the type of organization that owns the site (an organization, the government, an educational entity, or a company).

VLDB: Acronym for *very large database*, which is a database containing a large amount of data. (Note that *very large* is a subjective term whose meaning keeps changing.)

Waterfall development methodology: A development methodology that mandates every step of the process be fully completed before moving onto the subsequent step. This methodology isn't appropriate for developing anything that includes a possibility of new discovery after the discovery stage.

WWW: Acronym for *World Wide Web*, which is a huge body of information available through the Internet. Although *Web* and *Internet* are often used synonymously, *Web* actually refers to the software and related conventions that store information on the Internet.

XML: Acronym for *Extensible Markup Language*, a self-documenting representation of data in standard text form.

Index